W9-BDN-128

HISTORY OF ART FOR YOUNG PEOPLE

Fourth Edition HISTORY OF ART

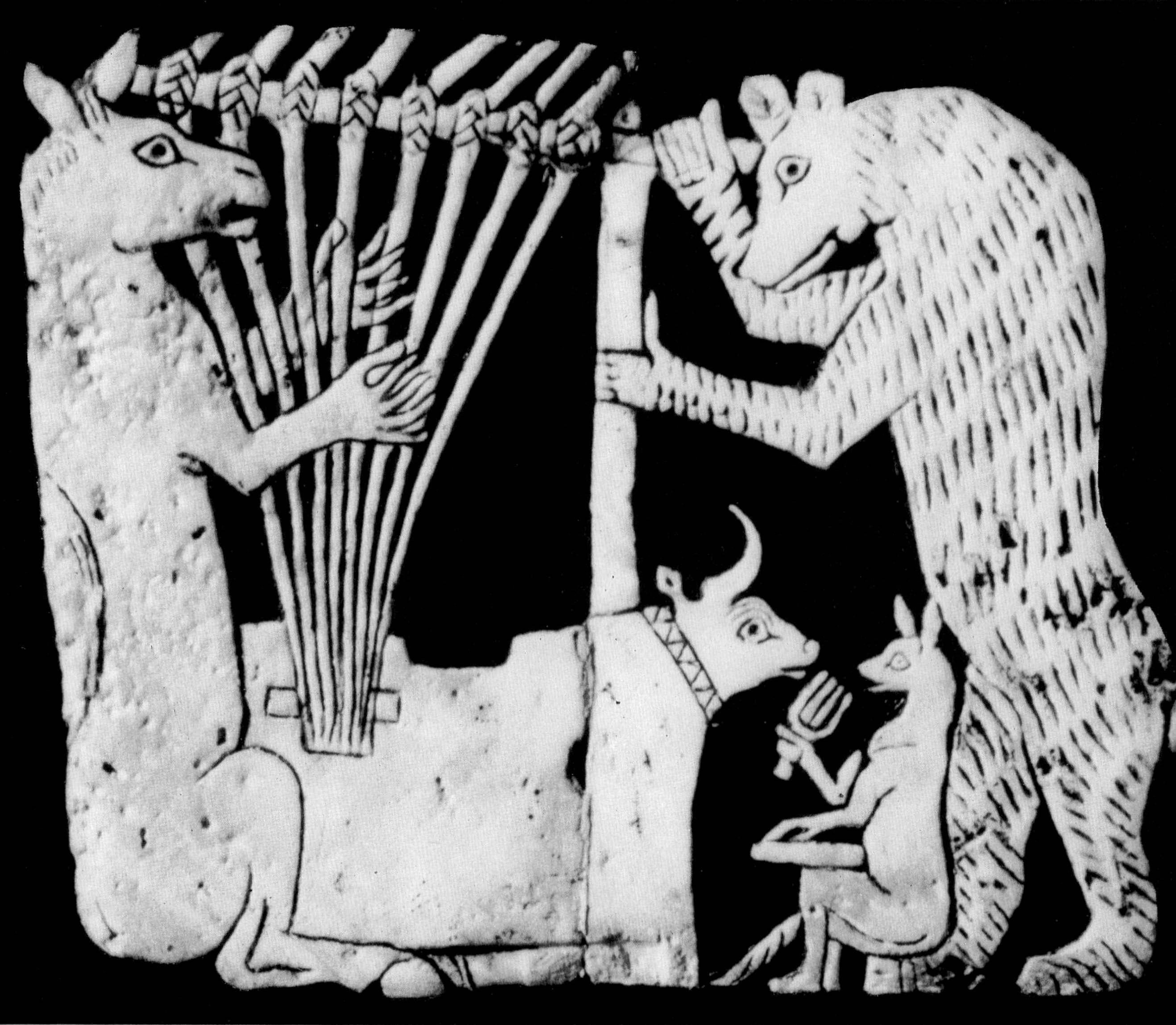

H. W. Janson and Anthony F. Janson

FOR YOUNG PEOPLE

HARRY N. ABRAMS, INC., PUBLISHERS, NEW YORK

Fourth Edition 1992

Project Director: Sheila Franklin Lieber
Editor: Diana Murphy
Designer: Ellen Nygaard Ford
Photo Research: Jennifer Bright, Colin Scott

Base maps by Paul Pugliese
Map typography by Julie Duquet

For identification of title page images,
see figure 44

Library of Congress
Cataloging-in-Publication Data

Janson, H. W. (Horst Woldemar), 1913–1982
History of art for young people /
H.W. Janson and Anthony F. Janson.—4th ed.
p. cm.
Includes bibliographical references and index.
Summary: Surveys the history of art, including painting, sculpture, architecture, and photography, from cave paintings to modern art.
ISBN 0-8109-3405-1
1. Art—History. [1. Art—History.]
I. Janson, Anthony F. II. Title.
N5300.J33 1992 91-2506
709—dc20 CIP
AC

Published in 1992 by Harry N. Abrams, Incorporated, New York
A Times Mirror Company

This book is also published by Abrams/Prentice Hall under the title *A Basic History of Art*

The original edition of *History of Art for Young People* was written by H. W. Janson with Samuel Cauman

Printed and bound in Japan

CONTENTS

PREFACE AND ACKNOWLEDGMENTS TO THE FOURTH EDITION

The fourth edition of H. W. Janson's *History of Art for Young People* has more changes and additions than any previous one. The book is now much more consistent in character with H. W. Janson's *History of Art,* from which it descends, yet preserves its own identity, appropriate to its different audience. Thus, the chapters on art between 1520 and 1750 differ appreciably from that volume.

Part Four, devoted to the modern world, has been completely reorganized. The distinction between Neoclassicism and Romanticism is now drawn more clearly. Twentieth-century painting now has a more straightforward chronological organization. A separate chapter is devoted to sculpture since 1900, which has followed a rather different path from painting. Modern architecture begins with Frank Lloyd Wright, while its antecedents, including the Chicago school and *Art Nouveau,* have been placed in earlier chapters where they properly belong. I have also taken the opportunity to bring the record of art history up-to-date and to add a number of artists.

There are many more illustrations in color, as well as several new illustrations showing works in situ. In addition, there are architectural drawings that have never appeared in the book, including improved diagrams and plans. The expanded Introduction now includes a brief discussion of line, color, light, composition, form, and space. This section is intended to help the beginner become more sensitive to visual components of art. The decision to incorporate basic elements of art appreciation—a subject that lies outside the traditional scope of art history—is based on the conviction that one must first learn how to look at art in order to understand it, since the works of art themselves remain the primary document. Most people who read this book do so to enhance their enjoyment of art, but often feel uneasy in looking at individual works of art. The new material addresses that obstacle by providing some general observations on viewing art, without resorting to formulaic guidelines that too often get in the way. In making these revisions, my primary aim has been to preserve the humanism that provided the foundation of this book, and to integrate my own views and writing style as seamlessly as possible into *History of Art for Young People* as it has evolved over more than twenty years.

This edition is dedicated to Diane Chalmers Johnson, who encouraged me to think more deeply about the process of looking at art. I am also indebted to two former curatorial colleagues: Michael McDonough for his helpful suggestions on modern architecture and Joseph Jacobs for his stimulating ideas about contemporary art. Diana Murphy has taken a fresh look at the entire text in the course of editing the book. Sheila Franklin Lieber, Project Manager at Harry N. Abrams, Inc., provided strong support and made consistently helpful suggestions throughout the revision process. Ellen Nygaard Ford redesigned the entire book with sensitivity and skill. Bob McKee also offered his experience in the design process. Jennifer Bright and Colin Scott provided their usual resourcefulness in securing new photographs and reproduction rights for the book. Shun Yamamoto brought his considerable expertise to bear on the book to ensure that the high production standards for which it is known would characterize the fourth edition as well.

A. F. J.
1991

INTRODUCTION

ART AND THE ARTIST

"What is art?" Few questions provoke such heated debate and provide so few satisfactory answers. If we cannot come to any definitive conclusions, there is still a good deal we can say. Art is first of all a *word,* one that acknowledges both the idea and the fact of art. Without it, we might well ask whether art exists in the first place. The term, after all, is not found in every society. Yet art is *made* everywhere. Art, therefore, is also an object, but not just any kind of object. Art is an *aesthetic object.* It is meant to be looked at and appreciated for its intrinsic value. Its special qualities set art apart, so that it is often placed away from everyday life, in museums, churches, or caves. What do we mean by aesthetic? By definition, aesthetic is "that which concerns the beautiful." Of course, not all art is beautiful to our eyes, but it is art nonetheless.

People the world over make much the same fundamental judgments, since our brains and nervous systems are the same. Taste, however, is conditioned solely by culture, which is so varied that it is impossible to reduce art to any one set of precepts. It would seem, therefore, that absolute qualities in art must elude us, that we cannot escape viewing works of art in the context of time and circumstance, whether past or present.

Imagination

We all dream. That is imagination at work. To imagine means simply to make an image—a picture—in our minds. Human beings are not the only creatures who have imagination. Even animals dream. There is, however, a profound difference between human and animal imagination. Humans are the only creatures who can tell one another about imagination in stories or pictures. The imagination is one of our most mysterious facets. It can be regarded as the connector between the conscious and the subconscious, where most of our brain activity takes place. It is the very glue that holds our personality, intellect, and spirituality together. Because the imagination responds to all three, it acts in lawful, if unpredictable, ways that are determined by the psyche and the mind.

The imagination is important, as it allows us to conceive of all kinds of possibilities in the future and to understand the past in a way that has real survival value. It is a fundamental part of our makeup, though we share it with other creatures. By contrast, the urge to make art is unique to us. It separates us from all other creatures across an evolutionary gap that is unbridgeable. The ability to make art must have been acquired relatively recently in the course of evolution. Human beings have been walking the earth for some

1. *Harpist,* so-called *Orpheus,* from Amorgos in the Cyclades. Latter part of the 3rd millennium B.C. Marble, height 8½″ (21.6 cm). National Archaeological Museum, Athens

two million years, but the oldest prehistoric art that we know of was made only about 35,000 years ago. It was undoubtedly the culmination of a long development no longer traceable, since the record of the earliest art is lost to us.

Who were the first artists? In all likelihood, they were shamans. Like the legendary Orpheus, they were believed to have divine powers of inspiration and to be able to enter the underworld of the subconscious in a deathlike trance, but, unlike ordinary mortals, they were then able to return to the realm of the living. Just such a figure seems to be represented by our *Harpist* (fig. 1) from nearly five thousand years ago. A work of unprecedented complexity for its time, it was carved by a remarkably gifted artist who makes us feel the visionary rapture of a bard as he sings his legend. With this artist-shaman's unique ability to penetrate the unknown and his rare talent for expressing it through art, he gained control over the forces hidden in human beings and nature. Even today the artist remains a magician whose work can mystify and move us—an embarrassing fact to civilized people, who do not readily relinquish their veneer of rational control.

Art plays a very special role in human personality. Like science and religion, art fulfills our innate urge to comprehend ourselves and the universe. This function makes art especially significant and, hence, worthy of our attention. Art has the power to penetrate to the core of our being, which recognizes itself in the creative act. For that reason, art represents its creators' deepest understanding and highest aspirations. At the same time, artists often act as the articulators of our shared beliefs and values, which they express through an ongoing tradition to us, their audience.

Creativity

What do we mean by making? If, in order to simplify our problem, we concentrate on the visual arts, we might say that a work of art must be a tangible thing shaped by human hands. This definition at least eliminates the confusion of treating as works of art such natural phenomena as flowers, seashells, or sunsets. It is a far from sufficient definition, to be sure, since human beings make many things other than works of art. Still, it will serve as a starting point. Now let us look at the striking *Bull's Head* by Pablo Picasso (fig. 2), which seems to consist of nothing but the seat and handlebars of an old bicycle. How meaningful is our formula here? Of course, the materials Picasso used are fabricated, but it would be absurd to insist that he must share the credit with the manufacturer, since the seat and handlebars in themselves are not works of art.

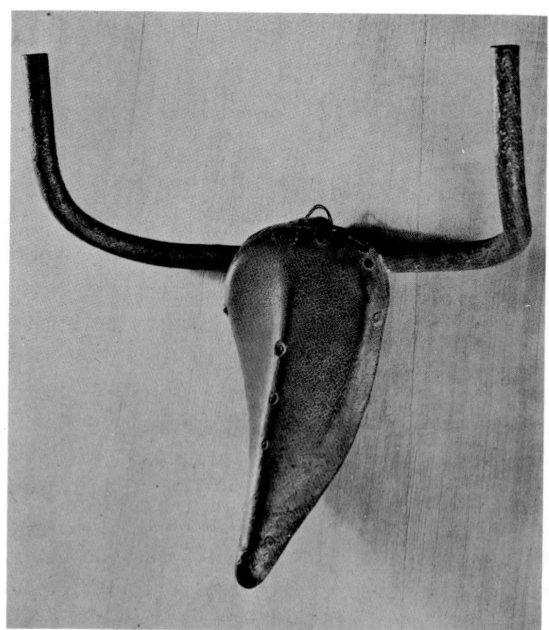

2. Pablo Picasso. *Bull's Head*. 1943. Bronze cast bicycle parts, height 16⅛″ (41 cm). Private collection

While we feel a certain jolt when we first recognize the ingredients of this visual pun, we also sense that it was a stroke of genius to put them together in this unique way, and we cannot very well deny that it is a work of art. Nevertheless, the actual handiwork of mounting the seat on the handlebars is ridiculously simple. What is far from simple is the leap of the imagination by which Picasso recognized a bull's head in these unlikely objects. The leap of the imagination is sometimes experienced as a flash of inspiration, but only rarely does a new idea emerge full-blown like Athena from the head of Zeus. Instead, it is usually preceded by a long gestation period in which all the hard work is done without finding the key to the solution to the problem. At the critical point, the imagination makes connections between seemingly unrelated parts and recombines them.

Our *Bull's Head* is, of course, an ideally simple case, involving only one leap of the imagination and a manual act in response to it. Once the seat had been properly placed on the handlebars and then cast in bronze, the job was done. Ordinarily, artists do not work with ready-made parts but with materials that have little or no shape of their own. The creative process consists of a long series of leaps of the imagination and the artist's attempts to give them form by shaping the material accordingly. In this way, by a constant flow of impulses back and forth between the artist's mind and the partly shaped material, he or she gradually defines more and more of the image, until at last all of it has been given visible form. Needless to say, artistic creation is too subtle and intimate an experience to permit an exact step-by-step description. Only artists can observe it fully, but they are so absorbed by it that they have great difficulty explaining it to us.

The creative process has been likened to birth, a metaphor that comes closer to the truth than would a description cast in terms of a transfer or projection of the image from the artist's mind. The making of a work of art is both joyous and painful, full of surprises, and in no sense mechanical. We have, moreover, ample testimony that artists themselves tend to look upon their creations as living things. Perhaps that is why creativity was once a concept reserved for God, as only He could give material form to an idea. Indeed, the artist's labors are much like the Creation told in the Bible.

This divine ability was not realized until Michelangelo, who described the anguish and glory of the creative experience when he spoke of "liberating the figure from the marble that imprisons it." We may translate this to mean that he started the process of carving a statue by trying to visualize a figure in the rough, rectilinear block as it came to him from the quarry. It seems fair to assume that at first Michelangelo did not see the figure any more clearly than one can see an unborn child inside the womb, but we may believe that he could see isolated "signs of life" within the marble. Once he started carving, every stroke of the chisel would commit him more and more to a specific conception of the figure hidden in the block, and the marble would permit him to free the figure whole only if his guess as to its shape was correct. Sometimes he did not guess well enough, and the stone refused to give up some essential part of its prisoner. Michelangelo, defeated, left the work unfinished, as he did with the *Captive* (fig. 3), whose very gesture seems to record the vain struggle for liberation. Looking at the block, we may get some inkling of Michelangelo's difficulties here. But could he not have finished the statue in *some* fashion? Surely there is enough material left for that. He probably could have, but perhaps not in the way he wanted. In that case the defeat would have been even more stinging.

Clearly, then, the making of a work of art has little in common with what we ordinarily mean by making. It is a strange and risky business in which the maker never quite knows what he or she is making until it has actually been made; or, to put it another way, it is a game of find-and-seek in which the seeker is not sure what he or she is looking for until it has been found. In the case of the *Bull's Head* it is the bold "finding" that impresses us most; in the *Captive*, the strenuous "seeking." To the non-artist, it seems hard to believe that this uncertainty, this need to take a chance, should be the essence of the artist's work. We all tend to think of "making" in terms of the craftsperson or manufacturer who knows exactly what he or she wants to produce from the very outset. There is thus comparatively little risk, but also little adventure, in such handiwork, which as a consequence tends to become routine. Whereas the artisan attempts only what is known to be possible, the artist is always driven to attempt the impossible, or at least the improbable or un-

3. Michelangelo. *Captive* (foreground). 1506.
Marble, height 8′11″ (2.72 m). Galleria dell'Accademia, Florence

imaginable. No wonder the artist's way of working is so resistant to any set rules, while the craftsperson's encourages standardization and regularity. We acknowledge this difference when we speak of the artist as *creating* instead of merely *making* something. Clearly, then, we must be careful not to confuse the making of a work of art with manual skill or craftsmanship. Some works of art may demand a great deal of technical discipline;

others do not. Even the most painstaking piece of craft does not deserve to be called a work of art unless it involves a leap of the imagination.

Needless to say, there have always been many more craftspeople than artists among us, since our need for the familiar and expected far exceeds our capacity to absorb the original but often deeply unsettling experiences we get from works of art. The urge to penetrate unknown realms, to achieve something original, may be felt by every one of us now and then. What sets the real artist apart is not so much the desire to *seek,* but that mysterious ability to *find,* which we call talent. We also speak of it as a "gift," implying that it is a sort of present from some higher power; or as "genius," a term that originally meant a higher power (a kind of "good demon") that inhabits and acts through the artist.

Originality and Tradition

Originality, then, ultimately distinguishes art from craft. We may say, therefore, that it is the yardstick of artistic greatness or importance. Unfortunately, it is also very hard to define. The usual synonyms—uniqueness, novelty, freshness—do not help us very much, and the dictionaries tell us only that an original work must not be a copy. No work of art can be entirely original. Each one is linked in a chain of relationships that arises somewhere out of the distant past and continues into the future. If it is true that "no man is an island," the same can be said of all works of art. The sum total of these chains makes a web in which every work of art occupies its own specific place; we call this *tradition.* Without tradition (the word means "that which has been handed down to us"), no originality would be possible. It provides, as it were, the firm platform from which the artist makes a leap of the imagination. The place where he or she lands will then become part of the web and serve as a point of departure for further leaps. And for us, too, the web of tradition is equally essential. Whether we are aware of it or not, tradition is the framework within which we inevitably form our opinions of works of art and assess their degree of originality.

Meaning and Style

Why do we create art? Surely one reason is an irresistible urge to adorn ourselves and decorate the world around us. Both are part of a larger desire, not to remake the world in our image but to recast ourselves and our environment in *ideal* form. Art is, however, much more than decoration, for it is laden with meaning, even if that content is sometimes slender or obscure. Art enables us to communicate our understanding in ways that cannot be expressed otherwise. Truly a painting (or any work of art) is worth a thousand words, not only in its descriptive value but also in its symbolic significance. In art, as in language, we are above all inventors of symbols that convey complex thoughts in new ways. However, we must think of art in terms not of everyday prose but of poetry, which is free to rearrange conventional vocabulary and syntax in order to convey new, often multiple, meanings and moods. A work of art likewise suggests much more than it states. It communicates partly by implying meanings through pose, facial expression, allegory, and the like. As in poetry, the value of art lies equally in what it says and how it says it.

But what is the *meaning* of art—its iconography? What is it trying to say? Artists often provide no clear explanation, since the work is the statement itself. Nonetheless, even the most private artistic statements can be understood on some level, even if only an intuitive one. The meaning, or content, of art is inseparable from its formal qualities, its *style.* The word *style* is derived from *stilus,* the writing instrument of the ancient Romans. Originally, it referred to distinctive ways of writing: the shape of the letters as well as the choice of words. In the visual arts, style means the particular way in which the forms that make up any given work of art are chosen and fitted together. To art historians the study of styles is of central importance. It not only enables them to find out, by means of careful analysis and comparison, when,

4. John De Andrea. *The Artist and His Model.* 1980. Polyvinyl polychromed in oil, lifesize. Collection Foster Goldstrom, Dallas and San Francisco. Courtesy O. K. Harris, New York

where, and often by whom a given work was produced, but it also leads them to understand the artist's intention as expressed through the style of the work. This intention depends on both the artist's personality and the context of time and place. Accordingly, we speak of "period styles." Thus art, like language, requires that we learn the style and outlook of a country, period, and artist if we are to understand it properly.

Self-Expression and Audience

Most of us are familiar with the famous Greek myth of the sculptor Pygmalion, who carved such a beautiful statue of the nymph Galatea that he fell in love with it and embraced her when Venus made his sculpture come to life. The myth has been given a fresh interpretation by John De Andrea's *The Artist and His Model* (fig. 4), which tells us a good deal about creativity by reversing the roles. Now it is the artist, lost in thought, who is oblivious to the statue's gaze. Clearly based on a real woman rather than an ideal conception, the model is still in the process of "coming to life" (the artist has not finished painting her white legs). The illusion is so convincing that we wonder which figure is real and which one is dreaming of the other, the artist or the sculpture? De Andrea makes us realize that to the artist, the creative act is a "labor of love" that brings art to life through self-expression. But can we not also say that it is the work of art that gives birth to the artist?

The birth of a work of art is an intensely private experience, so much so that many artists can work only when completely alone and refuse to show their unfinished pieces to anyone. Yet it must, as a final step, be shared by the public in order for the birth to be successful. Artists do not create merely for their own satisfaction, but want their work validated by others. In fact, the creative process is not complete until the work has found an audience. In the end, works of art exist in order to be liked rather than to be debated.

Perhaps we can resolve this seeming paradox once we understand what artists mean by "public." They are concerned not with *the* public as a statistical entity but with their particular public, their audience. Quality rather than wide approval is what matters to them. The audience whose approval is so important to artists is a limited and special one. Its members may be other artists as well as patrons, friends, critics, and interested beholders. The one quality they all have in common is an informed love of works of art, an attitude at once discriminating and enthusiastic that lends particular weight to their judgments. They are, in a word, experts, people whose authority rests on experience rather than theoretical knowledge. In reality, there is no sharp break, no difference in kind, between the expert and the public at large, only a difference in degree.

Tastes

Deciding what is art and rating a work of art are two separate problems. If we had an absolute method for distinguishing art from non-art, it would not necessarily enable us to measure quality. People tend to compound the two problems into one. Quite often when they ask, "Why is that art?" they mean, "Why is that *good* art?" Since the experts do not post exact rules, people are apt to fall back on the defense: "Well, I don't know anything about art, but I know what I like." It is a formidable roadblock, this stock phrase, in the path of understanding. Let us examine the roadblock and the various unspoken assumptions that buttress it.

Are there really people who know nothing about art? No, for art is so much a part of the fabric of our daily life that we encounter it all the time, even if our contacts with it are limited to magazine covers, advertising posters, war memorials, television, and the buildings where we live, work, and worship. When we say, "I know what I like," we really mean, "I like what I know (and I reject whatever fails to match the things I am familiar with)." Such likes are not in truth ours at all, for they have been imposed by habit and culture without any personal choice.

Why should so many of us cherish the illusion of having made a personal choice in art when in fact we have not? There is another unspoken assumption at work here: something must be wrong with a work of art if it takes an expert to appreciate it. But if experts appreciate art more than the uninformed, why should we not emulate them? The road to expertness is clear and wide, and it invites anyone with an open mind and a capacity to absorb new experiences. As our understanding grows, we find ourselves liking a great many more things than we had thought possible at the start. We gradually acquire the courage of our own convictions, until we are able to say, with some justice, that we know what we like.

LOOKING AT ART

The Visual Elements

We live in a sea of images conveying the culture and learning of modern civilization. Fostered by an unprecedented media explosion, this "visual background noise" has become so much a part of our daily lives that we take it for granted. In the process, we have become desensitized to art as well. Anyone can buy cheap paintings and reproductions to decorate a room, where they often hang virtually unnoticed, perhaps deservedly so. It is small wonder that we look at the art in museums with equal casualness. We pass rapidly from one object to another, sampling them like dishes in a smorgasbord. We may pause briefly before a famous masterpiece that we have been told we are supposed to admire, then ignore the gallery full of equally beautiful and important works around it. We will have seen the art but not really looked at it. Looking at great art is not such an easy task, for art rarely reveals its secrets readily. While the experience of a work can be immediately electrifying, we sometimes do not realize its impact until time has let it filter through the recesses of our imaginations. It even happens that something that at first repelled or confounded us emerges only many years later as one of the most important artistic events of our lives.

Understanding a work of art begins with a sensitive appreciation of its appearance. Art may be approached and appreciated for its purely visual elements: line, color, light, composition, form, and space. These may be shared by any work of art. Their effects, however, vary widely according to medium (the physical materials of which the artwork is made) and technique, which together help determine the possibilities and limitations of what the artist can achieve. For that reason, our discussion is merged with an introduction to four major arts: graphic arts, painting, sculpture, and architecture. (The technical aspects of the major mediums are treated in separate sections within the main body of the text and in the glossary at the back of the book.) Just because line is discussed with drawing, however, does not mean that it is not equally important in painting and sculpture. And while form is introduced with sculpture, it is just as essential to painting, drawing, and architecture.

Visual analysis can help us appreciate the beauty of a masterpiece, but we must be care-

5. Michelangelo. *Study for the Libyan Sibyl.* c. 1511. Red chalk on paper, 11⅜ × 8⅜″ (28.9 × 21.3 cm). The Metropolitan Museum of Art, New York. Purchase, 1924, Joseph Pulitzer Bequest

ful not to use a formulaic approach that would trivialize it. Every aesthetic "law" advanced so far has proven of dubious value and usually gets in the way of our understanding. Even if a valid "law" were to be found—and none has yet been discovered—it would probably be so elementary as to prove useless in the face of art's complexity. We must also bear in mind that art appreciation is more than mere enjoyment of aesthetics. It is learning to understand the meaning of a work of art. Finally, let us remember that no work can be understood outside its historical context.

Line. Line may be regarded as the most basic visual element. A majority of art is initially conceived in terms of contour line. Its presence is often implied even when it is not actually used to describe form. Because children generally start out by scribbling, line is often considered the most rudimentary component of art, although as anyone knows who has watched a youngster struggle to make a stick figure with pencil or crayon, drawing is by no means as easy as it seems. Line has traditionally been admired for its descriptive value, so that its expressive potential is easily overlooked, but line is capable of creating a broad range of effects.

6. Michelangelo. *Libyan Sibyl,* portion of the Sistine Ceiling. 1508–12. Fresco. Sistine Chapel, The Vatican, Rome

Drawings represent line in its purest form. The appreciation of drawings as works of art dates from the Renaissance, when the artist's creative genius first came to be valued and paper began to be made in quantity. Drawing style can be as personal as handwriting. In fact, the term graphic art, which designates drawings and prints, comes from the Greek word for writing, *graphos.* Collectors treasure drawings because they seem to reveal the artist's inspiration with unmatched freshness. Their role as records of artistic thought also makes drawings uniquely valuable to art historians, for they help in documenting the evolution of a work from its inception to the finished piece.

Artists themselves commonly treat drawings as a form of note-taking. Some of these notes are discarded as fruitless, while others are tucked away to form a storehouse of motifs and studies for later use. Once a basic idea is established, an artist may develop it into a more complete study. Michelangelo's study of the Libyan Sibyl (fig. 5) for the Sistine Chapel ceiling is a drawing of compelling beauty. For this sheet, he chose the softer medium of red chalk over the scratchy line of pen and ink, which he used in rough sketches. His chalk approximates the texture of flesh and captures the play of light and dark over the nude forms, giving the figure a greater sensuousness. The emphatic outline that defines each part of the form is so fundamental to the conceptual genesis and design process in all of Michelangelo's paintings and drawings that ever since his time, line has been closely associated with the "intellectual" side of art.

It was Michelangelo's habit to base his female figures on male nudes drawn from life. To him, only the heroic male nude possessed the physical monumentality necessary to express the awesome power of figures, such as this mythical prophetess. As in other sheets like this by Michelangelo, his focus here is on the torso; he studied the musculature at length before turning his attention to details, such as the hand and toes. Since there is no sign of hesitation in the pose, we can be sure that the artist already had the conception firmly in mind; probably he established it in a preliminary drawing. Why did he go to so much trouble when the finished sibyl is mostly clothed and must be viewed from a considerable distance below? Evidently Michelangelo believed that only by describing the anatomy completely could he be certain that the figure would be convincing. In the final painting (fig. 6) she communicates a superhuman strength, lifting her massive book of prophecies with the greatest ease.

Color. The world around us is alive with color, albeit even those of us who are not color-blind see only a relatively narrow band of the actual light spectrum. Whereas color is an adjunct element to graphics and sometimes sculpture, it is indispensable to virtually all forms of painting. This is true even of to-

7. Titian. *The Rape of Europa.* 1559–62. Oil on canvas, 70 × 80¾″ (177.8 × 205 cm). Isabella Stewart Gardner Museum, Boston

nalism, which emphasizes dark, neutral hues like gray and brown. Of all the visual elements, color is undoubtedly the most expressive, as well as the most intractable. Perhaps for that reason, it has attracted the wide attention of researchers and theorists since the mid-nineteenth century. We often read that red seems to advance, while blue recedes; or that the former is a violent or passionate color, the latter a sad one. Like a recalcitrant child, however, color in art refuses to be governed by any rules. They work only when the painter consciously applies them.

Notwithstanding this large body of theory, the role of color in art rests primarily on its sensuous and emotive appeal, in contrast to the more cerebral quality generally associated with line. The merits of line versus color have been the subject of a debate that first arose between partisans of Michelangelo and of Titian, his great contemporary in Venice. Titian himself was a fine draftsman and absorbed the influence of Michelangelo. He nevertheless stands at the head of the coloristic tradition that descends through Rubens and Van Gogh to the Abstract Expressionists of the twentieth century. *The Rape of Europa* (fig. 7), executed toward the end of Titian's long career, shows the painterly application of sonorous color that is characteristic of his style. Though he no doubt worked out the essential features of the composition in preliminary drawings, none have survived. Nor evidently did he transfer the design onto the canvas but worked directly on the surface, making numerous changes as he went along. By varying the consistency of his paints, the artist was able to capture the texture of Europa's flesh with uncanny accuracy, while distinguishing it clearly from her windswept dress and the shaggy coat of Zeus disguised as a bull. To convey these tactile qualities, Titian built up the surface of the painting in thin coats, known as glazes. The interaction between these layers produces a richness and complexity of color that are strikingly apparent in the orange drapery where it trails off into the green seawater, which has a delicious wetness. The medium is so filmy as to become nearly translucent in parts of the landscape background, which is painted with a deft, flickering brush.

8. Pablo Picasso. *Girl Before a Mirror.* March 1932. Oil on canvas, 64 × 51¼" (162.3 × 130.2 cm). Collection, The Museum of Modern Art, New York. Gift of Mrs. Simon Guggenheim

Color is so potent that it does not need a system to work its magic in art. From the heavy outlines, it is apparent that Picasso must have originally conceived *Girl Before a Mirror* (fig. 8) in terms of form; yet the picture makes no sense in black and white. He has treated his shapes much like the enclosed, flat panes of a stained-glass window to create a lively decorative pattern. The motif of a young woman contemplating her beauty goes all the way back to antiquity (see, for example, *The Toilet of Venus* by the French Baroque artist Simon Vouet, fig. 306), but rarely has it been depicted with such disturbing overtones. Picasso's girl is anything but serene. On the contrary, her face is divided into two parts, one with a somber expression, the other with a masklike appearance whose color nevertheless betrays passionate feeling. She reaches out to touch the image in the mirror with a gesture of longing and apprehension. Now, we all feel a jolt when we

9. Caravaggio. *David with the Head of Goliath.* 1607 or 1609/10. Oil on canvas, 49¼ × 39⅜" (125.1 × 100 cm). Galleria Borghese, Rome

unexpectedly see ourselves in a mirror, which often gives back a reflection that upsets our self-conception. Picasso here suggests this visionary truth in several ways. Much as a real mirror introduces changes of its own and does not merely give back the simple truth, so this one alters the way the girl looks, revealing a deeper reality. She is not so much examining her physical appearance as exploring her sexuality. The mirror is a sea of conflicting emotions signified above all by the color scheme of her reflection. Framed by strong blue, purple, and green hues, her features stare back at her with fiery intensity. Clearly discernible is a tear on her cheek. But it is the masterstroke of the green spot, shining like a beacon in the middle of her forehead, that conveys the anguish of the girl's confrontation with her inner self. Picasso was probably aware of the theory that red and green are complementary colors, which intensify each other. However, this "law" can hardly have dictated his choice of green to stand for the girl's psyche. That was surely determined as a matter of pictorial and expressive necessity.

Light. Except for modern light installations such as laser displays, art is concerned with reflected light effects rather than with radiant light. Artists have several ways of representing radiant light. Divine light, for example, is sometimes indicated by golden rays, at other times by a halo or aura. A candle or torch may be depicted as the source of light in a dark interior or night scene. The most common method is not to show radiant light directly but to suggest its presence through a change in the value of reflected light from dark to light. Sharp contrast (known as *chiaroscuro*, the Italian word for light-dark) is identified with the Baroque artist Caravaggio, who made it the cornerstone of his style. In *David with the Head of Goliath* (fig. 9), he employed it to heighten the drama. An intense raking light from an unseen source at the left is used to model forms and create textures. The selective highlighting endows the lifesize figure of David and the gruesome head with a startling presence. Light here serves as a device to create the convincing illusion that David is standing before us. The pictorial space, with its indeterminate depth, becomes continuous with ours, despite the fact that the frame cuts off the figure. Thus, the foreshortened arm with Goliath's head seems to extend out to the viewer from the dark background. For all its obvious theatricality, the painting is surprisingly muted: David seems to contemplate Goliath with a mixture of sadness and pity. According to contemporary sources, the severed head is a self-portrait, but although we may doubt the identification, this disturbing image communicates a tragic vision that was soon fulfilled. Not long after the *David* was painted, Caravaggio killed a man in a duel, which forced him to spend the rest of his short life on the run.

Composition. All art requires order. Otherwise its message would emerge as visually garbled. To accomplish this, the artist must control space within the framework of a unified composition. Moreover, pictorial space must work across the picture plane, as well as behind it. Since the Early Renaissance, viewers have become accustomed to experiencing

10. Jean-Baptiste-Siméon Chardin. *Blowing Bubbles.* c. 1745. Oil on canvas, 36⅝ × 29⅜″ (93 × 74.6 cm). The National Gallery of Art, Washington, D.C. Gift of Mrs. John Simpson

paintings as windows onto separate illusionistic realities. The Renaissance invention of one-point perspective (also called linear or scientific perspective) provided a geometric system for the convincing representation of architectural and open-air settings. By having the orthogonals (shown as diagonal lines) converge at a vanishing point on the horizon, the artist was able to gain command over every aspect of composition, including the rate of recession and placement of figures.

Artists usually dispense with aids like perspective and rely on their own eyes. This does not mean that they merely transcribe optical reality. *Blowing Bubbles* by the French painter Jean-Baptiste-Siméon Chardin (fig. 10) depends in good measure on the satisfying composition for its success. The motif had been popular in earlier Dutch genre scenes, where bubbles symbolized life's brevity and, hence, the vanity of all earthly things. No such meaning can be attached to Chardin's picture, which is disarming in its simplicity. The interest lies solely in the seemingly insignificant subject and in the sense of enchantment imparted by the children's rapt attention to the moment. We know from a contemporary source that Chardin painted the youth "carefully from life and . . . tried hard to give him an ingenuous air." The results are anything but artless, however. The triangular shape of the boy leaning on the ledge gives stability to the painting, which helps suspend the fleeting instant in time. To fill out the composition, the artist includes the toddler peering intently over the ledge at the bubble, which is about the same size as his head. Chardin has carefully thought out every aspect of his arrangement. The honeysuckle in the upper left-hand corner, for example, echoes the contour of the adolescent's back, while the two straws are virtually parallel to each other. Even the crack in the stone ledge has a purpose: to draw attention to the glass of soap by setting it slightly apart.

Often artists paint not what they see but what they imagine. Pictorial space, however, need not conform to either conceptual or visual reality. El Greco's *The Agony in the Garden* (fig. 11) uses contradictory, irrational space to help conjure up a mystical vision that represents a spiritual reality. Christ, isolated against a large rock that echoes His shape, is comforted by the angel bearing a golden cup, symbol of the Passion. The angel appears to kneel on a mysterious oval cloud, which envelops the sleeping disciples. In the distance to the right we see Judas and the soldiers coming to arrest the Lord. The composition is balanced by two giant clouds on either side. The entire landscape resounds with Christ's agitation, represented by the sweep of supernatural forces. The elongated forms, eerie moonlight, and expressive colors—all hallmarks of El Greco's style—help heighten our sense of identification with Christ's suffering.

Form. Every two-dimensional shape that we find in art is the counterpart to a three-dimensional form. There is nevertheless a vast difference between drawing or painting forms and sculpting them. The one transcribes, the other brings them to life, as it were. They require fundamentally different

11. El Greco. *The Agony in the Garden.* 1597–1600. Oil on canvas, 40¼ × 44¾" (102.2 × 113.7 cm). Toledo Museum of Art, Ohio. Gift of Edward Drummond Libbey

talents and attitudes toward material as well as subject matter. Although numerous artists have been competent in both painting and sculpture, only a handful have managed to bridge the gap between them with complete success.

Sculpture is categorized according to whether it is carved or modeled and whether it is a relief or free-standing. Relief remains tied to the background, from which it only partially emerges, in contrast to free-standing sculpture, which is fully liberated from it. A further distinction is made between low (*bas*) relief and high (*alto*) relief, depending on how much the carving projects. However, since scale as well as depth must be taken into account, there is no single guideline, so that a third category, middle (*mezzo*) relief, is sometimes cited.

Low reliefs often share characteristics with painting. In Egypt, where low-relief carving attained unsurpassed subtlety, many reliefs were originally painted and included elaborate settings. High reliefs largely preclude this kind of pictorialism. The figures on a column drum from a Greek temple (fig. 12) are so detached from the background that the addition of landscape or architectural elements would have been both unnecessary and unconvincing. The neutral setting, moreover, is in keeping with the mythological subject, which occurs in an indeterminate time and

12. *Alkestis Leaving Hades.* Lower column drum from the Temple of Artemis, Ephesus. c. 340 B.C. Marble, height 71″ (180.3 cm). British Museum, London

place. In compensation, the sculptor has treated the limited free space atmospherically, although the figures nonetheless remain imprisoned in stone.

Free-standing sculpture—that is, sculpture that is carved or modeled fully in the round—is generally made by either of two methods. One is carving. It is a subtractive process that starts with a solid block, usually stone, which is highly resistant to the sculptor's chisel. The brittleness of stone and the difficulty of cutting it tend to result in the compact, "closed" forms evident, for example, in Michelangelo's *Captive* (see fig. 3). Modeling is the very opposite of carving. It is an additive process using soft materials such as plaster, clay, or wax. Since these materials are not very durable, they are usually cast in a more lasting medium: anything that can be poured, including molten metal, cement, even plastic. Modeling encourages "open" forms created with the aid of metal armatures to support their extension into space. This technique and the development of lightweight hollow-bronze casting enabled the Greeks to experiment with daring poses in monumental sculpture before attempting them in marble. In contrast to the figure of Hades on the column drum (see fig. 12), the bronze *Standing Youth* (fig. 13) is free to move about, which lends him a lifelike presence that is further enhanced by his dancing pose. His inlaid eyes and soft patina, accentuated by oxidation and corrosion (he was found in the Aegean Sea off the coast of Marathon), make him even more credible in a way that marble statues, with their seemingly cold and smooth finish, rarely equal, despite their more natural color.

13. Praxiteles (attr.). *Standing Youth,* found in the sea off Marathon. c. 350–325 B.C. Bronze, height 51″ (129.5 cm). National Archaeological Museum, Athens

14. Frank Lloyd Wright. Solomon R. Guggenheim Museum, New York. 1956–59

15. Interior, Solomon R. Guggenheim Museum

Space. Architecture is the principal means of organizing space. Of all the arts, it is also the most practical. The parameters of architecture are defined by utilitarian function and structural system, but there is almost always an aesthetic component as well, even when it consists of nothing more than a decorative veneer. A building proclaims the architect's concerns by the way in which these elements are woven into a coherent program.

Architecture becomes memorable only when it expresses a transcendent vision, whether personal, social, or spiritual. Such buildings are almost always important public places that require the marshaling of significant resources and serve the purpose of bringing people together to share goals, pursuits, and values. An extreme case is the Solomon R. Guggenheim Museum in New York by Frank Lloyd Wright. Scorned when it was erected in the late 1950s, it is a brilliant, if idiosyncratic, creation by one of the most original architectural minds of the century. The sculptural exterior (fig. 14) announces that this can only be a museum, for it is self-consciously a work of art in its own right. As a piece of design, the Guggenheim Museum is remarkably willful. In shape it is as defiantly individual as the architect himself and refuses to conform to the boxlike apartments around it. From the outside, the structure looks like a gigantic snail, reflecting Wright's interest in organic shapes. The office area forming the "head" (to the left in our photograph) is connected by a narrow passageway to the "shell" containing the main body of the museum.

The outside gives us some idea of what to expect inside (fig. 15), yet nothing quite prepares us for the extraordinary sensation of light and air in the main hall after we have been ushered through the unassuming entrance. The radical design makes it clear that Wright had completely rethought the purpose of an art museum. The exhibition area is a kind of inverted dome with a huge glass-covered eye at the top. The vast, fluid space creates an atmosphere of quiet harmony while actively shaping our experience by determining how art shall be displayed. After taking an elevator to the top of the building, we begin a leisurely descent down the gently sloping ramp. The continuous spiral provides for uninterrupted viewing, conducive to studying art. At the same time, the narrow confines of the galleries prevent us from becoming passive observers by forcing us into a direct confrontation with the works of art. Sculpture takes on a heightened physical presence that demands we look at it. Even paintings acquire a new prominence by protruding slightly from the curved walls instead of receding into them. Viewing exhibitions at the Guggenheim is like being conducted through a predetermined stream of consciousness, where everything merges into a total unity. Whether one agrees with this approach or not, the building testifies to the strength of Wright's vision by precluding any other way of seeing the art.

Meaning

Art has been called a visual dialogue, for though the object itself is mute, it expresses its creator's intention just as surely as if the artist were speaking to us. For there to be a dialogue, however, our active participation is required. If we cannot literally talk to a work of art, we can learn how to respond to it and question it in order to fathom its meaning. Finding the right answers usually involves asking the right questions. Even if we aren't sure which question to ask, we can always start with, "What would happen if the artist had done it another way?" And when we are through, we must question our explanation according to the same test of adequate proof that applies to any investigation: have we taken into account *all* the available evidence, and arranged it in a logical and coherent way? There is, alas, no step-by-step method to guide us, but this does not mean the process is entirely mysterious. We can illustrate it by looking at some examples together. The demonstration will help us gain courage to try the same analysis the next time we enter a museum.

The great Dutch painter Jan Vermeer has been called The Sphinx of Delft, and with good reason, for all his paintings have a degree of mystery. In *Woman Holding a Balance* (fig. 16), a young woman, richly dressed in at-home wear of the day and with strings of pearls and gold coins spread out on the table before her, is contemplating a balance in her hand. The canvas is painted entirely in gradations of cool, neutral tones, except for a bit of the red dress visible beneath her jacket. The soft light from the partly open window is concentrated on her face and the cap framing it. Other beads of light reflect from the pearls and her right hand. The serene atmosphere is sustained throughout the stable composition. Vermeer places us at an intimate distance within the relatively shallow space, which has been molded around the figure. The underlying grid of horizontals and verticals is modulated by the gentle curves of the woman's form and the heap of blue drapery, as well as by the oblique angles of the mirror. The design is so perfect that we cannot move a single element without upsetting the delicate balance.

The composition is controlled in part by perspective. The vanishing point of the diagonals formed by the top of the mirror and the right side of the table lies at the juncture of the woman's little finger and the picture frame. If we look at the bottom of the frame, we see that it is actually lower on the right than on the left, where it lies just below her hand. The effect is so carefully calculated that the artist must have wanted to guide our eye to the painting in the background. Though difficult to read at first, it depicts Christ at the Last Judgment, when every soul is weighed. The parallel of this subject to the woman's activity tells us that, contrary to our initial impression, this cannot be simply a scene of everyday life. The meaning is nevertheless far from clear. Because Vermeer treated forms as beads of light, it was assumed until recently that the balance holds items of jewelry and that the woman is weighing the worthlessness of earthly possessions in the face of death; hence, the painting was generally called *The Pearl Weigher* or *The Gold Weigher.* But if we look closely, we can see that the pans contain nothing. This is confirmed by infrared photography, which also reveals that Vermeer changed the position of the balance: to make the composition more harmonious, he placed it parallel to the picture plane instead of allowing it to recede into space.

What, then, is she doing? If she is weighing temporal against spiritual values, it can be only in a symbolic sense, because nothing about the figure or the setting betrays a sense of conflict. What accounts for this inner peace? Perhaps it is self-knowledge, symbolized here by the mirror. It may also be the promise of salvation through her faith. In *Woman Holding a Balance*, as in Caravaggio's *The Calling of St. Matthew* (see fig. 271), light might therefore serve not only to illuminate the scene but also to represent religious revelation. In the end, we cannot be sure, because Vermeer's approach to his subject proves as subtle as his pictorial treatment. He avoids any anecdote or symbolism that might limit us to a single interpretation. There can be no

16. Jan Vermeer. *Woman Holding a Balance.* c. 1664. Oil on canvas, 16¾ × 15" (42.6 × 38.1 cm). The National Gallery of Art, Washington, D.C. Widener Collection, 1942

doubt, however, about his fascination with light. Vermeer's mastery of light's expressive qualities elevates his concern for the reality of appearance to the level of poetry, and subsumes its visual and symbolic possibilities. Here, then, we have found the real "meaning" of Vermeer's art.

The ambiguity in *Woman Holding a Balance* serves to heighten our interest and pleasure, while the carefully organized composition expresses the artist's underlying concept with singular clarity. But what are we to do when a work deliberately seems devoid of ostensible meaning? Modern artists can pose a gap between their intentions and the viewer's understanding. The gap is, however, often more apparent than real, for the meaning is usually intelligible to the imagination at some level. Still, we feel we must comprehend intellectually what we perceive intuitively. We can partially solve the personal code in Jasper Johns' *Target with Four Faces* (fig. 17) by treating it somewhat like a rebus. Where did he begin? Surely with the target, which stands alone as an object, unlike the long box at the top, particularly when its hinged door is closed. Why a target in the first place? The size, texture, and colors inform us that this is not to be interpreted as a real target. The design is nevertheless attractive in its own right, and Johns must have chosen it for that reason. When the wooden door is up, the assemblage is transformed from a neutral into a loaded image, bringing out the nascent connotations of the target. Johns has used the same plaster cast four times, which lends the faces a curious anonymity. He then cut them off at the eyes, "the windows of the soul," rendering them even more enigmatic. Finally, he crammed them into their compartments, so that they seem to press urgently out toward us. The results are disquieting, aesthetically as well as expressively.

Something so disturbing cannot be without significance. We may be reminded of prisoners trying to look out from small cell windows, or perhaps blindfolded targets of execution. Whatever our impression, the claustrophobic image radiates an aura of danger. Unlike Picasso's joining of a bicycle seat and handlebars to form a bull's head, *Target with Four Faces* combines two disparate components in an open conflict that we cannot reconcile, no matter how hard we try. The intrusion of this ominous meaning creates an extraordinary tension with the dispassionate investigation of the target's formal qualities. It is, then, this disparity between form and content that must have been Johns' goal.

How do we know we are right? After all, this is merely our personal interpretation, so we turn to the critics for help. We find them divided about the meaning of *Target with Four Faces*, although they agree it must have one.

17. Jasper Johns. *Target with Four Faces*. 1955. Assemblage: encaustic on newspaper and cloth over canvas, 26 × 26" (66 × 66 cm), surmounted by four tinted plaster faces in wood box with hinged front. Box, closed 3¾ × 26 × 3½" (9.5 × 66 × 8.9 cm); overall dimensions with box open, 33⅝ × 26 × 3" (85.4 × 66 × 7.6 cm). Collection, The Museum of Modern Art, New York. Gift of Mr. and Mrs. Robert C. Scull

Johns, on the other hand, has insisted that there is none! Whom are we to believe, the critics or the artist himself? The more we think about it, the more likely it seems that both sides may be right. Artists are not always aware of why they have made a work. That does not mean there were no reasons, only that they were unconscious ones. Under these circumstances, critics may well know artists' minds better than the artists do and explain their creations more clearly. We can now understand that to Johns the leap of his imagination in *Target with Four Faces* remains as mysterious as it first seemed to us. Our account reconciles the artist's aesthetic concerns and the critics' search for meaning, and while we realize that no ultimate solution is possible, we have arrived at a satisfactory explanation by looking and thinking for ourselves.

PART ONE

THE ANCIENT WORLD

Art history is more than a stream of art objects created over time. It is intimately related to history itself, that is, the recorded evidence of human events. For that reason, we must consider the *concept* of history, which, we are often told, begins with the invention of writing some 8,000 years ago. And indeed, the invention of writing was an early accomplishment of the "historic" civilizations of Mesopotamia and Egypt. Without writing, the growth we have known would have been impossible. We do not know the earliest phases of its development, but writing must have been several hundred years in the making—between 3300 and 3000 B.C., roughly speaking, with Mesopotamia in the lead—after the new societies were already past their first stage. Thus "history" was well under way by the time writing could be used to record events.

The invention of writing makes a convenient landmark, for the absence of written records is surely one of the key differences between prehistoric and historic societies. But as soon as we ask why this is so, we face some intriguing problems. First of all, how valid is the distinction between prehistoric and historic? Does it merely express a difference in our *knowledge* of the past? (Thanks to the invention of writing, we know a great deal more about history than about prehistory.) Or was there a genuine change in the way things happened—and in the kinds of things that happened—after history began? Obviously, prehistory was far from uneventful. Yet changes in the human condition that mark this road, decisive though they are, seem incredibly slow paced and gradual when measured against the events of the last 5,000 years. The beginning of history, then, means a sudden increase in the speed of events, a shifting from low gear into high gear, as it were. It also means a change in the *kinds* of events. Historic societies quite literally make history. They not only bring forth "great individuals and great deeds"—to cite one traditional definition—by demanding human effort on a large scale, but they make these achievements *memorable* as well. And for an event to be memorable, it must be more than "worth remembering." It must also be accomplished quickly enough to be grasped by human memory, and not spread over many centuries. Collectively, memorable events have caused the ever-quickening pace of change during the past five millenniums, which begin with what we call the ancient world.

NORTH SEA
BALTIC SEA
ENGLAND
Stonehenge
Salisbury
London
ATLANTIC OCEAN
GERMANY
BRITTANY
Carnac
Seine R.
Paris
Rhine R.
Elbe R.
Vistula R.
Loire R.
FRANCE
Vogelherd
Altamira
Dordogne R.
Lascaux
Les Eyzies
La Magdelaine
Garonne R.
Penne
La Madeleine
LAKE GENEVA
LAKE CONSTANCE
Willendorf
Danube R.
Vienna
AUSTRIA
CARPATHIANS
ALPS
PYRENEES
Rhone R.
Nimes
Venice
Po R.
APENNINES
Ravenna
Classe
Arno R.
Florence
Chiusi
Perugia
Vulci
Tiber R.
Tarquinia
Veii
Cerveteri
Tivoli
Rome
Ostia
Praeneste
SPAIN
YUGOSLAVIA
Split
ROMANIA
Cernavoda
ADRIATIC SEA
ITALY
MT. VESUVIUS
Naples
Boscoreale
ISCHIA
Pompeii
Herculaneum
Paestum
MEDITERRANEAN SEA
TYRRHENIAN SEA
BALKANS
Salonika
SAMOTHRACE
Constantinople
GREECE
MT. OLYMPUS
Addaura
MT. PELLEGRINO
CORFU
Troy
Palermo
AEGEAN SEA
Pergamum
SICILY
Naxos
Catana
MT. PARNASSUS
EUBOEA
LYDIA
CHIOS
Athens
Ephesus
IONIAN SEA
SAMOS
Tralles
Miletus
Sparta
Halicarna
Cnidus
AMORGOS
Heraklion
Knossos
CRETE
Mallia
RHODES
Palaikastro
Hagia Triada
Phaistos
Kato Zakro
Leptis Magna
MEDITERRANEAN SEA
NORTH AFRICA
Alexandr
LIBYA
THE FAIYU
LOWE
EGYP
PEPARETHUS
MT. PARNASSUS
PHOCIS
EUBOEA
Hosios Loukas
Delphi
BOEOTIA
Eretria
Plataea
ATTICA
Marathon
Daphnè
Eleusis
ARCADIA
Corinth
Athens
Mycenae
SALAMIS
Anavysos
Olympia
AEGINA
Epidaurus
DELOS
CYCLADES
NAXOS
Sparta
Vaphio
LACONIA
SIPHNOS
0 MILES 50
0 KM 50

THE ANCIENT WORLD
SITES AND CITIES
KOSTROMSKAYA
Moscow
RUSSIA
Ural R.
Don R.
Dnieper R.
Volga R.
ARAL SEA
CASPIAN SEA
BLACK SEA
ANATOLIA
Halys R.
Bogazköy
BACTRIA
TURKEY
Teheran
Dur Sharrukin
Catal Hüyük
Nineveh
Nimrud
PERSIA
ASIA MINOR
Issus
ASSYRIA
MESOPOTAMIA
Antioch
Assur
IRAN
Tigris R.
LURISTAN
Larissa
Dura-Europos
Tell Asmar
SYRIA
Baghdad
AKKAD
Ctesiphon
Susa
PHOENICIA
Baalbek
BABYLONIA
Babylon
ELAM
Lagash
Euphrates R.
Uruk
SUMER
Persepolis
Ur
Jerusalem
Jericho
Bethlehem
Naksh-i-Rustam
JORDAN
PALESTINE
Cairo
Saqqara
ARABIA
PERSIAN GULF
N
Beni Hasan
Tell el 'Amarna
W
E
Nile R.
S
Thebes
Luxor
Assuan
RED SEA
0
MILES
300
0
KM
300

MAGIC AND RITUAL: PREHISTORIC AND ETHNOGRAPHIC ART

THE OLD STONE AGE

When did human beings start creating works of art? What prompted them to do so? What did these earliest works of art look like? Every history of art must begin with these questions—and with the admission that we cannot answer them. Our earliest ancestors began to walk the earth on two feet about four million years ago, but how they were using their hands remains unknown to us. More than two million years later we meet the earliest evidence of toolmaking. Humans must have been *using* tools all along. After all, even apes will pick up a stick to knock down a banana or a stone to throw at an enemy. The *making* of tools is a more complex matter. It demands first of all the ability to think of sticks or stones as "fruit knockers" or "bone crackers," not only when they are needed for such purposes but at other times as well.

Once people were able to do that, they gradually discovered that some sticks or stones had a handier shape than others, and they put them aside for future use. They selected and "appointed" certain sticks or stones as tools because they had begun to connect *form* and *function*. The sticks, of course, have not survived, but a few of the stones have. They are large pebbles or chunks of rock that show the marks of repeated use for the same operation—whatever that may have been. The next step was to try chipping away at these tools-by-appointment so as to improve their shape. This is the first craft of which we have evidence, and with it we enter a phase of human development known as the Paleolithic, or Old Stone Age.

Cave Art

During the last stage of the Paleolithic, which began about 35,000 years ago, we meet the earliest works of art known to us. But these already show an assurance and refinement far removed from any humble beginnings. Unless we are to believe that they came into being in a single, sudden burst, we must assume that they were preceded by thousands of years of slow growth about which we know nothing at all. At that time the last Ice Age was drawing to a close in Europe (there had been at least three previous ones, alternating with periods of subtropical warmth, at intervals of about 25,000 years), and the climate between the Alps and Scandinavia resembled that of present-day Siberia or Alaska. Huge herds of reindeer and other large herbivores roamed the plains and valleys, preyed upon by the ferocious ancestors of today's lions and tigers—and by our own ancestors. These people liked to live in caves or in the shelter of overhanging rocks wherever they could find them. Many such sites have been discovered, mostly in Spain and in southwestern France. On the basis of differences among the tools and other remains found there, scholars have divided the "cave dwellers" into several groups, each named after a characteristic site, and of these it is especially the so-called Aurignacians and Magdalenians who stand out for the gifted artists they produced and for the important role art must have played in their lives.

The most striking works of Paleolithic art are the images of animals incised, painted, or sculpted on the rock surfaces of caves, such as

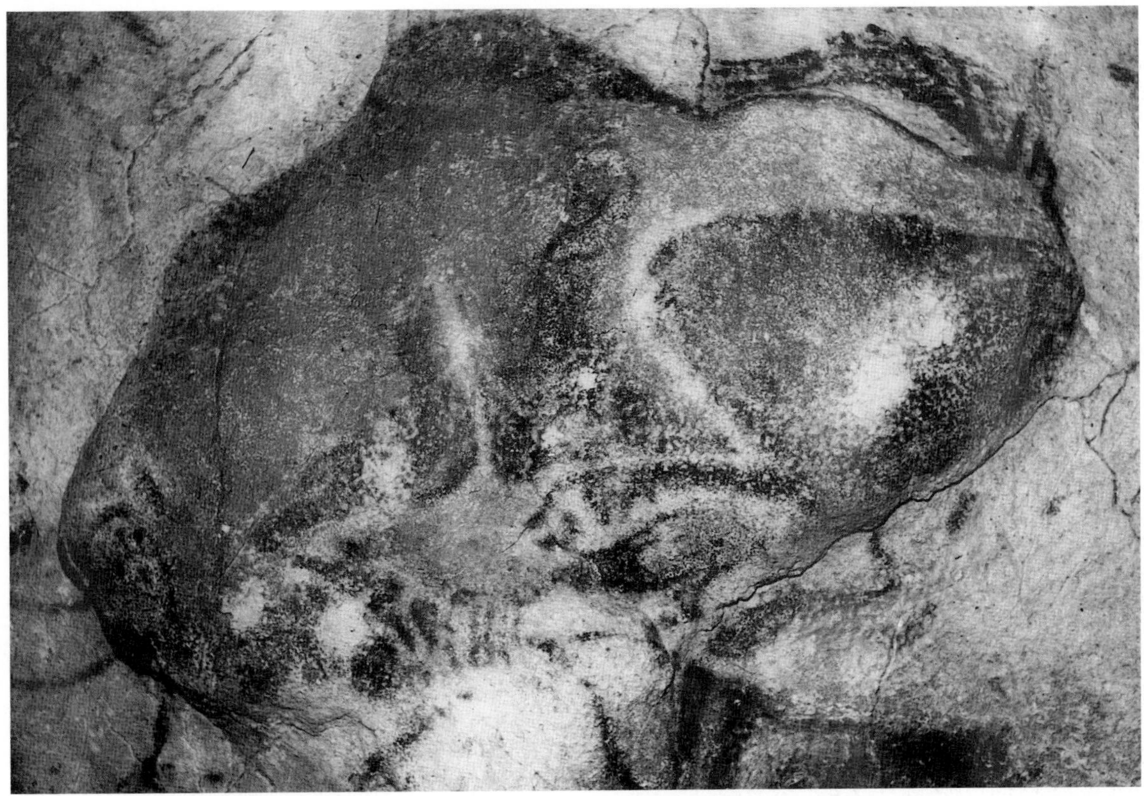

18. *Wounded Bison.* Cave painting. c. 15,000–10,000 B.C. Altamira, Spain

the wonderful *Wounded Bison* from the cave at Altamira in northern Spain (fig. 18). The dying animal has collapsed on the ground, its legs no longer able to carry the weight of the body, its head lowered in defense. What a vivid, lifelike picture it is! We are amazed not only by the keen observation, the assured, vigorous outlines, and the subtly controlled shading that lends bulk and roundness to the forms, but even more perhaps by the power and dignity of this creature in its final agony.

How did this extraordinary art develop? What purpose did it serve? And how did it happen to survive intact over so many thousands of years? The last question can be answered easily enough—for the pictures never occur near the mouth of a cave, where they would be open to easy view (and destruction), but only in the darkest recesses, as far from the entrance as possible. Some can be reached only by crawling on hands and knees, and the path is so intricate that one would soon be lost without an expert guide. The cave at Lascaux in southern France, characteristically enough, was discovered purely by chance in 1940 by some neighborhood boys whose dog fell into a hole that led to the underground chamber. Hidden away as they are in the bowels of the earth to protect them from the casual intruder, these images must have served a purpose far more serious than mere decoration. There can be little doubt, in fact, that they were produced as part of a magic ritual, perhaps to ensure a successful hunt. We gather this not only from their secret location and from the lines meant to represent spears or darts that are sometimes found pointing at the animals, but also from the peculiar, disorderly way the images are superimposed on one another, as in our example (fig. 19). Apparently, people of the Old Stone Age made no clear distinction between image and reality. By making a picture of an animal they meant to bring the animal itself within their grasp, and in "killing" the image they thought they had killed the animal's vital spirit. Hence

19. Cave paintings. 15,000–10,000 B.C. Lascaux (Dordogne), France

a "dead" image lost its potency after the killing ritual had been performed, and could be disregarded when the spell had to be renewed. The magic worked, too, we may be sure. Hunters whose courage was thus fortified were bound to be more successful when slaying these formidable beasts with their primitive weapons. Nor has the emotional basis of this kind of magic been lost even today. We carry snapshots of those we love in our wallets because this gives us a sense of their presence, and people have been known to tear up the photograph of someone they have come to hate.

Even so, there remains a good deal that puzzles us about the cave paintings. Why did they have to be in such inaccessible places? Couldn't the hunting magic they serve have been performed just as well out in the open? And why are they so marvelously lifelike? Would not the magic have been equally effective if the "killing" had been practiced upon less realistic images? We know of countless later instances of magic that require only the crudest and most schematic kind of representation, such as two crossed sticks for a human figure.

Perhaps we should regard the Magdalenian cave pictures as the final phase of a development that began as simple killing magic at a time when big game was plentiful but shifted its meaning when the animals became scarce (there is evidence that the big herds withdrew northward as the climate of Central Europe grew warmer). At Altamira and Lascaux, then, the main purpose may no longer have been to "kill" but to "make" animals—to increase their supply, perhaps through seasonal rituals repeated year after year. In some of the weapons associated with the animals, images of plants have recently been recognized. Could it be that the Magdalenians practiced their fertility magic in the bowels of the earth because they thought of the earth itself as a living thing from whose womb all other life springs? Such a notion is familiar to us from the cults of earth deities of later times; it is not impossible that its origin goes back to the Old Stone Age. If it does, this would help explain the admirable realism of the cave paintings, for an artist who believes that he is actually "creating" an animal is more likely to strive for this quality than one who merely sets up an image for the kill.

Some of the cave pictures may even provide a clue to the origin of this tradition of fertility magic. In a good many instances, the shape of the animal seems to have been suggested by the natural formation of the rock, so that its body coincides with a bump or its contour follows a vein or crack as far as possible. We all know how our imagination sometimes makes us see all sorts of images in chance formations such as clouds or blots. A Stone Age hunter, his mind filled with thoughts of the big game on which he depended for survival, would have been even more likely to recognize such animals as he stared at the rock surfaces of his cave and to attribute deep significance to his discovery. Perhaps at first he merely reinforced the outlines of such images with a charred stick from the fire, so that others, too, could see what he had found. It is tempting to think that those who proved par-

20. *Venus of Willendorf*, from Austria. c. 25,000–20,000 B.C. Stone, height 4⅜" (11.1 cm). Naturhistorisches Museum, Vienna

ticularly good at finding such images were given a special status as artist-magicians and were relieved of the dangers of the real hunt so that they could perfect their image-hunting, until finally they learned how to make images with little or no help from chance formations, though they continued to welcome such aid.

Carved Objects

Apart from large-scale cave art, the people of the Upper Paleolithic also produced small, hand-sized drawings and carvings in bone, horn, or stone, skillfully cut by means of flint tools. Some of these carvings suggest that the objects may have originated with the recognition and elaboration of some chance resemblance. At an earlier stage, it seems, Stone Age people were content to collect pebbles (as well as less durable small specimens) in whose natural shape they saw something that rendered them "magic." Echoes of this approach can sometimes be felt in later, more fully worked pieces. Thus the so-called *Venus of Willendorf* (fig. 20), one of many such female fertility figurines, has a bulbous roundness of form that recalls an egg-shaped "sacred pebble"; her navel, the central point of the design, is a natural cavity in the stone.

THE NEW STONE AGE

The art of the Old Stone Age in Europe as we know it today marks the highest achievements of a way of life that began to decline soon after. Adapted almost perfectly to the special conditions of the receding Ice Age, it could not survive beyond then. What brought the Old Stone Age to a close has been termed the Neolithic Revolution. And a revolution it was indeed, although its course extended over several thousand years. It began in the Near East sometime about 8000 B.C., with the first successful attempts to domesticate animals and food grains—one of the truly epoch-making achievements of human history. People in Paleolithic societies had led the unsettled life of the hunter and food gatherer, reaping where nature sowed and thus at the mercy of forces that they could neither understand nor control. But now, having learned how to assure a food supply by their own efforts, men and women settled down in permanent village communities. A new discipline and order entered their lives as well. There is, then, a very basic difference between the New Stone Age, or Neolithic, and the Old, or Paleolithic, despite the fact that all still depended on stone as the material of their main tools and weapons. The new mode of life brought forth a number of important new crafts and inventions long before the earliest appearance of metals: pottery, weaving and spinning, and basic methods of architectural construction in wood, brick, and stone.

We know all this from the tangible remains of Neolithic settlements that have been uncovered by excavation. Unfortunately, these remains tell us very little, as a rule, of the spiritual condition of Neolithic culture. They include stone implements of ever greater

21. Stonehenge (aerial view). c. 2000 B.C. Diameter of circle 97′ (29.6 m). Salisbury Plain (Wiltshire), England

technical refinement and beauty of shape, and a seemingly infinite variety of clay vessels covered with abstract ornamental patterns, but hardly anything comparable to the painting and sculpture of the Paleolithic. Yet the changeover from hunting to husbandry must have been accompanied by profound changes in the people's view of themselves and the world, and it seems impossible to believe that these did not find expression in art. There may be a vast chapter in the development of art here that is lost to us simply because Neolithic artists worked in wood or other impermanent materials. Or perhaps excavations in the future will help fill the gap.

One exception to this general rule is the great stone circle at Stonehenge in southern England (figs. 21, 22), the best preserved of several such megalithic, or large stone, monuments. Its purpose was religious. Apparently the sustained effort required to build Stonehenge could be compelled only by faith—faith that almost literally demanded the moving of mountains. The entire structure is oriented toward the exact point where the sun rises on the longest day of the year, and therefore it must have served a sun-worshiping ritual. Even today, Stonehenge has an awe-inspiring, superhuman quality, as if it were the work of a forgotten race of giants.

Whether a monument such as this should be termed architecture is a matter of definition. Nowadays, we tend to think of architecture in terms of enclosed interiors. Yet we also have landscape architects, the designers of gardens, parks, and playgrounds; nor would we want to deny the status of architecture to open-air theaters or sports stadiums. Perhaps we ought to consult the ancient Greeks, who coined the term. To them, "archi-tecture" meant something higher than ordinary "tecture" (that is, construction or building)—much as an archbishop ranks above a bishop or an archfiend above a fiend—a structure distinguished from the merely practical, everyday kind by its scale,

22. Stonehenge

order, permanence, or solemnity of purpose. A Greek, therefore, would certainly have acknowledged Stonehenge as architecture. And we, too, shall have no difficulty in doing so once we understand that it is not necessary to *enclose* space in order to define or articulate it. If architecture is "the art of shaping space to human needs and aspirations," then Stonehenge more than meets the test.

ETHNOGRAPHIC ART

There are few human groups for whom the Old Stone Age lasted until modern times. Modern survivors of the Neolithic are far easier to find. They include all the so-called primitive societies of tropical Africa, the islands of the South Pacific, and the Americas. "Primitive" is a somewhat unfortunate word: it suggests—quite wrongly—that these societies represent the original human condition, and has thus come to be burdened with many conflicting emotional overtones. The term "ethnographic" will serve us better. It stands for a way of life that has passed through the Neolithic Revolution but shows no signs of evolving in the direction of the "historic" civilizations. Ethnographic societies perpetuate themselves by custom and tradition; hence, the entire pattern of their life is static rather than dynamic.

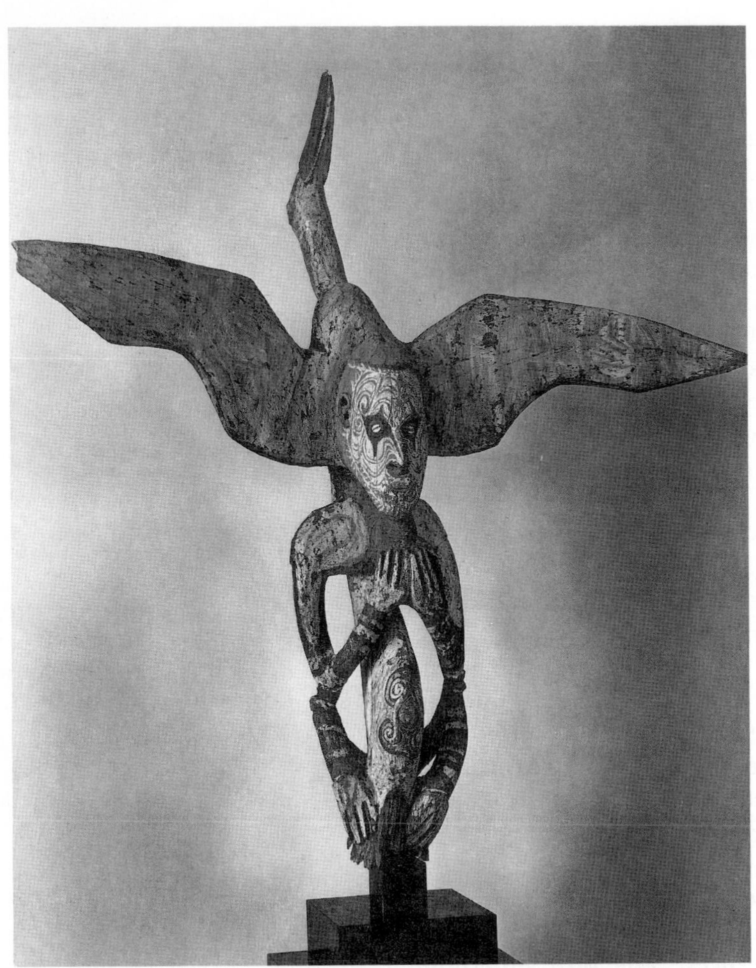

23. *Male Figure Surmounted by a Bird,* from the Sepik River, New Guinea. 19th–20th century. Wood, height 48″ (121.9 cm). Washington University Gallery of Art, St. Louis. University Purchase, Kende Sale Fund, 1945

Ethnographic art, despite its limitless variety, shares one dominant trait: the imaginative reshaping, rather than the careful observation, of the forms of nature. Its concern is not the visible world but the invisible, disquieting world of spirits. Such religious beliefs have been termed animism. To ethnographic peoples, a spirit exists in every living thing. An animist will feel that he must appease the spirit of a tree before he cuts it down, but the spirit of any particular tree is also part of a collective "tree spirit" which in turn merges into a general "life spirit." Other spirits dwell in the earth, in rivers and lakes, in the rain, in the sun and moon; still others demand to be appeased in order to promote fertility or cure disease.

24. Mask, from the Bamenda area, Cameroon. 19th–20th century. Wood, height 26½" (67.3 cm). Rietberg Museum, Zurich. E.v.d. Heydt Collection

Guardian Figures

Ancestor rituals are the most persistent feature of early religions and the strongest cohesive force in ethnographic societies. As a result of the animism that underlies their belief system, ethnographic peoples prefer to think of the spirits of their ancestors collectively, rather than in terms of separate individuals. Their dwelling places usually take human forms, known as guardian figures. Tribal secrets are not readily betrayed, hence the available accounts do not tell us very much about the exact significance of guardian figures. But since all spirits had to be appeased, it was the task of art to provide suitable dwelling places for them and thus to "trap" them. Such a trap is the splendid ancestor figure from New Guinea (fig. 23). The entire design is concentrated on the head, with its intensely staring shell-eyes, while the body has been reduced to a mere support. It seems reasonable to explain its extreme remoteness from nature—and the abstract tendency of ethnographic art generally—as an effort to convey the "otherness" of the spirit world, to divorce it as strictly as the artist's imagination would allow from the world of everyday appearances. The bird emerging from behind the head represents the ancestor's spirit or life force. Its soaring movement, contrasted with the rigidity of the human fig-

25. Mask, from the Gazelle Peninsula, New Britain. 19th–20th century. Bark cloth, height 18" (45.7 cm). Museo Nacional de Antropología, Mexico City

ure, forms a dramatic image—and a strangely familiar one, for our own tradition, too, includes the "soul bird," from the dove of the Holy Spirit to the albatross of the Ancient Mariner, so that we find ourselves responding to a work of art that at first glance might seem both puzzling and alien.

Masks

In dealing with the spirit world, people were not content to perform rituals or to present offerings before their spirit traps. They needed to act out their relations with the spirit world through dances and similar dramatic ceremonials in which they could themselves temporarily assume the role of the spirit trap by disguising themselves with elaborate masks and costumes. In these early societies, the costumes, always with a mask as the central feature, became correspondingly varied and elaborate. Nor has the fascination of the mask died out to this day. We still feel the thrill of a real change of identity when we wear one at Halloween or carnival time.

Masks form by far the richest chapter in ethnographic art. The proliferation of shapes, materials, and functions is almost limitless. Even the manner of wearing them varies surprisingly. There are also masks that are not made to be worn at all but to be displayed independently as images complete in themselves. Their meaning, more often than not, is impossible to ascertain. The ceremonies they served usually had elements of secrecy that were jealously guarded from the uninitiated, especially if the performers themselves formed a secret society. This emphasis on the mysterious and spectacular not only heightened the dramatic impact of the ritual, but also permitted the makers of masks to strive for imaginative new effects, so that masks in general are less subject to traditional restrictions than other kinds of ethnographic sculpture.

The few samples reproduced here can convey no more than the faintest suggestion of the wealth of the available material. African masks, such as the one in figure 24, are distinguished for symmetry of design and the precision and sharpness of their carving. In our example, the features of the human face have not been rearranged but restructured, so to speak, with the tremendous eyebrows rising above the rest like a protective canopy. The solidity of these shapes becomes strikingly evident as we turn to the fluid, ghostly features of the mask from the Gazelle Peninsula on the island of New Britain in the South Pacific made of bark cloth over a bamboo frame (fig. 25). It is meant to represent an animal spirit, said to be a crocodile, and was worn in nocturnal ceremonies by dancers carrying snakes. Even stranger is the Eskimo mask from southwest Alaska (fig. 26), with its nonsymmetrical design of seemingly unrelated elements, especially the dangling "leaves" attached to curved "branches." The single eye and the mouth full of teeth are the only recognizable details to the outsider; yet to those who know how to "read" this assembly of shapes it is the condensed representation of a tribal myth about a swan that drives white whales to the hunters.

26. Mask. Eskimo, from southwest Alaska. Early 20th century. Wood, height 22″ (55.9 cm). Museum of the American Indian, Heye Foundation, New York

27. Sand painting ritual for a sick child. Navajo. Arizona

Painting

Compared to sculpture, painting plays a subordinate role in ethnographic societies. Though the technique was widely known, its use was restricted in most areas to the coloring of wood carvings or of the human body, sometimes with intricate ornamental designs. As an independent art, however, painting could establish itself only when exceptional conditions provided suitable surfaces. Thus, the Indian tribes inhabiting the arid Southwest of the United States developed the unique art of sand painting (fig. 27). The technique, which demands considerable skill, consists of pouring powdered rock or earth of various colors on a flat bed of sand. Despite (or perhaps because of) the fact that they are impermanent and must be made fresh for each occasion that demands them, the designs are rigidly fixed by tradition. The various compositions are rather like recipes, prescribed by the medicine man and "filled" under his supervision by the painter, for the main use of sand paintings is in ceremonies of healing. That these ceremonies are sessions of great emotional intensity on the part of both doctor and patient is well attested by our illustration. Such a close union—or even, at times, identity—of priest, healer, and artist may be difficult to understand in modern Western terms. But for people trying to bend nature to their needs by magic and ritual, the functions appear as different aspects of a single process. And the success or failure of this process is to them virtually a matter of life and death.

ART FOR THE DEAD: EGYPT

FROM PREHISTORIC TO HISTORIC

The road from hunting to husbandry is long and arduous. The problems and pressures faced by historic societies are very different from those that confronted peoples in the Paleolithic or Neolithic eras. Prehistory was a phase of evolution during which humans as a species learned how to maintain themselves against a hostile environment; their achievements were responses to threats of physical extinction. With the domestication of animals and edible plants, people had won a decisive victory in this battle, assuring our survival on this planet. But the Neolithic Revolution placed us on a level at which we might well have remained indefinitely: the forces of nature—at least during that geological era—would never again challenge men and women as they had Paleolithic peoples. And in many parts of the globe, as we saw in the previous chapter, people were content to stay on a "Neolithic plateau."

In a few places, however, the Neolithic balance between humans and nature was upset by a new threat, posed not by nature but by people themselves, so that they began to build fortifications. What was the source of the human conflict that made them necessary? Competition for grazing land among tribes of herdsmen or for arable soil among farming communities? The basic cause, we suspect, was that the Neolithic Revolution had been too successful, permitting the local population to grow beyond the available food supply. This situation might have been resolved in a number of ways. Constant tribal warfare could have reduced the population; or the people could have united in larger and more disciplined social units for the sake of ambitious group efforts that no loosely organized tribal society would have been able to achieve. Such conflicts generated enough pressure to produce a new kind of society, very much more complex and efficient than had ever existed before.

First in Egypt and Mesopotamia, somewhat later in neighboring areas, and in the Indus valley and along the Yellow River in China, people were to live in a more dynamic world, where their capacity to survive was challenged not by the forces of nature but by human forces—by tensions and conflicts arising either within society or as the result of competition between societies. These efforts to cope with human environment have proved a far greater challenge than the earlier struggle with nature.

THE OLD KINGDOM

Egyptian civilization has long been regarded as the most rigid and conservative ever. Plato said that Egyptian art had not changed in 10,000 years. Perhaps "enduring" and "continuous" are better terms for it, although at first glance all Egyptian art between 3000 and 500 B.C. does tend to have a certain sameness. There is a kernel of truth in this: the basic pattern of Egyptian institutions, beliefs, and artistic ideas was formed during the first few centuries of that vast span of years and kept reasserting itself until the very end. We shall see, however, that as time went on this basic pattern went through ever more severe crises that challenged its ability to survive. Had it been as inflexible as supposed, it would have succumbed long before it finally did. Egyptian art alternates between conservatism and innovation but is never static. Some of its great achievements had a decisive influence on Greek and Roman art, and thus we can still feel ourselves linked to the Egypt of 5,000 years ago by a continuous, living tradition.

Dynasties

The history of Egypt is divided into dynasties of rulers, in accordance with ancient Egyptian practice, beginning with the First Dynasty, shortly after 3000 B.C. (the dates of the earliest rulers are difficult to translate exactly into our calendar). The transition from prehistory to the First Dynasty is known as the predynastic period. The Old Kingdom forms the first major division after that, ending about 2155 B.C. with the overthrow of the Sixth Dynasty. This method of counting historic time conveys at once the strong Egyptian sense of continuity and the overwhelming importance of the pharaoh (king), who was not only the supreme ruler but also a god. The pharaoh transcended all other people, for his kingship was not a duty or privilege derived from a superhuman source, but was absolute, divine. This belief remained the key feature of Egyptian civilization and largely determined the character of Egyptian art. We do not know exactly the steps by which the early pharaohs established their claim to divinity, but we know their historic achievements: molding the Nile valley from the first cataract at Assuan to the Delta into a single, effective state, and increasing its fertility by regulating the river waters through dams and canals.

Tombs and Religion

Of these vast public works nothing remains today, and very little has survived of ancient Egyptian palaces and cities. Our knowledge of Egyptian civilization rests almost entirely on the tombs and their contents. This is no accident, since the tombs were built to last forever; yet we must not make the mistake of concluding that the Egyptians viewed life on this earth mainly as a road to the grave. Their preoccupation with the cult of the dead is a link with the Neolithic past, but the meaning they gave it was quite new and different: the dark fear of the spirits of the dead that dominates primitive ancestor cults seems entirely absent. Instead, the Egyptian attitude was that each person must provide for his or her own happy afterlife. The ancient Egyptians would equip their tombs as a kind of shadowy replica of their daily environment for their spirits (*ka*) to enjoy, and would make sure that the *ka* had a body to dwell in (the individual's own mummified corpse or, if that should be destroyed, a statue of the person).

There is a curious blurring of the sharp line between life and death here, and perhaps that was the essential impulse behind these mock households. A man who knew that after death his *ka* would enjoy the same pleasures he did, and who had provided these pleasures in advance by his own efforts, could look forward to an active and happy life without being haunted by fear of the great unknown. In a sense, then, the Egyptian tomb was a kind of life insurance, an investment in peace of mind. Such, at least, is the impression one gains of Old Kingdom tombs. Later on, the serenity of this concept of death was disturbed by a tendency to subdivide the spirit or soul into two or more separate identities, and by the introduction of a sort of judgment, a weighing of souls. Only then do we also find expressions of the fear of death.

Sculpture

Palette of King Narmer. At the threshold of Egyptian history stands a work of art that is also a historic document: a carved palette (fig. 28) celebrating the victory of Narmer, king of Upper Egypt, over Lower Egypt, the oldest known image of a historic personage identified by name. It already shows most of the features characteristic of Egyptian art. But before we concern ourselves with these, let us first "read" the scene. The fact that we are able to do so is another indication that we

28. *Palette of King Narmer,* from Hierakonpolis. c. 3000 B.C. Slate, height 25″ (63.5 cm). Egyptian Museum, Cairo

have left prehistoric art behind. For the meaning of these reliefs is made clear and explicit not only by means of hieroglyphic labels, but also through the use of a broad range of visual symbols conveying precise messages to the beholder and—most important of all—through the disciplined, rational orderliness of the design.

In our view of the palette Narmer has seized a fallen enemy by the hair and is about to slay him with his mace. Two more defeated enemies are placed in the bottom compartment (the small rectangular shape next to the man on the left stands for a fortified town or citadel). Facing the king in the upper right we see a complex bit of picture writing: a falcon standing above a clump of papyrus plants holds a tether attached to a human head that "grows" from the same soil as the plants. This composite image actually repeats the main scene on a symbolic level: the head and papyrus plant stand for Lower Egypt, while the victorious falcon is Horus, the local god of Upper Egypt. The parallel is plain. Horus and Narmer are the same; a god triumphs over human foes. Hence, Narmer's gesture must not be taken as representing a real fight. The enemy is helpless from the very start, and the slaying is a ritual rather than a physical effort. We gather this from the fact that Narmer has taken off his sandals (the court official behind him carries them in his right hand), an indication that he is standing on holy ground. (The same notion recurs in the Old Testament, apparently as the result of Egyptian influence, when the Lord commands Moses to remove his shoes before He appears to him in the burning bush.)

The inner logic of the Narmer palette's style is readily apparent. The artist strives for clarity, not illusion, and therefore picks the most telling view in each case. But he imposes a strict rule on himself: when he changes his angle of vision, he must do so by ninety degrees, as if he were sighting along the edges of a cube. As a consequence, he acknowledges only two possible views: full face and strict profile (on the other side of the palette, he acknowledges a third, vertically from above). Any intermediate position embarrasses him (note the oddly rubberlike figures of the fallen enemies). Moreover, he is faced with the fact that the standing human figure, unlike that of an animal, does not have a single main profile but two competing profiles, so that, for the sake of clarity, he must combine these views. His method of doing this—a method that was to survive unchanged for 2,500 years—is clearly shown in the large figure of Narmer in our illustration: eye and shoulders in frontal view, head and legs in profile. Apparently this formula was worked out so as to show the pharaoh (and all persons of significance who move in the aura of his divinity) in the most complete way possible. And since the scenes depict solemn and, as it were, timeless rituals, our artist did not have to concern himself with the fact that this method of representing the human body made almost any kind of movement or action practically impossible. In fact, the frozen quality of the image would seem especially suited to the divine nature of the pharaoh. Ordinary mortals *act*, he simply *is*.

The Egyptian style of representing the human figure, then, seems to have been created specifically for the purpose of conveying in visual form the majesty of the divine king. It must have originated among the artists working for the royal court. And it never lost its ceremonial, sacred flavor, even when, in later times, it had to serve other purposes as well.

Tomb of Ti. This style was soon adopted for nonroyal tombs in the Old Kingdom. The hippopotamus hunt in figure 29, from the offering chambers of the architectural overseer Ti at Saqqara, is of special interest to us because of its landscape setting. A papyrus thicket is represented in the background of the relief. The stems of the plants make a regular, rippling pattern that erupts in the top zone into an agitated scene of nesting birds menaced by small predators. The water in the bottom zone, marked by a zigzag pattern, is equally crowded with struggling hippopotamuses and fish. All these, as well as the hunters in the first boat, are acutely observed and full of action. Only Ti himself, standing in the second boat, is immobile, as if he belonged to a different world. His pose is that of the funerary portrait reliefs and statues (compare fig. 30), and he towers above the other men, since he is more important than they.

His size also lifts him out of the context of the hunt—he neither directs nor supervises it but simply observes. His passive role is characteristic of the representations of the deceased in all such scenes from the Old Kingdom. It seems to be a subtle way of conveying the fact that the body is dead but the spirit is alive and aware of the pleasures of this world, though the man can no longer participate in them directly. We should also note that these scenes of daily life do not represent the dead man's favorite pastimes. If they did, he would be looking back, and such nostalgia is quite alien to the spirit of Old Kingdom tombs. It has been shown, in fact, that these scenes form a seasonal cycle, a sort of perpetual calendar of recurrent human activities for the spirit of the deceased to watch year in and year out. For the artist, on the other hand, these scenes offered a welcome opportunity to widen his powers of observation, so that in details we often find astounding bits of realism.

29. *Ti Watching a Hippopotamus Hunt.* Painted limestone relief. c. 2400 B.C. Tomb of Ti, Saqqara

Portraits. The "cubic" approach to the human form can be observed most strikingly in Egyptian sculpture in the round, such as the splendid group of the pharaoh Mycerinus and his queen (fig. 30). The artist must have started out by drawing the front and side views on the faces of a rectangular block and then worked inward until these views met. Only in this way could he have achieved figures of such overpowering three-dimensional firmness and immobility. What magnificent vessels for the *ka* to inhabit! Both have the left foot placed forward, yet there is no hint of a forward movement. The pair also affords an interesting comparison of male and female beauty as interpreted by a fine sculptor, who knew not only how to contrast the structure of the two bodies but also how to emphasize the soft, swelling form of the queen through a thin, close-fitting gown. The group must have originally shared with other statues a vivid coloring, which lent them a strikingly lifelike appearance but which has survived completely intact only in a few instances. According to the standard convention of Egyptian art, the king would have had a darker body color than the queen. Their eyes, too, would have been painted, and perhaps inlaid with shining quartz, to make them look as alive as possible and to emphasize the portrait character of the faces.

30. *Mycerinus and His Queen,* from Giza. 2599–2571 B.C. Slate, height 54½" (138.4 cm). Courtesy of Museum of Fine Arts, Boston

Architecture

When we speak of the Egyptians' attitude toward death and afterlife as expressed in their tombs, we must be careful to make it clear that we do not mean the attitude of the average Egyptian but only that of the small aristocratic caste clustered around the royal court. The tombs of the members of this class of high officials (who were often relatives of the royal family) are usually found near the pharaohs' tombs, and their shape and contents reflect, or are related to, the funerary monuments of the divine kings. We still have much to learn about the origin and significance of Egyptian tombs, but the concept of afterlife we find in the so-called private tombs did not apply to ordinary mortals, only to the privileged few because of their association with the immortal pharaohs. The standard form of these tombs was the mastaba, a squarish mound faced with brick or stone, above the burial chamber, which was deep underground and linked to the mound by a shaft. Inside the mastaba is a chapel for offerings to the *ka* and a secret cubicle for the statue of the deceased.

Pyramids. Royal mastabas grew to conspicuous size and soon developed into step pyramids. The earliest is probably that of King Zoser (fig. 31), a step pyramid suggestive of a stack of mastabas as against the smooth-sided later examples at Giza. Pyramids were not isolated structures in the middle of the desert, but rather were part of vast funerary districts, with temples and other buildings that were the scene of great religious celebrations during the pharaoh's lifetime as well as after. The funerary district around the Step Pyramid of King Zoser is the most elaborate of these: enough of its architecture has survived to make us understand why its creator, Imhotep, was deified in later Egyptian tradition. He is the first artist whose name has been recorded in history, and deservedly so, since his achievement is most impressive even today.

31. Imhotep. Step Pyramid of King Zoser, Saqqara. 3rd Dynasty, c. 2600 B.C.

Columns. Egyptian architecture had begun with structures made of mud bricks, wood, reeds, and other light materials. Imhotep used cut-stone masonry, but his repertory of architectural forms still reflected shapes or devices developed for less enduring materials. Thus we find columns of several kinds—always "engaged" rather than free-standing—which echo the bundles of reeds or the wooden supports that used to be set into mud-brick walls in order to strengthen them. But the very fact that these members no longer had their original functional purpose made it possible for Imhotep and his fellow architects to redesign them so as to make them serve a new, *expressive* purpose. The notion that architectural forms can express anything may seem difficult to grasp at first. Today we tend to assume that unless these forms have a clear-cut structural service to perform (such as supporting or enclosing), they are mere surface decoration. But let us look at the slender, tapering, fluted columns in figure 31, or the papyrus-shaped half-columns in figure 32: these do not simply decorate the walls to which they are attached, but interpret them and give them life. Their proportions, the feeling of strength or resilience they convey, their spacing, the degree to which they project, all share in this task.

32. Papyrus half-columns, North Palace, Funerary District of King Zoser, Saqqara

Giza. The development of the pyramid reaches its climax during the Fourth Dynasty in the famous triad of great pyramids at Giza (fig. 33), all of the familiar, smooth-sided shape. They originally had an outer casing of

33. The Pyramids of Mycerinus, c. 2470 B.C.; Chefren, c. 2500 B.C.; and Cheops, c. 2530 B.C., Giza

carefully dressed stone, which has disappeared except near the top of the Pyramid of Chefren. Clustered about the three great pyramids are several smaller ones and a large number of mastabas for members of the royal family and high officials, but the unified funerary district of Zoser has given way to a simpler arrangement. Adjoining each of the great pyramids to the east is a funerary temple, from which a processional causeway leads to a second temple at a lower level, in the Nile valley, at a distance of about a third of a mile.

Next to the valley temple of the Pyramid of Chefren stands the Great Sphinx carved from the live rock (fig. 34), perhaps an even more impressive embodiment of divine kingship than the pyramids themselves. The royal head rising from the body of a lion towers to a height of sixty-five feet and once bore, in all probability, the features of Chefren (damage inflicted upon it during Islamic times has obscured the details of the face). Its awesome majesty is such that a thousand years later it could be regarded as an image of the sun god.

Enterprises of this huge scale mark the high point of pharaonic power. After the end of the Fourth Dynasty (less than two centuries after Zoser) they were never attempted again, although pyramids on a much more modest scale continued to be built. The world has always marveled at the sheer size of the great pyramids as well as at the technical accomplishment they represent; but they have also come to be regarded as symbols of slave labor—thousands of men forced by cruel masters to serve the aggrandizement of absolute rulers. Such a picture may well be unjust: certain records have been preserved indicating that the labor was paid for, so that we are probably nearer the truth if we regard these monuments as vast public works providing economic security for a good part of the population.

34. The Great Sphinx, Giza. c. 2500 B.C.
Height 65′ (19.8 m)

THE MIDDLE KINGDOM

After the collapse of centralized pharaonic power at the end of the Sixth Dynasty, Egypt entered a period of political disturbances and ill fortune that was to last almost seven hundred years. During most of this time, effective authority lay in the hands of local or regional overlords, who revived the old rivalry of North and South. Many dynasties followed one another in rapid succession. Only two, the Eleventh and Twelfth, are worthy of note. These constitute the Middle Kingdom (2134–1785 B.C.), when a series of able rulers managed to reassert themselves against the provincial nobility. However, the spell of divine kingship, having once been broken, never regained its old effectiveness, and the authority of the Middle Kingdom pharaohs tended to be personal rather than institutional. Soon after the close of the Twelfth Dynasty, the weakened country was invaded by the Hyksos, a western Asiatic people of somewhat mysterious origin, who seized the Delta area and ruled it for 150 years until their expulsion by the princes of Thebes about 1570 B.C.

Tomb Decorations

A loosening of established rules also makes itself felt in Middle Kingdom painting and relief, where it leads to all sorts of interesting departures from convention. They occur most conspicuously in the decoration of the tombs of local princes at Beni Hasan, which have survived destruction better than most Middle Kingdom monuments because they are carved into the living rock. The mural *Feeding the Oryxes* (fig. 35) comes from one of these rock-cut tombs, that of Khnum-hotep. (As the emblem of the prince's domain, the oryx antelope seems to have been a sort of honored pet in his household.) According to the standards of Old Kingdom art, all the figures ought to share the same groundline, or the second oryx and its attendant ought to be placed above the first. Instead, the painter has introduced a secondary groundline only slightly higher than the primary one, and as a result the two groups are related in a way that closely approximates normal appearances. His interest in exploring spatial effects can also be seen in the awkward but quite bold foreshortening of the shoulders of the two attendants. If we cover up the hieroglyphic signs, which emphasize the flatness of the wall, we can "read" the forms in depth with surprising ease.

35. *Feeding the Oryxes*. c. 1920 B.C. Tomb of Khnum-hotep, Beni Hasan (modern copy)

THE NEW KINGDOM

The five hundred years following the expulsion of the Hyksos and comprising the Eighteenth, Nineteenth, and Twentieth dynasties represent a third Golden Age of Egypt. The country, once more united under strong and efficient kings, extended its frontiers far to the east, into Palestine and Syria (hence this period is also known as the Empire). New Kingdom art covers a vast range of styles and quality, from rigid conservatism to brilliant inventiveness, from oppressively massive ostentation to the most delicate refinement. As with the art of imperial Rome 1,500 years later, it is almost impossible to summarize in terms of a representative sampling. Different strands are interwoven into a fabric so complex that any choice of monuments is bound to seem arbitrary. All we can hope to accomplish is to convey some of the flavor of its variety.

Architecture

The divine kingship of the pharaohs was now asserted in a new way: by association with the god Amun, whose identity had been fused with that of the sun god Ra, and who became the supreme deity, ruling the lesser gods much as the pharaoh towered above the provincial nobility. During the climactic period of power and prosperity, between c. 1500 and the end of the reign of Ramesses III in 1162 B.C., vast architectural energies were devoted to building huge temples dedicated to Amun under royal sponsorship. The complex at Luxor (fig. 36) is characteristic of the general pattern of later Egyptian temples. The facade (at the far left in our illustration) consists of two massive walls with sloping sides that flank the entrance. This gateway, or pylon, leads to a series of courts and pillared halls, beyond which is the temple proper. The entire sequence was enclosed by high walls that shut off the outside world. Except for the pylon, such a structure is designed to be experienced from within. Ordinary worshipers were confined to the courts and could but marvel at the forest of columns that screened the dark recesses of the sanctuary. The columns had to be closely spaced, for they supported the stone lintels of the ceiling, and these had to be short to keep them from breaking under their own weight. Yet the architect has consciously exploited this condition by making the columns far heavier than they need be. As a result, the beholder feels almost crushed by their sheer mass. The effect is certainly impressive, but we need only compare the papyrus columns of the colonnade of Amenhotep III with their remote ancestors in Zoser's North Palace (see fig. 32) in order to realize how little of the genius of Imhotep has survived at Luxor.

Akhenaten; Tutankhamen

The growth of the Amun cult produced an unexpected threat to royal authority: the priests of Amun grew into a caste of such wealth and power that the pharaoh could maintain his position only with their consent. Amenhotep IV, the most remarkable figure of the Eighteenth Dynasty, tried to defeat them by proclaiming his faith in a single god, the sun disk Aten. He changed his name to Akhenaten, closed the Amun temples, and moved the capital to central Egypt, near the modern Tell el'Amarna. His attempt to place himself at the head of a new monotheistic faith, however, did not outlast his reign (1365–1347 B.C.), and under his successors

36. Court and pylon of Ramesses II, c. 1260 B.C., and colonnade and court of Amenhotep III, c. 1390 B.C., Temple of Amun-Mut-Khonsu, Luxor

ANCIENT NEAR EASTERN ART

SUMERIAN ART

It is an astonishing fact that human civilization should have emerged into the light of history in two separate places at just about the same time. Between 3500 and 3000 B.C., when Egypt was being united under pharaonic rule, another great civilization arose in Mesopotamia, the "land between the rivers." And for close to 3,000 years, the two rival centers retained their distinct characters, even though they had contact with each other from their earliest beginnings and their destinies were interwoven in many ways. The pressures that forced the inhabitants of both regions to abandon the pattern of Neolithic village life may well have been the same. But the valley of the Tigris and Euphrates rivers, unlike that of the Nile, is not a narrow fertile strip protected by deserts on either side. It resembles a wide, shallow trough with few natural defenses, crisscrossed by two great rivers and their tributaries, and easily encroached upon from any direction.

Thus the facts of geography tended to discourage the idea of uniting the entire area under a single head. As a consequence, the political history of ancient Mesopotamia has no underlying theme of the sort that divine kingship provides for Egypt. Local rivalries, foreign incursions, the sudden upsurge and equally sudden collapse of military power—these are its substance. Against such a disturbed background, the continuity of cultural and artistic traditions seems all the more remarkable. This common heritage is very largely the creation of the founders of Mesopotamian civilization, whom we call Sumerians after the region of Sumer, which they inhabited, near the confluence of the Tigris and Euphrates.

The origin of the Sumerians remains obscure. Their language is unrelated to any other known tongue. Sometime before 4000 B.C., they came to southern Mesopotamia from Persia, and there, within the next thousand years, they founded a number of city-states and developed their distinctive form of writing in cuneiform (wedge-shaped) characters on clay tablets. Unfortunately, the tangible remains of Sumerian civilization are extremely scanty compared to those of ancient Egypt. Building stone being unavailable in Mesopotamia, the Sumerians used mud brick and wood, so that almost nothing is left of their architecture except the foundations. Nor did they share the Egyptians' concern with the hereafter, although some richly endowed tombs—in the shape of vaulted chambers below ground—of the early dynastic period have been found in the city of Ur. Yet we have learned enough to form a general picture of the achievements of this vigorous, inventive, and disciplined people.

Each Sumerian city-state had its own local god, who was regarded as its "king" and owner. It also had a human ruler, the steward of the divine sovereign, who led the people in serving the deity. The local god, in return, was expected to plead the cause of his subjects among his fellow deities, who controlled the forces of nature, such as wind and weather, water, fertility, and the heavenly bodies. Nor was the idea of divine ownership treated as a mere pious fiction. The god was quite literally believed to own not only the territory of the city-state but also the labor power of the population and its products. All these were subject to his commands, transmitted to the people by his human steward. The result was an economic system that has been dubbed "theocratic socialism," a planned so-

ous turmoil. Central power was held by native rulers only from about 1760 to 1600 B.C. Hammurabi (c. 1792–1750 B.C.), the founder of the Babylonian dynasty, is by far the greatest figure of the age: combining military prowess with a deep respect for Sumerian tradition, he saw himself as "the favorite shepherd" of the sun god Shamash, whose mission was "to cause justice to prevail in the land." Under him and his successors, Babylon became the cultural center of Sumer. The city was to retain this prestige for more than a thousand years after its political power had waned.

Hammurabi's most memorable achievement is his law code, justly famous as the earliest uniform written body of laws and amazingly rational and humane in conception. He had it engraved on a tall diorite stele whose top shows Hammurabi confronting the sun god (fig. 45). The ruler's right arm is raised in a speaking gesture, as if he were reporting his work of codification to the divine king. The relief here is so high that the two figures almost give the impression of statues sliced in half. As a result, the sculptor has been able to render the eyes in the round, so that Hammurabi and Shamash gaze at each other with a force and directness unique in representations of this kind. They make us recall the statues from Tell Asmar, whose enormous eyes indicate an attempt to establish the same relationships between humans and god in an earlier phase of Sumerian civilization.

Assyria

The most copious archaeological finds date from the third major phase of Mesopotamian history, between c. 1000 and 500 B.C., which was dominated by the Assyrians. Under a series of able rulers, the Assyrian domain gradually expanded until it embraced not only Mesopotamia proper but the surrounding regions as well. At the height of its power, from about 1000 to 612 B.C., the Assyrian empire stretched from the Sinai peninsula to Armenia; even Lower Egypt was successfully invaded in 671 B.C.

The Assyrians, it has been said, were to the Sumerians what the Romans were to the Greeks. Assyrian civilization drew on the achievements of the south but reinterpreted them to fit its own distinctive character. Much of Assyrian art is devoted to glorifying the power of the king, either by detailed depictions of his military conquests or by showing him as the killer of lions. The latter were more in the nature of ceremonial contests than actual hunts: the animals were released from cages into a square formed by troops with shields for the king to kill. (Presumably, at a much earlier time, the hunting of lions in the field had been an important duty of Mesopotamian rulers as the "shepherds" of the communal flocks.) Here the Assyrian relief sculptor rises to his greatest heights. In figure 46, from the Palace of Ashurnasirpal II (died 860? B.C.) at Nimrud (Calah), the lion attacking the royal chariot from the rear is clearly the hero of the scene. Of magnificent strength and courage, the wounded animal seems to embody all the dramatic emotion of combat. The dying lion on the right is equally impressive in its agony. How differently the Egyptian artist had interpreted his scene of a hippopotamus hunt (see fig. 29)!

The Neo-Babylonians

The Assyrian empire came to an end in 612 B.C. when Nineveh fell before the combined onslaught of Medes and Scythians from the east. At that time the commander of the Assyrian army in southern Mesopotamia made himself king of Babylon. Under him and his successors the ancient city had a final brief flowering between 612 and 539 B.C., before it was conquered by the Persians. The best known of these Neo-Babylonian rulers was Nebuchadnezzar (died 562 B.C.), the builder of the Tower of Babel.

Whereas the Assyrians had used carved stone slabs, the Neo-Babylonians (who were farther removed from the sources of such slabs) substituted baked and glazed brick. This technique, too, had been developed in Assyria, but now it was used on a far larger scale, both for surface ornament and for ar-

45. Upper part of stele inscribed with the Law Code of Hammurabi. c. 1760 B.C. Diorite, height of stele c. 7′ (2.13 m); height of relief 28″ (71.1 cm). Musée du Louvre, Paris

46. *Ashurnasirpal II Killing Lions,* from the Palace of Ashurnasirpal II, Nimrud (Calah), Iraq. c. 850 B.C. Limestone, 3′3″ × 8′4″ (99.1 cm × 2.54 m). British Museum, London

47. Ishtar Gate (restored), from Babylon, Iraq. c. 575 B.C. Glazed brick. Vorderasiatisches Museum der Staatlichen Museen, Berlin

chitectural reliefs. Its distinctive effect is evident in the Ishtar Gate of Nebuchadnezzar's sacred precinct in Babylon, which has been rebuilt from the thousands of individual glazed bricks that covered its surface (fig. 47). The stately procession of bulls, dragons, and other animals of molded brick within a framework of vividly colored ornamental bands has a grace and gaiety that remind us again of that special genius of ancient Mesopotamian art for the portrayal of animals, which we noted in early dynastic times.

PERSIAN ART

Persia, the mountain-fringed high plateau to the east of Mesopotamia, takes its name from the people who occupied Babylon in 539 B.C. and became the heirs of what had been the Assyrian empire. Today the country is called Iran, its older and more suitable name, since the Persians, who put the area on the map of world history, were latecomers who had arrived on the scene only a few centuries before they began their epochal conquests. Inhabited continuously since prehistoric times, Iran seems always to have been a gateway for migratory tribes from the Asiatic steppes to the north as well as from India to the east. The new arrivals would settle down for a while, dominating or intermingling with the local population, until they in turn were forced to move on—to Mesopotamia, to Asia Minor, to southern Russia—by the next wave of migrants. These movements form a shadowy area of historical knowledge; all available information is vague and uncertain.

Animal Style

Since nomadic tribes leave no permanent monuments or written records, we can trace their wanderings only by a careful study of the objects they buried with their dead. Such objects, of wood, bone, or metal, represent a distinct kind of portable art which we call the nomad's gear: weapons, bridles for horses, buckles, fibulas and other articles of adornment, cups, bowls, and the like. They have been found over a vast area, from Siberia to Central Europe, from Iran to Scandinavia. They have in common not only a jewellike concentration of ornamental design but also a repertory of forms known as the "animal style." Its main feature, as the name suggests, is the decorative use of animal motifs in a rather abstract and imaginative manner. And one of the sources of the animal style appears to be ancient Iran. We find it in the small bronzes of the ninth to seventh centuries B.C. from the Luristan region, nomad's gear of a particularly resourceful kind. The pole-top ornament (fig. 48) consists of a symmetrical pair of rearing ibexes with vastly elongated necks and horns. Originally, we suspect, they were pursued by a pair of lions, but the bodies of the latter have been absorbed into those of the ibexes, whose necks have been pulled out to dragonlike slenderness.

48. Pole-top ornament, from Luristan. 9th–7th century B.C. Bronze, height 7½" (19.1 cm). British Museum, London

The Achaemenids

After conquering Babylon in 539 B.C., Cyrus (c. 600–529 B.C.) assumed the title King of Babylon along with the ambitions of the Assyrian rulers. The empire he founded continued to expand under his successors. Egypt as well as Asia Minor fell to them, and Greece escaped the same fate only by the narrowest margin. At its high tide, under Darius I (c. 550–486 B.C.) and Xerxes (519–465 B.C.), the Persian empire was far larger than its Egyptian and Assyrian predecessors together. Moreover, this vast domain endured for two centuries—it was toppled by Alexander the Great (356–323 B.C.) in 331 B.C.—and during most of its life it was ruled both efficiently and humanely. For an obscure tribe of nomads to have achieved all this is little short of miraculous. Within a single generation, the Persians not only mastered the complex machinery of imperial administration but also evolved a monumental art of remarkable originality to express the grandeur of their rule.

Despite their genius for adaptation, the Persians retained their own religious beliefs drawn from the prophecies of Zoroaster. This faith was based on the dualism of Good and Evil, embodied in Ahuramazda (Light) and Ahriman (Darkness). Since the cult of Ahuramazda centered on fire altars in the open air, the Persians had no religious architecture. Their palaces, on the other hand, were huge and impressive structures.

The most ambitious palace, at Persepolis, was begun by Darius I in 518 B.C. Assyrian traditions are the strongest single element

49. Audience Hall of Darius, Persepolis, Iran. c. 500 B.C.

throughout the vast complex. Yet they do not determine the character of the building, for they have been combined with influences from every corner of the empire in such a way that the result is a new, uniquely Persian style. Thus, at Persepolis columns are used on a grand scale. The Audience Hall of Darius, a room 250 feet square, had a wooden ceiling supported by thirty-six columns forty feet tall, a few of which are still standing (fig. 49). Such a massing of columns suggests Egyptian architecture (compare fig. 36), and Egyptian influence does indeed appear in the ornamental detail of the bases and capitals, but the slender, fluted shaft of the Persepolis columns is derived from the Ionian Greeks in Asia Minor, who are known to have furnished artists to the Persian court.

The double stairway leading up to the Audience Hall is decorated with long rows of solemnly marching figures in low relief. Their repetitive, ceremonial character emphasizes a subservience to the architectural setting that is typical of all Persian sculpture. Even here, however, we discover that the Assyrian-Babylonian heritage has been enriched by innovations stemming from the Ionian Greeks, who had created such figures in the course of the sixth century B.C., so that the style of the Persian carvings is a softer and more refined echo of the Mesopotamian tradition.

Persian art under the Achaemenids, then, is a remarkable synthesis of many diverse elements; yet it lacked a capacity for growth. The style formulated under Darius I about 500 B.C. continued without significant change until the end of the empire. The main reason for this failure, it seems, was the Persians' preoccupation with decorative effects regardless of scale, a carryover from their nomadic past that they never discarded.

AEGEAN ART

If we sail from the Nile Delta northwestward across the Mediterranean, our first glimpse of Europe will be the eastern tip of Crete. Beyond it, we find a scattered group of small islands, the Cyclades, and, a little farther on, the mainland of Greece, facing the coast of Asia Minor across the Aegean Sea. To archaeologists, "Aegean" is not merely a geographical term. They have adopted it to designate the civilizations that flourished in this area during the third and second millenniums B.C., before the development of Greek civilization proper. There are three of these, closely interrelated yet distinct from each other: that of the small islands north of Crete, known as Cycladic; that of Crete, called Minoan after the legendary Cretan King Minos; and that of the Greek mainland, called Helladic, which includes Mycenaean civilization. Each of them has in turn been divided into three phases, Early, Middle, and Late, which correspond, very roughly, to the Old, Middle, and New Kingdoms in Egypt. The most important remains, and the greatest artistic achievements, date from the latter part of the Middle phase and from the Late phase.

Aegean civilization was long known only from Homer's account of the Trojan War in the *Iliad* and from Greek legends centering on Crete. Since then, a great amount of fascinating material has been brought to light—far more than the literary sources would lead us to expect—but our knowledge of Aegean civilization even now is very much more limited than our knowledge of Egypt or the ancient Near East. We thus lack a great deal of the background knowledge necessary for an understanding of Aegean art. Its forms, although linked both to Egypt and the Near East on the one hand and to later Greek art on the other, are no mere transition between these two worlds. They have a haunting beauty of their own that belongs to neither. Among the many strange qualities of Aegean art, and perhaps the most puzzling, is its air of freshness and spontaneity, which makes us forget how little we know of its meaning.

CYCLADIC ART

The people who inhabited the Cycladic Islands between about 2600 and 1100 B.C. have left hardly any trace apart from their modest stone tombs. The things they buried with their dead are remarkable in one respect only: they include a large number of marble idols of a peculiarly impressive kind. Almost all of them represent a standing nude female figure with arms folded across the chest, presumably the mother and fertility goddess known to us from Asia Minor and the ancient Near East, whose ancestry reaches far back to the Old Stone Age. They also share a distinctive shape: the flat, wedge shape of the body, the strong, columnar neck, and the tilted oval shield of the face, featureless except for the long, ridgelike nose. Within this narrowly defined and stable type, however, the Cycladic idols show wide variations in scale (from a few inches to lifesize) as well as form.

The best of them, such as that in figure 50, have a disciplined refinement utterly beyond the range of Paleolithic or ethnographic art. The longer we study this piece, the more we come to realize that its qualities can only be defined as "elegance" and "sophistication," however incongruous such terms may seem in this context. What an extraordinary feeling for the organic structure of the body there is in the delicate curves of the outline, in the hints of convexity marking the knees and abdomen. Even if we discount its deceptively modern look, the figure seems a bold departure from anything we have seen before. There is no dearth of earlier fertility idols,

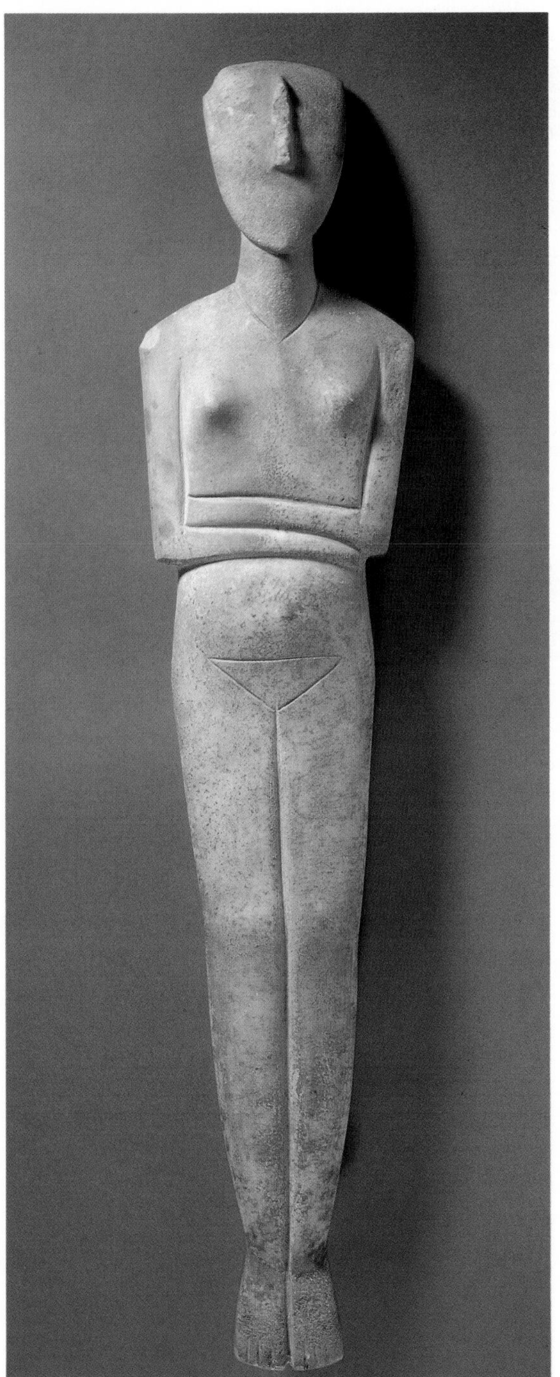

50. Idol, from Amorgos. 2500–1100 B.C. Marble, height 30″ (76.2 cm). The Ashmolean Museum, Oxford

but almost all of them betray their descent from the bulbous, heavy-bodied "Venus" figurines of the Old Stone Age (see fig. 20). In fact, the earliest Cycladic idols, too, were of that type. We do not know what made the Cycladic sculptors suppress the traditional fertility aspects of their female idols in favor of the lithe, "girlish" ideal of figure 50. Suffice it to say that the Cycladic sculptors of the second millennium B.C. produced the oldest lifesize figures of the female nude we know, and that for many hundreds of years they were the only ones to do so.

MINOAN ART

Minoan civilization is by far the richest, as well as the strangest, of the Aegean world. What sets it apart, not only from Egypt and the Near East but also from the Classical civilization of Greece, is a lack of continuity that appears to have deeper causes than archaeological accident. In surveying the main achievements of Minoan art, we cannot really speak of growth or development. They appear and disappear so abruptly that their fate must have been determined by external forces—volcanic eruptions or other sudden violent changes affecting the entire island—about which we know little or nothing. Yet the character of Minoan art, which is gay, even playful, and full of rhythmic motion, conveys no hint of such threats.

Architecture

The first of these unexpected shifts occurred about 2000 B.C. Until that time, during the eight centuries of the Early Minoan era, the Cretans had not advanced much beyond the Neolithic level of village life, even though they seem to have engaged in some overseas trade that brought them contact with Egypt. Then they created not only their own system of writing but an urban civilization as well, centering on several great palaces. At least three of them, at Knossos, Phaistos, and Mallia, were built in short order. Hardly anything is left today of this sudden spurt of large-scale building activity, for the three palaces were all destroyed at the same time, about 1700 B.C. After an interval of a hundred years, new and even larger structures began to appear on the

51. The Queen's Megaron, Palace of Minos, Knossos, Crete

same sites, only to suffer destruction, in their turn, about 1500 B.C.

These "new" palaces are our main source of information on Minoan architecture. The one at Knossos, called the Palace of Minos, was the most ambitious, covering a large territory and composed of so many rooms that it survived in Greek legend as the labyrinth of the Minotaur. It has been carefully excavated and partly restored. We cannot recapture the appearance of the building as a whole, but we can assume that the exterior probably did not look impressive compared with Assyrian or Persian palaces (see fig. 49). There was no striving for unified, monumental effect. The individual units are generally rather small and the ceilings low (fig. 51), so that even those parts of the structure that were several stories high could not have seemed very tall.

Nevertheless, the numerous porticoes, air shafts, and staircases must have given the palace a pleasantly open, airy quality. Some of the interiors, with their richly decorated walls, retain their atmosphere of intimate elegance to this day. The masonry construction of Minoan palaces is excellent throughout, but the columns were always of wood. Although none have survived, their characteristic form (the smooth shaft tapering downward, topped by a wide, cushion-shaped capital) is known from representations in painting and sculpture. About the origins of this type of column, which in some contexts could also serve as a religious symbol, or about its possible links with Egyptian architecture, we can say nothing at all.

Painting

After the catastrophe that had wiped out the earlier palaces, and a century of slow recovery, there was what seems to our eyes an explosive increase in wealth and an equally remarkable outpouring of creative energy. The most surprising aspect of this sudden efflorescence, however, is its great achievement in painting. Unfortunately, these paintings have survived only in small fragments, so that we hardly ever have a complete composition, let alone the design of an entire wall. A great many of them were scenes from nature showing animals and birds among luxuriant vegetation, or creatures of the sea.

Not only was marine life (as seen in the fish and dolphin fresco in fig. 51) a favorite subject of Minoan painting. The marine feeling pervades all Minoan art. We sense it even in "*The Toreador Fresco*," the largest and most dynamic Minoan mural recovered so far (fig. 52). (The darker patches are the original fragments on which the restoration is based.) The conventional title should not mislead us: what we see here is not a bullfight but a ritual game in which the performers vault over the back of the animal. Two of the slim-waisted athletes are girls, differentiated (as in Egyptian art) mainly by their lighter skin color. That the bull was a sacred animal and that bull-vaulting played an important role in Minoan religious life are beyond doubt. Scenes such as this still echo in the Greek legend of the youths and maidens sacrificed to the Minotaur. If we try, however, to "read" the fresco as a description of what actually went on during these performances, we find it strangely ambiguous. Do the three figures show successive phases of the same action? How did the youth in the center get onto the back of the bull, and in what direction is he moving? Scholars have even consulted rodeo experts without getting clear answers to these questions. All of which does not mean that the Minoan artist was deficient—it would be absurd to find fault for failing to accomplish what was never intended in the first place—but that fluid, effortless ease of movement was more important to him than factual precision or dramatic power. He has, as it were, idealized the ritual by stressing its harmonious, playful aspect to the point that the participants behave like dolphins gamboling in the sea.

MYCENAEAN ART

Along the southeastern shores of the Greek mainland there was during Late Helladic times (c. 1600–1100 B.C.) a number of settlements that corresponded in many ways to

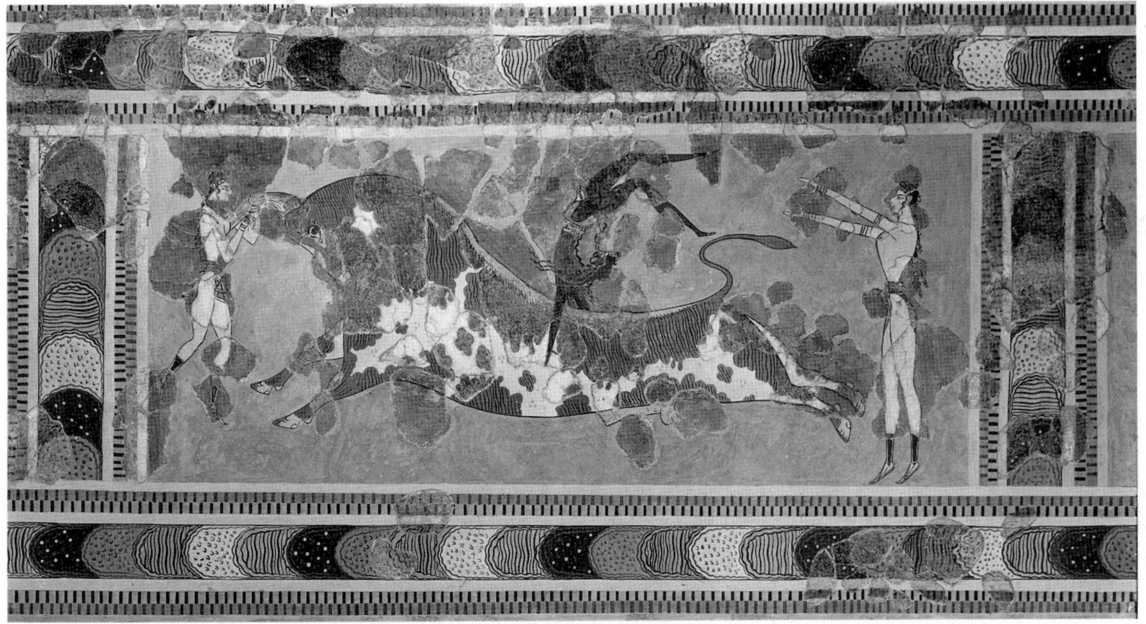

52. *"The Toreador Fresco."* c. 1500 B.C. Height including upper border c. 24½" (62.2 cm). Archaeological Museum, Heraklion, Crete

53. Interior, Treasury of Atreus, Mycenae, Greece. c. 1300–1250 B.C.

54. The Lion Gate, Mycenae, Greece. 1250 B.C.

those of Minoan Crete. They, too, were grouped around palaces. Their inhabitants have come to be called Mycenaeans, after Mycenae, the most important of these settlements. Since the works of art unearthed there by excavation often showed a strikingly Minoan character, the Mycenaeans were at first regarded as having come from Crete, but it is now agreed that they were the descendants of the earliest Greek tribes, who had entered the country soon after 2000 B.C.

For some four hundred years, these people had led an inconspicuous pastoral existence in their new homeland. Their modest tombs have yielded only simple pottery and a few bronze weapons. Toward 1600 B.C., however, they suddenly began to bury their dead in deep shaft graves and, a little later, in conical stone chambers, known as beehive tombs. This development reached its height toward 1300 B.C. in such impressive structures as the one shown in figure 53, built of concentric layers of precisely cut stone blocks. Its discoverer thought it far too ambitious for a tomb and gave it the misleading name Treasury of Atreus. Burial places as elaborate as this can be matched only in Egypt during the same period.

Apart from such details as the shape of the columns or decorative motifs of various sorts, Mycenaean architecture owes little to the Minoan tradition. The palaces on the mainland were hilltop fortresses surrounded by defensive walls of huge stone blocks, a type of construction quite unknown in Crete. The Lion Gate at Mycenae (fig. 54) is the most impressive remnant of these massive ramparts, which inspired such awe in the Greeks of later times that they were regarded as the work of the Cyclopes (a mythical race of one-eyed giants). Even the Treasury of Atreus, although built of smaller and more precisely shaped blocks, has a Cyclopean lintel (see fig. 53).

Another aspect of the Lion Gate foreign to the Minoan tradition is the great stone relief over the doorway. The two lions flanking a symbolic Minoan column have a grim, heraldic majesty. Their function as guardians of the gate, their tense, muscular bodies, and their symmetrical design again suggest an influence from the ancient Near East. We may at this point recall the Trojan War, which brought the Mycenaeans to Asia Minor soon after 1200 B.C. It seems likely, however, that they began to sally eastward across the Aegean, for trade or war, much earlier than that.

GREEK ART

The works of art we have come to know so far are like fascinating strangers: we approach them fully aware of their alien background and of the "language difficulties" they present. If it turns out that, after all, we can understand something of what they have to say, we are surprised and grateful. As soon as we reach the Greeks, our attitude undergoes a change: they are not strangers but relatives, we feel, older members of our own family whom we recognize immediately. It is just as well to remember, as we turn to these "ancestors" of ours, that the continuous tradition that links us to the ancient Greeks is a handicap as well as an advantage: we must be careful, in looking at Greek originals, not to let our memories of their countless later imitations get in the way.

The Mycenaeans and other clans described by Homer were the first Greek-speaking tribes to wander into the peninsula, around 2000 B.C. Then, around 1100 B.C., others came, overwhelming and absorbing those who were already there. Some of the late arrivals, the Dorians, settled on the mainland; others, the Ionians, spread out to the Aegean islands and Asia Minor. A few centuries later they ventured into the waters of the western Mediterranean, founding colonies in Sicily and southern Italy. Though the Greeks were united by language and religious beliefs, old tribal loyalties continued to divide them into

55. *Dipylon Vase.* 8th century B.C. Height 42⅝" (108.3 cm). The Metropolitan Museum of Art, New York. Rogers Fund, 1914

56. *The Blinding of Polyphemus* and *Gorgons,* on a Proto-Attic amphora. c. 675–650 B.C. Height 56" (142.2 cm). Archaeological Museum, Eleusis

city-states. The intense rivalry among these for power, wealth, and status stimulated the growth of ideas and institutions. In the end, they paid dearly for their inability to compromise. The Peloponnesian War (431–404 B.C.), in which the Spartans and their allies defeated the Athenians, was a catastrophe from which Greece never recovered.

PAINTING

The formative phase of Greek civilization embraces about four hundred years, from c. 1100 to 700 B.C. Of the first three centuries of this period we know very little, but after about 800 B.C. the Greeks rapidly emerge into the full light of history. The earliest specific dates that have come down to us are from that time: 776 B.C., the founding of the Olympic Games and the starting point of Greek chronology, as well as several slightly later dates recording the founding of various cities. That time also saw the full development of the oldest characteristically Greek style in the fine arts, the so-called Geometric. We know it only from painted pottery and small-scale sculpture (monumental architecture and sculpture in stone did not appear until the seventh century).

Geometric Style

At first the pottery had been decorated only with abstract designs—triangles, checkers, concentric circles—but toward 800 B.C. human and animal figures began to appear within the geometric framework, and in the most mature examples these figures could form elaborate scenes. Our specimen (fig. 55), from the Dipylon cemetery in Athens, belongs to a group of very large vases that served as grave monuments. Its bottom has holes through which liquid offerings could filter down to the dead below. On the body of the vessel we see the deceased lying in state, flanked by figures with their arms raised in a gesture of mourning, and a funeral procession of chariots and warriors on foot.

The most remarkable thing about this scene is that it contains no reference to an afterlife; its purpose is purely commemorative. Here lies a worthy man, it tells us, who was mourned by many and had a splendid funeral. Did the Greeks, then, have no conception of a hereafter? They did, but the realm of the dead to them was a colorless, ill-defined region where the souls, or "shades," led a feeble and passive existence without making any demands on the living.

Orientalizing Style

Representation and narrative, entirely absent from the *Dipylon Vase* of a hundred years earlier (see fig. 55), demand greater scope than the conservative tradition of the Geometric style could provide. The dam finally burst toward 725 B.C., when Greek art entered another phase, which we call the Orientalizing style, and new forms came flooding in. As its name implies, the new style reflects powerful influences from Egypt and the Near East, stimulated by increasing trade with these regions. Between c. 725 and 650 B.C. Greek art absorbed a host of Oriental motifs and ideas and was profoundly transformed in the process. The change becomes very evident if we compare the large amphora (a vase for storing wine or oil) from Eleusis (fig. 56) with the *Dipylon Vase*.

Geometric ornament has not disappeared from this vase altogether, but it is confined to the peripheral zones: the foot, the handles, and the lip. New, curvilinear motifs—such as spirals, interlacing bands, palmettes, and rosettes—are conspicuous everywhere. On the shoulder of the vessel we see a frieze of fighting animals, derived from the repertory of Near Eastern art. The major areas, however, are given over to narrative, which has become the dominant element. Ornament of any sort now belongs to a separate and lesser realm, clearly distinguishable from that of representation, so that the decorative patterns scattered among the figures can no longer interfere with their actions.

Narrative painting tapped a nearly inexhaustible source of subjects from Greek myths and legends. These tales were the result of mixing local Doric and Ionic deities and heroes into the pantheon of Olympian gods and Homeric sagas. They also represent a comprehensive attempt to understand the world. The Greeks grasped the internal meaning of events in terms of fate and human character rather than as the accidents of history, in which they had little interest before about 500 B.C. The main focus was on explaining why the legendary heroes of the past seemed incomparably greater than men of the present. Some were historical figures—Herakles, for example, was the king of Mycenaean Tiryns—but all were believed to be descendants of the gods, themselves often very human in behavior, who had children with mortals. This lineage explained the hero's extraordinary powers.

Such an outlook also helps us understand the strong appeal exerted on the Greek imagination by Oriental lions and monsters. These terrifying creatures embodied the unknown forces of life faced by the hero. This fascination is clearly seen on the Eleusis amphora. The figures are a far cry from the conventionalized forms of the Geometric style. They have gained greatly in both size and descriptive precision. As a result, the blinding of the giant Polyphemus by Odysseus and his companions—the scene on the neck of the amphora—is enacted with memorable directness and dramatic force. If these men lack the beauty we will later expect of epic heroes in art, their movements have an expressive vigor that makes them seem thoroughly alive. The slaying of another monstrous creature is depicted on the body of the vase, the main part of which has been badly damaged, so that only two figures have survived intact. They are Gorgons, the sisters of the snake-haired, terrible-faced Medusa, whom Perseus killed with the aid of the gods. Even here we notice an interest in the articulation of the body far beyond the limits of the Geometric style.

Archaic Style

The Orientalizing phase of Greek art was a period of experiment and transition, in contrast to the stable and consistent Geometric style. Once the new elements from the East had been fully assimilated, there emerged another style, as well defined as the Geometric but infinitely greater in range: the Archaic, which lasted from the later seventh century to about 480 B.C., the time of the famous Greek victories over the Persians at Salamis and Plataea. During the Archaic period, we witness the unfolding of the artistic genius of Greece not only in vase painting but also in monumental architecture and sculpture. While Archaic art lacks the balance, the sense of perfection of the Classical style of the later fifth century, it has a freshness that makes many people consider it the most vital phase of Greek art.

Black-Figure Style

By about the middle of the sixth century B.C., vase painters in particular were so highly esteemed that the best of them signed their works. The scene of Herakles killing the lion, on an amphora attributed to Psiax (fig. 57), is all grimness and violence. The two heavy bodies almost seem united forever in their grim struggle. Incised line and touches of colored detail have been kept to a minimum so as not to break up the compact black mass; yet both figures show such a wealth of anatomical knowledge and skillful use of foreshortening that they give an amazing illusion of existing in the round. The work of Psiax is the direct outgrowth of the forceful Orientalizing style of the blinding of Polyphemus in the Eleusis amphora. Herakles in his struggle reminds us of the hero on the sound box of the harp from Ur (see fig. 44). Both show humans facing the unknown forces of life embodied by terrifying mythical creatures. The Nemean lion likewise serves to underscore the hero's might and courage.

Red-Figure Style

Psiax must have felt that the silhouettelike black-figure technique made the study of foreshortening unduly difficult, for in some of his vases he tried the reverse procedure, leaving the figures red and filling in the back-

57. Psiax. *Herakles Strangling the Nemean Lion,* on an Attic black-figure amphora from Vulci, Italy. c. 525 B.C. Height 19½" (49.5 cm). Museo Civico, Brescia

58. The "Foundry Painter." *Lapith and Centaur.* Interior of an Attic red-figure kylix. c. 490–480 B.C. Staatliche Antikensammlungen, Munich

ground. This red-figure technique gradually replaced the older method toward 500 B.C. Its advantages are well shown in figure 58, a kylix (drinking cup) of c. 490–480 B.C. by an unknown master nicknamed the Foundry Painter. The details of the *Lapith and Centaur* are now freely drawn with the brush, rather than laboriously incised, so the artist depends far less on the profile view than before. Instead, he exploits the internal lines of communication that permit him to show boldly foreshortened and overlapping limbs, precise details of costume (note the pleated skirt), and interest in facial expressions. He is so fascinated by all these new effects that he has made the figures as large as he possibly could. They almost seem to burst from their circular frame, and a piece of the Lapith's helmet has actually been cut off. The Lapith and Centaur are counterparts to Herakles and the Nemean lion. But just as the style has changed, so has the meaning of this combat: the painting now stands for the victory of civilization over barbarianism and ultimately of humanity's rational and moral sides over its animal nature.

Classical Style

According to the literary sources, Greek painters of the Classical period, which began around 480 B.C., achieved a great breakthrough in mastering illusionistic space. Unhappily, we have no murals or panels to verify that claim, and vase painting by its very nature could echo the new concept of pictorial space only in rudimentary fashion. From the mid-fifth century on, the impact of monumental painting gradually transformed vase painting as a whole into a satellite art that

59. *The Battle of Issus* or *Battle of Alexander and the Persians.* Mosaic copy from Pompeii of a Hellenistic painting. 1st century B.C. 8′11″ × 16′9½″ (2.78 × 5.12 m). Museo Archeologico Nazionale, Naples

tried to reproduce large-scale compositions in a kind of shorthand dictated by its own limited technique. We can get some idea of what Greek wall painting looked like from later copies and imitations. According to the Roman writer Pliny, Philoxenus of Eretria at the end of the fourth century painted the victory of Alexander the Great over Darius at Issus. An echo of that work may survive in a famous Pompeian mosaic (fig. 59). The scene is far more complicated and dramatic than anything from earlier Greek art. And for the first time, we have a depiction of something that actually happened, without the symbolic overtones of *Herakles Strangling the Nemean Lion* or the *Lapith and Centaur.* In character and even in appearance, it is close to Roman reliefs commemorating specific historic events (see figs. 96, 97).

TEMPLES

Orders and Plans

In architecture, the Greek achievement has been identified since ancient Roman times with the creation of the three Classical architectural orders, Doric, Ionic, and Corinthian. Actually, there are only two, the Corinthian being a variant of the Ionic. The Doric (so named because its home is the region of Dōris on the Greek mainland) may well claim to be the basic order, since it is older and more sharply defined than the Ionic, which developed on the Aegean islands and the coast of Asia Minor.

What do we mean by "architectural order"? By common agreement, the term is used for Greek architecture only (and its descendants); and rightly so, for none of the other architectural systems known to us produced anything like it. Perhaps the simplest way to make clear the unique character of the Greek orders is this: there is no such thing as "the Egyptian temple" or "the Gothic church"—the individual buildings, however much they may have in common, are so varied that we cannot distill a generalized type from them—while "the Doric temple" is a real entity that inevitably forms in our minds as we examine the monuments themselves. We must be careful, of course, not to think of this abstraction as an ideal that permits us to measure the degree of perfection of any given Doric temple. It simply means that the elements of which a Doric temple is composed are extraordinarily constant in number, in kind, and in their relation to one another. As a result of this narrowly circumscribed repertory of forms, Doric temples all belong to the same clearly recognizable family, just as the Kouros statues do (see fig. 65). Like the Kouros statues, they show an internal consistency, a mutual adjustment of parts, that gives them a unique quality of wholeness and organic unity.

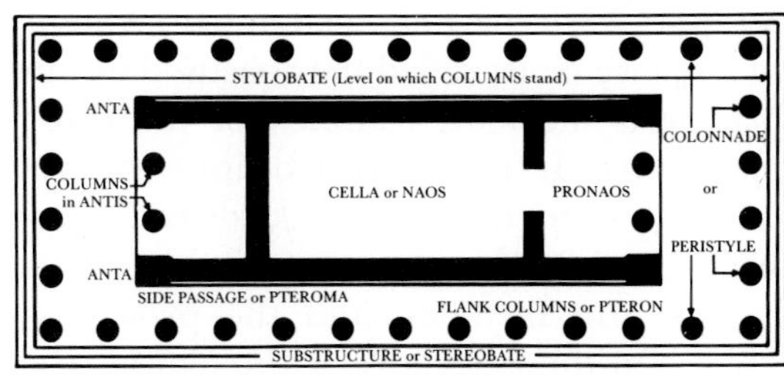

60. Ground plan of a typical Greek peripteral temple (after Grinnell)

Temple Plans

The plans of Greek temples are not directly linked to the orders, which concern only the elevation, or side view. They may vary according to the size of the building or regional preferences, but their basic features are so much alike that it is useful to study them from a generalized "typical" plan (fig. 60). The nucleus is the cella or naos (the room in which the image of the deity is placed) and the porch (pronaos) with its two columns flanked by pilasters (antae). Often we find a second porch added behind the cella to make the design more symmetrical. In the larger temples, the central unit is surrounded by a colonnade, called the peristyle, and the structure is then known as peripteral. The very largest temples of Ionian Greece may even have a double colonnade.

Doric Order

The term Doric order refers to the standard parts, and their sequence, constituting the exterior of any Doric temple (fig. 61). Let us first look at the three main divisions: the stepped platform, the columns, and the entablature (which includes everything that rests on the columns). The Doric column consists of the shaft, marked by shallow vertical grooves known as flutes, and the capital, which is

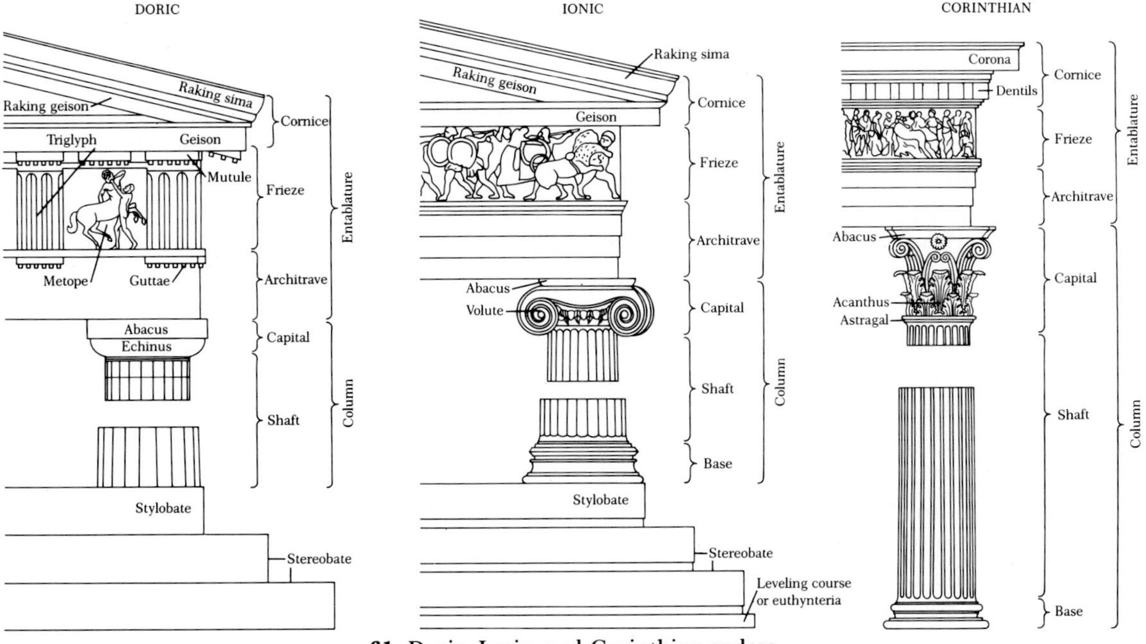

61. Doric, Ionic, and Corinthian orders

made up of the flaring, cushionlike echinus and a square tablet called the abacus. The entablature is the most complex of the three major units. It is subdivided into the architrave (a series of stone blocks directly supported by the columns), the frieze with its triglyphs and metopes, and the projecting cornice. On the long sides of the temple, the cornice is horizontal, while on the short sides (or facades), it is split open in such a way as to enclose the pediment between its upper and lower parts.

How did the Doric originate? Its essential features were already well established about 600 B.C., but how they developed and why they congealed so rapidly into a system remain a puzzle to which we have few reliable clues. The notion that temples ought to be built of stone, with large numbers of columns, must have come from Egypt; the fluted half-columns at Saqqara (see fig. 31) strongly suggest the Doric column. Egyptian temples, it is true, are designed to be experienced from the inside, while the Greek temple is arranged so that the exterior matters most (religious ceremonies usually took place out of doors, in front of the temple facade). But might not a Doric temple be interpreted as the columned hall of an Egyptian sanctuary turned inside out? The Greeks also owed something to the Mycenaeans—we have seen an elementary kind of pediment in the Lion Gate, and the capital of a Mycenaean column is rather like a Doric capital (compare fig. 54). There is, however, a third factor: to what extent can the Doric order be understood as a reflection of wooden structures? Our answer to this thorny question will depend on whether we believe that architectural form follows function and technique, or whether we accept the striving for beauty as a motivating force. The truth may well lie in a combination of these approaches. At the start, Doric architects certainly imitated in stone some features of wooden temples, if only because these features served to identify the building as a temple. But when they became enshrined in the Doric order, it was not from blind conservatism. By then, the wooden forms had been so thoroughly transformed that they were an organic part of the stone structure.

Paestum. We can see the evolution of temples in two examples near the southern Italian town of Paestum, where a Greek colony flourished during the Archaic period: the older is the "Basilica" (fig. 62, background); the "Temple of Poseidon"—it was probably dedicated to Hera—was erected about a hundred years later (fig. 62, foreground). How do the two temples differ? The "Basilica" looks low and sprawling—and not only because its roof is lost—while the "Temple of Poseidon," by comparison, appears tall and compact. The difference is partly psychological, produced by the outline of the columns which, in the "Basilica," are more strongly curved and are tapered to a relatively narrow top. This swelling effect, known as *entasis*, makes one feel that the columns bulge with the strain of supporting the superstructure, and that the slender tops, even though aided by the widely flaring cushionlike capitals, are just barely up to the task. The sense of strain has been explained on the grounds that Archaic architects were not fully familiar with their new materials and engineering procedures, but such a view judges the building by the standards of later temples—and overlooks the expressive vitality of the building, as of a living body, the vitality we also sense in the Archaic Kouros (see fig. 65).

In the "Temple of Poseidon" the exaggerated curvatures have been modified. This, combined with a closer ranking of the columns, literally as well as expressively brings the stresses between supports and weight into more harmonious balance. Perhaps because the architect took fewer risks, the building is better preserved than the "Basilica." Its air of self-contained repose parallels developments in the field of Greek sculpture.

Athens; The Parthenon. In 480 B.C., shortly before their defeat, the Persians had destroyed the temple and statues on the Acropolis, the sacred hill above Athens which had been a fortified site since Mycenaean times. The rebuilding of the Acropolis under the

62. The "Basilica," c. 550 B.C., and the "Temple of Poseidon," c. 460 B.C., Paestum, Italy

63. Ictinus and Callicrates. The Parthenon (view from the east), Acropolis, Athens. 448–432 B.C.

leadership of Pericles during the later fifth century, when Athens was at the height of its power, was the most ambitious enterprise in the history of Greek architecture, as well as its artistic climax. Individually and collectively, these structures represent the Classical phase of Greek art in full maturity.

The greatest temple, and the only one to be completed before the Peloponnesian War (431–404 B.C.), is the Parthenon (fig. 63), dedicated to the virginal Athena, the patron deity in whose honor Athens was named. The architects Ictinus and Callicrates erected it in 448–432 B.C., an amazingly brief span of time for a project of this size. Built of gleaming white marble on the most prominent site along the southern flank of the Acropolis, it dominates the entire city and the surrounding countryside, a brilliant landmark against the backdrop of mountains to the north of it.

As the perfect embodiment of Classical Doric architecture, the Parthenon makes an instructive contrast with the "Temple of Poseidon" (see fig. 62). Despite its greater size, it seems far less massive. Rather, the dominant impression it creates is one of festive, balanced grace within the austere scheme of the Doric order. This has been achieved by a general lightening and readjustment of the proportions. The entablature is lower in relation to its width and to the height of the columns; the cornice projects less; and the columns themselves are a good deal more slender, their tapering and entasis less pronounced and the capitals smaller and less flaring; yet the spacing of the columns is wider. We might say that the load carried by the columns has decreased, and as a consequence the supports can fulfill their task with a new sense of ease.

These so-called refinements, intentional departures from the strict geometric regularity of the design for aesthetic reasons, are another feature of the Classical Doric style that can be observed in the Parthenon better than anywhere else. Thus the stepped platform and the entablature are not absolutely straight but slightly curved, so that the center is a bit higher than the ends; the columns lean inward; and the interval between the corner column and its neighbors is smaller than the standard interval adopted for the colonnade as a whole. Such intentional departures from strict geometric regularity are not made of necessity. They give us visual reassurance that the points of greatest stress are supported, and provided with a counterstress as well.

Propylaea. Immediately after the completion of the Parthenon, Pericles commissioned another splendid and expensive edifice, the monumental entry gate at the western end of the Acropolis, called the Propylaea (fig. 64, left and center). It was begun in 437 B.C. under the architect Mnesicles, who completed the main part in five years; the remainder had to be abandoned because of the Peloponnesian War. Again the entire structure was built of marble and included refinements comparable to those of the Parthenon. It is fascinating to see how the familiar elements of a Doric temple have here been adapted to a totally different task and difficult terrain. Mnesicles has indeed acquitted himself nobly. His design not only fits the irregular and steeply rising hillside, but also transforms it from a rude passage among rocks into a splendid overture to the sacred precinct above.

Ionic Order

Next to the Propylaea is the elegant little Temple of Athena Nike (fig. 64, right), displaying the slenderer proportions and the scroll capitals of the Ionic order. The previous development of the order is known only in very fragmentary fashion. Of the huge Ionic temples that were erected in Archaic times on Samos and at Ephesus, little has survived except the plans. The Ionic vocabulary, however, seems to have remained fairly fluid, with strong affinities to the Near East, and it did not really become an order in the strict sense until the Classical period. Even then it continued to be rather more flexible than the Doric order. Its most striking feature is the column, which differs from the Doric not only in body but also, as it were, in spirit (see fig. 61). It rests on an ornately profiled base of its own. The shaft is more slender, and

64. Mnesicles. The Propylaea, 437–432 B.C., and the Temple of Athena Nike, 427–424 B.C. (view from the west), Acropolis, Athens

there is less tapering and entasis. The capital shows a large double scroll, or volute, between the echinus and abacus, which projects strongly beyond the width of the shaft.

That these details add up to an entity very distinct from the Doric column becomes clear as soon as we turn from the diagram to an actual building, such as the Temple of Athena Nike. How shall we define it? The Ionic column is, of course, lighter and more graceful than its mainland cousin; it lacks the latter's muscular quality. Instead, it evokes a growing plant, something like a formalized palm tree. And this vegetal analogy is not sheer fancy, for we have early ancestors, or relatives, of the Ionic capital that bear it out. If we were to pursue these plantlike columns all the way back to their point of origin, we would eventually find ourselves at Saqqara, where we encounter not only "proto-Doric" supports but also the wonderfully graceful papyrus half-columns of figure 32, with their curved, flaring capitals. It may well be, then, that the Ionic column, too, had its ultimate source in Egypt, but instead of reaching Greece by sea, as we suppose the proto-Doric column did, it traveled a slow and tortuous path by land through Syria and Asia Minor.

In the end, the greatest achievement of Greek architecture was much more than just beautiful buildings. Greek temples are governed by a structural logic that makes them look stable because of the precise arrangement of their parts. The Greeks tried to regulate their temples in accordance with nature's harmony by constructing them of measured units that were so proportioned that they would all be in perfect agreement. ("Perfect" was as significant an idea to the Greeks as "forever" was to the Egyptians.) Now architects could create organic unities, not by copying nature, not by divine inspiration, but by design. Thus their temples seem to be almost alive. They achieved this triumph chiefly by expressing the structural forces active in buildings. In the Classical period, expressions of force and counterforce in both Doric and Ionic temples were proportioned so exactly that their opposition produced the effect of a perfect balancing of forces and harmonizing of sizes and shapes. This is the real reason why, for so many centuries, the orders have been considered the only true basis for beautiful architecture. They are so perfect that they could not be surpassed, only equaled.

SCULPTURE

While enough examples of metalwork and ivory carvings of Near Eastern and Egyptian origin have been found on Greek soil to account for their influence on Greek vase painting, the origins of monumental sculpture and architecture in Greece are a different matter. To see such things, the Greeks had to go to Egypt or Mesopotamia. There is no doubt that they did so (we know that there were small colonies of Greeks in Egypt at the time), but this does not explain why the Greeks should have developed a sudden desire during the seventh century B.C., and not before, to create such things for themselves. The mystery may never be cleared up, for the oldest existing examples of Greek stone sculpture and architecture show that Egyptian tradition had already been well assimilated, and that skill to match was not long in developing.

Archaic Style

Let us compare a very early Greek statue of a nude youth of c. 600 B.C., called a Kouros (fig. 65), with the statue of Mycerinus (see fig. 30). The similarities are certainly striking: we note the block-conscious, cubic character of both sculptures, the slim, broad-shouldered silhouette of the figures, the position of their arms, their clenched fists, the way they stand with the left leg forward, the emphatic rendering of the kneecaps. The formalized, wiglike treatment of the hair is a further point of resemblance. Judged by Egyptian standards, the Archaic statue seems somewhat "primitive"—rigid, oversimplified, awkward, less close to nature. But the Greek statue also has virtues of its own that cannot be measured in Egyptian terms. First of all, it is truly free-standing—the earliest large stone image of the human form in the entire history of art of which this can be said. The Egyptian carver had never dared to liberate such figures completely from the stone. They remain immersed in it to some degree, as it were, so that the empty spaces between the legs and between the arms and the torso (or between two figures in a double statue, as in fig. 30) always remain partly filled. There are never any holes in Egyptian stone figures. In that sense, they do not rank as sculpture in the round but as an extreme case of high relief. The Greek carver, on the contrary, does not mind holes in the least. He separates the arms from the torso and the legs from each other, and goes to great lengths to cut away every bit of dead material (the only exceptions are the tiny bridges between the fists and the thighs). Apparently it is of the greatest importance to him that a statue consist only of stone that has representational meaning within an organic whole. The stone must be transformed; it cannot be permitted to remain inert, neutral matter.

This is not, we must insist, a question of technique but of artistic intention. The act of liberation achieved in our figure endows him with a spirit basically different from that of any of the Egyptian statues. While the latter seem becalmed by a spell that has released them from every strain for all time to come, the Greek image is tense, full of hidden life. The direct stare of his huge eyes offers the most telling contrast to the gentle, faraway gaze of the Egyptian figures.

The Kore, as the Greek female statue type is called, shows more variations than the Kouros. A clothed figure by definition, it poses a different problem—how to relate body and drapery. It is also likely to reflect changing habits or local differences of dress. The Kore of figure 66 was carved a full century after our Kouros. She, too, is blocklike, with a strongly accented waist. The heavy

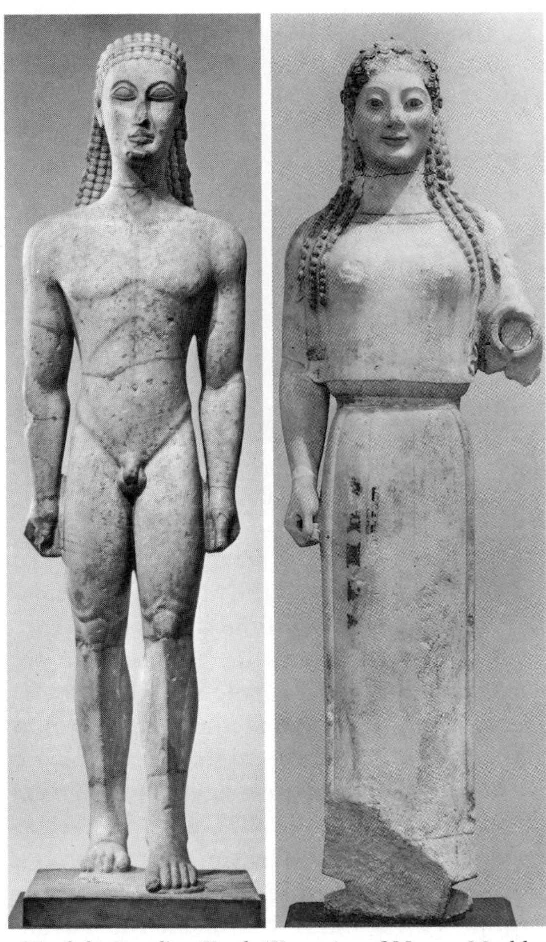

65. *(left) Standing Youth (Kouros).* c. 600 B.C. Marble, height 6′1½″ (1.88 m). The Metropolitan Museum of Art, New York. Fletcher Fund, 1932

66. *(right) Kore in Dorian Peplos.* c. 530 B.C. Marble, height 48″ (121.9 cm). Acropolis Museum, Athens

cloth of her garments forms a distinct, separate layer over the body, covering but not concealing the solidly rounded shapes beneath. As compared with the rigid wig of the Kouros, the treatment of the hair, which falls over the shoulders in soft, curly strands, is more organic. Most noteworthy of all is the full, round face with its enchantingly gay expression—the "Archaic smile."

Whom do they represent? The general names of Kore (Maiden) and Kouros (Youth) are noncommittal terms that gloss over the difficulty of identifying them further. Nor can we explain why the Kouros is always nude while the Kore is clothed. Whatever the reason, both types were produced in large numbers throughout the Archaic era, and their general outlines remained extraordinarily stable. Some are inscribed with the names of artists ("So-and-so made me") or with dedications to various deities. These, then, were votive offerings (the left hand of our Kore originally was extended forward, proffering a gift of some sort). But whether they represent the donor, the deity, or a divinely favored person such as a victor in athletic games remains uncertain in most cases. Others were placed on graves, yet they can be viewed as representations of the deceased only in the broadest (and a completely impersonal) sense. This odd lack of differentiation seems part of the essential character of the figures. They are neither gods nor mortals but something in between, an ideal of physical perfection and vitality shared by mortal and immortal alike, just as the heroes of the Homeric epics dwell in the realms of both history and mythology.

Architectural Sculpture

When the Greeks began to build their temples in stone, they also fell heir to the age-old tradition of architectural sculpture. The Egyptians had been covering the walls (and even the columns) of their buildings with reliefs since the time of the Old Kingdom, but these carvings were so shallow (for example, figs. 29, 37) that they left the continuity of the wall surface undisturbed. They had no weight or volume of their own, so that they were related to their architectural setting only in the same limited sense as Egyptian wall paintings (with which they were, in practice, interchangeable). This is also true of the reliefs on Assyrian, Babylonian, and Persian buildings (for example, figs. 46, 49). There existed, however, another kind of architectural sculpture in the ancient Near East: great guardian monsters protruding from the blocks that framed the gateways of fortresses or palaces. This tradition must have inspired, although perhaps indirectly, the carving over the Lion Gate at Mycenae (see fig. 54). We must nevertheless note one

67. *Battle of the Gods and Giants,* from the north frieze of the Treasury of the Siphnians, Delphi. c. 530 B.C. Marble, height 26″ (66 cm). Archaeological Museum, Delphi

important feature that distinguishes the Mycenaean guardian figures from their predecessors: although they are carved in high relief on a huge slab, this slab is thin and light compared to the enormously heavy, Cyclopean blocks around it. In building the gate, the Mycenaean architect left an empty triangular space above the lintel, for fear that the weight of the wall above would crush it, and then filled the hole with the comparatively lightweight relief panel. Here, then, we have a new kind of architectural sculpture—a work integrated with the structure yet also a separate entity rather than a modified wall surface or block.

The Greeks followed the Mycenaean example. In their temples, stone sculpture is confined to the pediment (the "empty triangle" between the ceiling and the sloping sides of the roof) and to the zone immediately below it (the "frieze"), but they retained the narrative wealth of Egyptian reliefs. The *Battle of the Gods and Giants* (fig. 67), part of a frieze from the Siphnian Treasury at Delphi, is executed in very high relief, with deep undercutting. The sculptor has taken full advantage of the spatial possibilities offered by this technique. He uses the projecting ledge at the bottom of the frieze as a stage on which he can place his figures in depth. The

68. *Dying Warrior,* from the east pediment of the Temple of Aphaia, Aegina. c. 490 B.C. Marble, length 72″ (182.9 cm). Staatliche Antikensammlungen, Munich

arms and legs of those nearest the beholder are carved completely in the round. In the second and third layer, the forms become shallower; yet even those farthest removed from us are never permitted to merge with the background. The result is a limited and condensed but very convincing space that permits a dramatic relationship between the figures such as we have never seen before in narrative reliefs. Any comparison with older examples (such as figs. 29, 46) will show us that Archaic art has indeed conquered a new dimension here, not only in the physical but also in the expressive sense.

Meanwhile, in pedimental sculpture, relief has been abandoned altogether. Instead, we find separate statues placed side by side in complex dramatic sequences designed to fit the triangular frame. The most ambitious ensemble of this kind, that of the east pediment of the Temple of Aphaia at Aegina, was created about 490 B.C., and thus brings us to the final stage in the evolution of Archaic sculpture. Among the most impressive figures is the fallen warrior from the left-hand corner (fig. 68), whose lean, muscular body seems marvelously functional and organic. That in itself, however, does not explain his great beauty, much as we may admire the artist's command of the human form in action. What really moves us is his nobility of spirit in the agony of dying. This man, we sense, is suffering—or carrying out—what fate has decreed with tremendous dignity and resolve. And this communicates itself to us in the very feel of the magnificently firm shapes of which he is composed.

Classical Style

Sometimes things that seem simple are the hardest to achieve. Greek sculptors of the late Archaic period were adept at representing battle scenes full of struggling, running figures in reliefs. To infuse the same freedom of movement into free-standing statues was a far greater challenge. Not only did it run counter to an age-old tradition that denied mobility to these figures, but also the unfreezing had to be done in such a way as to safeguard their all-around balance and self-sufficiency.

Early Greek statues have an unintentional military air, as if they were soldiers standing at attention. It took over a century after our Kouros was made before the Greeks discovered the secret to making a figure stand "at ease." *Kritios Boy* (fig. 69), named after the Athenian sculptor to whom it has been attributed, is the first statue we know that "stands" in the full sense of the term. Just as in military drill, this is simply a matter of allowing the

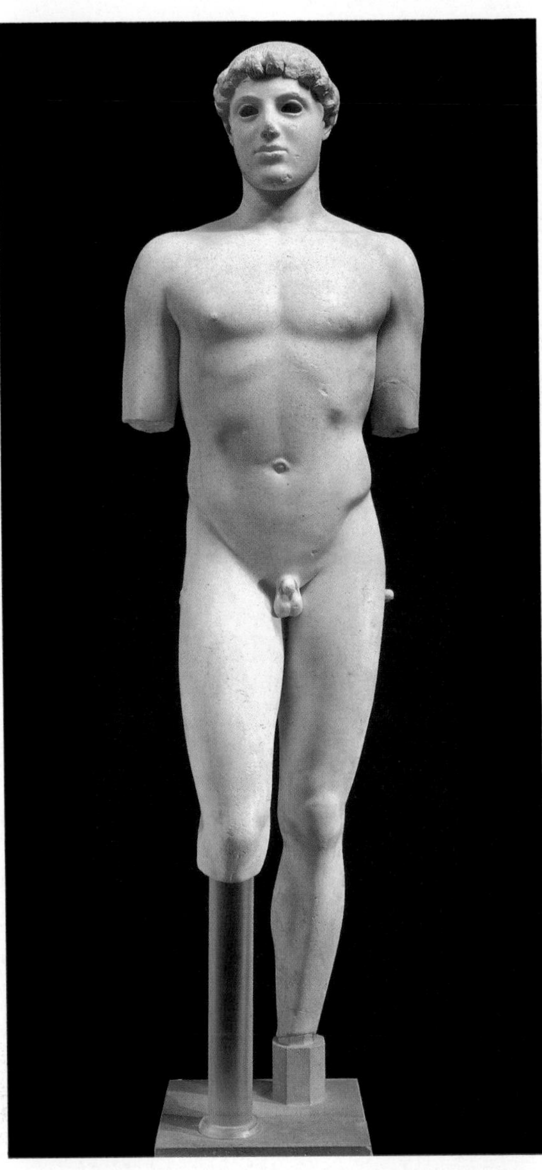

69. *Standing Youth (Kritios Boy).* c. 480 B.C. Marble, height 34" (86.4 cm). Acropolis Museum, Athens

70. *Poseidon (Zeus?).* c. 460–450 B.C. Bronze, height 6′10″ (2.08 m). National Archaeological Museum, Athens

weight of the body to shift from equal distribution on both legs (as is the case with the Kouros, even though one foot is in front of the other) to one leg. The resulting stance—called *contrapposto* (or counterpoise)—brings about all kinds of subtle curvatures: the bending of the "free" knee results in a slight swiveling of the pelvis, a compensating curvature of the spine, and an adjusting tilt of the shoulders. Like the refined details of the Parthenon, these variations have nothing to do with the statue's ability to maintain itself erect but greatly enhance its lifelike impression. In repose, it will still seem capable of movement; in motion, of maintaining its stability. Life now suffuses the entire figure. Hence, the Archaic smile, the "sign of life," is no longer needed and has given way to a serious, pensive expression. The forms, moreover, have a new naturalism and harmonious proportion which together provided the basis for the strong idealization characteristic of all subsequent Greek art.

Once the concept of *contrapposto* had been established, the solution to showing large, free-standing statues in motion no longer presented serious difficulties. Such figures are the most important achievement of the

Severe style. The finest one of this kind (fig. 70) was recovered from the sea near the coast of Greece: a magnificent nude bronze Poseidon (or Zeus?), almost seven feet tall, in the act of hurling his trident (or thunderbolt?). Here, stability in the midst of action becomes outright grandeur. The pose is that of an athlete, yet it is not so much the arrested moment in a continuous motion as an awe-inspiring gesture that reveals the power of the god. Hurling a weapon thus becomes a divine attribute, rather than an act aimed at a specific foe in the heat of battle.

Architectural Sculpture

The conquest of movement in a free-standing statue exerted a liberating influence on pedimental sculpture as well, endowing it with a new spaciousness, fluidity, and balance. The *Dying Niobid* (fig. 71), a work of the 440s, was carved for the pediment of a Doric temple but is so richly three-dimensional, so self-contained, that we hardly suspect her original context. Niobe, according to legend, had humiliated the mother of Apollo and Artemis by boasting of her seven sons and seven daughters, whereupon the two gods killed all of Niobe's children. Our Niobid has been shot in the back while running. Her strength broken, she sinks to the ground while trying to extract the fatal arrow. The violent movement of her arms has made her garment slip off. Her nudity is thus a dramatic device, rather than a necessary part of the story. The *Niobid* is the earliest known large female nude in Greek art. The artist's primary motive in devising it nevertheless was to display a beautiful female body in the kind of strenuous action hitherto reserved for the male nude. Still, we must not misread the intent: it was not a detached interest in the physical aspect of the event alone but the desire to unite motion and emotion and thus to make the beholder experience the suffering of this victim of a cruel fate. Looking at the face of the Niobid, we feel that here, for the first time, human feeling is expressed as eloquently in the features as in the rest of the figure.

A brief glance backward at the wounded warrior from Aegina (see fig. 68) will show us how very differently the agony of death had been conceived only half a century before. What separates the *Niobid* from the world of Archaic art is a quality summed up in the Greek word *pathos*, which means suffering, but particularly suffering conveyed with nobility and restraint so that it touches rather than horrifies us. Late Archaic art may approach it now and then, yet the full force of pathos can be felt only in Classical works such as the *Dying Niobid*.

The largest, as well as the greatest, group of Classical sculptures at our disposal consists of the remains of the marble decoration of the Parthenon, most of them, unfortunately, in battered and fragmentary condition. The east pediment represents various deities witnessing the birth of Athena from the head of

71. *Dying Niobid*. c. 450–440 B.C. Marble, height 59″ (149.9 cm). Museo delle Terme, Rome

72. *Three Goddesses,* from the east pediment of the Parthenon. c. 438–432 B.C. Marble, over lifesize. British Museum, London

Zeus (fig. 72). Here we marvel at the spaciousness, the complete ease of movement even in repose. There is neither violence nor pathos in them, indeed no specific action of any kind, only a deeply felt poetry of being. We find it in the soft fullness of the three goddesses, enveloped in thin drapery that seems to share the qualities of a liquid substance as it flows and eddies around the forms underneath. The figures are so freely conceived in depth that they create their own aura of space. Though all are seated or half-reclining, the turning of the bodies under the elaborate folds of their costumes makes them seem anything but static. In fact, they seem so capable of arising that it is hard to imagine them "shelved" upon the pediment. Evidently the sculptors who achieved such lifelike figures also found this incongruous. The sculptural decoration of later buildings tended to be placed in areas where they would seem less boxed in and be more readily visible.

73. Scopas (?). *Battle of the Greeks and Amazons,* from the east frieze of the Mausoleum, Halicarnassus. 359–351 B.C. Marble, height 35″ (88.9 cm). British Museum, London

Fourth-Century Sculpture

This Athenian style, so harmonious in both feeling and form, did not long survive the defeat of Athens by Sparta in the Peloponnesian War. Building and sculpture continued in the same tradition for another three centuries, but without the subtleties of the Classical age whose achievements we have just discussed. There is, unfortunately, no single word, like Archaic or Classical, that we can use to designate the third and final phase in the development of Greek art. The seventy-five-year span between the end of the Peloponnesian War and the rise of Alexander the Great used to be labeled "Late Classical," and the remaining two centuries and a half, "Hellenistic," a term meant to convey the spread of Greek civilization southeastward to Asia Minor and Mesopotamia, Egypt, and the borders of India. However, the history of style is not always in tune with political history. We have come to realize that there was no decisive break in the tradition of Greek art at the end of the fourth century, and that Hellenistic art was the direct outgrowth of developments that occurred well before the time of Alexander. The art of the years 400–325 B.C. nevertheless can be better understood if we view it as pre-Hellenistic rather than as Late Classical.

The contrast between Classical and pre-Hellenistic is strikingly demonstrated by the only project of the fourth century that corresponds to the Parthenon in size and ambition. It is not a temple but a huge tomb erected about 350 B.C. at Halicarnassus in Asia Minor by Mausolus, ruler of the area, from whose name comes the term mausoleum, used for all outsized funerary monuments. Scopas, who was very probably the sculptor of the main frieze showing the Greeks battling the Amazons (fig. 73), was familiar with the figure style of the Parthenon, but he has rejected its rhythmic harmony, its flow of action from one figure to the next. His sweeping, impulsive gestures require a lot of elbow room. What the composition lacks in continuity, it more than makes up for in bold innovation (note, for instance, the Amazon seated backward on her horse) and heightened expressiveness. In a sense, Scopas turned back as well to the scenes of violent action so popular in the Archaic period. We recognize its ancestor in the Siphnian *Battle of the Gods and Giants* (see fig. 67).

In many instances, unfortunately, the most famous works of Greek sculptors of the fifth and fourth centuries B.C. have been lost and only copies are preserved. There is some doubt whether the famous *Hermes* by Praxiteles (fig. 74) is the original, or a copy made some three centuries later. If the latter, how-

74. Praxiteles. *Hermes*. c. 330–320 B.C. (or copy?). Marble, height 7′1″ (2.16 m). Archaeological Museum, Olympia

ever, it is a very skillful copy, for it fits perfectly the qualities for which Praxiteles was admired in his own day; we also find many refinements that are ordinarily lost in a copy. The lithe proportions, the sinuous curve of the torso, the play of gentle curves, the sense of complete relaxation (enhanced by the use of an outside support for the figure to lean against)—all these are quite the opposite of Scopas' energetic innovations. The bland, lyrical charm of the *Hermes* is further enhanced by the caressing treatment of the marble: the faint smile, the meltingly soft, "veiled" modeling of the features, and even the hair, left comparatively rough for contrast, all share a misty, silken feel. Here, for the first time, there is an attempt to modify the stony look of a statue by giving to it this illusion of an enveloping atmosphere.

75. *Portrait Head,* from Delos. c. 80 B.C. Bronze, height 12¾" (32.4 cm). National Archaeological Museum, Athens

Hellenistic Style

Compared to Classical statues, the sculpture of the Hellenistic age often has a more pronounced realism and expressiveness, as well as a greater experimentation with drapery and pose, which often shows considerable torsion. These changes should be seen as a valid, even necessary, attempt to extend the subject matter and dynamic range of Greek art in accordance with a new temperament and outlook. The difference in psychology is suggested by the *Portrait Head* in figure 75. The serenity of Praxiteles' *Hermes* is replaced by a troubled look. And for the first time, we have an individual portrait, something that was inconceivable in earlier Greek art, which emphasized ideal, heroic types. It was not made as a bust but rather, in accordance with Greek custom, as part of a full-length statue. The identity of the sitter is unknown. Whoever he was, we get an intensely private view of him: the fluid modeling of the somewhat flabby features, the uncertain, plaintive mouth, the unhappy eyes under furrowed brows reveal an individual beset by doubts and anxieties, an extremely human, unheroic personality. There are echoes of noble pathos in these features, but it is a pathos translated into psychological terms. People of such inner turmoil certainly existed earlier in the Greek world, just as they do today. Yet it is significant that such complexity could be conveyed in art only when Greek independence, culturally as well as politically, was about to come to an end.

This more human conception is found again in the *Dying Gaul* (fig. 76), from a Roman copy in marble of the bronze groups dedicated by Attalus I of Pergamum (a city in northwestern Asia Minor) shortly before 200 B.C. to commemorate his victory over the invading Gauls. The sculptor who conceived the figure must have known the Gauls well, for he has carefully rendered the ethnic type in the facial structure and in the bristly shock of hair. The torque around the neck is another characteristically Celtic feature. Otherwise, however, the Gaul shares the heroic nudity of Greek warriors, such as those on the Aegina pediments (see fig. 68). If his agony seems infinitely more realistic in comparison, it still has considerable dignity and pathos. Clearly, the Gauls were not considered unworthy foes. "They knew how to die, barbarians though they were," is the idea conveyed by the statue. Yet we also sense something else, an animal quality that had never before been part of Greek images of men. Death, as we witness it here, is a very concrete physical process: no longer able to move his legs, the Gaul puts all his waning strength into his arms, as if to prevent some tremendous invisible weight from crushing him against the ground.

Two decades later, we find a second sculptural style flourishing at Pergamum. About 180 B.C., the son and successor of Attalus I had a mighty altar erected on a hill above the city to commemorate his father's victories. Much of the sculptural decoration has been recovered by excavation, and the entire west front of the altar is to be seen in Berlin. The subject of the frieze covering the base (fig. 77), the battle of the gods and giants, is traditional for Ionic friezes; we saw it before on the Siphnian Treasury (compare fig. 67). At Pergamum, however, it has a novel significance, since the victory of the gods is meant to symbolize the victories of Attalus I. Such a translation of history into mythology had been an established device in Greek art for a long time: victories over the Persians were habitually represented in terms of Lapiths battling Centaurs or Greeks fighting Amazons. But to place Attalus I in analogy with the gods themselves implies an exaltation of the ruler that is Oriental rather than Greek in origin. Since the time of Mausolus (see p. 85), who may have been the first to introduce it on Greek soil, the idea of divine kingship had been adopted by Alexander the Great, and it continued to flourish among the lesser sovereigns who divided his realm, such as the rulers of Pergamum. The huge figures, cut to such a depth that they are almost detached from the background, have the scale and weight of pedimental statues without the confining triangular frame—a unique compound of two separate traditions that represents a

76. *Dying Gaul.* Roman copy after a bronze original of c. 230–220 B.C. from Pergamum, Turkey. Marble, lifesize. Museo Capitolino, Rome

77. *Athena and Alcyoneus,* from the east side of the Great Frieze of the Altar of Zeus at Pergamum. c. 180 B.C. Marble, height 7′6″ (2.29 m). Pergamonmuseum, Berlin

thundering climax in the development of Greek architectural sculpture. The carving of the frieze, though not very subtle in detail, has tremendous dramatic force. The heavy, muscular bodies rushing at each other, the strong accents of light and dark, the beating wings and windblown garments are almost overwhelming in their dynamism, though today the pathos seems somewhat calculated and rhetorical. A writhing movement pervades the entire design, down to the last lock of hair, linking the victors and the vanquished in a single continuous rhythm. This sense of unity disciplines the physical and emotional violence of the struggle and thus keeps it—but just barely—from exploding its architectural frame.

Equally dramatic in its impact is another great victory monument of the early second century B.C., the *Nike of Samothrace* (fig. 78). The goddess has just descended to the prow of a ship. Her great wings spread wide, she is still partly airborne by the powerful head wind against which she advances. The invisible force of onrushing air here becomes a tangible reality. It not only balances the forward movement of the figure but also shapes every fold of the wonderfully animated drapery. As a result, there is an active relationship—indeed, an interdependence—between the statue and the space that envelops it, such as we have never seen before. Nor shall we see it again for a long time to come. The *Nike of Samothrace* deserves all of her fame as the greatest masterpiece of Hellenistic sculpture.

78. *Nike of Samothrace.* c. 200–190 B.C. Marble, height 8′ (2.44 m). Musée du Louvre, Paris

ETRUSCAN ART

We know surprisingly little about the early Etruscans. According to the Classical Greek historian Herodotus, they had left their homeland of Lydia in Asia Minor and settled in the area between Florence and Rome, which to this day is known as Tuscany. But their presence on Italian soil may go back much further. If so, the sudden flowering of Etruscan civilization from about 700 B.C. onward could have resulted from a fusion of this prehistoric Italian stock with small but powerful groups of seafaring invaders from Lydia in the course of the eighth century B.C. Be that as it may, the Italian peninsula did not emerge into the light of history until fairly late. The Bronze Age came to an end there only in the eighth century B.C., about the time the earliest Greeks began to settle along the southern shores of Italy and in Sicily. The seventh and sixth centuries B.C. saw the Etruscans at the height of their power, which extended over a large part of central Italy. But the Etruscans, like the Greeks, never formed a unified nation. They were no more than a loose federation of individual city-states given to quarreling among themselves and slow to unite against a common enemy. By the end of the third century B.C., all of them lost their independence to Rome, which had once been ruled by Etruscan kings. We would know practically nothing about the Etruscans at firsthand were it not for their elaborate tombs, which fortunately the Romans did not molest when they destroyed or rebuilt Etruscan cities and which therefore have survived intact until modern times.

Sculpture

The flowering of Etruscan civilization coincides with the Archaic age in Greece. During this period, especially near the end of the sixth and early in the fifth century B.C., Etruscan art showed its greatest vigor. Greek Archaic influence had displaced Orientalizing tendencies, but Etruscan artists did not simply imitate their Hellenic models. Working in a very different cultural setting, they retained

79. *Apollo,* from Veii. c. 510 B.C. Terra-cotta, height 69″ (175.3 cm). Museo Nazionale di Villa Giulia, Rome

80. *She-Wolf.* c. 500 B.C. Bronze, height 33½" (85.1 cm). Museo Capitolino, Rome

their own clear-cut identity, as we can see from the *Apollo* in figure 79, which has long been acknowledged as the masterpiece of Etruscan Archaic sculpture. His massive body, completely revealed beneath the ornamental striations of the drapery; the sinewy, muscular legs; the hurried, purposeful stride—all these betray an expressive power that has no counterpart in free-standing Greek statues of the same date. The bronze figure of the she-wolf that nourished Romulus and Remus, the legendary founders of Rome (fig. 80; the two babes are Renaissance additions), has the same wonderful ferocity of expression, the physical power of the body and legs, and the awesome quality we sense in the *Apollo.*

Tombs and Their Decoration

We do not know precisely what ideas the Archaic Etruscans held about the afterlife. They seem to have regarded the tomb as an abode not only for the body but for the soul as well (in contrast to the Egyptians, who thought of the soul as roaming freely and whose funerary sculpture therefore remained "inanimate"). Perhaps the Etruscans believed that by filling the tomb with banquets, dancing, games, and similar pleasures they could induce the soul to stay put in the city of the dead and therefore not haunt the realm of the living. How else are we to understand the purpose of the wonderfully rich array of murals in these funerary chambers? Figure 81 from the Tomb of the Lionesses in Tarquinia shows a pair of ecstatic dancers. As in the *Apollo,* the passionate energy of their movements strikes us as characteristically Etruscan rather than Greek in spirit. Of particular interest is the transparent garment of the woman, which lets the body shine through. The contrasting body color of the two figures continues a practice introduced by the Egyptians more than 2,000 years before (see p. 45). In Greece, this differentiation appears only a few years earlier, during the final phase of Archaic vase painting. Since nothing of the sort has survived in Greek territory, such paintings are uniquely important, not only as an Etruscan achievement but also as a possible reflection of Greek wall painting.

During the fifth century B.C., the Etruscan view of the hereafter must have become a good deal more complex and less festive. The change is reflected by the group in figure 82, a cinerary container carved of soft local stone soon after 400 B.C. A woman sits at the foot of the couch, but she is not the wife of the young man. Her wings indicate that she is the demon of death, and the scroll in her left hand records the fate of the deceased. The young

81. *Musician and Two Dancers.* Detail of a wall painting. c. 480–470 B.C.
Tomb of the Lionesses, Tarquinia, Italy

man is pointing to it as if to say, "Behold, my time has come." The thoughtful, melancholy air of the two figures may be due to some extent to the influence of Classical Greek art, which pervades the style of our group. At the same time, however, a new mood of uncertainty and regret is felt: human destiny is in the hands of inexorable supernatural forces, while death is the great divide rather than a continuation, albeit on a different plane, of life on earth. In later tombs, death gains an even more fearful aspect. Other, more terrifying demons enter the scene, often battling against benevolent spirits for possession of the soul of the deceased.

82. *Youth and Demon of Death.* Cinerary container.
Early 4th century B.C. Stone (pietra fetida),
length 47″ (119.4 cm).
Museo Archeologico Nazionale, Florence

Architecture

According to Roman writers, the Etruscans were masters of architectural engineering and of town planning and surveying. The Etruscans must also have taught the Romans how to build fortifications, bridges, drainage systems, and aqueducts, but very little remains of their vast enterprises in these fields. That the Romans learned a good deal from them can hardly be doubted, but exactly how much the Etruscans contributed to Roman architecture is difficult to say, since hardly anything of Etruscan or early Roman architecture remains standing above ground. The only impressive surviving monument is the Porta Augusta in Perugia, a fortified city gate of the second century B.C. (fig. 83). The gate itself, recessed between two massive towers, is not just an entry but a true architectural facade. The tall opening is spanned by a semicircular arch framed by a molding. Above is a balustrade of dwarf pilasters alternating with round shields, a pattern derived from the triglyphs and metopes of the Doric frieze; it supports a second arched opening (now filled in) flanked by two larger pilasters.

The arches here are true, which means they are constructed of wedge-shaped blocks, called voussoirs, each pointing toward the center of the semicircular opening. Although the true arch had been invented in Egypt as early as c. 2700 B.C., its use had been confined to underground structures or to simple gateways. The importance of the Porta Augusta is that this is the first instance we know of in which arches were integrated with the vocabulary of the Greek orders into a monumental whole. The Romans were to develop this combination in a thousand ways, but the merit of having invented it, of having made the arch respectable, as it were, seems to belong to the Etruscans.

83. Porta Augusta, Perugia. 2nd century B.C.

ROMAN ART

Among the civilizations of the ancient world, that of the Romans is far more accessible to us than any other. They have left a vast literary legacy which permits us to trace their history with a wealth of detail that never ceases to amaze us. Yet, paradoxically, there are few questions more difficult to answer than "What is Roman art?" The Roman genius, so clearly recognizable in every other sphere of human activity, becomes oddly elusive when we ask whether there was a characteristic Roman style in the fine arts. Why is this so? The most obvious reason is the great admiration the Romans had for Greek art of every period and variety. They imported originals of earlier date by the thousands, and had them copied in even greater numbers. In addition, their own production was clearly based on Greek sources, and many of their artists, from Republican times to the end of the Empire, were of Greek origin. But beyond the different subject matter, the fact remains that, as a whole, the art produced under Roman auspices does look distinctly different from Greek art, and has positive un-Greek qualities expressing different intentions. Thus, we must not insist on evaluating Roman art by the standards of Greek art. The Roman Empire was an extraordinarily complex and open society which absorbed national or regional traits into a common all-Roman framework that was homogeneous and diverse at the same time. The "Romanness" of Roman art must be found in this complex pattern, rather than in a single and consistent quality of form.

ARCHITECTURE

If the autonomy of Roman sculpture and painting has been questioned, Roman architecture is a creative feat of such magnitude as to silence all doubts of this sort. Its growth, moreover, from the very start reflected a specifically Roman way of public and private life, so that whatever elements had been borrowed from the Etruscans or Greeks were soon marked with an unmistakable Roman stamp. Greek models, though much admired, no longer sufficed to accommodate the sheer numbers of people in large public buildings necessitated by the Empire. And when it came to supplying the citizenry with everything it needed, from water to entertainment on a vast scale, radical new forms had to be invented, and cheaper materials and quicker methods had to be used.

From the beginning, the growth of the capital city of Rome is hardly thinkable without the arch and the vaulting systems derived from it: the barrel vault, a half-cylinder; the groin vault, which consists of two barrel vaults intersecting each other at right angles; and the dome. The same is equally true of concrete, a mixture of mortar and gravel with rubble (that is, small pieces of building stone and brick). Concrete construction had been invented in the Near East more than a thousand years earlier, but the Romans developed its potential until it became their chief building technique. The advantages of concrete are obvious: strong, cheap, and flexible, it alone made possible the vast architectural enterprises that are still the chief reminders of "the grandeur that was Rome." The Romans knew how to hide the unattractive concrete surface behind a facing of brick, stone, or marble or layers of smooth plaster. Today, this decorative skin has disappeared from the remains of most Roman buildings, leaving the concrete core exposed and thus depriving these ruins of the appeal that Greek ruins have for us. They speak to us in other ways, through massive size and boldness of conception.

Sanctuary of Fortuna Primigenia. The oldest monument in which these qualities are fully in evidence is the Sanctuary of Fortuna

84. Sanctuary of Fortuna Primigenia, Praeneste (Palestrina). Early 1st century B.C.

85. The Colosseum, Rome. 72–80 A.D.

Primigenia at Palestrina, in the foothills of the Apennines east of Rome. Here, in what was once an important Etruscan stronghold, a strange cult had been established since early times, dedicated to Fortuna (Fate) as a mother deity and combined with a famous oracle. The Roman sanctuary dates from the early first century B.C. A series of ramps and terraces (visible in fig. 84) leads up to a great colonnaded court, from which we ascend, on a flight of steps arranged like the seats of a Greek theater, to the semicircular colonnade that crowned the entire structure. Arched openings, framed by engaged columns and entablatures, play an important part, as do semicircular recesses. Except for the columns and architraves, all the surfaces now visible are of concrete, and it is indeed hard to imagine how a complex as vast as this could have been constructed otherwise.

What makes the sanctuary at Palestrina so imposing, however, is not merely its scale but the superb way it fits the site. An entire hillside, comparable to the Acropolis of Athens in its commanding position, has been transformed and articulated so that the architectural forms seem to grow out of the rock, as if human beings had simply completed a design laid out by nature itself. Such a molding of great open spaces had never been possible—or even desired—in the Classical Greek world; the only comparable projects are found in Egypt. Nor was it compatible with the spirit of the Roman Republic. Significantly enough, the Palestrina sanctuary dates from the time of Sulla, whose absolute dictatorship (82–79 B.C.) marked the transition from Republican government to the one-man rule of Julius Caesar and his imperial successors.

Colosseum. The arch and vault, which we encountered at Palestrina as an essential part of Roman monumental architecture, testify not only to the high quality of Roman engineering but also to the sense of order and permanence that inspired such efforts. These virtues impress us again in the Colosseum, the enormous amphitheater for gladiatorial games in the center of Rome (fig. 85). Completed in 80 A.D., it is, in terms of mass, one of the largest single buildings anywhere; when intact, it accommodated more than 50,000 spectators. The concrete core, with its miles of vaulted corridors and stairways, is a masterpiece of engineering efficiency devised to ensure the smooth flow of traffic to and from the arena. The exterior, dignified and monumental, reflects the interior articulation of the structure but clothes and accentuates it in cut stone. There is a fine balance between vertical and horizontal elements in the framework of engaged columns and entablatures that contains the endless series of arches. The three Classical orders are superimposed according to their intrinsic "weight": Doric, the oldest and most severe, on the ground floor, followed by Ionic and Corinthian. The

86. The Pantheon, Rome. 118–25 A.D.

87. *The Interior of the Pantheon.* Painting by Giovanni Paolo Pannini, c. 1740. The National Gallery of Art, Washington, D.C. Samuel H. Kress Collection

lightening of the proportions, however, is barely noticeable; the orders, in their Roman adaptation, are almost alike. Structurally, they have become ghosts; yet their aesthetic function continues unimpaired, for through them this enormous facade is related to human scale.

Arches, vaults, and concrete permitted the Romans, for the first time in the history of architecture, to create vast interior spaces. These were explored especially in the thermae, or great baths, which had become important centers of social life in imperial Rome. The experience gained there could then be applied to other, more traditional types of buildings, sometimes with revolutionary results.

Pantheon. Perhaps the most striking example of this process is the famous Pantheon in Rome, a very large round temple of the early second century A.D. whose interior is the best preserved as well as the most impressive of any surviving Roman structure (fig. 86). There had been round temples long before this time, but their shape is so different from that of the Pantheon that the latter could not possibly have been derived from them. On the outside, the cella of the Pantheon appears as an unadorned cylindrical drum, surmounted by a gently curved dome. The entrance is emphasized by a deep porch of a type standard to Roman temples. The junction of these two elements seems rather abrupt, but we no longer see the building as it was meant to be seen; today the level of the surrounding streets is a good deal higher than it was in antiquity.

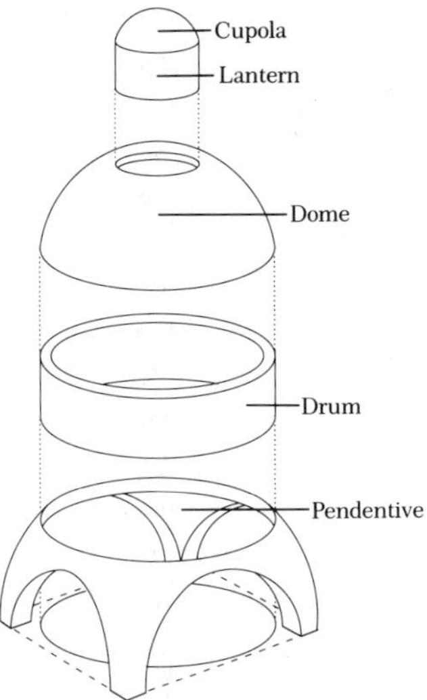

88. Parts of a dome

That the architects did not have an easy time with the engineering problems of supporting the huge hemisphere of a dome may be deduced from the heavy plainness of the exterior wall. Nothing on the outside, however, gives any hint of the airiness and elegance of the interior; photographs fail to capture it, and even the painting (fig. 87) that we use to illustrate it does not do it justice. The height from the floor to the opening of the dome (called the oculus, or eye) is exactly that of the diameter of the dome's base, thus giving the proportions perfect balance. The weight of the dome is concentrated on the eight solid sections of wall (fig. 88). Between them, with graceful columns in front, niches are daringly hollowed out of the massive concrete, and these, while not connected with each other, give the effect of an open space behind the supports, making us feel that the walls are less thick and the dome much lighter than is actually the case. The multicolored marble panels and paving stones are still essentially as they were, but originally the dome was gilded to resemble "the golden dome of heaven."

As its name suggests, the Pantheon was dedicated to all the gods or, more precisely, to the seven planetary gods (there are seven niches). It seems reasonable, therefore, to assume that the golden dome had a symbolic meaning, that it represented the Dome of Heaven. Yet this solemn and splendid structure grew from rather humble antecedents. The Roman architect Vitruvius, writing more than a century earlier, describes the domed steam chamber of a bathing establishment that anticipates (undoubtedly on a very much smaller scale) the essential features of the Pantheon: a hemispherical dome, a proportional relationship of height and width, and the circular opening in the center (which could be closed by a bronze shutter on chains to adjust the temperature of the steam room).

89. The Basilica of Constantine, Rome. c. 310–20 A.D.

Basilica of Constantine. The Basilica of Constantine, from the early fourth century A.D., is a similar example. Basilicas, long halls serving a variety of civic purposes, had first been developed in Hellenistic Greece. Under the Romans, they became a standard feature of every major town, where one of their chief functions was to provide a dignified setting for the courts of law, which dispensed justice in the name of the emperor. Unlike other basilicas, the Basilica of Constantine derives its shape from the main hall of the public baths built by two earlier emperors, Caracalla and Diocletian. But it is built on an even vaster scale. It must have been the largest roofed interior in all of Rome. Today only the north aisle—three huge barrel-vaulted compartments—is still standing (fig. 89). The upper walls of the center tract, or nave, were pierced by a row of large windows (called the clerestory), so that the interior of the basilica must have had a light and airy quality despite its enormous size (fig. 90). We meet its echoes in many later buildings, from churches to railway stations.

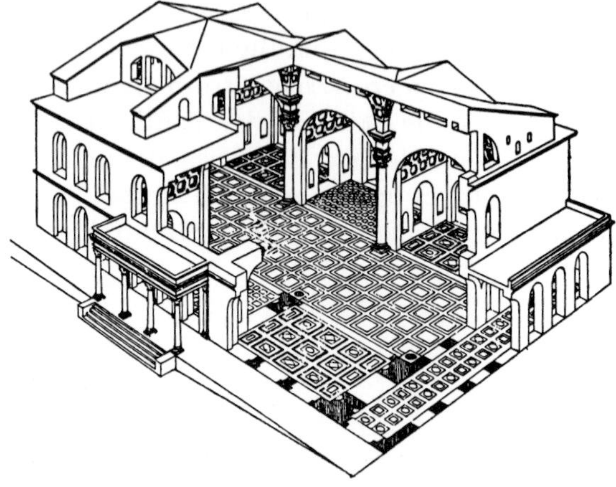

90. Reconstruction drawing of the Basilica of Constantine (after Huelsen)

SCULPTURE

The dispute over the question "Is there such a thing as a Roman style?" has centered largely on the field of sculpture, for understandable reasons. Even if we discount the wholesale importing and copying of Greek originals, the reputation of the Romans as imitators seems borne out by vast quantities of works that are most probably adaptations and variants of Greek models of every period. While the Roman demand for sculpture was tremendous, much of it may be attributed to antiquarianism and to a taste for sumptuous interior decoration. On the other hand, there can be no doubt that some kinds of sculpture had serious and important functions in ancient Rome. They represent the living sculptural tradition. We shall concern ourselves here with those aspects of Roman sculpture that are most conspicuously rooted in Roman society: portraiture and narrative relief.

Portraits

We know from literary accounts that, from early Republican times on, meritorious political or military leaders were honored by having their statues put on public display. The habit was to continue until the end of the Empire a thousand years later. Unfortunately, the first four hundred years of this Roman tradition are a closed book to us; not a single Roman portrait has yet come to light that can be dated before the first century B.C. with any degree of confidence. Apparently, however, the creation of a monumental, unmistakably Roman portrait style was achieved only in the time of Sulla, when Roman architecture, too, came of age (see p. 95). It arose from a patriarchal Roman custom of considerable antiquity. Upon the death of the head of the family, a waxen image was made of his face, which was then preserved in a special shrine, or family altar. At funerals, these ancestral images were carried in the procession. We have seen the roots of this kind of ancestor worship in ethnographic societies (compare fig. 23). The patrician families of Rome clung to it tenaciously well into imperial times. The desire to have these perishable wax records duplicated in marble perhaps came about because the patricians, feeling their traditional position of leadership endangered, wanted to make a greater public display of their ancestors, as a way of emphasizing their ancient lineage.

Ancestor Portraits

Such display certainly is the purpose of the statue in figure 91. It shows an unknown Roman holding two busts of his ancestors, presumably his father and grandfather. The impressive heads of the two ancestors are

91. *A Roman Patrician with Busts of His Ancestors.* Late 1st century B.C. Marble, lifesize. Museo Capitolino, Rome

later copies of the lost originals (differences in style and in the shape of the bust indicate that the original of the head on the left is about thirty years older than that of its companion). The work has little distinction, yet a peculiar "father-image" spirit can be felt here. This quality was not present in the wax images themselves. It came to the fore when they were translated into marble, a process that not only made the ancestral images permanent but monumentalized them in the spiritual sense as well.

Nevertheless, what mattered was only the facial "text," not the "handwriting" of the artist who recorded it. For that reason, these portraits are characterized by a serious, prosaically factual quality. The term "uninspired" suggests itself, not as a criticism but as a way to describe the basic attitude of the Roman artist in contrast to the attitude of Greek or even Etruscan portraitists. That seriousness was consciously intended as a positive value becomes clear when we compare the right-hand ancestral head in our group with the fine Hellenistic portrait from Delos in figure 75. A more telling contrast could hardly be imagined. Both are extremely persuasive likenesses, yet they seem worlds apart. Whereas the Hellenistic head impresses us with its subtle grasp of the sitter's psychology, the Roman may strike us at first glance as nothing but a detailed record of facial topography—the sitter's character emerges only incidentally, as it were. And yet this is not really the case: the features are true to life, no doubt, but the carver has treated them with a selective emphasis designed to bring out a specifically Roman personality—stern, rugged, iron-willed in its devotion to duty. It is a "father image" of frightening authority, and the minutely observed facial details are like individual biographical data that differentiate this father image from others.

Augustus of Primaporta. As we approach the reign of the emperor Augustus (27 B.C.–14 A.D.), we find a new trend in Roman portraiture that reaches its climax in the splendid statue of Augustus of Primaporta (fig. 92). At first glance, we may be uncertain whether it represents a god or a human being. This doubt is entirely appropriate, for the figure is meant to be both. Here, on Roman soil, we meet a concept familiar to us from Egypt and the ancient Near East: that of the divine ruler. It had entered the Greek world in the fourth century B.C. Alexander the Great made it his own, and so did his successors. They, in turn, transmitted it to Julius Caesar and the Roman emperors.

The idea of attributing superhuman stature to the emperor, thereby enhancing his authority, became official policy, and while Augustus did not carry it as far as his successors, the Primaporta statue clearly shows

92. *Augustus of Primaporta.* c. 20 B.C. Marble, height 6′8″ (2.03 m). Musei Vaticani, Rome

him enveloped in an air of divinity. Still, despite its heroic, idealized body, the statue has an unmistakably Roman flavor. The costume, including the rich allegorical program on the breastplate, has a concreteness of surface texture that conveys the actual touch of cloth, metal, and leather. The head, too, is idealized, or, better perhaps, "Hellenized." Small physiognomic details are suppressed, and the focusing of attention on the eyes gives it something of an "inspired" look. Nevertheless, the face is a definite likeness, elevated but clearly individual, as we can determine by comparison with the numerous other portraits of Augustus. The Primaporta statue, which was found in the villa of Augustus' wife, Livia, must have been made under his direct patronage. It has a high level of artistic quality rarely found in the ruler's portraits, which were mass-produced.

The output of portraits was vast, and the diversity of types and styles mirrors the ever more complex character of Roman society. If we regard the Republican ancestral image tradition and the Greek-inspired *Augustus of Primaporta* as opposite ends of the scale, we can find almost any variety of interbreeding between the two. Augustus still conformed to age-old Roman custom by being clean-shaven. His later successors, in contrast, adopted the Greek fashion of wearing beards as an outward sign of admiration for the Hellenic heritage. It is not surprising, therefore, to find a strong classicistic trend, often of a peculiarly cool, formal sort, in the sculpture of the second century A.D., especially during the reigns of Hadrian and Marcus Aurelius, both of them private men deeply interested in Greek philosophy.

Equestrian Monuments

We can sense this introspective quality in the sculpture of Marcus Aurelius on horseback (fig. 93), which is remarkable not only as the sole survivor of the imperial equestrian monuments but as one of the few Roman statues that remained on public view throughout the Middle Ages. The image showing the mounted emperor as the all-conquering lord of the earth had been a firmly established tradition ever since Julius Caesar permitted such a statue of himself to be erected in the Forum Julium. Marcus Aurelius, too, was meant to be seen as ever victorious, for beneath the right front leg of the horse (according to medieval accounts) there once crouched a small figure of a bound barbarian chieftain. The wonderfully spirited and powerful steed expresses this martial spirit. But the emperor himself, without weapons or armor, presents a picture of stoic detachment—a bringer of peace rather than a military hero. And so indeed he saw himself and his reign (161–180 A.D.).

93. *Equestrian Statue of Marcus Aurelius.* 161–80 A.D. Bronze, over lifesize. Piazza del Campidoglio, Rome

Portrait Heads

It was the calm before the storm. The third century saw the Roman Empire in almost perpetual crisis. Barbarians endangered its far-flung frontiers while internal conflicts undermined the authority of the imperial office. To retain the throne became a matter of naked force, succession by murder a regular habit. The "soldier emperors"—mercenaries from the outlying provinces of the realm—

94. *Philippus the Arab.* 244–49 A.D.
Marble, lifesize. Musei Vaticani, Rome

95. *Constantine the Great.* Early 4th century A.D.
Marble, height 8′ (2.44 m).
Palazzo dei Conservatori, Rome

followed one another at brief intervals. The portraits of some of these men, such as Philippus the Arab (fig. 94), who reigned from 244 to 249 A.D., are among the most powerful likenesses in all of art. Their facial realism is as uncompromising as that of Republican portraiture, but its aim is expressive rather than documentary: all the dark passions of the human mind—fear, suspicion, cruelty—suddenly stand revealed here, with a directness that is almost unbelievable. The face of Philippus mirrors all the violence of the time; yet in a strange way it moves us to pity: there is a psychological nakedness about it that recalls a brute creature, cornered and doomed.

The results will remind us of the head from Delos (see fig. 75). Let us note, however, the new plastic means through which the impact of the Roman portrait is achieved. We are struck, first of all, by the way expression centers on the eyes, which seem to gaze at some unseen but powerful threat. The engraved outline of the iris and the hollowed-out pupils, devices alien to earlier portraits, serve to fix the direction of the glance. The hair, too, is rendered in thoroughly un-Classical fashion as a close-fitting, textured cap. The face has been given a peculiar unshaven look, which results from roughing up the surfaces around the jaw and mouth with short chisel strokes.

Clearly, the agony of the Roman world was spiritual as well as physical. So, too, were the glories of its dwindling years—or so they must have seemed to Constantine the Great (fig. 95), reorganizer of the Roman state and the first Christian emperor (see p. 108). No mere bust, this head is one of several remaining fragments of a colossal statue (the head alone is over eight feet tall) that once stood in Constantine's gigantic basilica (see fig. 89). In this head everything is so out of proportion to the scale of ordinary people that we feel crushed by its immensity. The impression of being in the presence of some unimaginable power was deliberate, we may be sure, for it is reinforced by the massive, immobile features of the head, out of which the huge, radiant eyes stare with hypnotic intensity. All in all, it tells us less about the way Constantine looked than about his view of himself and his exalted office.

Reliefs

Imperial art was not confined to portraiture. The emperors also commemorated their outstanding achievements in narrative reliefs on monumental altars, triumphal arches, and columns. Similar scenes are familiar to us from the ancient Near East (see figs. 28, 45, and 46) but not from Greece. Historic events—that is, events that occurred only once, at a specific time and in a particular place—had not been dealt with in Classical Greek sculpture. If a victory over the Persians was to be commemorated, it would be represented indirectly, as a combat of Lapiths and Centaurs, or Greeks and Amazons—a mythical event outside any space-time context. Even in the Hellenistic era, this attitude persisted, although not quite as absolutely. When the kings of Pergamum celebrated their victories over the Gauls, the latter were represented faithfully but in typical poses of defeat rather than in the framework of a particular battle (see fig. 76).

Greek painters, on the other hand, had depicted historic subjects. The mosaic from Pompeii showing *The Battle of Issus* (see fig. 59) probably reflects a famous Greek painting of about 315 B.C. depicting the defeat of the Persian king Darius by Alexander the Great. In Rome, too, historic events had been painted from the third century B.C. on. Rendered on panels, these pictures seem to have had the fleeting nature of posters advertising a hero's triumphs. Sometime during the late years of the Republic the temporary representations of such events began to assume more monumental and permanent form by being carved and attached to structures intended to last indefinitely. They were thus a ready tool for the glorification of imperial rule, and the emperors did not hesitate to use them on a large scale.

Arch of Titus. Roman relief carving reached its greatest development in the two large narrative panels on the triumphal arch erected in 81 A.D. to commemorate the victories of the emperor Titus. One of them (fig. 96) shows part of the triumphal procession celebrating the conquest of Jerusalem; the booty displayed includes the seven-branched candlestick and other sacred objects. Despite the mutilated surface, the movement of a crowd of figures in depth is still conveyed with striking success. On the right, the procession turns away from us and disappears through a

96. *Spoils from the Temple in Jerusalem.* Relief in passageway, Arch of Titus, Rome. 81 A.D. Marble, height 7′10″ (2.39 m)

triumphal arch placed obliquely to the background plane so that only the nearer half actually emerges from the background—a radical but effective device.

Column of Trajan. The purposes of Imperial art, narrative or symbolic, were sometimes incompatible with a realistic treatment of space. In terms of the number of figures and the density of the narrative, the continuous spiral band of relief covering the Column of Trajan (fig. 97), erected in 106–113 A.D. to celebrate that emperor's victorious campaigns against the Dacians (the ancient inhabitants of Romania), is by far the most ambitious frieze composition attempted up to that time. It is also the most frustrating, for viewers must "run around in circles like a circus horse" (to borrow the apt description of one scholar) to follow the narrative, and can hardly see anything above the fourth or fifth turn without binoculars. The spiral frieze was a new and demanding framework for historic narrative which imposed a number of difficult conditions upon the sculptor. Since there could be no clarifying inscriptions, the pictorial account had to be as self-sufficient and explicit as possible, which meant that the spatial setting of each episode had to be worked out with great care; visual continuity had to be preserved without destroying the inner coherence of the individual scenes; and the actual depth of the carving had to be much shallower than in reliefs such as those on the Arch of Titus, otherwise the shadows cast by the projecting parts would make the scenes unreadable from below. Our artist has solved these problems with great success, but at the cost of sacrificing all but the merest remnants of illusionistic spatial depth. Landscape and architecture are reduced to abbreviated "stage sets," and the ground on which the figures stand is tilted upward. The scenes in our detail are a fair sampling of the events depicted on the column: among the more than a hundred fifty separate episodes, actual combat occurs only rarely, while the geographic, logistic, and political aspects of the campaign receive detailed attention, much as they do in Julius Caesar's famous account of his conquest of Gaul.

97. Lower portion of the Column of Trajan, Rome. 106–13 A.D. Marble, height of relief band c. 50″ (127 cm)

PAINTING

We know infinitely less about Roman painting than we do about Roman architecture or sculpture. Almost all of the surviving examples consist of wall paintings, and the great majority of these come from Pompeii, Herculaneum, and other settlements buried by the eruption of Mount Vesuvius in 79 A.D., or from Rome and its environs; their dates cover a span of less than two hundred years. That there was copying of Greek designs, and that Greek paintings as well as painters were imported, nobody will dispute. But *The Battle of Issus* (see fig. 59) is one of the few instances in which this link can be demonstrated.

98. The Ixion Room, House of the Vettii, Pompeii. 63–79 A.D.

Roman Illusionism

The style that prevailed at the time of the eruption of Mount Vesuvius can be seen in the painting that adorned a corner of the Ixion Room in the House of the Vettii at Pompeii (fig. 98): it combines imitation marble paneling, conspicuously framed mythological scenes intended to give the effect of panel pictures set into the wall, and fantastic architectural vistas seen through make-believe windows, creating the effect of a somewhat disjointed compilation of motifs from various sources. The architecture, too, has a strangely unreal and picturesque quality that is believed to reflect the architectural backdrops of the theaters of the time. The illusion of surface textures and distant views has an extraordinary degree of three-dimensional reality, but as soon as we try to analyze the relationship of the parts to each other, we quickly realize that the Roman painter has no systematic grasp of spatial depth, that his perspective is haphazard and inconsistent within itself. Apparently he never intended us to enter the space he has created. Like a promised land, it remains forever beyond us.

When landscape takes the place of architectural vistas, exact foreshortening becomes less important, and the virtues of the Roman painter's approach outweigh his limitations. This is most strikingly demonstrated by the famous *Odyssey Landscapes*, a continuous stretch of landscape subdivided into eight compartments by a framework of pilasters. Each section illustrates an episode of the adventures of Odysseus (Ulysses). One of the adventures with the Laestrygonians is reproduced in figure 99. The airy, bluish tones create a wonderful feeling of atmospheric, light-filled space that envelops and binds together all the forms within this warm Mediterranean fairyland, where the human figures seem to play no more than an incidental role. Only upon further reflection do we realize how frail the illusion of coherence is even here: if we were to try mapping this land-

99. *The Laestrygonians Hurling Rocks at the Fleet of Odysseus.* Wall painting from the *Odyssey Landscapes* series in a house on the Esquiline Hill, Rome. Late 1st century B.C. Musei Vaticani, Rome

100. *Scenes of a Dionysiac Mystery Cult.* Wall painting frieze. c. 50 B.C. Villa of the Mysteries, Pompeii

scape, we would find it just as ambiguous as the architectural perspective discussed above. Its unity is not structural but poetic.

Villa of the Mysteries. There exists one monument whose sweeping grandeur of design and coherence of style are unique in Roman painting: the great frieze in one of the rooms in the Villa of the Mysteries just outside Pompeii (fig. 100). The artist has placed his figures on a narrow ledge of green against a regular pattern of red panels separated by strips of black, a kind of running stage on which they enact their strange and solemn ritual. Who are they, and what is the meaning of the cycle? Many details remain puzzling, but the program as a whole represents various rites of the Dionysiac Mysteries, a semisecret cult of very ancient origin that had been brought to Italy from Greece. Human and mythical reality tend to merge into one. We sense the blending of these two spheres in the qualities all the figures have in common: their dignity of bearing and expression, the wonderful firmness of body and drapery, the rapt intensity with which they participate in the drama of the ritual. Many of the poses and gestures are taken from the repertory of Classical Greek art, yet they lack the studied and self-conscious quality we call classicism. An artist of exceptional greatness of vision has filled these forms with new life. Whatever his relation to the famous masters of Greek painting whose works are lost to us forever, he was their legitimate heir in the same sense that the finest Latin poets of the Augustan age were the legitimate heirs to the Greek poetic tradition.

Portraits

We know from Pliny that portrait painting was an established custom in Republican Rome, but none of these panels have survived. The only coherent group of painted portraits at our disposal comes instead from the Faiyum district in Lower Egypt. We owe them to the survival (or revival) of an ancient Egyptian custom, that of attaching a portrait of the deceased to the wrapped, mummified body. The amazing freshness of their color is due to the fact that they were done in a medium of great durability called encaustic, which means that the pigments are suspended in hot wax. The mixture can be opaque and creamy, like oil paint, or thin and translucent. At their best, these portraits, such as the very fine and well-preserved wooden panel reproduced in figure 101, have an immediacy and sureness of touch that have rarely been surpassed. Our dark-haired boy is as solid, sparkling, and lifelike a piece of reality as anyone might wish. The artist has emphasized certain features, for example, the eyes. But in this happy instance, the stylization has been made with the intention only of recalling the attractive personality of a beloved child.

101. *Portrait of a Boy,* from the Faiyum, Lower Egypt. 2nd century A.D. Encaustic on panel, 13 × 7¼" (33 × 18.4 cm). The Metropolitan Museum of Art, New York. Gift of Edward S. Harkness, 1918

EARLY CHRISTIAN AND BYZANTINE ART

In 323 A.D. Constantine the Great made a fateful decision, the consequences of which are still felt today—he resolved to move the capital of the Roman Empire to the Greek town of Byzantium, which thenceforth was to be known as Constantinople, and today as Istanbul. In taking this step, the emperor acknowledged the growing strategic and economic importance of the eastern provinces. The new capital also symbolized the new Christian basis of the Roman state. Constantine could hardly have foreseen that shifting the seat of imperial power would result in splitting the realm; yet within less than a hundred years the division had become an accomplished fact, even though the emperors at Constantinople did not relinquish their claim to the western provinces. The latter, ruled by western Roman emperors, soon fell prey to invading Germanic tribes. By the end of the sixth century, the last vestige of centralized authority had disappeared. The eastern, or Byzantine, Empire, in contrast, survived these onslaughts, and under Justinian (527–565) reached new power and stability.

The division of the Roman Empire soon led to a religious split as well. At the time of Constantine, the bishop of Rome, deriving his authority from St. Peter, was the acknowledged head, the pope, of the Christian Church. His claim to preeminence, however, soon came to be disputed by the patriarch of Constantinople; differences in doctrine began to develop; and eventually the division of Christendom into a Western, or Catholic, and an Eastern, or Orthodox, Church became all but final. The differences between them went very deep. Roman Catholicism maintained its independence from imperial or any other state authority and became an international institution reflecting its character as the Universal Church, while the Orthodox Church was based on the union of spiritual and secular authority in the person of the emperor, who appointed the patriarch. We will recognize this pattern as the Christian adaptation of a very ancient heritage, the divine kingship of Egypt and the Near East. If the Byzantine emperors, unlike their pagan predecessors, could no longer claim the status of gods, they retained an equally unique and exalted role by placing themselves at the head of the Church as well as of the State.

It is the religious even more than the political separation of East and West that makes it impossible to discuss the development of Christian art in the Roman Empire under a single heading. "Early Christian" does not, strictly speaking, designate a style. It refers, rather, to any work of art produced by or for Christians during the time prior to the splitting off of the Orthodox Church—or, roughly, the first five centuries of our era. "Byzantine," on the other hand, designates not only the art of the eastern Roman Empire but a specific quality of style as well. Since this style grew out of certain tendencies that can be traced back to the time of Constantine or even earlier, there is no sharp dividing line between Early Christian and Byzantine art. Thus the reign of Justinian has been termed the First Golden Age of Byzantine art. Yet the monuments he sponsored, especially those on Italian soil, may be viewed as either Early Christian or Byzantine, depending on which frame of reference we select.

Soon after, it is true, the political and religious cleavage between East and West became an artistic cleavage as well. In western Europe, Celtic and Germanic peoples fell heir to the civilization of late antiquity, of which Early Christian art had been a part, and trans-

102. Painted ceiling. 4th century A.D. Catacomb of SS. Pietro e Marcellino, Rome

formed it into that of the Middle Ages. The East, in contrast, experienced no such break. In the Byzantine Empire, late antiquity lived on, although the Greek and Oriental elements came increasingly to the fore at the expense of the Roman heritage. As a consequence, Byzantine civilization never became wholly medieval.

EARLY CHRISTIAN ART

There is little we know for certain about Christian art until we reach the reign of Constantine the Great. The painted decorations of the Roman catacombs, the underground burial places of the Christians, provide the only sizable and coherent body of material, but these are merely one among various possible kinds of Christian art. Before that time, Rome did not embody the faith. Older and larger Christian communities existed in the great cities of North Africa and the Near East, such as Alexandria and Antioch. They had probably developed separate artistic traditions of their own, but few traces of them survive. If the dearth of material from the eastern provinces of the Empire makes it difficult to trace the early development of Christian art, the catacomb paintings nevertheless tell us a good deal about the spirit of the communities that sponsored them.

Catacombs

The burial rite and the safeguarding of the tomb were of vital concern to the early Christian, whose faith rested on the hope of eternal life in paradise. The imagery of the catacombs, as can be seen in the painted ceiling in figure 102, clearly expresses this outlook, although the forms are in essence still those of pre-Christian mural decoration. Thus we recognize the division of the ceiling into compartments as a late and highly simplified echo of the illusionistic architectural schemes in Pompeian painting, and the modeling of the figures, as well as the landscape settings, betray their descent from the same Roman idiom, which here has become debased in the hands of an artist of very modest ability. But the catacomb painter has used this traditional vocabulary to convey a new, symbolic content, and the original meaning of the forms is of little interest to him. Even the geometric framework shares in this task, for the great circle suggests the Dome of Heaven, inscribed with the cross, the basic symbol of the faith. In the central medallion we see a youthful shepherd, with a sheep on his shoulders, in a pose that can be traced back as far as Greek Archaic art. He stands for Christ the Saviour, the Good Shepherd who gives His life for His flock.

The semicircular compartments tell the story of Jonah: on the left he is cast from the ship, on the right he emerges from the whale, and at the bottom he is safe again on dry land, meditating upon the mercy of the Lord. This Old Testament miracle, often juxtaposed with New Testament miracles, enjoyed great favor in Early Christian art as proof of the Lord's power to rescue the faithful from the jaws of death. The standing figures represent members of the Church, with their hands raised in prayer, pleading for divine help. The entire scheme, though small in scale and unimpressive in execution, has a consistency and clarity that set it apart from its pagan ancestors.

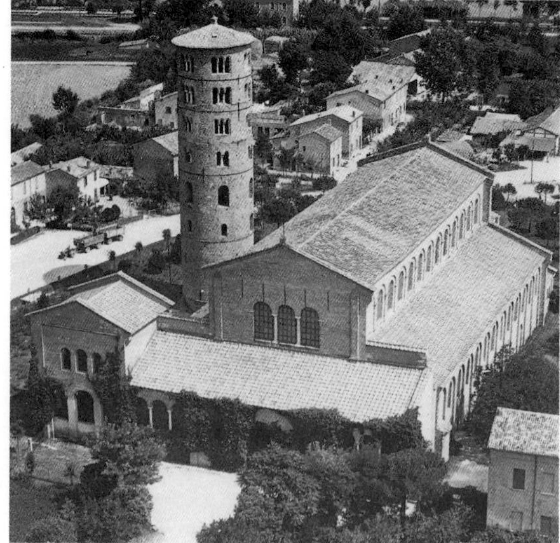

103. S. Apollinare in Classe, Ravenna. 533–49 A.D.

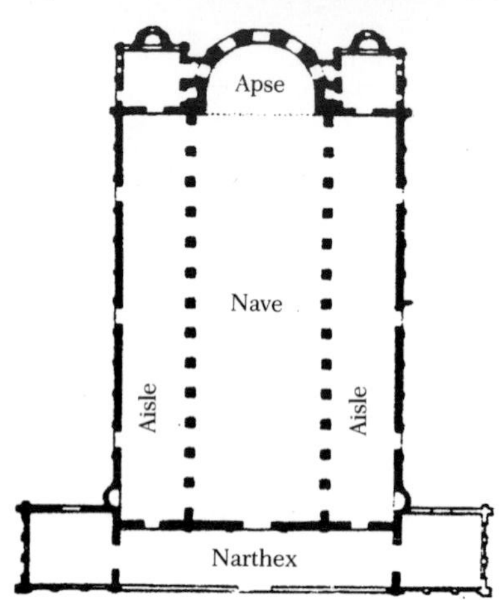

104. Plan of S. Apollinare in Classe (after De Angelis d'Ossat)

Architecture

Constantine's decision to make Christianity the state religion of the Roman Empire had a profound impact on Christian art. Until that time, congregations had been unable to meet for worship in public. Services were held covertly in the houses of the wealthier members. Now, almost overnight, an impressive architectural setting had to be created for the new official faith, so that the Church might be visible to all. Constantine himself devoted the full resources of his office to this task, and within a few years an astonishing number of large, imperially sponsored churches arose, not only in Rome but also in Constantinople, in the Holy Land, and at other important sites.

S. Apollinare in Classe. These structures were a new type, the Early Christian basilica, and they provided the basic model for the development of church architecture in western Europe. The Early Christian basilica, as seen in the sixth-century church of S. Apollinare in Classe near Ravenna (figs. 103, 104), is a synthesis of assembly hall, temple, and

105. Interior (view into the apse), S. Apollinare in Classe

private house. It also has the qualities of an original creation that cannot be wholly explained in terms of its sources. It owes to the Imperial basilicas of pagan times the long nave flanked by aisles and lit by clerestory windows, the apse, and the wooden roof. Our view, taken from the west, shows the entrance hall (narthex) but not the colonnaded court (atrium), which was torn down a long time ago; the round bell tower, or campanile, is a medieval addition. (Many basilican churches also include a transept, a separate compartment of space placed at right angles to the nave and aisles forming a cross plan, though this feature is frequently omitted, as here.) The pagan basilica was a uniquely suitable model for Constantinian churches, since it combined the spacious interior demanded by Christian ritual with imperial associations that proclaimed the privileged status of Christianity as the new state religion. But a church had to be more than an assembly hall. In addition to enclosing the community of the faithful, it was the sacred House of God, the Christian successor to the temples of old.

In order to express this function, the design of the pagan basilica had to be given a new focus, the altar, which was placed in front of the apse at the eastern end of the nave, and the entrances, which in pagan basilicas had usually been on the flanks, were shifted to the western end. The Christian basilica was thus oriented along a single, longitudinal axis that is curiously reminiscent of the layout of Egyptian temples (compare fig. 36).

S. Apollinare in Classe shows another essential aspect of Early Christian religious architecture: the contrast between exterior and interior. The plain brick exterior remains conspicuously unadorned. It is merely a shell whose shape reflects the interior space it encloses—the exact opposite of the Classical temple. This ascetic, antimonumental treatment of the exterior gives way to the utmost richness as we enter the church proper (fig. 105). Here, having left the everyday world behind, we find ourselves in a shimmering realm of light and color where precious marble surfaces and the brilliant glitter of mosaics evoke the spiritual splendor of the Kingdom of God. The steady rhythm of the nave arcade pulls us toward the great arch at the eastern end (called the triumphal arch), which frames the altar and the vaulted apse beyond.

Mosaics

The rapid growth of Christian architecture on a large scale must have had an almost revolutionary effect on the development of Early Christian painting. All of a sudden, huge wall surfaces had to be covered with images worthy of their monumental framework. The heritage of the past, however, was not only absorbed but also transformed to make it fit its new physical and spiritual environment. In the process, a great new art form emerged, the Early Christian wall mosaic, which to a large extent replaced the older and cheaper medium of mural painting. The Hellenistic Greeks and the Romans had produced mostly floor mosaics. The vast and intricate wall mosaics of Early Christian art thus are essentially without precedent. The same is true of their material, for they consist of small cubes of colored glass known as tesserae. These offered colors of far greater range and intensity than the marble employed in *The Battle of Issus* (see fig. 59), including gold, but lacked the fine gradations in tone necessary for imitating painted pictures. The shiny (and slightly irregular) faces of glass tesserae act as tiny reflectors, so that the overall effect is that of a glittering, immaterial screen rather than of a solid, continuous surface. All these qualities made glass mosaic the ideal complement of the new architectural aesthetic in Early Christian basilicas. The brilliant color, the light-filled, transparent brightness of gold, the severe geometric order of the images in a mosaic complex such as that of S. Apollinare in Classe fit the spirit of these interiors to perfection. One might say, in fact, that Early Christian and Byzantine churches *demand* mosaics the way Greek temples demand architectural sculpture.

In Early Christian mosaics the flatness of the wall surface is denied, not in order to suggest a reality beyond the surface of the wall, as in Roman mural painting, but for the purpose of achieving an "illusion of unreality," a luminous realm peopled by celestial beings or symbols. In narrative scenes, too, we see the illusionistic tradition of ancient painting being transformed by new content. Long sequences of scenes, selected from the Old and New Testaments, adorned the nave walls of Early Christian basilicas.

The Parting of Lot and Abraham (fig. 106) is taken from the oldest surviving cycle of this kind, executed about 430 in the church of Sta. Maria Maggiore in Rome. Abraham, his son Isaac, and the rest of his family occupy the left half of the composition; Lot and his clan, including his two small daughters, turn toward the city of Sodom on the right. The task of the artist who designed our panel is comparable to that faced by the sculptors of the Column of Trajan (see fig. 97): how to condense complex actions into a visual form that would permit them to be read at a distance. He has, in fact, employed many of the same "shorthand" devices, such as the abbreviative formulas for house, tree, and city, or the trick of showing a crowd of people as a "grape-cluster of heads" behind the foreground figures. But in the Trajanic reliefs, these devices could be used only to the extent that they were compatible with the realistic aim of the scenes, which re-create actual historic events. The mosaics in Sta. Maria Maggiore, on the other hand, depict the history of salvation. The reality they illustrate is the living word of the Scriptures (in this instance, Genesis 13), which is a *present* reality shared by artist and beholder alike, rather than something that happened only once in the space-and-time context of the external world.

Hence the artist need not clothe the scene with the concrete details of historic narrative. Glances and gestures are more important to him than dramatic movement or three-dimensional form. The symmetrical composition, with its cleavage in the center, makes clear the symbolic significance of this parting: the way of Abraham, which is that of righteousness and the Covenant, as against the way of Lot, destined for divine vengeance. And the contrasting fate of the two groups is further emphasized by the juxtaposition of Isaac and the daughters of Lot, whose future roles are thus called to mind.

106. *The Parting of Lot and Abraham.* c. 430 A.D. Mosaic. Sta. Maria Maggiore, Rome

Roll, Book, and Illustration

From what source did the designers of narrative mosaic cycles such as that of Sta. Maria Maggiore derive their compositions? For certain subjects, they could have found models among the catacomb murals, but their most important prototypes may have come from illustrated manuscripts, especially of the Old Testament. As a scriptural religion, founded on the Word of God as revealed in Holy Writ, the early Christian Church must have sponsored the duplicating of the sacred text on a vast scale. Every copy of it was handled with a reverence quite unlike the treatment of any book in Graeco-Roman civilization.

The history of books begins in Egypt—we do not know exactly when—with the discovery of a paperlike material, but rather more brittle, made from the papyrus plant. Books of papyrus were in the form of rolls. Not until late Hellenistic times did a better substance become available: parchment, or vellum (thin, bleached animal hide). Far more durable than papyrus, it was strong enough to be creased without breaking, and thus made possible the kind of bound book

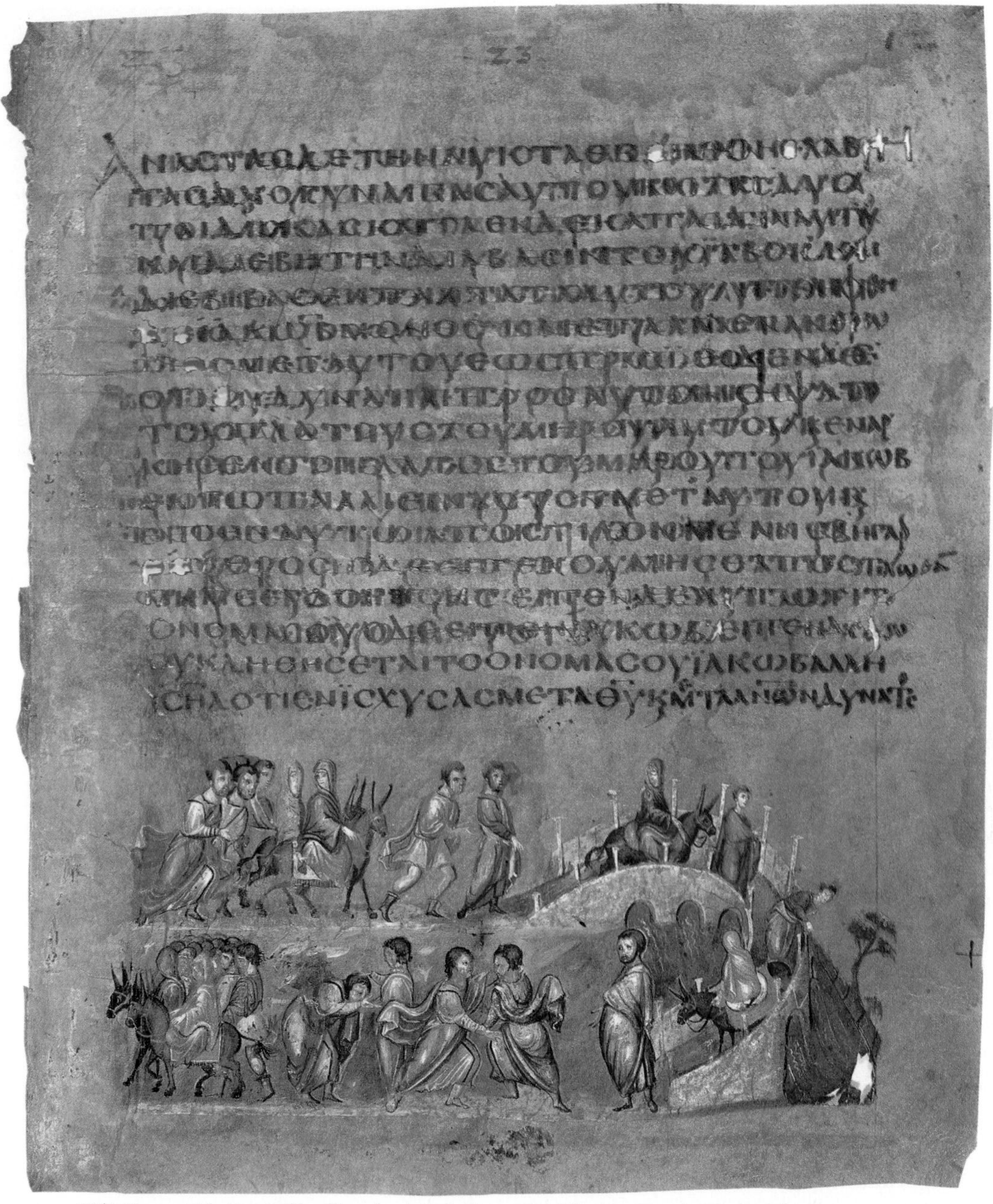

107. Page with *Jacob Wrestling the Angel,* from the *Vienna Genesis.* Early 6th century A.D. 13¼ × 9½" (33.7 × 24.1 cm). Österreichische Nationalbibliothek, Vienna

we know today, technically called a codex. Between the first and the fourth century A.D., the vellum codex gradually replaced the roll. This change had an important effect on the growth of book illustration. Only the vellum codex permitted the use of rich colors, including gold, that was to make book illustration—or, as we usually say, illumination—the small-scale counterpart of murals, mosaics, and panel pictures.

Vienna Genesis. One of the oldest extant examples of an Old Testament book, the *Vienna Genesis*, written in silver (now turned black) on purple vellum, was adorned with brilliantly colored miniatures that achieve a sumptuous effect not unlike that of the mosaics we have seen. Figure 107 shows several scenes from the story of Jacob; in the foreground, we see him wrestling with the angel and receiving the angel's benediction. The picture, then, does not show a single event but a whole sequence, strung out along a single U-shaped path, so that progression in space becomes progression in time. This method, known as continuous narration, may reflect earlier illustrations made for books in roll form. For manuscript illustration, the continuous method offers the advantage of spatial economy. It permits the painter to pack a maximum of narrative content into the area at his disposal. Our artist apparently thought of his picture as a running account to be read like lines of text, rather than as a window demanding a frame. The painted forms are placed directly on the purple background that holds the letters, emphasizing the importance of the page as a unified field.

Sculpture

Compared to painting and architecture, sculpture played a secondary role in Early Christian art. The biblical prohibition of graven images was thought to apply with particular force to large cult statues, the idols worshiped in pagan temples. If religious sculpture was to avoid the pagan taint of idolatry, it had to eschew lifesize representations of the human figure. It thus developed from the very start in an antimonumental direction: away from the spatial depth and massive scale of Graeco-Roman sculpture toward shallow, small-scale forms and lacelike surface decoration. The earliest works of Christian sculpture are marble sarcophagi, which were produced from the middle of the third century on for the more important members of the Church. Before the time of Constantine, their decoration consisted mostly of the same limited repertory of themes familiar from catacomb murals—the Good Shepherd, Jonah and the Whale, and so forth—but within a framework borrowed from pagan sarcophagi. Not until a century later do we find a significantly broader range of subject matter and form.

Sarcophagus of Junius Bassus. A key example for those years is the richly carved *Sarcophagus of Junius Bassus*, made for a prefect of Rome who died in 359 (fig. 108). Its colon-

108. *Sarcophagus of Junius Bassus.* c. 359 A.D. Marble, 3′10½″×8′ (1.18×2.44 m). Museo Petriano, St. Peter's, Rome

naded front, divided into ten square compartments, shows a mixture of Old and New Testament scenes: in the upper row (left to right), the Sacrifice of Isaac, St. Peter Taken Prisoner, Christ Enthroned Between Sts. Peter and Paul, Christ Before Pontius Pilate (two compartments); in the lower row, the Misery of Job, the Fall of Man, Christ's Entry into Jerusalem, Daniel in the Lions' Den, and St. Paul Led to His Martyrdom. This choice, somewhat strange to the modern beholder, is highly characteristic of the Early Christian way of thinking, which stresses the divine rather than the human nature of Christ. Hence His suffering and death are merely hinted at. He appears before Pilate as a youthful, long-haired philosopher expounding the true wisdom (note the scroll), and the martyrdom of the two apostles is represented in the same discreet, nonviolent fashion. The two central scenes are devoted to Christ the King: as Ruler of the Universe He sits enthroned above the personification of the firmament, and as an earthly sovereign He enters Jerusalem in triumph. Adam and Eve, the original sinners, denote the burden of guilt redeemed by Christ, the Sacrifice of Isaac is the Old Testament prefiguration of Christ's sacrificial death, while Job and Daniel carry the same message as Jonah—they fortify the hope of salvation. The figures in their deeply recessed niches betray a conscious attempt to recapture the statuesque dignity of the Greek tradition. Yet beneath this superimposed classicism we sense an oddly becalmed, passive air in the scenes calling for dramatic action. The events and personages confronting us are no longer intended to tell their own story, physically or emotionally, but to call to our minds a higher, symbolic meaning that binds them together.

Classicism

Classicizing tendencies of this sort seem to have been a recurrent phenomenon in Early Christian sculpture from the mid-fourth to the early sixth century. Their causes have been explained in various ways. On the one hand, during this period paganism still had many important adherents who may have fostered such revivals as a kind of rearguard action. Recent converts (such as Junius Bassus himself, who was not baptized until shortly before his death) often kept their allegiance to values of the past, artistic and otherwise. There were also important leaders of the Church who favored a reconciliation of Christianity with the heritage of classical antiquity. The imperial courts, too, both East and West, always remained aware of their institutional links with pre-Christian times, and could thus become centers for revivalist impulses. Whatever its roots in any given instance, classicism had its virtues in this age of transition, for it preserved—and thus helped transmit to the future—a treasury of forms and an ideal of beauty that might otherwise have been irretrievably lost.

Ivory Diptychs

This holds true particularly for a class of objects whose artistic importance far exceeds their physical size: ivory panels and other small-scale reliefs in precious materials. Designed for private ownership and meant to be enjoyed at close range, they often mirror a collector's taste, a refined aesthetic sensibility not found among the large, official enterprises sponsored by Church or State. The ivory leaf (fig. 109) done soon after 500 in the eastern Roman Empire is just such a piece. It shows a classicism that has become an eloquent vehicle of Christian content. The majestic archangel is clearly a descendant of the winged Victories of Graeco-Roman art, down to the richly articulated drapery (see fig. 78). Yet the power he heralds is not of this world; nor does he inhabit an earthly space. The architectural niche against which he appears has lost all three-dimensional reality. Its relationship to him is purely symbolic and ornamental, so that he seems to hover rather than to stand (notice the position of the feet on the steps). It is this disembodied quality, conveyed through classically harmonious forms, that gives him so compelling a presence.

109. *The Archangel Michael.* Leaf of a diptych. Early 6th century A.D. Ivory, 17 × 5½" (43.2 × 14 cm). British Museum, London

BYZANTINE ART

The First Golden Age

There is no clear-cut line of demarcation between Early Christian and Byzantine art before the reign of Justinian (527–565), when Constantinople not only reasserted its political dominance over the West but became the undisputed artistic capital as well. Justinian himself was an art patron on a scale unmatched since Constantine's day. The works he sponsored or promoted have an imperial grandeur that fully justifies the acclaim of those who have termed his era a golden age. They also display an inner unity of style, which links them more strongly with the future development of Byzantine art than with the art of the preceding centuries. Ironically, the richest array of monuments of the First Golden Age (526–726 A.D.) survives today not in Constantinople (where much has been destroyed) but in the Adriatic port of Ravenna, which, under Justinian, was the main stronghold of Byzantine rule in Italy.

S. Vitale, Ravenna. The most important church of that time, S. Vitale (fig. 110), built in 526–547, has an octagonal plan, with a domed central core, which marks it as the descendant of the elaborate Roman baths. The design of the Pantheon (see fig. 86) was derived from that source as well, but the intervening development seems to have taken place in the East. S. Vitale is notable for the richness of its spatial effect. Below the clerestory, the nave wall turns into a series of semicircular niches that penetrate into the aisle and thus link it to the nave in a new and intricate way. The aisle itself has been given a second story (the galleries were reserved for women). A new economy in the construction of the vaulting permits large windows on every level, which flood the interior with light. The complexity of the exterior is matched by the spatial richness of the interior (fig. 111), with its lavish decoration.

Remembering S. Apollinare in Classe (see fig. 103), built in Ravenna at the same time, we are particularly struck by the alien charac-

110. S. Vitale, Ravenna, 526–47 A.D.

111. Interior (view from the apse), S. Vitale

ter of S. Vitale. We find only the merest remnants of the longitudinal axis of the Early Christian basilica. From the time of Justinian, domed, central-plan churches were to dominate the world of Orthodox Christianity as thoroughly as the basilican plan dominated the architecture of the medieval West. How did it happen that the East favored a type of church building (as distinct from baptisteries and mausoleums) so radically different from the basilica and—from the Western point of view—so ill adapted to Christian ritual? After all, the design of the basilica had been backed by the authority of Constantine himself. Many different reasons have been suggested—practical, religious, political. All of them may be relevant; yet, if the truth be told, they fall short of a really persuasive explanation.

As for S. Vitale, its link with the Byzantine court is evidenced by the famous mosaics flanking the altar, whose design must have come directly from the imperial workshop. We see Justinian, accompanied by officials and the local clergy, attending the service as if this were a palace chapel (fig. 112). (The empress Theodora is shown with her ladies-in-waiting in the opposite panel.) Here we find an ideal of human beauty quite distinct from the squat, large-headed figures we encountered in the art of the fourth and fifth centuries: extraordinarily tall, slim figures, with tiny feet, small almond-shaped faces dominated by their huge, staring eyes, and bodies that seem to be capable only of slow ceremonial gestures and the display of magnificently patterned costumes. Justinian and his immediate neighbors were surely intended to be individual likenesses, and their features are indeed differentiated to a degree (those of the archbishop, Maximianus, more so than the rest), but the ideal has molded the faces as well as the bodies, so that they all have a curious family resemblance. The same large, dark eyes under curved brows, the same small mouths and long, narrow, slightly aquiline noses became the standard type from now on in Byzantine art.

If we turn from these mosaics to the interior space of the church, we discover that it, too, shares the quality of dematerialized, soaring slenderness that endows the figures with their air of mute exaltation. Every hint of movement or change is carefully excluded—the dimensions of time and earthly space have given way to an eternal present amid the golden translucency of Heaven, and the solemn, frontal images in the mosaics seem to present a celestial rather than a secular court. This union of political and spiritual authority

112. *Emperor Justinian and His Attendants.* c. 547 A.D. Mosaic. S. Vitale

accurately reflects the "divine kingship" of the Byzantine emperor. We are, in fact, invited to see Justinian as analogous to Christ. He is flanked by twelve companions (six are soldiers, crowded behind a shield with the monogram of Christ)—the imperial equivalent of the twelve apostles.

Hagia Sophia, Istanbul. Among the surviving monuments of Justinian's reign in Constantinople, the most important by far is Hagia Sophia (the Church of Holy Wisdom), the architectural masterpiece of that age and one of the great creative triumphs of any age (figs. 113, 114). Built in 532–537, it achieved such fame that the names of the architects, too, were remembered—Anthemius of Tralles and Isidorus of Miletus. After the Turkish conquest in 1453, it became a mosque (the four minarets were added then). The design of Hagia Sophia presents a unique combination of elements: it has the longitudinal axis of an Early Christian basilica, but the central feature of the nave is a square compartment crowned by a huge dome and abutted at either end by half domes, so that the nave becomes a great oval. Attached to these half domes are semicircular niches with open arcades, similar to those in S. Vitale. One might say, then, that the dome of Hagia Sophia has been inserted between the two halves of a central-plan church. The dome rests on four arches, which carry its weight to the great piers at the corners of the square, so that the walls below the arches have no supporting function at all. The transition from the square formed by these arches to the circular rim of the dome is achieved by spherical triangles called pendentives. This device permits the construction of taller, lighter, and more economical domes than the older method (as seen in the Pantheon and S. Vitale) of placing the dome on a round or polygonal base. The plan, the buttressing of the

113. Anthemius of Tralles and Isidorus of Miletus. Hagia Sophia, Istanbul. 532–37 A.D.

main piers, and the vast scale of the whole recall the Basilica of Constantine (see fig. 89), the most ambitious achievement of Imperial Roman vaulted architecture and the greatest monument associated with a ruler for whom Justinian had particular admiration. Hagia Sophia thus unites East and West, past and future, in a single overpowering synthesis.

Once we are inside, all sense of weight disappears, as if the material, solid aspects of the structure had been banished to the outside. Nothing remains but an expanding space that inflates, like so many sails, the apsidal recesses, the pendentives, and the dome itself. Here the architectural aesthetic we saw taking shape in S. Apollinare in Classe (see fig. 105) has achieved a new, magnificent dimension. Even more than previously, light plays a key role: the dome seems to float—"like the radiant heavens," according to a contemporary description of the building—because it rests upon a closely spaced ring of windows, and the nave walls are pierced by so many openings that they have the transparency of lace curtains. The golden glitter of the mosaics must have completed the "illusion of unreality."

The Second Golden Age

Byzantine architecture never produced another structure to match Hagia Sophia. The churches of the Second Golden Age (from the late ninth to the eleventh century) and after were modest in scale, and monastic rather than imperial in spirit.

The development of Byzantine painting and sculpture after the age of Justinian was disrupted by the Iconoclastic Controversy, which began with an imperial edict of 726 prohibiting religious images as idolatrous and raged for more than a hundred years. The

114. Interior, Hagia Sophia

roots of the conflict went very deep. On the plane of theology they involved the basic issue of the relationship of the human and the divine in the person of Christ. Socially and politically, they reflected a power struggle between State and Church, and between the Western and Eastern provinces. The Controversy also marked the final break between Catholicism and the Orthodox faith. The edict did succeed in reducing the production of sacred images very greatly, but failed to wipe it out altogether, so that there was a fairly rapid recovery after the victory of the Iconophiles in 843. While we know little for certain about how the Byzantine artistic tradition managed to survive from the early eighth to the mid-ninth century, Iconoclasm seems to have brought about a renewed interest in secular art, which was not affected by the ban. This interest may help explain the astonishing reappearance of Late Classical motifs in the art of the Second Golden Age.

115. *The Crucifixion.* 11th century. Mosaic. Monastery Church, Daphnē, Greece

Mosaics

The finest works of the Second Golden Age show a classicism that has been harmoniously merged with the spiritualized ideal of beauty we encountered in the art of Justinian's reign. Among these, the *Crucifixion* mosaic at Daphnē (fig. 115) enjoys special fame. Its Classical qualities are deeply felt, yet are also completely Christian. There is no attempt to re-create a realistic spatial setting, but the composition has a balance and clarity that are truly monumental. Classical, too, is the statuesque dignity of the figures, which seem extraordinarily organic and graceful compared to those of the Justinian mosaics at S. Vitale (see fig. 112).

The most important aspect of these figures' Classical heritage, however, is emotional rather than physical. It is the gentle pathos conveyed by their gestures and facial expressions, a restrained and noble suffering of the kind we first met in Greek art of the fifth century B.C. (see pp. 83–84). Early Christian art had been quite devoid of this quality. Its view of Christ stressed the Saviour's divine wisdom and power, but alongside it we now find a new emphasis on the Christ of the Passion, which exercises a strong appeal to the emotions of the beholder. To have introduced this compassionate quality into sacred art was perhaps the greatest achievement of the Second Golden Age, even though its full possibilities were to be exploited not in Byzantium but in the medieval West at a later date.

Late Byzantine Painting

During the Iconoclastic Controversy, one of the chief arguments in favor of sacred images was the claim that Christ Himself had permitted St. Luke to paint His portrait, and that other portraits of Christ or of the Virgin had miraculously appeared on earth by divine fiat. These original, "true" sacred images were supposedly the source for the later, man-made ones. Such pictures, or icons, had developed in early Christian times out of Graeco-Roman portrait panels (such as that in fig. 101). Because of the veneration in which they were held, icons had to conform to strict formal rules, with fixed patterns repeated over and over again. As a consequence, the majority of them are more conspicuous for exacting craftsmanship than for artistic inventiveness. The madonna in figure 116 shows this conservatism. Although painted in the thirteenth century, it reflects a type of several hundred years earlier. Echoes of the classicism of the Second Golden Age abound: the graceful pose, the rich play of drapery folds, the tender melancholy of the Virgin's face, the elaborate architectural perspective of the throne (which looks rather like a miniature replica of the Colosseum). But all these elements have become oddly abstract. The throne, despite its foreshortening, no longer functions as a three-dimensional object, and the highlights on the drapery resemble ornamental sunbursts, in strange contrast to the soft shading of hands and faces. The total effect is neither flat nor spatial but transparent, somewhat like that of a stained-glass window; the shapes look as if they were lit

116. *Madonna and Child on a Curved Throne.* Late 13th century. Tempera on wood panel, 32⅛ × 19⅜" (81.6 × 49.2 cm). The National Gallery of Art, Washington, D.C. Andrew W. Mellon Collection, 1937

from behind. And this is almost literally true, for they are painted in a thin film on a highly reflective gold surface, which forms the highlights, the halos, and the background, so that even the shadows never seem wholly opaque. This all-pervading celestial radiance, we will recall, is a quality first encountered in Early Christian mosaics. Panels such as ours, therefore, should be viewed as the aesthetic equivalent, on a smaller scale, of mosaics, and not simply as the descendants of the ancient panel painting tradition. In fact, the most precious Byzantine icons are miniature mosaics done on panels rather than paintings.

CHRONOLOGICAL CHART I

	POLITICAL HISTORY	RELIGION, LITERATURE	SCIENCE, TECHNOLOGY
B.C. 4000	Sumerians settle in lower Mesopotamia	Pictographic writing, Sumer, c. 3500	Wheeled carts, Sumer, c. 3500–3000 Sailboats used on Nile c. 3500 Potter's wheel, Sumer, c. 3250
3000	Old Kingdom, Egypt (dynasties I–VI), c. 3100–2155 Early dynastic period, Sumer, c. 3000–2340; Akkadian kings 2340–2180	Hieroglyphic writing, Egypt, c. 3000 Cuneiform writing, Sumer, c. 2900 Divine kingship of the pharaoh Theocratic socialism in Sumer	First bronze tools and weapons, Sumer
2000	Middle Kingdom, Egypt, 2134–1785 Hammurabi founds Babylonian dynasty c. 1760 Flowering of Minoan civilization c. 1700–1500 New Kingdom, Egypt, c. 1570–1085	Code of Hammurabi c. 1760 Monotheism of Akhenaten (r. 1372–1358) *Book of the Dead,* first papyrus book, XVIII Dynasty	Bronze tools and weapons in Egypt Canal from Nile to Red Sea Mathematics and astronomy flourish in Babylon under Hammurabi Hyksos bring horses and wheeled vehicles to Egypt c. 1725
1000	Jerusalem capital of Palestine; rule of David; of Solomon (died 926) Assyrian Empire c. 1000–612 Persians conquer Babylon 539; Egypt 525 Romans revolt against Etruscans, set up republic 509	Hebrews accept monotheism Phoenicians develop alphabetic writing c. 1000; Greeks adopt it c. 800 First Olympic games 776 Homer (fl. c. 750–700), *Iliad* and *Odyssey* Zoroaster, Persian prophet (born c. 660) Aeschylus, Greek playwright (525–456)	Coinage invented in Lydia (Asia Minor) c. 700–650; soon adopted by Greeks Pythagoras, Greek philosopher (fl. c. 520)
500	Persian Wars in Greece 499–478 Periclean Age in Athens c. 460–429 Peloponnesian War, Sparta against Athens, 431–404 Alexander the Great (356–323) occupies Egypt 333; defeats Persia 331; conquers Near East	Sophocles, Greek playwright (496–406) Euripides, Greek playwright (died 406) Socrates, philosopher (died 399) Plato, philosopher (427–347); founds Academy 386 Aristotle, philosopher (384–322)	Travels of Herodotus, Greek historian, c. 460–440 Hippocrates, Greek physician (born 469) Euclid's books on geometry (fl. c. 300–280) Archimedes, physicist and inventor (287–212)
200	Rome dominates Asia Minor and Egypt; annexes Macedonia (and thereby Greece) 147		Invention of paper, China
100	Julius Caesar dictator of Rome 49–44 Emperor Augustus (r. 27 B.C.–14 A.D.)	Golden Age of Roman literature: Cicero, Catullus, Vergil, Horace, Ovid, Livy	Vitruvius' *De architectura*
A.D. 1	Jewish rebellion against Rome 66–70 destruction of Jerusalem Eruption of Mt. Vesuvius buries Pompeii, Herculaneum 79	Crucifixion of Jesus c. 30 Paul (died c. 65) spreads Christianity to Asia Minor and Greece	Pliny the Elder, *Natural History,* dies in Pompeii 79 Seneca, Roman statesman
100	Emperor Trajan (r. 98–117) rules Roman Empire at its largest extent Emperor Marcus Aurelius (r. 161–80)		Ptolemy, geographer and astronomer (died 160)
200	Shapur I (r. 242–72), Sassanian king of Persia Emperor Diocletian (r. 284–305) divides Empire	Persecution of Christians in Roman Empire 250–302	
300	Constantine the Great (r. 324–37) Roman Empire split into Eastern and Western branches 395	Christianity legalized by Edict of Milan 313; state religion 395 St. Augustine (354–430), St. Jerome (c. 347–420)	
400	Rome sacked by Visigoths 410 Fall of Western Roman Empire 476 "Golden Age" of Justinian 527–65	St. Patrick (died c. 461) founds Celtic Church in Ireland 432 Split between Eastern and Western Churches begins 451	Silk cultivation brought to eastern Mediterranean from China

NOTE: Figure numbers of black-and-white illustrations are in (italics). Colorplate numbers are in **(bold face)**.
Duration of papacy or reign is indicated by the abbreviation r. *The abbreviation* fl. *stands for flourished.*

ARCHITECTURE	SCULPTURE	PAINTING	
"White Temple" and ziggurat, Uruk *(40, 41)*			**B.C. 4000**
Step pyramid and funerary district of Zoser, Saqqara, by Imhotep *(31, 32)* Sphinx, Giza *(34)* Pyramids at Giza *(33)*	Palette of Narmer *(28)* Statues from Abu Temple, Tell Asmar *(42)* Offering stand and harp from Ur (**43,** *44)* *Mycerinus and His Queen (30)* Cycladic idol from Amorgos (**50**)		**3000**
Stonehenge, England *(21, 22)* Palace of Minos, Knossos, Crete *(51)* Temple of Amun-Mut-Khonsu, Luxor *(36)* Treasury of Atreus, Mycenae *(53)*	Stele of Hammurabi *(45)* Heads of Akhenaten and Nofretete (**37, 38**) Coffin of Tutankhamen (**39**) Lion Gate, Mycenae *(54)*	*"Toreador Fresco" (52)*	**2000**
Ishtar Gate, Babylon (**47**) "Basilica," Paestum (**62**)	Pole-top ornament from Luristan *(48)* Relief from Nimrud (**46**) Standing Youth (Kouros) *(65)* *Kore in Dorian Peplos (66)* North frieze from Treasury of the Siphnians, Delphi *(67)* *Apollo* from Veii *(79)*	Dipylon vase (**55**) Black-figure amphora by Psiax (**57**)	**1000**
Palace, Persepolis *(49)* Temple of Poseidon, Paestum (**62**) Temples on Acropolis, Athens: Parthenon (**63**); Propylaea and Temple of Athena Nike *(64)*	She-Wolf from Rome *(80)* East pediment from Aegina *(68)* *Standing Youth (Kritios Boy)* (**69**) *Poseidon (Zeus?) (70)* East pediment from the Parthenon *(72)* East frieze from the Mausoleum, Halicarnassus *(73)* *Hermes* by Praxiteles (**74**) Cinerary container *(82)* *Dying Gaul (76)*	*Lapith and Centaur,* red-figure kylix (**58**) Tomb of Lionesses, Tarquinia (**81**) *The Battle of Issus (59)*	**500**
Porta Augusta, Perugia *(83)*	*Nike of Samothrace (78)*		**200**
	Roman Patrician (**91**) *Portrait Head* from Delos *(75)*	*Odyssey Landscapes* (**99**) Villa of the Mysteries, Pompeii (**100**)	**100**
Colosseum, Rome *(85)*	Arch of Titus, Rome *(96)*	House of the Vettii, Pompeii *(98)*	**A.D. 1**
Pantheon, Rome *(86,* **87**)	Column of Trajan, Rome *(97)* Equestrian statue of Marcus Aurelius, Rome *(93)*	*Portrait of a Boy,* the Faiyum (**101**)	**100**
	Philippus the Arab (**94**)		**200**
Basilica of Constantine, Rome *(89, 90)*	Colossal statue of Constantine *(95)* Sarcophagus of Junius Bassus, Rome *(108)*	Catacomb of SS. Pietro e Marcellino, Rome *(102)*	**300**
S. Vitale, Ravenna (**110,** *111)* Hagia Sophia, Istanbul *(113, 114)* S. Apollinare in Classe, Ravenna *(103, 104)*	*Archangel Michael,* diptych leaf *(109)*	Mosaics, Sta. Maria Maggiore, Rome *(106)* *Vienna Genesis* (**107**) Mosaics, S. Apollinare in Classe and S. Vitale, Ravenna (**105, 112**)	**400**

PART TWO

THE MIDDLE AGES

When we think of the great civilizations of our past, we tend to do so in terms of visible monuments that have come to symbolize the distinctive character of each: the pyramids of Egypt, the ziggurats of Babylon, the Parthenon of Athens, the Colosseum, Hagia Sophia. The Middle Ages, in such a review of climactic achievements, would be represented by a Gothic cathedral—Notre-Dame in Paris, perhaps, or Chartres, or Salisbury. We have many to choose from, but whichever one we pick, it will be well north of the Alps, although in territory that formerly belonged to the Roman Empire. And if we were to spill a bucket of water in front of the cathedral of our choice, this water would eventually make its way to the English Channel, rather than to the Mediterranean. Here, then, we have the most important single fact about the Middle Ages: the center of gravity of European civilization has shifted to what had been the northern boundaries of the Roman world. The Mediterranean, for so many centuries the great highway of commercial and cultural exchange binding together all the lands along its shores, has become a barrier, a border zone.

We have already observed some of the events that paved the way for this shift—the removal of the imperial capital to Constantinople, the growing split between the Catholic and Orthodox faiths, the decay of the western half of the Roman Empire under the impact of invasions by Germanic tribes. Yet these tribes, once they had settled in their new environment, accepted the framework of late Roman, Christian civilization, however imperfectly; the local kingdoms they founded—the Vandals in North Africa, the Visigoths in Spain, the Franks in Gaul, the Ostrogoths and Lombards in Italy—were all Mediterranean-oriented, provincial states on the periphery of the Byzantine Empire, subject to the pull of its military, commercial, and cultural power. As late as 630, after the Byzantine armies had recovered Syria, Palestine, and Egypt from the Sassanid Persians, the reconquest of the lost Western provinces remained a serious possibility. Ten years later, the chance had ceased to exist, for meanwhile a tremendous and completely unforeseen new force had made itself felt in the East: the Arabs, under the banner of Islam, were overrunning the Near Eastern and African provinces of Byzantium. By 732, within a century after the death of Mohammed, they had swallowed all of North Africa as well as Spain, and threatened to add southwestern France to their conquests.

It would be difficult to exaggerate the impact of the lightninglike advance of Islam on the Christian world. The Byzantine Empire, deprived of its western Mediterranean bases, had to concentrate all its efforts on keeping Islam at bay in the East. Its impotence in the West (where it retained only a precarious foothold on Italian soil) left the European shore of the western Mediterranean, from the Pyrenees to Naples, exposed to Arabic raiders from North Africa or Spain. Western Europe was thus forced to develop its own resources, political, economic, and spiritual. The Church in Rome broke its last ties with the East and turned for support to the Germanic north, where the Frankish kingdom, under the energetic leadership of the Carolingian dynasty, rose to the status of imperial power during the eighth century.

When the pope, in the year 800, bestowed the title of emperor upon Charlemagne, he solemnized the new order of things by placing himself and all of Western Christianity under the protection of the king of the Franks and Lombards. He did not, however, subordinate himself to the newly created Catholic emperor, whose legitimacy depended on the pope, whereas hitherto it had been the other way around (the emperor in Constantinople had formerly ratified the newly elected pope). This interdependent dualism of spiritual and political authority, of Church and State, was to distinguish the West from both the Orthodox East and the Islamic South. Its outward symbol was the fact that though the emperor had to be crowned in Rome, he did not reside there; Charlemagne built his capital at the center of his effective power, in Aachen, located, on the present-day map of Europe, in Germany and close to France, Belgium, and the Netherlands.

THE MIDDLE AGES

SITES AND CITIES

ASIA
BLACK SEA
CASPIAN SEA
ARAL SEA
NEAR EAST
CHINA
FAR EAST
PERSIA
KHURASAN
Damascus
Tigris R.
Indus R.
MEDITERRANEAN SEA
Euphrates R.
LURISTAN
AFGHANISTAN
PAKISTAN
HIMALAYAS
Cairo
PERSIAN GULF
Agra
Ganges R.
ARABIA
Nile R.
Mecca
INDIA
RED SEA
EGYPT
ARABIAN SEA
BAY OF BENGAL
Moscow
RUSSIA
Dnieper R.
CARPATHIANS
BLACK SEA
Danube R.
ARMENIA
Erzurum
Euphrates R.
Tigris R.
PERSIA
Constantinople (Istanbul)
TURKEY
ANATOLIA
NEAR EAST
MESOPOTAMIA
MT. ATHOS
Samarra
Baghdad
AEGEAN SEA
MT. PARNASSUS
Athens
SYRIA
Damascus
RHODES
CYPRUS
CRETE
Jerusalem
Mshatta
DEAD SEA
Cairo
ARABIA
Nile R.
N
W
E
S
EGYPT
RED SEA
0
MILES
300
0
KM
300
Mecca

EARLY MEDIEVAL ART

THE DARK AGES

The labels we use for historical periods tend to be like the nicknames of people: once established, they are almost impossible to change, even though they may no longer be suitable. Those who coined the term "Middle Ages" thought of the entire thousand years from the fifth to the fifteenth century as an age of darkness, an empty interval between classical antiquity and its rebirth, the Renaissance in Italy. Since then, our view of the Middle Ages has changed completely. We now think of the period as the "Age of Faith." With the spread of this positive conception, the idea of darkness has become confined more and more to the early part of the Middle Ages. Whereas a hundred years ago, the "Dark Ages" were generally thought to extend as far as the twelfth century, today the term covers no more than the two-hundred-year interval between the death of Justinian and the reign of Charlemagne. Perhaps we ought to pare down the Dark Ages even further. In the course of the century 650–750 A.D., the center of gravity of European civilization shifted northward from the Mediterranean, and the economic, political, and spiritual framework of the Middle Ages began to take shape. We shall now see that the same century also gave rise to some important artistic achievements.

Celtic-Germanic Style

The Germanic tribes that had entered western Europe from the east during the declining years of the Roman Empire carried with them, in the form of nomads' gear, an ancient and widespread artistic tradition, the so-called animal style (see p. 60). This style, with its combination of abstract and organic shapes, of formal discipline and imaginative freedom, became an important element in the Celtic-Germanic art of the Dark Ages, such as the gold-and-enamel purse cover (fig. 117) from the grave, at Sutton Hoo, of an East Anglian king who died between 625 and 633. On it are four pairs of symmetrical motifs: each has its own distinctive character, an indication that the motifs have been assembled from four different sources. One motif, the standing man between confronted animals, has a very long history indeed—we first saw it in Sumerian art more than 3,000 years earlier (see fig. 44). The eagles pouncing on ducks also date back a long way, to similar pairings of carnivore and victim. The design above them, on the other hand, is of more recent origin. It consists of fighting animals whose tails, legs, and jaws are elongated into bands forming a complex interlacing pattern. Interlacing bands as an ornamental device occur in Roman and Early Christian art, especially along the southern shore of the Mediterranean, but their combination with the animal style, as shown here, seems to be

117. Purse cover, from the Sutton Hoo Ship-Burial. 625–33 A.D. Gold with garnets and enamels, length 8″ (20.3 cm). British Museum, London

118. *Animal Head,* from the Oseberg Ship-Burial. c. 825 A.D. Wood, height c. 5" (12.7 cm). Institutt for Kunsthistorie og Klassisk Arkeologi, Universitetet i Oslo

an invention of the Dark Ages, not much before the date of our purse cover.

Metalwork, in a variety of materials and techniques and often of exquisitely refined craftsmanship, had been the principal medium of the animal style. Such objects, small, durable, and eagerly sought after, account for the rapid diffusion of this idiom's repertory of forms. During the Dark Ages, however, these forms migrated not only in the geographic sense but also technically and artistically, into wood, stone, and even manuscript illumination. Wooden specimens have not survived in large numbers. Most of them come from Scandinavia, where the animal style flourished longer than anywhere else. The splendid animal head in figure 118, of the early ninth century, is the terminal of a post that was found, along with much other equipment, in a buried Viking ship at Oseberg in southern Norway. Like the motifs on the Sutton Hoo purse cover, it shows a peculiarly composite quality: the basic shape of the head is surprisingly realistic, as are certain details (teeth, gums, nostrils), but the surface has been spun over with interlacing and geometric patterns that betray their derivation from metalwork. Snarling monsters such as this used to rise from the prows of Viking ships, which endowed them with the character of mythical sea dragons.

Hiberno-Saxon Style

The pagan Germanic version of the animal style was also reflected in the earliest Christian works of art north of the Alps. They were made by the Irish (Hibernians), who, during the Dark Ages, assumed the spiritual and cultural leadership of western Europe. The period 600–800 A.D. deserves, in fact, to be called the Golden Age of Ireland. Unlike their English neighbors, the Irish had never been part of the Roman Empire. Thus the missionaries who carried the Gospel to them from England in the fifth century found a Celtic society entirely barbarian by Roman standards. The Irish readily accepted Christianity, which brought them into contact with Mediterranean civilization, but they did not become Rome-oriented. Rather, they adapted what they had received in a spirit of vigorous local independence.

The institutional framework of the Roman Church, being essentially urban, was ill-suited to the rural character of Irish life. Irish Christians preferred to follow the example of the desert saints of Egypt and the Near East, who had left the temptations of the city to seek spiritual perfection in the solitude of the wilderness. Groups of such hermits, sharing the ideal of ascetic discipline, had founded the earliest monasteries. By the fifth century, monasteries had spread as far north as western Britain, but only in Ireland did monasticism take over the leadership of the Church from the bishops.

Irish monasteries, unlike their Egyptian prototypes, soon became seats of learning and the arts. They also developed a missionary fervor, which sent Irish monks to preach to the heathen and to found monasteries in northern Britain as well as on the European mainland, from Poitiers to Vienna. These Irishmen not only speeded the conversion to Christianity of Scotland, northern France, the Netherlands, and Germany; they also established the monastery as a cultural center

119. Cross Page from the *Lindisfarne Gospels*. c. 700 A.D. 13½ × 9¼" (34.3 × 23.5 cm). British Library, London

throughout the European countryside. Although their Continental foundations were taken over before long by the monks of the Benedictine order, who were advancing north from Italy during the seventh and eighth centuries, Irish influence was to be felt within medieval civilization for several hundred years to come.

Manuscripts

In order to spread the Gospel, the Irish monasteries had to produce copies of the Bible and other Christian books in large numbers. Their scriptoria (writing workshops) also became centers of artistic endeavor, for a manuscript containing the Word of God was looked upon as a sacred object whose visual beauty should reflect the importance of its contents. Irish monks must have known Early Christian illuminated manuscripts, but here again, as in so many other respects, they developed an independent tradition instead of simply copying their models. While pictures illustrating biblical events held little interest for them, they devoted great effort to decorative embellishment. The finest of these manuscripts belong to the Hiberno-Saxon style, combining Celtic and Germanic elements, which flourished in the monasteries founded by Irishmen in Saxon England.

The Cross Page from the *Lindisfarne Gospels* (fig. 119) is an imaginative creation of breathtaking complexity. The miniaturist, working with a jeweler's precision, has poured into the compartments of his geometric frame an animal interlace so dense and yet so full of controlled movement that the fighting beasts on the Sutton Hoo purse cover seem childishly simple in comparison. It is as if the world of paganism, embodied in these biting and clawing monsters, had suddenly been subdued by the superior authority of the Cross. In order to achieve this effect, our artist has had to impose an extremely severe discipline upon himself. His "rules of the game" demand, for instance, that organic and geometric shapes must be kept separate; also, that within the animal compartments every line must turn out to be part of an animal's body, if we take the trouble to trace it back to its point of origin. There are also rules, too complex to go into here, concerning symmetry, mirror-image effects, and repetitions of shapes and colors. Only by working these out for ourselves by intense observation can we hope to enter into the spirit of this strange, mazelike world.

Of the representational images they found in Early Christian manuscripts, the Hiberno-Saxon illuminators generally retained only the symbols of the four evangelists, since these could be translated into their ornamental idiom without much difficulty. The human figure, on the other hand, remained beyond the Celtic or Germanic artist's reach for a long time. The bronze plaque of the Crucifixion (fig. 120), probably made for a book cover, shows how helpless the artist was when faced with the image of a man. In his attempt to reproduce an Early Christian composition, he suffers from an utter inability to conceive of the human frame as an organic unit, so that the figure of Christ becomes disembodied in the most literal sense: the head, arms, and feet are all separate elements joined to a central pattern of whorls, zigzags, and interlacing bands. Clearly, there is a wide gulf between the Celtic-Germanic and the Mediterranean traditions, a gulf that the Irish artist who modeled the *Crucifixion* did not

120. *Crucifixion,* plaque from a book cover (?). 8th century A.D. Bronze, height 8¼" (21 cm). National Museum of Ireland, Dublin

know how to bridge. Much the same situation prevailed elsewhere during the Dark Ages; even the Lombards, on Italian soil, did not know what to do with human images.

CAROLINGIAN ART

The empire built by Charlemagne did not endure for long. His grandsons divided it into three parts, and proved incapable of effective rule even in these, so that political power reverted to the local nobility. The cultural achievements of his reign, in contrast, have proved far more lasting. This very page would look different without them, for it is printed in letters whose shapes derive from the script in Carolingian manuscripts. The fact that these letters are known today as "Roman" rather than Carolingian recalls another aspect of the cultural reforms sponsored by Charlemagne: the collecting and copying of ancient Roman literature. The oldest surviving texts of a great many classical Latin authors are to be found in Carolingian manuscripts, which, until not very long ago, were mistakenly regarded as Roman, hence their lettering, too, was called Roman.

This interest in preserving the classics was part of an ambitious attempt to restore ancient Roman civilization, along with the imperial title. Charlemagne himself took an active hand in this revival, through which he expected to implant the cultural traditions of a glorious past in the minds of the semibarbaric people of his realm. To an astonishing extent, he succeeded. Thus the "Carolingian revival" may be termed the first—and in some ways the most important—phase of a genuine fusion of the Celtic-Germanic spirit with that of the Mediterranean world.

Architecture

The fine arts played an important role in Charlemagne's cultural program from the very start. On his visits to Italy, he had become familiar with the architectural monuments of the Constantinian era in Rome and with those of the reign of Justinian in Ravenna. His own capital at Aachen, he felt, must convey the majesty of Empire through buildings of an equally impressive kind. His famous Palace Chapel (fig. 121) is, in fact, directly inspired by S. Vitale (see fig. 111). To erect such a structure on Northern soil was a difficult undertaking. Columns and bronze gratings had to be imported from Italy, and expert stonemasons must have been hard to find. The design, by Odo of Metz (probably the earliest architect north of the Alps known to us by name), is by no means a mere echo of S. Vitale but a vigorous reinterpretation, with piers and vaults of Roman massiveness and a geometric clarity of the spatial units very different from the fluid space of the earlier structure.

121. Odo of Metz. Interior of the Palace Chapel of Charlemagne, Aachen. 792–805 A.D.

Plan of a Monastery, St. Gall. The importance of monasteries and their close link with the imperial court are vividly suggested by a unique document of the period, the large drawing of a plan for a monastery preserved in the Chapter Library at St. Gall in Switzerland (fig. 122). Its basic features seem to have been determined at a council held near Aachen in 816–17; this copy was then sent to the abbot of St. Gall for his guidance in rebuilding the monastery. We may regard it, therefore, as a standard plan, intended to be modified according to local needs.

The monastery is a complex, self-contained unit, filling a rectangle about 500 by 700 feet. The main path of entrance, from the west, passes between stables and a hostelry toward a gate which admits the visitor to a colonnaded semicircular portico flanked by two round towers, a sort of strung-out westwork that looms impressively above the low outer buildings. It emphasizes the church as the center of the monastic community. The church is a basilica, with a transept and choir in the east but an apse and altar at either end. The nave and aisles, containing numerous other altars, do not form a single continuous space but are subdivided into compartments by screens. There are numerous entrances: two beside the western apse, others on the north and south flanks.

This entire arrangement reflects the functions of a monastery church, designed for the liturgical needs of the monks rather than for a lay congregation. Adjoining the church to the south is an arcaded cloister, around which are grouped the monks' dormitory (on the east side), a refectory and kitchen (on the south side), and a cellar. The three large buildings north of the church are a guest house, a school, and the abbot's house. To the east are the infirmary, a chapel and quarters for novices, the cemetery (marked by a large cross), a garden, and coops for chickens and geese. The south side is occupied by workshops, barns, and other service buildings. There is, needless to say, no monastery exactly like this anywhere—even in St. Gall the plan was not carried out as drawn—yet its layout conveys an excellent notion of such establishments throughout the Middle Ages.

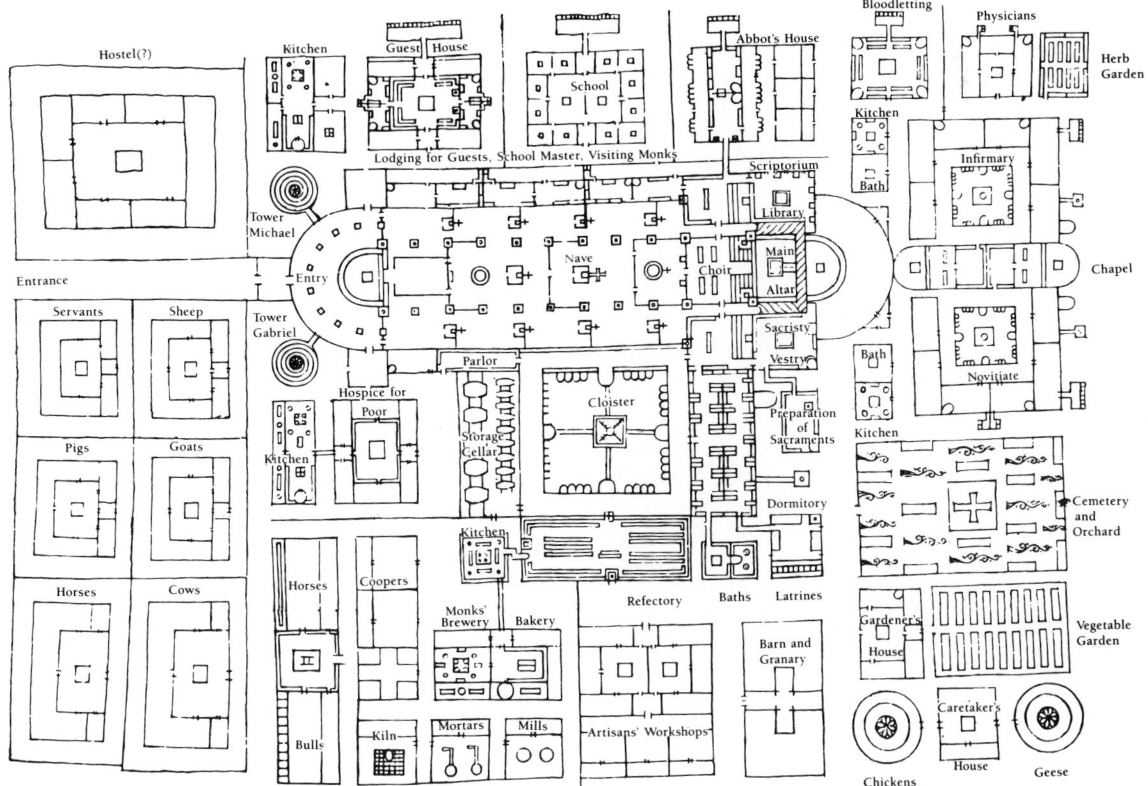

122. Plan of a monastery. Original c. 820 A.D. in red ink on parchment, 28×44⅛″ (71.1×112.1 cm). Stiftsbibliothek, St. Gall, Switzerland (inscriptions translated into English from Latin)

123. *St. Matthew,* from the *Gospel Book of Charlemagne.* c. 800–10 A.D. 13 × 10″ (33 × 25.4 cm). Kunsthistorisches Museum, Vienna

124. *St. Mark,* from the *Gospel Book of Archbishop Ebbo of Reims.* 816–35 A.D. Bibliothèque Municipale, Épernay, France

Manuscripts and Book Covers

We know from literary sources that Carolingian churches contained murals, mosaics, and relief sculpture, but these have disappeared almost entirely. Illuminated manuscripts, ivories, and goldsmiths' work, on the other hand, have survived in considerable numbers. They demonstrate the impact of the Carolingian revival even more strikingly than the architectural remains of the period. As we look at the picture of St. Matthew from a Gospel book said to have been found in the tomb of Charlemagne and, in any event, closely linked with his court at Aachen (fig. 123), we find it hard to believe that such a work could have been executed in northern Europe about the year 800. If it were not for the large golden halo, the Evangelist Matthew might almost be mistaken for a Classical author's portrait. Whoever the artist was—Byzantine, Italian, or Frankish—he plainly was fully conversant with the Roman tradition of painting, down to the acanthus ornament on the wide frame, which emphasizes the "window" treatment of the picture.

The *St. Matthew* represents the most orthodox phase of the Carolingian revival. It is the visual counterpart of copying the text of a Classical work of literature. A miniature of some three decades later for the *Gospel Book of Archbishop Ebbo of Reims* (fig. 124) shows the Classical model translated into a Carolingian idiom. The *St. Mark* will remind us of the Enthroned Christ from the sarcophagus of Junius Bassus (see fig. 108) made some five hundred years earlier in the seated "stance" with one foot advanced, the diagonal drape of the upper part of the toga, and the square outline of the face. The hands, too, are similar, with one holding a scroll or codex, the other a quill pen, which is added to what must once have been an expository gesture. And the throne on which Christ is seated in the earlier sculpture has exactly the same kind of animal legs as St. Mark's seat. But now the entire picture is filled with a vibrant energy that sets everything in motion: the drapery swirls about the figure, the hills heave upward, the vegetation seems to be tossed about

125. Upper cover of binding, *Lindau Gospels*. c. 870 A.D. Gold and jewels, 13¾ × 10½″ (34.9 × 26.7 cm). The Pierpont Morgan Library, New York

by a whirlwind, and even the acanthus pattern on the frame assumes a strange, flamelike character. The Evangelist himself has been transformed from a Roman author setting down his own thoughts into a man seized with the frenzy of divine inspiration, an instrument for recording the Word of God. His gaze is fixed not upon his book but upon his symbol (the winged lion with a scroll), which acts as the transmitter of the Sacred Text. This dependence on the Will of the Word, so powerfully expressed here, marks the contrast between Classical and medieval images of humanity. But the *means* of expression—

the dynamism of line that distinguishes our miniature from its predecessor—recalls the passionate movement in the ornamentation of Irish manuscripts of the Dark Ages (see fig. 119).

The style of the Reims school can still be felt in the reliefs of the jeweled front cover of the *Lindau Gospels* (fig. 125), a work of the third quarter of the ninth century. This masterpiece of the goldsmith's art shows how splendidly the Celtic-Germanic metalwork tradition of the Dark Ages adapted itself to the Carolingian revival. The clusters of semiprecious stones are not mounted directly on the gold ground but raised on claw feet or arcaded turrets, so that the light can penetrate beneath them to bring out their full brilliance. Interestingly enough, the crucified Christ betrays no hint of pain or death. He seems to stand rather than to hang, His arms spread out in a solemn gesture. To endow Him with the signs of human suffering was not yet conceivable, even though the means were at hand, as we can see from the eloquent expressions of grief among the small figures in the adjoining compartments.

OTTONIAN ART

In 870, about the time when the *Lindau Gospels* cover was made, the remains of Charlemagne's empire were ruled by his two surviving grandsons: Charles the Bald, the West Frankish king, and Louis the German, the East Frankish king, whose domains corresponded roughly to the France and Germany of today. Their power was so weak, however, that Continental Europe once again lay exposed to attack. In the south, the Moslems resumed their depredations; Slavs and Magyars advanced from the east; and Vikings from Scandinavia ravaged the north and west. These Norsemen (the ancestors of today's Danes and Norwegians) had been raiding Ireland and Britain by sea from the late eighth century on. Now they invaded northwestern France as well, occupying the area that ever since has been called Normandy. Once established there, they soon adopted Christianity and Carolingian civilization, and from 911 on their leaders were recognized as dukes nominally subject to the authority of the king of France. During the eleventh century, the Normans assumed a role of major importance in shaping the political and cultural destiny of Europe, with William the Conqueror becoming king of England while other Norman nobles expelled the Arabs from Sicily and the Byzantines from southern Italy (see p. 146).

In Germany, meanwhile, after the death of the last Carolingian monarch in 911, the center of political power had shifted north to Saxony. The Saxon kings (919–1024) reestablished an effective central government, and the greatest of them, Otto I, also revived the imperial ambitions of Charlemagne. After marrying the widow of a Lombard king, he extended his rule over most of Italy and had himself crowned emperor by the pope in 962. From then on the Holy Roman Empire was to be a German institution—or perhaps

126. *Gero Crucifix.* c. 975–1000 A.D.
Wood, height 6′2″ (1.88 m). Cologne Cathedral

130. *Christ Washing the Feet of Peter,* from the *Gospel Book of Otto III.* c. 1000. 13 × 9⅜″ (33 × 23.9 cm). Staatsbibliothek, Munich

markable for their classical Roman character, is part of the dedicatory inscription, with the date and Bernward's name. In these figures we find nothing of the monumental spirit of the *Gero Crucifix*: they seem far smaller than they actually are, so that one might easily mistake them for a piece of goldsmith's work such as the *Lindau Gospels* cover (compare fig. 125). The entire composition must have been derived from an illuminated manuscript; the oddly stylized bits of vegetation have a good deal of the twisting, turning movement we recall from Irish miniatures. Yet the story is conveyed with splendid directness and expressive force. The accusing finger of the Lord, seen against a great void of blank surface, is the focal point of the drama: it points to a cringing Adam, who passes the blame to his mate, while Eve, in turn, passes it to the serpent at her feet.

Manuscripts

The same intensity of glance and of gesture characterizes Ottonian manuscript painting, which blends Carolingian and Byzantine elements into a new style of extraordinary scope and power. The most important center of manuscript illumination at that time was the Reichenau Monastery, on an island in Lake Constance. Perhaps its finest achievement—and one of the great masterpieces of medieval art—is the *Gospel Book of Otto III*. The scene of Christ washing the feet of St. Peter (fig. 130) contains notable echoes of ancient painting, transmitted through Byzantine art. The soft pastel hues of the background recall the illusionism of Graeco-Roman landscapes (see fig. 99), and the architectural frame around Christ is a late descendant of the kind of architectural perspectives we saw in the House of the Vettii (see fig. 98). That these elements have been misunderstood by the Ottonian artist is obvious enough; but he has also put them to a new use, so that what was once an architectural vista now becomes the Heavenly City, the House of the Lord filled with golden celestial space as against the atmospheric earthly space without. The figures have undergone a similar transformation. In ancient art, this composition had been used to represent a doctor treating a patient. Now St. Peter takes the place of the sufferer, and Christ that of the physician (note that He is still the beardless young philosopher type here). As a consequence, the emphasis has shifted from physical to spiritual action, and this new kind of action is not only conveyed through glances and gestures, but it also governs the scale of things. Christ and St. Peter, the most active figures, are larger than the rest; Christ's "active" arm is longer than His "passive" one; and the eight disciples, who merely watch, have been compressed into a tiny space, so that we see little more than their eyes and hands. Even the Early Christian crowd-cluster from which this derives (see fig. 106) is not quite so literally disembodied.

ROMANESQUE ART

Looking back over the ground we have covered in this book so far, a thoughtful reader will be struck by the fact that almost all of our chapter headings and subheadings might serve equally well for a general history of civilization. Some are based on technology (for example, the Old Stone Age), others on geography, ethnology, religion. Whatever the source, they have been borrowed from other fields, even though in our context they also designate artistic styles. There are only two important exceptions to this rule: Archaic and Classical are primarily terms of style. They refer to qualities of form rather than to the setting in which these forms were created. Why don't we have more terms of this sort? We do, as we shall see—but only for the art of the past nine hundred years.

Those who first conceived the idea of viewing the history of art as an evolution of styles started out with the conviction that art in the ancient world developed toward a single climax: Greek art from the age of Pericles to that of Alexander the Great. This style they called Classical (that is, perfect). Everything that came before was labeled Archaic, to indicate that it was still old-fashioned and tradition-bound, not yet Classical but striving in the right direction, while the style of post-Classical times did not deserve a special term since it had no positive qualities of its own, being merely an echo or a decadence of Classical art.

The early historians of medieval art followed a similar pattern. To them, the great climax was the Gothic style, from the thirteenth century to the fifteenth. For whatever was not yet Gothic they adopted the label Romanesque. In doing so, they were thinking mainly of architecture. Pre-Gothic churches, they noted, were round-arched, solid, and heavy (as against the pointed arches and the soaring lightness of Gothic structures), rather like the ancient Roman style of building, and the term "Romanesque" was meant to convey just that. In this sense, all of medieval art before 1200, insofar as it shows any link with the Mediterranean tradition, could be called Romanesque.

Carolingian art, we will recall, was brought into being by Charlemagne and his circle as part of a conscious revival policy; even after his death, it remained strongly linked with his imperial court. Ottonian art, too, had this sponsorship, and a correspondingly narrow base. The Romanesque proper (that is, medieval art from about 1050 to 1200), in contrast, sprang up all over western Europe at about the same time. It consists of a large variety of regional styles, distinct yet closely related in many ways, and without a central source. In this respect, it resembles the art of the Dark Ages rather than the court styles that had preceded it, although it includes the Carolingian-Ottonian tradition along with a good many other, less clearly traceable ones, such as Late Classical, Early Christian, and Byzantine elements, some Islamic influence, and the Celtic-Germanic heritage.

What welded all these different components into a coherent style during the second half of the eleventh century was not any single force but a variety of factors that made for a new burgeoning of vitality throughout the West. There was a growing spirit of religious enthusiasm, reflected in the greatly increased pilgrimage traffic to sacred sites. Christianity had at last triumphed everywhere in Europe. The Vikings, still largely pagan in the ninth and tenth centuries when their raids terrorized the British Isles and the Continent, had entered the Catholic fold, not only in

Normandy but in Scandinavia as well. The Moslem threat subsided after 1031. And the Magyars settled in Hungary.

Equally important was the reopening of Mediterranean trade routes by the navies of Venice, Genoa, and Pisa; the revival of commerce and manufacturing; and the consequent growth of city life. During the turmoil of the early Middle Ages, the towns of the western Roman Empire had shrunk greatly in size (the population of Rome, about one million in 300 A.D., fell to less than 50,000 at one point); some were deserted altogether. From the eleventh century on, they began to regain their former importance. New towns sprang up everywhere, and an urban middle class of artisans and merchants established itself between the peasantry and the landed nobility as an important factor in medieval society.

In many respects, then, western Europe between 1050 and 1200 became a great deal more "Roman-esque" than it had been since the sixth century, recapturing some of the international trade patterns, the urban quality, and the military strength of ancient imperial times. The central political authority was lacking, to be sure (even the empire of Otto I did not extend much farther west than modern Germany does), but the central spiritual authority of the pope took its place to some extent as a unifying force. The international army that responded to Urban II's call in 1095 for the First Crusade to liberate the Holy Land from Moslem rule was more powerful than anything a secular ruler could have raised for the purpose.

ARCHITECTURE

The greatest difference between Romanesque architecture and that of the preceding centuries is the amazing increase in building activity. An eleventh-century monk, Raoul Glaber, summed it up well when he triumphantly exclaimed that the world was putting on a "white mantle of churches." These churches were not only more numerous than those of the early Middle Ages, they were also generally larger, more richly articulated, and more "Roman-looking." Their naves now had vaults instead of wooden roofs, and their exteriors, unlike those of Early Christian, Byzantine, Carolingian, and Ottonian churches, were decorated with both architectural ornament and sculpture. Geographically, Romanesque monuments of the first importance are distributed over an area that might well have represented the world—the Catholic world, that is—to Raoul Glaber: from northern Spain to the Rhineland, from the Scottish-English border to central Italy. The richest crop, the greatest variety of regional types, and the most adventurous ideas are to be found in France, but throughout Europe we are presented with a wealth of architectural invention unparalleled by any previous era.

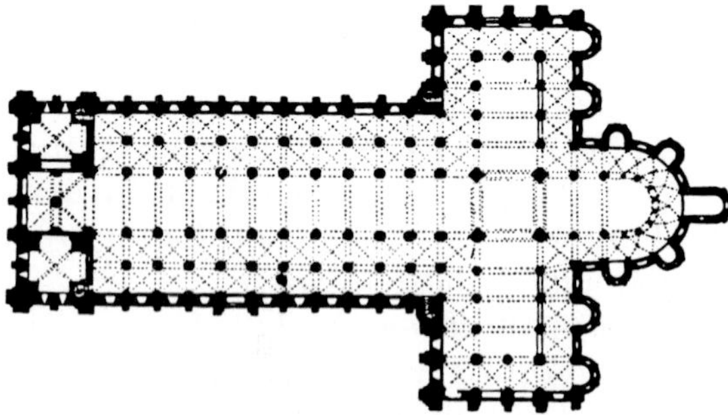

131. Plan of St.-Sernin, Toulouse (after Conant)

132. St.-Sernin (aerial view). c. 1080–1120

Southwestern France

We begin our sampling of Romanesque churches—it cannot be more than that—with St.-Sernin, in the southern French town of Toulouse (figs. 131–33), one of a group of great churches of the "pilgrimage type," so called because they were built along the roads leading to the pilgrimage center of Santiago de Compostela in northwestern Spain. The plan immediately strikes us as very much more complex and more fully integrated than those of earlier structures such as St. Michael's at Hildesheim (see fig. 128). It is an emphatic Latin cross, with the center of gravity at the eastern end. Clearly, this church was not designed to serve a monastic community only but to accommodate large crowds of lay worshipers as well in its long nave and transept.

The nave is flanked by two aisles on either side, the inner aisle continuing around the arms of the transept and the apse and thus forming a complete ambulatory circuit anchored to the two towers of the west facade. The ambulatory, we will recall, had developed as a feature of the crypts of earlier churches (as at St. Michael's). Now it has emerged above ground, is linked with the aisles of nave and transept, and is enriched with apsidal chapels that seem to radiate from the apse and continue along the eastern face of the transept. (Apse, ambulatory, and radiating chapels form a unit known as the pilgrimage choir.) The plan also shows that the aisles of St.-Sernin are groin-vaulted throughout. This, in conjunction with the features already noted, imposes a high degree of regularity upon the entire design: the aisles are made up of square bays, which serve as a basic unit, or module, for the other dimensions, so that the nave and transept bays equal two such units, the crossing and the facade towers four units.

133. Nave and choir, St.-Sernin

The exterior is marked by an equally rich articulation. The different roof levels set off the nave and transept against the inner and outer aisles, the apse, the ambulatory, and the radiating chapels. This is enhanced by the buttresses reinforcing the walls between the windows to contain the outward thrust of the vaults. The windows and portals themselves are further emphasized by decorative framing. The great crossing tower was completed in Gothic times and is taller than originally intended. The two facade towers, unfortunately, have remained stumps.

As we enter the nave, we are impressed with its tall proportions, the architectural elaboration of the nave walls, and the dim, indirect lighting, all of which create a sensation very different from the ample and serene interior of St. Michael's, with its simple and clearly separated "blocks" of space (see fig. 127). If the nave walls of St. Michael's look Early Christian (see fig. 105), those of St.-Sernin seem more akin to structures such as the Colosseum (see fig. 85). The syntax of ancient Roman architecture—vaults, arches, engaged columns, and pilasters firmly knit together into a coherent order—has indeed been recaptured here to a remarkable degree. Yet the forces whose interaction is expressed in the nave of St.-Sernin are no longer the physical, "muscular" forces of Graeco-Roman architecture but spiritual forces—spiritual forces of the kind we have seen governing the human body in Carolingian and Ottonian miniatures. The half-columns running the entire height of the nave wall would appear just as unnaturally drawn-out to an ancient Roman beholder as the arm of Christ in figure 130. They seem to be driven upward by some tremendous, unseen pressure, hastening to meet the transverse arches that subdivide the barrel vault of the nave. Their insistently repeated rhythm propels us toward the eastern end of the church, with its light-filled apse and ambulatory (now, unfortunately, obscured by a huge altar of later date).

In thus describing our experience we do not, of course, mean to suggest that the architect consciously set out to achieve this effect. For him, beauty and engineering were inseparable. Vaulting the nave so as to eliminate the fire hazard of a wooden roof was not only a practical aim; it also challenged him to make the House of the Lord grander and more impressive. And since a vault becomes more difficult to sustain the farther it is from the ground, he strained every resource to make the nave as tall as he dared. He had, however, to sacrifice the clerestory for safety's sake. Instead, he built galleries over the inner aisles to abut the lateral pressure of the nave vault, hoping that enough light would filter through them into the central space. St.-Sernin serves to remind us that architecture, like politics, is "the art of the possible," and that its success, here as elsewhere, is measured by the degree to which the architect has explored the limits of what was possible to him under those particular circumstances, structurally and aesthetically.

Burgundy and Western France

The builders of St.-Sernin would have been the first to admit that their answer to the problem of the nave vault was not a final one, impressive though it is on its own terms. The architects of Burgundy arrived at a more elegant solution, as evidenced by the Cathedral of Autun (fig. 134), where the galleries are replaced by a blind arcade (called a triforium, since it often has three openings per bay) and a clerestory. What made this three-story elevation possible was the use of the pointed arch for the nave vault, which produced a thrust more nearly downward than outward. For reasons of harmony, the pointed arch also appears in the nave arcade (it had probably reached France from Islamic architecture, where it had been employed for some time). Autun, too, comes close to straining the limits of the possible, for the upper part of the nave wall shows a slight but perceptible outward lean under the pressure of the vault, a warning against any further attempts to increase the height of the clerestory or to enlarge the windows.

134. Nave and choir, Autun Cathedral. c. 1120–32

Normandy and England

Farther north, architecture evolved in an entirely different direction. For example, on the west facade of the abbey church of St.-Étienne at Caen in Normandy (fig. 135), founded by William the Conqueror a year or two after his invasion of England (see p. 138), decoration is kept at a minimum. Four huge

135. West facade, St.-Étienne, Caen. Begun 1068

buttresses divide the front of the church into three vertical sections, and the vertical impetus continues triumphantly in the two splendid towers, whose height would be impressive enough even without the tall Early Gothic helmets. St.-Étienne is cool and composed: a structure to be appreciated, in all its refinement of proportions, by the mind rather than the eye.

The thinking that went into Norman architecture is responsible for the next great breakthrough in structural engineering, which took place in England, where William started to build as well. Durham Cathedral (fig. 136), begun in 1093, is among the largest churches of medieval Europe. Despite its great width, the nave may have been designed to be vaulted from the start. The vault over its eastern end had been completed by 1107, a remarkably short time, and the rest of the nave, following the same pattern, by 1130. This vault is of great interest, for it represents the earliest systematic use of a pointed-ribbed groin vault over a three-story nave, and thus marks a basic advance beyond the solution we saw at Autun. The aisles, which we can glimpse through the arcade, consist of the usual groin-vaulted compartments closely approaching a square, while the bays of the nave, separated by strong transverse arches, are decidedly oblong and groin-vaulted in such a way that the ribs form a double-X design, dividing the vault into seven sections rather than the conventional four. Since the nave bays are twice as long as the aisle bays, the transverse arches occur only at the odd-numbered piers of the nave arcade, and the piers therefore alternate in size, the larger ones being of compound shape (that is, bundles of column and pilaster shafts attached to a square or oblong core), the others cylindrical.

Perhaps the easiest way to visualize the origin of this peculiar system is to imagine that the architect started out by designing a barrel-vaulted nave with galleries over the aisles and without a clerestory, as at St.-Sernin. While he was doing so, it suddenly occurred to him that by putting groin vaults over the nave as well as the aisles, he would gain a semicircular area at the ends of each transverse vault, which could be broken through to make a clerestory because it had no essential supporting functions (fig. 137). Each nave bay contains a pair of Siamese-twin groined vaults, divided into seven compartments; the weight of the whole vault is concentrated at six securely anchored points on the gallery level. While the transverse arches at the crossing are round, those to the west of it are slightly pointed, indicating a continuous search for improvements. By eliminating the part of the round arch that responds the most to the pull of gravity, the two halves of a pointed arch brace each other. The pointed arch thus exerts less outward pressure than

136. Nave (looking east), Durham Cathedral. 1093–1130

the semicircular arch, and can be made as steep as possible. The potentialities of the engineering advances that grew out of this discovery were to make possible the soaring churches of the Gothic period. The ribs were necessary to provide a stable skeleton for the groined vault, so that the curved surfaces between them could be filled in with masonry of minimum thickness, thus reducing both weight and thrust. We do not know whether this ingenious scheme was actually invented at Durham, but it could not have been created much earlier, for it is still in an experimental stage. Aesthetically, the nave at Durham is among the finest in all Romanesque architecture: the wonderful sturdiness of the alternating piers makes a splendid contrast with the dramatically lighted, saillike surfaces of the vault.

Italy

We might have expected central Italy, which had been part of the heartland of the original Roman Empire, to have produced the noblest Romanesque of them all, since surviving Classical originals were close at hand. Such was not the case, however. All of the rulers having ambitions to revive "the grandeur that was Rome," with themselves in the role of emperor, were in the north of Europe. The spiritual authority of the pope, reinforced by considerable territorial holdings, made imperial ambitions in Italy difficult to achieve. New centers of prosperity, whether arising from seaborne commerce or local industries, tended to consolidate a number of small principalities, which competed among themselves or aligned themselves from time to time, if it seemed politically profitable, with the pope or the German emperor. Lacking the urge to

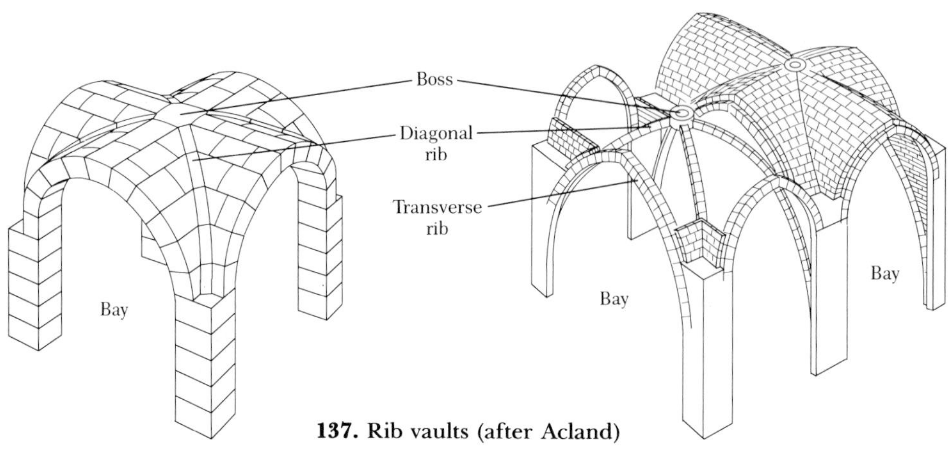

137. Rib vaults (after Acland)

138. Pisa Baptistery, Cathedral, and Campanile (view from the west). 1053–1272

re-create the old Empire, and furthermore having Early Christian church buildings as readily accessible as Classical Roman architecture, the Tuscans were content to continue what are basically Early Christian forms, but enlivened them with decorative features inspired by pagan architecture.

If we take one of the best preserved Tuscan Romanesque examples, the Cathedral complex of Pisa (fig. 138), and compare it on the one hand with S. Apollinare in Ravenna and on the other with St.-Sernin in Toulouse (see figs. 103, 132), we are left in little doubt as to which is its closer relation. True, it has grown taller than its ancestor, and a large transept has altered the plan to form a Latin cross, with the consequent addition of the tall lantern rising above the intersection. But the essential features of the earlier basilica type, with its files of flat arcades and even the detached bell tower (the famous Leaning Tower of Pisa, which was not planned that way but soon began to tilt because of weak foundations), still continue much as we see them in S. Apollinare.

The only deliberate revival of the antique Roman style in Tuscan architecture was in the use of a multicolored marble "skin" on the exteriors of churches (Early Christian examples tended to leave the outsides plain). Little of this is left in Rome, a great deal of it having literally been "lifted" for the embellishment of later structures. But the interior of the Pantheon (see fig. 87) still gives us some idea of it, and we can recognize the desire to emulate such marble inlay in the Baptistery in Florence (fig. 139), whose green and white marble paneling follows severely geometric lines. The blind arcades, too, are eminently classical in proportion and detail. The entire building, in fact, exudes such an air of classicism that the Florentines themselves came to

139. Baptistery of S. Giovanni, Florence. c. 1060–1150

believe a few years later that it was originally a temple of Mars, the Roman god of war.

SCULPTURE

The revival of monumental stone sculpture is even more astonishing than the architectural achievements of the Romanesque era, since neither Carolingian nor Ottonian art had shown any tendencies in this direction. Freestanding statues, we will recall, all but disappeared from Western art after the fifth century. Stone relief survived only in the form of architectural ornament or surface decoration, with the depth of the carving reduced to a minimum. Thus the only continuous sculptural tradition in early medieval art was that of sculpture-in-miniature: small reliefs and occasional statuettes in metal or ivory. Ottonian art, in works such as the bronze doors of Bishop Bernward (see fig. 129), had enlarged the scale of this tradition but not its spirit. Its truly large-scale sculptural efforts, represented by the impressive *Gero Crucifix* (see fig. 126), were limited almost entirely to wood.

Southwestern France

Just when and where the revival of stone sculpture began we cannot say with certainty, but it was probably along the pilgrimage roads, in southwestern France and northern Spain, leading to Santiago de Compostela. As in Romanesque architecture, the rapid development of stone sculpture between 1050 and 1100 reflects the growth of religious fervor among the general population in the decades before the First Crusade. Architectural sculpture, especially when applied to the exterior of a church, is meant to appeal to the lay worshiper rather than to the members of a closed monastic community.

St.-Sernin at Toulouse contains several important examples probably carved about 1090. The original location of the *Apostle* (fig. 140) within the church remains uncertain—perhaps it decorated the front of an altar. Where have we seen its like before? The solidity of the forms has a strongly classical air, indicating that our artist must have had a close look at late Roman sculpture (of which there are considerable remains in southern France). On the other hand, the design as a whole—the solemn frontality of the figure, its placement in the architectural frame—derives from a Byzantine source, in all likelihood an ivory panel descended from the *Archangel Michael* in figure 109. Yet in enlarging such a miniature, the carver of our relief has also reinflated it: the niche is a real cavity, the hair a round, close-fitting cap, the body severe and blocklike. Our *Apostle* has, in fact, much the same dignity and directness as the sculpture of Archaic Greece.

The figure (which is somewhat more than half lifesize) was not intended for viewing at close range only. Its impressive bulk and weight "carry" over a considerable distance. This emphasis on massive volume hints at what may well have been the main impulse behind the revival of large-scale sculpture: a stone-carved image, being tangible and three-dimensional, is far more "real" than a painted one. To the mind of a cleric steeped in the abstractions of theology, this might seem irrelevant, or even dangerous. St. Bernard of Clairvaux, writing in 1127, denounced the

140. *Apostle.* c. 1090. Stone. St.-Sernin, Toulouse

141. South portal (portion), St.-Pierre, Moissac. Early 12th century

sculptured decoration of churches as a vain folly and diversion that tempts us "to read in the marble rather than in our books." His was a voice not very much heeded, however. For the unsophisticated laity, any large piece of sculpture inevitably had something of the quality of an idol, and it was this very fact that gave it such great appeal.

Another important early center of Romanesque sculpture was the abbey at Moissac, some distance north of Toulouse. The south portal of its church, carved a generation later than the *Apostle* from St.-Sernin, displays a richness of invention that would have made St. Bernard wince. In figure 141 we see the magnificent *trumeau* (the center post supporting the lintel) and the western jamb. Both have a scalloped profile, and the shafts of the half-columns applied to jambs and *trumeau* follow this scalloped pattern, as if they had been squeezed from a giant pastry tube. Human and animal forms are treated with the same flexibility, so that the spidery prophet on the side of the *trumeau* seems perfectly adapted to his precarious perch. (Notice how he, too, has been fitted into the scalloped outline.) He even remains free to cross his legs in a dancelike movement and to turn his head toward the interior of the church as he unfurls his scroll.

But what of the crossed lions that form a symmetrical zigzag on the face of the *trumeau*—do they have a meaning? So far as we know, they simply "animate" the shaft as the interlacing beasts of Irish miniatures (whose descendants they are) animate the compartments assigned to them. In manuscript illumination, this tradition had never died out. Our sculpture has undoubtedly been influenced by it, just as the agitated movement of the prophet has its ultimate origin in miniature painting (see fig. 124). The crossed lions reflect another source as well: they can be traced back through Persian metalwork to the confronted animals of ancient Near Eastern art (see figs. 44, 54). Yet we cannot fully account for the presence of the crossed lions at Moissac in terms of their effectiveness as ornament. They belong to a vast family of savage or monstrous creatures in Romanesque art that retain their demoniacal vitality even though they are compelled—like our lions—to perform a supporting function. Their purpose is thus not merely decorative but expressive as well. They embody dark forces that have been domesticated into guardian figures or banished to a position that holds them fixed for all eternity, however much they may snarl in protest.

Burgundy

The tympanum (the lunette above the lintel) of the main portal of Romanesque churches is usually given over to a composition centered on the Enthroned Christ, most often the Apocalyptic Vision (or Last Judgment), the most awesome scene of Christian art. At Autun Cathedral, the latter subject has been visualized with singularly expressive force. Our detail (fig. 142) shows part of the right half of the tympanum, with the weighing of the souls. At the bottom, the dead rise from their graves in fear and trembling; some are already beset by snakes or gripped by huge, clawlike hands. Above, their fate quite literally hangs in the balance, with devils yanking at one end of the scales and angels at the other. The saved souls cling like children to the hem of the angel's garment for protection, while the condemned are seized by grinning devils and cast into the mouth of Hell. These devils betray the same nightmarish imagination we observed in the Romanesque animal world. They are composite creatures, human in general outline but with spidery, birdlike legs, furry thighs, tails, pointed ears, and enormous, savage mouths. Their violence, unlike that of the animal monsters, is unchecked; they enjoy themselves to the full in their grim occupation. No visitor, having "read in the marble" here (to speak with St. Bernard), could fail to enter the church in a chastened spirit.

142. *Last Judgment* (detail), west tympanum, Autun Cathedral. c. 1130–35

The Meuse Valley

The emergence of distinct artistic personalities in the twelfth century is a phenomenon that is rarely acknowledged, perhaps because it contravenes the widespread assumption that all medieval art is anonymous. It does not happen very often, of course, but it is no less significant for all that.

We find the revival of individuality in Italy and in one particular region of the north, the valley of the Meuse River, which runs from northeastern France into Belgium and Holland. This region had been the home of the Reims style in Carolingian times (see figs. 124, 125), and that awareness of classical sources pervades its art during the Romanesque period. Here again, interestingly enough, the revival of individuality is linked with the influence of ancient art, although this influence did not produce works on a monumental scale. "Mosan" Romanesque sculpture excelled in metalwork, such as the splendid baptismal font of 1107–18 in Liège (fig. 143), which is also the masterpiece of the earliest among the individually known artists of the region, Renier of Huy. The vessel rests on twelve oxen (symbols of the twelve apostles), like Solomon's basin in the Temple at Jerusalem, as described in the Bible. The reliefs make an instructive contrast with those of Bernward's doors (see fig. 129), since they are about the same height. Instead of the rough expressive power of the Ottonian panel, we find here a harmonious balance of design, a subtle control of the sculptured surfaces, and an understanding of organic structure that, in medieval terms, are amazingly classical. The figure seen from the back (beyond the tree on the left in our picture), with its graceful turning movement and Greek-looking drapery, might almost be taken for an ancient work.

143. Renier of Huy. Baptismal Font. 1107–18. Bronze, height 25″ (63.5 cm). St.-Barthélemy, Liège

144. Lion Monument. 1166. Bronze, length c. 6′ (1.83 m). Cathedral Square, Brunswick, Germany

Germany

The one monumental free-standing statue of Romanesque art—perhaps not the only one made, but the only one that has survived—is that of an animal, and in a secular rather than a religious context: the lifesize bronze lion on top of a tall shaft that Duke Henry the Lion of Saxony had placed in front of his palace at Brunswick in 1166 (fig. 144). The wonderfully ferocious beast (which, of course, personifies the duke, or at least that aspect of his personality that earned him his nickname) reminds us in a curious way of the archaic bronze she-wolf of Rome (see fig. 80). Perhaps the resemblance is not entirely coincidental, since the she-wolf was on public view in Rome at that time and must have had a strong appeal for Romanesque artists.

PAINTING AND METALWORK

Unlike architecture and sculpture, Romanesque painting shows no sudden revolutionary developments that set it apart immediately from Carolingian or Ottonian.

145. *St. John the Evangelist,* from the *Gospel Book of Abbot Wedricus.* Shortly before 1147. Société Archéologique et Historique, Avesnes-sur-Helpe, France

Nor does it look more "Roman" than Carolingian or Ottonian painting. This does not mean, however, that in the eleventh and twelfth centuries painting was any less important than it had been during the earlier Middle Ages; it merely emphasizes the greater continuity of the pictorial tradition, especially in manuscript illumination. Nevertheless, soon after the year 1000 we find the beginnings of a painting style that corresponds to—and often anticipates—the monumental qualities of Romanesque sculpture.

The Channel Region

While Romanesque painting, like architecture and sculpture, developed a wide variety of regional styles throughout western Europe, its greatest achievements emerged from the monastic scriptoria of northern France, Belgium, and southern England. The works produced in this area are so closely related in style that it is at times impossible to be sure on which side of the English Channel a given manuscript belongs. Thus the style of the wonderful miniature of St. John (fig. 145) has been linked with both Cambrai and Canterbury. The abstract linear draftsmanship of early medieval manuscripts (see fig. 124) has been influenced by Byzantine style (note the ropelike loops of drapery, whose origin can be traced back to such works as the relief in fig. 109), but without losing its energetic rhythm. It is the precisely controlled dynamics of every contour, both in the main figure and in the frame, that unite the varied elements of the composition into a coherent whole. This quality of line still betrays its ultimate source, the Celtic-Germanic heritage. If we compare our miniature with the *Lindisfarne Gospels* (see fig. 119), we see how much the interlacing patterns of the Dark Ages have contributed to the design of the St. John page. The drapery folds and the clusters of floral ornament have an impulsive yet disciplined aliveness that echoes the intertwined snakelike monsters of the animal style, even though the foliage is derived from the Classical acanthus and the human figures are based on Carolingian and Byzantine models. The unity of the entire page, however, is conveyed not only by the forms but by the content as well. The Evangelist "inhabits" the frame in such a way that we could not remove him from it without cutting off his ink supply (proffered by the donor of the manuscript, Abbot Wedricus), his source of inspiration (the dove of the Holy Spirit in the hand of

146. *The Battle of Hastings*. Detail of the *Bayeux Tapestry*. c. 1073–83. Wool embroidery on linen, height 20″ (50.8 cm). Centre Guillaume le Conquérant, Bayeux, France

147. *The Building of the Tower of Babel.* Detail of painting on the nave vault, St.-Savin-sur-Gartempe. Early 12th century

God), or his identifying symbol, the eagle. The other medallions, less directly linked with the main figure, show scenes from the life of St. John.

The linearity and the simple, closed contours of this painting style lent themselves readily to other mediums and to changes in scale: murals, tapestries, stained-glass windows, sculptured reliefs. The so-called *Bayeux Tapestry* is an embroidered frieze 230 feet long illustrating William the Conqueror's invasion of England. In our detail (fig. 146), portraying the Battle of Hastings, the main scene is enclosed by two border strips that perform a framing function. The upper tier with birds and animals is purely decorative, but the lower strip is full of dead warriors and horses and thus forms part of the story. Devoid of nearly all the pictorial refinements of Classical painting (see fig. 59), it nevertheless manages to give us an astonishingly vivid and detailed account of warfare in the eleventh century. The massed discipline of the Graeco-Roman scene is gone, but this is due not so much to the artist's ineptitude at foreshortening and overlapping, as to a new kind of individualism that makes of each combatant a potential hero, whether by dint of force or cunning. (Observe how the soldier who has fallen from the horse that is somersaulting with its hind legs in the air is, in turn, toppling his adversary by yanking at the saddle girth of his mount.)

Southwestern France

Firm outlines and a strong sense of pattern are equally characteristic of Romanesque wall painting. *The Building of the Tower of Babel* (fig. 147) is taken from the most impressive surviving cycle, on the nave vault of the church at St.-Savin-sur-Gartempe. It is an intensely dramatic design, crowded with strenuous action. The Lord Himself, on the far left, participates directly in the narrative as He addresses the builders of the colossal structure. He is counterbalanced, on the right, by the giant Nimrod, the leader of the enterprise, who frantically hands blocks of stone to the masons atop the tower, so that the entire scene becomes a great test of strength between God and man. The heavy, dark contours and the emphatic play of gestures make the composition eminently readable from a distance; yet the same qualities occur in the illuminated manuscripts of the region, which can be equally monumental despite their small scale.

148. Nicholas of Verdun. *The Crossing of the Red Sea,* from the *Klosterneuburg Altarpiece.* 1181. Enamel on gold plaque, height 5½″ (14 cm). Klosterneuburg Abbey, Austria

The Meuse Valley

Soon after the middle of the twelfth century, an important change of style began to make itself felt in Romanesque painting on either side of the English Channel. *The Crossing of the Red Sea* (fig. 148), one of many enamel plaques that make up a large altarpiece at Klosterneuburg by Nicholas of Verdun, shows that lines have suddenly regained their ability to describe three-dimensional forms instead of abstract patterns. The drapery folds no longer lead an ornamental life of their own but suggest the rounded volume of the body underneath. Here, at last, we meet the pictorial counterpart of that classicism we saw earlier in the baptismal font of Renier of Huy at Liège (see fig. 143). That the new style should have had its origin in metalwork (which includes not only casting and embossing but also engraving, enameling, and goldsmithing) is not as strange as it might seem, for its essential qualities are sculptural rather than pictorial. Moreover, metalwork had been a highly developed art in the Meuse valley area since Carolingian times. In these "pictures on metal," Nicholas straddles the division between sculpture and painting, as well as that between Romanesque and Gothic art. Although the *Klosterneuburg Altarpiece* was completed well before the end of the twelfth century, there is an understandable inclination to rank it as a harbinger of the style to come, rather than the culmination of a style that had been. Indeed, the altarpiece was to have a profound impact on the painting and sculpture of the next fifty years, when the astonishing maturity of Nicholas' art found a ready response in a Europe that was generally reawakening to an interest in humanity and the natural world.

GOTHIC ART

The term "Gothic" was first coined for architecture, and it is in architecture that the characteristics of the style are most easily recognized. For a century—from about 1150 to 1250, during the Age of the Great Cathedrals—architecture retained its dominant role. Gothic sculpture was at first severely architectural in spirit, but became less and less so after 1200; its greatest achievements occur between the years 1220 and 1420. Painting, in turn, reached a climax of creative endeavor between 1300 and 1350 in central Italy. North of the Alps, it became the leading art from about 1400 on. We thus find, in surveying the Gothic era as a whole, a gradual shift of emphasis from architecture to painting or, better perhaps, from architectural to pictorial qualities.

Overlying this broad pattern is another one: international diffusion as against regional independence. Starting as a local development in the Île-de-France, Gothic art radiates from there to the rest of France and to all Europe, where it comes to be known as *opus modernum* or *francigenum* (modern or French work). In the course of the thirteenth century, the new style gradually loses its imported flavor and regional variety begins to reassert itself. Toward the middle of the fourteenth century, we notice a growing tendency for these regional achievements to influence each other until, about 1400, a surprisingly homogeneous "International Gothic" style prevails almost everywhere. Shortly thereafter, this unity breaks apart: Italy, with Florence in the lead, creates a radically new art, that of the Early Renaissance, while north of the Alps, Flanders assumes an equally commanding position in the development of Late Gothic painting and sculpture. A century later, finally, the Italian Renaissance becomes the basis of another international style. With this skeleton outline to guide us, we can now explore the unfolding of Gothic art in greater detail.

ARCHITECTURE

France

St.-Denis and Abbot Suger. We can pinpoint the origin of no previous style as exactly as that of Gothic. It was born between 1137 and 1144 in the rebuilding, by Abbot Suger, of the royal Abbey Church of St.-Denis just outside the city of Paris. The only area ruled directly by the kings of France was the Île-de-France, and they often found their authority challenged even there by the nobles. Not until the early twelfth century did royal power begin to expand; Suger, as chief adviser to Louis VI, played a key role in this process. It was he who forged the alliance between the monarchy and the Church, which brought the bishops of France (and the cities under their authority) to the king's side, while the king, in turn, supported the papacy in its struggle against the German emperors.

Suger championed the monarchy not only on the plane of practical politics but also on that of "spiritual politics." By investing the royal office with religious significance and glorifying it as the strong right arm of justice, he sought to rally the nation behind the king. His architectural plans for the Abbey of St.-Denis must be understood in this context, for the church, founded in the late eighth century, enjoyed a dual prestige that made it ideally suitable for Suger's purpose: it was the shrine of the Apostle of France, the sacred protector of the realm, as well as the chief memorial of the Carolingian dynasty. Suger wanted to make the abbey the spiritual center

149. Ambulatory, Abbey Church of St.-Denis, Paris. 1140–44

of France, a pilgrimage church to outshine the splendor of all the others, the focal point of religious as well as patriotic emotion. But in order to become the visible embodiment of such a goal, the old edifice had to be enlarged and rebuilt. The great abbot himself has described the entire campaign in such eloquent detail that we know more about what he desired to achieve than we do about the final result, for the west facade and its sculpture are sadly mutilated today, and the choir, which Suger regarded as the most important part of the church, retains its original appearance only in the ambulatory (fig. 149).

The ambulatory and radiating chapels surrounding the apse are familiar elements from the Romanesque pilgrimage choir (compare fig. 133). Yet these elements have been integrated in strikingly novel fashion. The chapels, instead of remaining separate entities, are merged so as to form, in effect, a second ambulatory, and ribbed groin-vaulting based on the pointed arch is employed throughout. (In the Romanesque pilgrimage choir, only the ambulatory had been groin-vaulted.) As a result, we experience this double ambulatory not as a series of separate compartments but as a continuous (though articulated) space, whose shape is outlined for us by the network of slender arches, ribs, and columns that sustains the vaults.

What distinguishes this interior immediately from its predecessors is its lightness, in both senses. The architectural forms seem graceful, almost weightless as against the massive solidity of the Romanesque, and the windows have been enlarged to the point that they are no longer openings cut into a wall—they fill the entire wall area, so that they themselves become translucent walls. This abundance of light is made possible by heavy buttresses, visible only from the outside, jutting out between the chapels to contain the outward pressure of the vaults. No wonder, then, that the interior appears so amazingly airy and weightless, since the heaviest members of the structural skeleton are beyond our view.

In describing Suger's choir, we have also described the essentials of Gothic architecture; yet none of the individual elements that entered into its design were really new. They were taken from the various regional schools of the French and Anglo-Norman Romanesque, even though we never encounter them all combined in the same building until St.-Denis. The Île-de-France had failed to develop a Romanesque tradition of its own, so that Suger—as he himself tells us—had to bring together artisans from many different regions for his project. Gothic architecture originated as more than a synthesis of Romanesque traits, however. Suger's account of the rebuilding of his church insistently stresses strict geometric planning and the quest for luminosity as the highest values achieved in the new structure at St.-Denis. "Harmony" (that is, the perfect relationship among parts in terms of mathematical proportions or ratios) is the source of all beauty, since it exemplifies the laws according to which divine reason has constructed the universe. The "miraculous" light that floods the choir through the "most sacred" windows becomes the Light Divine, a mystic revelation of the spirit of God. This symbolic interpretation of numerical harmony and of light had been established over the centuries in Christian thought. For Suger, the light-and-number symbolism of this theology must have had a particularly strong appeal. His mind was steeped in it, and he wanted to give it visible expression when he rebuilt the church of the royal patron saint. That he succeeded is proved not only by the inherent qualities of his choir design but also by its extraordinary impact. Every visitor to St.-Denis, it seems, was overwhelmed by Suger's achievement, and within a few decades the new style had spread far beyond the confines of the Île-de-France.

The how and why of Suger's success are a good deal more difficult to explain. Here we encounter a controversy we have met several times before—that of form versus function. How could the theological ideas of Suger have led to these technical advances, unless we are willing to assume that he was an architect? Oddly enough, there is no contradiction here. The term architect was understood in a very different way from the modern sense, which derives from Greece and Rome by way of the Italian Renaissance. To the medieval mind, he was the overall leader of the project, not the master builder responsible for its construction. Professional training as we know it did not exist at the time.

It is perfectly true, of course, that the choir of St.-Denis is more rationally planned and constructed than any Romanesque church. The function of a church, however, is not merely to enclose a maximum of space with a minimum of material. For the master who built the choir of St.-Denis under Suger's supervision, the technical problems of vaulting must have been inextricably bound up with considerations of form (that is, of beauty, harmony, fitness, and so forth). As a matter of fact, his design includes various elements that *express* function without actually performing it, such as the slender shafts (called responds) that seem to carry the weight of the vaults to the church floor. But in order to know what constituted beauty, harmony, and fitness, the medieval architect needed the guidance of ecclesiastical authority. In the case of a patron as actively concerned with architectural aesthetics as Suger, it amounted to full participation in the design process. Thus Suger's desire to "build theology" is likely to have been a decisive factor from the very beginning: it shaped his mental image of the kind of structure he wanted, we may assume, and determined his choice of a master of Norman background. This man, a great artist, must have been singularly responsive to the abbot's ideas and instructions. Together, the two created the Gothic style.

Notre-Dame, Paris. Although St.-Denis was an abbey, the future of Gothic architecture lay in the towns rather than in rural monastic communities. There had been a vigorous revival of urban life, we will recall, since the early eleventh century. This movement continued at an accelerated pace, and the growing weight of the cities made itself felt not only economically and politically but in countless other ways as well. Bishops and the city clergy rose to new importance. That is why the Gothic is known as the Great Age of Cathedrals. (A cathedral is the principal church of a diocese, presided over by a bishop, usually in the leading city of the see.) Cathedral schools and universities took the place of monasteries as centers of learning, while the artistic efforts of the age culminated in the great cathedral churches.

Notre-Dame ("Our Lady," the Virgin Mary) at Paris, begun in 1163, reflects the salient features of Suger's St.-Denis more directly than any other cathedral. The plan (fig. 150), with its emphasis on the longitudinal axis, is extraordinarily compact and unified compared to that of major Romanesque churches. The double ambulatory of the choir continues directly into the aisles, and the stubby transept barely exceeds the width of the facade. The sexpartite nave vaults over squarish bays, although not identical with the "Siamese-twin" groin vaulting in Durham Ca-

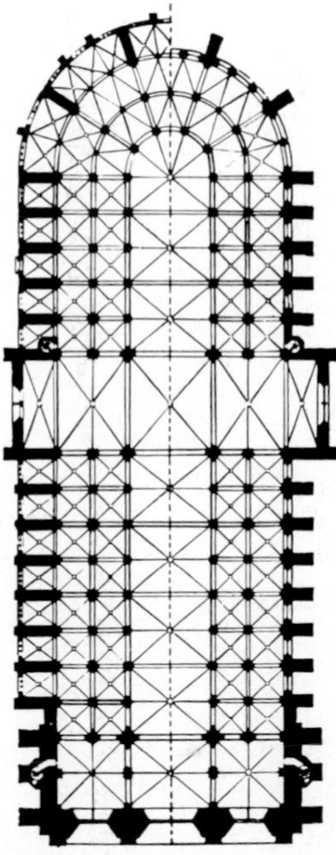

150. Plan of Notre-Dame, Paris. 1163–c. 1250

151. Nave and choir, Notre-Dame, Paris

thedral (see fig. 136), continue the kind of structural experimentation that was begun by the Norman Romanesque. Inside (fig. 151), we find other echoes of Norman Romanesque in the galleries above the inner aisles and the columns used in the nave arcade. Here, too, the use of pointed ribbed arches, which was pioneered in the western bays of the nave at Durham, has become systematic throughout the building. Yet the large clerestory windows and the lightness and slenderness of the forms, which reflect that of the ribs of the vault, create the "weightless" effect that we associate with Gothic interiors, and make the nave walls seem thin. Gothic, too, is the verticality of the interior space. This depends less on the actual proportions of the nave—for some Romanesque naves are equally tall, relative to their width—than on the constant accenting of the verticals and on the soaring ease with which the sense of height is attained. Romanesque interiors (such as that in fig. 133), by contrast, emphasize the great effort required in supporting the weight of the vaults.

In Notre-Dame, as in Suger's choir, the buttresses (the "heavy bones" of the structural skeleton) are not visible from the inside. The plan shows them as massive blocks of masonry that stick out from the building like a row of teeth. Above the aisles, these piers turn into flying buttresses—arched bridges that reach upward to the critical spots between the clerestory windows where the outward thrust of the nave vault is concentrated (figs. 152, 153). This method of anchoring vaults, a characteristic feature of Gothic architecture, certainly owed its origin to functional considerations. Even the flying buttress, however, soon became aesthetically important as well, and its shape could express support (apart from actually providing it) in a variety of ways, according to the designer's sense of style.

The most monumental aspect of the exterior of Notre-Dame is the west facade (fig. 154). Except for its sculpture, which suffered heavily during the French Revolution and is for the most part restored, it retains its original appearance. The design reflects the

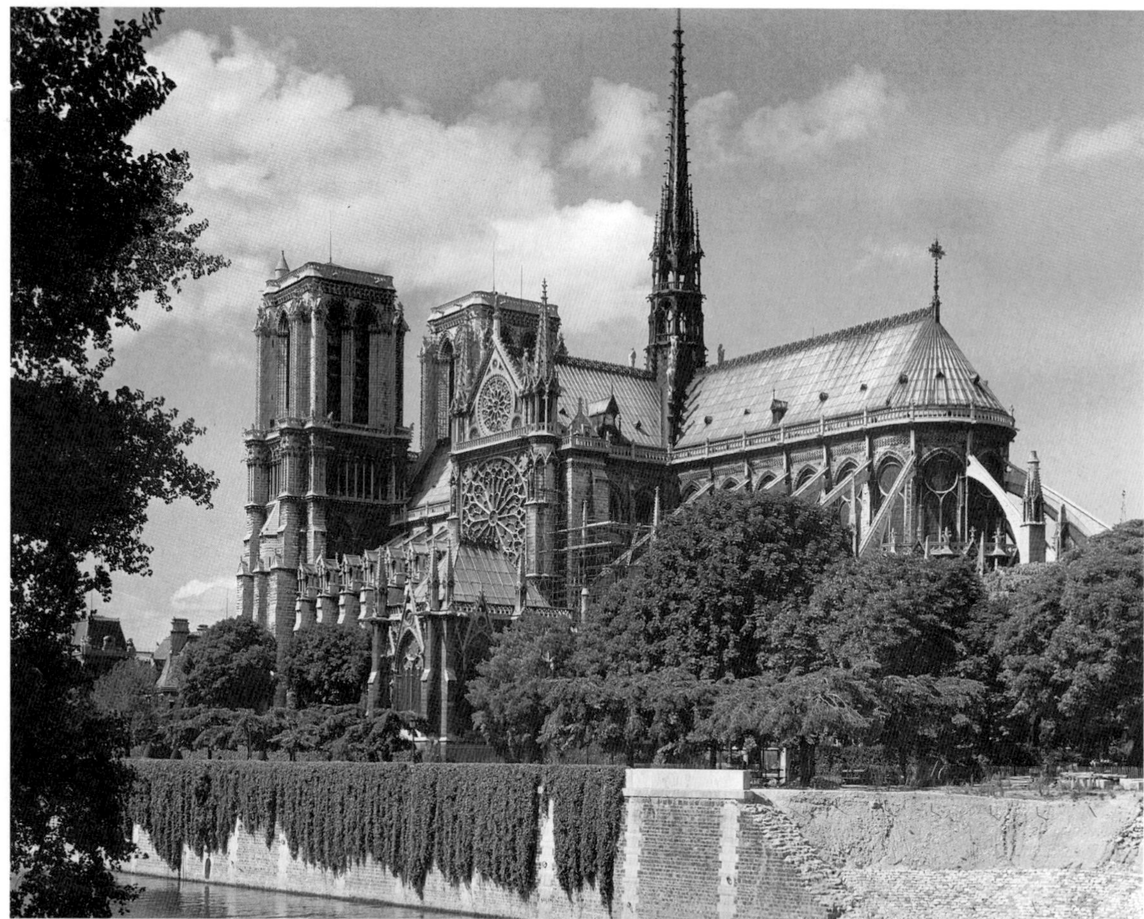

152. Notre-Dame (view from the southeast), Paris

general disposition of the facade of St.-Denis, which in turn had been derived from Norman Romanesque facades such as that of St.-Étienne at Caen (see fig. 135). Comparing the latter with Notre-Dame, we note the persistence of some basic features: the pier buttresses that reinforce the corners of the towers and divide the front into three main parts; the placing of the portals; and the three-story arrangement. The rich sculptural decoration, however, recalls the facades of western France and the elaborately carved portals of Burgundy (see fig. 142).

Much more important than these resemblances are the qualities that distinguish the facade of Notre-Dame from its Romanesque ancestors. Foremost among these is the way all the details have been integrated into a wonderfully balanced and coherent whole. The meaning of Suger's emphasis on harmony, geometric order, and proportion becomes evident here even more strikingly than in St.-Denis itself. This formal discipline also embraces the sculpture, which is no longer permitted the spontaneous (and often uncontrolled) growth so characteristic of the Romanesque but has been assigned a precisely defined role within the architectural framework. At the same time, the cubic solidity of the facade of St.-Étienne at Caen has been transformed into its very opposite. Lacelike arcades, huge portals, and windows dissolve the continuity of the wall surfaces, so that the total effect approximates that of a weightless openwork screen. How rapidly this tendency advanced during the first half of the thir-

153. Flying buttresses, Notre-Dame, Paris

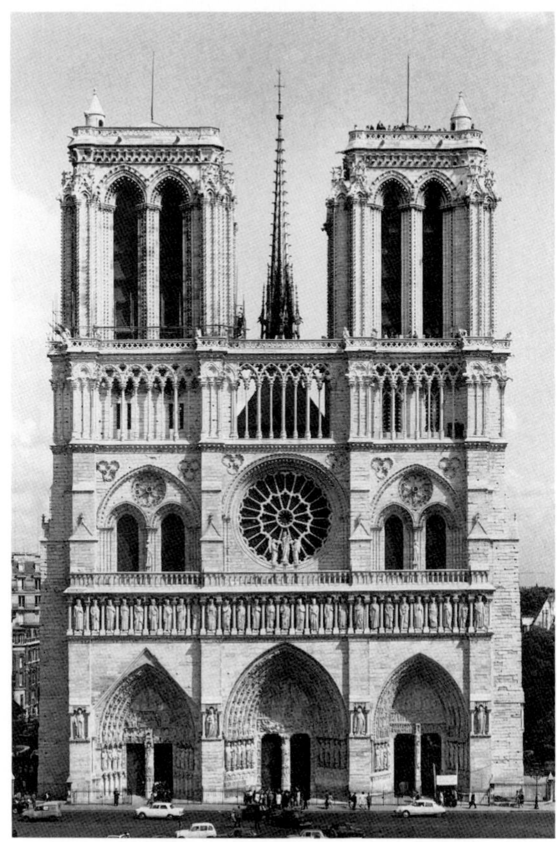
154. West facade, Notre-Dame, Paris

teenth century can be seen by comparing the west front of Notre-Dame with the somewhat later facade of the south transept, visible in the center of figure 152. In the west facade, the rose window in the center is still deeply recessed and, as a result, the stone tracery that subdivides the opening is clearly set off against the surrounding wall surface. On the transept facade, in contrast, we can no longer distinguish the rose window from its frame—a single network of tracery covers the entire area.

Chartres Cathedral. Alone among all major Gothic cathedrals, Chartres still retains most of its more than 180 original stained-glass windows. The magic of the colored light streaming down from the clerestory through the large windows is unforgettable to anyone who has experienced their intense, jewellike hues (fig. 155). The windows admit far less light than one might expect. They act mainly as multicolored diffusing filters that change the *quality* of ordinary daylight, endowing it with the poetic and symbolic values—the "miraculous light"—so highly praised by Abbot Suger. The sensation of ethereal light, which dissolves the physical solidity of the church and, hence, the distinction between the temporal and the divine realms, creates the intensely mystical experience that lies at the heart of Gothic spirituality.

The High Gothic style defined at Chartres reaches its climax a generation later. Breathtaking height becomes the dominant aim, both technically and aesthetically. Skeletal construction is carried to its most precarious limits. The inner logic of the system forcefully asserts itself in the shape of the vaults, taut and thin as membranes, and in the expanded window area, so that the entire wall above the nave arcade becomes a clerestory.

Reims Cathedral. The same emphasis on verticality and translucency can be traced in the development of the High Gothic facade. The most famous of these, at Reims Cathedral (fig. 156), makes an instructive contrast with the west facade of Notre-Dame in Paris, even though its basic design was conceived

155. Nave and choir, Chartres Cathedral. 1145–1220

only about thirty years later. Many elements are common to both, but in the younger structure they have been reshaped into a very different ensemble. The portals, instead of being recessed, are projected forward as gabled porches, with windows in place of tympanums above the doorways. The gallery of royal statues, which in Paris forms an incisive horizontal between the first and second stories, has been raised until it merges with the third-story arcade. Every detail except the rose window has become taller and narrower than before. A multitude of pinnacles further accentuates the restless upward-pointing movement. The sculptural decoration, by far the most lavish of its kind, no longer remains in clearly marked-off zones. It has now spread to so many hitherto unaccustomed perches, not only on the facade but on the flanks as well, that the exterior of the cathedral begins to look like a dovecote for statues. The progression toward verticality in French Gothic cathedral architecture occurred relatively swiftly: figure 157 shows how vast height and large expanses of window were achieved toward the end of this development.

156. West facade, Reims Cathedral. c. 1225–99

International Gothic. The High Gothic cathedrals of France represent a concentrated expenditure of effort such as the world has rarely seen before or since. They are truly national monuments, whose immense cost was borne by donations collected all over the country and from all classes of society—the tangible expression of that merging of religious and patriotic fervor that had been the goal of Abbot Suger. Among the astonishing things about Gothic art is the enthusiastic response this "royal French style of the Paris region" evoked abroad. Even more remarkable was its ability to acclimate itself to a variety of local conditions—so much so, in fact, that the Gothic monuments of England and Germany have become objects of intense national pride in modern times, and critics in both countries have acclaimed Gothic as a peculiarly "native" style. A number of factors contributed to the rapid spread of Gothic art: the superior skill of French architects and stone carvers; the vast intellectual prestige of

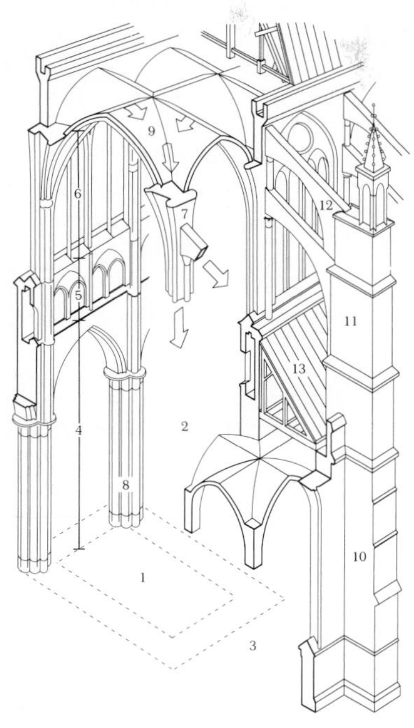

157. Axonometric projection of a High Gothic cathedral (after Acland). 1) Bay; 2) Nave; 3) Side aisle; 4) Nave arcade; 5) Triforium; 6) Clerestory; 7) Pier; 8) Compound pier; 9) Sexpartite vault; 10) Buttress; 11) Flying buttress; 12) Flying arch; 13) Roof

158. Salisbury Cathedral. 1220–70

French centers of learning; and the influence of the Cistercians, the reformed monastic order founded by St. Bernard of Clairvaux, which promulgated an austere version of the Gothic throughout western Europe. The ultimate reason for the international victory of Gothic art, however, seems to have been the extraordinary persuasive power of the style itself, its ability to kindle the imagination and to arouse religious feeling even among people far removed from the cultural climate of the Île-de-France.

England

That England should have proved particularly receptive to the new style is hardly surprising. Yet English Gothic did not grow directly from Anglo-Norman Romanesque but rather from the Gothic of the Île-de-

France (introduced in 1175 by the French architect who rebuilt the choir of Canterbury Cathedral) and of the Cistercians. Within less than fifty years, it developed a well-defined character of its own, known as the Early English style, which is best exemplified in Salisbury Cathedral (fig. 158). We realize immediately how different the exterior is from its counterparts in France—and how futile it would be to judge it by French Gothic standards. Compactness and verticality have given way to a long, low, sprawling look (the great crossing tower, which provides a dramatic unifying accent, was built a century later than the rest and is much taller than originally planned). Since there is no straining after height, flying buttresses have been introduced only as an afterthought. Characteristically enough, the west facade has become a screen wall, wider than the church itself and stratified by emphatic horizontal bands of ornament and statuary, while the towers have shrunk to stubby turrets.

English Gothic rapidly developed toward a more pronounced verticality. The choir of Gloucester Cathedral (fig. 159) is a striking example of the English Late Gothic, also called Perpendicular. The name certainly fits, since we now find the dominant vertical accent that is so conspicuously absent in the Early English style. In this respect Perpendicular Gothic is much more akin to French sources, yet it includes so many features we have come to know as English that it would look very much out of place on the Continent. The repetition of small uniform tracery panels recalls the bands of statuary on the west facade at Salisbury. The square end simulates the apses of earlier English churches, and the upward curve of the vault is as steep as in them. The ribs of the vaults, on the other hand, have assumed an altogether new role—they have been multiplied until they form an ornamental network that screens the boundaries between the bays and thus makes the entire vault look like one continuous surface. This, in turn, has the effect of emphasizing the unity of the interior space. Such decorative elaboration of the "classic" quadripartite vault is characteristic of the so-called

159. Choir, Gloucester Cathedral. 1332–57

Flamboyant style on the Continent as well, but the English started it earlier and carried it to greater lengths.

Germany

In Germany, Gothic architecture took root a good deal more slowly than in England. Until the mid-thirteenth century, the Romanesque tradition, with its persistent Ottonian reminiscences, remained dominant, despite the growing acceptance of Early Gothic features. From about 1250 on, the High Gothic of the Île-de-France had a strong impact on the Rhineland. Especially characteristic of German Gothic is the *Hallenkirche,* or hall church, with aisles and nave of the same height. In the large hall choir added in 1361–72 to the church of St. Sebald in Nuremberg (fig. 160), the space has a fluidity and expansiveness that enfold us as if we were standing under a huge canopy. There is no pressure, no directional command to prescribe our path. And

160. Choir, St. Sebald, Nuremberg. 1361–72

the unbroken lines of the pillars, formed by bundles of shafts which gradually diverge as they turn into ribs, seem to echo the continuous movement that we feel in the space itself.

Italy

Italian Gothic architecture stands apart from that of the rest of Europe. Judged by the formal criteria of the Île-de-France, most of it hardly deserves to be called Gothic at all. Yet the Gothic in Italy produced structures of singular beauty and impressiveness that cannot be understood as mere continuations of the local Romanesque. We must be careful, therefore, to avoid too rigid or technical a standard in approaching these monuments, lest we fail to do justice to their unique blend of Gothic qualities and Mediterranean tradition. It was the Cistercians, rather than the cathedral builders of the Île-de-France, who provided the chief exemplars on which Italian architects based their conception of the Gothic style. As early as the end of the twelfth century, Cistercian abbeys sprang up in both north and central Italy, their designs patterned directly after those of the French abbeys of the order.

Cistercian churches made a deep impression upon the Franciscans, the monastic order founded by St. Francis of Assisi in the early thirteenth century. As mendicant friars dedicated to poverty, simplicity, and humility, they were the spiritual kin of St. Bernard, and the severe beauty of Cistercian Gothic must have seemed to them to express an ideal closely related to theirs. From the first, the Franciscans' churches reflected Cistercian influence and thus played a leading role in establishing Gothic architecture in Italy.

Sta. Croce in Florence may well claim to be the greatest of all Franciscan structures (fig. 161). It is also a masterpiece of Gothic architecture, even though it has wooden ceilings instead of groined vaults except in the choir. There can be no doubt that this was a matter of deliberate choice, rather than of

161. Nave and choir, Sta. Croce, Florence. Begun c. 1295

162. Florence Cathedral (Sta. Maria del Fiore). Begun by Arnolfo di Cambio, 1296; dome by Filippo Brunelleschi, 1420–36

technical or economic necessity—a choice made not only on the basis of local practice (wooden ceilings were a feature of the Tuscan Romanesque) but also perhaps from a desire to evoke the simplicity of Early Christian basilicas and, in doing so, to link Franciscan poverty with the traditions of the early Church. Since the wooden ceilings do not require buttresses, there are none. This allows the walls to remain intact as continuous surfaces.

Why, then, do we speak of Sta. Croce as Gothic? Surely the use of the pointed arch is not sufficient to justify the term. A glance at the interior will dispel our misgivings. For we sense immediately that this space creates an effect fundamentally different from that of either Early Christian or Romanesque architecture. The nave walls have the weightless, "transparent" quality we saw in Northern Gothic churches, and the dramatic massing of windows at the eastern end conveys the dominant role of light as forcefully as Abbot Suger's choir at St.-Denis. Judged in terms of its emotional impact, Sta. Croce is Gothic beyond doubt. It is also profoundly Franciscan—and Florentine—in the monumental simplicity of the means by which this impact has been achieved.

If in Sta. Croce the architect's main concern was an impressive interior, Florence Cathedral was planned as a monumental landmark to civic pride towering above the entire city (fig. 162). The original design, by the sculptor Arnolfo di Cambio, dates from 1296, about the same time construction was begun at Sta. Croce; although somewhat smaller than the present building, it probably showed the same basic plan. The building as we know it, however, is based largely on a design by Francesco Talenti, who took over around 1343. The most striking feature is the great octagonal dome with its subsidiary half-domes, a motif ultimately of late Roman origin (see fig. 86). It forms a huge central pool of space that makes the nave look like an afterthought. The basic characteristics of the dome were set by a committee of leading painters and sculptors in 1367; the actual construction, however, belongs to the early fifteenth century (see p. 225).

Apart from the windows and the doorways, there is nothing Gothic about the exterior of Florence Cathedral. A separate campanile takes the place of the facade towers familiar to us in Northern Gothic churches. It was begun by the great painter Giotto, who managed to finish only the first story, and continued by the sculptor Andrea Pisano, son of Nicola Pisano (see p. 176), who was responsible for the niche zone. The rest represents the work of Talenti, who completed it by about 1360.

SCULPTURE

France

St.-Denis. Although Abbot Suger's story of the rebuilding of St.-Denis does not deal at length with the sculptural decoration of the church, he must have attached considerable importance to this aspect of the enterprise. The three portals of his west facade were far larger and more richly carved than those of Norman Romanesque churches. Unhappily, their condition today is so poor that they do not tell us a great deal about Suger's ideas of the role of sculpture within the total context of the structure he had envisioned.

Chartres Cathedral, West Portals. Suger's ideas paved the way for the admirable west portals of Chartres Cathedral (fig. 163), begun about 1145 under the influence of St.-

163. West portals, Chartres Cathedral. c. 1145–70

Denis, but even more ambitious. They probably represent the oldest full-fledged example of Early Gothic sculpture. Comparing them with a Romanesque portal (see fig. 141), we are impressed first of all with a new sense of order, as if all the figures had suddenly come to attention, conscious of their responsibility to the architectural framework. The dense crowding and the frantic movement of Romanesque sculpture have given way to an emphasis on symmetry and clarity. The figures on the lintels, archivolts, and tympanums are no longer entangled with each other but stand out as separate entities, so that the entire design carries much further than that of previous portals.

Particularly striking in this respect is the novel treatment of the jambs (fig. 164), which are lined with tall figures attached to columns. Instead of being treated essentially as reliefs carved into—or protruding from—the masonry of the doorway, the Chartres jamb figures are essentially statues, each with its own axis; they could, in theory at least, be detached from their supports. Here, then, we witness a development of truly revolutionary importance: the first basic step toward the reconquest of monumental sculpture in the round since the end of classical antiquity. Apparently, this step could be taken only by "borrowing" the rigid cylindrical shape of the column for the human figure, with the result that these statues seem more abstract than their Romanesque predecessors. Yet they will not retain their immobility and unnatural proportions for long. The very fact that they are round endows them with a more emphatic presence than anything in Romanesque sculpture, and their heads show a gentle, human quality that betokens the fundamentally realistic trend of Gothic sculpture.

Realism is, of course, a relative term whose meaning varies greatly according to circumstances. On the Chartres west portals, it appears to spring from a reaction against the fantastic and demoniacal aspects of Romanesque art, a reaction that may be seen not only in the calm, solemn spirit of the figures and their increased physical bulk, but also in the rational discipline of the symbolic program underlying the entire scheme. While the subtler aspects of this program are accessible only to those fully conversant with the theology of the Chartres Cathedral School, its main elements can be readily understood.

The jamb statues, a continuous sequence linking all three portals, represent the prophets, kings, and queens of the Bible. Their purpose is both to acclaim the rulers of

164. Jamb statues, west portal, Chartres Cathedral

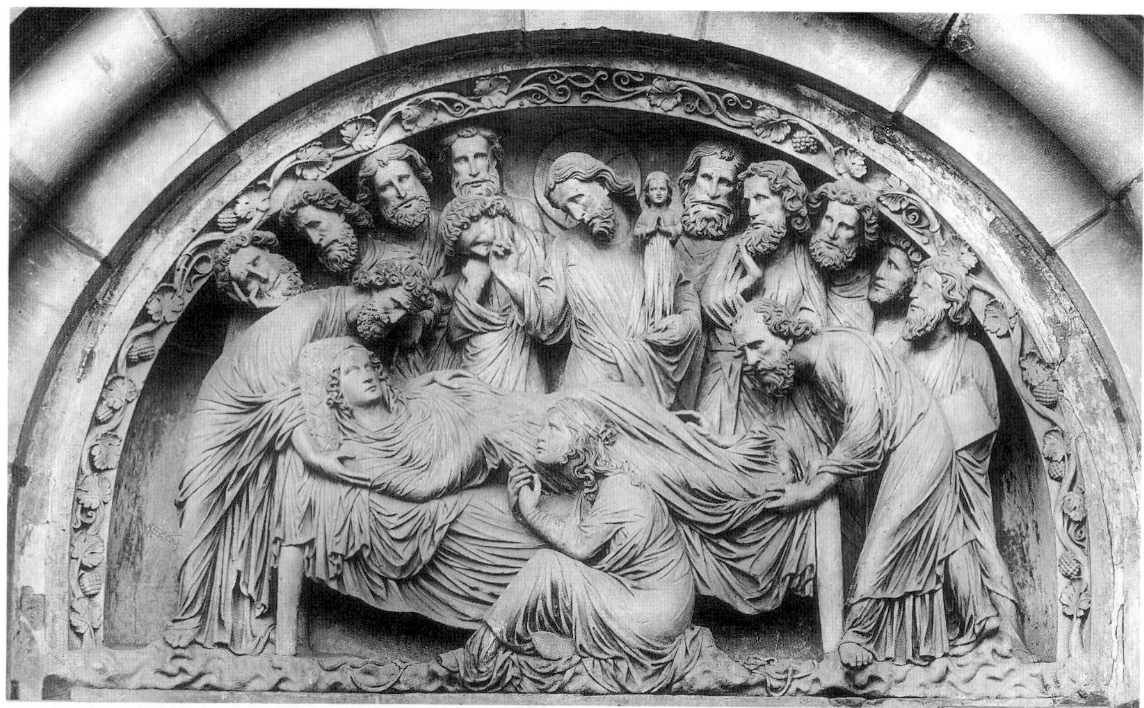

165. *The Death of the Virgin,* tympanum of south transept portal, Strasbourg Cathedral. c. 1220

France as the spiritual descendants of Old Testament royalty and to stress the harmony of secular and spiritual rule, of priests (or bishops) and kings—an ideal insistently put forward by Abbot Suger. Christ Himself appears enthroned above the main doorway as Judge and Ruler of the Universe, flanked by the symbols of the four evangelists, with the apostles assembled below and the twenty-four elders of the Apocalypse in the archivolts. The right-hand tympanum shows His incarnation—the Birth, the Presentation in the Temple, and the Infant Christ on the lap of the Virgin (who also stands for the Church)—while in the archivolts we see the personifications and representatives of the liberal arts: human wisdom paying homage to the divine wisdom of Christ. In the left-hand tympanum, we see the timeless Heavenly Christ (the Christ of the Ascension) framed by the ever-repeating cycle of the year: the signs of the zodiac and their earthly counterparts, the labors of the twelve months.

Gothic Classicism. Gothic sculpture came to incorporate another, equally important tradition: the classicism of the Meuse valley, which we traced in the previous chapter from Renier of Huy to Nicholas of Verdun (compare figs. 143, 148). At the end of the twelfth century this trend, hitherto confined to metalwork and miniatures, began to appear in monumental stone sculpture as well, transforming it from Early Gothic to Classic High Gothic. The link with Nicholas of Verdun is striking in *The Death of the Virgin* (fig. 165), a tympanum at Strasbourg Cathedral contemporary with the Chartres transept portals. Here the draperies, the facial types, and the movements and gestures have a classical flavor that immediately recalls the *Klosterneuburg Altarpiece* (see fig. 148).

What marks it as Gothic rather than Romanesque, on the other hand, is the deeply felt tenderness pervading the entire scene. We sense a bond of shared emotion among the figures, an ability to communicate by glance and gesture such as we have never met before. This quality of pathos, too, has classical roots—we recall its entering into Christian art during the Second Golden Age in Byzantium. But how much warmer and more eloquent it is at Strasbourg than at Daphnē (see fig. 115)!

The climax of Gothic classicism is reached in some of the statues at Reims Cathedral, of which the most famous is the Visitation group (fig. 166, right). To have a pair of jamb figures enact a narrative scene such as this would have been unthinkable in Early Gothic sculpture. The fact that they can do so now shows how far the sustaining column has receded into the background. Characteristically enough, the S-curve, resulting from the pronounced *contrapposto* (see p. 81), dominates the side view as well as the front view, and the physical bulk of the body is further emphasized by horizontal folds pulled across the abdomen. The relationship of the two women shows the same human warmth and sympathy we found in the Strasbourg tympanum, but their classicism is of a far more monumental kind. They make us wonder if the artist was inspired directly by large-scale Roman sculpture. The influence of Nicholas of Verdun alone could hardly have produced such firmly rounded, solid volumes.

The vast scale of the sculptural program for Reims Cathedral made it necessary to call upon the services of masters and workshops from various other building sites, and so we encounter several distinct styles among the Reims sculpture. Two of these styles, both clearly different from the classicism of the *Visitation,* appear in the Annunciation group (fig. 166, left). The Virgin exhibits a severe manner, with a rigidly vertical body axis and straight, tubular folds meeting at sharp angles, a style probably invented about 1220 by the sculptors of the west portals of Notre-Dame in Paris. The angel, in contrast, is conspicuously graceful: we note the tiny, round face framed by curly locks, the emphatic smile, the strong S-curve of the slender body, the ample, richly accented drapery. This "elegant style," created around 1240 by Parisian masters working for the royal court, was to spread far and wide during the following decades. It soon became, in fact, the standard formula for High Gothic sculpture.

166. *Annunciation* and *Visitation,* west portal, Reims Cathedral. c. 1225–45

Germany

The spread of the Gothic style in sculpture beyond the borders of France began only toward 1200—the style of the Chartres west portals had hardly any echoes abroad—but, once under way, it proceeded at an astonishingly rapid pace. England may well have led the way, as it did in evolving its own version of Gothic architecture. Unfortunately, so much English Gothic sculpture was destroyed during the Reformation that we can study its development only with difficulty. In Germany, the growth of Gothic sculpture can be traced more easily. From the 1220s on, German masters trained in the sculptural workshops of the great French cathedrals transplanted the new style to their homeland, although German architecture at that time was still predominantly Romanesque. However, even after the middle of the century, Germany failed to emulate the vast statuary cycles of France. As a consequence, German Gothic sculpture tended to be less closely linked with its architectural setting (the finest work was often done for the interiors rather than the exteriors of churches), and this, in turn, permitted it to develop an individuality and ex-

167. *Crucifixion,* on the choir screen, Naumburg Cathedral. c. 1240–50. Stone

pressive freedom greater than that of its French models.

The Naumburg Master. All these qualities are strikingly evident in the style of the Naumburg Master, an artist of real genius whose best-known work is the magnificent series of statues and reliefs he carved about 1240–50 for Naumburg Cathedral. The *Crucifixion* (fig. 167) forms the central feature of the choir screen; flanking it are statues of the Virgin and John the Baptist. Enclosed by a deep, gabled porch, the three figures frame the opening that links the nave with the sanctuary. Placing the group on the screen (rather than above it, in accordance with the usual practice), our sculptor has brought the sacred subject down to earth both physically and emotionally. The suffering of Christ becomes a human reality because of the emphasis on the weight and volume of the Saviour's body; Mary and John, pleading with the beholder, now convey their grief more eloquently than ever before. The pathos of these figures is heroic and dramatic, as against the lyricism of the Strasbourg tympanum or the Reims *Visitation* (see figs. 165, 166). If the Classic High Gothic sculpture of France evokes comparison with Phidias, the Naumburg Master might be termed the temperamental kin of Scopas (see p. 85).

The Pietà. Gothic sculpture, as we have come to know it so far, reflects a desire to endow the traditional themes of Christian art with an ever greater emotional appeal. Toward the end of the thirteenth century, this tendency gave rise to a new kind of religious imagery, designed to serve private devotion; it is often referred to by the German term *Andachtsbild,* since Germany played a leading part in its development. The most characteristic and widespread type of *Andachtsbild* was the *Pietà* (an Italian word derived from the Latin *pietas,*

168. *Pietà.* Early 14th century. Wood, height 34½" (87.6 cm). Provinzialmuseum, Bonn

the root word for both pity and piety), a representation of the Virgin grieving over the dead Christ. No such scene occurs in the scriptural account of the Passion. Rather, it was invented—we do not know exactly where or when—as a tragic counterpart to the familiar motif of the Madonna and Child.

The *Pietà* reproduced in figure 168 is carved of wood, with a vividly painted surface to enhance its impact. Realism here has become purely a vehicle of expression, reflected in the agonized faces. The blood-encrusted wounds of Christ are enlarged and elaborated to an almost grotesque degree. The bodies and limbs likewise are puppetlike in their thinness and rigidity. The purpose of the work, clearly, is to arouse so overwhelming a sense of horror and pity that we will identify our own feelings completely with those of the grief-stricken Mother of God.

The International Style in the North

The *Pietà* reaches an extreme in the negation of the physical aspects of the human figure. Only after 1350 do we again find an interest in weight and volume, coupled with a renewed impulse to explore tangible reality. The climax of this new trend came around 1400, during the period of the International Style (see pp. 177–78, 188–93). Its greatest exponent was Claus Sluter, a sculptor of Netherlandish origin working for the duke of Burgundy at Dijon. In the *Moses Well* (fig. 169), a symbolic well surrounded by statues of Old Testament prophets and once surmounted by a crucifix, he explores sculptural style in two new directions. In the majestic Moses, to the right in our picture, soft, lavishly draped garments envelop the heavyset body like an ample shell, and the swelling forms seem to reach out into the surrounding space, determined to capture as much of it as possible (note the outward curve of the scroll). In the Isaiah, facing left in our illustration, these aspects of our artist's style are less pronounced. What strikes us, rather, is the precise and masterful realism of every detail, from the minutiae of the costume to the texture of the wrinkled skin. The head, unlike that of Moses, has all the individuality of a portrait. Nor is this impression deceiving, for the sculptural development that culminated in Claus Sluter produced the first genuine portraits since late antiquity, including splendid examples by Sluter himself. This attachment to the tangible and specific distinguishes his realism from that of the thirteenth century.

169. Claus Sluter. *Moses Well.* 1395–1406. Stone, height of figures c. 6′ (1.88 m). Chartreuse de Champmol, Dijon

Italy

We have left a discussion of Italian Gothic sculpture to the last, for here, too, as in Gothic architecture, Italy stands apart from the rest of Europe. The earliest Gothic sculpture on Italian soil was probably produced in the extreme south, in Apulia and Sicily, the domain of the German emperor Frederick II, who employed Frenchmen and Germans along with native artists at his court. Of the works he sponsored little has survived, but there is evidence that his taste favored a strongly classical style derived from the Visitation group at Reims (see fig. 166). This style provided a fitting visual language for a ruler who saw himself as the heir of the Caesars of old.

170. Nicola Pisano. *Nativity,* detail of pulpit. 1259–60. Marble. Baptistery, Pisa

Nicola Pisano. Such was the background of Nicola Pisano, who went to Tuscany from southern Italy about 1250 (the year of Frederick II's death). His work has been well defined as that of "the greatest—and in a sense the last—of medieval classicists." In 1260 he completed the marble pulpit in the Baptistery of Pisa Cathedral, which was covered with reliefs of narrative scenes such as the *Nativity* (fig. 170). The classical flavor is so strong that the Gothic elements are hard to detect at first glance. They are there nonetheless. Most striking, perhaps, is the Gothic quality of human feeling in the figures. The dense crowding, on the other hand, has no counterpart in Northern Gothic sculpture. Aside from the Nativity, the panel shows the Annunciation and the shepherds in the fields receiving the glad tidings of the birth of Christ. This treatment of the relief as a shallow box filled almost to the bursting point with solid, convex shapes tells us that Nicola Pisano must have been thoroughly familiar with Roman sarcophagi (compare fig. 108).

171. Giovanni Pisano. *Nativity,* detail of pulpit. 1302–10. Marble. Pisa Cathedral

Giovanni Pisano. Half a century later Nicola's son Giovanni (1245/50–after 1314), who was an equally gifted sculptor, carved a marble pulpit for Pisa Cathedral. It, too, includes a *Nativity* (fig. 171). Both panels have a good many things in common, as we might well expect, yet they also offer a sharp—and instructive—contrast. Giovanni's slender, swaying figures, with their smoothly flowing draperies, recall neither classical antiquity nor the Visitation group at Reims. Instead, they reflect the elegant style of the royal court at Paris, which had become the standard Gothic formula during the later thirteenth century. And with this change there has come about a new treatment of relief: to Giovanni Pisano, space is as important as plastic form. The figures are no longer tightly packed together. They are now spaced far enough apart to let us see the landscape setting that contains them, and each figure has been allotted its own pocket of space. If Nicola's *Nativity* strikes us as essentially a sequence of bulging, rounded masses, Giovanni's appears to be made up mainly of cavities and shadows. Giovanni Pisano, then, follows the same trend toward "disembodiment" that we encountered north of the Alps around 1300, only he does so in a more limited way.

172. Lorenzo Ghiberti. *The Sacrifice of Isaac.* 1401–2. Gilt bronze, 21 × 17″ (53.3 × 43.2 cm). Museo Nazionale del Bargello, Florence

The International Style in the South

By about 1400, at the time of the International Style, French influence had been thoroughly assimilated in Italy. Its foremost representative was a Florentine, Lorenzo Ghiberti (c. 1381–1455), who as a youth must have had close contact with French art. We first encounter him in 1401–2, when he won a competition for a pair of richly decorated bronze doors for the Baptistery of S. Giovanni in Florence. (It took him more than two decades to complete these doors, on the north portal of the building.) Each of the competing artists had to submit a trial relief, in a Gothic quatrefoil frame, representing the Sacrifice of Isaac. Ghiberti's panel (fig. 172) strikes us first of all with the perfection of its craftsmanship, which reflects his training as a goldsmith. The silky shimmer of the surfaces, the wealth of beautifully articulated detail, make it easy to understand why this entry was awarded the prize. If the composition seems somewhat lacking in dramatic force, that is as characteristic of Ghiberti's calm, lyrical temper as of the taste of the period. The realism of the International Style did not extend to the realm of the emotions. The figures, in their softly draped, ample garments, retain an air of courtly elegance even when they enact scenes of violence.

However much his work may owe to French influence, Ghiberti proves himself thoroughly Italian in one respect: his admiration for ancient sculpture, as evidenced by the beautiful nude torso of Isaac. Here our artist revives a tradition of classicism that had reached its highest point in Nicola Pisano but had gradually died out during the fourteenth century. But Ghiberti is also the heir of Giovanni Pisano. In Giovanni's *Nativity* panel (see fig. 171) we noted a bold new emphasis on the spatial setting. The trial relief carries this same tendency a good deal further, achieving

173. *Iohel.* c. 1220. Stained-glass window, height c. 14′ (4.27 m). Bourges Cathedral

a far more natural sense of recession. For the first time since classical antiquity, we are made to experience the background of the panel not as a flat surface but as empty space from which the sculpted forms emerge toward the beholder, so that the angel in the upper right-hand corner seems to hover in midair. This "pictorial" quality relates Ghiberti's work to the painting of the International Style, where we find a similar concern with spatial depth and atmosphere (see pp. 177–78). While not a revolutionary himself, he prepares the ground for the great revolution that will mark the second decade of the fifteenth century in Florentine art and that we call the Early Renaissance.

PAINTING

Stained Glass

Although Gothic architecture and sculpture began so dramatically at St.-Denis and Chartres, Gothic painting developed at a rather slow pace in its early stages. The new architectural style sponsored by Abbot Suger gave birth to a new conception of monumental sculpture almost at once but did not demand any radical change of style in painting. Suger's account of the rebuilding of his church, to be sure, places a great deal of emphasis on the miraculous effect of stained-glass windows, whose "continuous light" flooded the interior. Stained glass was thus an integral element of Gothic architecture from the very beginning. Yet the technique of stained-glass painting had already been perfected in Romanesque times. The "many masters from different regions" whom Suger assembled to do the choir windows at St.-Denis may have faced a larger task and a more complex pictorial program than before, but the style of their designs remained Romanesque.

During the next half century, as Gothic structures became ever more skeletal and clerestory windows grew to vast size, stained glass displaced manuscript illumination as the leading form of painting. Since the production of stained glass was so intimately linked with the great cathedral workshops, the designers came to be influenced more and more by architectural sculpture, and in this way, about the year 1200, arrived at a distinctively Gothic style of their own.

The majestic *Iohel* (Joel) at Bourges Cathedral (fig. 173), one of a series of windows representing Old Testament prophets, is the direct kin of the *Visitation* at Reims. These works have a common ancestor, the classicizing style of Nicholas of Verdun (compare fig. 148), yet *Iohel* resembles a statue projected onto a translucent screen rather than an enlarged figure from the enamel plaques of the *Klosterneuburg Altarpiece*. The window consists not of large panes but of hundreds of small pieces of tinted glass bound together by strips of lead. The maximum size of these pieces was severely limited by the primitive methods of medieval glass manufacture, so that the artist who created this window could not simply "paint on glass." Rather, he painted *with* glass, assembling his design, somewhat the way one would a mosaic or a jigsaw puzzle, out of odd-shaped fragments that he cut to fit the contours of the forms. Only the finer details, such as eyes, hair, and drapery folds, were added by actually painting—or, better perhaps, drawing—in black or gray on the glass surfaces. Just as this process encourages an abstract, ornamental style, so it tends to resist any attempt to render three-dimensional effects. Yet, in the hands of a master, the maze of lead strips could resolve itself into figures having the looming monumentality of our *Iohel.*

Apart from the peculiar demands of their medium, the stained-glass workers who filled the windows of the great Gothic cathedrals had to face the difficulties arising from the enormous scale of their work. No Romanesque painter had ever been called upon to cover areas so vast—the *Iohel* window is more than fourteen feet tall—or so firmly bound into an architectural framework. The task required a technique of orderly planning for which the medieval painting tradition could offer no precedent. Only architects and stonemasons knew how to deal with this problem, and it was their methods that the stained-glass workers borrowed in mapping out their own compositions. Gothic architectural design, as we recall from our discussion of the choir of St.-Denis (see pp. 158–60), uses a system of geometric relationships to establish numerical harmony. The same rules could be used to control the design of stained-glass windows, through which shines the Light Divine.

The period 1200–1250 might be termed the golden age of stained glass. After that, as architectural activity declined and the demand for stained glass began to slacken, manuscript illumination gradually recaptured its former position of leadership. By then, however, miniature painting had been thoroughly affected by the influence of both stained glass and stone sculpture, the artistic pacemakers of the first half of the century.

Illuminated Manuscripts

The change of style is fully evident in figure 174, which shows a page from a psalter done about 1260 for King Louis IX (St. Louis) of France. The scene illustrates I Samuel 11:2, in which Nahash the Ammonite threatens the Jews at Jabesh. We notice first of all the careful symmetry of the framework, which consists of flat, ornamented panels very much like those in the *Iohel* window, and of an architectural setting remarkably similar to the choir screen by the Naumburg Master (see fig. 167). Against this emphatically two-dimensional background, the figures are "relieved" by smooth and skillful modeling. But their sculptural quality stops short at the outer contours, which are defined by heavy dark lines rather like the lead strips in stained-glass windows. The figures themselves show all the characteristics of the elegant style originated about twenty years before by the sculptors of the royal court: graceful gestures, swaying poses, smiling faces, neatly waved strands of hair. Of the expressive energy of Romanesque painting we find no trace (see fig. 145). Our miniature exemplifies the subtle and refined taste that made the court art of Paris the standard for all Europe.

174. *Nahash the Ammonite Threatening the Jews at Jabesh,* from the *Psalter of St. Louis.* c. 1260. 5 × 3½" (12.7 × 8.9 cm). Bibliothèque Nationale, Paris

Italy

At the end of the thirteenth century, Italian painting produced an explosion of creative energy as spectacular, and as far-reaching in its impact on the future, as the rise of the Gothic cathedral in France. As we inquire into the conditions that made it possible, we find that it arose from the same "old-fashioned" attitudes we met in Italian Gothic architecture and sculpture. Medieval Italy, although strongly influenced by Northern art from Carolingian times on, had always maintained close contact with Byzantine civilization. As a result, panel painting, mosaic, and mural painting—mediums that had never taken firm root north of the Alps—were kept alive on Italian soil. Indeed, a new wave of Byzantine influence overwhelmed the lingering Romanesque elements in Italian painting at the very time when stained glass became the dominant pictorial art in France. This neo-Byzantine style, or "Greek manner" as the Italians called it, prevailed almost until the end of the thirteenth century, so that Italian painters were able to absorb the Byzantine tradition far more thoroughly than ever before. During this same period, we recall, Italian architects and sculptors followed a very different course; untouched by the

Greek manner, they were assimilating the Gothic style. Eventually, toward 1300, Gothic influence spilled over into painting as well, and the interaction of this element with the neo-Byzantine produced the revolutionary new style.

Duccio. Among the painters of the Greek manner, the most important was Duccio of Siena (c. 1255–before 1319). His great altarpiece for Siena Cathedral, the *Maesta* (Majesty), includes many small compartments with scenes from the lives of Christ and the Virgin. Among these panels, the most mature works of Duccio's career, is *Christ Entering Jerusalem* (fig. 175). Here, the cross-fertilization of Gothic and Byzantine elements has given rise to a development of fundamental importance—a new kind of picture space. In Duccio's hands, the Greek manner has become unfrozen, as it were. The rigid, angular draperies have given way to an undulating softness; the abstract shading-in-reverse with lines of gold is reduced to a minimum; and the bodies, faces, and hands are beginning to swell with a subtle three-dimensional life. Clearly, the heritage of Hellenistic-Roman illusionism that had always been part of the Byzantine tradition, however dormant or submerged, is asserting itself once more. But there is also a half-hidden Gothic element here. We sense it in the fluency of the drapery folds, the appealing naturalness of the figures, and the tender glances by which they communicate with each other. The chief source of this Gothic influence must have been Giovanni Pisano (see p. 176), who was in Siena from 1285 to 1295 as the sculptor-architect in charge of the cathedral facade.

175. Duccio. *Christ Entering Jerusalem,* from the back of the *Maestà Altarpiece.* 1308–11. Tempera on panel, 40½ × 21⅛" (102.9 × 53.7 cm). Museo dell'Opera del Duomo, Siena

Christ Entering Jerusalem shows us something we have never seen before in the history of painting: Duccio's figures inhabit a space that is created and defined by the architecture. Northern Gothic painters, too, had tried to reproduce architectural settings, but they could do so only by flattening them out completely (as in the *Psalter of St. Louis*, fig. 174). The Italian painters of Duccio's generation, trained as they were in the Greek manner, had acquired enough of the devices of Hellenistic-Roman illusionism to let them render such a framework without draining it of its three-dimensional qualities. In *Christ Entering Jerusalem,* the architecture keeps its space-creating function. The diagonal movement into depth is conveyed not by the figures—which have the same scale throughout—but by the walls on either side of the road leading to the city, by the gate that frames the welcoming crowd, and by the structures beyond. Whatever the shortcomings of Duccio's perspective, his architecture has the capacity to contain and enclose, and for that reason strikes us as more intelligible than similar vistas in ancient art (compare fig. 98).

Giotto. Turning from Duccio to Giotto (1267?–1336/37), we meet an artist of far bolder and more dramatic temper. Ten to fifteen years younger, Giotto was less close to the Greek manner from the start, and he was a wall painter by instinct, rather than a panel painter. Of his surviving murals, those in the Arena Chapel in Padua, done in 1305–6, are the best preserved as well as the most characteristic. The decorations are devoted principally to scenes from the life of Christ, laid in a carefully arranged program consisting of three tiers of narrative scenes (fig. 176). Giotto depicts many of the same subjects that we find on the reverse of Duccio's *Maestà,* including Christ Entering Jerusalem (fig. 177). A single glance at Giotto's painting will convince us that we are faced with a truly revolutionary development. How, we wonder, could a work of such intense dramatic power be conceived by a contemporary of Duccio? To be sure, the two versions have many elements in common, since they both ultimately derive from the same Byzantine source. But where Duccio has enriched the traditional scheme, spatially as well as in narrative detail, Giotto subjects it to a radical simplification. The action proceeds parallel to the picture plane. Landscape, architecture, and figures have been reduced to the essential minimum. The sober medium of fresco painting (water-based paint applied to the freshly plastered wall), with its limited range and intensity of tones, further emphasizes the austerity of Giotto's art, as against the jewellike brilliance of Duccio's picture, which is executed in egg tempera on gold ground. Yet Giotto's work has by far the more powerful impact of the two: it makes us feel so close to the event that we have a sense of being participants rather than distant observers.

How does the artist achieve this extraordinary effect? He does so, first of all, by having the entire scene take place in the foreground

176. Interior, Arena (Scrovegni) Chapel, Padua

177. Giotto. *Christ Entering Jerusalem.* 1305–6. Fresco. Arena (Scrovegni) Chapel, Padua

and—even more important—by presenting it in such a way that the beholder's eye level falls within the lower half of the picture. Thus we can imagine ourselves standing on the same ground plane as these painted figures, even though we see them from well below, whereas Duccio makes us survey the scene from above, in bird's-eye perspective. The consequences of this choice of viewpoint are truly epoch-making. Choice implies conscious awareness—in this case, awareness of a relationship in space between the beholder and the picture—and Giotto may well claim to be the first to have established such a relationship. Duccio, certainly, does not yet conceive his picture space as continuous with the beholder's space; hence we have the sensation of vaguely floating above the scene, rather than of knowing where we stand. Even ancient painting at its most illusionistic provides no more than a pseudocontinuity in this respect (see fig. 98). Giotto, on the other hand, tells us where we stand, and he also endows his forms with a three-dimensional reality so forceful that they seem as solid and tangible as sculpture in the round.

With Giotto it is the figures, rather than the architectural framework, that create the picture space. As a result, this space is more limited than Duccio's—its depth extends no further than the combined volumes of the overlapping bodies in the picture—but within its limits it is very much more persuasive. To Giotto's contemporaries, the tactile quality of his art must have seemed a near miracle. It was this quality that made them praise him as equal, or even superior, to the greatest of the ancient painters, because his forms looked so lifelike that they could be mistaken for reality itself. Equally significant are the stories linking Giotto with the claim that painting is superior to sculpture—not an idle boast, as it turned out, for Giotto does indeed mark the start of what might be called "the era of painting" in Western art. The symbolic turning point is the year 1334, when he was appointed the head of the Florence Cathedral workshop, an honor and responsibility hitherto reserved for architects or sculptors.

Yet Giotto's aim was not simply to transplant Gothic statuary into painting. By creating a radically new kind of picture space, he had also sharpened his awareness of the picture surface. When we look at a work by Duccio (or his ancient and medieval predecessors), we tend to do so in installments, as it were. Our glance travels from detail to detail at a leisurely pace until we have surveyed the entire area. Giotto, on the contrary, invites us to see the whole at one glance. His large, simple forms, the strong grouping of his figures, the limited depth of his "stage," all these factors help endow his scenes with an inner coherence such as we have never found before. Notice how dramatically the massed verticals of the "block" of apostles on the left are contrasted with the upward slope formed by the welcoming crowd on the right; how Christ, alone in the center, bridges the gulf between the two groups. The more we study the composition, the more we come to realize its majestic firmness and clarity.

The art of Giotto is so daringly original that its sources are far more difficult to trace than those of Duccio's style. Apart from his Florentine background in the Greek manner, the young Giotto seems to have been familiar with the more monumental, albeit cruder neo-Byzantine style practiced by painters in Rome, partly under the influence of ancient Roman and Early Christian mural decorations, and it is likely that he became acquainted with such older monuments as well. Classical sculpture, too, left an impression on him. More fundamental than any of these, however, was the influence of the Pisanos—Nicola, and especially Giovanni—the founders of Italian Gothic sculpture. They were the chief intermediaries through whom Giotto first came in contact with the world of Northern Gothic art. And the latter remains the most important of all the elements that entered into Giotto's style. Without the knowledge, direct or indirect, of Northern works such as that in figure 165, he could never have achieved such powerful emotional impact.

Martini. There are few artists in the entire history of art who equal the stature of Giotto as a radical innovator. His very greatness, however, tended to dwarf the next generation of Florentine painters, which produced only followers rather than new leaders. Their contemporaries in Siena were more fortunate in this respect, since Duccio never had the same overpowering impact. As a consequence, it was they, not the Florentines, who took the next decisive step in the development of Italian Gothic painting. Simone Martini (c. 1284–1344) may well claim to be the most distinguished of Duccio's disciples. He spent the last years of his life in Avignon, the town in southern France that served as the residence-in-exile of the popes during most of the fourteenth century. *The Road to Calvary* (fig. 178), originally part of a small altar, was probably done there about 1340. In its sparkling colors, and especially in the architectural background, our tiny but intense panel still echoes the art of Duccio (see fig. 175). The vigorous modeling of the figures, on the other hand, as well as their dramatic gestures and expressions, betray the influence of Giotto. While Simone Martini is not much concerned with spatial clarity, he proves to be an extraordinarily acute observer. The sheer variety of costumes and physical types and the wealth of human incident create a sense

178. Simone Martini. *The Road to Calvary.* c. 1340. Tempera on panel, 9⅞ × 6⅛″ (25.1 × 15.6 cm). Musée du Louvre, Paris

179. Pietro Lorenzetti. *The Birth of the Virgin.* 1342. Tempera on panel, 6′1½″ × 5′11½″ (1.88 × 1.82 m). Museo dell'Opera del Duomo, Siena

of down-to-earth reality very different from both the lyricism of Duccio and the grandeur of Giotto.

The Lorenzettis. This closeness to everyday life also appears in the work of the brothers Pietro and Ambrogio Lorenzetti (both died 1348?), but on a more monumental scale and coupled with a keen interest in problems of space. The boldest spatial experiment is Pietro's triptych of 1342, *The Birth of the Virgin* (fig. 179), where the painted architecture has been correlated with the real architecture of the frame in such a way that the two are seen as a single system. Moreover, the vaulted chamber where the birth takes place occupies two panels: it continues unbroken behind the column that divides the center from the right wing. The left wing represents an anteroom which leads to a vast and only partially glimpsed architectural space suggesting the interior of a Gothic church.

What Pietro Lorenzetti achieved here is the outcome of a development that began three decades earlier in the work of Duccio, but only now does the picture surface assume the quality of a transparent window through which—not *on* which—we perceive the same kind of space we know from daily experience. Yet Duccio's work alone is not sufficient to explain Pietro's astonishing breakthrough. It became possible, rather, through a combination of the *architectural* picture space of Duccio and the *sculptural* picture space of Giotto.

The same procedure enabled Ambrogio Lorenzetti, in his frescoes of 1338–40 in the Siena city hall, to unfold a comprehensive view of the entire town before our eyes (fig. 180). Again we marvel at the distance that separates this precisely articulated "portrait" of Siena from Duccio's Jerusalem (see fig. 175). Ambrogio's mural forms part of an elaborate allegorical program depicting the contrast of good and bad government; hence the artist, in order to show the life of a well-ordered city-state, had to fill the streets and houses with teeming activity. The gay and busy crowd gives the architectural vista its striking reality by introducing the human scale.

The Black Death. The first four decades of the fourteenth century in Florence and Siena had been a period of political stability and economic expansion as well as of great artistic achievement. In the 1340s both cities suffered a series of catastrophes whose echoes were to be felt for many years: banks and merchants went bankrupt by the score, internal upheavals shook the government, there were repeated crop failures, and in 1348 the epidemic of bubonic plague that spread throughout Europe, the Black Death, wiped out more than half their urban population. Many people regarded these events as signs of divine wrath, warnings to a sinful humanity to forsake the pleasures of this earth; to others, the fear of sudden death merely intensified the desire to enjoy life while there

180. Ambrogio Lorenzetti. *The Commune of Siena* (left), *Good Government in the City* and *Good Government in the Country* (right), frescoes in the Sala della Pace, Palazzo Pubblico, Siena. 1338–40

181. Francesco Traini. *The Triumph of Death* (portion). c. 1325–50. Fresco. Camposanto, Pisa

was yet time. These conflicting attitudes are reflected in the pictorial theme of the Triumph of Death.

Traini. The most impressive treatment of this subject is an enormous fresco, attributed to the Pisan master Francesco Traini (documented c. 1321–1363), in the Camposanto, the cemetery building next to Pisa Cathedral. In a particularly dramatic detail from this work (fig. 181), the elegantly costumed men and women on horseback have suddenly come upon three decaying corpses in open coffins. Even the animals are terrified by the sight and smell of rotting flesh. Only the hermit, having renounced all earthly pleasures, calmly points out the lesson of the scene. But will the living accept the lesson, or will they turn away from the shocking spectacle more determined than ever to pursue their own hedonistic ways? The artist's own sympathies seem curiously divided. His style is far from being otherworldly, and recalls the realism of Ambrogio Lorenzetti, although the forms are harsher, more expressive.

Traini retains a strong link with the great masters of the second quarter of the century. The Tuscan painters who reached maturity after the Black Death, around the 1350s, cannot compare with the earlier artists whose work we have discussed. Their style, in comparison, seems dry and formula-ridden, although at its best it did express the somber mood of the time with memorable intensity.

North of the Alps

We are now in a position to turn once more to Gothic painting north of the Alps. What happened there during the latter half of the fourteenth century was determined in large measure by the influence of the great Italians. Toward the middle years of the fourteenth century, Italian influence becomes ever more important in Northern Gothic painting. Sometimes this influence was transmitted by

182. Bohemian Master. *The Death of the Virgin*. 1350–60.
Tempera on panel, 39⅜ × 28″ (100 × 71.1 cm). Museum of Fine Arts, Boston.
William Francis Warden Fund: Seth K. Sweetser Fund,
The Henry C. and Martha B. Angell Coll., Juliana Cheney Edwards Collection,
Gift of Martin Brimmer, and Mrs. Frederick Frothingham: by exchange

183. Melchior Broederlam. *Annunciation* and *Visitation*; *Presentation in the Temple*; and *Flight into Egypt*. 1394–99. Tempera on panel, 53¾ × 49¼" (136.5 × 125.1 cm). Musée des Beaux-Arts, Dijon

Italian artists working on Northern soil; an example is Simone Martini (see p. 184). Another gateway of Italian influence was the city of Prague, which in 1347 became the residence of Emperor Charles IV and rapidly developed into an international cultural center second only to Paris. *The Death of the Virgin* (fig. 182), made by an unknown Bohemian painter about 1360, again brings to mind the achievements of the great Sienese masters, although these were known to our artist only at second- or third-hand. Its glowing richness of color recalls Simone Martini (see fig. 178), and the carefully articulated architectural interior betrays its descent from such works as Pietro Lorenzetti's *The Birth of the Virgin* (see fig. 179), although it lacks the spaciousness of its Italian models. Italian, too, is the vigorous modeling of the heads and the overlapping of the figures, which reinforces the three-dimensional quality of the design but raises the awkward question of what to do with the halos. Still, the Bohemian master's picture is not a mere echo of Italian painting. The gestures and facial expressions convey an intensity of emotion that represents the finest heritage of Northern Gothic art. In this respect, our panel is far more akin to *The Death of the Virgin* at Strasbourg Cathedral (see fig. 165) than to any Italian work.

The International Style

Toward the year 1400, the merging of Northern and Italian traditions gave rise to a single dominant style throughout western Europe. This International Style was not confined to painting—we have used the same term for the sculpture of the period—but painters clearly played the main role in its development.

Broederlam. Among the most important was Melchior Broederlam (flourished c. 1387–1409), a Fleming who worked for the court of the duke of Burgundy in Dijon. Figure 183 shows the panels of a pair of shutters for an altar shrine that he did in 1394–99. Each

184. The Limbourg Brothers. *October,* from *Les Très Riches Heures du Duc de Berry.* 1413–16. 8⅞ × 5⅜" (22.5 × 13.7 cm). Musée Condé, Chantilly, France

185. Gentile da Fabriano. *The Adoration of the Magi.* 1423. Oil on panel, 9′10⅛″ × 9′3″ (3 × 2.88 m). Galleria degli Uffizi, Florence

wing presents two scenes. As a result, the temple of the *Presentation* and the landscape of the *Flight into Egypt* stand abruptly side by side, even though the artist has made a halfhearted effort to persuade us that the landscape extends around the building. Compared to paintings by Pietro Lorenzetti and Simone Martini, Broederlam's picture space still strikes us as naive in many ways—the architecture looks like a doll's house, and the details of the landscape are quite out of scale with the figures. Yet the panels convey a far stronger feeling of depth than we have found in any previous Northern work. The reason for this is the subtlety of the modeling. The softly rounded shapes and the dark, velvety shadows create a sense of light and air that more than makes up for any shortcomings of scale or perspective. The same soft, pictorial quality—a hallmark of the International

Style—appears in the ample, loosely draped garments with their fluid curvilinear patterns of folds, which remind us of Sluter and Ghiberti (see figs. 169, 172).

Our panels also exemplify another characteristic of the International Style: its "realism of particulars," the same kind of realism we encountered first in Gothic sculpture (see p. 175). We find it in the carefully rendered foliage and flowers, in the delightful donkey (obviously drawn from life), and in the rustic figure of St. Joseph, who looks and behaves like a simple peasant and thus helps emphasize the delicate, aristocratic beauty of the Virgin. This painstaking concentration on detail gives Broederlam's work the flavor of an enlarged miniature rather than of a large-scale painting, even though the panels are more than five feet tall.

The Limbourg Brothers. That book illumination remained the leading form of painting in northern Europe at the time of the International Style, despite the growing importance of panel painting, is well attested by the miniatures of *Les Très Riches Heures du Duc de Berry*. Produced for the brother of the king of France, a man of far from admirable character but the most lavish art patron of his day, this luxurious book of hours represents the most advanced phase of the International Style. The artists were Pol de Limbourg and his two brothers, a group of Flemings who, like Sluter and Broederlam, had settled in France early in the fifteenth century. They must have visited Italy as well, for their work includes numerous motifs and whole compositions borrowed from the great masters of Tuscany.

The most remarkable pages of *Les Très Riches Heures* are those of the calendar, with their elaborate depiction of the life of humans and nature throughout the months of the year. Such cycles, originally consisting of twelve single figures each performing an appropriate seasonal activity, had long been an established tradition in medieval art. The Limbourg brothers, however, integrated all these elements into a series of panoramas of human life *in* nature.

Figure 184 shows the sowing of winter grain during the month of October. Landscape and architecture are harmoniously united in deep, atmospheric space. It is a bright, sunny day, and the figures—for the first time since classical antiquity—cast visible shadows on the ground. We marvel at the wealth of realistic detail, such as the scarecrow in the middle distance or the footprints of the sower in the soil of the freshly plowed field. The sower is memorable in other ways as well. His tattered clothing, his unhappy air, go beyond mere description. He is meant to be a pathetic figure, to arouse our awareness of the miserable lot of the peasantry in contrast to the life of the aristocracy, as symbolized by the splendid castle on the far bank of the river. (The castle shown is the Gothic Louvre, the most lavish structure of its kind at that time; see pp. 283–84.)

Gentile da Fabriano. From Broederlam's panels it is but a step to the altarpiece with the three Magi and their train (fig. 185) by Gentile da Fabriano (c. 1370–1427), the greatest Italian painter of the International Style. The costumes here are as colorful, the draperies as ample and softly rounded, as in Northern painting. The Holy Family, on the left, almost seems in danger of being overwhelmed by the gay and festive pageant pouring down upon it from the hills in the distance. We admire the marvelously well observed animals, which now include not only the familiar ones but also hunting leopards, camels, and monkeys. (Such creatures were eagerly collected by the princes of the period, many of whom kept private zoos.) The Oriental background of the Magi is further emphasized by the Mongolian facial cast of some of their companions. It is not these exotic touches, however, that mark our picture as the work of an Italian master but something else, a greater sense of weight, of physical substance, than we could hope to find among the Northern representatives of the International Style. Gentile, despite his love of fine detail, is obviously a painter used to working on a monumental scale, rather than a manuscript illuminator at heart.

CHRONOLOGICAL CHART II

	POLITICAL HISTORY	RELIGION, LITERATURE	SCIENCE, TECHNOLOGY
600	Mohammed (570–632) Byzantium loses Near Eastern and African provinces to Muslims 642–732 Muslims invade Spain 711–18; defeated by Franks, Battle of Tours, 732 Independent Muslim state established in Spain 756	Isidore of Seville, encyclopedist (died 636) Koran 652 *Beowulf,* English epic, early 8th cent. Iconoclastic Controversy 726–843	Papermaking introduced into Near East from China Stirrup introduced into Western Europe c. 600
800	Charlemagne (r. 768–814) crowned emperor of Romans by pope 800 Alfred the Great (r. 871–99?), Anglo-Saxon king of England	Carolingian revival of Latin classics Earliest printed book, China, 868	Earliest documented church organ, Aachen, 822 Horse collar adopted in Western Europe, makes horses efficient draft animals
900	Otto I crowned emperor by pope 962 Otto II (r. 973–83) defeated by Muslims in southern Italy	Monastic order of Cluny founded 910 Conversion of Russia to Orthodox Church c. 990	Earliest application of waterpower to industry
1000	Normans arrive in Italy 1016 William the Conqueror defeats Harold at Battle of Hastings 1066 Reconquest of Spain from Muslims begins 1085 First Crusade (1095–99) takes Jerusalem	College of Cardinals formed to elect pope 1059 Cistercian order founded 1098 *Chanson de Roland,* French epic, c. 1098	Leif Ericsson sails to North America 1002
1100	King Henry II founds Plantagenet line in England 1154 Frederick Barbarossa (r. 1155–90) titles himself "Holy Roman Emperor," tries to dominate Italy	Rise of universities (Bologna, Paris, Oxford); faculties of law, medicine, theology Pierre Abélard, French philosopher and teacher (1079–1142) Flowering of French vernacular literature (epics, fables, chansons); age of the troubadours	Earliest manufacture of paper in Europe, by Muslims in Spain Earliest use of magnetic compass for navigation Earliest documented windmill in Europe 1180
1200	Fourth Crusade (1202–4) conquers Constantinople Latin Empire in Constantinople 1204–61 Magna Carta limits power of English kings 1215 Louis IX (r. 1226–70), king of France Philip IV (r. 1285–1314), king of France	St. Dominic (1170–1221) founds Dominican order; Inquisition established to combat heresy St. Francis of Assisi (died 1226) St. Thomas Aquinas, Italian scholastic philosopher (died 1274) Dante Alighieri, Italian poet (1265–1321)	Marco Polo travels to China and India c. 1275–93 Arabic (actually Indian) numerals introduced in Europe First documented use of spinning wheel in Europe 1298, replaces distaff and spindle
1300	Exile of papacy in Avignon 1309–76 Hundred Years' War between England and France begins 1337 Black Death throughout Europe 1347–50	John Wycliffe (died 1384) challenges church doctrine; translates Bible into English Petrarch, first humanist (1304–1374) *Canterbury Tales* by Chaucer c. 1387 *Decameron* by Boccaccio 1387	First large-scale production of paper in Italy and Germany Large-scale production of gunpowder; earliest known use of cannon 1326 Earliest cast iron in Europe
1400	Great Papal Schism (since 1378) settled 1417; pope returns to Rome	Jan Hus, Czech reformer, burned at stake for heresy 1415; Joan of Arc burned at stake for heresy and sorcery 1431	Gutenberg invents printing with movable type 1446–50

NOTE: Figure numbers of black-and-white illustrations are in (italics). Colorplate numbers are in **(bold face)**.
Duration of papacy or reign is indicated by the abbreviation r.

	ARCHITECTURE	SCULPTURE	PAINTING
600		Sutton Hoo ship-burial treasure *(117)* *Crucifixion* (plaque from a book cover?) (**120**)	*Lindisfarne Gospels* (**119**)
800	Palace Chapel of Charlemagne, Aachen *(121)* Monastery plan, St. Gall *(122)*	Oseberg ship-burial *(118)* Crucifixion relief, cover of *Lindau Gospels* (**125**)	*Gospel Book of Charlemagne* (**123**) *Gospel Book of Archbishop Ebbo of Reims* (**124**)
900		*Gero Crucifix,* Cologne Cathedral *(126)*	
1000	St. Michael's, Hildesheim *(127, 128)* Pisa Cathedral complex *(138)* Baptistery, Florence (**139**) St.-Étienne, Caen *(135)* St.-Sernin, Toulouse *(131,* **132,** *133)* Durham Cathedral *(136)*	Bronze doors of Bishop Bernward, Hildesheim *(129)* *Apostle,* St.-Sernin, Toulouse *(140)*	*Gospel Book of Otto III* (**130**) Mosaics, Daphnē *(115)* *Bayeux Tapestry (146)*
1100	St.-Denis, Paris *(149)* Notre-Dame, Paris *(150–54)* Chartres Cathedral *(155)* Reims Cathedral *(156)*	South portal, St.-Pierre, Moissac *(141)* Baptismal font, St. Barthélemy, Liège, by Renier of Huy *(143)* *Last Judgment* tympanum, Autun Cathedral *(142)* West portals, Chartres Cathedral *(163, 164)* *Klosterneuburg Altarpiece,* by Nicholas of Verdun *(148)*	Nave vault murals, St.-Savin-sur-Gartempe *(147)* *Gospel Book of Abbot Wedricus* (**145**)
1200	Salisbury Cathedral *(158)* Sta. Croce, Florence *(161)* Florence Cathedral *(162)*	West portal, Reims Cathedral *(166)* Choir screen, Naumburg Cathedral *(167)* Pulpit, Baptistery, Pisa, by Nicola Pisano *(170)*	Stained glass, nave clerestory, Bourges Cathedral *(173)* *Psalter of St. Louis (174)* *Madonna and Child on a Curved Throne,* icon (**116**)
1300	Gloucester Cathedral *(159)*	*Pietà,* Bonn *(168)* Pulpit, Pisa Cathedral, by Giovanni Pisano *(171)* *Moses Well,* Dijon, by Claus Sluter *(169)*	Arena Chapel frescoes, Padua, by Giotto (**176, 177**) *Maestà Altarpiece,* Siena, by Duccio (**175**) *Good Government* fresco, Palazzo Pubblico, Siena, by Ambrogio Lorenzetti (**180**) *Road to Calvary,* by Simone Martini (**178**) *Birth of the Virgin* triptych, Siena, by Pietro Lorenzetti (**179**) *Death of the Virgin,* by Bohemian Master (**182**) Altar wings, Dijon, by Melchior Broederlam (**183**)
1400		Competition relief for Baptistery doors, Florence, by Ghiberti (**172**)	*Les Très Riches Heures du Duc de Berry,* by Limbourg Brothers (**184**) *Adoration of the Magi* altarpiece, by Gentile da Fabriano (**185**)

PART THREE

THE RENAISSANCE, MANNERISM, AND THE BAROQUE

In discussing the transition from classical antiquity to the Middle Ages, we were able to point to the rise of Islam as a great crisis marking the separation between the two eras. No comparable event sets off the Middle Ages from the Renaissance. The fifteenth and sixteenth centuries, to be sure, witnessed far-reaching developments: the deep spiritual crisis of the Reformation and Counter Reformation, the fall of Constantinople and the Turkish conquest of southeastern Europe, and the journeys of exploration that led to the founding of overseas empires in the New World, Africa, and Asia, with the subsequent rivalry of Spain and England as the foremost colonial powers. None of these events, however vast their effects, can be said to have produced the new era. By the time they happened, the Renaissance was well under way. Even if we disregard the minority of scholars who would deny the existence of the animal altogether, we are left with an extraordinary diversity of views on the Renaissance. Perhaps the only essential point on which most experts agree is that the Renaissance had begun when people realized they were no longer living in the Middle Ages.

This statement brings out the undeniable fact that the Renaissance was the first period in history to be aware of its own existence and to coin a label for itself. Medieval people did not think they belonged to an age distinct from classical antiquity; the past, to them, consisted simply of "B.C." and "A.D.": the era "under the Law" (that is, of the Old Testament) and the era "of Grace" (that is, after the birth of Christ). From their point of view, history was made in Heaven rather than on earth. The Renaissance, by contrast, divided the past not according to the divine plan of salvation, but on the basis of human achievements. It saw classical antiquity as the era when civilization had reached the peak of its creative powers, an era brought to a sudden end by the barbarian invasions that destroyed the Roman Empire. During the thousand-year interval of "darkness" that followed, little was accomplished, but now, at last, this "time in between" or "Middle Age" had been superseded by a revival of all those arts and sciences that flourished in classical antiquity. The present, the "New Age," could thus be fittingly labeled a "rebirth": *rinascita* in Italian (from the Latin *renascere*, to be reborn), *renaissance* in French and, by adoption, in English.

The origin of this revolutionary view of history can be traced back to the 1330s in the writings of the Italian poet Francesco Petrarca, the first of the great individuals who made the Renaissance. Petrarch, as we call him, thought of the new era mainly as a "revival of the classics," limited to the restoration of Latin and Greek to their former purity and the return to the original texts of ancient authors. During the next two centuries, this concept of the rebirth of antiquity grew to embrace almost the entire range of cultural endeavor, including the visual arts. The latter, in fact, came to play a particularly important part in shaping the Renaissance, for reasons that we shall explore later.

That the new historic orientation should have had its start in the mind of one man is itself a telling comment on the new era. Individualism—a new self-awareness and self-assurance—enabled him to proclaim, against all established authority, his own conviction that the "age of faith" was actually an era of darkness, while the "benighted pagans" of antiquity really represented the most enlightened stage of history. Such readiness to question traditional beliefs and practices was to become profoundly characteristic of the Renaissance as a whole. Humanism, to Petrarch, meant a belief in the importance of what we still call the "humanities" or "humane letters," rather than divine letters, or the study of Scripture; that is, the pursuit of learning in languages, literature, history, and philosophy for its own end, in a secular rather than a religious framework.

We must not assume, however, that Petrarch and his successors wanted to revive classical antiquity lock, stock, and barrel. By interposing the concept of "a thousand years of darkness" between themselves and the ancients, they acknowledged (unlike the medieval classicists) that the Graeco-Roman world was irretrievably dead. Its glories could be revived only in the mind, by nostalgic and admiring contemplation across the barrier of the "dark ages," by rediscovering the full greatness of ancient achievements in art and thought, and by endeavoring to compete with these achievements on an ideal plane.

The humanists, however great their enthusiasm for classical philosophy, did not become neo-pagans but went to great lengths trying to reconcile the heritage of the ancient thinkers with Christianity. In the arts, the aim of the Renaissance was not to duplicate the works of antiquity but to equal and, if possible, to surpass them. In practice, this meant that the authority granted to the ancient models was far from unlimited. Writers strove to express themselves with Ciceronian eloquence and precision, but not necessarily in Latin. Architects continued to build the churches demanded by Christian ritual, not to duplicate pagan temples; their churches were designed *all'antica*, "in the manner of the ancients," using an architectural vocabulary based on the study of classical structures.

The people of the Renaissance, then, found themselves in the position of the legendary sorcerer's apprentice, who set out to emulate his master's achievements and in the process released far greater energies than he had bargained for. Since their master was dead, rather than merely absent, they had to cope with these unfamiliar powers as best they could, until they became masters in their own right. This process of forced growth was replete with crises and tensions. The Renaissance must have been an uncomfortable, though intensely exciting, time in which to live. These very tensions, it appears in retrospect, called forth an outpouring of creative energy such as the world had never experienced. It is a fundamental paradox that the desire to return to the classics, based on a rejection of the Middle Ages, brought to the new era not the rebirth of antiquity but the birth of modern civilization.

NORTH SEA
IRELAND
ENGLAND
OXFORDSHIRE
Woodstock
Oxford
Thames R.
London
Windsor
Amsterdam
Haarlem
Leyden
The Hague
Utrecht
Delft
Rotterdam
HOLLAND
's Hertogenbosch
NETHERLANDS
Bruges
Antwerp
Ghent
FLANDERS
Brussels
Tournai
Flémalle
Lille
BELGIUM
ENGLISH CHANNEL
Douai
ATLANTIC OCEAN
Caen
NORMANDY
Chantilly
Reims
Paris
Versailles
Maisons
BRITTANY
Chartres
Fontainebleau
Meuse R.
Seine R.
Strasbourg
ALSACE
Loire R.
Chambord
BERRY
Colmar
BURGUNDY
Dijon
LAKE GE
FRANCE
Geneva
BAY OF BISCAY
ALPS
SAVOY
Turin
Garonne R.
Rhone R.
Avignon
PROVENCE
PYRENEES
Marseilles
Duero R.
Ebro R.
SPAIN
PORTUGAL
Madrid
Toledo
Tagus R.
Guadalquivir R.
Seville
Granada
MEDITERRANEAN SEA

THE RENAISSANCE
SITES AND CITIES
LATE GOTHIC, RENAISSANCE, MANNERIST, BAROQUE
BALTIC SEA
Berlin
Elbe R.
Wittenberg
SAXONY
Naumburg
RUSSIA
burg
VARIA
Nuremberg
CARPATHIANS
Danube R.
Augsburg
Munich
Melk
Vienna
AUSTRIA
Pruth R.
Tisza R.
CONSTANCE
St. Wolfgang
TYROL
ALPS
avaggio
Vicenza
Verona
scia
Padua
Venice
Mantua
Po R.
Parma
Bologna
Ravenna
BLACK SEA
Danube R
Rimini
Vinci
Prato
Florence
Urbino
Arno R.
Arezzo
Volterra
Siena
Perugia
TUSCANY
Orvieto
UMBRIA
Tiber R.
ADRIATIC SEA
APENNINES
Rome
APULIA
ITALY
Naples
GREECE
ASIA MINOR
AEGEAN SEA
TYRRHENIAN SEA
IONIAN SEA
Athens
Messina
STRAIT OF MESSINA
SICILY
N
W
E
S
CRETE
0
MILES
200
0
KM
200

"LATE GOTHIC" PAINTING, SCULPTURE, AND THE GRAPHIC ARTS

RENAISSANCE VERSUS "LATE GOTHIC" PAINTING

As we narrow our focus from the Renaissance as a whole to the Renaissance in the fine arts, we are faced with many questions. When did it start? Did it, like Gothic art, originate in a specific center, or in several places at the same time? Should we think of it as one new, coherent style, or as a new "Renaissance-conscious" attitude that might be embodied in more than one style? When did this development get under way? So far as architecture and sculpture are concerned, modern scholarship agrees with the traditional view, first expressed more than five hundred years ago, that the Renaissance began soon after 1400. For painting, however, an even older tradition argues that the new era began with Giotto. We hesitate to accept such a claim at face value, for we must then assume that the Renaissance in painting dawned about 1300, a full generation before Petrarch. Nor, as we have seen, did Giotto himself reject the past.

Renaissance art was born of a second revolution, a century after Giotto, which began simultaneously and independently in Italy and in Flanders about 1420. We must think of two events, linked by a common aim—the conquest of the visible world—but sharply separated in almost every other respect. The Italian, or Southern, revolution was the more systematic and, in the long run, the more fundamental, since it included architecture and sculpture as well as painting. The movement that originated in Florence is called the Early Renaissance. The same term is not generally applied to the new style that emerged in the Netherlands. We have, in fact, no satisfactory name to designate the Northern branch of the revolution, for art historians are still of two minds about its scope and significance in relation to the Renaissance as a whole.

"Late Gothic"

We shall use the customary label, "Late Gothic," for the sake of convenience, with quotation marks to indicate its doubtful status. The term hardly does justice to the special character of Northern fifteenth-century painting, but it has some justification. It indicates, for instance, that the creators of the new style, unlike their Italian contemporaries, did not reject the International Style. Rather, they took it as their point of departure, so that the break with the past was less abrupt in the North than in the South. Moreover, their artistic environment was clearly "Late Gothic." Fifteenth-century architecture outside Italy remained firmly rooted in the Gothic tradition. How could they create a genuinely post-medieval style in such a setting, one wonders? Would it not be more reasonable to regard their work, despite its great importance, as the final phase of Gothic painting? Italian Renaissance art, after all, made very little impression north of the Alps during the fifteenth century.

If we treat Northern painters of this time as the counterpart of the Early Renaissance, it is because the great Flemish masters whose work we are about to examine had an impact that went far beyond their own region. In Italy they were as admired as the leading Italian artists of the period, and their intense realism had a conspicuous influence on Early Renaissance painting. The Italians themselves associated the exact imitation of nature in painting with a "return to the classics." To their eyes, "Late Gothic" painting appeared definitely post-medieval.

NETHERLANDISH PAINTING

The Master of Flémalle. The first phase, and perhaps the decisive one, of the pictorial revolution in Flanders is represented by an artist whose name we do not know for certain. We call him the Master of Flémalle (after the fragments of a large altarpiece from Flémalle), although he was probably identical with Robert Campin, the foremost painter of Tournai, whose career we can trace in documents from 1406 to his death in 1444. Among his finest works is the *Mérode Altarpiece* (fig. 186), which he must have done soon after 1425. Comparing it with one of its relatives among the Franco-Flemish pictures of the International Style (see fig. 183), we see that it belongs within that tradition and, at the same time, we recognize in it a new pictorial experience.

Here, for the first time, we have the sensation of actually looking *through* the surface of the panel into a spatial world that has all the essential qualities of everyday reality: unlimited depth, stability, continuity, and completeness. The painters of the International Style, even at their most adventurous, had never aimed at such consistency, and their commitment to reality was far from absolute. The pictures they created have the enchanting quality of fairy tales where the scale and relationship of things can be shifted at will, where fact and fancy mingle without conflict. The Master of Flémalle, in contrast, has undertaken to tell the truth, the whole truth, and nothing but the truth. To be sure, he does not yet do it with ease. His objects, overly foreshortened, tend to jostle each other in space. But with almost obsessive determination, he defines every last detail of every object to give it maximum concreteness: its individual shape and size; its color, material, surface textures; its degree of rigidity and way of responding to light. He even distinguishes between the diffused light creating soft shadows and delicate gradations of brightness, and the direct light entering through the two round windows, which produces the twin shadows sharply outlined in the upper part of the center panel and the twin reflections on the brass vessel and candlestick.

The *Mérode Altarpiece* transports us abruptly from the aristocratic world of the International Style to the household of a Flemish burgher. The Master of Flémalle was no court painter but a townsman catering to the tastes of such well-to-do fellow citizens as the two donors piously kneeling outside the Virgin's chamber. This is the earliest Annunciation in panel painting that occurs in a fully equipped domestic interior (compare fig. 179), as well as the first to honor Joseph, the humble carpenter, by showing him at work next door.

This bold departure from tradition forced upon our artist a problem no one had faced before: how to transfer supernatural events from symbolic settings to an everyday environment, without making them look either trivial or incongruous. He has met this challenge by the method known as "disguised symbolism," which means that almost any detail within the picture, however casual, may carry a symbolic message. Thus the flowers in the left wing and the center panel are associated with the Virgin: the roses denote her charity, the violets her humility, and the lilies her chastity. The shiny water basin and the towel on its rack are not ordinary household equipment but further tributes to Mary as the "vessel most clean" and the "well of living waters."

The significance of these well-established symbols would have been readily understood by the artist's patrons. Clearly, the entire wealth of medieval symbolism survives in our picture, but it is so completely immersed in the world of everyday appearances that we are often left to doubt whether a given detail demands symbolic interpretation. Perhaps the most intriguing symbol of this sort is the candle next to the vase of lilies. It was extinguished only moments before, as we can tell from the glowing wick and the curl of smoke. But why, in broad daylight, had it

186. Master of Flémalle (Robert Campin?). *Mérode Altarpiece*. c. 1425–30.
Oil on wood panels, center 25³⁄₁₆ × 24⅞" (64.1 × 63.2 cm), each wing c. 25⅜ × 10⅞" (64.5 × 27.6 cm).
The Metropolitan Museum of Art, New York. The Cloisters Collection, 1956

been lit, and what made the flame go out? Has the divine radiance of the Lord's presence overcome the material light? Or did the flame of the candle itself represent the divine light, now extinguished to show that God has become man, that in Christ "the Word was made flesh"? Equally mystifying is the little boxlike object on Joseph's workbench and a similar one on the ledge outside the open window. They have been identified as mousetraps intended to convey a specific theological message. According to St. Augustine, God had to appear on earth in human form so as to fool Satan: "the Cross of the Lord was the devil's mousetrap."

The freshly extinguished candle and the mousetrap are unusual symbols that the Master of Flémalle himself introduced into the visual arts. He must have been either a man of unusual learning, or had contact with theologians and other scholars who could supply him with references that suggested the symbolic meanings of everyday things. Our artist, then, did not merely continue the symbolic tradition of medieval art within the framework of the new realistic style. He expanded and enriched it by his own efforts.

Why, we wonder, did he pursue simultaneously what we tend to regard as two opposite goals, realism and symbolism? To him, apparently, the two were interdependent, rather than in conflict. For him to paint everyday reality, he had to "sanctify" it with a maximum of spiritual significance. This deeply reverential attitude toward the physical universe as a mirror of divine truths helps us understand why in the *Mérode* panels the smallest and least conspicuous details are rendered with the same concentrated attention as the sacred figures; potentially at least, everything is a symbol and thus merits an equally exacting scrutiny. The disguised symbolism of the Master of Flémalle and his successors was not an external device grafted onto the new realistic style, but ingrained in the creative process. Their Italian contemporaries must have sensed this, for they praised both the miraculous realism and the "piety" of the Flemish masters.

If we compare the *Mérode* Annunciation

187. Hubert and/or Jan van Eyck.
The Crucifixion and *The Last Judgment*. c. 1420–25.
Oil on canvas, transferred from panel; each panel 22¼ × 7¾" (56.5 × 19.7 cm). The Metropolitan Museum of Art, New York. Fletcher Fund, 1933

with an earlier panel painting (see fig. 183), we see that, all other differences aside, the Master of Flémalle's picture stands out for its distinctive tonality. The jewellike brightness of the older work, with its patterns of brilliant hues and lavish use of gold, has given way to a color scheme that is far less decorative but much more flexible and differentiated. The subdued palette of muted greens and bluish or brownish gray tints shows a new subtlety, and the scale of intermediate shades is smoother and has a wider range. All these effects are essential to the realistic style of the Master of Flémalle. They were made possible by the use of oil, the medium he was among the first to exploit.

Tempera and Oil Techniques. The basic medium of medieval panel painting had been tempera, in which the finely ground pigments were mixed ("tempered") with diluted egg yolk to produce a tough, quick-drying coat of colors that cannot be smoothly blended. Oil, a viscous, slow-drying medium, could produce a vast variety of effects, from thin, translucent films (called glazes) to a thick layer of creamy, heavy-bodied paint (called impasto). The tones could also yield a continuous scale of hues necessary for rendering three-dimensional effects, including rich, velvety dark shades previously unknown. The medium offers a unique advantage over egg tempera, encaustic, and fresco: oils give artists the unprecedented ability to change their minds almost at will. Without oil, the Flemish masters' conquest of visible reality would have been much more limited. Although oil was not unfamiliar to medieval artists, it was the Master of Flémalle and his contemporaries who discovered its artistic possibilities. Thus, from the technical point of view, too, they deserve to be called the "fathers of modern painting," for oil has been the painter's basic medium ever since.

Jan and Hubert van Eyck. The full range of effects made possible by oil was not discovered all at once, nor by any one individual. The actual "invention" of oil painting was long credited to Jan van Eyck, a somewhat younger and much more famous artist than the Master of Flémalle. We know a good deal about Jan's life and career. Born about 1390, he worked in Holland from 1422 to 1424, in Lille from 1425 to 1429, and thereafter in Bruges, where he died in 1441. He was both a townsman and a court painter, highly esteemed by Duke Philip the Good of Burgundy, who occasionally sent him on confidential diplomatic errands. After 1432, we can follow Jan's career through a number of signed and dated pictures.

Jan's earlier development, however, remains disputed. There are several "Eyckian" works that may have been painted by him or his older brother Hubert, a shadowy figure who died in 1426, or both. The most fascinating of these is a pair of panels showing the Crucifixion and the Last Judgment (fig. 187), which date from between 1420 and 1425. The style of these panels has many qualities in common with that of the *Mérode Altarpiece*: the all-embracing devotion to the visible world, the unlimited depth of space, the angular drapery folds, less graceful but far more realistic than the unbroken loops of the International Style. At the same time, the individual forms are not starkly tangible, like those characteristic of the Master of Flémalle, and seem less isolated, less "sculptural." The sweeping sense of space is the result not so much of violent foreshortening as of subtle changes of light and color. If we inspect the *Crucifixion* panel closely, we see a gradual decrease in the intensity of local colors and in the contrast of light and dark from the foreground figures to the far-off city of Jerusalem and the snow-capped peaks beyond. Everything tends toward a uniform tint of light bluish gray, so that the farthest mountain range merges imperceptibly with the color of the sky.

This optical phenomenon is known as "atmospheric perspective." The Limbourg brothers had already been aware of the effect (see fig. 184), but the Van Eycks were the first to utilize it fully and systematically. This phenomenon results from the fact that the atmosphere is never wholly transparent. Even on the clearest day, the air between us and the things we are looking at acts as a hazy screen that interferes with our ability to see distant shapes clearly; as we approach the limit of visibility, it swallows them altogether. Atmospheric perspective is more fundamental to our perception of deep space than linear perspective, which records the diminution in the apparent size of objects as their distance from us increases. It is effective not only in faraway vistas. In the *Crucifixion* panel, even the foreground seems enveloped in a delicate haze that softens contours, shadows, and colors, and thus the entire scene has a continuity and harmony quite beyond the pictorial range of the Master of Flémalle.

How did the Van Eycks accomplish this effect? Their exact technical procedure is difficult to reconstruct, but there can be no question that they used the oil medium with extraordinary refinement. By alternating opaque and translucent layers of paint, they were able to impart to their pictures a soft, glowing radiance of tone that has never been equaled, probably because it depends fully as much on their individual sensibilities as it does on their skillful craftsmanship.

Viewed as a whole, the *Crucifixion* seems singularly devoid of drama, as if the scene had been gently becalmed by some magic spell. Only when we concentrate on the details do we become aware of the violent emotions in the faces of the crowd beneath the cross, and the restrained but profoundly touching grief of the Virgin Mary and her companions in the foreground. In the *Last Judgment* panel, this dual aspect of the Eyckian style takes the form of two extremes. Above the horizon, all is order, symmetry, and calm; below it, on earth and in the subterranean realm of Satan, the opposite condition prevails. The two states thus correspond to Heaven and Hell, contemplative bliss as against physical and emotional turbulence. The lower half, clearly, was the greater challenge to the artist's imaginative powers. The dead rising from their graves with frantic gestures of fear and hope, the damned being torn apart by devilish monsters more frightful than any we have seen before, all have the awesome reality of a nightmare, but a nightmare "observed" with the same infinite care as the natural world of the *Crucifixion* panel.

188. Jan van Eyck. *Man in a Red Turban (Self-Portrait?)*. 1433. Oil on panel, $10\frac{1}{4} \times 7\frac{1}{2}''$ (26 × 19.1 cm). The National Gallery, London. Reproduced by courtesy of the Trustees

As observed above, donors' portraits, each of splendid individuality, occupy a conspicuous position in the *Mérode Altarpiece*. A renewed interest in realistic portraiture had developed in the mid-fourteenth century, but until about 1420 its best achievements were in sculpture. The portrait did not play a major role in Northern painting until the Master of Flémalle, the first artist since antiquity to have real command of a close-range view of the human face from a three-quarter angle, instead of in profile. In addition to donors' portraits, we now begin to encounter in growing numbers small, independent likenesses whose peculiar intimacy suggests that they were treasured keepsakes, pictorial substitutes for the real presence of the sitter. One of the most fascinating is Jan van Eyck's *Man in a Red Turban* of 1433 (fig. 188), which may well

189. Jan van Eyck. *Wedding Portrait.* 1434. Oil on panel, 33 × 22½" (83.8 × 57.2 cm). The National Gallery, London. Reproduced by courtesy of the Trustees

be a self-portrait (the slight strain about the eyes seems to come from gazing into a mirror). The sitter is bathed in a gentle, clear light, and every detail of shape and texture has been recorded with almost microscopic precision. Jan does not suppress the sitter's personality, yet this face, like all of Jan's portraits, remains a psychological puzzle. It might be described as "even-tempered" in the most exact sense of the term, its character traits balanced against each other so perfectly that none can assert itself at the expense of the rest. As Jan was fully capable of expressing emotion (we need only recall the faces of the crowd in the *Crucifixion*), the stoic calm of

190. Jan van Eyck. *Wedding Portrait* (detail)

191. Rogier van der Weyden. *Descent from the Cross*. c. 1435. Oil on panel, 7′2⅝″ × 8′7⅛″ (2.2 × 2.62 m). Museo del Prado, Madrid

his portraits surely reflects his conscious ideal of human character rather than indifference or lack of insight.

The Flemish cities of Tournai, Ghent, and Bruges, where the new style of painting flourished, were the rivals of Florence, Venice, and Rome as centers of international banking and trade. Their foreign residents included many Italian businessmen. For one of these, perhaps a member of the Arnolfini family, Jan van Eyck painted his remarkable *Wedding Portrait* (fig. 189). The young couple is solemnly exchanging marriage vows in the privacy of the bridal chamber. They seem to be quite alone, but in the mirror conspicuously placed behind them is the reflection of two other persons who have entered the room (fig. 190). One of them must be the artist, since the words above the mirror, in florid legal lettering, tell us that "Johannes de eyck fuit hic" (Jan van Eyck was here) in the year 1434.

Jan's role, then, is that of a witness. The picture claims to show exactly what he saw and has the function of a pictorial marriage certificate. Though persuasively realistic, the domestic setting is filled with disguised symbolism of the most subtle kind, conveying the sacramental nature of marriage. The single candle in the chandelier, burning in broad daylight, stands for the all-seeing Christ (the mirror frame is decorated with Passion scenes). The shoes the couple has taken off remind us that they are standing on "holy ground" (for the origin of the theme, see p. 43). Even the little dog is an emblem of marital faith, and the furnishings of the room invite similar interpretation. As in the *Mérode Altarpiece*, the natural world is made to contain the world of the spirit in such a way that the two actually become one.

Van der Weyden. In the work of Jan van Eyck, the exploration of the reality made visible by light and color had reached a limit that was not to be surpassed for another two centuries. Rogier van der Weyden (1399/1400–1464), the third great master of early Flemish painting, set himself a different though equally important task: to recapture, within the framework of the new style created by his predecessors, the emotional drama, the pathos, of the Gothic past. In the *Descent from the Cross* (fig. 191), his early masterpiece painted around the same time as Jan's *Wedding Portrait*, the modeling is sculpturally precise, with brittle, angular drapery folds recalling those of the Master of Flémalle. The soft half-shadows and rich, glowing colors show his knowledge of Jan van Eyck. However, Rogier is far more than a follower of the two older artists. Whatever he owes to them (and it is obviously a great deal) he uses for ends that are not theirs but his. The external events (in this case, the lowering of Christ's body from the cross) concern him less than the world of human feeling. This *Descent*, judged for its expressive content, could well be called a *Lamentation*.

The artistic ancestry of these grief-stricken gestures and faces is in sculpture rather than in painting. It descends from the Strasbourg *Death of the Virgin* and the Naumburg *Crucifixion* to the Bonn *Pietà* and Sluter's *Moses Well* (see figs. 165, 167–69). It therefore seems peculiarly fitting that Rogier should have staged his scene in a shallow architectural niche or shrine, as if his figures were colored statues, and not against a landscape background. This bold device gave him a double advantage in heightening the effect of the tragic event. It focused the viewer's entire attention on the foreground, and allowed him to mold the figures into a coherent, formal group. No wonder that Rogier's art, which has been well described as "at once physically barer and spiritually richer than Jan van Eyck's," set an example for countless other artists. When he died in 1464, after thirty years as the foremost painter of Brussels, his influence was supreme in European painting north of the Alps. Such was the authority of his style that its echoes continued to be discernible throughout Northern Europe until the end of the century.

Van der Goes. Few of the artists who came after Rogier van der Weyden succeeded in escaping from the great master's shadow. The most dynamic of these was Hugo van der Goes (c. 1440–1482), an unhappy genius

192. Hugo van der Goes. *Portinari Altarpiece* (open). c. 1476. Tempera and oil on panel, center 8′3½″ × 10′ (2.53 × 3.05 m), wings each 8′3½″ × 4′7½″ (2.53 × 1.41 m). Galleria degli Uffizi, Florence

whose tragic end suggests an unstable personality especially interesting to us today. After a spectacular rise to fame in the cosmopolitan atmosphere of Bruges, he decided in 1478, when he was near forty years of age, to enter a monastery as a lay brother. He continued to paint for some time, but increasing fits of depression drove him to the verge of suicide, and four years later he was dead.

Hugo van der Goes' most ambitious work, the huge altarpiece he completed about 1476 for Tommaso Portinari, is an awesome achievement (fig. 192). While we need not search here for hints of Hugo's future mental illness, it nonetheless evokes a nervous and restless personality. There is a tension between the artist's devotion to the natural world and his concern with the supernatural. Hugo has rendered a wonderfully spacious and atmospheric landscape setting, with a wealth of precise detail; yet the disparity in the size of the figures seems to contradict this realism. In the wings, the kneeling members of the Portinari family are dwarfed by their patron saints, whose gigantic size characterizes them as being of a higher order. The latter figures are not meant to be "larger than life," for they share the same huge scale with Joseph, the Virgin Mary, and the shepherds of the Nativity in the center panel, whose height is normal in relation to the architecture and to the ox and ass. The angels are drawn to the same scale as the donors and thus appear abnormally small.

This variation of scale, although its symbolic and expressive purpose is clear, stands outside the logic of everyday experience affirmed in the environment the artist has provided for his figures. There is another striking contrast between the frantic excitement of the shepherds and the ritual solemnity of all the other figures. These field hands, gazing in breathless wonder at the newborn Child, react to the dramatic miracle of the Nativity with a wide-eyed directness never attempted before. They aroused particular admiration in the Italian painters who saw the work after it arrived in Florence in 1483.

Geertgen tot Sint Jans. During the last quarter of the fifteenth century there were no painters in Flanders comparable to Hugo van der Goes, and the most original artists appeared farther north, in Holland. To one of these, Geertgen tot Sint Jans of Haarlem, who died about 1495, we owe the enchanting *Nativity* reproduced in figure 193, a picture as daring, in its quiet way, as the center panel of the *Portinari Altarpiece*. The idea of a nocturnal Nativity, illuminated mainly by radiance from the Christ Child, goes back to the Inter-

193. Geertgen tot Sint Jans. *Nativity*. c. 1490. Oil on panel, 13½ × 10" (34.3 × 25.4 cm). The National Gallery, London. Reproduced by courtesy of the Trustees

194. Hieronymus Bosch. *The Garden of Delights*. c. 1510. Oil on panel, center 86½ × 76¾" (219.7 × 195 cm), wings each 86½ × 38" (219.7 × 96.5 cm). Museo del Prado, Madrid

national Style (see fig. 185), but Geertgen, applying the pictorial discoveries of Jan van Eyck, gives new, intense reality to the theme. The magic effect of his little panel is greatly enhanced by the smooth, simplified shapes that record the play of light with striking clarity. The heads of the angels, the Infant, and the Virgin are all as round as objects turned on a lathe, while the manger is a rectangular trough.

Bosch. If Geertgen's uncluttered, "abstract" forms are especially attractive to us today, another Dutch artist, Hieronymus Bosch, appeals to our interest in the world of dreams. Little is known about Bosch except that he spent his life in the provincial town of 's Hertogenbosch and that he died, an old man, in 1516. His work, full of weird and seemingly irrational imagery, has proved difficult to interpret, despite research showing that some of it was derived from alchemy texts.

We can readily understand this problem when we study the triptych known as *The Garden of Delights* (fig. 194), the richest and most puzzling of Bosch's pictures. Of the three panels, only the left one has a clearly recognizable subject: the Garden of Eden, where the Lord introduces Adam to the newly created Eve. The landscape, almost Eyckian in

its airy vastness, is filled with animals, among them such exotic creatures as an elephant and a giraffe, and also hybrid monsters of odd and sinister kinds. Behind them, the distant rock formations are equally strange. The right wing, a nightmarish scene of burning ruins and fantastic instruments of torture, surely represents Hell. But what of the center, the Garden of Delights?

Here we see a landscape much like that of the Garden of Eden, populated with countless nude men and women performing a variety of peculiar actions. In the center, they parade around a circular basin on the backs of all sorts of beasts; many frolic in pools of water; most of them are closely linked with enormous birds, fruit, flowers, or marine animals. Only a few are openly engaged in lovemaking, but there can be no doubt that the delights in this "garden" are those of carnal desire, however oddly disguised. The birds, fruit, and the like are symbols or metaphors which Bosch uses to depict life on earth as an unending repetition of the Original Sin of Adam and Eve, which dooms us to be the prisoners of our appetites. Nowhere does he so much as hint at the possibility of Salvation. Corruption, on the animal level at least, had already asserted itself in the Garden of Eden before the Fall, and we are all destined for

195. Conrad Witz. *The Miraculous Draught of Fishes.* 1444. Oil on panel, 51 × 61" (129.5 × 154.9 cm). Musée d'Art et d'Histoire, Geneva

Hell, the Garden of Satan, with its grisly and refined instruments of torture.

Despite Bosch's profound pessimism, there is indeed an innocence, even a haunting poetic beauty, in this panorama of human sinfulness. Consciously, Bosch was a stern moralist who intended his pictures to be visual sermons, every detail packed with didactic meaning. Unconsciously, however, he must have been so enraptured by the sensuous appeal of the world of the flesh that the images he coined in such abundance tend to celebrate what they are meant to condemn. That, surely, is the reason why *The Garden of Delights* still evokes so strong a response today, even though we no longer understand every word of the pictorial sermon.

SWISS AND FRENCH PAINTING

The new realism of the Flemish masters began to spread after about 1430 into France and Germany until, by the middle of the century, its influence prevailed everywhere from Spain to the Baltic. Among the countless artists who turned out provincial adaptations of Netherlandish painting, many of them still anonymous today, only a few were gifted enough to impress us with a distinctive personality.

Witz. One of the earliest and most original masters was Conrad Witz of Basel (1400/10–1445/46), whose altarpiece for Geneva Cathedral, painted in 1444, includes the remarkable panel shown in figure 195. To judge from the drapery, with its tubular folds and sharp, angular breaks, he must have had close contact with the Master of Flémalle. But the setting, rather than the figures, attracts our interest, and here the influence of the Van Eycks seems dominant. Witz, however, did not simply follow these great pioneers. An explorer himself, he knew more about the optical appearances of water than any other painter of his time, as we can see from the reflections and especially the bottom of the lake in the foreground. The landscape, too, is an original contribution. Representing a specific part of the shore of Lake Geneva, it is among the earliest landscape "portraits" that have come down to us.

Avignon Pietà. A Flemish style, influenced by Italian art, also characterizes the most famous of all fifteenth-century French pictures, the *Avignon Pietà* (fig. 196). As its name indicates, the panel comes from the extreme south of France. It is attributed to an artist of that region, Enguerrand Quarton. He must have been thoroughly familiar with the art of Rogier van der Weyden, for the figure types and the expressive content of the *Avignon Pietà* could be derived from no other source. At the same time, the magnificently simple and stable design is Italian rather than Northern: these are qualities we first saw in the art of Giotto. Southern, too, is the bleak, featureless landscape emphasizing the monumental isolation of the figures. The distant buildings behind the donor on the left have an unmistakably Islamic flavor, suggesting that the artist meant to place the scene in an authentic Near Eastern setting. From these various features he has created an unforgettable image of heroic pathos.

"LATE GOTHIC" SCULPTURE

If we had to describe fifteenth-century art north of the Alps in a single phrase, we might label it "the first century of panel painting," for panel painting so dominated the art of the period between 1420 and 1500 that its standards apply to manuscript illumination, stained glass, and even, to a large extent, sculpture. It was the influence of the Master of Flémalle and Rogier van der Weyden that ended the International Style in Northern European sculpture. The carvers, who quite often were also painters, began to reproduce in stone or wood the style of those two masters, and continued to do so until about 1500.

Pacher. The most characteristic works of the "Late Gothic" carvers are wooden altar shrines, often large in size and incredibly intricate in detail. Such shrines were especially

196. Enguerrand Quarton. *Avignon Pietà*. c. 1470. Oil on panel, 63¾ × 85⅞" (161.9 × 218.1 cm). Musée du Louvre, Paris

popular in the Germanic countries. One of the richest examples is the *St. Wolfgang Altarpiece* (fig. 197) by the Tyrolean sculptor and painter Michael Pacher (c. 1435–1498). Its lavishly gilt and colored forms make a dazzling spectacle as they emerge from the shadowy depth of the shrine under spiky Flamboyant canopies. We enjoy it, but in pictorial rather than plastic terms. We have no experience of volume, either positive or negative. The figures and setting seem to melt into a single pattern of agitated, twisting lines that permits only the heads to stand out as separate entities.

If we compare this altarpiece with Rogier's *Descent from the Cross* (see fig. 191), we realize that the latter, paradoxically, is a far more "sculptural" scene. Did Pacher, the "Late Gothic" sculptor, feel unable to compete with the painter's rendering of three-dimensional bodies and therefore choose to meet him in the pictorial realm, by extracting the maximum of drama from contrasts of light and shade? Support for this view comes from Pacher's own work: some years after completing the St. Wolfgang shrine he made another altarpiece, this time with a painted center.

THE GRAPHIC ARTS

Printing

The development of printing, for pictures as well as books, north of the Alps was an important event that had a profound effect on Western civilization. Our earliest printed books in the modern sense were produced in the Rhineland soon after 1450 (we are not certain whether Gutenberg deserves the pri-

197. Michael Pacher. *St. Wolfgang Altarpiece*. 1471–81.
Carved wood, figures about lifesize. Church of St. Wolfgang, Austria

ority long claimed for him). The new technique quickly spread all over Europe and developed into an industry, ushering in the era of general literacy. Printed pictures had hardly less importance, for without them the printed book could not have replaced the work of the medieval scribe and illuminator so quickly and completely. The pictorial and the literary aspects of printing were, indeed, closely linked from the start.

Woodcut

The idea of printing pictorial designs from wood blocks onto paper seems to have originated in Northern Europe at the very end of the fourteenth century. Many of the oldest surviving examples of such prints, called woodcuts, are German, others are Flemish, and some may be French; but all show the familiar qualities of the International Style. The designs were probably furnished by painters or sculptors. The actual carving of the wood blocks was done by the specially trained artisans who also produced wood blocks for textile prints. As a result, early woodcuts, such as the *St. Dorothy* in figure 198, have a flat, ornamental pattern. Forms are defined by simple, heavy lines with little concern for three-dimensional effects, as there is no hatching or shading. Since the outlined shapes were meant to be filled in with color, these prints often recall stained glass (compare fig. 173) more than the miniatures they replaced. Despite their aesthetic appeal to modern eyes, we should remember that fifteenth-century woodcuts were popular art, on a level that did not attract artists of great ability until shortly before 1500. A single wood block yielded thousands of copies, to be sold for a few pennies apiece, bringing the individual ownership of pictures within everyone's reach for the first time in our history.

198. *St. Dorothy*. c. 1420. Woodcut, 10⅝ × 7½" (27 × 19.1 cm). Staatliche Graphische Sammlung, Munich

Engraving

The idea of making an engraved print apparently came from the desire for an alternative to woodcuts. In a woodcut, lines left by gouging out the block are ridges; hence, the thinner they are, the more difficult to carve. In an engraving, lines are incised with a tool (called a burin) into a metal plate, usually copper, which is relatively soft and easy to work, so that they are much more refined and flexible. Engravings appealed from the first to a smaller and more sophisticated public. The oldest examples we know, dating from about 1430, already show the influence of the great Flemish painters. Their forms are systematically modeled with fine hatched lines, and often convincingly foreshortened. Nor do engravings share the anonymity of early woodcuts. Individual hands can be distinguished almost from the beginning; dates and initials soon appear; and most of the important engravers of the last third of the fifteenth century are known to us by name. Even though the early engravers were usually goldsmiths by training, their prints are so closely linked to local painting styles that we may determine their geographic origin far more easily than

199. Martin Schongauer. *The Temptation of St. Anthony.* c. 1480–90. Engraving, 12¼ × 9″ (31.1 × 22.9 cm). The Metropolitan Museum of Art, New York. Rogers Fund, 1920

for woodcuts. Especially in the Upper Rhine region, we can trace a continuous tradition of fine engravers from the time of Conrad Witz to the end of the century.

Schongauer. The most accomplished of these is Martin Schongauer (c. 1430–1491), the first printmaker whom we also know as a painter, and the first to gain international fame. Schongauer might be called the Rogier van der Weyden of engraving. After learning the goldsmith's craft in his father's shop, he must have spent considerable time in Flanders, for he shows a thorough knowledge of Rogier's art. His prints are filled with Rogierian motifs and expressive devices and reveal a deep temperamental affinity to the great Fleming. Yet Schongauer had his own impressive powers of invention. His finest engravings have a complexity of design, spatial depth, and richness of texture that make them fully equivalent to panel paintings. In fact, lesser artists often found inspiration in them for large-scale pictures.

The Temptation of St. Anthony (fig. 199), one of Schongauer's most famous works, masterfully combines savage expressiveness and formal precision, violent movement and ornamental stability. The longer we look at it, the more we marvel at its range of tonal values, the rhythmic beauty of the engraved line, and the artist's ability to render every conceivable surface—spiky, scaly, leathery, furry—merely by varying the burin's attack upon the plate. In this respect he was not to be surpassed by any later engraver.

THE EARLY RENAISSANCE IN ITALY

We do not yet fully understand the link between the great Flemish painters and the social, political, and cultural setting in which they worked to explain why the new style of painting arose in Flanders about 1420. We have far more insight into the special circumstances that help explain why Early Renaissance art was born in Florence at the beginning of the fifteenth century, rather than somewhere else or at some other time. In the years around 1400, Florence faced an acute threat to its independence from the powerful duke of Milan, who was trying to bring all of Italy under his rule. He had already subjugated the Lombard plain and most of the Central Italian city-states; only Florence remained a serious obstacle to his ambition. The city put up a vigorous and successful defense on the military, diplomatic, and intellectual fronts. Of these three, the intellectual was by no means the least important. The duke had eloquent support as a new Caesar, bringing peace and order to the country. Florence, in its turn, rallied public opinion by proclaiming itself as the champion of freedom against unchecked tyranny. The humanist Leonardo Bruni concluded in *Praise of the City of Florence* (written in 1402–3) that it had assumed the same role of political and intellectual leadership as Athens at the time of the Persian Wars. The patriotic pride, the call to greatness, implicit in this image of Florence as the "new Athens," aroused a deep response throughout the city, and just when the forces of Milan threatened to engulf them, the Florentines embarked on an ambitious campaign to finish the great artistic enterprises begun a century before, at the time of Giotto. The huge investment was itself not a guarantee of artistic quality, but, stirred by such civic enthusiasm, it provided a splendid opportunity for the emergence of creative talent and the coining of a new style worthy of the "new Athens."

From the start, the visual arts were considered essential to the resurgence of the Florentine spirit. Throughout antiquity and the Middle Ages, they had been classed with the crafts, or "mechanical arts." It cannot be by chance that the first explicit statement claiming a place for them among the liberal arts occurs about 1400 in the writings of the Florentine chronicler Filippo Villani. A century later, this claim was to win general acceptance throughout the Western world. What does it imply? The liberal arts were defined by a tradition going back to Plato and comprised the intellectual disciplines necessary for a "gentleman's" education: mathematics (including musical theory), dialectics, grammar, rhetoric, and philosophy. The fine arts were excluded because they were "handiwork" lacking a theoretical basis. Thus, when artists gained admission to this select group, the nature of their work had to be redefined. They were acknowledged as people of ideas rather than mere manipulators of materials, and works of art came to be viewed more and more as the visible records of their creative minds. This meant that works of art need not—indeed, should not—be judged by fixed standards of craftsmanship. Soon everything that bore the imprint of a great master—drawings, sketches, fragments, unfinished pieces—was eagerly collected, regardless of its incompleteness.

The outlook of artists underwent important changes as well. Now in the company of scholars and poets, they themselves often became learned and literary. They might write poems, autobiographies, or theoretical treatises. As another consequence of this new social status, artists tended to develop into one of two contrasting personality types: the person of the world, self-controlled, polished, at ease in aristocratic society; or the solitary genius, secretive, idiosyncratic, subject to fits of melancholy, and likely to be in conflict with patrons. This remarkably modern view soon became a living reality in the Florence of the Early Renaissance. From there it spread to other centers in Italy and throughout Europe. However, such an attitude did not take immediate hold everywhere, nor did it apply equally to all artists: England, for example, was slow to grant them special status, and women in general were denied the professional training and opportunities available to men.

SCULPTURE

The first half of the fifteenth century became the heroic age of the Early Renaissance. Florentine art, dominated by the original creators of the new style, retained the undisputed leadership of the movement. To trace its beginnings, we must discuss sculpture first, for the sculptors had earlier and more plentiful opportunities than the architects and painters to meet the challenge of the "new Athens."

Di Banco. The artistic campaign had opened with the competition for the Baptistery doors, and for some time it consisted mainly of sculptural projects. Ghiberti's trial relief, we recall, does not differ significantly from the International Gothic (see fig. 172). His admiration for ancient art, evidenced by the torso of Isaac, merely recaptures what Nicola Pisano had done a century before (see fig. 170). A decade after the trial relief, we find that this limited medieval classicism has been surpassed by a somewhat younger artist, Nanni di Banco (c. 1384–1421). The *Quattro Coronati* or *Four Saints* (fig. 200), which he made about

200. Nanni di Banco. *Four Saints (Quattro Coronati).* c. 1410–14. Marble, about lifesize. Or San Michele, Florence

1410–14 for one of the niches on the exterior of the church of Or San Michele, demand to be compared not with the work of Nicola Pisano but with the Reims *Visitation* (see fig. 166). The figures in both groups are approximately lifesize, yet Nanni's give the impression of being a good deal larger than those at Reims. Their quality of mass and monumentality was quite beyond the range of medieval sculpture. This is so, even though Nanni depended less directly on ancient models than had the sculptor of the *Visitation* or Nicola Pisano. Only the heads of the second and third of the *Coronati* recall specific examples of Roman sculpture. Nanni was obviously much impressed by their realism and their agonized expression (see fig. 94). His ability to retain the essence of both these qualities indicates a new attitude toward ancient art, which unites classical form and content, no longer separating them as medieval classicists had done.

Donatello. Early Renaissance art, in contrast to "Late Gothic," sought an attitude toward the human body similar to that of classical antiquity. The man who did most to reestablish this attitude was Donatello (1386–1466), the greatest sculptor of his time. We have clearly entered a new epoch when we look at his *St. George* (fig. 201), carved in marble for another niche of the Church of Or San Michele around 1415. Here is the first statue we have seen since ancient times that can stand by itself; or, put another way, the first to recapture the full meaning of classical *contrapposto* (see p. 82). The artist has mastered at one stroke the central achievement of ancient sculpture: he has treated the human body as an articulated *structure* capable of movement. The armor and drapery are a secondary structure shaped by the body underneath. Unlike any Gothic statue, this *St. George* can take off his clothes. Also unlike any Gothic statue, he can be taken away from his architectural setting and lose none of his immense authority. His stance, with his weight placed on the forward leg, conveys the idea of readiness for combat (the right hand originally held a weapon). The controlled energy of his body is echoed in his eyes, which seem to scan the horizon for the approaching enemy. For this *St. George*, slayer of dragons, is a proud and heroic defender of the "new Athens."

201. Donatello. *St. George Tabernacle,* from Or San Michele, Florence. c. 1415–17. Marble, height of statue 6′10″ (2.08 m). Museo Nazionale del Bargello, Florence

The unidentified prophet (fig. 202), nicknamed *Zuccone* ("Pumpkinhead") for obvious reason, was carved some eight years later for the bell tower of Florence Cathedral. It has long enjoyed fame as a striking example of the master's realism. There can be no question that it is indeed realistic—far more so than any ancient statue or its nearest rivals, the prophets on Sluter's *Moses Well* (see fig. 169). But what *kind* of realism is this? Donatello has not followed the conventional image of a prophet (a bearded old man in Oriental-looking costume, holding a scroll). Rather, he has invented an entirely new type, and it is difficult to account for his impulse in terms of realism. Why did he not reinterpret the old image from a realistic point of view, as Sluter had done? Donatello obviously felt that the established type was inadequate for his own conception of the subject. But how did he conceive it anew? Surely not by observing the people around him. More likely, he imagined the personalities of the prophets from what he had read about them in the Old Testament. He gained an impression, we may assume, of divinely inspired orators haranguing the multitude; this, in turn, reminded him of the Roman orators he had seen in ancient sculpture. Hence, the classical costume of the *Zuccone*, whose mantle falls from one shoulder like those of the toga-clad patricians in figure 91. Hence, also, the fascinating head, ugly yet noble, like Roman portraits of the third century A.D. (compare fig. 94).

202. *(left)* Donatello. *Prophet (Zuccone),* on the campanile of Florence Cathedral. 1423–25. Marble, height 6′5″ (1.96 m). Original now in the Museo dell'Opera del Duomo, Florence

203. *(right)* Donatello. *David.* c. 1425–30. Bronze, height 62¼″ (158.1 cm). Museo Nazionale del Bargello, Florence

To shape all these elements into a coherent whole was a revolutionary feat, an almost visible struggle. Donatello himself seems to have regarded the *Zuccone* as a particularly hard-won achievement. It is the first of his surviving works to carry his signature. He is said to have sworn "by the *Zuccone*" when he wanted to emphasize a statement and to have shouted at the statue, during his work, "Speak, speak, or the plague take you!"

Donatello had learned the technique of bronze sculpture as a youth working under Ghiberti on the first Baptistery doors. By the 1420s, he began to rival his former teacher in that medium, which he used to make *David* (fig. 203). This is the first free-standing lifesize nude statue since antiquity. *David,* moreover, is nude in the full classical sense. Donatello has clearly rediscovered the sensuous beauty of the unclothed body. Medieval nudes, even the most accomplished, are devoid of that appeal, which we take for granted in every nude of classical antiquity. It was purposely avoided rather than unattainable, for to the medieval mind the physical beauty of the ancient "idols," especially nude statues, embodied the insidious attraction of paganism. The Middle Ages would surely have condemned *David* as an idol, and Donatello's contemporaries, too, must have felt uneasy about it; for many years it remained the only work of its kind.

The statue must be understood as a civic-patriotic public monument identifying David—weak but favored by the Lord—with Florence, and Goliath with Milan. David's nudity is most readily explained as a reference to the classical origin of Florence, and his wreathed hat as the opposite of Goliath's elaborate helmet: peace versus war. Donatello chose to model an adolescent boy, not a full-grown youth like the athletes of Greece, so

204. Donatello. *Equestrian Monument of Gattamelata.* 1445–50. Bronze, c. 11 × 13′ (3.1 × 3.96 m). Piazza del Santo, Padua

that the skeletal structure here is less fully enveloped in swelling muscles; nor does he articulate the torso according to the classical pattern (compare fig. 74). In fact his *David* resembles an ancient statue only in its beautifully poised *contrapposto*. If the figure nevertheless conveys a profoundly classical air, the reason lies beyond its anatomical perfection. As in ancient statues, the body speaks to us more eloquently than the face, which by Donatello's standards is strangely devoid of individuality.

Donatello was invited to Padua in 1443 to produce the *Equestrian Monument of Gattamelata* (fig. 204), portraying the recently deceased commander of the Venetian armies. This statue, the artist's largest free-standing work in bronze, still occupies its original position on a tall pedestal near the facade of the church dedicated to St. Anthony of Padua. Without directly imitating the mounted *Marcus Aurelius* in Rome (see fig. 93), the *Gattamelata* shares its material, its impressive scale, and its sense of balance and dignity. Donatello's horse, a heavyset animal fit to carry a man in full armor, is so large that the rider must dominate it by his authority of command, rather than by physical force. The *Gattamelata*, in the new Renaissance fashion, is not part of a tomb; it was designed solely to immortalize the fame of a great soldier. Nor is it the self-glorifying statue of a sovereign, but a monument authorized by the Republic of Venice in special honor of distinguished and faithful service. To this purpose, Donatello has coined an image that is a complete union of ideal and reality. The head is powerfully individual, yet endowed with a truly Roman nobility of character. The general's armor likewise combines modern construction with classical detail.

Ghiberti. One of the few important sculptors left in Florence following Donatello's departure was Lorenzo Ghiberti. After the great success of his first Baptistery doors, he was commissioned to do a second pair, which were to be dubbed the "Gates of Paradise." Its reliefs, unlike those of the first doors (see fig. 172), were large and set in simple square frames (fig. 205). The hint of spatial depth we saw in *The Sacrifice of Isaac* has grown in *The Story of Jacob and Esau* into a complete setting for the figures that goes back as far as the eye can reach. We can imagine the figures leaving the scene, for the deep, continuous space of this "pictorial relief" in no way depends on their presence. How did Ghiberti achieve this effect? In part by varying the degree of relief, with the forms closest to us being modeled almost in the round, a method familiar from ancient art (see figs. 67, 96). Far more important is the carefully controlled recession of figures and architecture, which causes their apparent size to diminish systematically (rather than haphazardly as before) as their distance from us increases. This system, known as linear perspective, was invented by Filippo Brunelleschi, whose architectural achievements will occupy us soon. It is a geometric procedure for projecting space onto a plane, analogous to the way the lens of a photographic camera projects a perspective image on the film. Its central feature is the vanishing point, toward which all parallel lines will seem to converge. If these lines are perpendicular to the picture plane, their vanishing point will be on the horizon, corre-

205. Lorenzo Ghiberti. *The Story of Jacob and Esau*, panel of the *"Gates of Paradise."* c. 1435. Gilt bronze, 31¼" (79.4 cm) square. Baptistery of S. Giovanni, Florence

206. Luca della Robbia. *Singing Angels,* from the *Cantoria.* c. 1435. Marble, c. 38 × 24″ (96.5 × 61 cm). Museo dell'Opera del Duomo, Florence

sponding exactly to the position of the beholder's eye. Brunelleschi's discovery in itself was scientific rather than artistic, but it immediately became highly important to Early Renaissance artists because it enabled them to gain command over every aspect of composition. Unlike the perspective practices of the past, it was objective, precise, and rational. In fact, it soon became an argument for upgrading the fine arts into the liberal arts.

Della Robbia. Ghiberti aside, the only significant sculptor in Florence after Donatello left was Luca della Robbia (1400–1482). He had made his reputation in the 1430s with the marble reliefs of his *Cantoria* (singers' pulpit) in the Cathedral. The *Singing Angels* panel reproduced here (fig. 206) shows the beguiling mixture of sweetness and gravity characteristic of all of Luca's work. Its style, we realize, has very little to do with Donatello. Instead, it recalls the classicism of Nanni di Banco (see fig. 200), with whom Luca may have worked as a youth. We also sense a touch of Ghiberti here and there, as well as the powerful influence of Roman reliefs (see fig. 96). Luca, despite his great gifts, lacked a capacity for growth. He never, so far as we know, did a free-standing statue, and the *Cantoria* remained his most ambitious achievement.

Because of Luca's almost complete withdrawal from the domain of carving, there was a real shortage of capable marble sculp-

207. Bernardo Rossellino. *Tomb of Leonardo Bruni.* c. 1445–50. Marble, height to top of arch 20′ (6.1 m). Sta. Croce, Florence

tors in the Florence of the 1440s. This gap was filled by a group of younger men from the little hill towns to the north and east of Florence that had long supplied the city with stonemasons and carvers; now, the most gifted of them developed into artists of considerable importance.

Bernardo Rossellino. The oldest of these, Bernardo Rossellino (1409–1464), seems to have begun as a sculptor and architect in Arezzo. He established himself in Florence about 1436, but received no commissions of real consequence until some eight years later, when he was entrusted with the tomb of Leonardo Bruni (fig. 207). This great humanist and statesman had played a vital part in the city's affairs ever since the beginning of the century (see p. 217). When he died in 1444, he received a grand funeral "in the manner of the ancients." His monument was probably ordered by the city governments of both Florence and Arezzo, where he and Rossellino were born.

Although the Bruni monument is not the earliest Renaissance tomb, nor even the earliest large-scale tomb of a humanist, it can claim to be the first memorial that fully expresses the spirit of the new era. Echoes of Bruni's funeral *all'antica* are everywhere: the deceased reclines on a bier supported by Roman eagles, his head wreathed in laurel and his hands enfolding a volume (presumably his own *History of Florence,* rather than a prayer book). The monument is a fitting tribute to the man who, more than any other, had helped establish the new historical perspective of the Florentine Early Renaissance. On the classically severe sarcophagus, two winged genii display an inscription very different from those on medieval tombs. Instead of recording the name, rank, and age of the deceased and the date of his death, it refers only to his timeless accomplishments: "At Leonardo's passing, history grieves, eloquence is mute, and it is said that the Muses, Greek and Latin alike, cannot hold back their tears." The religious aspect of the tomb is confined to the lunette, where the Madonna is adored by angels. The entire monument may thus be viewed as an attempt to reconcile two contrasting attitudes toward death—the retrospective, commemorative outlook of the ancients (see pp. 99–100), and the Christian concern with afterlife and salvation. Bernardo's design is admirably suited to such a program, balancing architecture and sculpture within a compact and self-contained framework.

Pollaiuolo. By 1450 the great civic campaign of art patronage came to an end, and Florentine artists had to depend mainly on private commissions. This put the sculptors at a disadvantage because of the high costs involved in their work. Since the monumental tasks were few, they concentrated on works of moderate size and price for individual pa-

208. Antonio del Pollaiuolo. *Hercules and Antaeus.* c. 1475. Bronze, height with base 18″ (45.7 cm). Museo Nazionale del Bargello, Florence

trons, such as bronze statuettes. The collecting of sculpture, widely practiced in ancient times, had apparently ceased during the Middle Ages. The taste of kings and feudal lords—those who could afford to collect for personal pleasure—ran to precious objects. The habit was reestablished in fifteenth-century Italy as an aspect of the revival of antiquity. Humanists and artists first collected ancient sculpture, especially small bronzes, which were numerous and of convenient size. Before long, contemporary artists began to cater to the spreading vogue, with portrait busts and small bronzes of their own "in the manner of the ancients."

A particularly fine piece of this kind is *Hercules and Antaeus* (fig. 208) by Antonio del Pollaiuolo (1431–1498), who represents a sculptural style very different from that of the marble carvers we discussed above. Trained as a goldsmith and metalworker, probably in the Ghiberti workshop, he was deeply impressed by the late styles of Donatello and Andrea del Castagno (see fig. 218), as well as by ancient art. From these sources, he evolved the distinctive manner that appears in our statuette. To create a free-standing group of two figures in violent struggle, even on a small scale, was a daring idea in itself. Even more astonishing is the way Pollaiuolo has endowed his composition with a centrifugal impulse. Limbs seem to radiate in every direction from a common center, and we see the full complexity of their movements only when we examine the statuette from all sides. Despite its strenuous action, the group is in perfect balance. To stress the central axis, Pollaiuolo in effect grafted the upper part of Antaeus onto the lower part of his adversary. There is no precedent for this design among earlier statuary groups of any size, ancient or Renaissance. Our artist has simply given a third dimension to a composition from the field of drawing or painting. He himself was a painter and engraver as well as a bronze sculptor, and we know that about 1465 he did a large picture of Hercules and Antaeus, now lost, for the Medici Palace (our statuette also belonged to the Medici).

209. Andrea del Verrocchio. *Putto with Dolphin.* c. 1470. Bronze, height without base 27" (68.6 cm). Palazzo Vecchio, Florence

Verrocchio. During the late years of his career, Pollaiuolo did two monumental bronze tombs for St. Peter's in Rome, but he never had an opportunity to execute a large-scale free-standing statue. For such works we must turn to his slightly younger contemporary Andrea del Verrocchio (1435–1488), the greatest sculptor of his day and the only one to share some of Donatello's range and ambition. A modeler as well as a carver—we have works of his in every medium—he combined elements from Bernardo Rossellino and Antonio del Pollaiuolo into a unique synthesis. He was also a respected painter and the teacher of Leonardo da Vinci (something of a misfortune, for he has been overshadowed ever since).

Putto with Dolphin (fig. 209) owes its popularity to its enduring charm. It was designed as the center of a fountain for one of the Medici villas near Florence: the dolphin spouts a jet of water, as if responding to the hug it has to endure. The term "putto" (plural, "putti") designates one of the nude, often winged children that accompany more weighty subjects in ancient art. They personify spirits (such as the spirit of love, in which case we call them cupids), usually in a merry and playful way. They were reintroduced during the Early Renaissance, both in their original identity and as child angels. The dolphin associates Verrocchio's *Putto* with the classical kind (note the small putto and dolphin in fig. 92). Artistically, however, he is closer to Pollaiuolo's *Hercules and Antaeus* than to ancient art, despite his larger size and greater sense of volume. Again the forms fly out in every direction from a central axis, but here the movement is graceful and continuous rather than jagged and broken. The stretched-out leg, the dolphin, and the arms and wings fit into an upward spiral, making the figure seem to revolve before our eyes.

ARCHITECTURE

Brunelleschi. Although Donatello was its greatest and most daring master, he did not create the Early Renaissance style in sculpture all by himself. The new architecture, on the other hand, did owe its existence to one man, Filippo Brunelleschi (1377–1446). Ten years older than Donatello, he too had begun his career as a sculptor. After failing to win the competition of 1401–2 for the first Baptistery doors, Brunelleschi reportedly went to Rome with Donatello. He studied the architectural monuments of the ancients, and seems to have been the first to take exact measurements of these structures. His discovery of scientific perspective (see pp. 221–22) may well have grown out of his search for an accurate method of recording their appearance on paper. What else he did during this long "gestation period" we do not know, but in 1417–19 we again find him competing with Ghiberti, this time for the job of building the Florence Cathedral dome (see fig. 162). Its design had been established half a century earlier and could be altered only in details, but its vast size posed a difficult problem of construction. Brunelleschi's proposals, although contrary to all traditional practice, so impressed the authorities that this time he won out over his rival. Thus the dome deserves to be called the first work of post-medieval architecture, as an engineering feat if not for style.

In 1419, while he was working out the final plans for the dome, Brunelleschi received his first opportunity to create buildings entirely of his own design. It came from the head of the Medici family, one of the leading merchants and bankers of Florence, who asked him to develop a new design for the church of S. Lorenzo. The construction, begun in 1421, was often interrupted, so that the interior was not completed until 1469, more than twenty years after the architect's death (the exterior remains unfinished to this day). Nevertheless, the building in its present form is essentially what Brunelleschi had envisioned about 1420, and thus represents the first full statement of his architectural aims (figs. 210, 211). The plan may not seem very novel, at first glance. The unvaulted nave and transept link it to Sta. Croce (see fig. 161). What distinguishes it is a new emphasis on symmetry and regularity. The entire design consists of square units: four large squares form the choir, the crossing, and the arms of the transept; four more are combined into the nave; other squares, one-fourth the size of the large ones, make up the aisles and the chapels attached to the transept (the oblong chapels outside the aisles were not part of the original design). We notice, however, some small deviations from this scheme. The transept arms are slightly longer than they are wide, and the length of the nave is not four but four and one-half times its width. These apparent inconsistencies are easily explained: Brunelleschi in his scheme made no allowance for the thickness of the walls. In other words, he conceived S. Lorenzo as a grouping of abstract "space blocks," the larger ones being simple multiples of the standard unit. Once we understand this, we realize how revolutionary he was, for his clearly defined, separate space

210. Filippo Brunelleschi. S. Lorenzo, Florence. 1469

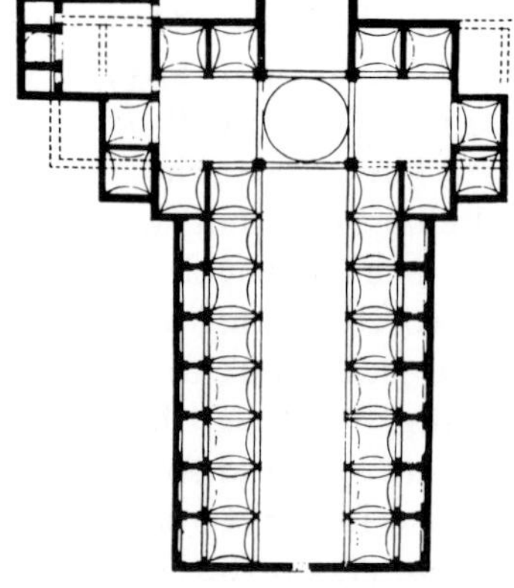

211. Plan of S. Lorenzo

compartments represent a radical departure from the Gothic architect's way of thinking.

The interior bears out our expectations. Cool, static order has replaced the emotional warmth, the flowing spatial movement of Gothic church interiors. The total effect recalls the "old-fashioned" Tuscan Romanesque, such as the Baptistery of S. Giovanni in Florence (see fig. 139), and Early Christian basilicas (compare figs. 89, 90). These monuments, to Brunelleschi, exemplified the church architecture of classical antiquity. They inspired his return to the use of the round arch and of columns, rather than piers, in the nave arcade. Yet these earlier buildings lack the transparent lightness, the wonderfully precise articulation of S. Lorenzo. Clearly then, Brunelleschi did not revive the architectural vocabulary of the ancients out of mere antiquarian enthusiasm. The very quality that attracted him to the component parts of classical architecture must have seemed, from the medieval point of view, their chief drawback: inflexibility. Not that the classical vocabulary is completely rigid; but the disciplined spirit of the Greek orders, which can be felt even in the most original Roman buildings, demands regularity and consistency, and discourages sudden, arbitrary departures from the norm.

Architectural Proportions. If Renaissance architecture found a standard vocabulary in the revival of classical forms, the theory of harmonious proportions provided it with the kind of syntax that had been mostly absent from medieval architecture. This controlling principle is what makes the interior of S. Lorenzo seem so beautifully integrated, and accounts for the harmonious, balanced character of its design. The secret of good architecture, Brunelleschi was convinced, lay in giving the "right" proportions—that is, proportional ratios expressed in simple whole numbers—to all the significant measurements of a building. The ancients had possessed this secret, he believed, and he tried to rediscover it by painstakingly surveying the remains of their monuments. What he found, and how he applied his theory to his own designs, we do not know for sure. He may have been the first to think out what would be explicitly stated a few decades later in Leone Battista Alberti's *Treatise on Architecture*: that the mathematical ratios determining musical harmony must also govern architecture, for they recur throughout the universe and are thus divine in origin.

Even Brunelleschi's faith in the universal validity of harmonious proportions did not tell him how to allot these ratios to the parts of any given building. It left him many alternatives, and his choice among them was necessarily subjective. We may say, in fact, that the main reason S. Lorenzo strikes us as the product of a single great mind is the very individual sense of proportion permeating every detail.

Alberti. The death of Brunelleschi in 1446 brought to the fore Leone Battista Alberti (1404–1472), whose career as a practicing architect, like Brunelleschi's, had been long delayed. Until he was forty, Alberti seems to have been interested in the fine arts only as an antiquarian and theorist. He was close to the leading artists of his day: *On Painting,* one of three treatises he wrote, is dedicated to Brunelleschi and refers to "our dear friend" Donatello. Alberti began to practice art as a dilettante, and eventually he became a professional architect of outstanding ability. Highly educated in classical literature and philosophy, as an artist he exemplifies both the humanist and the person of the world.

212. Leone Battista Alberti. S. Andrea, Mantua. Designed 1470

In the Church of S. Andrea in Mantua (fig. 212), his last work, Alberti accomplished the seemingly impossible feat of superimposing a classical temple front on the traditional basilican church facade. To harmonize this marriage, he used pilasters, which are flat, instead of columns, thus emphasizing the continuity of the wall surface. They are of two sizes. The smaller ones sustain the arch over the huge center niche; the larger ones form what is known as a colossal order spanning all three stories of the facade wall, balancing exactly the horizontal and vertical impulses within the design. So intent was Alberti on stressing the inner cohesion of the facade that he inscribed the entire design within a square, even though it is appreciably lower in height than the nave of the church. (The effect of the west wall protruding above the pediment is more disturbing in photographs than at street level, where it is nearly invisible.) The facade offers an exact "preview" of the interior, where the same colossal order, the same proportions, and the same triumphal-arch motif reappear on the nave walls.

Alberti's facade design interprets his classical models freely. They no longer embody an absolute authority that must be quoted literally, but serve as a valuable store of motifs to be utilized at will. With this sovereign attitude toward his sources, he was able to create a structure that truly deserves to be called a "Christian temple." Nevertheless, S. Andrea, which occupies the site of an older basilican church, does not conform to the ideal shape of sacred buildings as defined in Alberti's *Treatise on Architecture*. There he explains that the plan of such structures should be either circular, or of a shape derived from the circle (square, hexagon, octagon, and so forth), because the circle is the perfect, as well as the most natural, figure and therefore a direct image of divine reason. This argument rests, of course, on Alberti's faith in the God-given validity of mathematically determined proportions.

Alberti's ideal church demands a design so harmonious that it would be a revelation of divinity, and would arouse pious contemplation in the worshiper. It should stand alone, elevated above the surrounding everyday life, and light should enter through openings

213. Giuliano da Sangallo. Sta. Maria delle Carceri, Prato. 1485

placed high, for only the sky should be seen through them. A church, he believed, must be a visible embodiment of "divine proportion," which the central plan alone could attain. That such an isolated, central-plan structure was ill adapted to the requirements of Catholic ritual made no difference to Alberti. But how could he reconcile it with the historical evidence? Alberti arbitrarily disregarded the standard longitudinal form of both ancient temples and Christian churches, and relied instead on the Pantheon and similar structures.

Giuliano da Sangallo. When Alberti formulated these ideas in his treatise, about 1450, he could not yet cite any modern example of them. Toward the end of the century, after his treatise became widely known, the central-plan church gained general acceptance, and between 1500 and 1525 it became a vogue reigning supreme in High Renaissance architecture. It is no coincidence that Sta. Maria delle Carceri in Prato (fig. 213), an early and distinguished example of this trend, was begun in 1485, the date of the first printed edition of Alberti's treatise. Its architect, Giuliano da Sangallo (c. 1443–1516), must have been an admirer of Brunelleschi, but the basic shape of his structure conforms closely to Alberti's ideal. Except for the dome, the entire church would fit neatly inside a cube, since its height (up to the drum) equals its length and width. By cutting into the corners of this cube, as it were, Giuliano has formed a Greek cross (a plan he preferred for its symbolic value). The dimensions of the four arms stand in the simplest possible ratio to those of the cube: their length is one-half their width, their width one-half their height. The arms are barrel-vaulted, and the dome rests on these vaults, yet the dark ring of the drum does not quite touch the supporting arches, making the dome seem to hover, weightlessly, like the pendentive domes of Byzantine architecture (compare fig. 114). There can be no doubt that Giuliano wanted his dome to accord with the age-old tradition of the Dome of Heaven: the single round opening in the center and the twelve on the perimeter clearly refer to Christ and the apostles.

PAINTING

Florence

Masaccio. Early Renaissance painting did not appear until the early 1420s, a decade later than Donatello's *St. George* and some six years after Brunelleschi's first designs for S. Lorenzo. Its inception, however, was the most extraordinary of all. This new style was launched single-handedly by a young genius named Masaccio (1401–1428), who was only twenty-one years old at the time he painted *The Holy Trinity* fresco in Sta. Maria Novella (fig. 214). Because the Early Renaissance was already well established in sculpture and architecture, Masaccio's task was easier than it would have been otherwise, but his achievement remains stupendous nevertheless.

Here, as in the case of the *Mérode Altarpiece,* we seem to plunge into a new environment. But Masaccio's world is a realm of monumental grandeur rather than the concrete, everyday reality of the Master of Flémalle. It seems hard to believe that only two years

214. Masaccio. *The Holy Trinity with the Virgin, St. John, and Two Donors*. 1425. Fresco. Sta. Maria Novella, Florence

215. Left wall of Brancacci Chapel, with frescoes by Masaccio. Sta. Maria del Carmine, Florence. c. 1427

before, in this city of Florence, Gentile da Fabriano had completed *The Adoration of the Magi* (see fig. 185), one of the masterpieces of the International Gothic. What the *Trinity* fresco brings to mind is not the style of the immediate past, but Giotto's art, with its sense of large scale, its compositional severity and sculptural volume. Masaccio's renewed allegiance to Giotto was only a starting point, however. For Giotto, body and drapery form a single unit, as if both had the same substance. In contrast, Masaccio's figures are "clothed nudes," like Donatello's, their drapery falling like real fabric.

The setting, equally up-to-date, reveals a complete command of Brunelleschi's new architecture and of scientific perspective. For the first time in history, we are given all the data needed to measure the depth of this painted interior, to draw its plan, and to duplicate the structure in three dimensions. It is, in short, the earliest example of a *rational* picture space. For Masaccio, like Brunelleschi, it must have also been a symbol of the universe ruled by divine reason. This barrel-vaulted chamber is no mere niche, but a deep space wherein the figures could move freely if they wished. Thus, in Masaccio's *Trinity,* as well as in Ghiberti's later relief panel *The Story of Jacob and Esau* (see fig. 205), the picture space is independent of the figures: they inhabit it but do not create it. Take away the architecture and you take away the figures' space. We could go even further and say that geometric perspective depends not just on architecture, but on this particular kind of architecture, so different from Gothic.

The largest group of Masaccio's works to come down to us are frescoes in the Brancacci Chapel in Sta. Maria del Carmine (fig. 215).

The Tribute Money, in the upper tier, is the most renowned of these. It illustrates, by the age-old method known as "continuous narration" (see p. 115), the story in the Gospel of Matthew (17:24–27): in the center, Christ instructs Peter to catch a fish, whose mouth will contain the tribute money for the tax collector; on the far left, in the distance, Peter takes the coin from the fish's mouth; on the right, he gives it to the tax collector. Since the lower edge of the fresco is almost fourteen feet above the floor of the chapel, Masaccio expects us to imagine that we are looking directly at the central vanishing point, which is located behind the head of Christ. Oddly enough, this feat is remarkably easy. The illusion depends to only a minor degree on Brunelleschian perspective. Masaccio's weapons here are exactly those employed by the Master of Flémalle and the Van Eycks. He controls the flow of light (which comes from the right, where the window of the chapel is actually located), and he uses atmospheric perspective in the subtly changing tones of the landscape.

The figures in *The Tribute Money,* even more than those in the *Trinity* fresco, display Masaccio's ability to merge the weight and volume of Giotto's figures with the new functional view of body and drapery. All stand in beautifully balanced *contrapposto,* and close inspection reveals fine vertical lines scratched in the plaster by the artist, establishing the gravitational axis of each figure from the head to the heel of the engaged leg. In accord with a dignified approach, the narrative is conveyed by intense glances and a few emphatic gestures, rather than by physical movement.

Veneziano. Masaccio died too young (he was only twenty-seven) to found a "school," and his style was too bold to be taken up immediately by his contemporaries. Their work, for the most part, combines his influence with lingering elements of the International Style. Then, in 1439 a gifted painter from Venice, Domenico Veneziano, settled in Florence. We can only guess at his age (he was probably born about 1410 and he died in 1461), training, and previous work. He must, however, have been in sympathy with the spirit of Early Renaissance art, for he quickly became a thoroughgoing Florentine-by-choice, and a master of great importance in his new home. His *Madonna and Child with Saints,* shown in figure 216, is one of the earliest examples of a new type of altar panel that was to prove popular from the mid-fifteenth century on, the so-called *sacra conversazione* ("sacred conversation"). The scheme includes an enthroned Madonna framed by architecture and flanked by saints, who may converse with her, with the beholder, or among themselves.

Looking at Domenico's panel, we can understand the wide appeal of the *sacra conversazione.* The architecture and the space it defines are supremely clear and tangible, yet elevated above the everyday world. The figures, while echoing the formal solemnity of their setting, are linked with each other and with us by a thoroughly human awareness. But although we are admitted to their presence, they do not invite us to join them; like spectators in a theater, we are not allowed "onstage." In Flemish painting, by contrast, the picture space seems a direct extension of the viewer's everyday environment (compare fig. 186).

The basic elements of our panel were already present in Masaccio's *Holy Trinity* fresco. Domenico must have studied it carefully, for his St. John looks at us while pointing toward the Madonna, repeating the glance and gesture of Masaccio's Virgin. Domenico's perspective setting is worthy of the earlier master, although the slender proportions and colored inlays of his architecture are less severely Brunelleschian. His figures, too, are balanced and dignified like Masaccio's, but without the same weight and bulk. The slim, sinewy bodies of the male saints, with their highly individualized, expressive faces, show Donatello's influence (see fig. 202).

Like Masaccio, Domenico treats color as an integral part of his work, and the *sacra conversazione* is quite as remarkable for its color scheme as for its composition. The blond tonality, its harmony of pink, light green, and white set off by strategically placed spots of red, blue, and yellow, reconciles the decora-

216. Domenico Veneziano. *Madonna and Child with Saints*. c. 1455. Oil on panel, 6′7½″ × 6′11⅞″ (2.02 × 2.13 m). Galleria degli Uffizi, Florence

tive brightness of Gothic panel painting with the demands of perspective space and natural light. Ordinarily, a *sacra conversazione* is an indoor scene, but this one takes place in a kind of loggia (a covered open-air arcade) flooded with sunlight streaming in from the right, as we can tell from the cast shadow behind the Madonna. The surfaces of the architecture reflect the light so strongly that even the shadowed areas glow with color. Masaccio had achieved a similar quality of light in one of his paintings, which Domenico surely knew. In this *sacra conversazione,* the discovery has been applied to a far more complex set of forms, and integrated with Domenico's exquisite color sense. The influence of its distinctive tonality can be felt throughout Florentine painting of the second half of the century.

Piero della Francesca. When Domenico Veneziano settled in Florence, he had as an assistant a young man from southeastern Tuscany named Piero della Francesca (c. 1420–1492), who became his most important disci-

217. Piero della Francesca. *The Discovery and Proving of the True Cross.* c. 1460. Fresco. S. Francesco, Arezzo

ple and one of the truly great artists of the Early Renaissance. Surprisingly enough, Piero left Florence after a few years, never to return. The Florentines seem to have regarded his work as somewhat provincial and old-fashioned, and from this point of view they were right. Piero's style, even more strongly than Domenico's, reflected the aims of Masaccio. He retained this allegiance to the founder of Italian Renaissance painting throughout his long career.

Piero's most impressive achievement is the fresco cycle in the choir of S. Francesco in Arezzo, which he painted from about 1452 to 1459. Its many scenes represent the legend of the True Cross (that is, the story of the cross used for Christ's crucifixion). The section in figure 217 shows the empress Helena, the mother of Constantine the Great, discovering the True Cross and the two crosses of the thieves who died beside Christ (all three had been hidden by enemies of the Faith). On the left, they are being lifted out of the ground, and on the right, the True Cross is identified by its power to bring a dead youth back to life.

Piero's link with Domenico Veneziano is readily apparent from his colors. The tonality of this fresco, although less luminous than in Domenico's *Madonna and Child with Saints,* is similarly blond, evoking early morning sunlight in much the same way. Since the light enters the scene at a low angle, in a direction almost parallel to the picture plane, it serves both to define the three-dimensional character of every shape and to lend drama to the narrative. But Piero's figures have a harsh grandeur that recalls Masaccio, or even Giotto, more than Domenico. These men and women seem to belong to a lost heroic race, beautiful and strong—and silent. Their inner life is conveyed by glances and gestures, not by facial expressions. Above all, they have a gravity, both physical and emotional, that makes them seem kin to Greek sculpture of the Severe style (see fig. 70).

How did Piero arrive at these memorable images? Using his own testimony, we may say that they were born of his passion for perspective. More than any artist of his day, Piero believed in scientific perspective as the basis of painting. In a rigorous mathematical treatise, the first of its kind, he demonstrated how it applied to stereometric bodies and architectural shapes, and to the human form. This mathematical outlook permeates all his work. When he drew a head, an arm, or a piece of drapery, he saw them as variations or compounds of spheres, cylinders, cones, cubes, and pyramids, thus endowing the visible world with some of the impersonal clarity and permanence of stereometric bodies. In this respect, he may be called the earliest ancestor of the abstract artists of our own time, for they, too, work with systematic simplifications of natural forms. It is hardly surprising that Piero's fame is greater today than ever before.

Castagno. Florentine taste developed in a different direction after 1450. We see it in the remarkable *David* (fig. 218) by Andrea del Castagno (c. 1423–1457), which was executed shortly before Piero's Arezzo frescoes. It is painted on a leather shield that was to be used for display, not protection, and its owner probably wanted to convey an analogy between himself and the biblical hero, since David is here defiant as well as victorious. Solid volume and statuesque immobility have given way to graceful movement, conveyed by both the pose and the windblown hair and drapery. The modeling of the figure has been minimized, so that the *David* seems to be in relief rather than in the round, the forms now defined mainly by their outlines.

218. Andrea del Castagno. *David*. c. 1450–57
Leather, surface curved, height 45½" (115.6 cm).
The National Gallery of Art,
Washington, D.C. Widener Collection

Botticelli. This dynamic linear style was to dominate the second half of the century. Its climax comes in the final quarter of the century, in the art of Sandro Botticelli (1444/45–1510), who soon became the favorite painter of the so-called Medici circle: those patricians, literati, scholars, and poets surrounding Lorenzo the Magnificent, the head of the Medici family and, for all practical purposes, the real ruler of the city. For one member of this group, Botticelli did *The Birth of Venus* (fig. 219), his most famous picture. The shallow modeling and the emphasis on outline produce an effect of low relief rather than of solid, three-dimensional shapes. We note, too, a lack of concern with deep space. The grove on the right-hand side of Venus, for example, functions as an ornamental screen. Bodies are attenuated and drained of all weight and muscular power; they seem to float even when they touch the ground. All this seems to deny the basic values of the founders of Early Renaissance art, yet the picture does not look medieval. The bodies, ethereal though they be, retain their voluptuousness. They are genuine nudes enjoying full freedom of movement.

Neo-Platonism. *The Birth of Venus,* in fact, contains the first monumental image since Roman times of the nude goddess in a pose derived from classical statues of Venus. Moreover, the subject of the picture is clearly meant to be serious, even solemn. How could such images be justified in a Christian civilization, without subjecting both artist and patron to the accusation of neo-paganism?

To understand this paradox, we must consider the meaning of our picture, and the general use of classical subjects in Early Renaissance art. During the Middle Ages, classical form had become divorced from classical subject matter. Artists could only draw upon the ancient repertory of poses, gestures, expressions, and types by changing the identity of their sources: philosophers became apostles, Orpheus turned into Adam, Hercules was now Samson. When medieval artists had occasion to represent the pagan gods, they based their pictures on literary descriptions rather than visual models. In the Middle Ages, moreover, classical myths were at times interpreted didactically, however remote the analogy, as allegories of Christian precepts. Europa abducted by the bull, for instance, could be declared to signify the soul redeemed by Christ. But such pallid constructions were hardly an adequate excuse for reinvesting the pagan gods with their ancient beauty and strength.

To fuse the Christian faith with ancient mythology, rather than merely relate them, required a more sophisticated argument. This was provided by the Neo-Platonic philosophers, whose foremost representative, Marsilio Ficino, enjoyed tremendous prestige during the later years of the fifteenth century and after. Ficino's thought was based as much on the mysticism of Plotinus as on the authentic works of Plato. He believed that the life of the universe, including human life, was linked to God by a spiritual circuit continuously ascending and descending, so that all revelation, whether from the Bible, Plato, or classical myths, was one. Similarly, he proclaimed that beauty, love, and beatitude, being phases of this same circuit, were one. Thus Neo-Platonists could invoke the "celestial Venus" (that is, the nude Venus born of the sea, as in our picture) interchangeably with the Virgin Mary, as the source of "divine love" (meaning the cognition of divine beauty). This celestial Venus, according to Ficino, dwells purely in the sphere of Mind, while her twin, the ordinary Venus, engenders "human love."

Once we understand that Botticelli's picture has this quasi-religious meaning, it seems less astonishing that the two wind gods on the left look so much like angels and that the personification of Spring on the right, who welcomes Venus ashore, recalls the traditional relation of St. John to the Saviour in the Baptism of Christ (compare fig. 143). As baptism is a "rebirth in God," the birth of

219. Sandro Botticelli. *The Birth of Venus*. c. 1480. Tempera on canvas, 5′8⅞″ × 9′1⅞″ (1.75 × 2.79 m). Galleria degli Uffizi, Florence

220. Piero di Cosimo. *The Discovery of Honey*. c. 1499. Tempera on wood panel, 31¼ × 50⅝″ (79.4 × 128.6 cm). Worcester Art Museum, Massachusetts

Venus evokes the hope for "rebirth" from which the Renaissance takes its name. Thanks to the fluidity of Neo-Platonic doctrine, the number of possible associations to be linked with our painting is vast. All of them, however, like the celestial Venus herself, "dwell in the sphere of Mind," and Botticelli's deity would hardly be a fit vessel for them if she were less ethereal.

Neo-Platonic philosophy and its expression in art were obviously too complex to become popular outside the select and highly educated circle of its devotees. In 1494, the suspicions of ordinary people were confirmed by the friar Girolamo Savonarola, an ardent advocate of religious reform, who gained a huge following with his sermons attacking the "cult of paganism" in the city's ruling circle. Botticelli himself was perhaps a follower of Savonarola and reportedly burned a number of his "pagan" pictures. In his last works—he seems to have stopped painting entirely after 1500—he returned to traditional religious themes but with no essential change in style.

Piero di Cosimo. *The Discovery of Honey* (fig. 220) by Botticelli's younger contemporary Piero di Cosimo (1462–1521) illustrates a view of pagan mythology diametrically opposed to that of the Neo-Platonists. Instead of "spiritualizing" the pagan gods, it brings them down to earth as beings of flesh and blood. In this alternate theory, humanity had slowly risen from a barbaric state through the discoveries and inventions of a few exceptionally gifted individuals. Gratefully remembered by posterity, these were finally accorded the status of gods. St. Augustine subscribed to such a view (which can be traced back to Hellenistic times) without facing all of the implications expressed by ancient authors. The complete theory, which was not revived until the late fifteenth century, postulates a gradual evolution from the animal level, and so conflicts with the scriptural account of Creation. This could be glossed over, however, by making a happy idyll out of the achievements of these pagan "culture heroes" to avoid the impression of complete seriousness, which is exactly what Piero di Cosimo has done in our picture.

Its title refers to the central episode, a group of satyrs busying themselves about an old willow tree. They have discovered a swarm of bees, and are making as much noise as possible with their pots and pans to induce the bees to cluster on one of the branches. The satyrs will then collect the honey, from which they will produce mead. Behind them, to the right, some of their companions are about to discover the source of another fermented beverage; they are climbing trees to collect wild grapes. Beyond is a barren rock, while on the left are gentle hills and a town. This contrast does not imply that the satyrs are city dwellers. It merely juxtaposes civilization, the goal of the future, with untamed nature. Here the "culture hero" is Bacchus, who appears in the lower right-hand corner, a tipsy grin on his face, next to his ladylove, Ariadne. Despite their classical appearance, Bacchus and his companions do not in the least resemble the frenzied revelers of ancient mythology. They have an oddly domestic air, suggesting a fun-loving family clan on a picnic. The brilliant sunlight, the rich colors, and the far-ranging landscape make the scene a still more plausible extension of everyday reality. We can well believe that Piero di Cosimo, in contrast to Botticelli, admired the great Flemish masters, for this landscape would be inconceivable without the strong influence of the *Portinari Altarpiece* (compare fig. 192).

Ghirlandaio. Piero was not the only Florentine painter receptive to the realism of the Flemings. Domenico Ghirlandaio (1449–1494), another contemporary of Botticelli, shared this attitude. His touching panel *An Old Man and His Grandson* (fig. 221), though lacking the pictorial delicacy of Flemish portraits (compare fig. 188), reflects their precise attention to surface texture and facial detail. But no Northern painter could have rendered the tender relationship between the little boy and his grandfather with Ghirlandaio's human understanding. Psychologically, our panel plainly bespeaks its Italian origin.

221. Domenico Ghirlandaio. *An Old Man and His Grandson.* c. 1480. Tempera and oil on wood panel, 24⅛ × 18″ (61.3 × 45.7 cm). Musée du Louvre, Paris

Northern Italy

Mantegna. Florentine masters had been carrying the new style of Early Renaissance art to Venice and to the neighboring city of Padua in northern Italy since the 1420s. Their presence, however, evoked only rather timid local responses until, shortly before 1450, the young Andrea Mantegna (1431–1506) emerged as an independent master. He was first trained by a minor Paduan painter, but his early development was decisively shaped by the impressions he received from locally available Florentine works and (we may assume) by personal contact with Donatello. Next to Masaccio, Mantegna was the most important painter of the Early Renaissance. He, too, was a precocious genius, fully capable at seventeen of executing commissions of his own. Within the next decade, he reached artistic maturity. His greatest achievement, the frescoes in the Church of the Eremitani in Padua, was almost entirely destroyed by acci-

222. Andrea Mantegna. *St. James Led to His Execution.* c. 1455. Fresco. Ovetari Chapel, Church of the Eremitani, Padua. Destroyed 1944

dental bombing during World War II. The scene we reproduce in figure 222, *St. James Led to His Execution,* is the most dramatic of the cycle because of its daring "worm's-eye view" perspective, which is based on the beholder's actual eye-level (the central vanishing point is below the bottom of the picture, somewhat to the right of center). The architectural setting consequently looms large, as in Masaccio's *Trinity* fresco (see fig. 214). Its main feature, a huge triumphal arch, although not a copy of any known Roman monument, looks so authentic in every detail that it might as well be.

Here Mantegna's devotion to the visible remains of antiquity, almost like an archaeologist's, shows his close association with the learned humanists at the University of Padua, who had the same reverence for every word of ancient literature. No Florentine painter or sculptor of the time could have transmitted such an attitude to him. The same desire for authenticity can be seen in the costumes of the Roman soldiers (compare fig. 97); it even extends to the use of "wet" drapery patterns, inherited by the Romans from Classical Greek sculpture (see fig. 72). But the tense figures, lean and firmly constructed, and especially their dramatic interaction, clearly derive from Donatello. Mantegna's subject hardly demands this agitated staging. The saint, on the way to his execution, blesses a paralytic and commands him to walk. Many of the bystanders express by glance and gesture how deeply the miracle has stirred them. The large crowd generates an extraordinary emotional tension that erupts into real physical violence on the far right, as the great spiral curl of the banner echoes the turbulence below.

Bellini. If Mantegna was a master of powerful drama, his brother-in-law in Venice, Giovanni Bellini (c. 1431–1516), was a poet of light and color. Bellini was slow to mature; his finest pictures, such as *St. Francis in Ecstasy* (fig. 223), date from the final decades of the century and later. The saint is here so small in comparison to the setting that he seems almost incidental, yet his mystic rapture before the beauty of the visible world sets our own response to the view that is spread out before us, ample and intimate at the same time. He has left his wooden pattens behind and stands barefoot on holy ground (see p. 43). The contours in Bellini's work are less brittle than those in Mantegna's, the colors are softer and the light more glowing. Bellini's interest in lyrical, light-filled landscape testifies to the impact of the great Flemish painters; they were much admired in Venice, which had strong trade links with the North. Bellini surely knew their work, and he shares their tender regard for every detail of nature. Unlike the Northerners, however, he can define the beholder's spatial relationship to the landscape. The rock formations of the foreground are structurally clear and firm, like architecture rendered by the rules of scientific perspective.

223. Giovanni Bellini. *St. Francis in Ecstasy*. c. 1485. Oil and tempera on panel, 49 × 55⅞" (124.5 × 141.9 cm). The Frick Collection, New York (Copyright)

224. Pietro Perugino. *The Delivery of the Keys.* 1482. Fresco. Sistine Chapel, The Vatican, Rome

Rome

Perugino. Rome, long neglected during the papal exile in Avignon (see p. 184), once more became an important center of art patronage. In the later fifteenth century, as the papacy regained its political power on Italian soil, the occupants of the Chair of St. Peter began to beautify both the Vatican and the city, in the conviction that the monuments of Christian Rome must outshine those of the pagan past. The most ambitious pictorial project of those years was the decoration of the walls of the Sistine Chapel around 1482. Among the artists who carried out this large cycle of Old and New Testament scenes we encounter most of the important painters of Central Italy, including Botticelli and Ghirlandaio, although these frescoes do not, on the whole, represent their best work.

There is, however, one exception: *The Delivery of the Keys* (fig. 224) by Pietro Perugino (c. 1450–1523) ranks as his finest achievement. Born near Perugia in Umbria (the region southeast of Tuscany), he maintained close ties with Florence. His early development was decisively influenced by Verrocchio, as the statuesque balance and solidity of the figures in *The Delivery of the Keys* suggest. The gravely symmetrical design conveys the special importance of the subject in this setting: the authority of St. Peter as the first pope, and that of all his successors, rests on his having received the keys to the Kingdom of Heaven from Christ Himself. Several contemporaries, with powerfully individualized features, witness the solemn event. Equally striking is the vast expanse of the background, its two Roman triumphal arches flanking a domed structure in which we recognize the ideal church of Alberti's *Treatise on Architecture*. The spatial clarity, achieved by the mathematically exact perspective of this view, is the heritage of Piero della Francesca, who spent much of his later life working for Umbrian clients, notably the duke of Urbino. And also from Urbino, shortly before 1500, Perugino received a pupil whose fame would soon outshine his own: Raphael, the most classic master of the High Renaissance.

THE HIGH RENAISSANCE IN ITALY

It used to be taken for granted that the High Renaissance followed upon the Early Renaissance as naturally and inevitably as noon follows morning. The great masters of the sixteenth century—Leonardo, Bramante, Michelangelo, Raphael, Giorgione, Titian—were thought to have shared the ideals of their predecessors, but to have expressed them so completely that their names became synonyms for perfection. They brought Renaissance art to a climax, its classic phase, just as the Periclean age represented the art of ancient Greece at its highest point. Such a view could also explain why these two classic phases were so short: if art is assumed to develop along the pattern of a ballistic curve, its highest point cannot be expected to last more than a moment.

Since the 1920s, art historians have come to realize the limitations of this scheme. When we apply it literally, the High Renaissance becomes so absurdly brief that we wonder whether it happened at all. Moreover, we hardly increase our understanding of the Early Renaissance if we regard it as a "not-yet-perfect High Renaissance," any more than an Archaic Greek statue can be satisfactorily viewed from a classical standpoint. Nor is it very useful to insist that the subsequent post-classical phase, whether Hellenistic or "Late Renaissance," must be decadent. The image of the ballistic curve has now been abandoned, and we have gained a less assured, but also less arbitrary, estimate of what, for lack of another term, we still call the High Renaissance.

In some fundamental respects, we shall find that the High Renaissance was indeed the culmination of the Early Renaissance, while in other respects it represented a departure. Certainly the tendency to view the artist as a sovereign genius, rather than as a devoted artisan, was never stronger than during the first half of the sixteenth century. Plato's concept of genius—the spirit that causes the poet to compose in a "divine frenzy"—had been broadened by Marsilio Ficino and his fellow Neo-Platonists to include the architect, the sculptor, and the painter. Individuals of genius were thought to be set apart from ordinary mortals by the divine inspiration guiding their efforts, and worthy of being called "divine," "immortal," and "creative" (before 1500, *creating*, as distinct from *making*, was the privilege of God alone).

This cult of the genius had a profound effect on the artists of the High Renaissance. It spurred them to vast and ambitious goals, and prompted their awed patrons to support such enterprises. Since these ambitions often went beyond the humanly possible, they were apt to be frustrated by external as well as internal difficulties, leaving artists with a sense of having been defeated by a malevolent fate. At the same time, their faith in the divine origin of inspiration led artists to rely on subjective, rather than objective, standards of truth and beauty. If Early Renaissance artists felt bound by what they believed to be universally valid rules, such as the numerical ratios of musical harmony and the laws of scientific perspective, their High Renaissance successors were less concerned with rational order than with visual effectiveness. They evolved a new drama and a new rhetoric to engage the emotions of the beholder, whether sanctioned or not by classical precedent. In fact, the works of the great High Renaissance masters immediately became classics in their own right, their authority equal to that of the most renowned monuments of antiquity.

Here we encounter a paradox. If the creations of genius are viewed as unique by definition, they cannot be successfully imitated by lesser artists, however worthy they may seem of such imitation. Indeed, unlike the founders of the Early Renaissance, the leading artists of the High Renaissance did not set the pace for a broadly based "period style" that could be practiced on every level of quality. The High Renaissance produced astonishingly few minor masters. It died with those who had created it, or even before.

Leonardo da Vinci

The key monuments of the High Renaissance were all produced between 1495 and 1520, despite the great differences in age of the artists creating them. Bramante, the oldest, was born in 1444, and Titian, the youngest, about 1488–90. Of the six great personalities mentioned above, only Michelangelo and Titian lived beyond 1520. The distinction of being the earliest High Renaissance master belongs to Leonardo da Vinci (1452–1519), not to Bramante. Born in the little Tuscan town of Vinci, Leonardo was trained in Florence by Verrocchio. Conditions there must not have suited him. At the age of thirty he went to work for the duke of Milan as a military engineer, and only secondarily as an architect, sculptor, and painter.

225. Leonardo da Vinci. *The Virgin of the Rocks.* c. 1485. Oil on panel, 75 × 43½″ (190.5 × 110.5 cm). Musée du Louvre, Paris

The Virgin of the Rocks. Soon after arriving in Milan, Leonardo painted *The Virgin of the Rocks* (fig. 225). The figures emerge from the semidarkness of the grotto, enveloped in a moisture-laden atmosphere that delicately veils their forms. This fine haze (called *sfumato*), more pronounced than similar effects in Flemish and Venetian painting, lends a peculiar warmth and intimacy to the scene. It also creates a remote, dreamlike quality, and makes the picture seem a poetic vision rather than an image of reality. The subject of the infant St. John adoring the Infant Christ in the presence of the Virgin and an angel is without immediate precedent, and Leonardo's treatment is mysterious in many ways. The secluded, rocky setting, the pool in front, and the plant life, carefully chosen and exquisitely rendered, all hint at symbolic meanings that are somehow hard to define. On what level, or levels, of significance are we to interpret the relationships among the four figures? Perhaps the key is the interplay of gestures. Protective, pointing, blessing, they tellingly convey the wonderment of St. John's recognition of Christ as the Saviour, but with a tenderness that raises the scene above the merely doctrinal.

The Last Supper. Despite its originality, *The Virgin of the Rocks* does not yet differ clearly in conception from the aims of the Early Renaissance. Leonardo's *The Last Supper* (fig. 226),

226. Leonardo da Vinci. *The Last Supper.* c. 1495–98. Tempera wall mural, 15′2″ × 28′10″ (4.62 × 8.79 m). Sta. Maria delle Grazie, Milan

later by a dozen years, has always been recognized as the first classic statement of the ideals of High Renaissance painting. Unhappily, the famous mural began to deteriorate a few years after its completion. The artist was dissatisfied with the limitations of the traditional fresco technique, and experimented in an oil-tempera medium that did not adhere well to the wall. We thus need some effort to imagine its original splendor. What remains is sufficient to account for its tremendous impact. Viewing the composition as a whole, we are struck at once by its balanced stability. Only afterward do we discover that this balance has been achieved by the reconciliation of competing, even conflicting, claims that no previous artist had attempted.

Leonardo began with the figure composition, and the architecture had merely a supporting role from the start. Hence, it is the very opposite of the rational pictorial space of the Early Renaissance. The central vanishing point, which governs our view of the interior, is located behind the head of Christ in the exact middle of the picture, and thus becomes charged with symbolic significance. Equally plain is the symbolic function of the main opening in the back wall: its projecting pediment acts as the architectural equivalent of a halo. We thus tend to see the perspective framework of the scene almost entirely in relation to the figures, rather than as a preexisting entity. How vital this relationship is can be seen by covering the upper third of the picture. The composition then takes on the character of a frieze, and the grouping of the apostles is less clear. Above all, the calm triangular shape of Christ becomes merely passive, instead of acting as a physical and spiritual force.

The Saviour, presumably, has just spoken the fateful words, "One of you shall betray me," and the disciples are asking, "Lord, is it I?" We actually see nothing that contradicts this interpretation, but to view the scene as one particular moment in a psychological drama hardly does justice to Leonardo's intentions. These went well beyond a literal rendering of the biblical narrative, for he crowded together all the disciples on the far side of the table, in a space quite inadequate for so many people. He clearly wanted to condense his subject physically by the compact, monumental grouping of the figures, and spiritually by presenting several levels of meaning at one time. The gesture of Christ is one of submission to the divine will, and of offering. It is a hint at Christ's main act at the Last Supper, the institution of the Eucharist: "And as they were eating, Jesus took bread

227. Leonardo da Vinci. *Mona Lisa.* c. 1503–5.
Oil on panel, 30¼ × 21″ (76.8 × 53.3 cm). Musée du Louvre, Paris

. . . and gave it to the disciples, and said, Take and eat; this is my body. And he took the cup . . . saying, Drink ye all of it; for this is my blood. . . ." The apostles do not merely react to these words. Each of them reveals his own personality, his own relationship to the Saviour. For example, although Judas is not segregated from the rest, his dark, defiant profile sets him apart well enough. They exemplify what the artist wrote in one of his notebooks, that the highest and most difficult aim of painting is to depict "the intention of man's soul" through gestures and movements of the limbs. This dictum is to be interpreted as referring not to momentary emotional states but to the inner life as a whole.

Mona Lisa. In 1499, the duchy of Milan fell to the French, and Leonardo, after brief trips to Mantua and Venice, returned to Florence. He must have found the cultural climate very different from his recollections of it. The Medici had been expelled, and the city was briefly a republic again, until their return.

There Leonardo painted his most famous portrait, the *Mona Lisa* (fig. 227). The delicate *sfumato* of *The Virgin of the Rocks* is here so perfected that it seemed miraculous to the artist's contemporaries. The forms are built from layers of glazes so gossamer-thin that the entire panel seems to glow with a gentle light from within. But the fame of the *Mona Lisa* comes not from this pictorial subtlety alone. Even more intriguing is the psychological fascination of the sitter's personality. Why, among all the smiling faces ever painted, has this particular one been singled out as "mysterious"? Perhaps the reason is that, as a portrait, the picture does not fit our expectations. The features are too individual for Leonardo to have simply depicted an ideal type. The sitter has recently been identified as the wife of a Florentine merchant; yet the element of idealization is so strong that it blurs her character. Once again the artist has brought two opposites into harmonious balance. The smile, also, may be read in two ways: as the echo of a momentary mood, and as a timeless, symbolic expression, akin to the "Archaic smile" of the Greeks (see fig. 66). The *Mona Lisa* seemingly embodies a quality of maternal tenderness, which was to Leonardo the essence of womanhood. Even the landscape in the background, composed mainly of rocks and water, suggests elemental generative forces.

Architecture. Contemporary sources attest that Leonardo was esteemed as an architect. Actual building seems to have concerned him less, however, than problems of structure and design. The numerous architectural projects in his drawings were intended, for the most part, to remain on paper. Nonetheless, these sketches, especially those of his Milanese period, have great historic importance, for only in them can we trace the transition from the Early to the High Renaissance in architecture.

The domed, centrally planned churches of the type illustrated in figure 228 hold particular interest for us. The plan recalls Early Renaissance structures, but the new relationship of the spatial units is more complex,

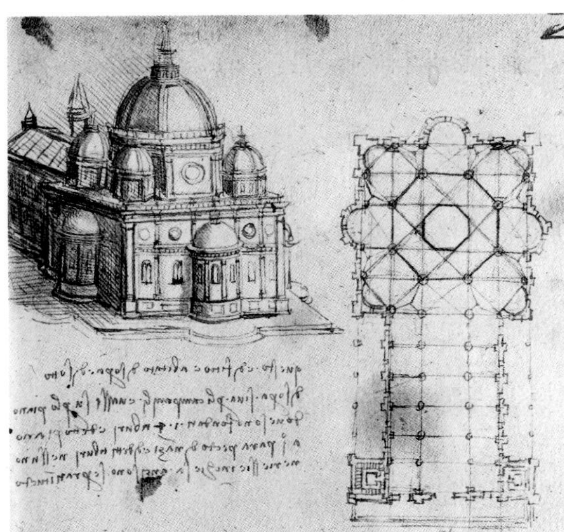

228. Leonardo da Vinci. *Project for a Church* (Ms. B). c. 1490. Pen drawing. Bibliothèque de l'Arsenal, Paris

while the exterior, with its cluster of domes, is more monumental than any earlier fifteenth-century building. In conception, this design stands halfway between the dome of Florence Cathedral and the most ambitious structure of the sixteenth century, the new basilica of St. Peter's in Rome (compare figs. 162, 229, and 230). It gives evidence, too, of Leonardo's close contact during the 1490s with the architect Donato Bramante (1444–1514), who was then also working for the duke of Milan. After Milan fell to the French, Bramante went to Rome where, during the last fifteen years of his life, he became the creator of High Renaissance architecture.

Bramante

St. Peter's. Most of the great achievements that made Rome the center of Italian art during the first quarter of the sixteenth century belong to the decade 1503–13, which corresponded to the papacy of Julius II. It was he who decided to replace the old basilica of St. Peter's, which had long been in precarious condition, with a church so magnificent as to overshadow all the monuments of ancient imperial Rome. The task fell to Bramante, who had established himself as the foremost architect in the city. His original design, of 1506, is

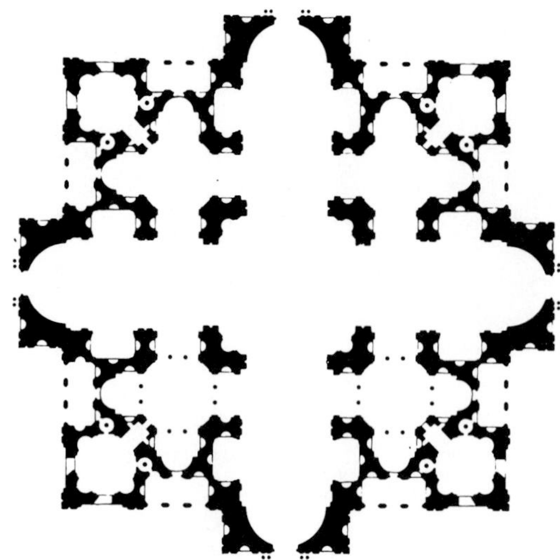

229. Donato Bramante. Original plan for St. Peter's, Rome. 1506 (after Geymuller)

230. Caradosso. Bronze medal showing Bramante's design for St. Peter's. 1506. British Museum, London

known to us only from a plan (fig. 229) and from the medal commemorating the start of the building campaign (fig. 230), which shows the exterior in rather imprecise perspective. These, however, bear out the words Bramante reportedly used to define his aim: "I shall place the Pantheon on top of the Basilica of Constantine."

The goal of surpassing the two most famous structures of Roman antiquity with a Christian edifice of unexampled grandeur testifies to the vast ambition of Julius II, who wanted to unite all Italy under his command and thus to gain temporal power matching the spiritual authority of his office. Bramante's design is indeed of truly imperial magnificence. A huge, hemispherical dome crowns the crossing of the barrel-vaulted arms of a Greek cross, with four lesser domes and tall corner towers filling the angles. This plan fulfills all the demands laid down by Alberti for sacred architecture (see p. 226). Based entirely on the circle and the square, it is so rigidly symmetrical that we cannot tell which apse was to hold the high altar. Bramante envisioned four identical facades like that on the medal of 1506, dominated by severely classical forms—domes, half-domes, colonnades, pediments.

These simple geometric shapes, however, do not prevail inside the church. Here the "sculptured wall" reigns supreme. The plan shows no continuous surfaces, only great, oddly shaped "islands" of masonry that have been well described by one critic as giant pieces of toast half-eaten by a voracious space. The huge size of these "islands" can be visualized only when we realize that each arm of the Greek cross has about the dimensions of the Basilica of Constantine (see figs. 89, 90). Bramante's reference to the Pantheon and the Basilica of Constantine was, then, no idle boast. His plan dwarfs these monuments, as well as every Early Renaissance church.

Michelangelo

The concept of genius as divine inspiration, a superhuman power granted to a few rare individuals and acting through them, is nowhere exemplified more fully than in the life and work of Michelangelo (1475–1564). Not only his admirers viewed him in this light. He himself, steeped in the tradition of Neo-Platonism (see pp. 235–37), accepted the idea of his genius as a living reality, although it seemed to him at times a curse rather than a blessing. The element that brings continuity to his long and stormy career is the sovereign power of his personality, his faith in the subjective rightness of everything he created.

Conventions, standards, and traditions might be observed by lesser spirits, but he could acknowledge no authority higher than the dictates of his genius.

Unlike Leonardo, for whom painting was the noblest of the arts because it embraced every visible aspect of the world, Michelangelo was a sculptor to the core; more specifically, he was a carver of marble statues. Art, for him, was not a science but "the making of men," analogous (however imperfectly) to divine creation. Hence, the limitations of sculpture that Leonardo condemned were essential virtues in Michelangelo's eyes. Only the "liberation" of real, three-dimensional bodies from recalcitrant matter could satisfy his urge (for his procedure, see p. 11). Painting, for him, should imitate the roundness of sculptured forms, and architecture, too, must partake of the organic qualities of the human figure.

Michelangelo's faith in the human image as the supreme vehicle of expression gave him the strongest sense of kinship with Classical sculpture of any Renaissance artist. Among recent masters he admired Giotto, Masaccio, and Donatello, more than the men he knew as a youth in Florence. Nevertheless, his mind was decisively shaped by the cultural climate of Florence during the 1480s and 1490s. Both the Neo-Platonism of Marsilio Ficino and the religious reforms of Savonarola affected him profoundly. These conflicting influences reinforced the tensions within Michelangelo's personality, his violent changes of mood, his sense of being at odds with himself and with the world. As he conceived his statues to be human bodies released from their marble prison, so the body was the earthly prison of the soul—noble, surely, but a prison nevertheless. This dualism of body and spirit endows his figures with their extraordinary pathos. Outwardly calm, they seem stirred by an overwhelming psychic energy that has no release in physical action.

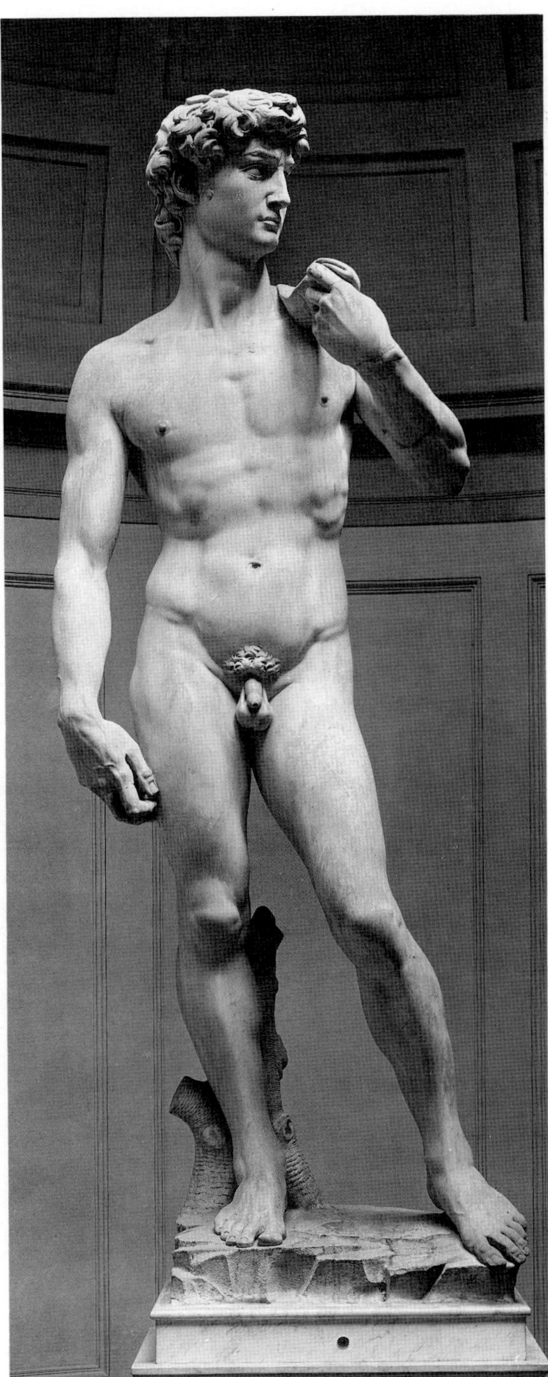

231. Michelangelo. *David.* 1501–4. Marble, height of figure 13′5″ (4.09 m). Galleria dell'Accademia, Florence

David. The unique qualities of Michelangelo's art are fully present in his *David* (fig. 231), the earliest monumental statue of the High Renaissance. Commissioned in 1501, when the artist was twenty-six, the huge figure was designed to be placed high above the ground, on one of the buttresses of Florence Cathedral. The city fathers chose instead to put it in front

232. Interior of the Sistine Chapel showing Michelangelo's ceiling fresco. The Vatican, Rome

of the Palazzo Vecchio, the fortresslike palace of the Medici near the center of town, as the civic-patriotic symbol of the Florentine republic (it has since been replaced by a modern copy).

We can well understand their decision. By omitting the head of Goliath, Michelangelo transforms his *David* from a victorious hero into the champion of a just cause. Vibrant with pent-up energy, he faces the world like Donatello's *St. George* (see fig. 201), although his nudity links him as well to the older master's bronze *David* (see fig. 203). The style of the figure nonetheless proclaims an ideal very different from the wiry slenderness of Donatello's youths. Michelangelo had just spent several years in Rome, where he had been deeply impressed with the emotion-charged,

233. Michelangelo. *The Creation of Adam,* portion of the Sistine Ceiling. 1508–12. Fresco

muscular bodies of Hellenistic sculpture. Their heroic scale, their superhuman beauty and power, and the swelling volume of their forms became part of Michelangelo's own style and, through him, of Renaissance art in general. The *David* could never be taken for an ancient statue, however. In Hellenistic statues (compare fig. 77) the body "acts out" the spirit's agony, while the *David,* at once calm and tense, shows the action-in-repose so characteristic of Michelangelo.

The Sistine Chapel. Soon after, Michelangelo was called to Rome by Pope Julius II, the greatest and most ambitious of Renaissance popes, for whom he designed an enormous tomb. After a few years, the pope changed his mind and set the reluctant artist to work instead on the ceiling fresco of the Sistine Chapel (fig. 232). Driven by his desire to resume work on the tomb, as well as by pressure from Julius II, Michelangelo completed the entire ceiling in four years, 1508–12. He produced a masterpiece of truly epochal importance. The ceiling is a huge organism with hundreds of figures rhythmically distributed within the painted architectural framework, dwarfing the earlier murals (see fig. 224) by its size, and still more by its compelling inner unity. In the central area, subdivided by five pairs of girders, are nine scenes from Genesis, from the Creation of the World to the Drunkenness of Noah (at the far end of the chapel in our illustration).

The theological scheme of these scenes is accompanied by a complex array of nude youths, prophets, sibyls (see figs. 5, 6), medallions, and scenes in the spandrels. This rich program has not been fully explained, but we know that it links early history and the coming of Christ, the beginning of time and its end. We do not know how much responsibility Michelangelo had for the program, but he was not a man to submit to dictation. The subject matter of the ceiling, moreover, fits his cast of mind so perfectly that his own desires cannot have conflicted strongly with those of his patron. What greater theme could he wish than the Creation of the World, the Fall of Man, and our ultimate reconciliation with the Lord?

The Creation of Adam (fig. 233) must have stirred Michelangelo's imagination most deeply. It shows not the physical molding of Adam's body but the passage of the divine spark—the soul—and thus achieves a dramatic juxtaposition of Man and God unrivaled by any other artist. The dynamism of Michelangelo's design contrasts the earthbound Adam and the figure of God rushing through the sky. This relationship becomes even more meaningful when we realize that

Adam strains not only toward his Creator but also toward Eve, whom he sees, yet unborn, in the shelter of the Lord's left arm. Michelangelo has been called a poor colorist, quite unjustly as the recently undertaken cleaning of the frescoes has revealed. *The Creation of Adam* shows the bold, intense hues typical of the whole ceiling. The range of Michelangelo's palette is astonishing. Contrary to what had been thought, the heroic figures have anything but the quality of painted sculpture. Full of life, they act out their epic roles in illusionistic "windows" that puncture the architectural setting. Michelangelo does not simply color the areas within the contours but builds up his forms from broad and vigorous brushstrokes in the tradition of Giotto and Masaccio.

The Last Judgment. When Michelangelo returned to the Sistine Chapel in 1534, over twenty years later, the Western world was enduring the spiritual and political crisis of the Reformation (see pp. 281–82). We perceive with shocking directness how the mood has changed as we turn from the radiant vitality of Michelangelo's ceiling fresco to the somber vision of his *Last Judgment.* The Blessed and Damned alike huddle together in tight clumps, pleading for mercy before a wrathful God. Straddling a cloud just below the Lord is the Apostle Bartholomew, holding a human skin to represent his martyrdom by flaying (fig. 234). The face on that skin, however, is not the saint's but Michelangelo's own. In this grimly sardonic self-portrait, so well hidden that it was recognized only in modern times, the artist has left his personal confession of guilt and unworthiness.

234. Michelangelo. *The Last Judgment* (detail, with self-portrait). 1534–41. Fresco. Sistine Chapel, The Vatican, Rome

The Medici Chapel. The interval between the Sistine Ceiling and *The Last Judgment* coincides with the papacies of Leo X (1513–21) and Clement VII (1523–34). Both were members of the Medici family and preferred to employ Michelangelo in Florence. His activities centered on S. Lorenzo, the Medici church, where Leo X decided to build a chapel to house four tombs. Michelangelo took early charge of this project and worked on it for fourteen years, completing the architecture and two of the tombs. The design of the tomb of Giuliano (fig. 235) still shows some kinship with such Early Renaissance tombs as that of Leonardo Bruni (see fig. 207), but the differences weigh more heavily. There is no inscription, and the effigy has been replaced by two allegorical figures: *Day* on the right, *Night* on the left. The statue of Giuliano, in classical military garb, bears no resemblance to the deceased Medici. ("A thousand years from now, nobody will know what he looked like," Michelangelo is said to have remarked.) What is the meaning of this triad? The question, put countless times, has never found a satisfactory answer. Michelangelo's plans for the Medici tombs underwent so many changes of form and program while the work was under way that the present state of the monuments can hardly be the final solution. In fact, the dynamic process of design was halted by the artist's departure for Rome in 1534. *Day* and *Night* were certainly designed to rest on horizontal surfaces, not the curved,

235. Michelangelo. Tomb of Giuliano de'Medici. 1524–34. Marble, height of central figure 71″ (180.3 cm). New Sacristy, S. Lorenzo, Florence

sloping lid of the present sarcophagus. Perhaps they were not even intended for this particular tomb. Nevertheless, the tomb of Giuliano remains a compelling visual unit. The great triangle of the statues is held in place by a network of verticals and horizontals whose slender, sharp-edged forms heighten the roundness and weight of the sculpture. *Giuliano,* the ideal image of the prince, is a counterpart of the *David.* The reclining figures contrast in mood, embodying the quality of action-in-repose more dramatically than any other works by Michelangelo. In the brooding menace of *Day,* and in the disturbed slumber of *Night,* the dualism of body and soul is expressed with unforgettable grandeur.

St. Peter's. The construction of St. Peter's progressed at so slow a pace that in 1514, when Bramante died, only the four crossing piers had actually been built. For the next three decades the campaign was carried on hesitantly by architects trained under Bramante, who modified his design in a number of ways. A new and decisive phase in the history of St. Peter's began only in 1546, when Michelangelo took charge. The present appearance of the church (fig. 236) is largely shaped by his ideas. Michelangelo simplified Bramante's complex plan without changing its centralized character. He also redesigned the exterior. Unlike Bramante's many-layered elevation (see fig. 230), Michelangelo's uses a colossal order of pilasters to emphasize the compact body of the structure, thereby setting off the dome more dramatically. We have encountered the colossal order before, on the facade of Alberti's S. Andrea (see fig. 212), but it was Michelangelo who welded it into a fully coherent system. The same desire for compactness and organic unity led Michelangelo to simplify the interior, again without changing its basic character. The dome, although largely built after his death, reflects his ideas in every important respect.

236. Michelangelo. St. Peter's (view from the west), Rome. 1546–64 (dome completed by Giacomo della Porta, 1590)

237. Raphael. *The School of Athens.* 1510–11. Fresco. Stanza della Segnatura, Vatican Palace, Rome

Bramante had planned his dome as a stepped hemisphere above a narrow drum, which would have seemed to press down on the church below. Michelangelo's conveys the opposite sensation, a powerful thrust that draws energy upward from the main body of the structure. The high drum, the strongly projecting buttresses accented by double columns, the ribs, the raised curve of the cupola, the tall lantern—all contribute to this verticality. Michelangelo borrowed both the double-shell construction and the Gothic profile from the Florence Cathedral dome (see fig. 162), but to immensely different effect. The smooth planes of Brunelleschi's dome give no hint of the internal stresses, while Michelangelo finds a sculptured shape for these contending forces and relates them to those in the rest of the building. (The impulse of the paired colossal pilasters below is taken up by the double columns of the drum, continues in the ribs, and culminates in the lantern.) The logic of this design is so persuasive that few domes built between 1600 and 1900 fail to acknowledge it in some way.

Raphael

If Michelangelo exemplifies the solitary genius, Raphael (1483–1520) belongs just as surely to the opposite type: the artist as a person of the world. The contrast between the two was as clear to their contemporaries as it is to us. Although each had his partisans, they enjoyed equal fame. Today our sympathies are less evenly divided:

> In the room the women come and go
> Talking of Michelangelo.
>
> *(T. S. Eliot)*

So do a lot of us, including the authors of historical novels and fictionalized biographies, while Raphael is usually discussed only by historians of art. The younger master's career is too much a success story, his work too marked by seemingly effortless grace, to match the tragic heroism of Michelangelo. As an innovator, Raphael seems to contribute less than Leonardo, Bramante, and Michelangelo, the three artists whose achievements were basic to his. Nevertheless, he is the central painter of the High Renaissance. Our conception of the entire style rests more on his work than on any other master's.

The genius of Raphael was a unique power of synthesis that enabled him to merge the qualities of Leonardo and Michelangelo, creating an art at once lyric and dramatic, pictorially rich and sculpturally solid. The full force of Michelangelo's influence can be felt only in Raphael's Roman works, rather than in the early ones from Perugia and Florence. At the time Michelangelo began to paint the Sistine Ceiling, Julius II summoned the younger artist to Rome and commissioned him to decorate a series of rooms in the Vatican Palace. The first room, the Stanza della Segnatura, may have housed the pope's library, and Raphael's cycle of frescoes on its walls and ceiling refers to the four domains of learning: theology, philosophy, law, and the arts.

The School of Athens. Of these frescoes, *The School of Athens* (fig. 237) has long been acknowledged as Raphael's masterpiece and the

238. Raphael. *Galatea.* 1513. Fresco. Villa Farnesina, Rome

perfect embodiment of the classical spirit of the High Renaissance. Its subject is "the Athenian school of thought," a group of famous Greek philosophers gathered around Plato and Aristotle, each in a characteristic pose or activity. Raphael must have already seen the Sistine Ceiling, then nearing completion. He evidently owes to Michelangelo the expressive energy, the physical power, and the dramatic grouping of his figures. Raphael has not simply borrowed Michelangelo's repertory of gestures and poses. He has absorbed it into his own style, and thereby given it different meaning.

Body and spirit, action and emotion, are now balanced harmoniously, and every member of this great assembly plays his role with magnificent, purposeful clarity. The total conception of *The School of Athens* suggests the spirit of Leonardo's *The Last Supper* (see fig. 226) rather than the Sistine Ceiling. This holds true of the way Raphael makes each philosopher reveal "the intention of his soul," distinguishes the relations among individuals and groups, and links them in formal rhythm. Also Leonardesque is the centralized, symmetrical design, and the interdependence of the figures and their architectural setting. With its lofty dome, barrel vault, and colossal statuary, Raphael's classical edifice shares far more of the compositional burden than the hall of *The Last Supper.* Inspired by Bramante, it seems like an advance view of the new St. Peter's. Its geometric precision and spatial grandeur bring to a climax the tradition begun by Masaccio, continued by Domenico Veneziano and Piero della Francesca, and transmitted to Raphael by his teacher Perugino.

Galatea. Raphael never again set so splendid an architectural stage. To create pictorial space, he relied increasingly on the movement of human figures, rather than perspective vistas. In the *Galatea* of 1513 (fig. 238), the subject is again classical—the beautiful nymph Galatea, vainly pursued by the cyclops Polyphemus, belongs to Greek mythology—but here the exuberant and sensuous aspect of antiquity is celebrated, in contrast to the austere idealism of *The School of Athens.* Its composition recalls *The Birth of Venus* (see fig. 219) by Botticelli, a picture Raphael knew from his Florentine days; yet their very resemblance emphasizes their profound dissimilarity. Raphael's full-bodied, dynamic figures take on their expansive spiral movement from the vigorous *contrapposto* of Galatea, whereas in Botticelli's picture, the movement is not generated by the figures but imposed on them from without, so that it never detaches itself from the surface of the canvas.

Giorgione

The distinction between Early and High Renaissance art, so marked in Florence and Rome, is far less sharp in Venice. Giorgione (1478–1510), the first Venetian painter to belong to the new, sixteenth century, left the orbit of Giovanni Bellini only during the final years of his short career. Among his very few mature works, *The Tempest* (fig. 239) is both the most individual and the most enigmatic. Our first glance may show us little more than a particularly charming reflection of Bellinesque qualities, familiar from the *St. Francis in Ecstasy* (see fig. 223). The difference is one of mood, and in *The Tempest* this mood is subtly, pervasively pagan. Bellini's landscape is meant to be seen through the eyes of St. Francis, as a piece of God's creation. Giorgione's figures, by contrast, do not interpret the scene for us. Belonging themselves to nature, they are passive witnesses of the thunderstorm about to engulf them. Who are they? So far, the young soldier and the nude mother with her baby have refused to disclose their identity, and the subject of the picture remains unknown. The present title is a confession of embarrassment, but it is not inappropriate, for the only "action" is that of the tempest. Whatever its intended meaning, the scene is like an enchanted idyll, a dream of pastoral beauty soon to be swept away. Only poets had hitherto captured this air of nostalgic reverie. Now, it entered the repertory of the painter. Thus, *The Tempest* initiates what was to become an important new tradition.

239. Giorgione. *The Tempest.* c. 1505. Oil on canvas, 31¼ × 28¾" (79.4 × 73 cm). Galleria dell'Accademia, Venice

Titian

Giorgione died before he could explore in full the sensuous, lyrical world he had created in *The Tempest.* He bequeathed this task to Titian (1488/90–1576), who was decisively influenced by Giorgione and surely worked in his studio. An artist of extraordinary gifts, Titian dominated Venetian painting for the next half-century.

Bacchanal. Titian's *Bacchanal* of about 1518 (fig. 240) is frankly pagan, inspired by an ancient author's description of such a revel.

240. Titian. *Bacchanal.* c. 1518. Oil on canvas, 5′8⅞″ × 6′4″ (1.75 × 1.93 m). Museo del Prado, Madrid

The landscape, rich in contrasts of cool and warm tones, has all the poetry of Giorgione's *The Tempest,* but the figures are of another breed. Active and muscular, they move with a joyous freedom that recalls Raphael's *Galatea* (see fig. 238). By this time, many of Raphael's compositions had been engraved (see fig. 368), and from these reproductions Titian became familiar with the High Renaissance in Rome, which he was soon to absorb at firsthand. A number of the celebrants in his *Bacchanal* also reflect the influence of classical art. Titian's approach to antiquity, however, is very different from Raphael's. He visualizes the realm of classical myths as part of the natural world, inhabited not by animated statues but by beings of flesh and blood. The figures of the *Bacchanal* are idealized beyond everyday reality just enough to persuade us that they belong to a long-lost golden age. They invite us to share their blissful state in a way that makes Raphael's *Galatea* seem cold and remote by comparison.

Portraits. Titian's prodigious gifts made him the most sought-after portraitist of the age. The dreamy intimacy of *Man with a Glove* (fig. 241), with its soft outline and deep shadows, still reflects the style of Giorgione. Lost in thought, the young man seems quite

241. Titian. *Man with a Glove*. c. 1520. Oil on canvas, 39½×35″ (100.3×88.9 cm). Musée du Louvre, Paris

242. Titian. *Christ Crowned with Thorns*. c. 1570. Oil on canvas, 9′2″×6′ (2.79×1.83 m). Pinakothek, Munich

unaware of us. The slight melancholy in his features conjures up the poetic appeal of *The Tempest*. The breadth and power of form, however, goes far beyond Giorgione. In Titian's hands, the possibilities of oil technique now are fully realized: rich, creamy highlights, deep dark tones that are transparent and delicately modulated. The separate brushstrokes, hardly visible before, become increasingly free, so that the personal rhythms of the artist's "handwriting" are an essential element of the finished work. In this respect, Titian seems infinitely more "modern" than Leonardo, Michelangelo, or Raphael.

Late Works. A change of pictorial technique is no mere surface phenomenon. It always reflects a change of the artist's aim. This correspondence of form and technique is especially clear in *Christ Crowned with Thorns* (fig. 242), a masterpiece of Titian's old age. The shapes emerging from the semidarkness now consist wholly of light and color. Despite the heavy impasto, the shimmering surfaces have lost every trace of material solidity and seem translucent, aglow from within. In consequence, the violent physical action has been miraculously suspended. What lingers in our minds is not the drama but the strange mood of serenity engendered by deep religious feeling. The painting participates in a visionary tendency that was widely shared by other late-sixteenth-century Venetian artists. We shall meet it again in the work of Tintoretto and El Greco.

MANNERISM AND OTHER TRENDS

What happened after the High Renaissance? Eighty years ago the answer would have been that the High Renaissance was followed by the Late Renaissance, which lasted from about 1520 until the Baroque style emerged at the end of the century. This span was regarded as a period only in the negative sense of an interval between two high points, much as the Renaissance viewed the Middle Ages. According to such an interpretation, this interim was dominated by shallow imitators of the great masters of the previous generation. Today we have a far more positive attitude toward the artists who reached maturity after 1520, and generally discard the term "Late Renaissance" as misleading, but we have yet to agree on a name for the eighty years separating the High Renaissance from the Baroque. We have run into this difficulty before, in dealing with the problem of Late Classical versus Hellenistic art (see pp. 85–89). Our dilemma is that any label implies that the period has only a single style, but nobody has succeeded in defining one for the years 1520–1600. This period was a time of crisis that gave rise to several competing tendencies rather than one dominant ideal. And because it was full of inner contradictions, not unlike the present, it remains peculiarly fascinating to us.

PAINTING

Mannerism in Florence and Rome

Among the various trends in art in the wake of the High Renaissance, Mannerism is the most significant, as well as the most problematic. In scope, the original meaning of the term was narrow and derogatory, designating a group of mid-sixteenth-century painters in Rome and Florence whose self-consciously "artificial," mannered style was derived from certain aspects of Raphael and Michelangelo. Mannerism was the assertion of a purely aesthetic ideal. Through formulaic abstraction, it translated form and expression into a style of the utmost refinement that emphasized grace, variety, and virtuoso display at the expense of content, clarity, and unity. This taste for affected elegance and bizarre conceits necessarily appealed to a small but sophisticated audience, but in a larger sense Mannerism signifies a major change in Italian culture. The quest for originality as a projection of the individual's personality had a liberating influence that gave artists license to explore their imaginations freely. This investigation of new modes was ultimately healthy, although the style itself came to be regarded as decadent. Given such subjective freedom, it is hardly surprising that Mannerism produced extreme personalities which today seem the most "modern" of all sixteenth-century artists.

The seemingly cold and barren formalism of their work has been recognized as a special form of a wider movement that placed "inner vision," however private or fantastic, above the twin standard of nature and the ancients. Hence, some scholars have broadened the definition of Mannerism to include the later style of Michelangelo, who could himself acknowledge no authority higher than his genius. Ironically, Mannerism is often considered a reaction against the ideals created by

243. Rosso Fiorentino. *The Descent from the Cross.* 1521. Panel, 11′ × 6′5½″ (3.1 × 1.92 m). Pinacoteca Communale, Volterra

the High Renaissance as well. Save for a brief initial phase, however, Mannerism did not consciously reject the tradition from which it stemmed. Although the subjectivity inherent in this aesthetic was necessarily unclassical, it was not deliberately anticlassical, except in its more extreme manifestations. The relation of Mannerism to religious trends was equally paradoxical. Despite the continuing importance of religious painting, it has rightly been observed that Mannerism represents the spiritual bankruptcy of the age. Moreover, its extreme worldliness was fundamentally antithetical to both the Reformation, with its stern morality, and the Counter Reformation, which demanded a strict adherence to doctrine. After mid-century, however, the subjective latitude of Mannerism became valued for its visionary power as part of a larger shift in religious sensibility.

244. Parmigianino. *Self-Portrait.* 1524. Oil on panel, diameter 9⅝" (24.5 cm). Kunsthistorisches Museum, Vienna

Rosso. The first signs of disquiet in the High Renaissance appear shortly before 1520 in Florence. Art had been left in the hands of a younger generation that could refine but not further develop the styles of the great innovators who had spent their early careers there. Having absorbed the lessons of the leading masters at one remove, the first generation of Mannerists was free to apply High Renaissance formulas to a new aesthetic divorced from its previous content. By 1521, Rosso Fiorentino (1495–1540), the most eccentric member of this group, expressed the new attitude with full conviction in *The Descent from the Cross* (fig. 243). Nothing has prepared us for the shocking impact of this latticework of spidery forms set against the dark sky. The figures are agitated yet rigid, as if frozen by a sudden, icy blast. Even the draperies have brittle, sharp-edged planes. The acid colors and the light, brilliant but unreal, reinforce the nightmarish effect of the scene. Here is clearly a full-scale revolt against the classical balance of High Renaissance art: a profoundly disquieting, willful, visionary style that indicates a deep inner anxiety.

Parmigianino. The first phase of Mannerism, exemplified by Rosso, was soon replaced by one less overtly anticlassical, less laden with subjective emotion, but equally far removed from the confident, stable world of the High Renaissance. The *Self-Portrait* (fig. 244) by Parmigianino (1503–1540) suggests no psychological turmoil. The artist's appearance is bland and well groomed, veiled by a delicate Leonardesque *sfumato.* The distortions, too, are objective, not arbitrary, for the picture records what Parmigianino saw as he gazed at his reflection in a convex mirror. Why was he so fascinated by this view "through the looking glass"? Earlier painters who used the mirror as an aid to observation had "filtered out" the distortions (see fig. 188), except when the mirror image was contrasted with a direct view of the same scene (see figs. 189, 190). But Parmigianino substitutes his painting for the mirror itself, even employing a specially prepared convex panel. Did he perhaps want to demonstrate that there is no single "correct" reality, that distortion is as natural as the normal appearance of things?

His scientific detachment soon changed into its very opposite. Giorgio Vasari, the artist's biographer, tells us that Parmigianino, as he neared the end of his brief career (he died at thirty-seven), was obsessed with alchemy and became "a bearded, long-haired, neglected, and almost savage or wild man." Certainly his strange imagination is evident in his most famous work, *The Madonna with the Long Neck* (fig. 245), painted after he had returned to his native Parma after several years in Rome. He had been deeply impressed with the rhythmic grace of Raphael's art, but he has transformed the older master's figures into a remarkable new breed. Their limbs, elongated and ivory-smooth, move with effortless languor, embodying an ideal of beauty as remote from nature as any Byzantine figure. Their setting is equally arbitrary, with a gigantic (and apparently purposeless) row of columns looming behind the tiny figure of a prophet. Parmigianino seems determined to prevent us from measuring anything in this picture by the standards of ordinary experience. Here we have approached that "artificial" style for which the term Mannerism was originally coined. *The Madonna with the Long Neck* is a vision of unearthly perfection, its cold elegance no less compelling than the violence in Rosso's *Descent*.

Bronzino. Keyed to a sophisticated, even rarefied taste, the elegant phase of Italian Mannerism appealed particularly to aristocratic patrons like the grand duke of Tuscany and the king of France, and soon became international. The style produced splendid portraits, like that of Eleanora of Toledo (fig. 246), the wife of Cosimo I de'Medici, by his court painter Agnolo Bronzino (1503–1572). The sitter here appears as the member of an exalted social caste, not as an individual personality. Congealed into immobility behind the barrier of her lavishly ornate costume, Eleanora seems more akin to Parmigianino's *Madonna* (compare the hands) than to ordinary flesh and blood.

Mannerism in Venice

Tintoretto. Mannerism did not appear in Venice until the middle of the century; there it became allied to the visionary tendencies already manifest in Titian's late work (see fig. 242). Its leading exponent, Jacopo Tintoretto (1518–1594), was an artist of prodigious energy and inventiveness, who combined qualities of both its anticlassical and elegant phases in his work. He reportedly wanted "to paint like Titian and to design like Michelangelo," but his relationship to these two masters, though real enough, was as peculiar as Parmigianino's was to Raphael. Tintoretto's last major work, *The Last Supper* (fig. 247), is also his most spectacular. This canvas denies in every possible way the classic values of Leonardo's version (see fig. 226), painted almost exactly a century before. Christ, to be sure, still occupies the center of the composition, but now the table is placed at a sharp angle to the picture plane in exaggerated perspective. His small figure in the middle distance is distinguishable mainly by the brilliant halo. Tintoretto has gone to great lengths to give the event an everyday setting, cluttering the scene with attendants, containers of food and drink, and domestic animals. There are also celestial attendants that converge upon Christ just as He offers His body and blood, in the form of bread and wine, to the disciples. The smoke from the blazing oil lamp miraculously turns into clouds of angels, blurring the distinction between the natural and the supernatural and turning the scene into a magnificently orchestrated vision. Tintoretto's main concern has been to make visible the miracle of the Eucharist—the transubstantiation of earthly into divine food—the institution central to Catholic doctrine, which was reasserted during the Counter Reformation. He barely hints at the human drama of Judas' betrayal, so important to Leonardo: Judas can be seen isolated on the near side of the table, but his role is so insignificant that he could almost be mistaken for an attendant.

El Greco. The last, and today most famous, Mannerist painter was also a member of the Venetian school for a while. Domenikos Theotocopoulos (1541–1614), nicknamed El Greco, came from Crete, which was then under Venetian rule. His earliest training must have been from a Cretan artist still working in

245. Parmigianino. *The Madonna with the Long Neck.* c. 1535. Oil on panel, 7′1″ × 4′4″ (2.16 × 1.32 m). Galleria degli Uffizi, Florence

246. Agnolo Bronzino. *Eleanora of Toledo and Her Son Giovanni de'Medici.* c. 1550. Oil on panel, 45¼ × 37¾" (114.9 × 95.9 cm). Galleria degli Uffizi, Florence

the Byzantine tradition. Soon after 1560 El Greco arrived in Venice and quickly absorbed the lessons of Titian, Tintoretto, and other masters. A decade later, in Rome, he came to know the art of Raphael, Michelangelo, and the Central Italian Mannerists. In 1576/77 he went to Spain, settling in Toledo for the rest of his life. There he became established in the leading intellectual circles of the city, then a major center of learning as well as the seat of Catholic reform in Spain. Although it provides the content of his work, Counter Reformation theology does not account for the exalted emotionalism that informs his painting. The spiritual tenor of El Greco's mature work was primarily a response to mysticism, which was especially intense in Spain. Contemporary Spanish painting, however, was too provincial to affect him. His style had already been formed before he arrived in Toledo; nor did he forget his Byzantine background (until the very end of his career, he signed his pictures in Greek).

The largest, most resplendent of El Greco's

247. Jacopo Tintoretto. *The Last Supper.* 1592–94. Oil on canvas, 12′ × 18′8″ (3.66 × 5.69 m). S. Giorgio Maggiore, Venice

248. Chapel with *The Burial of Count Orgaz* by El Greco. 1586. Oil on canvas, 16′ × 11′10″ (4.88 × 3.61 m). S. Tomé, Toledo, Spain

major works, and the only one for a public chapel, is *The Burial of Count Orgaz* (fig. 248) in the church of Santo Tomé. The program, which was given at the time of the commission, emphasizes the traditional role of good works in salvation and of the saints as intercessors with heaven. This huge canvas honors a medieval benefactor so pious that St. Stephen and St. Augustine miraculously appeared at his funeral and themselves lowered the body into its grave. The burial took place in 1323, but El Greco represents it as a contemporary event, portraying among the attendants many of the local nobility and clergy. The dazzling display of color and texture in the armor and vestments could hardly have been surpassed by Titian himself. Directly above, the count's soul (a small, cloudlike figure akin to the angels in Tintoretto's *The Last Supper*) is carried to Heaven by an angel. The celestial assembly filling the upper half of the picture is painted very differently from the lower half: every form—clouds, limbs, draperies—takes part in the sweeping, flamelike movement toward the distant figure of Christ. Here, even more than in Tintoretto's art, the full range of Mannerism fuses into a single ecstatic vision.

Because of its location within the original setting, we must look sharply upward to see the upper half of the picture. El Greco's violent foreshortening is calculated to achieve an illusion of boundless space above, while the lower foreground figures appear as on a stage (their feet are cut off by the molding just below the picture). A large stone plaque set into the wall also belongs to the ensemble, representing the front of the sarcophagus into which the two saints lower the body of the count; it thus explains the action within the picture. The beholder, then, perceives three levels of reality: the grave itself, supposedly set into the wall at eye level and closed by an actual stone slab; the contemporary reenactment of the miraculous burial; and the vision of celestial glory witnessed by some of the participants. El Greco's task here was analogous to Masaccio's in his *Trinity* mural (see fig. 214). But whereas the Renaissance master creates the illusion of reality through his command of rational pictorial space which appears continuous with ours, El Greco summons an apparition that remains essentially separate from its architectural surroundings.

El Greco has created a spiritual counterpart to his imagination, in contrast to Counter Reformation images of saints, which were given a convincing physical presence. Every passage is alive with his peculiar religiosity, which is felt as a nervous exaltation occurring as the dreamlike vision is conjured up. This kind of mysticism is very similar in character to the Spiritual Exercises of St. Ignatius of Loyola, the Spanish priest who founded the Jesuits in 1534 and spearheaded the Counter Reformation following the Council of Trent in 1545. St. Ignatius sought to make visions so real that they would seem to appear before the very eyes of the faithful. Such mysticism could be achieved only through strenuous devotion. That effort is mirrored in the intensity of El Greco's work, which fully retains a feeling of spiritual struggle.

Realism

Although it spread to Venice and other cities, Mannerism failed to establish dominance outside Florence and Rome. Elsewhere it competed with other tendencies. In towns along the northern edge of the Lombard plain, such as Brescia and Verona, we find a number of artists who worked in a style based on those of Giorgione and Titian, but with a stronger interest in everyday reality.

Savoldo. One of the earliest and most attractive of these North Italian realists was Girolamo Savoldo (c. 1480–1550) from Brescia. His masterpiece, *St. Matthew and the Angel* (fig. 249), must be contemporary with Parmigianino's *The Madonna with the Long Neck* (see fig. 245). The broad, fluid manner of painting reflects the dominant influence of Titian, but the great Venetian master would never have placed the Evangelist in so thoroughly domestic an environment. The humble scene in the background shows the saint's milieu to be lowly indeed, and makes the presence of the angel doubly miraculous. This tendency to visualize sacred events among ramshackle buildings and simple people had been characteristic of "Late Gothic" painting, and Savoldo must have acquired it from that source. The nocturnal lighting, too, recalls such Northern pictures as the *Nativity* by Geertgen tot Sint Jans (see fig. 193). But the main source of illumination in Geertgen's panel is the divine radiance of the Child,

249. Girolamo Savoldo. *St. Matthew and the Angel.* c. 1535. Oil on canvas, 36¾ × 49″ (93.4 × 124.5 cm). The Metropolitan Museum of Art, New York. Marquand Fund, 1912

whereas Savoldo uses an ordinary oil lamp for his similarly magic and intimate effect.

Veronese. In the work of Paolo Veronese (1528–1588), North Italian realism attains the splendor of pageantry. Born and trained in Verona, Veronese became, after Tintoretto, the most important painter in Venice. Both found favor with the public, though they were utterly unlike each other in style. The contrast is strikingly evident if we compare Tintoretto's *The Last Supper* (see fig. 247) and Veronese's *Christ in the House of Levi* (fig. 250), which have similar subjects. Veronese avoids all reference to the supernatural. His symmetrical composition harks back to paintings of Leonardo and Raphael, while the festive mood of the scene reflects examples by Titian, so that at first glance the picture looks like a High Renaissance work born fifty years too late. Missing is one essential element: the elevated, ideal conception of humanity underlying the High Renaissance. Veronese paints a sumptuous banquet, a true feast for the eyes, but not "the intention of man's soul."

Significantly, we are not even sure which event from the life of Christ he originally meant to depict, for he gave the canvas its present title only after he had been summoned by the religious tribunal of the Inquisition on the charge of filling his picture with "buffoons, drunkards, Germans, dwarfs, and similar vulgarities" unsuited to its sacred character. The tribunal thought the painting represented the Last Supper, but Veronese's testimony never made clear whether it was the Last Supper, or the Supper in the House

250. Paolo Veronese. *Christ in the House of Levi.* 1573. Oil on canvas, 18′2″ × 42′ (5.54 × 12.8 m). Galleria dell'Accademia, Venice

251. Correggio. *The Assumption of the Virgin* (portion). c. 1525. Fresco. Dome, Parma Cathedral

of Simon. To him, apparently, this distinction made little difference. In the end, he settled on a convenient third title, *The Supper in the House of Levi,* which permitted him to leave the offending incidents in place. He argued that they were no more objectionable than the nudity of Christ and the Heavenly Host in Michelangelo's *Last Judgment,* but the tribunal failed to see the analogy on the grounds that "in the Last Judgment it was not necessary to paint garments, and there is nothing in those figures that is not spiritual."

The Inquisition, of course, considered only the impropriety of Veronese's art, not its lack of concern with spiritual depth. His dogged refusal to admit the justice of the charge, his insistence on his right to introduce directly observed details, however "improper," and his indifference to the subject of the picture spring from an attitude so startlingly "extroverted" that it was not generally accepted until the nineteenth century. The painter's domain, Veronese seems to say, is the entire visible world, and here he acknowledges no authority other than his senses.

Proto-Baroque

A third trend that emerges about 1520 in northern Italy has been labeled Proto-

252. Correggio. *Jupiter and Io.* c. 1532. Oil on canvas, 64½ × 27¾" (163.8 × 70.5 cm). Kunsthistorisches Museum, Vienna

Baroque, as much because it eludes convenient categories as because it anticipates so many features of the Baroque style. This tendency centers largely on Correggio, although later in the century it has a counterpart in architecture (see pp. 271–72).

Correggio. Correggio (1489/94–1534), a phenomenally gifted painter, spent most of his brief career in Parma, which lies to the west along the Lombard plain. Consequently, he absorbed a wide range of influences, of Leonardo and the Venetians as a youth, then of Michelangelo and Raphael, but their ideal of classical balance did not attract him. Correggio's work partakes of North Italian realism but applies it with the imaginative freedom of the Mannerists, though we do not find any hint of his fellow townsman Parmigianino in his style. His largest commission, the fresco of *The Assumption of the Virgin* in the dome of Parma Cathedral (fig. 251), is a masterpiece of illusionistic perspective, a vast, luminous space filled with soaring figures. They move with such exhilarating ease that the force of gravity seems not to exist for them. They are healthy, energetic beings of flesh and blood, not the disembodied spirits of El Greco, and they frankly delight in their weightless condition.

For Correggio, there was little difference between spiritual and physical ecstasy, as we may judge by comparing *The Assumption of the Virgin* with his *Jupiter and Io* (fig. 252), one in a series of canvases illustrating the loves of the classical gods. The nymph, swooning in the embrace of a cloudlike Jupiter, is the direct kin of the jubilant angels in the fresco. Leonardesque *sfumato*, combined with a Venetian sense of color and texture, produces an effect of exquisite voluptuousness that exceeds even Titian's in his *Bacchanal* (see fig. 240). Correggio had no immediate successors or any lasting influence on the art of his century, but toward 1600 his work began to be widely appreciated. For the next century and a half, he was admired as the equal of Raphael and Michelangelo, while the Mannerists, so important before, were largely forgotten.

253. Benvenuto Cellini. *Saltcellar of Francis I.* 1539–43. Gold with enamel, 10¼ × 13⅛" (26 × 33.3 cm). Kunsthistorisches Museum, Vienna

SCULPTURE

Italian sculptors of the later sixteenth century failed to match the achievements of the painters. Perhaps Michelangelo's overpowering personality discouraged new talent in this field, but the dearth of challenging new tasks is a more plausible reason. The "anticlassical" phase of Mannerism, represented by the style of Rosso, has no sculptural counterpart, but the second, elegant phase of Mannerism appears in countless sculptural examples in Italy and abroad.

Cellini. The best-known representative of the style is Benvenuto Cellini (1500–1571), the Florentine goldsmith and sculptor who owes much of his fame to his picaresque autobiography. The gold saltcellar for King Francis I of France (fig. 253), Cellini's only major work in precious metal to escape destruction, displays the virtues and limitations of his art. To hold condiments is obviously the lesser function of this lavish conversation piece. Because salt comes from the sea and pepper from the land, Cellini placed the boat-shaped salt container under the guardianship of Neptune, while the pepper, in a tiny triumphal arch, is watched over by a personification of Earth. On the base are figures representing the four seasons and the four parts of the day.

The entire object thus reflects the cosmic significance of the Medici tombs (compare fig. 235), but on this miniature scale Cellini's program turns into playful fancy. He wants to impress us with his ingenuity and skill, and to charm us with the grace of his figures. The allegorical significance of the design is simply a pretext for this display of virtuosity. When he tells us, for instance, that Neptune and Earth each have a bent and a straight leg to signify mountains and plains, form is completely divorced from content. Despite his boundless admiration for Michelangelo, Cellini here has created elegant figures as elongated, smooth, and languid as Parmigianino's (see fig. 245).

Giovanni Bologna. The plague of 1522 and, above all, the Sack of Rome in 1527 by the forces of Charles V had the effect of disrupting the development of Mannerism and displacing it abroad, where its next phase took place. In 1530, Rosso was called to France by Francis I to decorate the palace at Fontainebleau. He was soon followed by Cellini and other leading Mannerists, who made Mannerism the dominant style in sixteenth-century France. Their influence went far beyond the royal court. It reached Jean de Bologne (1529–1608), a gifted young sculptor from Douai in northern France, who went to Italy about 1555 for further training; he stayed and became, under the Italianized name of Giovanni Bologna, the most important sculptor in Florence during the last third of the century. His over-lifesize marble group, *The Rape of the Sabine Woman* (fig. 254), won particular acclaim, and still has its place of honor near the Palazzo Vecchio.

254. Giovanni Bologna. *The Rape of the Sabine Woman*. Completed 1583. Marble, height 13′6″ (4.11 m). Loggia dei Lanzi, Florence

Actually, the artist designed the group with no specific subject in mind, to silence those critics who doubted his ability as a monumental sculptor in marble. He selected what seemed to him the most difficult feat, three figures of contrasting character united in a common action. Their identities were disputed among the learned connoisseurs of the day, who finally settled on *The Rape of the Sabine Woman* as the most suitable title. Here, then, is another artist who is noncommittal about subject matter, although his unconcern had a different motive than Veronese's. Like Cellini's, Bologna's purpose was virtuoso display. His self-imposed task was to carve in marble, on a massive scale, a sculptural composition that was to be seen not from one but from all sides; this had hitherto been attempted only in bronze and on a much smaller scale (see figs. 208, 209). He has solved this formal problem, but at the cost of insulating his group from the world of human experience. The figures, spiraling upward as if confined inside a tall, narrow cylinder, perform their well-rehearsed choreographic exercise with ease; yet, like much Hellenistic sculpture (compare fig. 77), it is finally devoid of emotional meaning. We admire their discipline but find no trace of genuine pathos.

ARCHITECTURE

Mannerism

The term Mannerism was first coined to describe painting of the period. We have not encountered any difficulty in applying it to sculpture. But can it usefully be extended to architecture as well? And if so, what qualities must we look for? These questions have proved surprisingly difficult to answer precisely. Only a few buildings are generally acknowledged today as Mannerist, because of their reliance on idiosyncratic gestures that depart from Renaissance norms, but this does not provide a viable definition of Mannerism as an architectural period style. Mannerist architecture lacks a consistent integration between elements. It places an emphasis on encrusted decoration in order to create picturesque effects, with the occasional distortion of form and novel, even illogical rearrangement of space. By this standard, most late-sixteenth-century architecture can hardly be called Mannerist at all. Indeed, the work of Andrea Palladio (1518–1580), next to Michelangelo the most important architect of the century, stands in the tradition of the humanist and theoretician Leone Battista Alberti (see pp. 226–28).

Palladio. Although his career centered on his native town of Vicenza, Palladio's buildings and theoretical writings soon brought him international status. Palladio insisted that architecture must be governed both by reason and by certain universal rules that were perfectly exemplified by the buildings of the ancients. He thus shared Alberti's basic outlook and his firm faith in the cosmic significance of numerical ratios (see p. 226). The two differed in how each related theory and practice, however. With Alberti, this relationship had been loose and flexible, whereas Pal-

255. Andrea Palladio. Villa Rotonda, Vicenza. c. 1567–70

256. Giacomo della Porta. Facade of Il Gesù, Rome. c. 1575–84

ladio believed quite literally in practicing what he preached. His architectural treatise, *The Four Books of Architecture*, is consequently more practical than Alberti's (this helps explain its huge success), while his buildings are linked more directly with his theories. It has even been said that Palladio designed only what was, in his view, sanctioned by ancient precedent. Indeed, the usual term for both Palladio's work and theoretical attitude is "classicistic," to denote a conscious striving for classic qualities, though the results are not necessarily classical in style.

The Villa Rotonda (fig. 255), one of Palladio's finest buildings, perfectly illustrates the meaning of his classicism. An aristocratic country residence near Vicenza, it consists of a square block surmounted by a dome and is faced on all four sides with identical porches in the shape of temple fronts. Alberti had defined the ideal church as such a completely symmetrical, centralized design (see pp. 227–28), and it is evident that Palladio found in the same principles the ideal country house. How could he justify a context so purely secular for the solemn motif of the temple front? Like Alberti, he sought support in a selective interpretation of the historical evidence. He was convinced, on the basis of ancient literary sources, that Roman private houses had porticoes like these (excavations have since proved him wrong). But Palladio's use of the temple front here is not mere antiquarianism. He probably persuaded himself that it was legitimate because he regarded this feature as desirable for both beauty and utility. Beautifully correlated with the walls behind, the porches of the Villa Rotonda are an organic part of his design that lend the structure an air of serene dignity and festive grace.

Proto-Baroque

Vignola and Della Porta. When it came to church design, Palladio was less successful. Because of his allegiance to the antique orders, he was unable to solve the problem of how to fit a classical facade onto a basilican church, although he was undoubtedly familiar with Alberti's compromise at S. Andrea (see fig. 212). The first church in which this union was accomplished was Il Gesù (Jesus) in Rome, designed by Giacomo Vignola (1507–1573) and Giacomo della Porta (c. 1540–1602), architects who had assisted Michelangelo at St. Peter's and were still using his architectural vocabulary. Il Gesù is a building whose importance for subsequent church architecture can hardly be exaggerated. Since Il Gesù was the mother church of the Jesuits, its design must have been closely supervised so as to conform to the aims of the militant new order. We may thus view it as the architectural embodiment of the spirit of the Counter Reformation. The planning stage of the structure began in 1550, only five years after the Council of Trent (see p. 265). Michelangelo himself once promised a design, but never furnished it. The present plan, by Vignola, was adopted in 1568.

Della Porta was responsible for the bold facade (fig. 256). The paired pilasters and broken architrave on the lower story are clearly derived from the colossal order on the exterior of St. Peter's (see fig. 236), and with good reason, for it was Della Porta who completed Michelangelo's dome. In the upper story the same pattern recurs on a somewhat smaller scale, with four instead of six pairs of supports. The difference in width is bridged by a pair of scroll-shaped buttresses. This novel device, taken from Michelangelo, forms a graceful transition to the large pediment crowning the facade, which retains the classic proportions of Renaissance architecture (the height equals the width).

What is fundamentally new here is the integration of all the parts into one whole. Della Porta, freed from classicistic scruples by his allegiance to Michelangelo, gave the same vertical rhythm to both stories of the facade. This rhythm is obeyed by all the horizontal members (note the broken entablature), but the horizontal divisions in turn determine the size of the vertical members (hence no colossal order). Equally important is the emphasis on the main portal: its double frame—two pediments resting on coupled pilasters and columns—projects beyond the rest of the facade and gives strong focus to the entire design. Not since Gothic architecture has the entrance to a church received such a dramatic concentration of features, attracting the attention of the beholder outside the building much as the concentrated light beneath the dome channels that of the worshiper inside.

What are we to call the style of Il Gesù? Obviously, it has little in common with Palladio. The label Mannerist will not serve us either. As we shall see, the design of Il Gesù will become basic to Baroque architecture; by calling it Proto-Baroque, we suggest both its special place in relation to the past and its seminal importance for the future.

THE RENAISSANCE IN THE NORTH

Most fifteenth-century artists north of the Alps remained indifferent to Italian forms and ideas. Since the time of the Master of Flémalle and the Van Eycks they looked to Flanders rather than to Tuscany for leadership. This relative isolation ended suddenly, toward the year 1500. As if a dam had burst, Italian influence flowed northward in an ever wider stream, and Northern Renaissance art began to replace "Late Gothic." Northern Renaissance, however, has a less well-defined meaning than "Late Gothic," which refers to a single, clearly recognizable stylistic tradition. The diversity of trends north of the Alps is even greater than in Italy in the sixteenth century. Nor does Italian influence provide a common denominator, for this influence is itself diverse: Early Renaissance, High Renaissance, and Mannerist, all in regional variants from Lombardy, Venice, Florence, and Rome. Its effects, too, may vary greatly. They may be superficial or profound, direct or indirect, specific or general.

The "Late Gothic" tradition remained much alive, if no longer dominant, and its encounter with Italian art resulted in a kind of Hundred Years' War among styles that ended only when, in the early seventeenth century, the Baroque emerged as an international movement. Its course, moreover, was decisively affected by the Reformation, which had a far more immediate impact on art north of the Alps than in Italy. Our account necessarily emphasizes the heroic phases of the struggle at the expense of the lesser skirmishes.

GERMANY

Let us begin with Germany, the home of the Reformation, where the main battles of the "war of styles" took place during the first quarter of the century. Between 1475 and 1500, it had produced such important masters as Michael Pacher and Martin Schongauer (see figs. 197, 199), but these hardly prepare us for the astonishing burst of creative energy that was to follow. The range of achievements of this period, which was comparable in its brevity and brilliance to the Italian High Renaissance, is measured by the contrasting personalities of its greatest artists: Matthias Grünewald and Albrecht Dürer. Both died in 1528, probably at about the same age, although we know only Dürer's birth date (1471). Dürer quickly became internationally famous, while Grünewald, who was born about 1470–80, remained so obscure that his real name, Mathis Gothart Nithart, was discovered only at the end of the nineteenth century.

Grünewald. Grünewald's fame, like that of El Greco, has developed almost entirely within our own century. His main work, the *Isenheim Altarpiece*, is unique in the Northern art of his time in its ability to overwhelm us with something like the power of the Sistine Ceiling. Long believed to be by Dürer, it was painted between 1509/10 and 1515 for the monastery church of the Order of St. Anthony at Isenheim, in Alsace, and is now in the museum of the nearby town of Colmar.

This extraordinary altarpiece is a carved shrine with two sets of movable wings, which give it three stages, or "views"; two of them are shown here. The first, visible when all the wings are closed, shows *The Crucifixion* (fig. 257)—probably the most impressive ever painted. In one respect it is very medieval: Christ's terrible agony and the desperate grief of the Virgin, St. John, and Mary Magdalen recall the older German *Andachtsbild* (see fig. 168). But the pitiful body on the cross, with its twisted limbs, its countless lacerations, its rivulets of blood, is on a heroic scale that raises it beyond the human, and thus reveals the two natures of Christ. The same message is conveyed by the flanking figures. The three historic witnesses on the left mourn Christ's death as a man, while John the Baptist, on the right, points with calm emphasis to Him as the Saviour. Even the background suggests this duality. Golgotha here is not a hill outside Jerusalem, but a mountain towering above lesser peaks. The Crucifixion, lifted from its familiar setting, thus becomes a lonely event silhouetted against a deserted, ghostly landscape and a blue black sky. Darkness is over the land, in accordance with the Gospel, yet brilliant light bathes the foreground with the force of sudden revelation. This union of time and eternity, of reality and symbolism, gives Grünewald's *Crucifixion* its awesome grandeur.

When the outer wings are opened, the mood of the *Isenheim Altarpiece* changes dramatically (fig. 258). All three scenes in this second "view"—the Annunciation, the Angel Concert for the Madonna and Child, and the Resurrection—celebrate events as jubilant in spirit as the Crucifixion is austere. Most striking in comparison with "Late Gothic" painting is the sense of movement pervading these panels. Everything twists and turns as though it had a life of its own. The angel of the Annunciation enters the room like a gust of wind that blows the Virgin backward; the canopy over the Angel Concert seems to writhe in response to the heavenly music; and the Risen Christ shoots from His grave with explosive force. This vibrant energy has thoroughly reshaped the brittle, spiky contours and angular drapery patterns of "Late Gothic" art. Grünewald's forms are soft, elastic, fleshy. His light and color show a corresponding change. Commanding all the resources of the great Flemish masters, he employs them with unexampled boldness and flexibility. His color scale is richly iridescent, its range matched only by the Venetians. Grünewald's exploitation of colored light was altogether without parallel at that time. His genius achieved miracles through light that to this day remain unsurpassed in the luminescent angels of the Concert, the apparition of God the Father and the Heavenly Host above the Madonna, and, most spectacularly, the rainbow-hued radiance of the Risen Christ.

How much did Grünewald owe to Italian art? Nothing at all, we are first tempted to reply, yet he must have learned from the Renaissance in more ways than one. His knowledge of perspective (note the low horizons) and the physical vigor of some of his figures cannot be explained by the "Late Gothic" tradition alone, and occasionally his pictures show architectural details of Southern origin. Perhaps the most important effect of the Renaissance on him, however, was psychological.

We know little about his career, but he apparently did not lead the settled life of a craftsman-painter controlled by the rules of his guild. He was also an architect, an engineer, something of a courtier, and an entrepreneur; he worked for many different patrons and stayed nowhere for very long. He was in sympathy with Martin Luther (who frowned upon religious images as "idolatrous"), even though, as a painter, he depended on Catholic patronage. In a word, Grünewald seems to have shared the free, individualistic spirit of Italian Renaissance artists. The daring of his pictorial vision likewise suggests a reliance on his own resources. The Renaissance, then, had a liberating influence on him but did not change the basic cast of his imagination. Instead, it helped him epitomize the expressive aspects of the "Late Gothic" in a style of unique intensity and individuality.

Dürer. For Dürer (1471–1528), the Renaissance held a richer meaning. Attracted to Italian art while still a young journeyman, he visited Venice in 1494/95 and returned to his native Nuremberg with a new conception of the world and the artist's place in it. The unbridled fantasy of Grünewald's art was to him "a wild, unpruned tree" (a phrase he used for painters who worked by rules of thumb, without theoretical foundations) that needed the discipline of the objective, rational standards

257. Matthias Grünewald. *The Crucifixion,* from the *Isenheim Altarpiece* (closed). c. 1510–15. Oil on panel, 8′10″ × 10′1″ (2.69 × 3.07 m). Musée Unterlinden, Colmar, France

258. Matthias Grünewald. *The Annunciation, The Angel Concert for the Madonna and Child,* and *The Resurrection,* from the *Isenheim Altarpiece* (open). c. 1510–15. Oil on panel, each wing 8′10″ × 4′8″ (2.69 × 1.42 m); center panel 8′10″ × 11′2½″ (2.69 × 3.42 m)

259. Albrecht Dürer. *Self-Portrait.* 1500.
Oil on panel, 26¼ × 19¼″ (66.7 × 48 cm). Pinakothek, Munich

of the Renaissance. Taking the Italian view that the fine arts belong among the liberal arts, he also adopted the ideal of the artist as a gentleman and humanistic scholar. By steadily cultivating his intellectual interests he came to encompass in his lifetime a vast variety of subjects and techniques. And since he was the greatest printmaker of the time, Dürer had a wide influence on sixteenth-century art through his woodcuts and engravings, which circulated everywhere in Europe.

The first artist to be fascinated by his own image, Dürer was in this respect more of a Renaissance personality than any Italian artist. His earliest known work, a drawing made at thirteen, is a self-portrait, and he continued to produce self-portraits throughout his career. Most impressive, and uniquely revealing, is the panel of 1500 (fig. 259). Pictorially, it belongs to the Flemish tradition (compare Jan van Eyck's *Man in a Red Turban*, fig. 188), but the solemn, frontal pose and the Christlike idealization of the features assert an authority quite beyond the range of ordinary portraits. The picture reflects not so much Dürer's vanity as the seriousness with which he regarded his mission as an artistic reformer. (One thinks of Martin Luther's "Here I stand; I cannot do otherwise.")

The didactic aspect of Dürer's art is clearest perhaps in the engraving *Knight, Death, and Devil* (fig. 260), one of his finest prints. The knight on his beautiful mount, poised and confident as an equestrian statue, embodies an ideal both aesthetic and moral. He is the Christian Soldier steadfast on the road of faith toward the Heavenly Jerusalem, undeterred by the hideous horseman threatening to cut him off, or the grotesque devil behind him. The dog, another symbol of virtue, loyally follows his master despite the lizards and skulls in his path. Italian Renaissance form, united with the heritage of "Late Gothic" symbolism (whether open or disguised), here takes on a new, characteristically Northern significance.

The subject of *Knight, Death, and Devil* seems to have been derived from the *Manual of the Christian Soldier* by Erasmus of Rotterdam, the greatest of the Northern humanists. Dürer's own convictions were essentially those of Christian humanism. They made him an early and enthusiastic follower of Martin Luther, although, like Grünewald, he continued to work for Catholic patrons. Nevertheless, his new faith can be sensed in the growing austerity of style and subject in his religious works after 1520. The climax of this trend is represented by *The Four Apostles* (fig. 261), paired panels containing what has rightly been termed Dürer's artistic testament.

Dürer presented the panels in 1526 to the city of Nuremberg, which had joined the Lutheran camp the year before. The chosen apostles are basic to Protestant doctrine: John and Paul face one another in the foreground, with Peter and Mark behind. Quotations from their writings, inscribed below in Luther's translation, warn the city government not to mistake human error and pretense for the will of God; they plead against Catholics and ultrazealous Protestant radicals alike. But in another, more universal sense, the four figures represent the Four Temperaments—and, by implication, the other cosmic quartets: the seasons, the elements, the times of day, and the ages of man—encircling, like the cardinal points of the compass, the Deity who is at the invisible center of this "triptych." In keeping with their role, the apostles have a cubic severity and grandeur such as we have

260. Albrecht Dürer. *Knight, Death, and Devil.* 1513. Engraving, 9⅞ × 7½″ (25.1 × 19.1 cm). Museum of Fine Arts, Boston

not encountered since Masaccio and Piero della Francesca.

Cranach the Elder. Dürer's hope for a monumental art embodying the Protestant faith remained unfulfilled. Other German painters also tried to cast Luther's doctrines into visual form, but created no viable tradition. Such efforts were doomed, since the spiritual leaders of the Reformation often looked upon them with outright hostility. Martin Luther himself seems to have been indifferent to religious art, even though he developed a close relationship with Lucas Cranach the Elder (1472–1553), court painter to Frederick the Wise, Elector of Saxony, in Wittenberg, where he had nailed his ninety-five theses to the castle church doors in 1517. Like Grünewald and Dürer, Cranach continued to rely on Catholic patronage, but some of his altars have a Protestant content; ironically, they lack the fervor of those he painted before converting to Protestantism. He is best remembered

261. Albrecht Dürer. *The Four Apostles.* 1523–26. Oil on panel, each 85 × 30″ (215.9 × 76.2 cm). Pinakothek, Munich

today for his portraits and his delightfully incongruous mythological scenes, which embody a peculiarly Northern adaptation of humanism. In *The Judgment of Paris* (fig. 262), nothing could be less classical than the wriggly nakedness of these three coquettish damsels. Paris is a German knight clad in fashionable armor, indistinguishable from the nobles at the court of Saxony who were the artist's patrons. The playful eroticism, small size, and precise, miniaturelike detail of the picture make it plainly a collector's item, attuned to the refined tastes of a provincial aristocracy.

Altdorfer. As remote from the classic ideal, but far more impressive, is *The Battle of Issus* (fig. 263) by Albrecht Altdorfer (c. 1480–1538), a Bavarian painter somewhat younger than Cranach. Without the text on the tablet suspended in the sky, and the other inscriptions, we could not possibly identify the subject, Alexander's victory over Darius. The artist has tried to follow ancient descriptions of the actual number and kind of combatants in the battle, but this required him to adopt a bird's-eye view whereby the two protagonists are lost in the antlike mass of their own armies (contrast the Hellenistic representation of the same subject in fig. 59). Moreover, the soldiers' armor and the fortified town in the distance are unmistakably of the sixteenth century.

The picture might well show some contemporary battle, except for one feature: the spectacular sky, with the sun triumphantly breaking through the clouds and "defeating" the moon. The celestial drama above a vast Alpine landscape, obviously correlated with the human contest below, raises the scene to the cosmic level. This is strikingly similar to the vision of heavenly glory above the Virgin and Child in the *Isenheim Altarpiece* (see fig. 258). Altdorfer may indeed be viewed as a later, albeit lesser, Grünewald. Although Altdorfer, too, was an architect, well acquainted with perspective and the Italian stylistic vocabulary, his paintings show the same unruly imagination as the older master's. But Altdorfer is also unlike Grünewald: he makes the human figure incidental to its spatial setting, whether natural or architectural. The tiny soldiers of *The Battle of Issus* have their counterpart in his other pictures, and he painted at least one landscape with no figures at all, the earliest known "pure" landscape.

Holbein. Gifted though they were, Cranach and Altdorfer both evaded the main challenge of the Renaissance so bravely faced (if not always mastered) by Dürer: the human image. Their style, antimonumental and miniaturelike, set the pace for dozens of lesser masters. Perhaps the rapid decline of German art after Dürer's death was due to a failure of ambition, among artists and patrons alike. The career of Hans Holbein the Younger (1497–1543), the one painter of whom this is not true, confirms the general rule. Born and raised in Augsburg, a center of international commerce in southern Germany particularly open to Renaissance ideas, he left

262. Lucas Cranach the Elder. *The Judgment of Paris*. 1530.
Oil on panel, 13½ × 8¾" (34.3 × 22.2 cm). Staatliche Kunsthalle, Karlsruhe

263. Albrecht Altdorfer. *The Battle of Issus.* 1529.
Oil on panel, 62×47" (157.5×119.4 cm). Pinakothek, Munich

at the age of eighteen for Switzerland. By 1520, he was firmly established in Basel as a designer of woodcuts, a splendid decorator, and an incisive portraitist. Holbein's likeness of Erasmus of Rotterdam (fig. 264), painted soon after the famous author had settled in Basel, gives us a truly memorable image of this doctor of humane letters: intimate yet monumental, he has an intellectual authority formerly reserved for the doctors of the Church.

Holbein must have felt confined in Basel, for in 1523–24 he traveled to France, apparently intending to offer his services to Francis

264. Hans Holbein the Younger. *Erasmus of Rotterdam.* c. 1523. Oil on panel, 16½ × 12½" (41.9 × 31.8 cm). Musée du Louvre, Paris

265. Hans Holbein the Younger. *Henry VIII.* 1540. Oil on panel, 32½ × 29" (82.6 × 73.7 cm). Galleria Nazionale d'Arte Antica, Rome

I; two years later, Basel was in the throes of the Reformation crisis, and he went to England, hoping for commissions at the court of Henry VIII. (Erasmus, recommending Holbein to Thomas More, wrote: "Here [in Basel] the arts are out in the cold.") On his return to Basel in 1528, he saw fanatical mobs destroying religious images as "idols." Four years later he settled permanently in London as court painter to Henry VIII. His portrait of the king (fig. 265) shares the rigid frontality of Dürer's self-portrait (see fig. 259), but its purpose is to convey the almost divine authority of the absolute ruler. The monarch's physical bulk creates an overpowering sensation of his ruthless, commanding presence. Holbein's style now has gained an international flavor: the portrait shares with Bronzino's *Eleanora of Toledo* (see fig. 246) the immobile pose, the air of unapproachability, and the precisely rendered costume and jewels. While Holbein's picture, unlike Bronzino's, does not yet reflect the Mannerist ideal of elegance, both clearly belong to the same species of court portrait.

THE NETHERLANDS

The Netherlands in the sixteenth century had the most turbulent and painful history of any country north of the Alps. When the Reformation began, they were part of the far-flung empire of the Hapsburgs under Charles V, who was also king of Spain. Protestantism quickly became powerful in the Netherlands, and the attempts of the crown to suppress it led to open revolt against foreign rule. After a bloody struggle, the northern provinces (today's Holland) emerged at the end of the century as an independent state, while the southern ones (roughly corresponding to modern Belgium) remained in Spanish hands.

The religious and political strife might have had catastrophic effects on the arts, yet this, astonishingly, did not happen. Sixteenth-century Netherlandish painting, to be sure, does not equal that of the fifteenth in brilliance, nor did it produce any pioneers of

266. Pieter Bruegel the Elder. *The Blind Leading the Blind.* c. 1568. Oil on panel, 34½ × 60⅝" (87.6 × 154 cm). Museo di Capodimonte, Naples

the Northern Renaissance comparable to Dürer and Holbein. This region absorbed Italian elements more slowly than Germany, but more steadily and systematically, so that instead of a few isolated peaks of achievement we find a continuous range. Between 1550 and 1600, their most troubled time, the Netherlands produced the major painters of Northern Europe; these artists in turn paved the way for the great Dutch and Flemish masters of the next century.

Two main concerns, sometimes separate, sometimes interwoven, characterized sixteenth-century Netherlandish painting. One was to assimilate Italian art from Raphael to Tintoretto (though this was often accomplished in a dry and didactic manner). The other was to develop a repertory that would supplement the traditional religious subjects. All the secular themes that loom so large in Dutch and Flemish painting of the Baroque era—landscape, still life, genre (scenes of everyday life)—were first defined between 1500 and 1600. The process was gradual, shaped less by the achievements of individual artists than by the need to cater to popular taste as church commissions became steadily scarcer in the Netherlands, where Protestant iconoclastic zeal was particularly widespread.

Bruegel the Elder. Pieter Bruegel the Elder (1525/30–1569), the only genius among these Netherlandish painters, explored landscape, peasant life, and moral allegory. Although his career was spent in Antwerp and Brussels, he may have been born near 's Hertogenbosch. Certainly the work of Hieronymus Bosch deeply impressed him, and he is in many ways as puzzling to us as the older master. What were his religious convictions, his political sympathies? We know little about him, but his preoccupation with folk customs and the daily life of humble people seems to have sprung from a complex philosophical attitude. Bruegel was highly educated, the friend of humanists, and patronized by the Hapsburg court. Yet he apparently never worked for the Church, and when he dealt with religious subjects he did so in an oddly ambiguous way.

The Blind Leading the Blind (fig. 266), one of Bruegel's last pictures, shows a philosophical detachment from religious and political fanaticism. Its source is the Gospels (Matt. 15:12–19): Christ says, speaking of the Pharisees, "And if the blind lead the blind, both shall fall into the ditch." This parable of human folly recurs in humanist literature, and we know it in at least one earlier representation, but the tragic depth of Bruegel's forceful image gives new urgency to the theme. Perhaps he found the biblical context of the parable especially relevant to his time: the Pharisees had asked why Christ's disciples, violating religious traditions, did not wash their hands before meals; He answered, "Not that which goeth into the mouth defileth a man; but that which cometh out of the mouth." When this offended the Pharisees, He called them the blind leading the blind, explaining that "whatsoever entereth in at the mouth goeth into the belly, and is cast out. . . . But those things which proceed out of the mouth come forth from the heart; and they defile the man. For out of the heart proceed evil thoughts, murders . . . blasphemies." Perhaps Bruegel thought that this applied to the controversies then raging over details of religious ritual.

His attitude toward Italian art is also hard to define. A trip to the South in 1552–53 took him to Rome, Naples, and the Strait of Messina, but the famous monuments admired by other Northerners seem not to have interested him. He returned instead with a sheaf of magnificent landscape drawings, especially Alpine views. He was probably much impressed by landscape painting in Venice, particularly its integration of figures and scenery and the progression in space from foreground to background (see figs. 239, 240). Out of these memories came sweeping landscapes in Bruegel's mature style. *The Return of the Hunters* (fig. 267) is one of a set depicting

267. Pieter Bruegel the Elder. *The Return of the Hunters*. 1565. Oil on panel, 46½ × 63¾" (118.1 × 161.9 cm). Kunsthistorisches Museum, Vienna

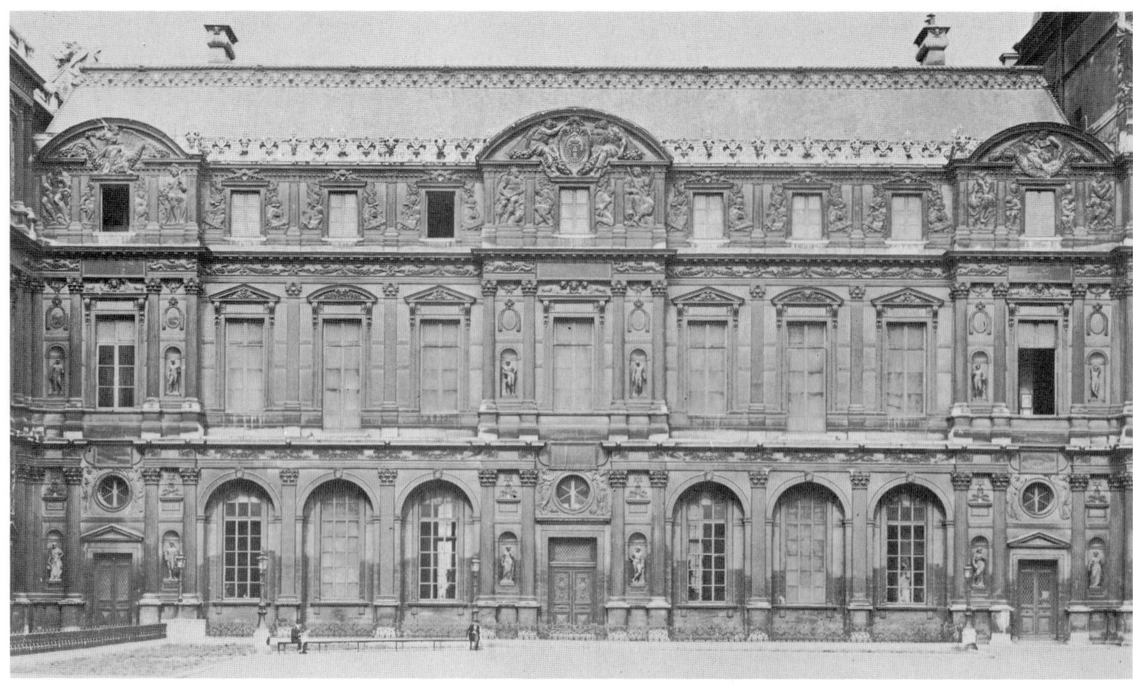

268. Pierre Lescot. Square Court of the Louvre, Paris. Begun 1546

the months. Such series, we recall, had begun with medieval calendar illustrations, and Bruegel's scene still shows its descent from the *Très Riches Heures du Duc de Berry* (see fig. 184). Now, however, nature is more than a setting for human activities: it is the main subject of the picture. Men and women in their seasonal occupations are incidental to the majestic annual cycle of death and rebirth that is the breathing rhythm of the cosmos.

FRANCE

In architecture and sculpture, it took the Northern countries longer to assimilate Italian forms than in painting. France, more closely linked with Italy than the rest (France, we will recall, had conquered Milan in 1499), was the first to achieve an integrated Renaissance style. In 1546 King Francis I, who had shown his admiration for Italian art earlier by inviting first Leonardo in 1517 and then the Mannerists to France (see p. 269), decided to replace the old Gothic royal castle, the Louvre (see fig. 184), with a new and much larger structure on the same site. The project, barely begun at the time of his death, was not completed until more than a century later; but its oldest portion, by Pierre Lescot (c. 1515–1578), is the finest surviving example of Northern Renaissance architecture.

Lescot. The details of Lescot's facade (fig. 268) have an astonishing classical purity, yet we would not mistake it for an Italian structure. Its distinctive quality comes not from Italian forms superficially applied, but from a genuine synthesis of the traditional French château with the Renaissance palace. Italian, of course, are the superimposed classical orders, the pedimented window frames, and the arcade on the ground floor. But the continuity of the facade is interrupted by three projecting pavilions that have supplanted the château turrets, and the high-pitched roof is also traditionally French. The vertical accents thus overcome the horizontal ones, and their effect is reinforced by the tall, narrow windows.

269. Francesco Primaticcio and Germain Pilon. Tomb of Henry II and Catherine de'Medici. 1563–70. Abbey Church of St.-Denis, Paris

270. Germain Pilon. *Gisants* of the king and queen, detail of the Tomb of Henry II and Catherine de'Medici. Marble

Pilon. The greatest sculptor of the later sixteenth century was Germain Pilon (c. 1535–1590). In his early years he learned a good deal from Francesco Primaticcio, Cellini's rival at the court of Francis I (see p. 268), but he soon developed his own idiom by merging the Mannerism of Fontainebleau with elements taken from ancient sculpture, Michelangelo, and the Gothic tradition. His main works are monumental tombs, of which the earliest and largest was for Henry II and Catherine de'Medici (fig. 269). Primaticcio built the architectural framework, an oblong, free-standing chapel on a platform decorated with bronze and marble reliefs. Four large bronze statues of Virtues, their style reminiscent of Fontainebleau, mark the corners. On the top of the tomb are bronze figures of the king and queen kneeling in prayer; inside the chapel, the couple reappear recumbent as marble *gisants*, or nude corpses (fig. 270).

This contrast of such effigies had been a characteristic feature of fourteenth-century Gothic tombs: the *gisant* expressed the transient nature of the flesh, usually showing the body in an advanced stage of decomposition, with vermin sometimes crawling through its open cavities. How could this gruesome image take on Renaissance form without losing its emotional significance? Pilon's solution is brilliant: by idealizing the *gisants* he reverses their former meaning. The recumbent queen in the pose of a classical Venus and the king in that of the dead Christ evoke neither horror nor pity but, rather, the pathos of a beauty that persists even in death. The shock effect of their predecessors has given way to a poignancy that is no less intense.

Remembering our earlier distinction between the classical and medieval attitudes toward death (see p. 223), we may define this sentiment as follows. The Gothic *gisant,* which emphasizes physical decay, represents the future state of the body, in keeping with the whole "prospective" character of the medieval tomb. Pilon's *gisants*, however, are "retrospective," yet do not deny the reality of death. In this union of opposites (never to be achieved again, even by Pilon himself) lies the greatness of these figures.

THE BAROQUE IN ITALY AND SPAIN

What is Baroque? Like Mannerism, the term was originally coined to disparage the very style it designates: it meant "irregular, contorted, grotesque." Art historians otherwise remain divided over its definition. Should Baroque be used only for the dominant style of the seventeenth century, or should it include other tendencies, such as classicism, to which it bears a problematic relationship? Should the time frame be extended to cover the period 1700–1750, known as the Rococo? More important, is the Baroque an era distinct from both Renaissance and modern, or the final phase of the Renaissance? On this last question, we have chosen the first alternative as a matter of convenience, while admitting that a good case can be made for the second. Which position we adopt on all these issues is perhaps less important than an understanding of the forces underlying the Baroque.

The fact is that the Baroque eludes simple classification; rather, it incorporates an extreme range of contradictions. Hence, we run into a series of paradoxes typical of the conflicting nature of the Baroque. It has been claimed that the Baroque style expresses the spirit of the Counter Reformation; yet the Counter Reformation had already done its work by 1600. Catholicism had recaptured much of its former territory, and Protestantism was on the defensive, so that neither side any longer had the power to upset the new balance. As if to signify the triumph of the old faith, in 1622 the heroes of the Counter Reformation—Ignatius of Loyola, Francis Xavier (both Jesuits), Theresa of Avila, Filippo Neri, and Isidoro Agricola—were named saints (Carlo Borromeo had been made one in 1610), beginning a wave of canonizations that lasted through the mid-eighteenth century. In contrast to the piety and good deeds of these reformers, the new princes of the Church were known primarily for worldly splendor.

Another reason why we should guard against overemphasizing the Baroque's ties to the Counter Reformation is that, unlike Mannerism, the new style was not specifically Italian (although historians generally agree that it was born in Rome during the final years of the sixteenth century), nor was it confined to religious art. Baroque elements quickly penetrated the Protestant North, where they were applied primarily to other subjects.

Equally problematic is the assertion that the Baroque is "the style of absolutism," reflecting the centralized state ruled by an autocrat of unlimited powers. Although absolutism reached its climax during the reign of Louis XIV in the later seventeenth century, it had been in the making since the 1520s, under Francis I in France and the Medici dukes in Tuscany. Moreover, Baroque art flourished in bourgeois Holland no less than in the absolutist monarchies, and the style officially sponsored under Louis XIV was a notably subdued, classicistic kind of Baroque.

We encounter similar difficulties when we try to relate Baroque art to the science and philosophy of the period. A direct link did exist in the Early and High Renaissance, when an artist could also be a humanist and a scientist. During the seventeenth century, however, scientific and philosophical thought became too complex, abstract, and systematic for the artist to share. Gravitation and calculus could not stir the artist's imagination any more than Descartes' motto *Cogito, ergo sum* ("I think, therefore I am").

There is nevertheless a relationship between Baroque art and science which, though subtle, is essential to an understanding of the

271. Caravaggio. *The Calling of St. Matthew.* c. 1599–1602. Oil on canvas, 11′1″ × 11′5″ (3.38 × 3.48 m). Contarelli Chapel, S. Luigi dei Francesi, Rome

entire age. The medieval outlook, which had persisted through the Renaissance, was gradually overthrown by Baroque science. The complex metaphysics of the Neo-Platonists, which endowed everything with religious import, was replaced by a new cosmology, beginning with Nicolaus Copernicus and Galileo Galilei and culminating in René Descartes and Sir Isaac Newton. In addition to placing the sun, not the earth (and humanity), at the center of the universe, they defined underlying relationships in mathematical and geometrical terms as part of the simple, orderly system of mechanics. The attack on Renaissance science and philosophy, which could trace their origins (and authority) back to antiquity, also had the effect of supplanting natural magic, a precursor of modern science that included both astrology and alchemy. The difference was that natural magic sought to exercise practical control of the world through prediction and manipulation, by uncovering nature's "secrets" instead of its laws. To be sure, the magical world view, linked as it was to traditional religion and morality, continued to live on in popular literature and folklore long afterward. We may nevertheless say that, thanks to advances in optical physics and physiology, the Baroque literally saw with new eyes, for its understanding of visual reality was forever altered by the new science.

In the end, Baroque art is not simply the result of religious, political, or intellectual developments. Let us therefore think of the Baroque style as one among other basic features that distinguish the period from what had gone before: the refortified Catholic faith, the absolutist state, and the new role of science. These factors are combined in volatile mixtures that give the Baroque its fascinating variety. Such diversity was perfectly suited to express the expanding view of humanity. What ultimately unites this refractory era is a reevaluation of people and their relation to the universe. Central to this image is the new psychology reflected quite clearly in Baroque art, where the tensions of the era often erupt into open conflict. A prominent role was now assigned by philosophers to human passion, which encompasses a wider range of emotions and social levels than ever before. The scientific revolution culminating in Newton's unified mechanics responded to the same impulses, for it assumes a more active role for the individual in his or her ability to understand and in turn affect the surrounding world. Remarkably, the Baroque remained an age of great religious faith, however divided it may have been in its loyalties. The counterpoint between passions, intellect, and spirituality may be seen as forming a dialogue which has never been truly brought to a close.

PAINTING IN ITALY

Around 1600 Rome became the fountainhead of the Baroque, as it had of the High Renaissance a century before, by gathering artists from other regions to perform challenging new tasks. The papacy patronized art on a large scale with the aim of making Rome the most beautiful city of the Christian world "for the greater glory of God and the Church." This campaign had begun as early as 1585, but the artists then on hand were late Mannerists of feeble distinction. Soon, however, it attracted ambitious young masters, especially from northern Italy, and they created the new style.

Caravaggio. Foremost among these northerners was a painter of genius, Michelangelo Merisi (1571–1610), called Caravaggio after his birthplace near Milan. *The Calling of St. Matthew* (fig. 271), part of a series of monumental canvases he painted for a chapel in S. Luigi dei Francesi from 1599 to 1602, is remote from both Mannerism and the High Renaissance. The only antecedent of this extraordinary picture is the North Italian realism of artists like Savoldo (see fig. 249). Caravaggio's realism, however, is such that a new term, "naturalism," is needed to distinguish it from the earlier kind.

Never have we seen a sacred subject depicted so entirely in terms of contemporary low life. Matthew, the tax gatherer, sits with some armed men (evidently his agents) in what is a common Roman tavern as two figures approach from the right. The arrivals are poor people, their bare feet and simple garments contrasting strongly with the colorful costumes of Matthew and his companions. Why do we sense a religious quality in this scene and not mistake it for an everyday event? The answer is that Caravaggio's North Italian realism is wedded to elements derived from his study of Renaissance art in Rome, which lend the scene its surprising dignity. His style, in other words, is classical, without being classicizing. The composition, for example, is disposed across the picture surface, its forms sharply highlighted, much as in a relief (see fig. 96). For Caravaggio, moreover, naturalism is not an end in itself but a means of conveying profoundly religious content. What identifies one of the figures as Christ? It is surely not the Saviour's halo, the only supernatural feature in the picture, which is an inconspicuous gold band that we might well overlook. Our eyes fasten instead upon His commanding gesture, borrowed from Michelangelo's *The Creation of Adam* (see fig. 233), which "bridges" the gap between the two groups and is echoed by Matthew, who points questioningly at himself.

Most decisive is the strong beam of sunlight

272. Artemisia Gentileschi. *Judith and Her Maidservant with the Head of Holofernes*. c. 1625. Oil on canvas, 72½ × 55¾" (184.2 × 141.6 cm). The Detroit Institute of Arts. Gift of Leslie H. Green

above Christ that illuminates His face and hand in the gloomy interior, thus carrying His call across to Matthew. Without this light, so natural yet so charged with symbolic meaning, the picture would lose its magic, its power to make us aware of the divine presence. Caravaggio here gives moving, direct form to an attitude shared by certain great saints of the Counter Reformation: that the mysteries of faith are revealed not by intellectual speculation but spontaneously, through an inward experience open to all people. What separates the Baroque from the later Counter Reformation is the externalization of the mystic vision, which appears to us complete, without any signs of the spiritual struggle in El Greco's art.

Caravaggio's paintings have a "lay Christianity," untouched by theological dogma, which appealed to Protestants no less than Catholics. This quality made possible his strong, though indirect, influence on Rembrandt, the greatest religious artist of the Protestant North. In Italy, Caravaggio fared less well. His work was acclaimed by artists and connoisseurs, but the ordinary people for whom it was intended, as well as some conservative critics, regarded it as lacking propriety and reverence. They resented meeting their own kind in these paintings, preferring religious imagery of a more idealized and rhetorical sort. For that reason, Caravaggism largely ran its course by 1630, when it was assimilated into other Baroque tendencies.

Gentileschi. We have not yet discussed a woman artist, although this does not mean that there were none. Pliny, for example, mentions in his *Natural History* (bk. XXXV) the names and describes the work of women artists in Greece and Rome, and there are records of women manuscript illuminators during the Middle Ages and the Renaissance. We must remember, however, that the vast majority of all artists remained anonymous until the "Late Gothic" period, so that all but a few works by women have proved impossible to identify. Women began to emerge as distinct artistic personalities about 1550. Until the middle of the nineteenth century, however, women artists were largely restricted to painting portraits, genre scenes, and still lifes. Many nevertheless carved out successful careers, often emerging as the equals or superiors of the men in whose styles they were trained. The obstacles they met in getting instruction in figure drawing and anatomy effectively barred them from painting narrative subjects. The exceptions to this general rule were several Italian women born into artistic families who were encouraged to cultivate their talents, though they did not receive the same training as men. Their major role began in the seventeenth century with Artemisia Gentileschi (1593–c.1653).

The daughter of painter Orazio Gentileschi, she was born in Rome and became one of the leading painters and personalities of her day. Her characteristic subjects are Bathsheba, the unfortunate object of King David's obsessive passion, and Judith, who saved her people by beheading the Assyrian general Holofernes. Both subjects were popular during the Baroque era, which delighted in erotic and violent scenes. While Gentileschi's early paintings of Judith take her father's and Caravaggio's work as their points of departure, our example (fig. 272) is a fully mature, independent work. The inner drama is uniquely hers, and no less powerful for its restraint in immortalizing Judith's courage. Rather than the decapitation itself, the artist shows the instant after. Momentarily distracted, Judith gestures theatrically as her servant stuffs Holofernes' head into a sack. The object of their attention remains hidden from view, heightening the air of intrigue. The hushed, candlelit atmosphere in turn establishes a mood of exotic mystery that conveys Judith's complex emotions with unsurpassed understanding.

Annibale Carracci. The conservative wishes of the simpler people in Italy were met by artists less radical, and less talented, than Caravaggio. They took their lead instead from another recent arrival in Rome, Annibale Carracci (1560–1609). Annibale came from Bologna where, since the 1580s, he and two other members of his family had evolved an anti-Mannerist style based on North Italian realism and Venetian art. He was a reformer rather than a revolutionary. Like Caravaggio, who apparently admired him, it was Annibale's experience of Roman classicism that transformed his art. He, too, felt that art must return to nature, but his approach was less single-minded, balancing studies from life with a revival of the classics, which to him meant the art of antiquity, and of Raphael, Michelangelo, Titian, and Correggio. At his best, he succeeded in fusing these diverse elements, although their union always remained somewhat precarious.

Between 1597 and 1604 Annibale produced the ceiling fresco in the gallery of the Palazzo Farnese, his most ambitious and important work. Our illustration (fig. 273) shows Annibale's rich and intricate design: the narrative scenes, like those of the Sistine Ceiling, are surrounded by painted architecture, simulated sculpture, and nude youths holding garlands. The Farnese Gallery does not rely solely on Michelangelo's masterpiece, however. The style of the main subjects, the Loves of the Classical Gods, is reminiscent of Raphael's *Galatea* (see fig. 238), and the whole is held together by an illusionistic scheme that reflects Annibale's knowledge of Correggio and the great Venetians. Carefully foreshortened and illuminated from below (as we can judge from the shadows), the nude youths and the simulated sculpture and architecture appear real. Against this background the mythologies are presented as simulated easel pictures. Each of these levels of reality is handled with consummate skill, and the entire ceiling has an exuberance that sets it apart from both Mannerism and High Renaissance art.

Reni; Guercino. To artists who were inspired by it, the Farnese Gallery seemed to offer two alternatives. Pursuing the Raphaelesque style of the mythological panels, they could arrive at a deliberate, "official" classicism; or they could take their cue from the sensuous illusionism present in the framework. Among the earliest responses to the first alternative is the ceiling fresco *Aurora* (fig. 274) by Guido Reni (1575–1642), showing Apollo in his chariot (the Sun) led by Aurora (Dawn). Despite its rhythmic grace, this relieflike design would seem like little more than a pallid reflection of High Renaissance art were it not for the glowing and dramatic light that gives it an emotional force that the figures alone could never achieve. The *Aurora* ceiling (fig. 275) painted less than ten years later by Guercino (1591–1666) is the very opposite of Reni's. Here architectural perspective, combined with the pictorial illusionism of Correggio and the intense light and color of Titian, converts the entire surface into one limitless space, in which the figures sweep past as if propelled by stratospheric winds. With this work, Guercino started what soon became a veritable flood of similar visions.

Da Cortona. The most overpowering of these is the ceiling fresco by Pietro da Cortona (1596–1669) in the great hall of the Palazzo Barberini in Rome, which presents a glorification of the reign of the Barberini pope, Urban VIII (fig. 276). As in the Farnese Gallery, the ceiling area is subdivided by a painted framework simulating architecture and sculpture and filled with figural scenes; but beyond it we now see the unbounded sky, as in Guercino's *Aurora*. Clusters of figures, perched on clouds or soaring freely, swirl above as well as below this framework, creating a dual illusion: some figures appear to hover well inside the hall, perilously close to our heads, while others recede into a light-filled, infinite distance. Cortona's source of inspiration was surely Correggio's *The Assumption of the Virgin* (see fig. 251), in which a similar effect is achieved. In the Barberini ceiling, the dynamism of the Baroque style reaches a resounding climax.

Cortona's frescoes provided the focal point for the rift between the High Baroque and Baroque classicism. The classicists asserted that art serves a moral purpose and must observe the principles of clarity, unity, and decorum. And supported by a long tradition reaching back to Horace's famous dictum *ut pictura poesis*, they further maintained that painting should follow the example of tragic poetry in conveying meaning through a minimum of figures whose movements, gestures, and expressions can be easily read. Cortona, though not anticlassical, presented the case for art as epic poetry, with many actors and episodes that elaborate on the central theme and create a magnificent effect. He was also the first to argue that art has a sensuous appeal which exists as an end in itself.

Although it took place on a largely theoretical level, the debate over illusionistic ceiling painting represented more than fundamentally divergent approaches to telling a story and expressing ideas in art. The issue lay at the very heart of the Baroque. Illusionism enabled artists to overcome the apparent contradictions of the era by fusing separate levels of reality into a pictorial unity of such overwhelming grandeur as to sweep aside any differences between them. Despite the intensity of the argument, in actual practice the two sides rarely came into conflict over easel paintings, where the differences between

273. Annibale Carracci. Ceiling fresco. 1597–1601.
Gallery, Palazzo Farnese, Rome

274. Guido Reni. *Aurora.* Ceiling fresco. 1613. Casino Rospigliosi, Rome

275. Guercino. *Aurora.* Ceiling fresco. 1623. Villa Ludovisi, Rome

Cortona and the classicism of Carracci's followers were not always so clear-cut. Nevertheless, the leader of the reaction against what were regarded as the excesses of the High Baroque was neither a fresco painter, nor was he an Italian, but a French artist living in Rome: Nicolas Poussin (see pp. 317–19).

276. Pietro da Cortona. *The Glorification of the Reign of Urban VIII.* Portion of ceiling fresco. 1633–39. Palazzo Barberini, Rome

277. St. Peter's (aerial view), Rome. Nave and facade by Carlo Maderno, 1607–15; colonnade by Gianlorenzo Bernini, designed 1657

ARCHITECTURE AND SCULPTURE IN ITALY

St. Peter's. In architecture, the beginnings of the Baroque style cannot be defined as precisely as in painting. In the vast ecclesiastical building program that got under way in Rome toward the end of the sixteenth century, the most talented young architect to emerge was Carlo Maderno (1556–1629). In 1603 he was given the task of completing, at long last, the church of St. Peter's. The pope had decided to add a nave to Michelangelo's building (see fig. 236), converting it into a basilica. The change of plan (which may have been prompted by the example of Il Gesù) made it possible to link St. Peter's with the Vatican Palace (to the right of the church in figure 277).

Maderno's design for the facade follows the pattern established by Michelangelo for the exterior of the church. It consists of a colossal order supporting an attic, but with a dramatic emphasis on the portals. There is what can only be described as a crescendo effect that builds from the corners toward the center. The spacing of the supports becomes closer, pilasters turn into columns, and the facade wall projects step-by-step. This quickened rhythm had been hinted at a generation earlier in Giacomo della Porta's facade of Il Gesù (see fig. 256). Maderno made it the dominant principle of his facade designs, not only for St. Peter's but for smaller churches as well. In the process, he replaced the traditional concept of the church facade as one continuous wall surface, which was not yet challenged by the facade of Il Gesù, with the "facade-in-depth," dynamically related to the open space before it. The possibilities implicit in this new concept were not to be exhausted until a hundred and fifty years later.

Bernini. Maderno's work at St. Peter's was completed by Gianlorenzo Bernini (1598–1680), the greatest sculptor-architect of the century. It was he who molded the open space in front of the facade into a magnificent oval "forecourt" framed by colonnades, which Bernini himself likened to the motherly, all-embracing arms of the Church. For sheer impressiveness, this integration of the building with such a grandiose setting of "molded" open space can be compared only with the ancient Roman sanctuary at Palestrina (see fig. 84).

This is not the only instance of an affinity between Baroque and ancient art. A similar relationship can be discovered between Hellenistic and Baroque sculpture. If we compare Bernini's *David* (fig. 278) with Michelangelo's and ask which is closer to the Pergamum frieze (see figs. 231, 77), our vote must go to Bernini. His figure shares with Hellenistic works that unison of body and spirit, of motion and emotion, which Michelangelo so conspicuously avoids. This does not mean Bernini is more classical than Michelangelo. It indicates, rather, that both the Baroque and the High Renaissance acknowledged the authority of ancient art, but each period drew inspiration from a different aspect of antiquity.

278. Gianlorenzo Bernini. *David.* 1623. Marble, lifesize. Galleria Borghese, Rome

Bernini's *David,* obviously, is in no sense an echo of the Pergamum altar. What makes it Baroque is the implied presence of Goliath. Unlike earlier statues of David, including Donatello's (see fig. 203), Bernini's is conceived not as one self-contained figure but as half of a pair, his entire action focused on his adversary. Did Bernini, we wonder, plan a statue of Goliath to complete the group? He never did, for his *David* tells us clearly enough where *he* sees the enemy. Consequently, the space between David and his invisible opponent is charged with energy: it "belongs" to the statue.

Bernini's *David* shows us what distinguishes Baroque sculpture from the sculpture of the two preceding centuries: its new, active relationship with the space it inhabits. It rejects self-sufficiency for the illusion of presences or forces that are implied by the behavior of the statue. Because it so often presents an "invisible complement" (like the Goliath of Bernini's *David*), Baroque sculpture is a tour de force, attempting essentially pictorial effects that were traditionally outside its province. Such a charging of space with active energy is, in fact, a key feature of all Baroque art. Caravaggio had achieved it in his *St. Matthew,* with the aid of a sharply focused beam of light. Indeed, Baroque art acknowledges no sharp distinction between sculpture and painting. The two may even be combined with architecture to form a compound illusion, like that of the stage.

In fact, Bernini, who had a passionate interest in the theater, was at his best when he could merge architecture, sculpture, and painting. His masterpiece in this vein is the Cornaro Chapel, containing the famous group called *The Ecstasy of St. Theresa* (fig. 279), in the church of Sta. Maria della Vittoria. Theresa of Avila, one of the great saints of the Coun-

279. Gianlorenzo Bernini. *The Ecstasy of St. Theresa.* 1645–52. Marble, lifesize. Cornaro Chapel, Sta. Maria della Vittoria, Rome

ter Reformation (see p. 286), had described how an angel pierced her heart with a flaming golden arrow: "The pain was so great that I screamed aloud; but at the same time I felt such infinite sweetness that I wished the pain to last forever. It was not physical but psychic pain, although it affected the body as well to some degree. It was the sweetest caressing of the soul by God."

Bernini has made this visionary experience as sensuously real as Correggio's *Jupiter and Io* (see fig. 252). In a different context, the angel would be indistinguishable from Cupid, and the saint's ecstasy is palpable. The two figures, on their floating cloud, are illuminated (from a hidden window above) in such a way as to seem almost dematerialized in their gleaming whiteness. The beholder experiences them as visionary. The "invisible complement" here, less specific than David's but equally important, is the force that carries the figures heavenward, causing the turbulence of their drapery. Its divine nature is suggested by the golden rays, which come from a source high above the altar: in an illusionistic fresco by Guidebaldo Abbatini on the vault of the chapel, the glory of the heavens is revealed as a dazzling burst of light from which tumble clouds of jubilant angels (fig. 280). This celestial "explosion" gives force to the thrusts of the angel's arrow and makes the ecstasy of the saint believable.

To complete the illusion, Bernini even provides a built-in audience for his "stage": on the sides of the chapel are balconies resembling theater boxes, where we see marble figures, representing members of the Cornaro family, who also witness the ecstasy (fig. 280). Their space and ours are the same, and thus part of everyday reality, while the ecstasy,

280. *The Cornaro Chapel.* Anonymous 18th-century painting. Staatliches Museum, Schwerin, Germany

housed in a strongly framed niche, occupies a space that is real but beyond our reach. Finally, the ceiling fresco represents the infinite, unfathomable space of Heaven.

We may recall that *The Burial of Count Orgaz* and its setting also form a whole embracing three levels of reality (see p. 265). There is nevertheless a profound difference between the two chapels. El Greco's Mannerism evokes an ethereal vision in which only the stone slab of the sarcophagus is "real," in contrast to Bernini's Baroque theatricality, where the distinction nearly breaks down altogether. It would be all too easy to dismiss *The Ecstasy of St. Theresa* as a superficial, melodramatic display, but Bernini also was a devout Catholic who believed (as did Michelangelo) that he received his inspiration directly from God. Like the Spiritual Exercises of St. Ignatius, which he practiced, his religious sculpture is intended to help the viewer achieve complete identification with miraculous events through a vivid appeal to the senses.

Bernini was steeped in Renaissance humanism and theory. Central to his sculpture is the role played by gesture and expression in arousing emotion. While no less important to the Renaissance (compare Leonardo), these devices have an apparent abandon that seems anticlassical in Bernini's hands. However, he essentially adhered to the Renaissance concept of decorum, and calculated his effects very carefully, varying them in accordance with his subject. Unlike the Frenchman Nicolas Poussin (whom he admired), Bernini did this for the sake of expressive impact rather than conceptual clarity. Their approaches were diametrically opposed as well. For Bernini, antique art served as no more than a point of departure for his own fertile inventiveness, whereas for classicists like Poussin it provided a reference point that acted as a standard of comparison. It is nevertheless characteristic of the paradoxical Baroque that Bernini's theories should be far more orthodox than his art, and that he sometimes sided with classicists against his fellow High Baroque artists, despite the fact that his sculpture has much in common with the paintings of Pietro da Cortona.

281. Francesco Borromini. Facade, S. Carlo alle Quattro Fontane, Rome. 1665–67

Borromini. As a personality, Bernini represents a type we first met among the artists of the Early Renaissance, a self-assured, expansive person of the world. His great rival in architecture, Francesco Borromini (1599–1667), was the opposite type: a secretive and emotionally unstable genius who died by suicide. The Baroque heightened the tension between the two types. The temperamental contrast between the two masters would be evident from their works alone, even without the testimony of contemporary witnesses. Both exemplify the climax of Baroque architecture in Rome, yet Bernini's design for the colonnade of St. Peter's is dramatically simple and unified, while Borromini's structures are extravagantly complex. Bernini himself agreed with those who denounced Borromini

282. Dome, S. Carlo alle Quattro Fontane

the world. This is attested by the foreigners who . . . try to procure copies of the plan. We have been asked for them by Germans, Flemings, Frenchmen, Italians, Spaniards, and even Indians. . . ."

Guarini. The wealth of new ideas that Borromini introduced was to be exploited not in Rome but in Turin, the capital of Savoy, which became the creative center of Baroque architecture in Italy toward the end of the seventeenth century. In 1666, that city attracted Borromini's most brilliant successor, Guarino Guarini (1624–1683), a monk whose architectural genius was deeply grounded in philosophy and mathematics. His design for the facade of the Palazzo Carignano (fig. 283) repeats on a larger scale the undulating movement of S. Carlo alle Quattro Fontane, using a highly individual vocabulary. Incredibly, the exterior of the building is entirely of brick, down to the last ornamental detail.

for flagrantly disregarding the classical tradition, enshrined in Renaissance theory and practice, that architecture must reflect the proportions of the human body.

In Borromini's first major project, the church of S. Carlo alle Quattro Fontane (fig. 281), it is the syntax, not the vocabulary, that is new and disquieting. The ceaseless play of concave and convex surfaces makes the entire structure seem elastic, "pulled out of shape" by pressures that no previous building could have withstood. The inside of the dome (fig. 282), like the plan which it echoes, looks as if it had been drawn on rubber and would snap back to normal if the tension were relaxed. The facade was designed almost thirty years later, and the pressures and counterpressures here reach their maximum intensity. Borromini merges architecture and sculpture in a way that must have shocked Bernini, as no such fusion had been ventured since Gothic art. S. Carlo alle Quattro Fontane established Borromini's local and international fame. "Nothing similar," wrote the head of the religious order for which the church was built, "can be found anywhere in

283. Guarino Guarini. Facade of Palazzo Carignano, Turin. Begun 1679

PAINTING IN SPAIN

During the sixteenth century, at the height of its political and economic power, Spain had produced great saints and writers, but no artists of the first rank. Nor did El Greco's presence prove a stimulus to native talent. The impetus came, rather, from Caravaggio. We do not know exactly how his style was transmitted, for his influence was felt in Spain by the second decade of the century, even before he fled Rome for Naples, then under Spanish rule, after slaying a man in a duel (see p. 120).

284. Francisco de Zurbarán. *St. Serapion.* 1628. Oil on canvas, 47½ × 41" (120.7 × 104.1 cm). Wadsworth Atheneum, Hartford, Connecticut. Ella Gallup Sumner and Mary Catlin Sumner Collection

Zurbarán. Seville was the home of the leading Spanish Baroque painters before 1640. Francisco de Zurbarán (1598–1664) stands out among them for his quiet intensity. This artist's most important works were done for monastic orders, and consequently are filled with an ascetic piety that is uniquely Spanish. *St. Serapion* (fig. 284) shows an early member of the Mercedarians (Order of Mercy) who was brutally murdered by pirates in 1240 but canonized only a hundred years after this picture was painted. The canvas was appropriately placed as a devotional image in the funerary chapel of the order, which was originally dedicated to self-sacrifice.

The painting will remind us of Caravaggio's *David with the Head of Goliath* (see fig. 9). Each shows a single, three-quarter-length figure in life size; but Zurbarán's saint is both hero and martyr, and it is the viewer who now contemplates the slain monk with a mixture of compassion and awe. The sharp contrast between the white habit and dark background lends the motionless figure a heightened visual and expressive presence. Here pictorial and spiritual purity become one. The hushed stillness creates a reverential mood that counteracts the stark realism, so that we identify with the strength of St. Serapion's faith rather than his physical suffering. The very absence of rhetorical pathos makes this timeless image profoundly moving.

Velázquez. Diego Velázquez (1599–1660), too, painted in a Caravaggesque vein during his early years in Seville, but his interests centered on genre and still life rather than religious themes. In the late 1620s Velázquez was appointed court painter and moved to Madrid, where he mainly did portraits of the royal family. During one of his visits to the Spanish court, the Flemish painter Peter Paul Rubens helped him discover the beauty of the many Titians in the king's collection, from which he developed a new fluency and richness.

The Maids of Honor (fig. 285) displays Velázquez' mature style at its fullest. It is at once a group portrait and a genre scene. It might be subtitled "the artist in his studio," for Velázquez shows himself at work on a huge canvas. In the center is the little Princess Margarita, who has just posed for him, among her playmates and maids of honor. The faces of her parents, the king and queen, appear in the mirror on the back wall. Have they just stepped into the room, to see the scene exactly as we do, or does the mirror reflect part of the canvas (presumably a full-length portrait of the royal family) on which the artist

285. Diego Velázquez. *The Maids of Honor.* 1656. Oil on canvas, 10′5″ × 9′ (3.18 × 2.74 m). Museo del Prado, Madrid

has been working? This ambiguity shows Velázquez' fascination with light. The artist challenges us to find the varieties of direct and reflected light in *The Maids of Honor.* We are expected to match the mirror image against the paintings on the same wall, and against the "picture" of the man in the open doorway.

Although the side lighting and strong contrasts of light and dark still suggest the influence of Caravaggio, Velázquez' technique is far more varied and subtle, with delicate glazes setting off the impasto of the highlights. The glowing colors have a Venetian richness, but the brushwork is even freer and sketchier than Titian's. Velázquez was concerned with the optical qualities of light rather than its metaphysical mysteries; these he penetrated more completely than any other painter of his time. His aim is to show the movement of light itself and the infinite range of its effects on form and color. For Velázquez, as for Jan Vermeer in Holland (see pp. 25–26), light *creates* the visible world.

THE BAROQUE IN FLANDERS AND HOLLAND

In 1581, the six northern provinces of the Netherlands, led by William the Silent of Nassau, declared their independence from Spain, capping a rebellion that had begun fifteen years earlier against Catholicism and the attempt by Philip II to curtail local power. The southern Netherlands, called Flanders (now divided between France and Belgium), were soon recovered; but after a long struggle the United Provinces (today's Holland) gained their autonomy, which was recognized by the truce declared in 1609. Although hostilities broke out again in 1621, the freedom of the Dutch was ratified by the Treaty of Münster, which ended the Thirty Years' War in 1648.

The division of the Netherlands had very different consequences for the economy, social structure, culture, and religion of the north and the south. After being sacked by marauding Spanish troops in 1576, Antwerp lost half its population. The city gradually regained its position as Flanders' commercial and artistic capital, as well as its leading port, until the Scheldt River leading to its harbor was closed permanently to shipping as part of the Treaty of Münster, thereby crippling trade for the next two centuries. (Only then did Brussels, the seat of the Spanish regent, come to play a major role in the country's cultural life.) Because Flanders continued to be ruled by the Spanish monarchy, which was staunchly Catholic and viewed itself as the defender of the true faith, its artists relied heavily on commissions from Church and State, although the patronage of the aristocracy and wealthy merchants was also of considerable importance.

Holland was proud of its hard-won freedom. While the cultural links with Flanders remained strong, several factors encouraged the quick development of Dutch artistic traditions. Unlike Flanders, where all artistic activity radiated from Antwerp, Holland had a number of flourishing local schools. Besides Amsterdam, the commercial capital, we find important groups of painters in Haarlem, Utrecht, Leyden, Delft, and other towns. Thus, Holland produced a bewildering variety of masters and styles.

The new nation was one of merchants, farmers, and seafarers, and its religion was Reformed Protestant. Hence, Dutch artists did not have the large-scale commissions sponsored by State and Church that were available throughout the Catholic world. While municipal authorities and civic bodies provided a certain amount of art patronage, their demands were limited, so that the private collector now became the painter's chief source of support. This condition had already existed to some extent before (see p. 282), but its full effect can be seen only after 1600. There was no shrinkage of output; on the contrary, the general public developed so insatiable an appetite for pictures that the whole country became gripped by a kind of collectors' mania. Pictures became a commodity, and their trade followed the law of supply and demand. Many artists produced "for the market" rather than for individual patrons. The collectors' mania in seventeenth-century Holland caused an outpouring of artistic talent comparable only to Early Renaissance Florence. Many Dutch were lured into becoming painters by hopes of success that failed to materialize, and even the greatest masters were sometimes hard-pressed. (It was not unusual for an artist to keep an inn, or run a small business on the side.) Yet they survived—less secure, but freer.

FLANDERS

Rubens. In Flanders, all of art was overshadowed by the majestic personality of the great painter Peter Paul Rubens (1577–1640). It might be said that he finished what Dürer had started a hundred years earlier: the breakdown of the artistic barriers between North and South. Rubens' father was a prominent Antwerp Protestant who fled to Germany to escape Spanish persecution during the war of independence. The family returned to Antwerp after his death, when Peter Paul was ten years old, and the boy grew up a devout Catholic. Trained by local painters, Rubens became a master in 1598, but developed a personal style only when, two years later, he went to Italy.

During his eight years in the South, he eagerly studied ancient sculpture, the masterpieces of the High Renaissance, and the work of Caravaggio and Annibale Carracci, absorbing the Italian tradition far more thoroughly than had any Northerner before him. He competed with the best Italians of his day on even terms, and could well have made his career in Italy. When in 1608 his mother's illness brought him back to Flanders, he received a special appointment as court painter to the Spanish regent, which permitted him to establish a workshop in Antwerp, exempt from local taxes and guild regulations. Rubens had the best of both worlds. Like Jan van Eyck before him (see p. 204), he was valued at court not only as an artist, but also as a confidential adviser and emissary. Diplomatic errands gave him entrée to the royal households of the major powers, where he procured sales and commissions. Aided by a small army of assistants, he also carried out a vast amount of work for the city of Antwerp, for the Church, and for private patrons.

In his life, Rubens epitomized the extroverted Baroque ideal of the virtuoso for whom the entire universe is a stage. He was, on the one hand, a devoutly religious person and, on the other, a person of the world who succeeded in every arena by virtue of his character and ability. Rubens resolved the contradictions of the era through humanism, that union of faith and learning attacked by the Reformation and Counter Reformation alike. In his paintings as well, Rubens reconciled seemingly incompatible opposites. His enormous intellect and vitality enabled him to synthesize his sources into a unique style that unites the natural and supernatural, reality and fantasy, learning and spirituality. Thus, his epic canvases defined the scope and the style of High Baroque painting. They possess a seemingly boundless energy and inventiveness, which, like his heroic nudes, express life at its fullest. The presentation of this heightened existence required the expanded arena that only Baroque theatricality, in the best sense of the term, could provide, and Rubens' sense of drama was as highly developed as Bernini's.

The Raising of the Cross (fig. 286), the first major altarpiece Rubens produced after his return to Antwerp, shows just how much he owed to Italian art. The muscular figures, modeled to display their physical power and passionate feeling, recall those in Michelangelo's Sistine Ceiling and Annibale Carracci's Farnese Gallery, while the lighting suggests Caravaggio's (see figs. 233, 273, and 271). The panel nevertheless owes much of its success to Rubens' remarkable ability to unite Italian influences with Netherlandish ideas, updating them in the process. The painting is more heroic in scale and conception than any previous Northern work, yet it is unthinkable without Rogier van der Weyden's *Descent from the Cross* (see fig. 191). Rubens is also a meticulous Flemish realist in such details as the foliage, the armor of the soldier, and the curly haired dog in the foreground. These varied elements, integrated with sovereign mastery, form a composition of tremendous dramatic force. The unstable pyramid of bodies, swaying precariously, bursts the limits

286. Peter Paul Rubens. *The Raising of the Cross.* 1609–10. Center panel of a triptych, oil on panel, 15′ × 11′2″ (4.57 × 3.4 m). Antwerp Cathedral

287. Peter Paul Rubens. *Marie de'Medici, Queen of France, Landing in Marseilles.* 1622–23. Oil on panel, 25 × 19¾″ (63.5 × 50.2 cm). Pinakothek, Munich

of the frame in a characteristically Baroque way, making the beholder feel like a participant in the action.

In the decade of the 1620s, Rubens' dynamic style reached its climax in his huge decorative schemes for churches and palaces. The most famous is the cycle in the Luxembourg Palace in Paris, glorifying the career of Marie de'Medici, the widow of Henry IV and mother of Louis XIII. Our illustration shows the artist's oil sketch for one episode, the young queen landing in Marseilles (fig. 287). Rubens has turned what is hardly an exciting subject into a spectacle of unprecedented splendor. As Marie de'Medici walks down the gangplank, Fame flies overhead sounding a triumphant blast on two trumpets, and Neptune rises from the sea with his fish-tailed crew; having guarded the queen's journey, they rejoice at her arrival. Everything flows together here in swirling movement: heaven and earth, history and allegory, even drawing and painting, for Rubens used oil sketches like this one to prepare his compositions. Unlike earlier artists, he preferred to design his pictures in terms of light and color from the very start (most of his drawings are figure studies or portrait sketches). This unified vision, initiated but never fully achieved by the great Venetians, was Rubens' most precious legacy to subsequent painters.

Around 1630, the turbulent drama of Rubens' preceding work changes to a late style of lyrical tenderness inspired by Titian, whom Rubens rediscovered in the royal palace while he visited Madrid. *The Garden of Love* (fig. 288) is one result of this encounter, as glowing a tribute to life's pleasures as Titian's *Bacchanal* (see fig. 240). But these celebrants belong to the present, not to a golden age of the past, though they are playfully assaulted by swarms of cupids. The picture must have had special meaning for him, since he had just married a beautiful girl of sixteen (his first wife died in 1626). The Garden of Love had been a feature of Northern painting ever since the courtly style of the International Gothic. The early versions of the subject, however, were pure

288. Peter Paul Rubens. *The Garden of Love.* c. 1638. Oil on canvas, 6′6″ × 9′3½″ (1.98 × 2.83 m). Museo del Prado, Madrid

genre scenes which merely showed groups of fashionable young lovers in a garden. By combining this tradition with Titian's classical mythologies, Rubens has created an enchanted realm where myth and reality become one.

Van Dyck. Besides Rubens, only one Flemish Baroque artist won international stature. Anthony van Dyck (1599–1641) was that rarity among painters, a child prodigy. Before he was twenty, he had become Rubens' most valued assistant. Although he lacked the older master's vitality and inventiveness, his gifts were ideally suited to portraits. Those he painted in England as court painter to Charles I between 1632 and 1641 represent the crowning achievement of his career. *Portrait of Charles I Hunting* (fig. 289) shows the king standing near a horse and two grooms against a landscape backdrop. Repre-

289. Anthony van Dyck. *Portrait of Charles I Hunting.* c. 1635. Oil on canvas, 8′11″ × 6′11½″ (2.72 × 2.12 m). Musée du Louvre, Paris

290. Jacob Jordaens. *The Nurture of Jupiter.* c. 1630–35. Oil on canvas, 59 × 80" (149.9 × 203.2 cm). Musée du Louvre, Paris

senting the sovereign at ease, it might be called a "dismounted equestrian portrait," less rigid than a formal state portrait but hardly less grand. The fluid Baroque movement of the setting contrasts oddly with the self-conscious elegance of the king's pose, which still suggests the stylized grace of Mannerist portraits (compare fig. 246). Van Dyck has brought the Mannerist court portrait up-to-date, rephrasing it in the pictorial language of Rubens and Titian. He created a new aristocratic portrait tradition that continued in England until the late eighteenth century, and had considerable influence on the Continent as well.

Jordaens. Jacob Jordaens (1593–1678) was the successor to Rubens and Van Dyck as the leading artist in Flanders. He preceded Van Dyck as Rubens' assistant and continued to turn to Rubens for inspiration long after leaving his studio. His most characteristic subjects are mythological themes. Throughout his career, Jordaens emulated Rubens in depicting the revels of nymphs and satyrs. Like his eating and drinking scenes, which illustrate popular parables of an edifying or moralizing sort, they reveal him to be a close observer of people and epitomize the Flemish gusto for life. These denizens of the woods, however, inhabit an idyllic realm, untouched by the cares of human affairs. While the painterly execution in *The Nurture of Jupiter* (fig. 290) acknowledges a strong debt to Rubens, the monumental figures possess a calm dignity that dispenses with Rubens' rhetoric and lends them a character all their own.

HOLLAND

Hals. The Baroque style came to Holland from Antwerp through the work of Rubens,

291. Frans Hals. *The Jolly Toper.* c. 1628–30. Oil on canvas, 31⅞ × 26¼″ (81 × 66.7 cm). Rijksmuseum, Amsterdam

and from Rome through direct contact with Caravaggio and his followers, some of whom were Dutch. One of the first artists to profit from this experience was Frans Hals (1580/85–1666), the great portrait painter of Haarlem. He was born in Antwerp, and what little is known of his early work suggests the influence of Rubens. However, his fully developed style, as seen in *The Jolly Toper* (fig. 291), combines Rubens' robustness and breadth with a concentration on the "dramatic moment" that must be derived from Caravaggio. Everything here conveys complete spontaneity: the twinkling eyes and half-open mouth, the raised hand, and the teetering wineglass. Most important of all is the quick way of setting down the forms. Hals works in dashing brushstrokes, each so clearly visible as a separate entity that we can almost count the total number of "touches." With this open, split-second technique, the completed picture has the immediacy of a sketch by Rubens (com-

292. Frans Hals. *The Women Regents of the Old Men's Home at Haarlem.* 1664. Oil on canvas, 67 × 98″ (170.2 × 248.9 cm). Frans Halsmuseum, Haarlem

pare fig. 287). The impression of a race against time is, of course, deceptive. Hals spent hours, not minutes, on this lifesize canvas, but he maintains the illusion of having done it all in the wink of an eye.

In the artist's last canvases these pictorial fireworks are transformed into an austere style of great emotional depth. His group portrait *The Women Regents of the Old Men's Home at Haarlem* (fig. 292), the institution where he spent his final years, has an insight into human character matched only in Rembrandt's late style (compare fig. 296). The daily experience of suffering and death has so etched the faces of these women that they

293. Judith Leyster. *Boy Playing a Flute*. 1630–35. Oil on canvas, 28$\frac{3}{8}$ × 24$\frac{3}{8}$″ (72.1 × 61.9 cm). Nationalmuseum, Stockholm

294. Rembrandt. *The Blinding of Samson*. 1636. Oil on canvas, 7′9″ × 9′11″ (2.36 × 3.02 m). Städelsches Kunstinstitut, Frankfurt

295. Rembrandt. *The Night Watch (The Company of Captain Frans Banning Cocq)*. 1642. Oil on canvas, 12'2" × 14'7" (3.71 × 4.45 m). Rijksmuseum, Amsterdam

seem themselves to have become images of death—gentle, inexorable, and timeless.

Leyster. Hals' virtuosity was such that it could not be imitated readily, and his followers were necessarily few. The only one of importance was Judith Leyster (1609–1660). The enchanting *Boy Playing a Flute* (fig. 293) is her masterpiece. The rapt musician is a memorable expression of a gentle activity. To convey this spirit, Leyster investigated the poetic quality of light with a quiet intensity that anticipates the work of Jan Vermeer a generation later (see fig. 301).

Rembrandt. Like Hals, Rembrandt (1606–1669), the greatest genius of Dutch art, was stimulated at the beginning of his career by indirect contact with Caravaggio. His earliest pictures are small, sharply lit, and intensely realistic. Many deal with Old Testament subjects, a lifelong preference. They show both his greater realism and his new emotional attitude as compared with the Italian's style. Rembrandt viewed the stories of the Old Testament in the same lay Christian spirit that governed Caravaggio's approach to the New Testament: as direct accounts of God's ways with His human creations. How strongly these stories affected him is evident from *The Blinding of Samson* (fig. 294). Painted in the full-blown High Baroque style he developed in the 1630s, it shows us the Old Testament world in Oriental splendor and violence. The flood of brilliant light pouring into the dark tent is unabashedly theatrical, heightening

296. Rembrandt. *Self-Portrait.* 1658. Oil on canvas, 52⅝ × 40⅞" (133.7 × 103.8 cm). The Frick Collection, New York (Copyright)

the drama to the pitch of *The Raising of the Cross* (see fig. 286) by Rubens, whose work Rembrandt sought to rival.

Rembrandt was at this time an avid collector of Near Eastern paraphernalia, which serve as props in these pictures. He was now Amsterdam's most sought-after portrait painter, as well as a man of considerable wealth. This prosperity petered out in the 1640s. The turning point may have been his famous group portrait known as *The Night Watch* (fig. 295). The huge canvas (originally it was even larger) shows a military company, whose members had each contributed toward the cost. But Rembrandt did not do them equal justice. Anxious to avoid a mechanically regular design, he made the picture a virtuoso performance of Baroque movement and lighting; in the process some of the figures were plunged into shadow, and some were hidden by overlapping.

The decline in Rembrandt's fortunes after 1642 was less sudden and complete than his romantic admirers would have us believe. Certain important people in Amsterdam continued to be his steadfast friends and supporters, and he received some major public commissions in the 1650s and 1660s. His financial difficulties resulted largely from poor management. Still, the 1640s were a period of crisis, of inner uncertainty and external troubles. Rembrandt's outlook changed profoundly. After about 1650, his style foregoes the rhetoric of the High Baroque for lyric subtlety and pictorial breadth. Some exotic trappings from the earlier years remain, but they no longer create an alien world.

We can trace this change in the many self-portraits Rembrandt painted over his long career. His view of himself reflects every stage of his inner development: experimental in the early Leyden years, theatrically disguised in the 1630s, frank toward the end of his life. Our late example (fig. 296), while partially indebted to Titian's sumptuous portraits (compare fig. 241), shows Rembrandt scrutinizing himself with the same typically Northern candor found in Jan van Eyck's *Man in a Red Turban* (see fig. 188). This self-analytical approach helps account for the simple dignity we see in the religious scenes that play so large a part in Rembrandt's work in his later years.

Rembrandt's prints, such as *Christ Preaching* (fig. 297), show his depth of feeling. The sensuous beauty of *The Blinding of Samson* has now yielded to a humble world of bare feet and ragged clothes. The scene is full of the artist's great compassion for the poor and outcast who make up Christ's audience. Rembrandt had a special sympathy for Jews, who were often his models. To him, they were the heirs of the biblical past and patient victims of persecution. This print strongly suggests some corner in the Amsterdam ghetto, and surely incorporates observations of life from the drawings he habitually made throughout his career. Here, as in Caravaggio's *The Calling of St. Matthew* (see fig. 271), it is the magic of light that endows *Christ Preaching* with spiritual significance.

Etching and Drypoint. Rembrandt's importance as a graphic artist is second only to

297. Rembrandt. *Christ Preaching*. c. 1652. Etching, 6⅛ × 8⅛" (15.6 × 20.6 cm). The Metropolitan Museum of Art, New York. Bequest of Mrs. H. O. Havemeyer, 1929

Dürer's, although we get no more than a hint of this from our single example. Like other creative printmakers of the day, he preferred etching, often combined with drypoint, to the techniques of woodcut and engraving, which were employed mainly to reproduce other works. An etching is made by coating a copperplate with resin to make an acid-resistant "ground," through which the design is scratched with a needle, laying bare the metal surface underneath. The plate is then bathed in an acid that etches (or "bites") the lines into the copper. To scratch a design with a needle into the resinous ground is, of course, an easier task than to gouge it using a burin (see p. 215); hence, an etched line is smoother and more flexible than an engraved line, and preserves a sketchlike immediacy. As a result of its greater density of line, etching permits a wide tonal range, including velvety dark shades not possible in engraving or woodcut. Drypoint is made by scratching the design directly into the copperplate itself with a needle, which leaves a raised "burr" (the metal displaced by the needle) along the shallow line. Since the burr quickly breaks down, a drypoint plate yields far fewer prints than an etched plate.

Landscape and Still Life Painters

Rembrandt's religious pictures demand an insight that was beyond the capacity of all but a few collectors. Most art buyers in Holland preferred subjects within their own experience: landscapes, architectural views, still lifes, everyday scenes. These various types, we recall, originated in the latter half of the sixteenth century (see p. 283). As they became fully defined, an unheard-of specialization began. The trend was not confined to Holland, and is found throughout Europe to some degree. In both volume and variety, however, Dutch painters produced far more subtypes within each major division than anyone else.

Van Ruisdael. The richest of the newly developed "specialties" was landscape, both as a portrayal of familiar views and as an imaginative vision of nature. *The Jewish Cemetery* (fig. 298) by Jacob van Ruisdael (1628/29–1682), the greatest Dutch landscape painter, is frankly imaginary. Natural forces dominate the scene. The thunderclouds passing over a wild, deserted mountain valley, the medieval ruin, the torrent that has forced its way between ancient graves, all create a mood of deep melancholy. Nothing endures on this earth, the artist tells us: time, wind, and water grind all to dust, the feeble works of human hands as well as the trees and rocks. Ruisdael's vision of nature in relation to civilization inspires that awe on which the Romantics, a century later, were to base their concept of the Sublime.

298. Jacob van Ruisdael. *The Jewish Cemetery.* 1655–60. Oil on canvas, 4′6″ × 6′2½″ (1.37 × 1.89 m). The Detroit Institute of Arts. Gift of Julius H. Haass in memory of his brother Dr. Ernest W. Haass

299. Willem Claesz. Heda. *Still Life.* 1634. Oil on panel, 16⅞ × 22⅞″ (42.9 × 58.1 cm). Boymans-van Beuningen Museum, Rotterdam

Heda. Still lifes are meant above all to delight the senses, but even they can be tinged with

300. Jan Steen. *The Feast of St. Nicholas.* c. 1660–65. Oil on canvas, 32¼ × 27¾" (81.9 × 70.5 cm). Rijksmuseum, Amsterdam

a melancholy air. As a result of Holland's conversion to Calvinism, these visual feasts became vehicles for teaching moral lessons. In them, the disguised symbolism of "Late Gothic" painting lives on in a new form. Most Dutch Baroque still lifes treat the theme of *Vanitas* (the vanity of all earthly things), either overtly or implicitly: they preach the virtue of temperance, frugality, and hard work by admonishing the viewer to contemplate the brevity of life, the inevitability of death, and the passing of all earthly pleasures. The imagery

301. Jan Vermeer. *The Letter.* 1666. Oil on canvas, 17¼ × 15¼" (43.8 × 38.7 cm). Rijksmuseum, Amsterdam

derives in part from emblem books, as well as other popular literature and prints, which encompass the prevailing ethic in words and pictures. The stern Calvinist sensibility is exemplified by homilies like, "A fool and his money are soon parted," and illustrated by flowers, shells, and other exotic luxuries. The presence in *Vanitas* still lifes of precious goods, scholarly books, and objects appealing to the senses suggests an ambivalent attitude toward their subject. Such symbols, moreover, usually take on multiple meanings. In their most elaborate form, these moral allegories become visual riddles that rely on the very learning they sometimes ridicule.

The banquet (or breakfast) piece, showing the remnants of a meal, had *Vanitas* connotations almost from the beginning. The message may lie in such established symbols as death's-heads and extinguished candles, or be conveyed by less direct means. Willem Claesz. Heda's *Still Life* (fig. 299) belongs to this widespread type. Food and drink are less emphasized here than luxury objects, such as crystal goblets and silver dishes, which are carefully juxtaposed for their contrasting shape, color, and texture. Virtuosity was not Heda's only aim: he reminds us that all is vanity. Heda's "story," the human context of these grouped objects, is suggested by the broken glass, the half-peeled lemon, the overturned silver dish. The unstable composition, with its signs of a hasty departure, is itself a reference to transience: whoever sat at this table has been suddenly forced to abandon the meal. The curtain that time has lowered on the scene, as it were, invests the objects with a strange pathos.

Genre Painters

Steen. The vast class of pictures termed genre is as varied as that of landscapes and still lifes. It ranges from tavern brawls to refined domestic interiors. *The Feast of St. Nicholas* (fig. 300) by Jan Steen (1625/26–1679) is midway between. St. Nicholas has just paid his pre-Christmas visit to the household, leaving toys, candy, and cake for the children. Everybody is jolly except the bad boy on the left, who has received only a birch rod. Steen tells this story with relish, embroidering it with many delightful details. Of all the Dutch painters of daily life, he was the sharpest, and the most good-humored, observer. To supplement his earnings he kept an inn, which perhaps explains his keen insight into human behavior. His sense of timing and his characterization often remind us of Frans Hals (compare fig. 291), while his storytelling stems from the tradition of Pieter Bruegel the Elder (compare fig. 266).

Vermeer. In the genre scenes of Jan Vermeer (1632–1675), by contrast, there is hardly any narrative. Single figures, usually women, engage in simple, everyday tasks; when there are two, as in *The Letter* (fig. 301), they do no more than exchange glances. They exist in a timeless "still life" world, seemingly calmed by some magic spell. The cool, clear light that filters in from the left in our picture is the only active element, working its miracles upon all the objects in its path. As we look at *The Letter*, we feel as if a veil had been pulled from our eyes. The everyday world shines with jewellike freshness, beautiful as we have never seen it before. No painter since Jan van Eyck *saw* as intensely as this.

Unlike his predecessors, Vermeer perceives reality as a mosaic of colored surfaces; perhaps more accurately, he translates reality into a mosaic as he puts it on canvas. We see *The Letter* as a perspective "window," and as a plane, a "field" composed of smaller fields. Rectangles predominate, carefully aligned with the picture surface; there are no "holes," no undefined empty spaces. These interlocking shapes give Vermeer's work a uniquely modern quality. The carefully "staged" entrance serves to establish our relation to the scene. We are more than privileged bystanders: we become the bearer of the letter that has just been delivered to the young woman. Dressed in sumptuous clothing, she has been playing the lute, as if awaiting our visit. This instrument, laden with erotic meaning, traditionally signifies the harmony between lovers, who play each other's heartstrings. Are we, then, her lover? The amused expression of the maid suggests just such an anecdotal interest. Moreover, the lover in Dutch art and literature is often compared to a ship at sea, whose calm waters depicted in the painting here indicate smooth sailing. As usual with Vermeer, however, the picture refuses to yield a final answer (see p. 25), since the artist has concentrated on the moment before the letter is opened.

THE BAROQUE IN FRANCE: THE AGE OF VERSAILLES

Under Louis XIV, France became the most powerful nation of Europe, militarily and culturally. By the late seventeenth century, Paris was vying with Rome as the world capital of the major and minor arts, a position the Holy City had held for centuries. How did this change come about? We are tempted to think of French art in the age of Louis XIV as the expression of absolutism, because of the Palace of Versailles and other vast projects glorifying the king of France. This is true of the climactic phase of Louis' reign, 1660–85, but by that time seventeenth-century French art had already attained its distinctive style.

The French are reluctant to call this manner Baroque. To them, it is the Style of Louis XIV. They often describe the art and literature of the period as "classic." In this context, the word has three meanings. It is first of all a synonym for "highest achievement," which implies that the Style of Louis XIV corresponds to the High Renaissance in Italy or the age of Pericles in ancient Greece. The term also refers to the emulation of the form and subject matter of classical antiquity. Finally, "classic" suggests qualities of balance and restraint, shared by ancient art and the Renaissance. The second and third of these meanings describe what could more accurately be called "classicism." Since the Style of Louis XIV reflects Italian Baroque art, we may label it "Baroque classicism."

The origin of this classicism was primarily artistic, not political. Sixteenth-century architecture in France, and to a lesser extent sculpture, were more intimately linked with the Italian Renaissance than in any other northern country, although painting continued to be dominated by the Mannerist style of the later school of Fontainebleau until after 1600 (see pp. 268–70). Classicism was also nourished by French humanism, with its intellectual heritage of reason and Stoic virtue. These factors retarded the spread of the Baroque in France, and modified its interpretation. Rubens' Medici Cycle (see fig. 287), for example, had no effect on French art until the very end of the century. In the 1620s, when he painted it, the young artists in France were still assimilating the Early Baroque.

PAINTING

De La Tour. Many of these painters were influenced by Caravaggio, although how they

302. Georges de La Tour. *Joseph the Carpenter.* c. 1645. Oil on canvas, 51⅛ × 39¾″ (129.9 × 101 cm). Musée du Louvre, Paris

303. Nicolas Poussin. *The Rape of the Sabine Women.* c. 1636–37. Oil on canvas, 60⅞ × 82⅝" (154.6 × 209.9 cm). The Metropolitan Museum of Art, New York. Harris Brisbane Dick Fund, 1946

absorbed his style is far from clear. They were for the most part minor artists toiling in the provinces, but a few developed highly original styles. The finest of them was Georges de La Tour (1593–1652), whose importance was recognized only two hundred years later. His *Joseph the Carpenter* (fig. 302) might be mistaken for a genre scene, were it not for its devotional spirit, which has the power of Caravaggio's *The Calling of St. Matthew* (see fig. 271). The boy Jesus holds a candle, a favorite device with De La Tour, which lights the scene with an intimacy and tenderness reminiscent of Geertgen tot Sint Jans (compare fig. 193). De La Tour also shares Geertgen's tendency to reduce his forms to geometric simplicity.

Poussin. Why was De La Tour so quickly forgotten? The reason is simply that after the 1640s, classicism was supreme in France. The clarity, balance, and restraint of De La Tour's art might be termed "classical," especially when measured against other Caravaggesque painters, but he was certainly not a "classicist." The artist who did the most to bring the rise of classicism about was Nicolas Poussin (1593/94–1665). The greatest French painter of the century, and the first French painter in history to win international fame, Poussin nevertheless spent almost his entire career in Rome. There, under the inspiration of Raphael, he formulated the style that was to become the ideal model for French painters of the second half of the century.

The Rape of the Sabine Women (fig. 303) shows the severe discipline of Poussin's intellectual style. The strongly modeled figures are "frozen in action" like statues, and many are, in fact, derived from Hellenistic sculpture. Poussin has placed them before reconstructions of Roman architecture that he

304. Nicolas Poussin. *The Birth of Bacchus.* c. 1657. Oil on canvas, 48⅜ × 70½" (123 × 179 cm). Fogg Art Museum, Harvard University Art Museums, Cambridge, Massachusetts. Gift of Mrs. Samuel Sachs in memory of her husband, Mr. Samuel Sachs

believed to be archaeologically correct. The composition has an air of theatricality, and with good reason: it was worked out by moving clay figurines around a miniature stage-like setting until it looked right to the artist. Emotion is abundantly displayed, but it is so lacking in spontaneity that it fails to touch us. Clearly, the attitude reflected here is Raphael's. More precisely, it is Raphael as filtered through Annibale Carracci and his school (compare figs. 273, 274). Venetian qualities, which asserted themselves early in his career, have been consciously suppressed.

Poussin may strike us as a man who knew his own mind only too well, an impression confirmed by the numerous letters in which he expounded his views to friends and patrons. The highest aim of painting, he believed, is to represent noble and serious human actions. These must be shown in a logical and orderly way; that is, not as they really happened, but as they would have happened if nature were perfect. To this end, the artist must strive for the general and typical. In appealing to the mind rather than the senses, he should suppress such incidentals as color, and stress form and composition. In a good picture, the beholder must be able to "read" the exact emotions of each figure, and relate them to the story. These ideas were not new. We recall the ancient dictum *ut pictura poesis* and Leonardo's statement that the highest aim of painting is to depict "the intention of man's soul" (see pp. 244, 291). Before Poussin, however, no one made the analogy between painting and literature so close, nor put it into practice so single-mindedly. His method accounts for the cold and overexplicit rhetoric in *The Rape of the Sabine Women* that makes the picture seem so remote, much as we may admire its rigor.

Poussin also painted "ideal landscapes" according to this theoretical view, with surprisingly impressive results, for they have an austere beauty and somber calm. This severe rationalism lasted until about 1650, when he began to paint a series of landscapes that return to the realm of mythology he had abandoned in middle age. These unite the Titianesque style of his early work with his later, Raphaelesque classicism to produce a new kind of mythological landscape, close in spirit to Claude Lorraine's (see below) but rich in personal associations that lend them multiple levels of meaning. Indeed, the artist's late ruminations have rightly been called transcendental meditations, for they contain archetypal imagery of universal significance. *The Birth of Bacchus* (fig. 304), among his most profound statements, takes up the great Stoic theme (which Poussin had treated twice already as a young man) that death is to be found even in the happiest realm. The painting shows the moment when the infant, created by Jupiter's union with the moon goddess Semele and born from his thigh, is delivered for safekeeping by Mercury to the river goddess Dirce, while the satyr Pan plays the flute in rapt inspiration. (Jupiter himself had been raised by sylvan deities; see fig. 290.) The picture is not beautifully executed; the act of painting became difficult for the artist in old age, so that the brushwork is shaky. He nevertheless turned this liability to his advantage, and *The Birth of Bacchus* represents the purest realization of expressive intent in painted form. It is full of serene lyricism conveying the joy of life on the one hand, and dark forebodings of death on the other: to the right, the nymph Echo weeps over the dead Narcissus, the beautiful youth who spurned her love and instead drowned kissing his reflection.

Claude Lorraine. If Poussin developed the heroic qualities of the "ideal landscape," the great French landscapist Claude Lorraine (1600–1682) brought out its idyllic aspects. He, too, spent almost his entire career in Rome. Like many Northerners, Claude explored the countryside outside that city (the Campagna) more thoroughly and affectionately than any Italian. Countless drawings made on the spot bear witness to his extraordinary powers of observation. He is also documented as having sketched in oils from nature, the first artist known to have done so. Sketches, however, were only the raw material for his paintings, which do not aim at topographic exactitude but evoke the poetic essence of a countryside filled with echoes of antiquity. Often, as in *A Pastoral Landscape* (fig. 305), the compositions are suffused with the hazy, luminous atmosphere of early morning or late afternoon. The space expands serenely, rather than receding step-by-step as in Poussin's ideal landscapes. An air of nostalgia hangs over such vistas, of past experience gilded by memory. Hence, they appealed especially to the English who had seen Italy only briefly or even not at all.

Vouet. At an early age Simon Vouet (1590–1649), too, went to Rome, where he became the leader of the French Caravaggesque painters; unlike Poussin and Claude, he returned to France. Upon settling in Paris, he quickly shed all vestiges of Caravaggio's manner and formulated a colorful style based on Carracci's, which won such acclaim that Vouet was named first painter to the king. He also brought with him memories of the great North Italian precursors of the Baroque. *The Toilet of Venus* (fig. 306) depicts a subject popular in Venice from Titian to Veronese. Vouet's figure looks back as well to Correggio's Io (see fig. 252), but without her frank eroticism. Instead, she has been given an elegant sensuousness that could hardly be further removed from Poussin's disciplined art. Ironically, *The Toilet of Venus* was painted around 1640, toward the beginning of Poussin's ill-fated sojourn in Paris, where he had gone at the invitation of Louis XIII. He met with no more success than Bernini was to have thirty years later (see pp. 323–24); after several years Poussin left bitterly disappointed by his cool reception at the court, whose taste and politics Vouet understood far better. In one sense, their rivalry was to continue long afterward. Vouet's decorative manner provided the foundation for the Rococo, but it was Poussin's classicism that soon dominated art in France. The two tradi-

305. Claude Lorraine. *A Pastoral Landscape*. c. 1650. Oil on copper, 15⅞ × 21⅝″ (40.3 × 54.9 cm). Yale University Art Gallery, New Haven, Connecticut. Leo C. Hanna, Jr., Fund

306. Simon Vouet. *The Toilet of Venus*. c. 1640. Oil on canvas, 65¼ × 45″ (165.7 × 114.3 cm). Carnegie Institute, Pittsburgh

tions vied with each other through the Romantic era, alternating in succession without gaining the upper hand for long.

The Royal Academy

When young Louis XIV took over the reins of government in 1661, Jean-Baptiste Colbert, his chief adviser, built the administrative apparatus to support the power of the absolute monarch. In this system, aimed at subjecting the thoughts and actions of the entire nation to strict control from above, the visual arts had the task of glorifying the king, and the official "royal style," in both theory and practice, was classicism. Centralized control over the visual arts was exerted by Colbert and the artist Charles Lebrun (1619–1690), and not only through the power of the purse. It also included a new system of educating artists in the officially approved style. Throughout antiquity and the Middle Ages, artists had been trained by apprenticeship, and this time-honored practice still prevailed in the Renaissance. As painting, sculpture, and architecture gained the status of liberal arts, artists wished to supplement their "mechanical" training with theoretical knowledge. For this purpose, "art academies" were founded, patterned on the academies of the humanists (the name academy is derived from the term for the Athenian grove where Plato met with his disciples). Art academies appeared first in Italy in the later sixteenth century. They seem to have been private associations of artists who met periodically to draw from the model and discuss questions of art theory. These academies later became formal institutions that took over some functions from the guilds, but their teaching was limited and far from systematic.

This was the case as well with the Royal Academy of Painting and Sculpture in Paris, founded in 1648. But when Lebrun became its director in 1663, he established a rigid curriculum of compulsory instruction in practice and theory, based on a system of "rules." This set the pattern for all later academies, including their successors, the art schools of today. Much of this doctrine was derived from Poussin's views, but it was carried to rationalistic extremes. The Academy even devised a method for tabulating, in numerical grades, the merits of artists past and present in such categories as drawing, expression, and proportion. The ancients received the highest marks, needless to say, then came Raphael and his school, and Poussin. The Venetians, who "overemphasized" color, ranked low, the Flemish and Dutch even lower. Subjects were similarly classified, from "history" at the top (that is, narrative subjects, be they classical, biblical, or mythological) to still life at the bottom.

ARCHITECTURE

The Louvre. Baroque classicism as the official royal style extended to architecture. We know that the choice was deliberate from the history of the first great project Colbert directed, the completion of the Louvre. Work on the palace had proceeded intermittently for over a century, along the lines of Lescot's design (see fig. 268). What remained to be done was to close the square court on the east side with an impressive facade. Colbert, dissatisfied with the proposals of French architects, invited Bernini to Paris in the hope that the most famous master of the Roman Baroque would do for the French king what he had already done so magnificently for the Church. Bernini spent several months in Paris in 1665 and submitted three designs, all on a scale that would completely engulf the existing palace. After much argument and intrigue, Louis XIV rejected these plans, and turned over the problem of a final solution to a committee of three: Louis Le Vau (1612–1670), his court architect, who had worked on the project before; Charles Lebrun, his court painter; and Claude Perrault (1613–1688), who was a student of ancient architecture, not a professional architect. All three were responsible for the structure that was actually built (fig. 307), although Perrault is usually credited with the major share.

The design in some ways suggests the mind of an archaeologist, but one who knew how to select those features of classical architecture that would link Louis XIV with the glory of the Caesars and still be compatible with the older parts of the palace. The center pavilion is a Roman temple front, and the wings look like the flanks of that temple folded outward. The temple theme demanded a single order of free-standing columns, but the Louvre had three stories. This difficulty was skillfully resolved by treating the ground story as the podium of the temple, and recessing the upper two behind the screen of the colonnade. The combination of grandeur and elegance fully justifies the design's fame. The East Front of the Louvre signaled the victory of French classicism over Italian Baroque as the

307. Claude Perrault. East Front of the Louvre, Paris. 1667–70

royal style. Ironically, this great example proved too pure, and Perrault soon faded from favor.

Palace of Versailles. The king's greatest enterprise was the Palace of Versailles, just over eleven miles from the center of Paris. It was begun in 1669 by Le Vau, who died within a year, then turned over to Jules Hardouin-Mansart (1646–1708), who expanded the entire project enormously to accommodate the ever-growing royal household. The Garden Front (fig. 308), intended by Le Vau to be the principal view of the palace, was stretched to an enormous length with no modification of the architectural membering, so that his original facade design, a less severe variant of the East Front of the Louvre, now looks repetitious and out of scale. The whole center block contains a single room, the famous Galerie des Glaces (Hall of Mirrors), with the Salon de la Guerre (War) and its counterpart, the Salon de la Paix (Peace), at either end.

Baroque features, although not officially acknowledged, reappeared inside the palace. This difference corresponded to the king's own taste. Louis XIV was interested less in architectural theory and monumental exteriors than in the lavish interiors that would make suitable settings for himself and his court. Thus the man to whom he really listened was not an architect, but the painter Lebrun, who became supervisor of all the king's artistic projects. As chief dispenser of royal art patronage, he commanded so much power that for all practical purposes he was the dictator of the arts in France. Lebrun had spent several years studying under Poussin in Rome; but the great decorative schemes of the Roman Baroque must also have impressed him, for they stood him in good stead twenty years later, both in the Louvre and at Versailles. He became a superb decorator, utilizing the combined labors of architects, sculptors, painters, and artisans for ensembles of unheard-of splendor. To subordinate all the arts to the single goal of glorifying Louis XIV was in itself Baroque. Lebrun drew freely on his memories of Rome for the Salon de la Guerre (fig. 309), which seems close in many ways to the Cornaro Chapel (compare fig. 280), although Lebrun obviously emphasized surface decoration far more than did Bernini. As in so many Italian Baroque interiors, the separate ingredients are less impressive than the effect of the whole.

Apart from the magnificent interior, the most impressive aspect of Versailles is the park extending west of the Garden Front for several miles (the view in figure 308 shows only a small part of it). Its design, by André Le Nôtre (1613–1700), is so strictly correlated with the plan of the palace that it becomes a

308. Louis Le Vau and Jules Hardouin-Mansart. Garden Front, center block, Palace of Versailles. 1669–85

309. Hardouin-Mansart, Lebrun, and Coysevox. Salon de la Guerre, Palace of Versailles. Begun 1678

continuation of the architectural space. Like the interiors, these formal gardens, with their terraces, basins, clipped hedges, and statuary, were meant to provide an appropriate setting for the king's appearances in public. They form a series of "outdoor rooms" for the splendid fêtes and spectacles that Louis XIV so enjoyed. The spirit of absolutism is even more striking in this geometric regularity imposed upon an entire countryside than it is in the palace itself.

SCULPTURE

Sculpture arrived at the official royal style in much the same way as architecture. While in Paris, Bernini carved a marble bust of Louis XIV and was commissioned to do an equestrian statue of him. The latter project shared

310. Antoine Coysevox. *Charles Lebrun.* 1676. Terra-cotta, height 26″ (66 cm). The Wallace Collection, London. Reproduced by permission of the Trustees

the fate of Bernini's Louvre designs. Although he portrayed the king in classical military garb, the statue was rejected; apparently it was too dynamic to safeguard the dignity of Louis XIV. This decision was far-reaching, for equestrian statues of the king were later erected throughout France as symbols of royal authority, and Bernini's design, had it succeeded, might have set the pattern for these monuments.

Coysevox. Bernini's influence can nevertheless be felt in the work of Antoine Coysevox (1640–1720), one of the sculptors Lebrun employed at Versailles. The victorious Louis XIV in Coysevox's large stucco relief for the Salon de la Guerre (see fig. 309) retains the pose of Bernini's equestrian statue, albeit with a certain restraint. Coysevox is the first of a long line of distinguished French portrait sculptors. His bust of Lebrun (fig. 310) likewise repeats the general outlines of Bernini's bust of Louis XIV. The face, however, shows a realism and a subtlety of characterization that are Coysevox's own.

Puget. Coysevox approached the Baroque in sculpture as closely as Lebrun would permit. Pierre-Paul Puget (1620–1694), the most talented and most Baroque of seventeenth-century French sculptors, had no success at court until after Colbert's death, when the power of Lebrun was on the decline. *Milo of Crotona* (fig. 311), Puget's finest statue, bears comparison to Bernini's *David* (see fig. 278). Puget's composition is more contained than Bernini's, but the agony of the hero has such force that its impact on the beholder is almost physical. The internal tension fills every particle of marble with an intense life that also recalls Hellenistic sculpture (see fig. 77).

311. Pierre-Paul Puget. *Milo of Crotona.* 1671–83. Marble, height 8′10½″ (2.71 m). Musée du Louvre, Paris

ROCOCO

Much as the Baroque is often considered the final phase of the Renaissance, so the Rococo has been treated as the end of the Baroque: a long twilight, delicious but decadent, that was cleaned away by the Enlightenment and Neoclassicism. In France, the Rococo is linked with the reign of Louis XV (1715–65), with which it corresponds roughly in date. However, it cannot be identified with the absolutist state or the Church any more than can the Baroque, even though these continued to provide the main patronage. Moreover, the essential characteristics of Rococo style were created before the king was born: its first symptoms begin as much as fifty years earlier, during the lengthy transition that constitutes the Late Baroque. Nevertheless, the view of the Rococo as the final phase of the Baroque is not without basis: as the philosopher François-Marie Voltaire acknowledged, the eighteenth century lived in the debt of the past. In art, Poussin and Rubens cast their long shadows over the Rococo. The controversy between their partisans, in turn, goes back much further to the debate between the supporters of Michelangelo and of Titian over the merits of design versus color (see p. 19). In this sense, the Rococo, like the Baroque, still belongs to the Renaissance world.

To overemphasize the similarities and stylistic debt of the Rococo to the Baroque, however, risks ignoring a fundamental difference between them. What is it? In a word, it is fantasy. If the Baroque presents theater on a grand scale, the Rococo stage is smaller, more intimate. At the same time, the Rococo is both more lighthearted and tenderminded, marked equally by playful whimsy and wistful nostalgia. Its artifice conjures up an enchanted realm that presents a temporary diversion from real life. Because the modern age is the product of the Enlightenment, it is still fashionable to denigrate the Rococo for its unabashed escapism and eroticism. To its credit, however, the Rococo discovered the world of love and broadened the range of human emotion in art to include, for the first time, the family as a major theme.

PAINTING

France

"Poussinistes" versus "Rubénistes." It is hardly surprising that the straightjacket system of the French Academy (see pp. 320–21) produced no significant artists. Even Lebrun, as we have seen, was far more Baroque in his practice than we would expect from his classicistic theory. The absurd rigidity of the official doctrine generated, moreover, a counterpressure that vented itself as soon as Lebrun's authority began to decline. Toward the end of the century, the members of the Academy formed two warring factions over the issue of drawing versus color: the "*Poussinistes*" (or conservatives) against the "*Rubénistes.*" The conservatives defended Poussin's view that drawing, which appealed to the mind, was superior to color, which appealed to the senses. The *Rubénistes* advocated color, rather than drawing, as being more true to nature. They also pointed out that drawing, admittedly based on reason, appeals only to the expert few, whereas color appeals to everyone. This argument had revolutionary implications, for it proclaimed the layperson to be the ultimate judge of artistic values, and challenged the Renaissance notion that painting, as a liberal art, could be appreciated only by the educated mind.

Watteau. By the time Louis XIV died in 1715, the dictatorial powers of the Academy

312. Jean-Antoine Watteau. *A Pilgrimage to Cythera*. 1717. Oil on canvas, 4′3″ × 6′4½″ (1.3 × 1.94 m). Musée du Louvre, Paris

had already been overcome, and the influence of Rubens and the great Venetians was everywhere. Two years later the *Rubénistes* scored their final triumph when the painter Jean-Antoine Watteau (1684–1721) was admitted to the Academy on the basis of his *A Pilgrimage to Cythera* (fig. 312). This picture violated all academic canons, and its subject did not conform to any established category. To accommodate Watteau, the Academy invented the new category of *fêtes galantes* (elegant fêtes or entertainments). The term refers less to this one canvas than to the artist's work in general, which mainly shows scenes of elegant society or comedy actors in parklike settings. He characteristically interweaves theater and real life so that no clear distinction can be made between the two. *A Pilgrimage to Cythera* includes yet another element: classical mythology. These young couples have come to Cythera, the island of love, to pay homage to Venus, whose garlanded image appears on the far right. They are about to board the boat, accompanied by swarms of cupids.

The scene at once recalls Rubens' *The Garden of Love* (see fig. 288), but Watteau has added a touch of poignancy, lending it a poetic subtlety reminiscent of Giorgione (see fig. 239). His figures, too, lack the robust vitality of Rubens'. Slim and graceful, they move with the studied assurance of actors who play their roles so superbly that they touch us more than reality ever could. They recapture an earlier ideal of "mannered" elegance.

Boucher. The work of Watteau signals a shift in French art as a whole to the Rococo. The term originally applied to the decorative arts (see p. 332), but it suits the playful character of French painting before 1765 equally well. By about 1720 even history painting becomes intimate in scale and delightfully ebullient in style and subject. The finest painter in this vein is François Boucher (1703–1770), who epitomizes the age of Madame de Pompadour, the mistress of Louis XV. *The Toilet of Venus* (fig. 313), painted for her private retreat, is full of silk and perfume. If Watteau elevated human love to the level of mythology, Boucher raised playful eroticism to the realm of the divine. What Boucher lacks in the emotional depth that distinguishes Watteau's art, he makes up for in unsurpassed understanding of the world of fantasies that enrich people's lives.

Yet, compared to Vouet's goddess (see fig. 306), from which she is descended, Boucher's has been reduced to a coquette. In this cosmetic never-never land, she has become ageless in her adolescent beauty, for she has the same soft, rosy skin as the cherubs who attend her. Trapped in eternal youth, she is a Venus who seems strangely incapable of passion.

313. François Boucher. *The Toilet of Venus.* 1751. Oil on canvas, 42⅝ × 33½" (108.3 × 85.1 cm). The Metropolitan Museum of Art, New York. Bequest of William K. Vanderbilt, 1920

Chardin. The style of Jean-Baptiste-Siméon Chardin (1699–1779) can be called Rococo only with reservations. The *Rubénistes* had cleared the way for a renewed interest in still life and genre by Dutch and Flemish masters as well. This revival was facilitated by the presence of numerous artists from the Netherlands, especially Flanders, who settled in France in growing numbers after about 1550 while maintaining artistic ties to their native countries. Chardin is the finest French painter in this vein. He is nevertheless far removed in spirit and style, if not in subject matter, from any Dutch or Flemish painter. His paintings act as moral exemplars, not by conveying symbolic messages as Baroque still lifes often do (see pp. 312–15), but by affirming the rightness of the existing social order and its values. To the rising middle class who were the artist's patrons, his genre scenes and kitchen still lifes proclaimed the virtues of hard work, frugality, honesty, and devotion to family.

Back from the Market (fig. 314) shows life in a Parisian middle-class household with such feeling for the beauty hidden in the commonplace, and so clear a sense of spatial order, that we can compare him only to Vermeer, but his remarkable technique is quite unlike

314. Jean-Baptiste-Siméon Chardin. *Back from the Market.* 1739. Oil on canvas, 18½ × 14¾" (47 × 37.5 cm). Musée du Louvre, Paris

315. Jean-Baptiste-Siméon Chardin. *Kitchen Still Life*. c. 1731. Oil on canvas, 12½ × 15⅜" (31.8 × 39.1 cm). The Ashmolean Museum, Oxford. Bequeathed by Mrs. W. F. R. Weldon

any Dutch artist's. Devoid of bravura, his brushwork renders the light on colored surfaces with a creamy touch that is both analytical and subtly lyrical. To reveal the inner nature of things, he summarizes forms, subtly altering their appearance and texture, rather than describing them in detail. Chardin discovered a hidden poetry in even the most humble objects and endowed them with timeless dignity. His still lifes usually depict the same modest environment, eschewing the "object appeal" of their Dutch predecessors. In *Kitchen Still Life* (fig. 315), we see only the common objects that belong in any kitchen: earthenware jugs, a casserole, a copper pot, a piece of raw meat, smoked herring, two eggs. But how important they seem, each so firmly placed in relation to the rest, each so worthy of the artist's—and our—scrutiny! Despite his concern with formal problems, evident in the beautifully balanced design, Chardin treats these objects with a respect close to reverence. Beyond their shapes, colors, and textures, they are to him symbols of the life of common people.

Vigée-Lebrun. It is from portraits that we can gain the clearest understanding of the French Rococo, for the transformation of the human image lies at the heart of the age. In portraits of the aristocracy, individuals were endowed with the illusion of character as a natural attribute of their station in life, stemming from their noble birth. The finest achievements of Rococo portraiture were reserved for depictions of women, hardly a surprising fact in a society that idolized the cult of love and feminine beauty. Indeed, one of the best practitioners in this vein was a woman: Marie-Louise-Élisabeth Vigée-Lebrun (1755–1842).

Throughout Vigée's long life she enjoyed great fame, which took her to every corner of Europe, including Russia, when she fled the French Revolution. *The Duchesse de Polignac* (fig. 316) was painted a few years after Vigée had become the portraitist for Queen Marie Antoinette, and it amply demonstrates her ability. The *duchesse* has the eternally youthful loveliness of Boucher's Venus (see fig. 313), made all the more persuasive by the artist's ravishing treatment of her clothing. At the

316. Marie-Louise-Élisabeth Vigée-Lebrun. *The Duchesse de Polignac*. 1783. Oil on canvas, 38¾ × 28" (98.4 × 71.1 cm). The National Trust Waddesdon Manor

317. William Hogarth. *The Orgy,* Scene III of *The Rake's Progress.* c. 1734. Oil on canvas, 24½ × 29½" (62.2 × 74.9 cm). Sir John Soane's Museum, London

same time, there is a sense of transience in the engaging mood that exemplifies the Rococo's whimsical theatricality. Interrupted in her singing, the lyrical *duchesse* becomes a real-life counterpart to the poetic creatures in Watteau's *A Pilgrimage to Cythera* (see fig. 312), by way of the delicate sentiment she shares with the girl in Chardin's *Back from the Market* (see fig. 314).

England

French Rococo painting from Watteau onward had a decisive, though unacknowledged, effect across the Channel and, in fact, helped bring about the first school of English painting since the Middle Ages that had more than local importance.

Hogarth. The earliest of these painters, William Hogarth (1697–1764), made his mark in the 1730s with a new kind of picture, which he described as "modern moral subjects . . . similar to representations on the stage." He wished to be judged as a dramatist, he said, even though his "actors" could only "exhibit a dumb show." These pictures, and the engravings he made from them for popular sale, came in sets, with details recurring in each scene to unify the sequence. Hogarth's "morality plays" teach, by horrid example, the solid middle-class virtues. They show a country girl who succumbs to the temptations of fashionable London; the evils of corrupt elections; aristocratic rakes who live only for ruinous pleasure, marrying wealthy women of lower status for their fortunes, which they

318. Thomas Gainsborough. *Robert Andrews and His Wife*. c. 1748–50. Oil on canvas, 27½ × 47" (69.9 × 119.4 cm). The National Gallery, London. Reproduced by courtesy of the Trustees

soon dissipate. He is probably the first artist in history to become a social critic in his own right.

In *The Orgy* (fig. 317), from *The Rake's Progress,* the young wastrel is overindulging in wine and women. The scene is so full of visual clues that a full account would take pages, plus constant references to the adjoining episodes. However literal-minded, the picture has great appeal. Hogarth combines some of Watteau's sparkle with Steen's narrative gusto (compare figs. 312, 300), and entertains us so well that we enjoy his sermon without being overwhelmed by its message.

Gainsborough. Portraiture remained the only constant source of income for English painters. Here, too, the eighteenth century produced a style that differed from the continental traditions that had dominated this field. Its greatest master, Thomas Gainsborough (1727–1788), began by painting landscapes, but ended as the favorite portraitist of British high society. His early portraits, such as *Robert Andrews and His Wife* (fig. 318),

319. Thomas Gainsborough. *Mrs. Siddons.* 1785. Oil on canvas, 49½ × 39" (125.7 × 99.1 cm). The National Gallery, London. Reproduced by courtesy of the Trustees

320. Sir Joshua Reynolds. *Sarah Siddons as the Tragic Muse.* 1784. Oil on canvas, 93 × 57½" (236.2 × 146.1 cm). Henry E. Huntington Library and Art Gallery, San Marino, California

have a lyrical charm that is not always found in his later pictures. Compared to Van Dyck's artifice in *Portrait of Charles I Hunting* (see fig. 289), this country squire and his wife are unpretentiously at home in their setting. The landscape, although derived from Ruisdael and his school, has a sunlit, hospitable air never achieved (or desired) by the Dutch masters. The casual grace of the two figures indirectly recalls Watteau's style. Later portraits by Gainsborough, such as the very fine one of the famous actress Mrs. Siddons (fig. 319), have other virtues: a cool elegance that translates Van Dyck's aristocratic poses into late-eighteenth-century terms, and a fluid, translucent technique reminiscent of Rubens.

Reynolds. Gainsborough painted *Mrs. Siddons* in conscious opposition to his great rival on the London scene, Sir Joshua Reynolds (1723–1792), who just before had portrayed the same sitter as the Tragic Muse (fig. 320). Reynolds, the president of the Royal Academy since its founding in 1768, was the champion of the academic approach to art, which he had acquired during two years in Rome. In his famous *Discourses* he formulated what he felt were necessary rules and theories. His views were essentially those of Lebrun, tempered by British common sense. Like Lebrun, he found it difficult to live up to his theories in actual practice. Although he preferred history painting in the grand style, the vast majority of his works are portraits "enabled," whenever possible, by allegorical additions or disguises like those in his picture of Mrs. Siddons. His style owed a good deal more to the Venetians, the Flemish Baroque, and even to Rembrandt (note the lighting in *Sarah Siddons*) than he conceded in theory, though he often recommended following the example of earlier masters. Reynolds was generous enough to give praise to Gainsborough, whom he outlived by a few years, and whose instinctive talent he must have envied. He eulogized him as one who saw with the eye of a painter rather than a poet.

ARCHITECTURE

France

After the death of Louis XIV, the centralized administrative machine that Colbert had created ground to a stop. The nobility, hitherto attached to the court at Versailles, were now freer of royal surveillance. Many of them chose not to return to their ancestral châteaux in the provinces, but to live instead in Paris, where they built elegant town houses, known as hôtels. As state-sponsored building activity was declining, the field of "design for private living" took on new importance. These city sites were usually cramped and irregular, so that they offered scant opportunity for impressive exteriors. Hence, the layout and decor of the rooms became the architects' main concern. The hôtels demanded a style of interior decoration less grandiloquent and cumbersome than Lebrun's. They required an intimate, flexible style that would give greater scope to individual fancy uninhibited by classicistic dogma.

321. Germain Boffrand. Salon de la Princesse, Hôtel de Soubise, Paris. Begun 1732

Boffrand. French designers created the Rococo ("the Style of Louis XV," as it is often called in France) in response to this need. The name fits well, although it was coined as a caricature of *rocaille* (echoing the Italian *barocco*), which meant the playful decoration of grottoes with irregular shells and stones. Indeed, the walls and ceiling of the Salon de la Princesse in the Hôtel de Soubise by Germain Boffrand (fig. 321) are encrusted with ornamentation and adorned with elaborately carved furniture. In such a setting there is no clear distinction between decoration and function, as in the clock and the statuette on the mantle in our illustration. French Rococo sculpture usually takes the form of small groups in a "miniature Baroque" style. Designed to be viewed at close range, they are playful echoes of the ecstasies of Bernini and Puget.

Germany and Austria

Rococo was a refinement in miniature also of the curvilinear, "elastic" Baroque of Borromini and Guarini, and thus could be happily united with architecture in Austria and Germany, where the Italian style had taken firm root. Rococo architecture in Central Europe is larger in scale and more exuberant than in France. Moreover, painting and sculpture are more closely linked with their settings. Palaces and churches are decorated with ceiling frescoes and decorative sculpture unsuited to domestic interiors, however lavish, although they reflect the same taste that produced the Hôtel de Soubise.

It is not surprising that the style invented in Italy should have achieved its climax north of the Alps, where such a synthesis of Gothic and Renaissance was sure of a particularly warm response (see pp. 298–99). In Austria and southern Germany, ravaged by the Thirty Years' War (1618–48), the number of new buildings erected remained small until near the end of the seventeenth century. Baroque was an imported style, practiced mainly by visiting Italians. Not until the 1690s did native designers come to the fore. There followed a period of intense activity that lasted more than fifty years and gave rise to some of the most imaginative creations in the history of architecture. These monuments were erected for the glorification of princes and prelates who, generally speaking, deserve to be remembered only as lavish patrons of the arts.

Fischer von Erlach. Johann Fischer von Erlach (1656–1723), the first great architect of the Rococo in Central Europe, is a transitional figure linked most directly to the Italian tradition. His design for the church of St. Charles Borromaeus in Vienna (fig. 322) combines a thorough understanding of Borromini (compare fig. 281) with reminiscences of St. Peter's and the Pantheon portico (see figs. 277 and 86). Here a pair of huge columns derived from the Column of Trajan (see fig. 97) substitutes for facade towers, which have become corner pavilions, reminiscent of the Louvre court (compare fig. 268). With these inflexible elements of Roman Imperial art embedded into the elastic curvatures of his church, Fischer von Erlach expresses, more boldly than any Italian Baroque architect, the power of the Christian faith to absorb and transfigure the splendors of antiquity.

322. Johann Fischer von Erlach. Facade of St. Charles Borromaeus (Karlskirche), Vienna. 1716–37

Neumann. The architects of the next generation favored a tendency toward lightness and elegance. The Episcopal Palace in Würzburg by Balthasar Neumann (1687–1753) includes the breathtaking Kaisersaal (fig. 323), a great oval hall decorated in the favorite color scheme of the mid-eighteenth century: white, gold, and pastel shades. The number and aesthetic role of structural members such as columns, pilasters, and architraves is now minimized. Windows and vault segments are framed by continuous, ribbonlike moldings, and the white surfaces are spun over with irregular ornamental designs. This repertory of lacy, curling motifs, the hallmark of the French style (see fig. 321), is happily combined with German Rococo architecture. The abundant illumination, the play of curves and countercurves, and the weightless grace of the stucco sculpture give the Kaisersaal an airy lightness far removed from the Roman

324. Giovanni Battista Tiepolo. Ceiling fresco (detail), 1751. The Kaisersaal, Residenz, Würzburg

Baroque. The vaults and walls seem thin and pliable, like membranes easily punctured by the expansive power of space.

Tiepolo. Just as the style of architecture invented in Italy achieved its climax north of the Alps, so the last, and most refined, stage of Italian illusionistic ceiling decoration is represented in Würzburg by its greatest master, Giovanni Battista Tiepolo (1696–1770). Venetian by birth and training, he blended that city's tradition of High Baroque illusionism with the pageantry of Veronese. His mastery of light and color, the grace and felicity of his touch, made him famous far beyond his home territory. When Tiepolo painted the Würzburg frescoes (fig. 324), his powers were at their height. The tissuelike ceiling so often gives way to illusionistic openings of every sort that we no longer feel it to be a spatial boundary. These openings do not reveal, however, avalanches of figures propelled by dramatic bursts of light, like those of Roman ceilings (compare fig. 276), but rather blue sky and sunlit clouds, and an occasional winged creature soaring in this limitless expanse. Only along the edges are there solid clusters of figures. Tiepolo proved himself a worthy successor to Pietro da Cortona, and followed in his footsteps to Madrid, where he spent his later years decorating the Royal Palace.

323. Balthasar Neumann. The Kaisersaal, Residenz, Würzburg. 1719–44. Frescoes by Giovanni Battista Tiepolo, 1751

CHRONOLOGICAL CHART III

	POLITICAL HISTORY	RELIGION, LITERATURE	SCIENCE, TECHNOLOGY
1400	Great Papal Schism (since 1378) settled 1417; pope returns to Rome Cosimo de'Medici leading citizen of Florence 1434–64	Leonardo Bruni (c. 1374–1444), *History of Florence* Leone Battista Alberti (1404–1472), *On Architecture*; *On Painting* Jan Hus, Czech reformer, burned at stake for heresy 1415; Joan of Arc burned at stake for heresy and sorcery 1431 Council of Florence attempts to reunite Catholic and Orthodox faiths 1439	Prince Henry the Navigator of Portugal (1394–1460) promotes geographic exploration Gutenberg invents printing with movable type 1446–50
1450	Hapsburg rule of Holy Roman Empire begins 1452 End of Hundred Years' War 1453 Constantinople falls to Turks 1453 Lorenzo de'Medici, "the Magnificent," virtual ruler of Florence 1469–92 Ferdinand and Isabella unite Spain 1469 Spain and Portugal divide southern New World 1493–94 Charles VIII of France invades Italy 1494–99 Henry VII (r. 1485–1509), first Tudor king of England	Marsilio Ficino, Italian Neo-Platonic philosopher (1433–1499) Pius II, humanist pope (r. 1458–64) Sebastian Brant's *Ship of Fools* 1494 Savonarola virtual ruler of Florence 1494; burned at stake for heresy 1498	Bartholomeu Diaz rounds Cape of Good Hope 1488 Christopher Columbus discovers America 1492 Vasco da Gama reaches India, returns to Lisbon 1497–99
1500	Charles V elected Holy Roman Emperor 1519; Sack of Rome 1527 Hernando Cortés wins Aztec Empire in Mexico for Spain 1519; Francisco Pizarro conquers Peru 1532 Henry VIII of England (r. 1509–47) founds Anglican Church 1534 Wars of Lutheran vs. Catholic princes in Germany; Peace of Augsburg (1555) lets each sovereign decide religion of his subjects	Erasmus of Rotterdam's *In Praise of Folly* 1511 Thomas More's *Utopia* 1516 Martin Luther (1483–1546) posts 95 theses 1517; excommunicated 1521 Castiglione's *Courtier* 1528 Machiavelli's *Prince* 1532 Ignatius of Loyola founds Jesuit order 1534 John Calvin's *Institutes of the Christian Religion* 1536	Vasco de Balboa sights Pacific Ocean 1513 First circumnavigation of the globe by Ferdinand Magellan and crew 1520–22 Copernicus refutes geocentric view of universe

NOTE: Figure numbers of black-and-white illustrations are in (italics). Colorplate numbers are in **(bold face)**.
Duration of papacy or reign is indicated by the abbreviation r.

ARCHITECTURE	SCULPTURE	PAINTING	
Brunelleschi begins career as architect 1419; Florence Cathedral dome *(162)*; S. Lorenzo, Florence *(210, 211)*	Donatello, *St. George* (**201**); *Prophet (Zuccone) (202)*; *David (203)* Ghiberti, "Gates of Paradise," Baptistery, Florence *(205)* Donatello, Equestrian statue of Gattamelata, Padua *(204)*	*St. Dorothy* woodcut *(198)* Hubert and/or Jan van Eyck, *Crucifixion* and *Last Judgment* (**187**) Masaccio, *Holy Trinity* fresco, Sta. Maria Novella, Florence (**214**); Brancacci Chapel frescoes, Sta. Maria del Carmine, Florence (**215**) Master of Flémalle, *Mérode Altarpiece* (**186**) Jan van Eyck, *Man in a Red Turban (188)*; *Wedding Portrait* (**189, 190**) Rogier van der Weyden, *Descent from the Cross* (**191**) Conrad Witz, Geneva Cathedral altarpiece *(195)* Domenico Veneziano, *Madonna and Child with Saints* (**216**)	**1400**
Alberti, S. Andrea, Mantua *(212)* Giuliano da Sangallo, Sta. Maria delle Carceri, Prato (**213**)	Verrocchio, *Putto with Dolphin,* Florence *(209)* Pollaiuolo, *Hercules and Antaeus* (**208**)	Castagno, *David* (**218**) Mantegna, Ovetari Chapel frescoes, Padua *(222)* Piero della Francesca, Arezzo frescoes (**217**) Hugo van der Goes, *Portinari Altarpiece (192)* Botticelli, *Birth of Venus* (**219**) Ghirlandaio, *Old Man and His Grandson* (**221**) Schongauer, *Temptation of St. Anthony* engraving *(199)* Perugino, *Delivery of the Keys,* Sistine Chapel, Rome (**224**) Leonardo, *Virgin of the Rocks (225)* Giovanni Bellini, *St. Francis in Ecstasy* (**223**) Geertgen tot Sint Jans, *Nativity (193)* Leonardo, *Last Supper,* Sta. Maria delle Grazie, Milan *(226)* Piero di Cosimo, *Discovery of Honey* (**220**)	**1450**
Bramante, design for St. Peter's, Rome *(229)* Michelangelo becomes architect of St. Peter's, Rome, 1546 *(236)* Lescot, Square Court of Louvre, Paris *(268)*	Michelangelo, *David (231)*; Tomb of Giuliano de'Medici, Florence *(235)* Cellini, Saltcellar of Francis I *(253)*	Dürer, *Self-Portrait (259)* Bosch, *Garden of Delights* (**194**) Leonardo, *Mona Lisa* (**227**) Giorgione, *The Tempest (239)* Michelangelo, Sistine Chapel ceiling, Rome (**6, 232, 233**) Grünewald, *Isenheim Altarpiece* (**257, 258**) Raphael, *School of Athens* fresco, Stanza della Segnatura, Rome (**237**); *Galatea* fresco, Villa Farnesina, Rome (**238**) Dürer, *Knight, Death, and Devil* engraving *(260)* Titian, *Bacchanal* (**240**); *Man with a Glove (241)* Rosso Fiorentino, *Descent from the Cross* (**243**) Holbein, *Erasmus of Rotterdam (264)* Parmigianino, *Self-Portrait (244)* Correggio, *Assumption of the Virgin* fresco, Parma Cathedral (**251**) Altdorfer, *Battle of Issus (263)* Cranach, *Judgment of Paris* (**262**) Michelangelo, *Last Judgment* fresco, Sistine Chapel, Rome *(234)* Parmigianino, *Madonna with the Long Neck* (**245**)	**1500**

	POLITICAL HISTORY	RELIGION, LITERATURE	SCIENCE, TECHNOLOGY
1550	Ivan the Terrible of Russia (r. 1547–84) Charles V retires 1556; son Philip II becomes king of Spain, Netherlands, New World Elizabeth I of England (r. 1558–1603) Lutheranism becomes state religion in Denmark 1560, in Sweden 1593 Netherlands revolt against Spain 1586 Spanish Armada defeated by English 1588 Henry IV of France (r. 1589–1610); Edict of Nantes establishes religious toleration 1598	Montaigne, French essayist (1533–1592) Council of Trent for Catholic reform 1545–63 St. Theresa of Avila, Spanish saint (1515–1582) Giorgio Vasari's *Lives* 1564 William Shakespeare, English dramatist (1564–1616)	
1600	Jamestown, Virginia, founded 1607; Plymouth, Massachusetts, 1620 Thirty Years' War 1618–48 Cardinal Richelieu, adviser to Louis XIII, consolidates power of king 1624–42 Cardinal Mazarin governs France during minority of Louis XIV 1643–61 (civil war 1648–53) Charles I of England beheaded 1649; Commonwealth under Cromwell 1649–53	Miguel de Cervantes' *Don Quixote* 1605–16 John Donne, English poet (1572–1631) King James Bible 1611 René Descartes, French mathematician and philosopher (1596–1650)	Johannes Kepler establishes planetary system 1609–19 Galileo (1564–1642) invents telescope 1609; establishes scientific method William Harvey describes circulation of the blood 1628
1650	Charles II restores English monarchy 1660 English Parliament passes Habeas Corpus Act 1679 Frederick William, the Great Elector (r. 1640–88), founds power of Prussia Louis XIV absolute ruler of France (r. 1661–1715); revokes Edict of Nantes 1685 Glorious Revolution against James II of England 1688; Bill of Rights	Molière, French dramatist (1622–1673) Blaise Pascal, French scientist and philosopher (1623–1662) Spinoza, Dutch philosopher (1632–1677) Racine, French dramatist (1639–1699) John Milton's *Paradise Lost* 1667 John Bunyan's *Pilgrim's Progress* 1678 John Locke's *Essay Concerning Human Understanding* 1690	Isaac Newton (1642–1727), theory of gravity 1687
1700	Peter the Great (r. 1682–1725) westernizes Russia, defeats Sweden English defeat French at Blenheim 1704 Robert Walpole first prime minister 1721–42 Frederick the Great of Prussia defeats Austria 1740–45	Alexander Pope's *Rape of the Lock* 1714 Daniel Defoe's *Robinson Crusoe* 1719 Jonathan Swift's *Gulliver's Travels* 1726 Wesley brothers found Methodism 1738 Voltaire, French author (1698–1778)	Carolus Linnaeus, Swedish botanist (1707–1778)
1750	Seven Years' War (1756–63): England and Prussia vs. Austria and France, called French and Indian War in America; French defeated in Battle of Quebec 1769 Catherine the Great (r. 1762–96) extends Russian power to Black Sea	Thomas Gray's *Elegy* 1750 Diderot's *Encyclopedia* 1751–72 Samuel Johnson's *Dictionary* 1755 Edmund Burke, English reformer (1729–1797) Jean-Jacques Rousseau, French philosopher and writer (1712–1778)	James Watt patents steam engine 1769 Priestley discovers oxygen 1774 Coke-fed blast furnaces for iron smelting perfected c. 1760–75 Benjamin Franklin's experiments with electricity c. 1750

	ARCHITECTURE	SCULPTURE	PAINTING
1550	Palladio, Villa Rotonda, Vicenza (**255**) Della Porta, Facade of Il Gesù, Rome *(256)*	Giovanni Bologna, *Rape of the Sabine Woman,* Florence *(254)*	Bronzino, *Eleanora of Toledo and Her Son Giovanni de'Medici* (**246**) Bruegel, *Return of the Hunters* (**267**) Titian, *Christ Crowned with Thorns* (**242**) Veronese, *Christ in the House of Levi* (**250**) El Greco, *Burial of Count Orgaz (248)* Tintoretto, *Last Supper* (**247**) Caravaggio, *Calling of St. Matthew,* Contarelli Chapel, Rome (**271**) Annibale Carracci, Farnese Gallery ceiling, Rome (**273**)
1600	Maderno, Nave and facade of St. Peter's, Rome; Bernini's colonnade *(277)* Borromini, S. Carlo alle Quattro Fontane, Rome *(281, 282)*	Bernini, *David (278)*; Cornaro Chapel, Rome (**279,** *280)*	Rubens, *Raising of the Cross (286)*; *Marie de'Medici, Queen of France, Landing in Marseilles* (**287**) Artemisia Gentileschi, *Judith and Her Maidservant with the Head of Holofernes* (**272**) Zurbarán, *St. Serapion* (**284**) Hals, *Jolly Toper (291)* Leyster, *Boy Playing a Flute (293)* Pietro da Cortona, Palazzo Barberini ceiling, Rome *(276)* Heda, *Still Life* (**299**) Van Dyck, *Portrait of Charles I Hunting* (**289**) Rembrandt, *Blinding of Samson* (**294**) Poussin, *Rape of the Sabine Women* (**303**) Rubens, *Garden of Love* (**288**) De La Tour, *Joseph the Carpenter* (**302**)
1650	Perrault, East front of Louvre, Paris *(307)* Hardouin-Mansart and Le Vau, Palace of Versailles, begun 1669 *(308)*; with Coysevox, Salon de la Guerre *(309)* Guarini, Palazzo Carignano, Turin *(283)*	Puget, *Milo of Crotona (311)* Coysevox, *Charles Lebrun (310)*	Lorraine, *Pastoral Landscape* (**305**) Rembrandt, *Christ Preaching (297)* Ruisdael, *Jewish Cemetery* (**298**) Velázquez, *Maids of Honor* (**285**) Rembrandt, *Self-Portrait (296)* Steen, *Feast of St. Nicholas* (**300**) Hals, *Women Regents of the Old Men's Home at Haarlem (292)* Vermeer, *The Letter (301)*
1700	Fischer von Erlach, St. Charles Borromaeus, Vienna (**322**) Neumann, Episcopal Palace, Würzburg *(323)* Burlington and Kent, Chiswick House, London *(332)* Boffrand, Hôtel de Soubise, Paris *(321)*		Watteau, *Pilgrimage to Cythera* (**312**) Chardin, *Kitchen Still Life (315)* Hogarth, *Rake's Progress (317)* Gainsborough, *Robert Andrews and His Wife* (**318**)
1750			Tiepolo, Würzburg ceiling fresco (**324**) Boucher, *Toilet of Venus* (**313**) Vigée-Lebrun, *Duchesse de Polignac (316)* Reynolds, *Sarah Siddons as the Tragic Muse* (**320**)

PART FOUR

THE MODERN WORLD

The era to which we ourselves belong has not yet acquired a name of its own. Perhaps this does not strike us as peculiar at first. We are, after all, still in midstream. Considering how promptly the Renaissance coined a name for itself, we may well wonder why no key concept comparable to the "rebirth of antiquity" has emerged for the modern era since it began two hundred and twenty-five years ago. It is tempting to call ours "the age of revolution," because rapid and violent change has indeed characterized the modern world. Yet we cannot discern a common impulse behind these developments, for the modern era began with revolutions of two kinds: the Industrial Revolution, symbolized by the invention of the steam engine, and the political revolution, under the banner of democracy, in America and France.

Both of these revolutions are still going on. Industrialization and democracy are sought as goals over most of the world. Western science and Western political thought (and, in their wake, all the other products of modern civilization—food, dress, art, music, literature) will soon belong to all peoples, although they have been challenged by nationalism, religion, and other ideologies that command allegiance. These two movements are so closely linked today that we tend to think of them as different aspects of one process, with effects more far-reaching than any since the Neolithic Revolution ten thousand years ago. Still, the twin revolutions of modern times are not the same. The more we try to define their relationship and trace their historic roots, the more paradoxical they seem. Both are founded on the idea of progress; but whereas progress in science during the past two centuries has been continuous and measurable, we can hardly make this claim for our pursuit of happiness, however we choose to define it.

Here, then, is the conflict fundamental to our era. Today, having cast off the framework of traditional authority which confined and sustained us before, we can act with a latitude both frightening and exhilarating. In a world where all values may be questioned, we search constantly for our own identity and for the meaning of human existence, individual and collective. Our knowledge about ourselves is now vastly greater, but this has not reassured us as we had hoped. Modern civilization lacks the cohesiveness of the past. It no longer proceeds by readily identifiable periods; nor are there clear period styles to be discerned in art or in any other form of culture.

Instead, we find a continuity of another kind: movements and countermovements. Spreading like waves, these "isms" defy national, ethnic, and chronological boundaries. Never dominant anywhere for long, they compete or merge with each other in endlessly shifting patterns. Hence our account of modern art is guided more by movements than by countries. Only in this way can we hope to do justice to the fact that modern art, all regional differences notwithstanding, is as international as modern science.

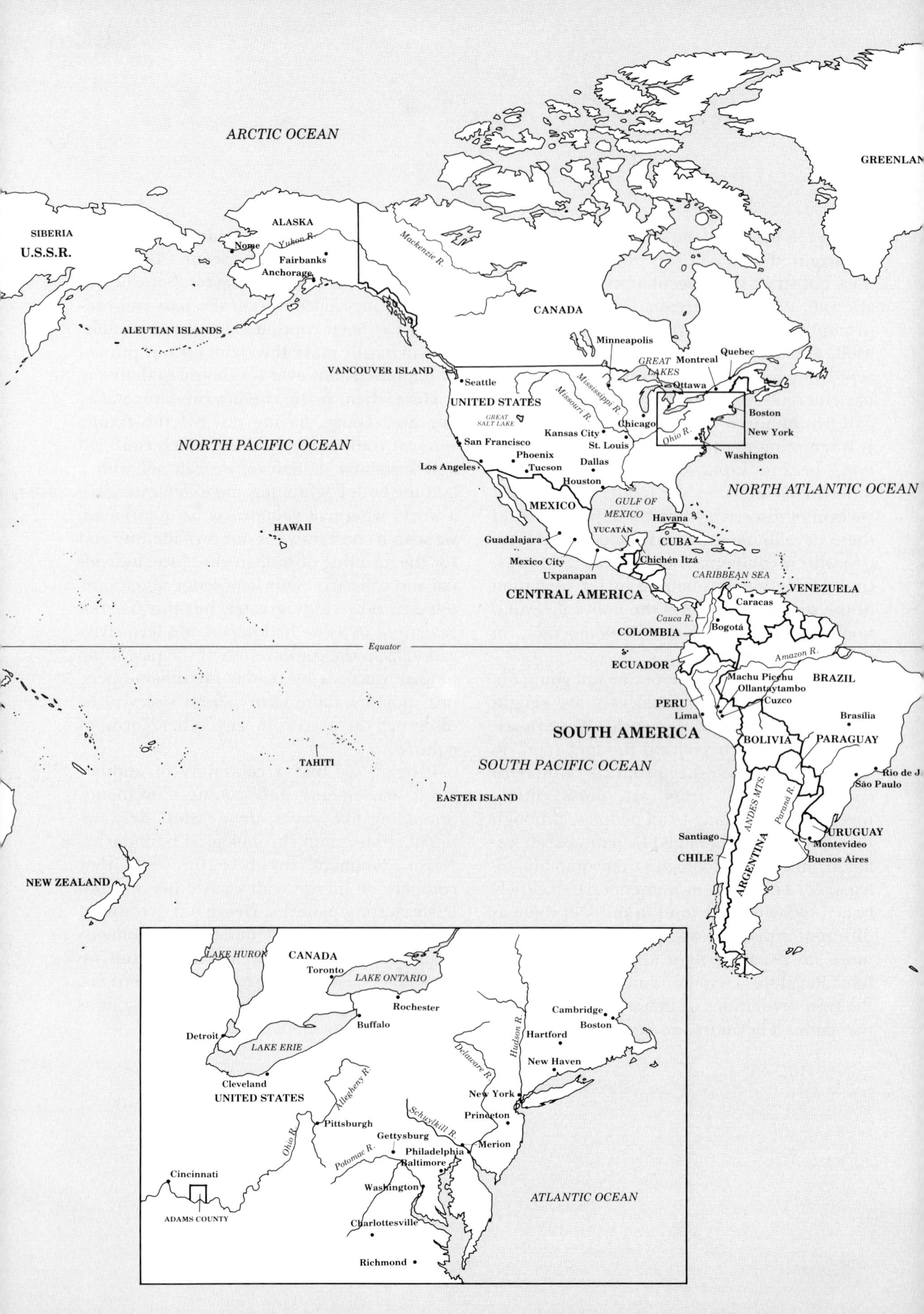
ARCTIC OCEAN
GREENLAN
SIBERIA
U.S.S.R.
ALASKA
Nome
Yukon R.
Fairbanks
Anchorage
Mackenzie R.
CANADA
ALEUTIAN ISLANDS
Minneapolis
VANCOUVER ISLAND
Seattle
GREAT LAKES
Montreal
Quebec
Ottawa
Mississippi R.
Missouri R.
UNITED STATES
GREAT SALT LAKE
Boston
New York
Chicago
Kansas City
St. Louis
Ohio R.
Washington
NORTH PACIFIC OCEAN
San Francisco
Phoenix
Los Angeles
Tucson
Dallas
Houston
NORTH ATLANTIC OCEAN
MEXICO
GULF OF MEXICO
HAWAII
YUCATÁN
Havana
CUBA
Guadalajara
Mexico City
Chichén Itzá
Uxpanapan
CARIBBEAN SEA
CENTRAL AMERICA
VENEZUELA
Caracas
Cauca R.
Bogotá
COLOMBIA
Equator
Amazon R.
ECUADOR
Machu Picchu
Ollantaytambo
BRAZIL
Cuzco
PERU
Lima
Brasília
SOUTH AMERICA
BOLIVIA
PARAGUAY
TAHITI
SOUTH PACIFIC OCEAN
Rio de J
São Paulo
EASTER ISLAND
ANDES MTS.
Paraná R.
URUGUAY
Santiago
Montevideo
CHILE
Buenos Aires
ARGENTINA
NEW ZEALAND
LAKE HURON
CANADA
Toronto
LAKE ONTARIO
Rochester
Cambridge
Boston
Buffalo
Detroit
Hudson R.
Hartford
LAKE ERIE
Delaware R.
New Haven
Allegheny R.
Cleveland
UNITED STATES
New York
Princeton
Ohio R.
Pittsburgh
Schuylkill R.
Gettysburg
Merion
Philadelphia
Potomac R.
Baltimore
Cincinnati
Washington
ATLANTIC OCEAN
ADAMS COUNTY
Charlottesville
Richmond

THE WORLD

SITES AND CITIES

ARCTIC OCEAN
ICELAND
NORWAY
SWEDEN
FINLAND
Oslo
Leningrad
NORTH SEA
BALTIC SEA
Volga R.
Moscow
ENGLAND
THE NETHERLANDS
GERMANY
ELGIUM
FRANCE
BAY OF BISCAY
SPAIN
ITALY
BLACK SEA
CASPIAN SEA
NEAR EAST
TURKEY
CHIOS
MEDITERRANEAN SEA
MOROCCO
ALGERIA
LIBYA
EGYPT
Cairo
ISRAEL
SYRIA
JORDAN
IRAQ
Tigris R.
Euphrates R.
PERSIAN GULF
SAUDI ARABIA
RED SEA
Teheran
IRAN
AFGHANISTAN
MIDDLE EAST
GANDHARA
PAKISTAN
Indus R.
Mohenjo-Daro
Lahore
Mathura
Ganges R.
Sanchi
Sarnath
Ajanta
Ellora
INDIA
Calcutta
BANGLADESH
ARABIAN SEA
BAY OF BENGAL
SRI LANKA
ITANIA
Niger R.
AFRICA
Nile R.
NIGERIA
Ife
CAMEROON
BENIN
GULF OF GUINEA
Equator
GABON
CONGO
Congo R.
Kinshasa
ZAIRE
ETHIOPIA
SOMALIA
KENYA
TANZANIA
ANGOLA
ZAMBIA
MADAGASCAR
MOZAMBIQUE
SOUTH AFRICA
UTH ATLANTIC OCEAN
INDIAN OCEAN
U.S.S.R.
Ob R.
Yenisey R.
Lena R.
SIBERIA
KAMCHATKA
MONGOLIA
CHINA
Peking
Yellow R. (Hwang Ho)
Yangtze R.
SZECHWAN
Shanghai
FAR EAST
Hong Kong
KOREA
Kyoto
JAPAN
Tokyo
Nara
Osaka
YELLOW SEA
EAST CHINA SEA
TAIWAN
PACIFIC OCEAN
PHILIPPINES
VIETNAM
SOUTH CHINA SEA
MALAYSIA
INDONESIA
GAZELLE PENINSULA
NEW BRITAIN
Sepik R.
PAPUA NEW GUINEA
WESTERN ARNHEM LAND
AUSTRALIA
Perth
Sydney
Canberra
Melbourne

NEOCLASSICISM

Neoclassicism Versus Romanticism

The history of the two movements to be dealt with in this and the next chapter covers roughly a century, from about 1750 to 1850. Paradoxically, Neoclassicism has been seen as the opposite of Romanticism on the one hand and as no more than one aspect of it on the other. The difficulty is that the two terms are not evenly matched—any more than are "quadruped" and "carnivore." Neoclassicism is a new revival of classical antiquity, more consistent than earlier classicisms, and one that was linked, at least initially, to Enlightenment thought. Romanticism, by contrast, refers not to a specific style but to an attitude of mind that may reveal itself in any number of ways, including classicism. Romanticism, therefore, is a far broader concept and is correspondingly harder to define. To compound the difficulty, the Neoclassicists and early Romantics were exact contemporaries who in turn overlapped the preceding generation of Rococo artists. David and Goya, for example, were born within a few years of each other. And in England the leading representatives of the Rococo, Neoclassicism, and Romanticism—Reynolds, West, and Fuseli—shared many of the same ideas, although they were otherwise separated by clear differences in style and approach.

The Enlightenment

If the modern era was born during the American Revolution of 1776 and the French Revolution of 1789, these cataclysmic events were preceded by a revolution of the mind that had begun half a century earlier. Its standard-bearers were those thinkers of the Enlightenment in England, France, and Germany—David Hume, François-Marie Voltaire, Jean-Jacques Rousseau, Heinrich Heine, and others—who proclaimed that all human affairs ought to be ruled by reason and the common good, rather than by tradition and established authority. In the arts, as in everything else, this rationalist movement turned against the prevailing practice: the ornate and aristocratic Rococo. In the mid-eighteenth century, the call for a return to reason, nature, and morality in art meant a return to the ancients—after all, had not the classical philosophers been the original "apostles of reason"? The first to formulate this view was Johann Joachim Winckelmann, the German art historian and theorist who popularized the famous phrase about the "noble simplicity and calm grandeur" of Greek art (in his *Thoughts on the Imitation of Greek Works* of 1755). Because Classical art offered little specific guidance, to most painters a return to the classics meant the style and "academic" theory of Poussin, combined with a maximum of archaeological detail newly gleaned from ancient sculpture and the excavations of Herculaneum and Pompeii.

PAINTING

France

Greuze. In France, the thinkers of the Enlightenment, who were the intellectual forerunners of the Revolution, strongly fostered the anti-Rococo trend in painting. This reform, at first a matter of content rather than style, accounts for the sudden fame around 1760 of Jean-Baptiste Greuze (1725–1805). *The Village Bride* (fig. 325), like his other pictures of those years, is a scene of lower-class family life. What distinguishes it from earlier genre paintings (compare fig. 300) is its contrived, stagelike character, borrowed from Hogarth's "dumb show" narratives (see fig. 317). But Greuze had neither wit nor sat-

325. Jean-Baptiste Greuze. *The Village Bride.* 1761. Oil on canvas, 36 × 46½" (91.4 × 118.1 cm). Musée du Louvre, Paris

ire. His pictorial sermon illustrates the social gospel of Jean-Jacques Rousseau: that the poor, in contrast to the immoral aristocracy, are full of "natural" virtue and honest sentiment. Everything is intended to remind us of this, from the declamatory gestures and expressions of the actors to the smallest detail, such as the hen with her chicks in the foreground: one chick has left the brood and sits alone on a saucer, like the bride who is about to leave her "brood." *The Village Bride* was acclaimed a masterpiece, and the loudest praise came from Denis Diderot, that apostle of Reason and Nature. Here at last was a painter with a social mission who appealed to the beholder's moral sense, instead of merely giving pleasure like the frivolous artists of the Rococo! In his first flush of enthusiasm, Diderot accepted the narrative of Greuze's pictures as "noble and serious human action" in Poussin's sense.

David. Diderot modified his views later, when a far more gifted and rigorous "Neo-Poussinist" appeared on the scene: Jacques-Louis David (1748–1825). In *The Death of Socrates* (fig. 326), of 1787, David seems more *Poussiniste* than Poussin himself (see fig. 303). The composition unfolds like a relief, parallel to the picture plane, and the figures are as solid, and as immobile, as statues. David has added one unexpected element: the lighting, sharply focused and casting precise shadows. It is derived from Caravaggio, and so is the firmly realistic detail. Consequently, the picture has a quality of life rather astonishing in so doctrinaire a statement of the new ideal style. The very harshness of the design suggests that its creator was passionately engaged in the issues of his age, artistic as well as political. Socrates, refusing to compromise his principles, was convicted of a trumped-up

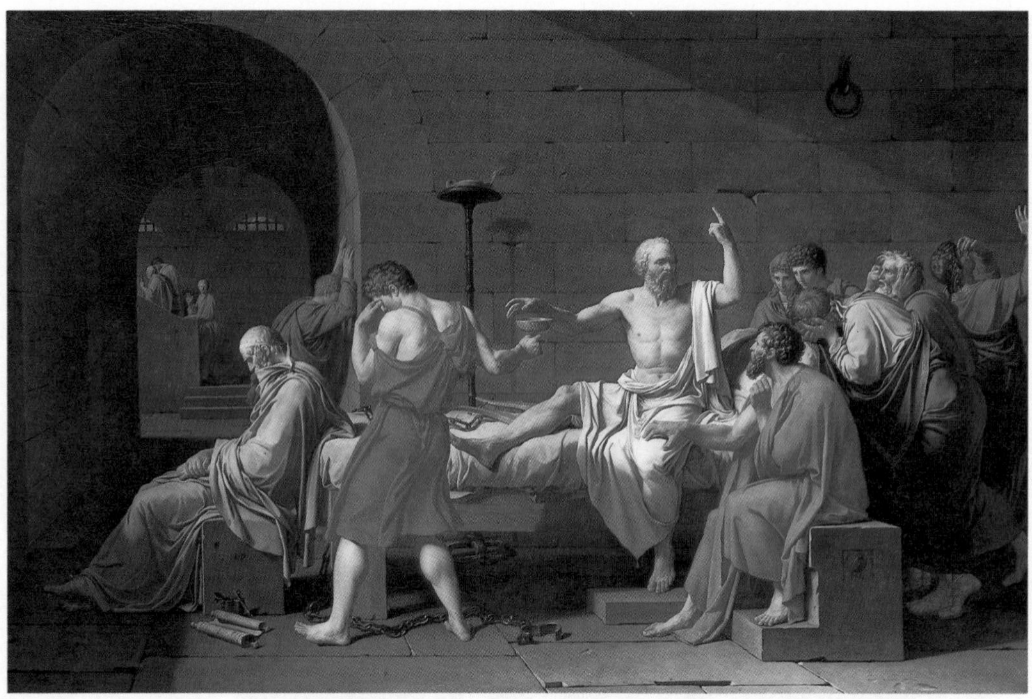

326. Jacques-Louis David. *The Death of Socrates.* 1787. Oil on canvas, 51 × 77¼" (129.5 × 196.2 cm). The Metropolitan Museum of Art, New York. Wolfe Fund, 1931. Catherine Lorillard Wolfe Collection

charge and sentenced to death. About to drink the poison cup, he is shown not only as an example of Ancient Virtue, but also as the founder of the "religion of Reason." He is here a Christlike figure amid his twelve disciples.

David took an active part in the French Revolution, and for some years he had controlling power over the artistic affairs of the nation. During this time he painted his greatest picture, *The Death of Marat* (fig. 327). David's deep emotion has made a masterpiece from a subject that would have embarrassed any lesser artist, for Marat, one of the political leaders of the Revolution, had been murdered in his bathtub. A painful skin condition required immersion, and he did his work there, with a wooden board serving as his desk. One day a young woman named Charlotte Corday burst in with a personal petition, and plunged a knife into his chest while he read it. David has composed the scene with a stark directness that is awe inspiring. In this canvas, which was planned as a public memo-

327. Jacques-Louis David. *The Death of Marat.* 1793. Oil on canvas, 65 × 50½" (165.1 × 128.3 cm). Musées Royaux des Beaux-Arts de Belgique, Brussels

328. Benjamin West. *The Death of General Wolfe.* 1770. Oil on canvas, 59½ × 84″ (151.1 × 213.4 cm). National Gallery of Canada, Ottawa. Gift of the Duke of Westminster

rial to the martyred hero, classical art coincides with devotional image and historical account. Here, far more than in *The Death of Socrates*, the artist has drawn on the Caravaggesque tradition of religious art. It is no accident that his *Marat* reminds us so strongly of Zurbarán's *St. Serapion* (see fig. 284).

England

West. The martyrdom of a contemporary secular hero was first immortalized by Benjamin West (1738–1820) in *The Death of General Wolfe* (fig. 328). West traveled to Rome from Pennsylvania in 1760 and caused something of a sensation, since no American painter had appeared in Europe before. He relished his role of frontiersman: on being shown a famous Greek statue he reportedly exclaimed, "How like a Mohawk warrior!" He also quickly absorbed the lessons of Neoclassicism, so that when he went to London a few years later, he was in command of the most up-to-date style. He became first a founding member of the Royal Academy, then, after the death of Reynolds, its president. His career was thus European rather than American, but he always took pride in his New World background.

We can sense this in *The Death of General Wolfe*, his most famous work. Wolfe's death in 1759, which occurred in the siege of Quebec during the French and Indian War, had aroused considerable feeling in London. When West, among others, decided to represent this event, two methods were open to him. He could give a factual account with the maximum of historic accuracy; or he could use "the grand manner," Poussin's ideal conception of history painting (see p. 318), with figures in "timeless" classical costume. Although he had absorbed the influence of the Neo-Poussinists in Rome, he did not follow them in this painting—he knew the American

329. John Singleton Copley. *Watson and the Shark.* 1778.
Oil on canvas, 72½ × 90¼″ (184.2 × 229.2 cm).
Museum of Fine Arts, Boston. Gift of Mrs. George von Lengerke Meyer.
Courtesy, Museum of Fine Arts, Boston

scene too well for that. Instead, he merged the two approaches. His figures wear contemporary dress, and the conspicuous figure of the Indian places the event in the New World for those unfamiliar with the subject; yet all the attitudes and expressions are "heroic." The composition, in fact, recalls an old and hallowed theme, the lamentation over the dead Christ (see fig. 191), dramatized by Baroque lighting (see fig. 286). West thus endowed the death of a modern military hero both with the rhetorical pathos of "noble and serious human actions," as defined by academic theory, and with the trappings of a real event. He created an image that expresses a phenomenon basic to modern times: the shift of emotional allegiance from religion to nationalism. No wonder his picture had countless successors during the nineteenth century.

Copley. West's gifted compatriot, John Singleton Copley of Boston (1738–1815), moved to London just two years before the American Revolution. Already an accomplished portraitist, Copley now turned to history painting in the manner of West. His most memorable effort in that field is *Watson and the Shark* (fig. 329). As a young man, Watson had been dramatically rescued from a shark attack while swimming in Havana harbor, but not until he met Copley did he decide to have this gruesome event memorialized. Perhaps he thought that only a painter newly arrived from America would do full justice to the exotic flavor of the incident. Copley, in turn, must have been fascinated by the task of translating the story into pictorial terms. Following West's example, he made every detail as authentic as possible (here the black man has the purpose of the Indian in *The Death of General Wolfe*) and utilized all the expressive resources of Baroque painting to invite the beholder's participation. Copley may have remembered representations of Jonah and the Whale, which include the elements of his scene, except that the action is reversed (the prophet is thrown overboard into the jaws of the sea monster). The shark becomes a monstrous embodiment of evil; the man with the boat hook resembles an Archangel Michael fighting Satan; and the nude youth, recalling a fallen gladiator, flounders helplessly between the forces of doom and salvation. This kind of moral allegory is typical of Neoclassicism as a whole: despite its charged emotion, the picture has the same logic and clarity found in David's *The Death of Socrates.*

330. Angelica Kauffmann. *The Artist in the Character of Design Listening to the Inspiration of Poetry.* 1782. Oil on canvas, circular, 24″ diameter (61 cm). The Iveagh Bequest, Kenwood, London (English Heritage)

Kauffmann. One of the leading Neoclassicists in England was Swiss-born Angelica Kauffmann (1741–1807). A founding member of the Royal Academy, she spent fifteen years in London among the group that included Reynolds and West, whom she had met in Winckelmann's circle in Rome (see p. 331). From the antique she developed a delicate style admirably suited to the interiors of Robert Adam (see pp. 351–52), which she was often commissioned to adorn. Nevertheless, Kauffmann's most ambitious works are narrative paintings, of which the artist John Henry Fuseli (see p. 363) observed, "Her heroines are herself." *The Artist in the Character of Design Listening to the Inspiration of Poetry* (fig. 330), one of her most appealing pictures, combines both aspects of her art. The subject must have held particular meaning for her,

331. Jean-Antoine Houdon. *Voltaire.* 1781. Terra-cotta model for marble, height 47" (119.4 cm). Musée Fabre, Montpellier, France

for it is eloquent testimony to women's struggle to gain recognition in the arts: the artist has assumed the guise of Design, who bears her features, suggesting her strong sense of identification with the muse.

SCULPTURE

Unlike painters, Neoclassical sculptors were overwhelmed by the authority accorded, since Winckelmann, to ancient statues. How could a modern artist compete with these works, which were acclaimed as the acme of sculptural achievement?

Houdon. As we might expect from what has just been said, portraiture proved the most viable field for Neoclassical sculpture. Its most distinguished practitioner, Jean-Antoine Houdon (1741–1828), still retains the acute sense of individual character introduced by Coysevox (see fig. 310). His fine statue of Voltaire (fig. 331) does full justice to the sitter's skeptical wit and wisdom, and the classical drapery enveloping the famous sage, to stress his equivalence to ancient philosophers, is not disturbing, for he wears it as casually as a dressing gown.

ARCHITECTURE

The Palladian Revival

England was the birthplace of Neoclassicism in architecture. The earliest sign of this attitude was the Palladian revival in the 1720s, sponsored by a wealthy amateur, Lord Burlington. Chiswick House (fig. 332), adapted from the Villa Rotonda (see fig. 255), is compact, simple, and geometric—the antithesis of Baroque pomp. What distinguishes this style from earlier classicisms is less its external appearance than its motivation. Instead of merely reasserting the superior authority of the ancients, it claimed to satisfy the demands of reason, and thus to be more "natural" than the Baroque. This rationalism explains the abstract, segmented look of Chiswick House. The surfaces are flat and unbroken, the ornament is meager, the temple portico juts out abruptly from the blocklike body of the structure.

Soufflot. The rationalist movement came somewhat later in France, indicating England's new importance for continental architects. Its first great monument, the Panthéon in Paris (fig. 333), by Jacques-Germain Soufflot (1713–1780), was built as the church of Ste.-Geneviève, but secularized during the Revolution. The smooth, sparsely decorated surfaces are abstractly severe, akin to those of Chiswick House, while the huge portico is modeled directly on ancient Roman temples.

Neoclassicism and the Antique

The mid-eighteenth century was greatly stirred by two experiences: the rediscovery of Greek art as the original source of classic style, and the excavations at Herculaneum and Pompeii, which for the first time revealed

332. Lord Burlington and William Kent. Chiswick House, near London. Begun 1725

333. Jacques-Germain Soufflot. The Panthéon (Ste.-Geneviève), Paris. 1755–92

the daily life of the ancients and the full range of their arts and crafts. Richly illustrated books about the Acropolis at Athens, the temples at Paestum, and the finds at Herculaneum and Pompeii were published in England and France. Archaeology caught everyone's imagination.

Adam. From this came a new style of interior decoration, seen at its finest in the works of the Englishman Robert Adam (1728–1792), such as the front drawing room of Home House (fig. 334). Adapted from Roman stucco ornament, it echoes the delicacy of Rococo interiors but with a characteristically

greatest creative achievement of Romanticism in the visual arts precisely because it was less dependent than architecture or sculpture on public approval. It held a correspondingly greater appeal for the individualism of the Romantic artist. Moreover, it could better accommodate the themes and ideas of Romantic literature. Romantic painting was not essentially illustrative. But literature, past and present, now became a more important source of inspiration for painters than ever before and provided them with a new range of subjects, emotions, and attitudes. Romantic poets, in turn, often saw nature with a painter's eye. Many had a strong interest in art criticism and theory. Some, notably Johann Wolfgang von Goethe and Victor Hugo, were capable draftsmen, and William Blake cast his visions in both pictorial and literary form (see fig. 349). Art and literature thus have a complex, subtle, and by no means one-sided relationship within the Romantic movement.

Goya. We begin our account with the great Spanish painter Francisco Goya (1746–1828), David's contemporary and the only artist of the age who may be called, unreservedly, a genius. His early works, in a delightful late Rococo vein, reflect the influence of Tiepolo and the French masters (Spain had produced no painters of significance for over a century). During the 1780s, Goya became more of a libertarian. He surely sympathized with

336. Francisco Goya. *The Family of Charles IV.* 1800. Oil on canvas, 9′2″ × 11′ (2.79 × 3.35 m). Museo del Prado, Madrid

337. Francisco Goya. *The Third of May, 1808.* 1814–15. Oil on canvas, 8′9″ × 13′4″ (2.67 × 4.06 m). Museo del Prado, Madrid

the Enlightenment and the Revolution, and not with the king of Spain, who had joined other monarchs in war against the young French Republic; yet Goya was much esteemed at court, especially as a portrait painter. He abandoned the Rococo for a Neo-Baroque style based on Velázquez and Rembrandt, the masters he had come to admire most. It is this Neo-Baroque style that announces the arrival of Romanticism.

The Family of Charles IV (fig. 336), Goya's largest royal portrait, deliberately echoes Velázquez' *The Maids of Honor* (see fig. 285). The entire clan has come to visit the artist, who is painting in one of the picture galleries of the palace. As in the earlier work, shadowy canvases hang behind the group and the light pours in from the side, although its subtle gradations owe as much to Rembrandt as to Velázquez. The brushwork, too, has an incandescent sparkle rivaling that of *The Maids of Honor.* Goya does not utilize the Caravaggesque Neoclassicism of David, yet his painting has more in common with David's work than we might think. Like David, he practices a revival style and, in his way, is equally devoted to the unvarnished truth: he uses the Neo-Baroque of Romanticism to unmask the royal family.

Psychologically, *The Family of Charles IV* is almost shockingly modern. No longer shielded by the polite conventions of Baroque court portraiture, the inner being of these individuals has been laid bare with pitiless candor. They are like a collection of ghosts: the frightened children, the bloated king, and—in a master stroke of sardonic humor—the grotesquely vulgar queen, posed like Velázquez' Princess Margarita (note the left arm and the turn of the head). How could Goya get away with this? Was the royal family so dazzled by the splendid painting of their costumes that they failed to realize what he had done to them? Goya, we realize, must have painted them as they saw themselves, while unveiling the truth for all the world to see.

When Napoleon's armies occupied Spain in 1808, Goya and many of his fellow Spaniards hoped that the conquerors would bring the liberal reforms so badly needed. The savage behavior of the French troops crushed these hopes and generated a popular resistance of equal savagery. Many of Goya's works from 1810–15 reflect this bitter experience. The greatest is *The Third of May, 1808* (fig. 337), commemorating the execution of a group of Madrid citizens. Here the blazing color, broad, fluid brushwork, and dramatic nocturnal light are more emphatically Neo-Baroque than ever. The picture has all the emotional intensity of religious art, but these martyrs are dying for Liberty, not the Kingdom of Heaven. Nor are their executioners the agents of Satan but of political tyranny—a formation of faceless automatons, impervious to their victims' despair and defiance. The same scene was to be reenacted countless times in modern history. With the clairvoyance of genius, Goya created an image that has become a terrifying symbol of our era.

Finally, in 1824, Goya went into voluntary exile; after a brief stay in Paris, he settled in Bordeaux, where he died. His importance for the Neo-Baroque Romantic painters of France is well attested by the greatest of them, Eugène Delacroix (see pp. 359–61), who said that the ideal style would be a combination of Michelangelo's and Goya's art.

France

Gros. The reign of Napoleon, with its glamour and its adventurous conquests in remote parts of the world, gave rise to French Romantic painting. It emerged from the studio of Jacques-Louis David, who became an ardent admirer of Napoleon and executed several large pictures glorifying the emperor. As a portrayer of the Napoleonic myth, however, he was partially eclipsed by artists who had been his students. They felt the style of David too confining and fostered a Baroque revival to capture the excitement of the age. David's favorite pupil, Antoine-Jean Gros (1771–1835), shows us Napoleon as a twenty-seven-year-old general leading his troops at the Battle of Arcole in northern Italy (fig. 338). Painted in Milan soon after the series of victories that gave the French the Lombard plain, it conveys Napoleon's magic as an irresistible "man of destiny," with a Romantic enthusiasm David could never match.

338. Antoine-Jean Gros. *Napoleon at Arcole.* 1796. Oil on canvas, 29½ × 23" (74.9 × 58.4 cm). Musée du Louvre, Paris

After Napoleon's empire collapsed, David spent his last years in exile in Brussels, where his major works were playfully amorous subjects drawn from ancient myths or legends and painted in a coolly sensuous Neo-Mannerist style he had initiated in Paris. He turned his pupils over to Gros, urging him to return to Neoclassical orthodoxy. Much as Gros respected his teacher's doctrines, his emotional nature impelled him toward the color and drama of the Baroque. He remained torn between his pictorial instincts and these academic principles. Consequently, he never achieved David's authority and ended his life by suicide.

Géricault. The Neo-Baroque trend initiated in France by Gros aroused the imagination of many talented younger artists. For them, politics no longer had the force of a faith. The chief heroes of Théodore Géricault (1791–1824), apart from Gros, were Michelangelo and the great Baroque masters. Géricault painted his most ambitious work, *The Raft of the "Medusa"* (fig. 339), in response to a political scandal and a modern tragedy of epic proportions. The *Medusa,* a government vessel, had foundered off the West African coast with hundreds of men on board; only a handful were rescued, after many days on a makeshift raft, which had been set adrift by the ship's cowardly captain and officers. The event attracted Géricault's attention because it was a political scandal—like many French liberals, he opposed the monarchy that was restored after Napoleon—and a modern tragedy of epic proportions. Géricault went to extraordinary lengths in trying to achieve a maximum of authenticity. He interviewed survivors, had a model of the raft built, even studied corpses in the morgue. This search for uncompromising truth is like David's, and *The Raft* is indeed remarkable for its powerfully realistic detail. Yet these preparations were subordinate in the end to the spirit of heroic drama that dominates the work. Géricault depicts the exciting moment when the rescue ship is first sighted. From the prostrate bodies of the dead and dying in the foreground, the composition is built up to a climax in the group that supports the frantically waving black man, so that the forward surge of the survivors parallels the movement of the raft itself.

Ingres. The mantle of David finally descended upon his pupil Jean-Auguste-Dominique Ingres (1780–1867). Too young

339. Théodore Géricault. *The Raft of the "Medusa."* 1818–19. Oil on canvas, 16′1″ × 23′6″ (4.9 × 7.16 m). Musée du Louvre, Paris

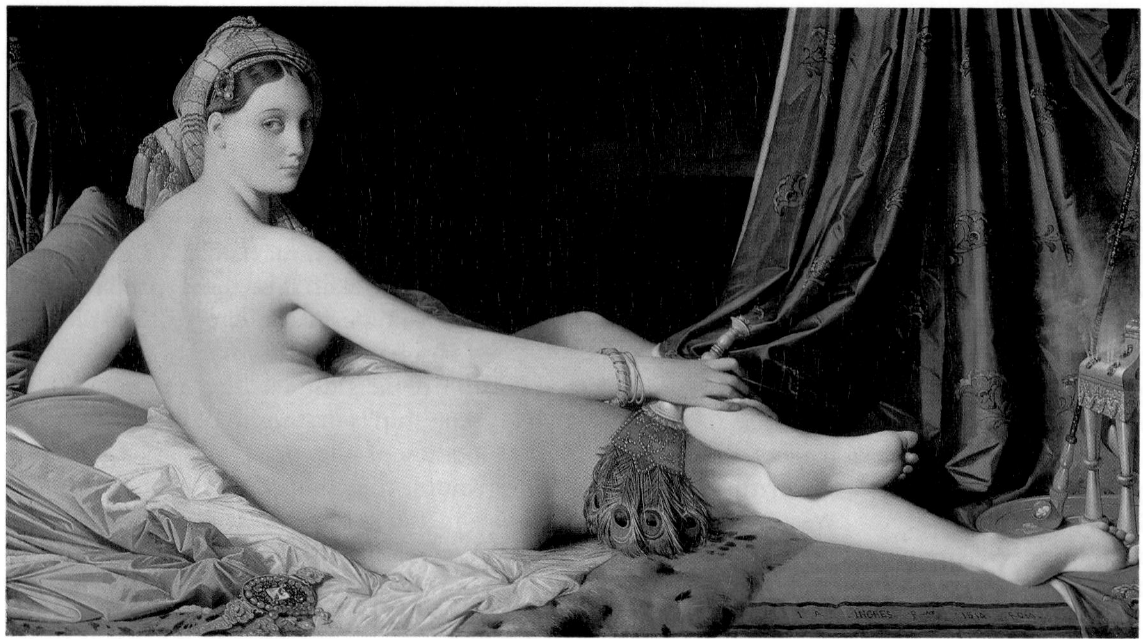

340. Jean-Auguste-Dominique Ingres. *Odalisque*. 1814. Oil on canvas, 35¼ × 63¾" (89.5 × 161.9 cm). Musée du Louvre, Paris

to share in the political passions of the Revolution, Ingres never was an enthusiastic Bonapartist. In 1806 he went to Italy and remained for eighteen years. Only after his return did he become the high priest of the Davidian tradition, defending it from the onslaughts of younger artists. What had been a revolutionary style only half a century before now congealed into rigid dogma, endorsed by the government and backed by the weight of conservative opinion.

Ingres is usually called a Neoclassicist, and his opponents Romantics. Actually, both factions stood for aspects of Romanticism after 1800: the Neoclassical phase, with Ingres as the last important survivor, and the Neo-Baroque, first announced in France by Gros' *Napoleon at Arcole*. Indeed, the two seem so interdependent that we should prefer a single name for both if we could find a suitable one. ("Romantic Classicism," which is appropriate only to the classical camp, has not won wide acceptance.) The two sides seemed to revive the old quarrel between *Poussinistes* and *Rubénistes* (see p. 325). The original *Poussinistes* had never quite practiced what they preached, and Ingres' views, too, were far more doctrinaire than his pictures. He always held that drawing was superior to painting, yet a canvas such as his *Odalisque* (fig. 340)

341. Jean-Auguste-Dominique Ingres. *Louis Bertin*. 1832. Oil on canvas, 46 × 37½" (116.8 × 95.3 cm). Musée du Louvre, Paris

342. Eugène Delacroix. *The Massacre at Chios.* 1822–24. Oil on canvas, 13′10″ × 11′7″ (4.22 × 3.53 m). Musée du Louvre, Paris

reveals an exquisite sense of color. Instead of merely tinting his design, he sets off the petal-smooth limbs of this Oriental Venus ("odalisque" is a Turkish word for a harem slave girl) with a dazzling array of rich tones and textures. The exotic subject, redolent of the enchantment of the *Thousand and One Nights*, is itself characteristic of the Romantic movement. Despite Ingres' professed worship of Raphael, this nude embodies no classical ideal of beauty. Her proportions, languid grace, and strange mixture of coolness and voluptuousness remind us, rather, of Parmigianino (compare fig. 245).

History painting as defined by Poussin remained Ingres' lifelong ambition, but he had great difficulty with it, while portraiture, which he pretended to dislike, was his strongest gift and his steadiest source of income. He was, in fact, the last great professional in a field soon to be dominated by the camera. Ingres' *Louis Bertin* (fig. 341) at first glance looks like a kind of "super-photograph," but this impression is deceptive. The artist applies the Caravaggesque Neoclassicism he had inherited from David to introduce slight changes of light and emphasis in the face, subtly altering its expression, which manifests an almost frightening intensity. Among the Romantics, only Ingres could so unify psychological depth and physical accuracy, while his followers concentrated on physical accuracy alone, competing vainly with the camera.

Delacroix. The year 1824 was crucial for French painting. Géricault died after a riding accident; Ingres returned to France from Italy and had his first public success; the first showing in Paris of works by the English Romantic painter John Constable was a revelation to many French artists (see pp. 364–65); and *The Massacre at Chios* (fig. 342) established Eugène Delacroix as the foremost Neo-Baroque Romantic painter. An admirer of both Gros and Géricault, Delacroix (1798–1863) had been exhibiting for some years, but *The Massacre* made his reputation: conservatives called it "the massacre of painting," others acclaimed it enthusiastically.

Like *The Raft of the "Medusa," The Massacre at Chios* was inspired by a contemporary

343. Eugène Delacroix. *Frédéric Chopin.* 1838. Oil on canvas, 18 × 15″ (45.7 × 38.1 cm). Musée du Louvre, Paris

event: the Greek war of independence against the Turks, which stirred a wave of sympathy throughout Western Europe (the full title is *Scenes of the Massacre at Chios: Greek Families Awaiting Death or Slavery*). Delacroix, however, aimed at "poetic truth" rather than at recapturing a specific, actual event. He shows us an intoxicating mixture of sensuousness and cruelty, but he does not succeed in forcing us to suspend our disbelief. While we revel in the sheer splendor of the painting, we do not quite accept the human experience as authentic. We react, instead, much as we do to J. M. W. Turner's *The Slave Ship* (see fig. 351). One reason may be the discontinuity of the foreground, with its dramatic contrasts of light and shade, and the luminous sweep of the landscape behind (Delacroix is said to have hastily repainted part of the background after viewing Constable's *The Haywain*; see fig. 350).

Sonorous color and the energetically fluid brushwork show Delacroix to be a *Rubéniste* of the first order. In the *Odalisque* (see fig. 340), Ingres had also celebrated the exotic world of the Near East—alien, seductive, and violent—but how different the result! No wonder that for the next quarter-century, he and Delacroix were acknowledged rivals, and their polarity, fostered by partisan critics, dominated the artistic scene in Paris. The same contrast persists in the portraiture of these perennial antagonists. Delacroix rarely painted portraits on commission. He felt at ease only when portraying his friends and fellow victims of the "Romantic agony." Like other Neo-Baroque Romantics, he emphasized the psychological aspect to such a degree that his portraits tended to become records of his personal relationship with the sitter. In a painting of the famous Polish composer Frédéric Chopin (fig. 343), we see the Romantic hero

344. Honoré Daumier. *The Third-Class Carriage*. c. 1862. Oil on canvas, 26 × 35½" (66 × 90.2 cm). The Metropolitan Museum of Art, New York. Bequest of Mrs. H. O. Havemeyer, 1929. The H. O. Havemeyer Collection

at his purest, consumed by the fire of his genius, like Gros' *Napoleon at Arcole*.

Daumier. The work of Delacroix reflects the attitude that eventually doomed the Romantic movement: its growing detachment from contemporary life. History, literature, the Near East—these were the domains of the imagination where he sought refuge from the turmoil of the Industrial Revolution. It is ironic that Honoré Daumier (1808–1879), the one Romantic artist who did not shrink from reality, remained in his day practically unknown as a painter. A biting political cartoonist, he contributed satirical drawings to various Paris weeklies for most of his life. He turned to painting in the 1840s but found no public for his work. Only a few friends encouraged him and, a year before his death, arranged his first one-person show. Daumier's mature paintings have the full pictorial range of the Neo-Baroque, but the subjects of many of them are scenes of daily life like those he treated in his cartoons. *The Third-Class Carriage* (fig. 344) is such a work. Daumier's forms reflect the compactness of François Millet's (see p. 362), but are painted so freely that they must have seemed raw and "unfinished" even by Delacroix's standards. Yet Daumier's power derives from this very freedom. His concern is not for the tangible surface of reality but for the emotional meaning behind it. In this picture, he has captured a peculiarly modern human condition: "the lonely crowd." These people have in common only that they are traveling together in a railway car. Though they are physically crowded, they take no notice of one another—each is alone with his or her own thoughts. Daumier explores this state with an insight into character and a breadth of human sympathy worthy of Rembrandt, whose work he revered.

French Landscape Painting. Thanks to the cult of nature, landscape painting became the most characteristic form of Romantic art. The Romantics believed that God's laws could be seen written in nature. While it arose out of the Enlightenment, their faith, known as pantheism, was based not on rational

345. Camille Corot. *Papigno*. 1826. Oil on canvas, 13 × 15¾" (33 × 40 cm). Private collection

thought but on subjective experience, and the appeal to the emotions rather than the intellect made those lessons all the more compelling. In order to express the feelings inspired by nature, the Romantics sought to transcribe landscape as faithfully as possible, in contrast to the Neoclassicists, who subjected landscape to prescribed ideas of beauty and linked it to historical subjects. At the same time, the Romantics felt equally free to modify nature's appearance to evoke heightened states of mind in accordance with the dictates of the imagination, the only standard they ultimately recognized. Landscape inspired the Romantics with passions so exalted that only in the hands of the greatest history painters could humans equal nature in power as protagonists. Hence, the Romantic landscape lies outside the descriptive and emotional range of the eighteenth century.

Corot. The first and surely the greatest French Romantic landscape painter was Camille Corot (1796–1875). In 1825 he went to Italy for two years and explored the countryside around Rome, as did Claude Lorraine. What Claude recorded only in his drawings—the quality of a particular place at a particular time—Corot made into paintings, small canvases done on the spot in an hour or two (fig. 345). In size and immediacy, these pictures are akin to Constable's oil sketches (see p. 365); yet they stem from different traditions. If Constable's view of nature, which emphasizes the sky as "the chief organ of sentiment," is derived from seventeenth-century Dutch landscapes, Corot's instinct for architectural clarity and stability again recalls Claude. But he, too, insists on "the truth of the moment." His exact observation and readiness to seize on any view that attracted him during his excursions show the same commitment to direct visual experience that we find in Constable. The Neoclassicists had also painted oil sketches out-of-doors. Unlike them, Corot did not initially transform his sketches into idealized pastoral visions, though he was to do so later in his career. His willingness to accept them as independent works of art marks him unmistakably as a Romantic.

Millet. Corot's fidelity to nature was an important model for the Barbizon school, though he was not actually a member. This group of painters, all younger than Corot, settled in the village of Barbizon near Paris to paint landscapes and scenes of rural life. Enthused, however, by Constable, whose work had been exhibited in Paris in 1824, they turned to the Northern Baroque landscape as an alternative to the Neoclassical tradition. Their landscapes are filled with a simple veneration that admirably reflects the rallying cry of the French Romantics: sincerity. *The Sower* (fig. 346) by François Millet (1814–1875), one of the artists of the Barbizon school, has a somewhat self-conscious flavor. Blurred in the hazy atmosphere, this "hero of the soil" is nevertheless a timeless image. (Could Millet have known the pathetic sower from the October page of the *Très Riches Heures du Duc de Berry*? Compare fig. 184.) Ironically, the

346. François Millet. *The Sower*. c. 1850. Oil on canvas, 40 × 32½" (101.6 × 82.6 cm). Museum of Fine Arts, Boston. Gift of Quincy Adams Shaw through Quincy A. Shaw, Jr., and Mrs. Marion Shaw Haughton

347. Rosa Bonheur. *Plowing in the Nivernais.* 1849.
Oil on canvas, 5′9″ × 8′8″ (1.75 × 2.64 m). Musée d'Orsay, Paris

painting monumentalizes a rural way of life that was rapidly disappearing under the pressure of the Industrial Revolution.

Bonheur. Millet and the Barbizon school advocated a return to nature as a way of fleeing the ills arising from industrialization and urbanization. Despite their conservative outlook, the popular revolution of 1848 elevated them to a new prominence in French art. That same year Rosa Bonheur (1822–1899), also an artist who worked out-of-doors, received a French government commission that led to her first great success and helped establish her as a leading painter of animals—and eventually as the most famous woman artist of her time. Her painting *Plowing in the Nivernais* (fig. 347) was exhibited the following year, after a winter spent making studies from life. The theme of humanity's union with nature had already been popularized in, among other works, the country romances of George Sand. Bonheur's picture shares Millet's reverence for peasant life, but the real subject here, as in all her paintings, is the animals within the landscape; these she depicts with a convincing naturalism that later placed her among the most influential Realists.

England

Fuseli. England was as precocious in nurturing Romanticism as it had been in promoting Neoclassicism. In fact, one of its first representatives, John Henry Fuseli (1741–1825), was a contemporary of West and Copley. This Swiss-born painter (originally named Füssli) had an extraordinary impact on his time, more perhaps because of his adventurous and forceful personality than the merits of his work. Fuseli based his style on Michelangelo and the Mannerists, not on Poussin and the antique. A German acquaintance of those years described him as "extreme in everything, Shakespeare's painter." Fuseli was a transitional figure. He espoused many of the same Neoclassical theories as Reynolds, West, and Kauffmann, but bent their rules virtually to the breaking point. We see this in *The Nightmare* (fig. 348). The sleeping woman, more Mannerist than Michelangelesque, is Neoclassical. The grinning devil and the luminescent horse, however, come from the demon-ridden world of medieval folklore, while the Rembrandtesque lighting reminds us of Reynolds (compare fig. 320). Here the Romantic quest for terrifying experiences

348. John Henry Fuseli. *The Nightmare.* c. 1790. Oil on canvas, 29½ × 25¼" (74.9 × 64.1 cm). Frankfurter Goethe-Museum, Frankfurt

349. William Blake. *The Ancient of Days,* frontispiece of *Europe, A Prophesy.* 1794. Metal relief etching, hand-colored. Library of Congress, Washington, D.C. Lessing J. Rosenwald Collection

leads not to physical violence but to the dark recesses of the mind.

Blake. Later, in London, Fuseli befriended the poet-painter William Blake (1757–1827), who possessed an even greater creativity and stranger personality than his own. A recluse and visionary, Blake produced and published his own books of poems with engraved text and hand-colored illustrations. Though he never left England, he acquired a large repertory of Michelangelesque and Mannerist motifs from engravings and through the influence of Fuseli. He also conceived a tremendous admiration for the Middle Ages, and came closer than any other Romantic artist to reviving pre-Renaissance forms (his books were meant to be the successors of illuminated manuscripts).

These elements are all present in Blake's memorable image *The Ancient of Days* (fig. 349). The muscular figure, radically foreshortened and fitted into a circle of light, is derived from Mannerism, while the symbolic compasses come from medieval representations of the Lord as Architect of the Universe. With these precedents, we would expect the Ancient of Days to signify Almighty God, but in Blake's esoteric mythology, he stands rather for the power of reason, which the poet regarded as ultimately destructive, since it stifles vision and inspiration. To Blake, the "inner eye" was all-important; he felt no need to observe the visible world around him.

Constable. It was in landscape rather than in narrative scenes that English painting reached its fullest expression. In the eighteenth century, landscape paintings had been, for the most part, imaginative exercises conforming to Northern and Italian examples. John Constable (1776–1837) admired Ruisdael and Claude, yet he strenuously opposed all flights of fancy. Landscape painting, he believed, must be based on observable facts; it should aim at "embodying a pure apprehension of natural effect." All of Constable's pictures show familiar views of the English countryside. It was, he later claimed, the scenery around his native Stour Valley that made him a painter. Although he painted the final versions in his studio, he prepared them by making oil sketches from nature. The sky, to him, remained "the key note, standard scale, and the chief organ of sentiment," as a mirror of those sweeping forces so dear to the Romantic view of nature. In *The Haywain* (fig. 350), he has caught a particularly splendid moment—a great sweep of wind, sunlight, and clouds playing over the spacious landscape. The earth and sky seem to have become organs of sentiment informed with the artist's poetic sensibility. At the same time, there is an intimacy in this monumental composition that reveals Constable's deep love of the countryside. This new, personal note is characteristically Romantic. Since Constable has painted the landscape with such conviction, we see the scene through his eyes and believe him, even though it perhaps did not look quite this way in reality.

Turner. Joseph Mallord William Turner (1775–1851) arrived at a style that Constable deprecatingly but acutely described as "airy visions, painted with tinted steam." Turner began as a watercolorist, and the use of translucent tints on white paper may help explain his preoccupation with colored light. Like Constable, he made copious studies from nature (though not in oils), but the scenery he selected satisfied the Romantic taste for the picturesque and the sublime: mountains, the sea, or sites linked with historic events. In his full-scale pictures he often changed these views so freely that they became quite unrecognizable. Many of Turner's landscapes are related to literary themes. When they were exhibited, he would add appropriate quotations from ancient or modern authors to the catalogue, or he would make up some lines himself and claim to be "citing" his own unpublished poem, "Fallacies of Hope." These canvases are nevertheless the opposite of history painting as defined by Poussin: the titles indeed indicate "noble and serious human actions," but the tiny figures, lost in the seething violence of nature, suggest the ultimate defeat of all endeavor—the "fallacies of hope."

The Slave Ship (fig. 351), one of Turner's most spectacular visions, illustrates how he translated his literary sources into "tinted steam." First entitled *Slavers Throwing Overboard the Dead and Dying—Typhoon Coming On*, the painting contains several levels of meaning. Like Géricault's *The Raft of the "Medusa"* (see fig. 339), which had been exhibited in England in 1820, it has to do, in part, with a specific incident about which Turner had recently read: when an epidemic broke out on a slave ship, the captain jettisoned his human cargo because he was insured against the loss of slaves at sea, but not by disease. Turner also thought of a relevant passage from *The Seasons*, by the eighteenth-century poet James Thompson, which describes how sharks follow a slave ship during a typhoon, "lured by the scent of steaming crowds, or rank disease, and death." But what is the relation between the slaver's action and the typhoon? Are the dead and dying slaves being cast into the sea against the threat of the storm, perhaps to lighten the ship? Is the typhoon nature's retribution for the captain's greed and cruelty? Of the many storms at sea that Turner painted, none has quite this apocalyptic quality. A cosmic catastrophe seems about to engulf everything, not merely the "guilty" slaver but the sea itself with its crowds of fantastic and oddly harmless-looking fish.

While we still feel the force of Turner's imagination, most of us enjoy, perhaps with a twinge of guilt, the tinted steam for its own sake rather than as a vehicle of the awesome emotions the artist meant to evoke. Even in terms of the values he himself acknowledged, Turner strikes us as "a virtuoso of the Sublime" led astray by his very exuberance. He must have been pleased by praise from the theorist John Ruskin, that protagonist of the moral superiority of Gothic style, who saw in *The Slave Ship*, which he owned, "the true, the beautiful, and the intellectual"—all qualities that raised Turner above older landscape painters. Still, Turner may have come to wonder if his tinted steam had its intended effect on all beholders. Soon after finishing *The Slave Ship*, he could have read in his copy of Goethe's *Color Theory*, recently translated into English, that yellow has a "gay, softly exciting

350. John Constable. *The Haywain*. 1821. Oil on canvas, 51¼ × 73″ (130.2 × 185.4 cm). The National Gallery, London. Reproduced by courtesy of the Trustees

351. Joseph Mallord William Turner. *The Slave Ship*. 1840. Oil on canvas, 35¾ × 48″ (90.8 × 121.9 cm). Museum of Fine Arts, Boston. Henry Lillie Pierce Fund (Purchase)

352. Caspar David Friedrich. *The Polar Sea.* 1824. Oil on canvas, 38½ × 50½" (97.8 × 128.2 cm). Kunsthalle, Hamburg

character," while orange red suggests "warmth and gladness." Would these be the emotions aroused by *The Slave Ship* in a viewer who did not know its title?

Germany

Friedrich. In Germany, as in England, landscape was the finest achievement of Romantic painting, and the underlying ideas, too, were often strikingly similar. When Caspar David Friedrich (1774–1840), the most important German Romantic artist, painted *The Polar Sea* (fig. 352), he may have known of Turner's "Fallacies of Hope," for in an earlier picture on the same theme (now lost) he had inscribed the name "Hope" on the crushed vessel. In any case, he shared Turner's attitude toward human fate. The painting, as so often before, was inspired by a specific event which the artist endowed with symbolic significance: a dangerous moment in William Parry's Arctic expedition of 1819–20.

One wonders how Turner might have depicted this scene. Perhaps it would have been too static for him, but Friedrich was attracted by this immobility. He has visualized the piled-up slabs of ice as a kind of megalithic monument to human defeat built by nature itself. Infinitely lonely, it is a haunting reflection of the artist's own melancholy. There is no hint of tinted steam—the very air seems frozen—nor any subjective handwriting. We look right through the paint-covered surface at a reality that seems created without Friedrich's intervention. This technique, impersonal and meticulous, is peculiar to German Romantic painting. It stems from the early Neoclassicists, but the Germans, whose tradition of Baroque painting was weak, adopted it more wholeheartedly than the English or the French.

United States

Bingham. The New World, too, had its Romantic landscape artists. At first, Americans were far too busy carving out homesteads to pay much attention to the poetry of nature's moods. The attitude toward landscape began

353. George Caleb Bingham. *Fur Traders Descending the Missouri.* c. 1845. Oil on canvas, 29 × 36" (73.7 × 91.4 cm). The Metropolitan Museum of Art, New York. Morris K. Jesup Fund, 1933

to change only as the surrounding wilderness was gradually tamed, allowing people for the first time to see nature as the escape from civilization that inspired European painters. Pantheism virtually became a national religion during the Romantic era. Spurred by the poets, who by 1825 were calling on them to depict the wilderness as the most conspicuous feature of the New World and its emerging civilization, American painters elevated the forests and mountains to symbols of the United States. While it could be frightening, nature was everywhere, and was believed to play a special role in determining the American character.

Fur Traders Descending the Missouri (fig. 353) by George Caleb Bingham (1811–1879) shows this close identification with the land. The picture, which is both a landscape and a genre scene, is full of the vastness and silence of the wide-open spaces. The two trappers in their dugout canoe, gliding downstream in the misty sunlight, are entirely at home in this idyllic setting. The assertion of a human presence portrays the United States as a benevolent Eden in which settlers assume their rightful place. Rather than being dwarfed by a vast and often hostile continent, these hardy pioneers live in an ideal state of harmony with nature, symbolized by the waning daylight. The picture carries us back to the river life of Mark Twain's childhood. At the same time, it reminds us of how much Romantic adventurousness went into the westward expansion of the United States. The scene owes a good deal of its haunting charm to the silhouette of the black cub chained to the prow and its reflection in the water. This masterstroke adds a note of primitive mystery that we shall not meet again until the work of Henri Rousseau (see p. 404).

SCULPTURE

The development of Romantic sculpture follows the pattern of painting. However, we shall find it much less venturesome than either painting or architecture. The unique virtue of sculpture—its solid, space-filling reality (its "idol" quality)—was not congenial to the Romantic temperament. The rebellious and individualistic urges of Romanticism could find expression in rough, small-scale sketches but rarely survived the laborious process of translating them into permanent, finished monuments. Moreover, the new standard of uncompromising, realistic "truth" was embarrassing to the sculptor. When a painter renders clothing, anatomical detail, or furniture with photographic precision, he or she does not produce a duplicate of reality but a representation of it. To do so in sculpture comes dangerously close to mechanical reproduction, making it a handmade equivalent of the plaster cast. Sculpture thus underwent a crisis that was resolved only toward the end of the nineteenth century.

Canova. At the beginning of the Romantic era, we find at first an adaptation of the Neoclassical style to new ends by sculptors, especially older ones. The most famous of them, Antonio Canova (1757–1822), produced a colossal nude statue of Napoleon inspired by portraits of ancient rulers whose nudity indicates their status as divinities. The elevation of the emperor to a god marks a shift away from the lofty ideals of the Enlightenment that had given rise to Neoclassicism. The glorification of the hero as a noble example, such as in Houdon's statue of Voltaire (see fig. 331), is abandoned in favor of the Romantic cult of the individual. There is no longer any higher authority—neither religion nor reason is invoked. Only the imperative of Greek art remains unquestioned as a style divorced from content. Not to be outdone, Napoleon's sister Pauline Borghese permitted Canova to sculpt her as a reclining Venus (fig. 354). The statue is so obviously idealized as to still any gossip. We recognize it as a precursor, more classically proportioned, of Ingres' *Odalisque* (see fig. 340). Both exemplify early Romanticism, which incorporated Rococo eroticism but in a less sensuous form. Strangely enough, *Pauline Borghese as Venus* seems less three-dimensional than the painting. She is designed for front and back view only, like a "relief in the round," and her considerable charm radiates almost entirely from the fluid grace of her contours. Here we

354. Antonio Canova. *Pauline Borghese as Venus.* 1808. Marble, lifesize. Galleria Borghese, Rome

355. François Rude. *La Marseillaise.* 1833–36. Stone, c. 42 × 26′ (12.8 × 7.93 m). Arc de Triomphe, Paris

356. Jean-Baptiste Carpeaux. *The Dance.* 1867–69. Plaster model, c. 15′ × 8′6″ (4.57 × 2.64 m). Musée de l'Opéra, Paris

also encounter the problem of representation versus duplication, not in the figure itself but in the pillows, mattress, and couch. This dilemma could be resolved in two ways: by reviving a preclassical style sufficiently abstract to restore the autonomous reality of sculpture, or by a return to the frankly theatrical Baroque. At the time, only the latter alternative proved generally feasible.

Rude. By the 1830s, Neo-Baroque sculpture had produced a masterpiece: the splendidly rhetorical *La Marseillaise* (fig. 355) by François Rude (1784–1855), on the Arc de Triomphe in Paris, would be worthy of Bernini and Puget (see figs. 278, 311). The soldiers, volunteers of 1792 rallying to defend the Republic, are still in classical guise (see figs. 68, 97), but the Genius of Liberty above them imparts her great forward-rushing movement to the entire group, lending it an irresistible Romantic sweep.

Carpeaux. Rude's successor in the field of architectural sculpture was Jean-Baptiste Carpeaux (1827–1875). The plaster model for his famous group *The Dance* for the facade of the Paris Opéra (fig. 356) is both livelier and more precise than the final stone group, which may be seen in the bottom right of figure 360. Its coquettish gaiety, inspired by the Rococo (see fig. 313), perfectly matches Charles Garnier's Neo-Baroque architecture. Unlike *Pauline Borghese as Venus*, Carpeaux's figures look undressed rather than nude. So photographically realistic in detail are they that we do not accept them as legitimate denizens of the realm of mythology. "Truth" here has destroyed the ideal reality that was still intact in Canova.

ARCHITECTURE

Given the individualistic nature of Romanticism, we might expect the range of revival styles to be widest in painting, the most personal and private of the visual arts, and narrowest in architecture, the most communal and public—yet the opposite is true. Painters

357. Horace Walpole, with William Robinson and others. Strawberry Hill, Twickenham. 1749–77

and sculptors were unable to abandon Renaissance habits of representation, and never really revived medieval art or ancient art before the Classical Greek era. Architects were not subject to this limitation, and the revival styles persisted longer in architecture than in the other arts.

It is characteristic of Romanticism that at the time architects launched the classical revival, they also started a Gothic revival. England was far in advance here, as it was in the development of Romantic literature and painting. Gothic forms had never wholly disappeared in England. They were used on occasion for special purposes, but these were survivals of an authentic, if outmoded, tradition. The conscious revival, by contrast, was linked with the cult of the picturesque, and with the vogue for medieval (and pseudomedieval) romances.

Walpole. In this spirit Horace Walpole (1717–1797) enlarged and "gothicized" his country house, Strawberry Hill (figs. 357, 358) midway in the eighteenth century. Despite its studied irregularity, the rambling structure has dainty, flat surfaces that remind us strongly of Robert Adam (compare fig. 334): the interior looks almost as if it were decorated with lace-paper doilies. This playfulness, so free of dogma, gives Strawberry Hill its special charm. Gothic here is still an "exotic" style. It appeals because it is strange, but for that very reason it must be "translated," like a medieval romance, or the Chinese motifs that crop up in Rococo decoration.

358. Interior, Strawberry Hill

After 1800, the choice between the classical and Gothic modes was more often resolved in favor of Gothic. Nationalist sentiments, strengthened in the Napoleonic wars, became important factors. England, France, and Germany each tended to think that Gothic expressed its particular national genius. Certain theorists (notably John Ruskin) also regarded Gothic as superior for ethical or religious reasons on the grounds that it was "honest" and "Christian."

Barry and Pugin. All these considerations lie behind the design, by Sir Charles Barry

359. Sir Charles Barry and A. N. Welby Pugin. The Houses of Parliament, London. Begun 1836

(1785–1860) and A. N. Welby Pugin (1812–1852), for the Houses of Parliament in London, the largest monument of the Gothic revival (fig. 359). As the seat of a vast and complex governmental apparatus, but at the same time as a focus of patriotic feeling, it presents a curious mixture: repetitious symmetry governs the main body of the structure and picturesque irregularity its silhouette.

Garnier. Meanwhile, the stylistic alternatives for architects were continually increased by other revivals. When the Renaissance, and then the Baroque, returned to favor, the revival movement had come full circle: Neo-Renaissance and Neo-Baroque replaced the Neoclassical. This final phase of Romantic architecture, which dominated the years 1850–75 and lingered through 1900, is epitomized in the Paris Opéra (fig. 360), designed by Charles Garnier (1825–1898). Its Neo-Baroque quality derives more from the profusion of sculpture—including Carpeaux's *The Dance* (see fig. 356)—and ornament than from its eclectic architectural vocabulary: the paired columns of the facade, for example, are "quoted" from the East Front of the Louvre (see fig. 307). The whole building looks "overdressed," its luxurious vulgarity so naive as to be disarming. It reflects the taste of the beneficiaries of the Industrial Revolution, newly rich and powerful, who saw themselves as the heirs of the old aristocracy and thus found the styles predating the French Revolution more appealing than classical or Gothic.

360. Charles Garnier. The Opéra, Paris. 1861–74

PHOTOGRAPHY

Is photography art? The fact that we still pose the question testifies to the continuing debate. The answers have varied with the changing definition and understanding of art. In itself, of course, photography is simply a medium, like oil paint or pastel, used to make art but having no inherent claim to being art. After all, what distinguishes an art from a craft is why, not how, it is done. But photography shares creativity with art because, by its very nature, its performance necessarily involves the imagination. Any photograph, even a casual snapshot, represents both an organization of experience and the record of a mental image. The subject and style of a photograph thus tell us about the photographer's inner and outer worlds. Furthermore, like painting and sculpture, photography participates in aspects of the same process of seek-and-find. Photographers may not realize what they respond to until after they see the image that has been printed.

Like woodcut, etching, engraving, and lithography, photography is a form of printmaking that is dependent on mechanical processes. But in contrast to the other graphic mediums, photography has always been tainted as the product of a new technology. For this reason, the camera has usually been considered little more than a recording device. Photography, however, is by no means a neutral medium; its reproduction of reality is never completely faithful. Whether we realize it or not, the camera alters appearances. Photographs reinterpret the world around us, making us literally see it in new terms.

Photography and painting represent parallel responses to their times and have generally expressed the same world view. Sometimes the camera's power to extend our way of seeing has been realized first by the painter's creative vision. The two mediums nevertheless differ fundamentally in their approach and temperament: painters communicate their understanding through techniques that represent their cumulative response over time; photographers recognize the moment when the subject before them corresponds to the mental image they have formed of it. It is hardly surprising that photography and art have enjoyed an uneasy relationship from the start. Artists have generally treated the photograph something like a preliminary sketch. Photography has in turn been heavily influenced throughout its history by the painter's medium, and photographs may still be judged according to how well they imitate paintings and drawings. To understand photography's place in the history of art, we must learn to recognize the medium's particular strengths and inherent limitations.

The Founders of Photography

In 1822 a French inventor named Joseph Nicéphore Niépce (1765–1833) succeeded in making the first permanent photographic image, although his earliest surviving example (fig. 361) dates from four years later. He then joined forces with a younger man, Louis-Jacques-Mandé Daguerre (1789–1851), who had devised an improved camera. After ten more years of chemical and mechanical research, the daguerreotype, using positive exposures, was unveiled publicly in 1839 and the age of photography was born. The announcement spurred the Englishman William Henry Fox Talbot (1800–1877) to complete his own photographic process, involving a paper negative from which positives could be made, that he had been pursuing independently since 1833.

What motivated the earliest photographers? They were searching for an artistic medium, not for a device of practical utility. Though Niépce was a research chemist rather than an artist, his achievement was an outgrowth of his efforts to improve the lithographic process. Daguerre was a skilled painter, and he probably turned to the camera to heighten the illusionism in his huge painted dioramas, which were the sensation of Paris during the 1820s and 1830s. Fox Talbot saw in photography a substitute for drawing, as well as a means of reproduction, after using a camera obscura as a tool to sketch landscapes while on a vacation.

361. Joseph Nicéphore Niépce. *View from His Window at Le Gras.* 1826. Heliograph, 6½ × 7⅞" (16.5 × 20 cm). Gernsheim Collection, University of Texas at Austin

That the new medium should have a mechanical aspect was particularly appropriate. It was as if the Industrial Revolution, having forever altered civilization's way of life, had now to invent its own method for recording itself, although the transience of modern existence was not captured by "stopping the action" until the 1870s. Photography underwent a rapid series of improvements, including inventions for better lenses, glass plate negatives, and new chemical processes, which provided faster emulsions and more stable images. Since many of the initial limitations of photography were overcome around mid-century, it would be misleading to tell the early history of the medium in terms of technological developments, important though they were.

The basic mechanics and chemistry of photography, moreover, had been known for a long time. The camera obscura, a box with a small hole in one end, dates back to antiquity. In the sixteenth century it was widely used for visual demonstrations. The camera was fitted with a mirror and then a lens in the Baroque period, which saw major advances in optical science culminating in Newtonian physics. By the 1720s it had become an aid in drawing architectural scenes; at the same time, silver salts were discovered to be light-sensitive.

Why, then, did it take another hundred years for someone to put this knowledge together? Much of the answer lies in the nature of scientific revolutions, which as a rule involve combining old technologies and concepts with new ones. (They do this in response to changing world views that they, in turn, influence.) Photography was neither inevitable in the history of technology, nor necessary to the history of art; yet it was an idea whose time had clearly come. If we try for a moment to imagine that photography was invented a hundred years earlier, we will find this to be impossible simply on artistic, apart from technological, grounds: the eighteenth century was too devoted to fantasy to be interested in the literalness of photography. Rococo portraiture, for example, was more concerned with providing a flattering image than an accurate likeness, and the camera's straightforward record would have been totally out of place. Even in architectural painting, extreme liberties were willingly taken with topographical truth.

The invention of photography was a response to the artistic urges and historical forces that underlie Romanticism. Much of the impulse came from a quest for the True and the Natural. The desire for "images made by Nature" can already be seen in the late-eighteenth-century vogue for silhouette portraits (traced from the shadow of the sitter's profile), which led to attempts to record such shadows on light-sensitive materials. David's harsh realism in *The Death of Marat* (see fig. 327) had already proclaimed the cause of unvarnished truth. So did Ingres' *Louis Bertin* (see fig. 341), which established the standards of physical reality and character portrayal that photographers would follow.

Portraiture

Like lithography, which was invented only in 1797, photography met the growing middle-class demand for images of all kinds. By 1850, large numbers of the bourgeoisie were having their likenesses painted, and it was in portraiture that photography found its readiest acceptance. Soon after the daguerreotype was introduced, photographic studios sprang

362. Nadar. *Sarah Bernhardt.* 1859. George Eastman House, Rochester, New York

up everywhere, especially in America. Anyone could have a portrait taken cheaply and easily. In the process, the average person became memorable. Photography thus became an outgrowth of the democratic values fostered by the American and French revolutions. There was also keen competition among photographers to get the famous to pose for portraits.

Gaspard Félix Tournachon (1820–1910), better known as Nadar, managed to attract most of France's leading personalities to his studio. Like many early photographers, he started out as an artist but came to prefer the lens to the brush. He initially used the camera to capture the likenesses of the 280 sitters whom he caricatured in an enormous lithograph, *Le Panthéon Nadar.* The actress Sarah Bernhardt posed for him several times, and his photographs of her (fig. 362) are the direct ancestors of modern glamour photography. With her romantic pose and expression, she is a counterpart to the soulful maidens who inhabit much of nineteenth-century painting. Nadar has treated her in remarkably sculptural terms: indeed, the play of light and sweep of drapery are reminiscent of the sculptured portrait busts that were so popular with collectors at the time.

The Restless Spirit; Stereophotography

Early photography reflected the outlook and temperament of Romanticism, and indeed the entire nineteenth century had a pervasive curiosity and an abiding belief that everything could be discovered. While this fascination sometimes manifested a serious interest in science—witness Darwin's voyage on the *Beagle* from 1831 to 1836—it more typically took the form of a restless quest for new experiences and places. Photography had a remarkable impact on the imagination of the period by making the rest of the world widely available, or by simply revealing it in a new way.

A love of the exotic was fundamental to Romantic escapism, and by 1850 photographers had begun to cart their equipment to faraway places. The unquenchable thirst for vicarious experiences accounts for the expanding popularity of stereoscopic daguerreotypes. Invented in 1849, the two-lens camera produced two photographs that correspond to the slightly different images perceived by our two eyes; when seen through a special viewer called a stereoscope, the stereoptic photographs fuse to create a remarkable illusion of three-dimensional depth. Two years later, stereoscopes became the rage at the Crystal Palace exposition in London (see fig. 389). Countless thousands of double views were taken, such as that in figure 363. Virtually every corner of the earth became accessible to practically any household, with a vividness second only to being there.

Stereophotography was an important breakthrough, for its binocular vision marked a distinct departure from perspective in the pictorial tradition and demonstrated for the first time photography's potential to enlarge vision. Curiously enough, this success waned, except for special uses. People were simply too habituated to viewing pictures as if with one eye. When the halftone plate was

363. *Tsar Cannon Outside the Spassky Gate, Moscow* (cast 1586; world's largest caliber, 890 mm; presently inside Kremlin). Second half 19th century. Stereophotograph. Courtesy Culver Pictures

invented in the 1880s for reproducing pictures on a printed page, stereophotographs revealed another drawback: as our illustration shows, they were unsuitable for this process of reproduction. From then on, single-lens photography was inextricably linked with the mass media of the day.

Photojournalism

Fundamental to the rise of photography was the pervasive nineteenth-century sense that the present was already history in the making. Only with the advent of the Romantic hero did great acts other than martyrdom become popular subjects for contemporary painters and sculptors, and it can hardly be surprising that photography was invented a year after the death of Napoleon, who had been the subject of more paintings than any secular leader ever before. At about the same time, Géricault's *The Raft of the "Medusa"* and Delacroix's *The Massacre at Chios* (see figs. 339, 342) signaled a decisive shift in the Romantic attitude, toward representing contemporary events. This outlook brought with it a new kind of photography: photojournalism.

Its first great representative was Mathew Brady (1823–1896), who covered the Civil War. Other wars had already been photographed, but Brady and his twenty assistants, using cameras too slow and cumbersome to show actual combat, managed to bring home its horrors with unprecedented directness. *Home of a Rebel Sharpshooter, Gettysburg* (fig. 364) by Alexander Gardner (1821–1882), who left Brady to form his own team, is a landmark in the history of art. Never before had both the grim reality and, above all, the significance of death on the battlefield been conveyed so inexorably in a single image. Compared with the heroic act celebrated by Benjamin West (see fig. 328), this tragedy is as anonymous as the slain soldier himself. The photograph is all the more persuasive for having the same harsh realism of David's *The Death of Marat* (see fig. 327), and the limp figure, hardly visible between the rocks framing the scene, is no less poignant.

364. Alexander Gardner. *Home of a Rebel Sharpshooter, Gettysburg*. July 1863. Wet-plate photograph. Chicago Historical Society

REALISM AND IMPRESSIONISM

PAINTING

France

"Can Jupiter survive the lightning rod?" asked Karl Marx, not long after the middle of the century. The question implies that the ancient god of thunder and lightning was now in jeopardy through science. We felt a similar dilemma between art and life in *The Dance* by the sculptor Carpeaux. The French poet and art critic Charles Baudelaire was addressing himself to the same problem when, in 1846, he called for paintings that expressed "the heroism of modern life." At that time only one painter was willing to make an artistic creed of this demand: Baudelaire's friend Gustave Courbet (1819–1877).

Courbet and Realism. Courbet was born in Ornans, a village near the French-Swiss border, and remained proud of his rural background. A socialist in politics, he had begun as a Neo-Baroque Romantic in the early 1840s. By 1848, under the impact of the revolutionary upheavals then sweeping over Europe, he came to believe that the Romantic emphasis on feeling and imagination was merely an escape from the realities of the time. The modern artist must rely on direct experience and be a Realist. "I cannot paint an angel," he said, "because I have never seen one." As a descriptive term, "realism" is not very precise. For Courbet, it meant something akin to the "naturalism" of Caravaggio (see p. 288). As an admirer of Rembrandt he had, in fact, strong links with the Caravaggesque tradition, and his work, like Caravaggio's, was denounced for its supposed vulgarity and lack of spiritual content.

The storm broke in 1849 when he exhibited *The Stone Breakers* (fig. 365), the first canvas fully embodying his programmatic Realism. Courbet had seen two men working on a road, and had asked them to pose for him in his studio. He painted them lifesize, solidly and matter-of-factly, with none of Millet's overt pathos or sentiment: the young man's face is averted, the old one's half hidden by a hat. He cannot have picked them casually, however; their contrast in age is significant—one is too old for such heavy work, the other too young. Endowed with the dignity of their symbolic status, they do not turn to us for sympathy. Courbet's friend the socialist Pierre-Joseph Proudhon likened them to a parable from the Gospels. Courbet's Realism, then, was a revolution of subject matter more than of style. The conservatives' rage at him as a dangerous radical is understandable nonetheless. He treated everyday life with the gravity and monumentality traditionally reserved for narrative painting. His sweeping condemnation of all traditional subjects drawn from religion, mythology, and history spelled out what many others had begun to feel, but had not dared to put into words or pictures.

During the Paris Exposition of 1855, where works by Ingres and Delacroix were prominently displayed, Courbet brought his pictures to public attention by organizing a private exhibition in a large wooden shed and by distributing a "manifesto of Realism." The show centered on a huge canvas, the most ambitious of his career, entitled *Studio of a Painter: A Real Allegory Summarizing My Seven Years of Life as an Artist* (fig. 366). "Real allegory" is something of a teaser; allegories, after all, are unreal by definition. Courbet meant either an allegory couched in the terms of his particular Realism, or one that did not conflict with the "real" identity of the figures

365. Gustave Courbet. *The Stone Breakers.* 1849. Oil on canvas, 5′3″ × 8′6″ (1.6 × 2.6 m). Formerly Gemäldegalerie, Dresden. Destroyed 1945

366. Gustave Courbet. *Studio of a Painter: A Real Allegory Summarizing My Seven Years of Life as an Artist.* 1854–55. Oil on canvas, 11′10″ × 19′7″ (3.6 × 5.79 m). Musée d'Orsay, Paris

or objects embodying it. The framework is familiar. Courbet's composition clearly belongs to the type of Velázquez' *The Maids of Honor* and Goya's *The Family of Charles IV* (see figs. 285, 336). Now the artist has moved to the center, and his visitors are here as his guests, not royal patrons who enter whenever they wish. He has invited them specially, for a purpose that becomes evident only upon thoughtful reflection. The picture does not yield its full meaning unless we take the title seriously and inquire into Courbet's relation to this assembly.

There are two main groups. On the left are "the people," who are types rather than individuals, drawn largely from the artist's home environment at Ornans—hunters, peasants, workers, a Jew, a priest, a young mother with her baby. On the right, in contrast, we see groups of portraits representing the Parisian side of Courbet's life—clients, critics, intellectuals (the man reading is Baudelaire). All of these people are strangely passive, as if they were waiting for we know not what. Some are quietly conversing among themselves, others seem immersed in thought; hardly anybody looks at Courbet. They are not his audience, but rather a representative sampling of his social environment. Only two people watch the artist at work: a small boy, intended to suggest "the innocent eye," and a nude model. What is her role? In a more conventional picture, we would identify her as Inspiration, or Courbet's Muse, but she is no less "real" than the others here. Courbet probably meant her to be Nature: that undisguised Truth which he proclaimed to be the guiding principle of his art (note the emphasis on the clothing she has just taken off). Significantly enough, the center group is illuminated by clear, sharp daylight but the background and the lateral figures are veiled in semidarkness, to underline the contrast between the artist—the active creator—and the world around him that waits to be brought to life.

367. Marcantonio Raimondi, after Raphael. *The Judgment of Paris* (detail). c. 1520. Engraving, 11⅝ × 17¼" (29.5 × 43.8 cm). The Metropolitan Museum of Art, New York. Rogers Fund, 1919

Manet and the "Revolution of the Color Patch." Courbet's *Studio* helps us understand a picture that shocked the public even more: *Luncheon on the Grass* (fig. 368), showing a nude model accompanied by two gentlemen in frock coats, by Édouard Manet (1832–1883). He was the first to grasp Courbet's full importance; his *Luncheon* is, among other things, a tribute to the older artist. Manet particularly offended contemporary morality by juxtaposing the nude and nattily attired figures in an outdoor setting, the more so since the noncommittal title offered no "higher" significance. The group has so formal a pose, however, that Manet certainly did not intend to depict an actual event. In fact, the main figures were borrowed from a print after Raphael (see fig. 367). Perhaps the meaning of the canvas lies in this denial of plausibility, for the scene fits neither the plane of everyday experience nor that of allegory.

The *Luncheon* is a visual manifesto of artistic freedom far more revolutionary than Courbet's. It asserts the painter's privilege to combine elements for aesthetic effect alone. The nudity of the model is "explained" by the contrast between her warm, creamy flesh tones and the cool black-and-gray of the men's attire. Or, to put it another way, the world of painting has "natural laws" that are distinct from those of familiar reality, and the painter's first loyalty is to the canvas, not to the outside world. Here begins an attitude that was later summed up in the doctrine of

368. Édouard Manet. *Luncheon on the Grass (Le Déjeuner sur l'herbe).* 1863. Oil on canvas, 7′ × 8′10″ (2.13 × 2.64 m). Musée d'Orsay, Paris

"art for art's sake" and became a bone of contention between progressives and conservatives for the rest of the century (see p. 386). Manet himself disdained such controversies, but his work attests to his lifelong devotion to "pure painting"—to the belief that brushstrokes and color patches themselves, not what they stand for, are the artist's primary reality. Among painters of the past, he found that Hals, Velázquez, and Goya had come closest to this ideal. He admired their broad, open technique, their preoccupation with light and color values. Many of his canvases are, in fact, "pictures of pictures": they translate into modern terms older works that particularly challenged him. Manet always took care to filter out the expressive or symbolic content of his models, lest the beholder's attention be distracted from the pictorial structure itself. His paintings, whatever their subject, have an emotional reticence that can easily be mistaken for emptiness unless we understand its purpose.

369. Édouard Manet. *The Fifer.* 1866. Oil on canvas, 63 × 38¼″ (160 × 97.2 cm). Musée d'Orsay, Paris

370. Claude Monet. *The River (Au Bord de l'eau, Bennecourt).* 1868. Oil on canvas, 32⅛ × 39⅝" (81.6 × 100.7 cm). The Art Institute of Chicago. Potter Palmer Collection

371. Auguste Renoir. *Le Moulin de la Galette.* 1876. Oil on canvas, 51½ × 69" (130.8 × 175.3 cm). Musée d'Orsay, Paris

Courbet is said to have remarked that Manet's pictures were as flat as playing cards. Looking at *The Fifer* (fig. 369), we can see what he meant. Done three years after the *Luncheon,* it is a painting without shadows, modeling, or depth. The figure looks three-dimensional only because its contour renders the forms in realistic foreshortening. Otherwise, Manet neglects all the methods devised since Giotto's time for transforming a flat surface into pictorial space. The undifferentiated light-gray background seems as near to us as the figure, and just as solid. If the fifer stepped out of the picture, he would leave a hole, like the cutout shape of a stencil.

Here, then, the canvas itself has been redefined. It is no longer a "window," but rather a screen made up of flat patches of color. How radical a step this was can be readily seen if we match *The Fifer* against Delacroix's *The Massacre at Chios* or even Courbet's *The Stone Breakers* (see figs. 342, 365), which still follow the "window" tradition of the Renaissance. We realize in retrospect that the revolutionary qualities of Manet's art were already to be seen, if not yet so obviously, in the *Luncheon.* The three figures lifted from Raphael's group of river gods form a unit nearly as shadowless and stencillike as in *The Fifer.* They would be more at home on a flat screen, for the chiaroscuro of their present setting, which is inspired by the landscapes of Courbet, no longer fits them.

What brought about this "revolution of the color patch"? We do not know, and Manet himself surely did not reason it out beforehand. It is tempting to think that he was impelled to create the new style by the challenge of photography. The "pencil of nature," then known for a quarter century, had demonstrated the objective truth of Renaissance perspective, but it established a standard of representational accuracy that no handmade image could hope to rival. Painting needed to be rescued from competition with the camera. This Manet accomplished by insisting that a painted canvas is, above all, a material surface covered with pigments—that we must look *at* it, not *through* it. Unlike Courbet, he gave no name to the style he had created. When his followers began calling themselves Impressionists, he refused to accept the term for his own work.

Monet and Impressionism. The term Impressionism was coined in 1874, after a hostile critic had looked at a picture entitled *Impression: Sunrise* by Claude Monet (1840–1926), and it certainly fits Monet better than it does Manet. Monet had adopted Manet's concept of painting and applied it to landscapes done out-of-doors. Monet's *The River* of 1868 (fig. 370) is flooded with sunlight so bright that conservative critics claimed it made their eyes smart. In this flickering network of color patches, the reflections on the water are as "real" as the banks of the Seine. Even more than *The Fifer,* Monet's painting is a "playing card." Were it not for the woman and the boat in the foreground, the picture would be almost as effective upside down. The mirror image here serves a purpose contrary to that of earlier mirror images (compare fig. 195): instead of adding to the illusion of real space, it strengthens the unity of the actual painted surface. This inner coherence sets *The River* apart from Romantic "impressions" such as Corot's *Papigno* (see fig. 345), even though both have the same on-the-spot immediacy and fresh perception.

Renoir. Scenes from the world of entertainment—dance halls, cafés, concerts, the theater—were favorite subjects for Impressionist painters. Auguste Renoir (1841–1919), another important member of the group, filled his work with the *joie de vivre* of a singularly happy temperament. The flirting couples in *Le Moulin de la Galette* (fig. 371), dappled with sunlight and shadow, radiate a human warmth that is utterly entrancing, even though the artist permits us no more than a fleeting glance at any of them. Our role is that of the casual stroller, who takes in this slice of life in passing.

Degas. By contrast, Edgar Degas (1834–1917) makes us look steadily at the disenchanted pair in his café scene *The Glass of Absinthe* (fig. 372), but out of the corner of our

372. Edgar Degas. *The Glass of Absinthe.* 1876. Oil on canvas, 36 × 27" (91.4 × 68.6 cm). Musée d'Orsay, Paris

373. Edgar Degas. *The Tub.* 1886. Pastel, 23½ × 32½" (59.7 × 82.6 cm). Musée d'Orsay, Paris

eye, so to speak. The design of this picture at first seems as unstudied as a snapshot (Degas himself practiced photography). A longer look shows us that everything dovetails precisely: the zigzag of empty tables between us and the luckless couple reinforces their brooding loneliness, for example. Compositions as boldly calculated as this set Degas apart from other Impressionists. A wealthy aristocrat by birth, he had been trained in the tradition of Ingres, whom he greatly admired. Like Ingres, he despised portraiture as a trade but, unlike him, he acted on his conviction and portrayed only friends and relatives, people with whom he had emotional ties. His profound sense of human character lends weight even to seemingly casual scenes such as that in *The Glass of Absinthe.*

The Tub (fig. 373), of a decade later, is again an oblique view, but now severe, almost geometric in design. The tub and the crouching woman, both vigorously outlined, form a circle within a square. The rest of the rectangular format is filled by a shelf so sharply tilted that it almost shares the plane of the picture. Yet on this shelf Degas has placed two pitchers that are hardly foreshortened at all (note, too, how the curve of the small one fits the handle of the other). Here the tension between "two-D" surface and "three-D" depth comes close to the breaking point. *The Tub* is Impressionist only in its shimmering, luminous colors. Its other qualities are more characteristic of the 1880s, the first Post-Impressionist decade, when many artists showed a renewed concern with problems of form (see the next chapter).

Morisot. The Impressionists' ranks included several women of great ability. Berthe Morisot (1841–1895), a member of the group from its inception, was influenced at first by Manet, whose brother she later married, but it is clear that he in turn was affected by her work. Her subject matter was the world she knew: the domestic life of the French upper middle class, which she depicted with sensitive understanding. Morisot's early paintings, centering on her mother and her sister Edma, have a subtle but distinct sense of alienation. Her mature work is altogether different in character. The birth of her daughter in 1878 signaled a change in Morisot's art, which reached its height a decade later. Her painting of a little girl reading in a room overlooking the artist's garden (fig. 374) shows a light-filled style of her own making. Morisot applied her virtuoso brushwork with a

374. Berthe Morisot. *La Lecture (Reading).* 1888. Oil on canvas, 29¼ × 36½" (74.3 × 92.7 cm). Museum of Fine Arts, St. Petersburg, Florida. Gift of Friends of Art in Memory of Margaret Acheson Stuart

sketchlike brevity throughout the scene, so as to fully integrate the figure into the setting. Thanks in part to the pastel hues she favored, Morisot's painting radiates an air of contentment free of the sentimentality that often affects genre paintings of the period.

Cassatt. In 1877, the American painter Mary Cassatt (1845–1926) joined the Impressionists, after receiving a standard academic training in her native Philadelphia. Like Morisot, she was able to pursue her career as an artist, an occupation regarded as unsuitable for women, only because she was independently wealthy. A tireless champion of the Impressionists, Cassatt was instrumental in gaining early acceptance of their paintings in the United States through her social contacts with wealthy private collectors. Maternity provided the thematic and formal focus of most of her work. From her mentor Degas, as well as her study of Japanese prints, Cassatt developed an individual and highly accomplished style. The oblique view, simplified color forms, and flat composition in *The Bath* (fig. 375) show Cassatt at her best, after she reached her full artistic maturity around 1890.

Monet's Later Works. Among the major figures of the movement, Monet alone remained faithful to the Impressionist view of nature. Nevertheless, his work became more subjective over time, although he never ventured into fantasy, nor did he abandon the basic approach of his earlier landscapes. About 1890, Monet began to paint pictures in series, showing the same subject under various conditions of light and atmosphere. These tended increasingly to resemble Turner's "airy visions, painted with tinted steam" as Monet concentrated on effects of colored light (he had visited London, and knew Turner's work). *Water Lilies* (fig. 376) is a fascinating sequel to *The River* (see fig. 370) across a span of almost fifty years. The surface of the water now takes up the entire canvas, so that the effect of a weightless screen is stronger than ever. The artist's brushwork, too, has greater variety and a more individual rhythm. While the scene is still based on nature, this is no ordinary landscape but one

375. *(opposite)* Mary Cassatt. *The Bath.* 1891. Oil on canvas, 39½ × 26" (100.3 × 66 cm). The Art Institute of Chicago. Robert A. Waller Collection

376. Claude Monet. *Water Lilies.* 1914–17. Oil on canvas, 70⅞ × 57½" (180 × 146.1 cm). The Fine Arts Museum of San Francisco (Legion of Honor); Mildred Anna Williams Fund

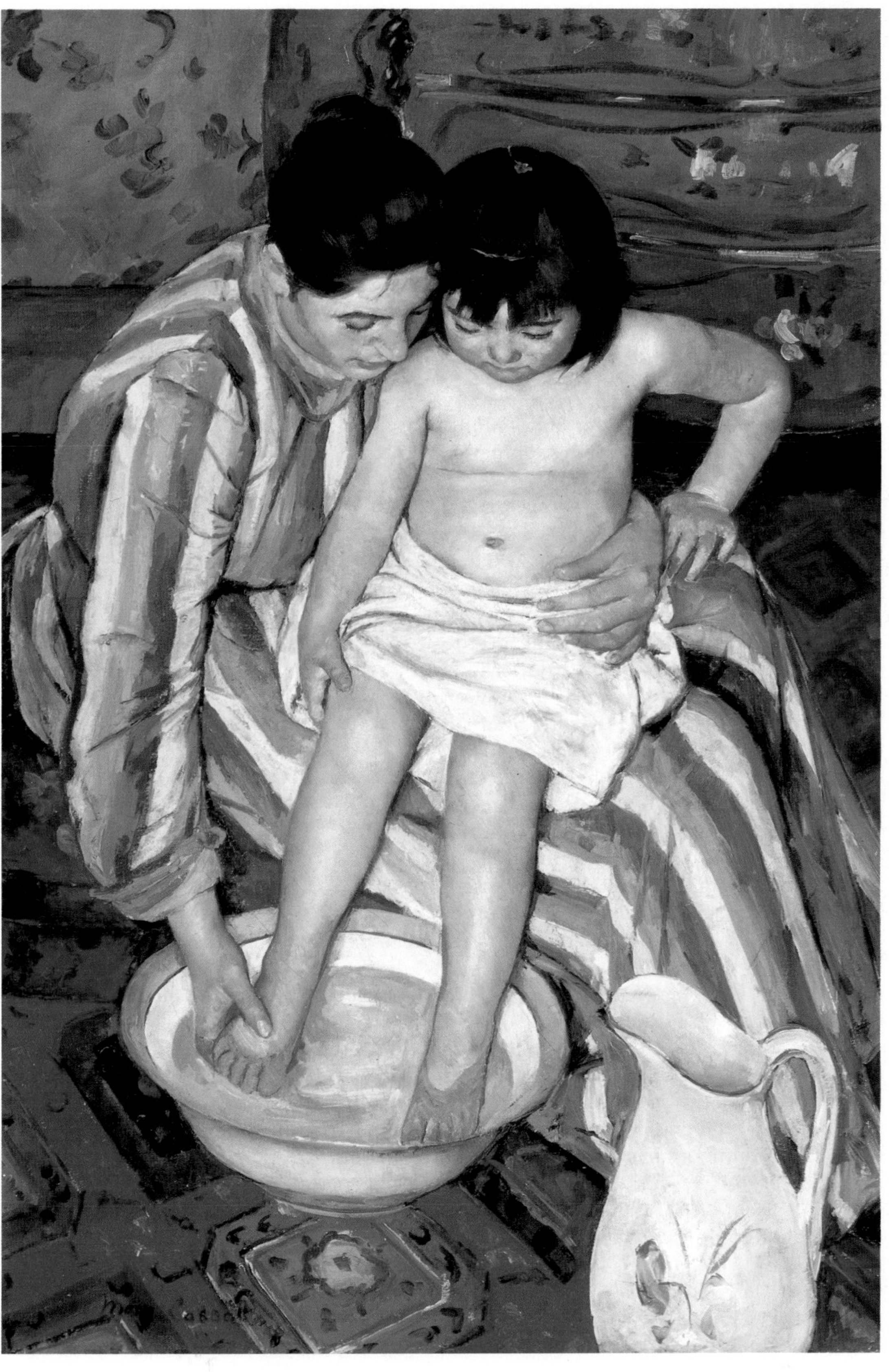

entirely of the painter's making. On the estate at Giverny given to him late in life by the French government, Monet created a self-contained world for purely personal and artistic purposes. The subjects he painted there are as much reflections of his imagination as they are of reality. They convey a different sense of time as well. Instead of the single moment captured in *The River,* his *Water Lilies* summarizes a shifting impression of the pond in response to the changing water as the breezes play across it.

England

The Pre-Raphaelites. By the time Monet came to admire his work, Turner's reputation was at a low ebb in his own country. In 1848 the painter and poet Dante Gabriel Rossetti (1828–1882) helped found an artists' society called the Pre-Raphaelite Brotherhood. Their basic aim: to do battle against the frivolous art of the day by producing "pure transcripts . . . from nature" and by having "genuine ideas to express." As the name of the Brotherhood proclaims, its members took their inspiration from the "primitive" masters of the fifteenth century. To that extent, they belong to the Gothic revival, which had long been an important aspect of the Romantic movement. What set the Pre-Raphaelites apart from Romanticism was an urge to reform the ills of modern civilization through their art. Rossetti himself was not concerned with social problems, however; he thought of himself as a reformer of aesthetic sensibility. His early masterpiece, *Ecce Ancilla Domini* (fig. 377), though naturalistic in detail, is full of self-conscious archaisms such as the pale tonality, the limited range of colors, the awkward perspective, and the stress on the verticals, not to mention the title in Latin. At the same time, this Annunciation radiates an aura of repressed eroticism, which became the hallmark of Rossetti's work and exerted a powerful influence on other Pre-Raphaelites.

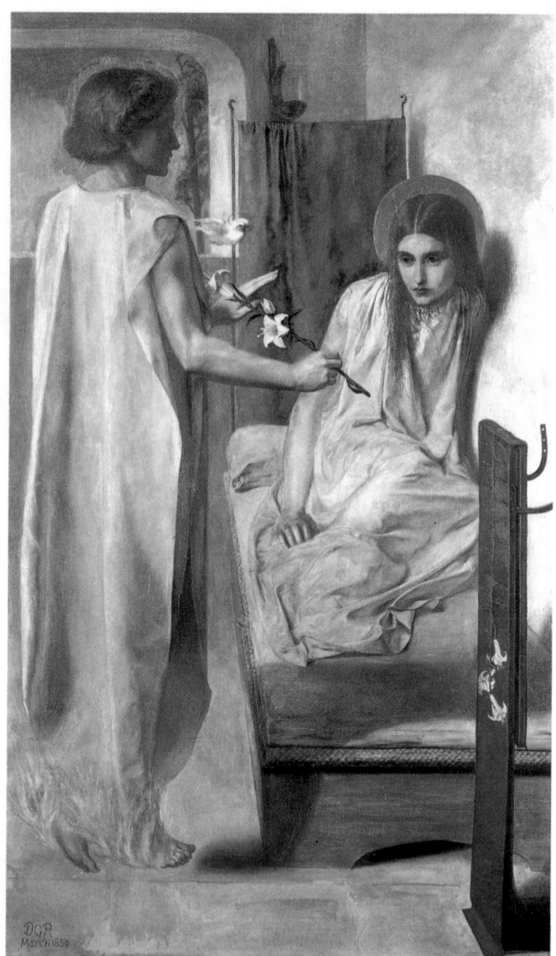

377. Dante Gabriel Rossetti. *Ecce Ancilla Domini (The Annunciation).* 1849–50. Oil on canvas, 28½ × 16½" (72.4 × 41.9 cm). The Tate Gallery, London

Morris. William Morris (1834–1896) started out as a Pre-Raphaelite painter but soon shifted his interest to "art for use": domestic architecture and interior decoration such as furniture, tapestries, and wallpapers. He wanted to displace the shoddy products of the machine age by reviving the handicrafts of the preindustrial past, an art "made by the people, and for the people, as a happiness to the maker and the user." Through the many enterprises he sponsored, as well as his skill as a writer and publicist, Morris became a tastemaker without peer in his day. Nor was he content to reform the arts of design alone; he saw them as a lever by which to reform modern society as a whole.

Morris was an apostle of simplicity. Architecture and furniture ought to be designed in accordance with the nature of their materials

378. William Morris (Morris and Co.). Green Dining Room. 1867. Victoria and Albert Museum, London. Crown copyright reserved

and working processes. Surface decoration likewise ought to be flat rather than illusionistic. His interiors (fig. 378) are total environments that create an effect of quiet intimacy. Despite Morris' self-proclaimed championship of the medieval tradition, he never imitated its forms directly but instead sought to capture its spirit. He invented the first original system of ornament since the Rococo—no small achievement.

United States

Whistler. American painters were among the earliest followers of Manet and his circle. James Abbott McNeill Whistler (1834–1903) went to Paris in 1855 to study painting. Four years later he moved to London, where he spent the rest of his life, but he visited France during the 1860s and was in close touch with the rising Impressionist movement. *Arrangement in Black and Gray: The Artist's Mother* (fig. 379), his best-known picture, reflects the influence of Manet in its emphasis on flat areas, and the likeness has the austere precision of Degas' portraits. Its fame as a symbol of our latter-day "mother cult" is a paradox of popular psychology that would have dismayed Whistler: he wanted the canvas to be appreciated for its formal qualities alone.

A witty, sharp-tongued advocate of art for art's sake, he thought of his pictures as analogous to pieces of music and called them "symphonies" or "nocturnes." The boldest example, painted about 1874, is *Nocturne in Black and Gold: The Falling Rocket* (fig. 380). Without an explanatory subtitle, we would have real difficulty making it out. No French painter had yet dared to produce a picture so "nonrepresentational," so reminiscent of Turner's "tinted steam" (see fig. 351). It was this canvas, more than any other, that prompted John Ruskin to accuse Whistler of "flinging a pot of paint in the public's face." (Since the same critic had highly praised Turner's *The Slave Ship*, we must conclude that what Ruskin really liked was not the tinted steam itself but the Romantic sentiment behind it.) During Whistler's successful libel suit against Ruskin, he defined his aims in terms that apply well to *The Falling Rocket*: "I have perhaps meant rather to indicate an artistic interest alone in my work, divesting the picture from any outside sort of interest. . . . It is an arrangement of line, form, and color, first, and I make use of any incident of it which shall bring about a symmetrical result." The last phrase has special significance, since Whistler acknowledges

379. James Abbott McNeill Whistler. *Arrangement in Black and Gray: The Artist's Mother.* 1871. Oil on canvas, 57 × 64½" (144.8 × 163.8 cm). Musée d'Orsay, Paris

380. James Abbott McNeill Whistler. *Nocturne in Black and Gold: The Falling Rocket.* c. 1874. Oil on wood panel, 23¾ × 18⅜" (60.3 × 46.7 cm). The Detroit Institute of Arts. Gift of Dexter M. Ferry, Jr.

that in utilizing chance effects, he does not look for resemblances but for a purely formal harmony. While he rarely practiced what he preached to quite the same extent as he did in *The Falling Rocket,* his statement reads like a prophecy of American abstract painting (see fig. 446).

Homer. Whistler's gifted contemporary in America Winslow Homer (1836–1910) also went to Paris as a young man, but left too soon to receive the full impact of Impressionism. He was a pictorial reporter throughout the Civil War and continued as a magazine illustrator until 1875, but he was also a remarkable painter. The fresh delicacy of the sunlit scene in *The Morning Bell* (fig. 381) might be called "pre-Impressionist." The picture is halfway between Corot and Monet (compare figs. 345, 370). It has an extraordinarily subtle design as well. The dog, the girl at the center, and those at the right turn the footpath into a seesaw, its upward slant balanced by the descending line of treetops. At the same time, the tilted walkway emphasizes the reluctance of the trudging figure, echoed by the little dog, to enter the mill where she will spend the rest of the day. The painting documents the early Industrial Revolution, before the advent of child labor laws, when young people often toiled long hours at difficult jobs.

Eakins. Thomas Eakins (1844–1916) arrived in Paris from Philadelphia about the time Homer painted *The Morning Bell*; he went home four years later, after receiving a conventional academic training, with decisive impressions of Courbet and Velázquez. Elements of both these artists' styles are combined in *William Rush Carving His Allegorical Figure of the Schuylkill River* (fig. 382; compare figs. 366, 285). Eakins had encountered stiff opposition for advocating traditional life studies at the Pennsylvania Academy of the Fine Arts. To him, Rush was a hero for basing his 1809 statue for the Philadelphia Water Works on the nude model, though the figure itself was draped in a classical robe. Eakins no doubt knew contemporary European paintings of sculptors carving from the nude; these were related to the theme of Pygmalion and Galatea, which was popular at the time among academic artists. Conservative critics denounced *William Rush Carving His Allegorical Figure of the Schuylkill River* for its nudity, despite the presence of the chaperon knitting quietly to the right. Nevertheless, to us the painting's declaration of honest truth seems an apposite fulfillment of Baudelaire's demand for pictures that express the heroism of modern life.

Tanner. Thanks in large part to Eakins' enlightened attitude, Philadelphia became the leading center of minority artists in the United States. Eakins encouraged women and blacks to study art seriously at a time when professional careers were closed to them. African Americans had no chance to enter the arts before Emancipation, and after the Civil War the situation improved only

381. Winslow Homer. *The Morning Bell.* c. 1870. Oil on canvas, 24 × 38″ (61 × 96.5 cm). Yale University Art Gallery, New Haven, Connecticut. Stephen C. Clark Collection

382. Thomas Eakins. *William Rush Carving His Allegorical Figure of the Schuylkill River.* 1877. Oil on canvas, 20⅛ × 26½″ (51.1 × 67.3 cm). The Philadelphia Museum of Art. Given by Mrs. Thomas Eakins and Miss Mary A. Williams

383. Henry O. Tanner. *The Banjo Lesson.* c. 1893. Oil on canvas, 49 × 35½" (124.5 × 90.2 cm). Hampton University Museum, Hampton, Virginia

gradually. Henry O. Tanner (1859–1937), the first important black painter, studied with Eakins in the early 1880s. Tanner's masterpiece, *The Banjo Lesson* (fig. 383), painted after he moved permanently to Paris, avoids the mawkishness of similar subjects by other American painters. The scene is rendered with the same direct realism as Eakins' *William Rush Carving His Allegorical Figure of the Schuylkill River.*

SCULPTURE

Impressionism, it is often said, revitalized sculpture no less than painting. The statement is at once true and misleading. Auguste Rodin, the first sculptor of genius since Bernini, redefined sculpture during the same years that Manet and Monet redefined painting. In so doing, however, he did not follow these artists' lead. How indeed could the effect of such pictures as *The Fifer* or *The River* be reproduced in three dimensions and without color?

Rodin. What Rodin (1840–1917) did accomplish is strikingly visible in *The Thinker* (fig. 384), originally conceived as part of a large unfinished project called *The Gates of Hell.* The welts and wrinkles of the vigorously creased surface produce, in polished bronze, an ever-changing pattern of reflections. But is this effect borrowed from Impressionist

384. Auguste Rodin. *The Thinker.* 1879–89. Bronze, height 27½″ (69.9 cm). The Metropolitan Museum of Art, New York. Gift of Thomas F. Ryan, 1910

painting? Does Rodin dissolve three-dimensional form into flickering patches of light and dark? The fiercely exaggerated shapes pulsate with sculptural energy, and they retain this quality under whatever conditions the piece is viewed. For Rodin did not work directly in bronze; he modeled in wax or clay. How could he calculate in advance the reflections on the bronze surfaces of the casts that would ultimately be made from these models?

He worked as he did, we must assume, for an altogether different reason: not to capture elusive optical effects, but to emphasize the process of "growth"—the miracle of inert matter coming to life in the artist's hands. As the color patch for Manet and Monet is the primary reality, so are the malleable lumps from which Rodin builds his forms. By insisting on this "unfinishedness," he rescued sculpture from mechanical reproduction just as Manet rescued painting from photographic realism.

Who is *The Thinker*? Partly Adam, no doubt (though there is also a different Adam by Rodin, another "outgrowth" of the *Gates*), partly Prometheus, and partly the brute imprisoned by the passions of the flesh. Rodin wisely refrained from giving him a specific name, for the statue fits no preconceived identity. In this new image of a man, form and meaning are one, instead of cleaving apart as in Carpeaux's *The Dance* (see fig. 356). Carpeaux produced naked figures that pretend to be nude, while *The Thinker,* like the nudes of Michelangelo, and whose action-in-repose he shares, is free from subservience to the undressed model.

Rodin, however, was by instinct a modeler, not a carver like Michelangelo. His greatest works were intended to be cast in bronze. Yet

385. Auguste Rodin. *Monument to Balzac.* 1897–98. Bronze (cast 1954), height 9′3″ (2.82 m). Collection, The Museum of Modern Art, New York. Presented in memory of Curt Valentin by his friends

even these reveal their full strength only when we see them in plaster casts made directly from Rodin's clay originals. The *Monument to Balzac,* his most daring creation (fig. 385), remained in plaster for many years, rejected by the committee that had commissioned it. The figure is larger than life, physically and spiritually. It has the overpowering presence of a specter; like a huge monolith, the man of genius towers above the crowd. He shares "the sublime egotism of the gods" (as the Romantics put it). Rodin has minimized the articulation of the body, so that from a distance we see only its great bulk. As we approach, we become aware that Balzac is wrapped in a long, shroudlike cloak. From this mass the head thrusts upward—one is tempted to say, erupts—with elemental force. When we are close enough to make out the features clearly, we sense beneath the disdain an inner agony that stamps *Balzac* as the kin of *The Thinker.*

Degas. It is significant of the fundamental difference between painting and modeling that only Degas among the Impressionists tried his hand at sculpture, producing dozens of small-scale wax figurines that explore the same themes as his paintings and drawings. These are private works made for his own interest. Few were exhibited during the artist's lifetime, and none were cast until after his death early in this century. During the 1870s, there was a growing taste for casts made from artists' working models, reflecting the same appreciation for the qualities of spontaneity and inspiration found in drawings and oil sketches, which had long appealed to collectors. For the first time sculptors felt emboldened to violate time-honored standards of naturalism and craftsmanship for statuettes, and to leave the impress of their fingers on the soft material as they molded it. Nevertheless, when Degas showed the wax original of *The Little Fourteen-Year-Old Dancer* (fig. 386) at the Impressionist exhibitions of 1880 and 1881, the public was scandalized by its lack of traditional finish and uncompromising adherence to unvarnished truth, although the response from critics was less harsh. The sculpture is nearly as rough in texture as the slightly smaller nude study from life on which it is based. Instead of sculpting her costume, Degas used real gauze and satin, a revolutionary idea for the time but something the Romantics, with their emphatic naturalism, must often have felt tempted to do. The ungainliness of the young adolescent's body is subtly emphasized by her pose, a standard ballet position that is nonetheless difficult to assume. Yet, rather than awkwardness, the statuette conveys a simple dignity and grace that are irresistible. The openness of the stance, with hands clasped behind the back and legs pointing in opposite directions, demands that we walk around the dancer to arrive at a complete image of it. As we view the sculpture from different angles, the surface provides a constantly shifting impression of light comparable to that in Degas' numerous paintings and pastels of the ballet.

386. Edgar Degas. *The Little Fourteen-Year-Old Dancer.* 1878–80. Bronze with gauze tutu and satin hair ribbon, height 38″ (96.5 cm). Norton Simon Art Foundation, Pasadena

ARCHITECTURE

Industrial Architecture and the Machine Aesthetic

For more than a century, from the mid-eighteenth to the late nineteenth, architecture had been dominated by a succession of revival styles (see p. 353). This term, we will recall, does not imply that earlier forms were slavish copies. On the contrary, the best work of the time has both individuality and high distinction. Nevertheless, the architectural wisdom of the past, however freely interpreted, proved in the long run to be inadequate for the practical demands of the Industrial Age—the factories, warehouses, stores, and city apartments that formed the bulk of building construction. For it is after about 1800, in the world of commercial architecture, that we find the gradual introduction of new materials and techniques that were to have a profound effect on architectural style by the end of the century. The most important was iron, never before used as a structural member. Within a few decades of their first appearance, cast-iron columns and arches became the standard means of supporting roofs over the large spaces required by railroad stations, exhibition halls, and public libraries.

387. Henri Labrouste. Bibliothèque Ste.-Geneviève, Paris. 1843–50

388. Henri Labrouste. Reading Room, Bibliothèque Ste.-Geneviève

Labrouste. A famous early example is the Bibliothèque Ste.-Geneviève in Paris by Henri Labrouste (1801–1875). The exterior (fig. 387) represents the historicism prevailing at mid-century. Its style is drawn chiefly from Italian Renaissance banks, libraries, and churches. To identify the building as a library, Labrouste used the simple but ingenious device of inscribing the names of great writers around the facade. The reading room (fig. 388), on the other hand, recalls the nave of a French Gothic cathedral (compare fig. 155). Why did Labrouste choose cast-iron columns and arches, hitherto used exclusively for railroad stations? Cast iron was not necessary to provide structural support for the two barrel roofs—this could have been done using other materials—but to complete the building's symbolic program. The library, Labrouste suggests to us, is a storehouse of something even more precious and sacred than material wealth: the world's literature, which takes us on journeys not to faraway places but of the mind.

Labrouste chose to leave the interior iron skeleton uncovered, and to face the difficulty of relating it to the massive Renaissance revival style of the exterior of his building. If his solution does not fully integrate the two systems, it at least lets them coexist. His architectural (as against merely technical) use of exposed iron members has a fanciful and delicate quality that links it, indirectly, to the Gothic revival. Cast iron was later superseded

389. Sir Joseph Paxton. The Crystal Palace (interior view looking north), London. 1851; reerected in Sydenham 1852; destroyed 1936 (lithograph by Joseph Nash). Victoria and Albert Museum, London. Crown copyright reserved

by structural steel and ferroconcrete. Its use here is a peculiarly appealing final chapter in the history of Romantic architecture.

Paxton. Within a year of the completion of the Bibliothèque Ste.-Geneviève, the Crystal Palace (fig. 389) was built in London. A pioneering achievement far bolder in conception than Labrouste's library, the Crystal Palace was designed to house the first of the great international expositions that continue today. Its designer, Sir Joseph Paxton (1801–1865), was an engineer and builder of greenhouses. The Crystal Palace was, in fact, a gigantic greenhouse—so large that it enclosed some old trees growing on the site—with its iron skeleton freely displayed. Still, the notion that there might be beauty, and not merely utility, in the products of engineering made headway very slowly, even though the doctrine "form follows function" found advocates from the mid-nineteenth century on.

The authority of historic modes had to be broken if the industrial era was to produce a truly contemporary style. It nevertheless proved extraordinarily persistent. The "architecture of conspicuous display" espoused by Garnier (see p. 372) was divorced, even more than previous revival styles, from the needs of the present. And Labrouste, pioneer though he was of cast-iron construction, could not think of architectural supports as anything but columns having proper capitals and bases, rather than as metal rods or pipes (see p. 393). It was only in structures that were not considered "architecture" at all that new building materials and techniques could be explored without these inhibitions. In this regard, Paxton's Crystal Palace was a harbinger of things to come.

POST-IMPRESSIONISM

PAINTING

In 1882, just before his death, Manet was made a chevalier of the Legion of Honor by the French government; four years later, the Impressionists, who had been exhibiting together since 1874, held their last group show. These two events mark the turn of the tide. Impressionism had gained wide acceptance among artists and the public, but by the same token it was no longer a pioneering movement. The future now belonged to the "Post-Impressionists." This colorless label designates a group of artists who passed through an Impressionist phase in the 1880s but became dissatisfied with the style and extended it in various directions. Because they did not have a common goal, it is difficult to find a more descriptive term for them than Post-Impressionists. They certainly were not "anti-Impressionists." Far from trying to undo the effects of the "Manet Revolution," they wanted to carry it further. Post-Impressionism is in essence just a later stage, though a very important one, of the development that had begun in the 1860s with such pictures as Manet's *Luncheon on the Grass.*

Cézanne. Paul Cézanne (1839–1906), the oldest of the Post-Impressionists, was born in Aix-en-Provence, near the Mediterranean coast. A man of intensely emotional temperament, he went to Paris in 1861 imbued with enthusiasm for the Romantics. Delacroix was his first love among painters, and he never lost his admiration for him. Cézanne quickly grasped the nature of the "Manet Revolution" as well. After passing through a Neo-Baroque phase, he began to paint bright outdoor scenes, but did not share his fellow Impressionists' interest in "slice-of-life" subjects, in movement and change. Instead, his goal was "to make of Impressionism something solid and durable, like the art of the museums." This quest for the "solid and durable" can be seen in Cézanne's still lifes, such as *Still Life with Apples* (fig. 390). Not since Chardin have simple everyday objects assumed such importance in a painter's eye. The ornamental backdrop is integrated with the three-dimensional shapes, and the brushstrokes have a rhythmic pattern that gives the canvas its shimmering texture. We also notice another aspect of Cézanne's style that may puzzle us at first. The forms are deliberately simplified and outlined with dark colors, and the perspective is incorrect for both the fruit bowl and the horizontal surfaces, which seem to tilt upward. Yet the longer we study the picture, the more we realize the rightness of these apparently arbitrary distortions. When Cézanne took these liberties with reality, his purpose was to uncover the permanent qualities beneath the accidents of appearance. All forms in nature, he believed, are based on the cone, the sphere, and the cylinder. This order underlying the external world was the true subject of his pictures, but he had to interpret it

390. Paul Cézanne. *Still Life with Apples.* 1879–82. Oil on canvas, 17⅛ × 21¼" (43.5 × 54 cm). Ny Carlsberg Glyptotek, Copenhagen

391. Paul Cézanne. *Mont Sainte-Victoire Seen from Bibémus Quarry*. c. 1897–1900. Oil on canvas, 25⅛ × 32" (63.8 × 81.3 cm). The Baltimore Museum of Art. The Cone Collection, formed by Dr. Claribel Cone and Miss Etta Cone of Baltimore, Maryland

to fit the separate, closed world of the canvas.

To apply this method to landscape became the greatest challenge of Cézanne's career. From 1882 on, he lived in isolation near his hometown of Aix-en-Provence, exploring its environs as Claude Lorraine and Corot had explored the Roman countryside. One motif, the distinctive shape of the mountain called Mont Sainte-Victoire, seemed almost to obsess him. Its craggy profile looming against the blue Mediterranean sky appears in a long series of compositions culminating in the monumental late works such as that in figure 391. There are no hints of human presence here; houses and roads would only disturb the lonely grandeur of the view. Above the wall of rocky cliffs that bars our way like a chain of fortifications, the mountain rises in triumphant clarity, infinitely remote, yet as solid and palpable as the shapes in the foreground. For all its architectural stability, the scene is alive with movement; but the forces at work here have been brought into equilibrium, subdued by the greater power of the artist's will. This disciplined energy, distilled from the trials of a stormy youth, gives the mature style of Cézanne its enduring strength.

Seurat. Georges Seurat (1859–1891) shared Cézanne's aim to make Impressionism "solid and durable," but he went about it very differently. His career was as brief as those of Masaccio, Giorgione, and Géricault, and his achievement just as astonishing. Seurat devoted his main efforts to a few very large paintings, spending a year or more on each of them. He made endless series of preliminary studies before he felt sure enough to tackle the definitive version. This painstaking method reflects his belief that art must be based on a system. Like Degas, he had studied with a follower of Ingres, and his theoretical interests came from this experience. But, as with all artists of genius, Seurat's theories do not really explain his pictures; it is the

392. Georges Seurat. *A Sunday Afternoon on the Grande Jatte*. 1884–86. Oil on canvas, 6′9¼″ × 10′ (2.06 × 3.05 m). The Art Institute of Chicago (Helen Birch Bartlett Memorial Collection)

pictures, rather, that explain the theories.

The subject of *A Sunday Afternoon on the Grande Jatte* of 1884–86 (fig. 392) is of the sort that had long been popular among Impressionist painters. Impressionist, too, are the brilliant colors and the effect of intense sunlight. Otherwise, however, the picture is the very opposite of a quick "impression." The firm, simple contours and the relaxed, immobile figures give the scene a timeless stability that recalls Piero della Francesca (see fig. 217). Even the brushwork demonstrates Seurat's passion for order and permanence: the canvas surface is covered with systematic, impersonal dots of brilliant color that were supposed to merge in the beholder's eye and produce intermediary tints more luminous than anything obtainable from pigments mixed on the palette. This procedure was variously known as Neo-Impressionism, Pointillism, or Divisionism (the term preferred by Seurat). The actual result, however, did not conform to the theory. Looking at *A Sunday Afternoon on the Grande Jatte* from a comfortable distance (seven to ten feet for the original), we find that the mixing of colors in the eye remains incomplete. The dots do not disappear, but are as clearly visible as the tesserae of a mosaic (compare fig. 112). Seurat himself must have liked this unexpected effect, which gives the canvas the quality of a shimmering, translucent screen; otherwise, he would have reduced the size of the dots.

The bodies have little weight or bulk. Modeling and foreshortening are reduced to a minimum, and the figures appear mostly in either strict profile or frontal views, as if Seurat had adopted the rules of ancient Egyptian art (see pp. 43–44). The machinelike quality of Seurat's forms, achieved through rigorous abstraction, is the first expression of a peculiarly modern outlook that would lead to Futurism (see pp. 423–24). Seurat's systematic approach to art has the internal logic of modern engineering, which he and his followers hoped would transform society for the better. This social consciousness was allied to a form of anarchism descended from Courbet's friend Pierre-Joseph Proudhon, and contrasts with the general political indifference of the Impressionists.

Van Gogh. While Cézanne and Seurat were converting Impressionism into a more severe, classical style, Vincent van Gogh (1853–1890) pursued the opposite direction. He believed that Impressionism did not provide artists with enough freedom to express their emotions. Since this was his main concern, he is sometimes called an Expressionist, although the term ought to be reserved for certain twentieth-century painters (see the next chapter). Van Gogh, the first great Dutch master since the seventeenth century, did not become an artist until 1880; since he died only ten years later, his career was even briefer than that of Seurat. His early interests were in literature and religion. Profoundly dissatisfied with the values of industrial society and imbued with a strong sense of mission, he worked for a while as a lay preacher among poverty-stricken coal miners. This intense feeling for the poor dominates the paintings of his pre-Impressionist period, 1880–85. In 1886 he went to Paris, where he met Degas, Seurat, and other leading French artists through his brother Theo, who had a gallery devoted to modern art. Their effect on him was electrifying: his pictures now blazed with color, and he even experimented briefly with the Divisionist technique of Seurat. This Impressionist phase, however, lasted less than two years. Although it was vitally important for his development, he had to integrate it with the style of his earlier years before his genius could fully unfold. Paris had opened his eyes to the sensuous beauty of the visible world and had taught him the pictorial language of the color patch, but painting continued to be nevertheless a vessel for his personal emotions. To investigate this spiritual reality with the new means at his command, he went to Arles, in the south of France. There, between 1888 and 1890, he produced his greatest pictures.

394. Vincent van Gogh. *Self-Portrait.* 1889. Oil on canvas, 22½ × 17" (57.2 × 43.2 cm). Collection Mrs. John Hay Whitney, New York

393. Vincent van Gogh. *Wheat Field and Cypress Trees.* 1889. Oil on canvas, 28½ × 36" (72.4 × 91.4 cm). The National Gallery, London. Reproduced by courtesy of the Trustees

Like Cézanne, Van Gogh now devoted his main energies to landscape painting, but the sun-drenched Mediterranean countryside evoked a very different response in him. He saw it filled with ecstatic movement, not architectural stability and permanence. In *Wheat*

Field and Cypress Trees (fig. 393), both earth and sky show an overpowering turbulence. The wheat field resembles a stormy sea, the trees spring flamelike from the ground, and the hills and clouds heave with the same undulant motion. The dynamism contained in every brushstroke makes of each one not merely a deposit of color, but an incisive graphic gesture. The artist's personal "handwriting" is here an even more dominant factor than in the canvases of Daumier (compare fig. 344). To Van Gogh himself it was the color, not the form, that determined the expressive content of his pictures. The letters he wrote to his brother include many eloquent descriptions of his choice of hues and the emotional meanings he attached to them. Although he acknowledged that his desire "to exaggerate the essential and to leave the obvious vague" made his colors look arbitrary by Impressionist standards, he nevertheless remained deeply committed to the visible world.

Compared to Monet's *The River* (see fig. 370), the colors of *Wheat Field and Cypress Trees* are stronger, simpler, and more vibrant, but in no sense "unnatural." They speak to us of that "kingdom of light" Van Gogh had found in the South, and of his mystic faith in a creative force animating all forms of life—a faith no less ardent than the sectarian Christianity of his early years. The missionary had now become a prophet. We see him in that role in the *Self-Portrait* (fig. 394). Dürer had portrayed himself as a Christlike reformer (see fig. 259); but how much greater is the visionary intensity of Van Gogh's luminous head, with its emaciated features and burning eyes, set off against a whirlpool of darkness! "I want to paint men and women with that something of the eternal which the halo used to symbolize," Van Gogh had written, groping to define for his brother the human essence that was his aim in pictures such as this. At the time of the *Self-Portrait,* he had already begun to suffer fits of a mental illness that made painting increasingly difficult for him. Despairing of a cure, he committed suicide a year later, for he felt very deeply that art alone made his life worth living.

395. Paul Gauguin. *The Vision After the Sermon (Jacob Wrestling with the Angel).* 1888. Oil on canvas, $28\frac{3}{4} \times 36\frac{1}{2}''$ (73 × 92.7 cm). The National Galleries of Scotland, Edinburgh

396. Paul Gauguin. *Offerings of Gratitude (Maruru).* c. 1891–93. Woodcut, printed in black, $8\frac{1}{16} \times 14''$ (20.4 × 35.5 cm). Collection, The Museum of Modern Art, New York. Lillie P. Bliss Collection

Gauguin and Symbolism. The quest for religious experience also played an important part in the work, if not in the life, of another great Post-Impressionist, Paul Gauguin (1848–1903). He began as a prosperous stockbroker in Paris and an amateur painter and collector of modern pictures. At the age of thirty-five, he became convinced that he must devote himself entirely to art. He abandoned his business career, separated from his family, and by 1889 was the central figure of a new movement called Synthetism or Symbolism.

Gauguin began as a follower of Cézanne and once owned one of his still lifes. He then developed a style that, though less intensely personal than Van Gogh's, was in some ways an even bolder advance beyond Impressionism. Gauguin believed that Western civilization was spiritually bankrupt, because industrial society had forced people into an incomplete life dedicated to material gain, while their emotions lay neglected. To rediscover for himself this hidden world of feeling, Gauguin left Paris to live among the peasants of Brittany, in western France. He noticed particularly that religion was still part of the everyday life of the country people, and in pictures such as *The Vision After the Sermon (Jacob Wrestling with the Angel)* (fig. 395), he tried to depict their simple, direct faith. Here at last is what no Romantic painter had achieved: a style based on pre-Renaissance sources. Modeling and perspective have given way to flat, simplified shapes outlined heavily in black, and the brilliant colors are equally unnatural. This style, inspired by folk art and medieval stained glass, is meant to re-create both the imagined reality of the vision, and the trancelike rapture of the peasant women. Yet we sense that although Gauguin tried to share this experience, he remained an outsider. He could paint pictures *about* faith, but not *from* faith.

Two years later, Gauguin's search for the unspoiled life led him even farther afield. He voyaged to Tahiti as a sort of "missionary in reverse," to learn from the natives instead of teaching them. Although he spent the rest of his life in the South Pacific (he returned home only once for a few years), none of his Tahitian canvases are as daring as those he had painted in Brittany. His strongest works of this period are woodcuts. *Offerings of Gratitude* (fig. 396) again presents the theme of religious worship, but the image of a local god now replaces the biblical subject of the *Vision*. In its frankly "carved" look and its bold white-on-black pattern, we can feel the influences of the native art of the South Seas and of other non-European styles. The renewal of Western art and Western civilization as a whole, Gauguin believed, must come from "the Primitives." He advised other Symbolists to shun the Greek tradition and to turn instead to Persia, the Far East, and ancient Egypt. The idea of primitivism itself was not new. It stems from the Romantic myth of the Noble Savage, propagated by the thinkers of the Enlightenment more than a century before, and its ultimate source is the age-old belief in an earthly paradise where human societies once dwelled, and might one day live again, in a state of nature and innocence. No artist before Gauguin had gone as far to put the doctrine of primitivism into practice. His pilgrimage to the South Pacific had more than a purely private meaning: it symbolized the end of the four hundred years of colonial expansion, which had brought most of the globe under Western domination. The "white man's burden," once so cheerfully, and ruthlessly, shouldered by the empire builders, was becoming unbearable.

The Nabis. Gauguin's Symbolist followers called themselves Nabis, from the Hebrew

397. Gustave Moreau. *The Apparition (Dance of Salome)*. c. 1876. Oil on canvas, 21¼ × 17½" (54 × 44.5 cm). Fogg Art Museum, Harvard University Art Museums, Cambridge, Massachusetts. Grenville L. Winthrop Bequest

word for prophet. They were less remarkable for their creative talent than for their ability to spell out and justify the aims of Post-Impressionism in theoretical form. One of them, Maurice Denis, made the statement that was to become the first article of faith for modernist painters of the twentieth century: "A picture—before being a war horse, a female nude, or some anecdote—is essentially a flat surface covered with colors in a particular order." The Symbolists also discovered that there were some older artists, descendants of the Romantics, whose work, like their own, placed inner vision above the observation of nature.

Moreau. One of the Symbolists was Gustave Moreau (1826–1898), a recluse who admired Delacroix. He created a world of personal fantasy that has much in common with the medieval reveries of some of the English Pre-Raphaelites. *The Apparition* (fig. 397) shows one of his favorite themes: the head of John the Baptist, in a blinding radiance of light, appears to the dancing Salome. Her odalisquelike sensuousness, the stream of blood pouring from the severed head, the mysterious space of the setting, suggestive of an exotic temple rather than of Herod's palace—these summon up all the dreams of Oriental splendor and cruelty so dear to the Romantic imagination, combined with an insistence on the reality of the supernatural.

Only late in life did Moreau achieve a measure of recognition; suddenly, his art was in tune with the times. During his last six years, he even held a professorship at the conservative École des Beaux-Arts, the successor of the official art academy founded under Louis XIV (see pp. 320–21). There he attracted the most gifted students, among them such future modernists as Henri Matisse and Georges Rouault.

Beardsley. How prophetic Moreau's work was of the taste prevailing at the end of the century is evident from a comparison with Aubrey Beardsley (1872–1898), a gifted young Englishman whose black-and-white drawings were the very epitome of that taste.

398. Aubrey Beardsley. *Salome*. 1892. Pen drawing, 10 15/16 × 5 13/16" (27.8 × 14.8 cm). Princeton University Library, New Jersey

They include an illustration for Oscar Wilde's *Salome* (fig. 398) that might well be the final scene of the drama depicted by Moreau: Salome has taken up John's severed head and triumphantly kissed it. Beardsley's erotic meaning is plain: Salome is passionately in love with John and has asked for his head because she could not have him in any other way. Moreau's intent, however, remains ambiguous. Did his Salome perhaps conjure up the vision of the head? Is she, too, in love with John? Nevertheless, the parallel is striking, and there are formal similarities as well, such as the "stem" of trickling blood from which John's head rises like a flower. Beardsley's *Salome* cannot be said to derive from Moreau's. The sources of his style are English—specifically, the art of the Pre-Raphaelites (see fig. 377)—with a strong element of Japanese influence.

Redon. Another solitary artist whom the Symbolists discovered and claimed as one of their own was Odilon Redon (1840–1916). Like Moreau, he had a haunted imagination, but his imagery was even more personal and disturbing. A master of etching and lithography, he drew inspiration from Goya as well as Romantic literature. The lithograph shown in figure 399 is one of a set he issued in 1882 and dedicated to Edgar Allan Poe. The American poet had been dead for thirty-three years, but his tormented life and his equally tormented imagination made him the very model of the *poète maudit,* the doomed poet. His works, excellently translated by Charles Baudelaire and Stéphane Mallarmé,

399. Odilon Redon. *The Eye Like a Strange Balloon Mounts Toward Infinity,* plate I from *Edgar A. Pöe,* a portfolio of 6 lithographs and a frontispiece, published by G. Fischbacher, Paris, 1882. Lithograph, printed in black, $10\frac{1}{4} \times 7\frac{11}{16}''$ (25.9 × 19.6 cm). Collection, The Museum of Modern Art, New York. Gift of Peter H. Deitsch

400. Henri de Toulouse-Lautrec. *At the Moulin Rouge.* 1892. Oil on canvas, $48\frac{3}{8} \times 55\frac{1}{4}''$ (122.9 × 140.3 cm). The Art Institute of Chicago. Helen Birch Bartlett Memorial Collection

401. Edvard Munch. *The Scream.* 1893. Tempera and casein on cardboard, 36 × 29" (91.4 × 73.7 cm). Nasjonalgalleriet, Oslo

were greatly admired in France. Redon's lithographs do not illustrate Poe. They are, rather, "visual poems" in their own right, evoking the macabre, hallucinatory world of Poe's imagination. In our example, the artist has revived a very ancient device, the single eye representing the all-seeing mind of God. But, in contrast to the traditional form of the symbol, Redon shows the whole eyeball removed from its socket and converted into a balloon that drifts aimlessly in the sky. Disquieting visual paradoxes of this kind were to be exploited on a large scale by the Dadaists and Surrealists in our own century (see figs. 430, 437).

Toulouse-Lautrec. Van Gogh's and Gauguin's discontent with the spiritual ills of

Western civilization was part of a sentiment widely shared at the end of the nineteenth century. A self-conscious preoccupation with decadence, evil, and darkness pervaded the artistic and literary climate. Even those who saw no escape analyzed their predicament in fascinated horror. Paradoxically, this very awareness proved to be a source of strength (the truly decadent, we may assume, are unable to realize their plight). The most remarkable instance of this strength was Henri de Toulouse-Lautrec (1864–1901). An ugly dwarf, he was an artist of superb talent who led a dissolute life in the night spots of Paris and died of alcoholism. *At the Moulin Rouge* (fig. 400) shows his great admiration for Degas: the zigzag form recalls Degas' *The Glass of Absinthe* (see fig. 372). Yet this view of the well-known nightclub is no Impressionist "slice of life." Toulouse-Lautrec sees through the gay surface of the scene, viewing performers and customers with a pitilessly sharp eye for their character, including his own: he is the tiny bearded man next to the very tall one in the back of the room. The large areas of flat color, however, and the emphatic, smoothly curving outlines reflect the influence of Gauguin. Although Toulouse-Lautrec was no Symbolist, the Moulin Rouge that he shows here has an atmosphere so joyless and oppressive that we have to wonder if the artist did not regard it as a place of evil, for all its fascination.

Munch. Something of the same macabre quality pervades the early work of Edvard Munch (1863–1944), a gifted Norwegian who went to Paris in 1889 and based his starkly expressive style on those of Toulouse-Lautrec, Van Gogh, and Gauguin. He settled in Berlin, where the controversy raised by his paintings led to the Secession movement. *The Scream* (fig. 401) is an image of fear, the terrifying, unreasoned fear we feel in a nightmare. Unlike Fuseli (see fig. 348), Munch visualizes this experience without the aid of frightening apparitions, and his achievement is the more persuasive for that very reason. The rhythm of the long, wavy lines seems to carry the echo of the scream into every corner of the picture, making of earth and sky one great sounding board of fear.

Picasso's Blue Period. Pablo Picasso (1881–1974), arrived in Paris in 1900, and felt the spell of the same artistic atmosphere that had generated the style of Munch. His so-called Blue Period (the term refers to the prevailing color of his canvases as well as to their mood) consists almost exclusively of pictures of beggars, derelicts, and other outcasts or victims of society whose pathos reflects the artist's own sense of isolation. Yet these figures, such as that in *The Old Guitarist* (fig. 402), convey poetic melancholy more than outright despair. The aged musician accepts his fate with a resignation that seems almost saintly, and the attenuated grace of his limbs reminds us of El Greco (compare fig. 248). *The Old Guitarist* is a strange amalgam of Mannerism and the art of Gauguin and Toulouse-Lautrec, imbued with the personal gloom of a twenty-two-year-old genius.

Rousseau. A few years later, Picasso and his friends discovered a painter who until then had attracted no attention, although he had been exhibiting his work since 1886. He was Henri Rousseau (1844–1910), a retired customs collector who had started to paint in his middle age without training of any sort. His ideal—which, fortunately, he never achieved—was the arid academic style of Ingres' followers. Rousseau is that paradox, a folk artist of genius. How else could he have done a picture like *The Dream* (fig. 403)? What goes on in the enchanted world of this canvas needs no explanation, because none is possible. Perhaps for that very reason its magic becomes believably real to us. Rousseau himself described the scene in a little poem:

> Yadwigha, peacefully asleep
> Enjoys a lovely dream:
> She hears a kind snake charmer
> Playing upon his reed.
> On stream and foliage glisten
> The silvery beams of the moon.
> And savage serpents listen
> To the gay, entrancing tune.

402. Pablo Picasso. *The Old Guitarist.* 1903. Oil on panel, 47¾ × 32½" (121.3 × 82.6 cm). The Art Institute of Chicago. Helen Birch Bartlett Memorial Collection

403. Henri Rousseau. *The Dream.* 1910. Oil on canvas, 6′8½″ × 9′9½″ (2.05 × 2.99 m). Collection, The Museum of Modern Art, New York. Gift of Nelson A. Rockefeller

Here at last was an innocent directness of feeling that Gauguin thought was so necessary for the age. Picasso and his friends were the first to recognize this quality in Rousseau's work. They revered him as the godfather of twentieth-century painting.

Modersohn-Becker. The inspiration of primitivism that Gauguin had traveled so far to find was discovered by Paula Modersohn-Becker (1876–1907) in the small village of Worpswede, near her family home in Bremen, Germany. Among the artists and writers who congregated there was the Symbolist lyric poet Rainer Maria Rilke, Rodin's friend and briefly his personal secretary. Rilke had visited Russia and been deeply impressed with what he viewed as the purity of Russian peasant life. His influence on the colony at Worpswede certainly affected Modersohn-Becker, whose last works are direct precursors of modern art. Her gentle yet powerful *Self-Portrait* (fig. 404), painted the year before

404. Paula Modersohn-Becker. *Self-Portrait.* 1906. Oil on canvas, 24 × 19¾″ (61 × 50.2 cm). Öffentliche Kunstsammlung, Kunstmuseum, Basel

her early death, presents a transition from the Symbolism of Gauguin and his followers, which she absorbed during several stays in Paris, to Expressionism. The color has the intensity of Matisse and the *Fauves* (see pp. 416–18). At the same time, her deliberately simplified treatment of forms parallels the experiments of Picasso, which were to culminate in *Les Demoiselles d'Avignon* (see fig. 422).

SCULPTURE

Maillol. No tendencies equal to Post-Impressionism appear in sculpture until about 1900. Sculptors in France of a younger generation had by then been trained under the dominant influence of Rodin, and were ready to go their own ways. The finest of these, Aristide Maillol (1861–1944), began as a Symbolist painter, although he did not share Gauguin's anti-Greek attitude. Maillol might be called a "classical primitivist." Admiring the simplified strength of early Greek sculpture, he rejected its later phases. The *Seated Woman* (fig. 405) evokes memories of the Archaic and Severe styles (compare figs. 68, 69) rather than of Praxiteles. The solid forms and clearly defined volumes also recall Cézanne's statement that all natural forms are based on the cone, the sphere, and the cylinder. But the most notable quality of the figure is its harmonious, self-sufficient repose, which the outside world cannot disturb. A statue, Maillol thought, must above all be "static," structurally balanced like a piece of architecture. It must further represent a state of being that is detached from the stress of circumstance, with none of the restless, thrusting energy of Rodin's work. In this respect, the *Seated Woman* is the exact opposite of *The Thinker* (see fig. 384). Maillol later gave it the title *Méditerranée* (The Mediterranean) to suggest the source from which he drew the timeless serenity of his figure.

405. Aristide Maillol. *Seated Woman (Méditerranée).* c. 1901. Stone, height 41″ (104.1 cm). Collection Oskar Reinhart, Winterthur, Switzerland

406. Ernst Barlach. *Man Drawing a Sword.* 1911. Wood, height 31″ (78.7 cm). Private collection

Barlach. Ernst Barlach (1870–1938), an important German sculptor who reached maturity in the years before World War I, seems the very opposite of Maillol; he is a "Gothic primitivist." What Gauguin had experienced in Brittany and the tropics, Barlach found by going to Russia: the simple humanity of a preindustrial age. His figures, such as *Man Drawing a Sword* (fig. 406), embody elementary emotions—wrath, fear, grief—that seem imposed upon them by invisible presences.

When they act, they are like somnambulists, unaware of their own impulses. Human beings, to Barlach, are humble creatures at the mercy of forces beyond their control; they are never masters of their fate. Characteristically, these figures do not fully emerge from the material substance (often, as here, a massive block of wood) of which they are made. Their clothing is like a hard chrysalis that hides the body, as in medieval sculpture. Barlach's art has a mute intensity that is not easily forgotten.

ARCHITECTURE

The search for a modern architecture began in earnest around 1880. It required wedding the ideas of William Morris and the machine aesthetic, first explored tentatively some fifteen years earlier, to new construction materials and techniques. The process itself took several decades, during which architects experimented with a variety of styles. It is significant that the symbol of modern architecture was the skyscraper, and that its first home was Chicago. The fire of 1871 that destroyed much of the city opened vast opportunities to architects. Chicago was rebuilt as a burgeoning metropolis not yet encumbered by allegiance to the styles of the past.

Sullivan. Chicago was home to Louis Sullivan (1856–1924), although the Wainwright Building, his first skyscraper, was erected in St. Louis (fig. 407). The organization of the exterior expresses the internal steel skeleton in the slender, continuous brick piers that rise between the windows from the base to the attic. Their collective effect is that of a vertical grating encased by the corner piers and by the emphatic horizontals of attic and mezzanine. This is, of course, only one of the many possible "skins" that could be stretched over the structural frame. What counts is that we immediately feel that this wall is derived from the skeleton underneath, that it is not self-sustaining. "Skin" is perhaps too weak a term to describe this brick sheathing. To Sullivan, who often thought of buildings as analogous to the human body, it was more like the "flesh" and "muscle" that are organically attached to the "bone" yet capable of an infinite variety of expressive effects. When he insisted that "form follows function," he meant a flexible relationship, not rigid dependence.

407. Louis Sullivan. Wainwright Building, St. Louis. 1890–91

Art Nouveau

In Europe, meanwhile, the authority of the revival styles was being undermined by a movement now usually called by its French name, *Art Nouveau*, although it was known by various terms in other countries as well. It was primarily a new style of decoration based on linear patterns of sinuous curves that often suggest water lilies and other natural forms. Its ancestor was the ornament of William Morris. *Art Nouveau* is also related to the styles of such artists as Gauguin, Beardsley, and Munch (see figs. 395, 398, and 401). During the 1890s and early 1900s its pervasive influence on the applied arts may be seen in wrought-iron work, furniture, jewelry, glass, typography, and even women's fashion. It had a profound effect on public taste, but did not lend itself easily to architectural designs on a large scale.

Gaudí. The most remarkable instance is the Casa Milá in Barcelona (fig. 408), a large apartment house by Antoní Gaudí (1852–1926). It shows an almost maniacal avoidance of all flat surfaces, straight lines, and symmetry of any kind, so that the building looks as if it had been freely modeled of some malleable substance. (The material is not stucco or cement, as we might expect, but cut stone.) The softly rounded openings anticipate the "eroded" shapes of Henry Moore's sculpture (see fig. 467); the roof has the rhythmic motion of a wave; and the chimneys seem to have been squeezed from a pastry tube. The Casa Milá expresses one man's fanatical devotion to the ideal of "natural" form; it could never be repeated, let alone developed further. Structurally, it is a tour de force of old-fashioned craftsmanship, an attempt at architectural reform from the periphery, rather than from the center. Gaudí and Sullivan stand at opposite poles, although they strove for the same goal—a contemporary style independent of the past.

Van de Velde. One of the founding fathers of *Art Nouveau* was the Belgian Henri van de Velde (1863–1957). Trained as a painter, Van de Velde fell under the influence of William Morris. He became a designer of posters, furniture, silverware, and glass, then after 1900 worked mainly as an architect. It was he who founded the Weimar School of Arts and Crafts in Germany, which became famous after World War I as the Bauhaus (see p. 477). His most ambitious building, the theater he designed in Cologne for an exhibition sponsored by the Werkbund (arts and crafts asso-

408. Antoní Gaudí. Casa Milá, Barcelona. 1905–7

409. Henri van de Velde. Theater, Werkbund Exhibition, Cologne. 1914. Destroyed

ciation) in 1914 (fig. 409), makes a telling contrast with the Paris Opéra (see fig. 360), completed only forty years before. Whereas the older building tries to evoke the splendors of the Louvre Palace, Van de Velde's exterior is a tautly stretched "skin" that both covers and reveals the individual units of which the internal space is composed. The Werkbund exhibition was a watershed in the development of modern architecture. It provided a showcase for a whole generation of young German architects who were to achieve prominence after World War I. Many of the buildings they designed for the fairgrounds anticipate ideas of the 1920s.

REALIST PHOTOGRAPHY

Documentary Photography

During the second half of the nineteenth century, the press played a leading role in the social movement that brought the harsh realities of poverty to the public's attention. The camera became an important instrument of reform through the photodocumentary, which tells the story of people's lives in a pictorial essay. The press reacted to the same conditions that had stirred Courbet (see p. 377), and its factual reportage likewise fell within the Realist tradition—only its response came a quarter century later. Hitherto, photographers had been content to present the romanticized image of the poor like those in genre paintings of the day. The first photodocumentary was John Thomson's illustrated sociological study *Street Life in London,* published in 1877. To get his pictures, he had to pose his figures.

Riis. The invention of gunpowder flash ten years later allowed Jacob Riis (1849–1914) to rely for the most part on the element of surprise. Riis was a police reporter in New York City, where he learned firsthand about the crime-infested slums and their appalling living conditions. He kept up a steady campaign of illustrated newspaper exposés, books, and lectures which in some cases led to major revisions of the city's housing codes and labor laws. The unflinching realism of his photographs has lost none of its force. It would be difficult to imagine a more nightmarish scene than *Bandits' Roost* (fig. 410). With good reason we sense a pervasive air of danger in the eerie light. The notorious gangs of New York City's Lower East Side sought their victims by night, killing them without hesitation. The motionless figures seem to look us over with the practiced casualness of hunters coldly sizing up potential prey.

410. Jacob Riis. *Bandits' Roost, Mulberry Street.* c. 1888. Gelatin-silver print. The Jacob A. Riis Collection. Museum of the City of New York

Pictorialism

The raw subject matter and realism of documentary photography had little impact on art and were shunned by most other photographers as well. England, through such organizations as the Photographic Society of London, founded in 1853, became the leader of the movement to convince doubting critics that photography, by imitating painting and printmaking, could indeed be art. To Victorian England, beauty above all meant art with a high moral purpose or noble sentiment, preferably in a classical style.

Rejlander. *The Two Paths of Life* (fig. 411) by Oscar Rejlander (1818–1875) fulfills these ends by presenting an allegory clearly descended from Hogarth's *The Rake's Progress* (see fig. 317). This tour de force, almost three feet wide, combines thirty negatives through composite printing. A young man (in two images) is choosing between the paths of virtue or of vice, the latter represented by a half

411. Oscar Rejlander. *The Two Paths of Life.* 1857. Combination albumen print, 16 × 31″ (40.6 × 78.7 cm). George Eastman House, Rochester, New York

dozen nudes. The picture created a sensation in 1857 and Queen Victoria herself purchased a print. Rejlander, however, never enjoyed the same success again. He was the most adventurous photographer of his time and soon turned to other subjects less in keeping with prevailing taste.

Cameron. The photographer who pursued ideal beauty with the greatest passion was Julia Margaret Cameron (1815–1879). An intimate of leading poets, scientists, and artists, she took up photography at age forty-eight when given a camera and went on to create a remarkable body of work. In her own day Cameron was known for her allegorical and narrative pictures, but now she is remembered primarily for her portraits of the men who shaped Victorian England. Many of her finest photographs, however, are of the women who were married to her closest friends. An early study of the actress Ellen Terry (fig. 412) has the lyricism and grace of the Pre-Raphaelite aesthetic that shaped Cameron's style (compare fig. 377).

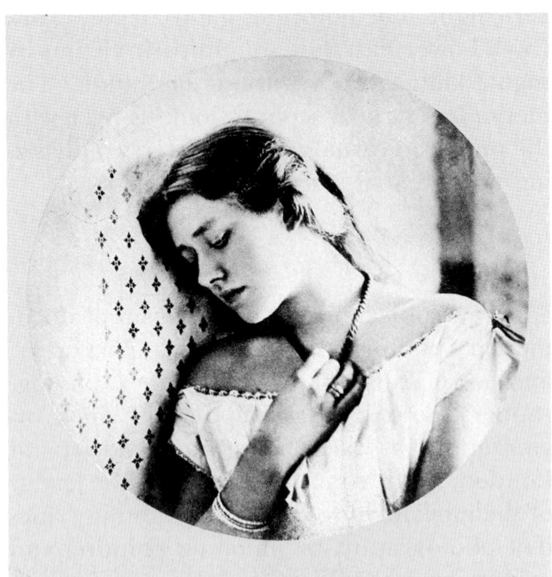

412. Julia Margaret Cameron. *Portrait of Ellen Terry.* 1863. Carbon print, diameter 9 7/16" (240 mm). The Metropolitan Museum of Art, New York. The Alfred Stieglitz Collection, 1949

Photo-Secession. The issue of whether photography could be art came to a head in the early 1890s with the Secession movement, which was spearheaded in 1893 by the founding in London of the Linked Ring, a rival group to the Royal Photographic Society of Great Britain. In seeking a pictorialism independent of science and technology, the Secessionists steered a course between academicism and naturalism by imitating every form of late Romantic art that did not involve narrative. Equally antithetical to their aims were Realist and Post-Impressionist painting, then at their zenith. In the group's art-for-art's-sake approach to photography, the Secession had the most in common with Whistler's aestheticism.

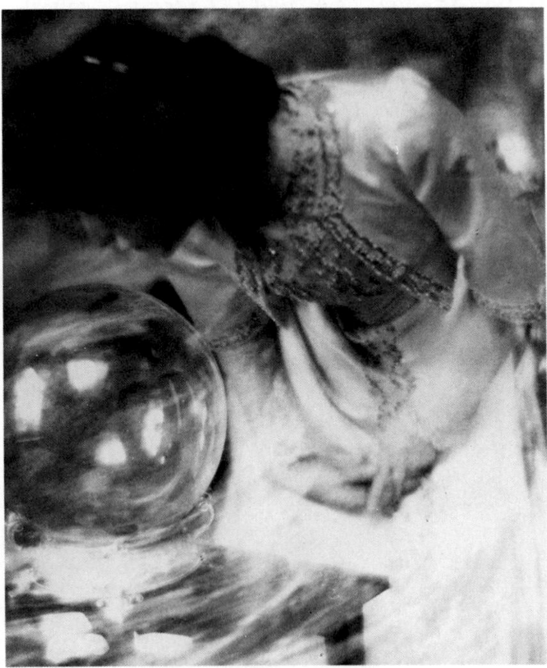

413. Gertrude Käsebier. *The Magic Crystal.* c. 1904. Platinum print. Royal Photographic Society, Bath

To resolve the dilemma between art and mechanics, the Secessionists tried to make their photographs look as much like paintings as possible. Rather than resorting to composite or multiple images, however, they exercised total control over the printing process, chiefly by adding special materials to their printing paper to create different effects. Pigmented gum brushed on coarse drawing paper yielded a warm toned, highly textured print that in its way approximated

414. Edward Steichen. *Rodin with His Sculptures "Victor Hugo" and "The Thinker."* 1902. Gum print. The Art Institute of Chicago, Alfred Stieglitz Collection

Impressionist painting. Paper impregnated with platinum salts was especially popular among the Secessionists for the clear grays in their prints. Their subtlety and depth lend a remarkable ethereality to *The Magic Crystal* (fig. 413) by Gertrude Käsebier (1854–1934), in which spiritual forces almost visibly sweep across the photograph.

Steichen. Through Käsebier and Alfred Stieglitz, the Linked Ring had close ties with America, where Stieglitz opened his Photo-Secession gallery in New York in 1905. Among his protégés was the young Edward Steichen (1879–1973), whose photograph of Rodin in his sculpture studio (fig. 414) is without doubt the finest achievement of the entire Photo-Secession movement. The head in profile contemplating *The Thinker* expresses the essence of the confrontation between the sculptor and his work of art. His brooding introspection hides the inner turmoil evoked by the ghostlike monument to Victor Hugo, which rises dramatically like a genius in the background. Not since *The Creation of Adam* by Michelangelo (see fig. 233), who was Rodin's ideal artist, have we seen a more telling use of space or an image that penetrates the mystery of creativity so deeply.

Motion Photography

An entirely new direction was charted by Eadweard Muybridge (1830–1904), the father of motion photography. He wedded two different technologies, devising a set of cam-

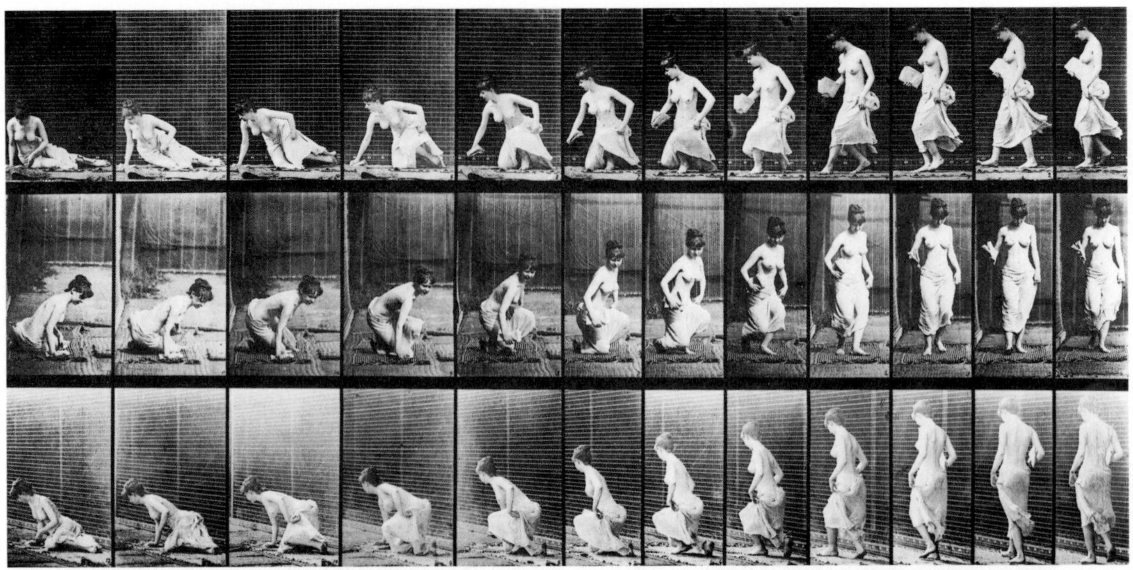

415. Eadweard Muybridge. *Female Semi-Nude in Motion,* from *Human and Animal Locomotion,* vol. 2, pl. 271. 1887. George Eastman House, Rochester, New York

eras capable of photographing action at successive points. Photography had grown from such marriages; another instance had occurred earlier when Nadar used a hot-air balloon to take aerial shots of Paris. After some trial efforts, Muybridge managed in 1877 to produce a set of pictures of a trotting horse which forever changed artistic depictions of the horse in movement. Of the 100,000 photographs he devoted to the study of animal and human locomotion, the most remarkable were those taken from several vantage points at once (fig. 415). The idea was surely in the air, for the art of the period occasionally shows similar experiments, but Muybridge's photographs must nevertheless have come as a revelation to artists. The simultaneous views present an entirely new treatment of motion across time and space that challenges the imagination. Like a complex visual puzzle, they can be combined in any number of ways that are endlessly fascinating. Muybridge's photographs convey a peculiarly modern sense of dynamics, reflecting the new tempo of life in the machine age. However, because the gap was then so great between scientific fact on the one hand and visual perception and artistic representation on the other, their far-reaching aesthetic implications were to be realized only by the Futurists (see pp. 423–24).

TWENTIETH-CENTURY PAINTING

PAINTING BEFORE WORLD WAR I

In our account of art in the modern era, we have already discussed a succession of "isms": Neoclassicism, Romanticism, Realism, Impressionism, Post-Impressionism, Divisionism, Symbolism. There are many more to be found in twentieth-century art. These "isms" can form a serious obstacle to understanding: they may make us feel that we cannot hope to comprehend the art of our time unless we immerse ourselves in a welter of esoteric doctrines. Actually, we can disregard all but the most important "isms." Like the terms we have used for the styles of earlier periods, they are merely labels to help us sort things out. If an "ism" fails the test of usefulness, we need not retain it. This is true of many "isms" in contemporary art. The movements they designate either cannot be seen very clearly as separate entities, or have so little importance that they can interest only the specialist. It has always been easier to invent new labels than to create a movement in art that truly deserves a new name.

Still, we cannot do without "isms" altogether. Since the start of the modern era, the Western world (and, increasingly, the rest of the world) has faced the same basic problems everywhere, and local artistic traditions have steadily given way to international trends. Among these we can distinguish three main currents, each comprising a number of "isms," that began among the Post-Impressionists and have developed greatly in our own century: Expressionism, Abstraction, and Fantasy. Expressionism stresses artists' emotional attitudes toward themselves and the world. Abstraction stresses the formal structure of the work of art. Fantasy explores the realm of the imagination, especially its spontaneous and irrational qualities. We must not forget, however, that feeling, order, and imagination are all present in every work of art. Without imagination, art would be deadly dull; without some degree of order, it would be chaotic; without feeling, it would leave us unmoved.

These currents, then, are not mutually exclusive by any means. We shall find them interrelated in many ways, and the work of one artist may belong to more than one current. Moreover, each current embraces a wide range of approaches, from the realistic to the completely nonrepresentational (or nonobjective). Thus these three currents correspond to general attitudes rather than to specific styles. The primary concern of the Expressionist is the human community; of the Abstractionist, the structure of reality; and of the artist of Fantasy, the labyrinth of the individual human mind. And we shall find that Realism, which is concerned with the appearance of reality, has continued to exist independently of the other three, especially in the United States, where art has often pursued a separate course from that of Europe. These currents bear a shifting relation to each other that reflects the complexity of modern life. To be understood, they must be seen in their proper historical context. After 1945, it is no longer meaningful to trace the evolution of these strands separately. The art of our times has become too complex for that.

In addition, we will encounter modernism, a concept peculiar to the twentieth century, though its roots can be traced to Romanticism. To artists it is a trumpet call that both asserts their freedom to create in a new style and provides them with the mission to define the meaning of their times, and even to reshape society through their art. This is a role

416. Henri Matisse. *The Joy of Life*. 1905–6. Oil on canvas, 68½ × 93¾" (174 × 238.1 cm). Copyright Barnes Foundation, Merion, Pennsylvania

for which the problematic term "avant-garde" (literally, vanguard) is hardly sufficient. Of course, artists have always responded to the changing world around them, but rarely have they risen to the challenge as now, or with so fervent a sense of personal cause.

Expressionism

The twentieth century may be said to have begun five years late, so far as painting is concerned. Between 1901 and 1906, several comprehensive exhibitions of the work of Van Gogh, Gauguin, and Cézanne were held in Paris. For the first time the achievements of these masters became accessible to a broad public.

The Fauves. The young painters who had grown up in the "decadent," morbid mood of the 1890s (see p. 401) were profoundly impressed by what they saw, and several of them developed a radical new style, full of violent color and bold distortions. When their work first appeared in 1905, it so shocked critical opinion that they were dubbed the *Fauves* (wild beasts), a label they wore with pride. Actually, it was not a common program that brought them together, but their shared sense of liberation and experiment. As a movement, Fauvism comprised a number of loosely related individual styles, and the group dissolved after a few years.

Matisse. Its leading member was Henri Matisse (1869–1954), the oldest of the founders of twentieth-century painting. *The Joy of Life* (fig. 416) sums up the spirit of Fauvism better than any other single work. It derives its flat planes of color, heavy undulating outlines, and the "primitive" flavor of its forms from Gauguin (see fig. 395). Even its subject suggests the vision of humanity in a state of Nature that Gauguin had pursued in Tahiti (see fig. 396). But we soon realize that Matisse's figures are not Noble Savages under the spell of a native god. The subject is a pagan scene in the classical sense: a bacchanal like Titian's (compare fig. 240). Even the poses of the figures have for the most part a classical origin, and in the apparently careless draftsmanship resides a profound knowledge of the human body (Matisse had been trained in the academic tradition). What makes the picture so revolutionary is its radical simplicity, its "genius of omission." Everything that possibly can be has been left out or stated by implication only, yet the scene retains the essentials of plastic form and spatial depth.

Painting, Matisse seems to say, is the rhythmic arrangement of line and color on a flat plane, but it is not only that. How far can the image of nature be pared down without destroying its basic properties and thus reducing it to mere surface ornament? "What I am after, above all," he once explained, "is expression. . . . [But] . . . expression does not consist of the passion mirrored upon a human face. . . . The whole arrangement of my picture is expressive. The placement of figures or objects, the empty spaces around them, the proportions, everything plays a part." What, we wonder, does *The Joy of Life* express? Exactly what its title says. Whatever his debt to Gauguin, Matisse was never stirred by the same agonized discontent with the decadence of our civilization. He was concerned above all with the act of painting. This to him was an experience so profoundly joyous that he wanted to transmit it to the beholder.

Matisse's "genius of omission" is again at work in *The Red Studio* (fig. 417). By reducing the number of tints to a minimum, he makes color an independent structural element. The result is to emphasize the radical new balance he struck between the "two-D" and "three-D" aspects of painting. Matisse spreads the same flat red color on the tablecloth and wall as on

417. Henri Matisse. *The Red Studio.* 1911. Oil on canvas, 5′11¼″ × 7′2¼″ (1.81 × 2.19 m). Collection, The Museum of Modern Art, New York. Mrs. Simon Guggenheim Fund

the floor, yet he distinguishes the horizontal from the vertical planes with complete assurance using only a few lines. Equally bold is Matisse's use of pattern. By repeating a few basic shapes, hues, and decorative motifs in seemingly casual, but perfectly calculated, array around the edges of the canvas, he harmonizes the relation of each element with the rest of the picture. Cézanne had pioneered this integration of surface ornament into the design of a picture (see fig. 390), but Matisse here makes it a mainstay of his composition.

Rouault. Another member of the *Fauves*, Georges Rouault (1871–1958), would hardly have agreed with Matisse's definition of "expression." For him this had still to include, as it had in the past, "the passion mirrored upon a human face." Rouault was the true heir of Van Gogh's and Gauguin's concern for the corrupt state of the world. However, he hoped for spiritual renewal through a revitalized Catholic faith, and his pictures are personal statements of that ardent hope. Trained in his youth as a stained-glass worker, he was better prepared than the other *Fauves* to share Gauguin's enthusiasm for medieval art. Rouault's mature work, such as *The Old King* (fig. 418), has glowing colors and compartmented, black-bordered shapes inspired by Gothic stained-glass windows (compare fig. 173). Within this framework he retains a good deal of pictorial freedom, which he uses to express his deep compassion for the human condition. Thus, the old king's face conveys a mood of resignation and inner suffering that reminds us of Rembrandt and Daumier (see figs. 296, 344).

418. Georges Rouault. *The Old King.* 1916–37. Oil on canvas, 30¼ × 21¼" (76.8 × 54 cm). Carnegie Institute, Pittsburgh

419. Emil Nolde. *The Last Supper.* 1909. Oil on canvas, 32½ × 41¾" (82.6 × 106.1 cm). Stiftung Seebüll Ada und Emil Nolde, Neukirchen (Schleswig), Germany

Die Brücke; Nolde. Fauvism had its most enduring impact in Germany, especially among the members of *Die Brücke* (The Bridge), a group of like-minded painters who lived in Dresden in 1905. Their early works not only reflect Matisse's simplified, rhythmic line and loud color, but also clearly reveal the direct influence of Van Gogh and Gauguin. One *Brücke* artist, Emil Nolde (1867–1956), stands somewhat apart. Older than the rest, he shared Rouault's predilection for religious themes. The deliberately clumsy draftsmanship of his *The Last Supper* (fig. 419) shows that Nolde, too, rejected pictorial refinement in favor of a primeval, direct expression inspired by Gauguin. The thickly encrusted surfaces of Rouault's canvases also come to mind, as does the mute intensity of Barlach's peasants (see fig. 406).

Kandinsky. The most daring and original step beyond Fauvism was taken in Germany by a Russian, Wassily Kandinsky (1866–1944), the leading member of a group of Munich artists called *Der Blaue Reiter* (The Blue Rider). Kandinsky began to forsake representation as early as 1910 and abandoned it altogether several years later. Using the rainbow colors and the free, dynamic brushwork of the Paris *Fauves,* he created a completely nonobjective style. These works have titles as abstract as their forms: our example, one of the most striking, is called *Sketch I for "Composition VII"* (fig. 420).

Perhaps we should avoid the term "abstract," because it is often taken to mean that the artist has analyzed and simplified the shapes of visible reality (compare Cézanne's dictum that all natural forms are based on the cone, sphere, and cylinder). Kandinsky's aim, however, was to charge form and color with a purely spiritual meaning (as he put it) by eliminating all resemblance to the physical world. Whistler, too, had spoken of "divesting the picture from any outside sort of interest"; he even anticipated Kandinsky's "musical" titles (see fig. 380). The liberating influence of the *Fauves* permitted Kandinsky to put this theory into practice, for the possibility was clearly implicit in Fauvism from the start.

How valid is the analogy between painting and music? When a painter like Kandinsky carries it through so uncompromisingly, does he really lift his art to another plane? Or could it be that his declared independence from representational images now forces him instead to "represent music," which limits him even more severely? Kandinsky's advocates like to point out that representational painting has a "literary" content, and they deplore such dependence on another art; but they do not explain why the "musical" content of nonobjective painting should be more desirable. Is painting less alien to music than to literature? They seem to think music is a higher art than literature or painting because it is inherently nonrepresentational. This is a point of view with a tradition that goes back to Plato and includes Plotinus, St. Augustine, and their medieval successors. The attitude of the nonobjectivists might thus be termed "secular iconoclasm": they do not condemn images as wicked, but denounce them as non-art.

The case is difficult to argue, and it does not matter whether this theory is right or wrong; the proof of the pudding is in the eating, not in the recipe. Any artist's ideas are not important to us unless we are convinced of the significance of the work itself. Kandinsky undoubtedly created a viable style, though his work admittedly demands an intuitive response that may be hard for some of us. The painting reproduced here has density and vitality, and a radiant freshness of feeling that impresses us even though we may be uncertain what exactly was the artist's intent.

Hartley. Americans became familiar with the *Fauves* through exhibitions from 1908 on. After the pivotal Armory Show of 1913, which introduced the latest European art to New York, there was a growing interest in the German Expressionists as well. The driving force behind the modernist movement in the United States was the photographer Alfred Stieglitz (see pp. 485–88), who almost singlehandedly supported many of its early members. To him, modernism meant abstraction and its related concepts. Among the most significant achievements of the Stieglitz group are the canvases painted by Marsden Hartley (1887–1943) in Munich during the early years of World War I under the direct influence of Kandinsky. *Portrait of a German Officer* (fig. 421) is a masterpiece of design from 1915, the year Hartley was invited to exhibit with *Der Blaue Reiter.* He had already been introduced to Futurism and several offshoots of Cubism (see pp. 422–25), which he used to discipline Kandinsky's supercharged surface. The emblematic portrait is testimony to the militarism Hartley encountered everywhere in Germany. It incorporates the insignia, epaulets, Maltese cross, and other details from an officer's uniform of the day.

420. Wassily Kandinsky. *Sketch I for "Composition VII."* 1913. India ink, 30¾ × 39⅜″ (78.1 × 100 cm). Kunstmuseum, Bern, Switzerland. Collection Felix Klee

421. Marsden Hartley. *Portrait of a German Officer.* 1914. Oil on canvas, 68¼ × 41⅜″ (173.4 × 105.1 cm). The Metropolitan Museum of Art, New York. The Alfred Stieglitz Collection, 1949

Abstraction

The second of our main currents is Abstraction. When discussing Kandinsky, we said that the term is usually taken to mean the process (or the result) of analyzing and simplifying observed reality. Literally, it means "to draw away from, to separate." If we have ten apples, and then separate the ten from the apples, we get an "abstract number," a number that no longer refers to particular things. "Apples," too, is an abstraction, since it places ten apples in one class, without regard for their individual qualities. The artist who sets out to paint ten apples will find no two of them alike, but it is impossible to take all their differences into account, so that even the most painstakingly realistic portrayal of these particular pieces of fruit is bound to be some

422. Pablo Picasso. *Les Demoiselles d'Avignon.* 1907. Oil on canvas, 8′ × 7′8″ (2.44 × 2.34 m). Collection, The Museum of Modern Art, New York. Acquired through the Lillie P. Bliss Bequest

sort of an abstraction. Abstraction, then, goes into the making of any work of art, whether the artist knows it or not. The process was not conscious and controlled, however, until the Early Renaissance, when artists first analyzed the shapes of nature in terms of mathematical bodies (see p. 233). Cézanne and Seurat revitalized this approach and explored it further. They are the direct ancestors of the abstract movement in twentieth-century art.

Picasso's *Demoiselles d'Avignon.* It is difficult to imagine the birth of modern abstraction without Pablo Picasso. About 1905, stimulated as much by the *Fauves* as by the retrospective exhibitions of the great Post-Impressionists, he gradually abandoned the melancholy lyricism of his Blue Period (see pp. 404–5) for a more robust style. He shared Matisse's enthusiasm for the work of Gauguin and Cézanne, but he viewed these masters very differently. In 1907 he produced his own counterpart to *The Joy of Life* (see fig. 416), a monumental canvas so challenging that it outraged even Matisse (fig. 422). The title, *Les Demoiselles d'Avignon* ("The Young Ladies of Avignon"), does not refer to the town of that name, but to Avignon Street in a notorious section of Barcelona. When Picasso started the picture, it was to be a temptation scene in a brothel, but he ended up with a composition of five nudes and a still life. But what nudes! Matisse's generalized figures in *The Joy of Life* seem utterly innocuous compared to this savage aggressiveness.

The three on the left are angular distortions of classical figures, but the violently dislocated features and bodies of the other two have all the barbaric qualities of certain types of ethnographic art (compare figs. 24, 25). Following Gauguin's lead, the *Fauves* had discovered the aesthetic appeal of African and Oceanic sculpture and had introduced Picasso to this material. Nonetheless it was Picasso, not the *Fauves*, who used primitivist art as a battering ram against the classical conception of beauty. Not only the proportions, but also the organic integrity and continuity of the human body are denied here, so that the canvas (in the apt description of one critic) "resembles a field of broken glass."

Picasso, then, has destroyed a great deal. What has he gained in the process? Once we recover from the initial shock, we begin to see that the destruction is quite methodical. Everything—the figures as well as their setting—is broken up into angular wedges or facets. These are not flat, but shaded in a way that gives them a certain three-dimensionality. We cannot always be sure whether they are concave or convex. Some look like chunks of solidified space, others like fragments of translucent bodies. They constitute a unique kind of matter, which imposes a new integrity and continuity on the entire canvas. The *Demoiselles,* unlike *The Joy of Life,* can no longer be read as an image of the external world. Its world is its own, analogous to nature but constructed along different principles. Picasso's revolutionary "building material," compounded of voids and solids, is hard to describe with any precision. The early critics, who saw only the prevalence of sharp edges and angles, dubbed the new style Cubism.

423. Pablo Picasso. *Portrait of Ambroise Vollard.* 1910. Oil on canvas, 36¼ × 25⅝" (92.1 × 65.1 cm). The Pushkin State Museum of Fine Arts, Moscow

Analytic Cubism. That the *Demoiselles* owes anything to Cézanne may at first seem incredible. However, Picasso had studied Cézanne's late work (see fig. 391) with great care, finding in Cézanne's abstract treatment of volume and space the translucent structural units from which to derive the faceted shapes of Analytic (or Facet) Cubism. The link is clearer in Picasso's *Portrait of Ambroise Vollard* (fig. 423), painted three years later. The facets are now small and precise, more like prisms, and the canvas has the balance and refinement of a fully mature style.

Contrasts of color and texture, so pronounced in the *Demoiselles,* are now reduced to a minimum; the subdued tonality of the picture approaches monochrome, so as not

to compete with the design. The structure has become so complex and systematic that it would seem wholly cerebral if the "imprismed" sitter's face did not emerge with such dramatic force. Of the "barbaric" distortions in the *Demoiselles* there is no trace; they had served their purpose. Cubism has become an abstract style within the purely Western sense, but its distance from observed reality has not significantly increased. Picasso may be playing an elaborate game of hide-and-seek with nature, but he still needs the visible world to challenge his creative powers. The nonobjective realm held no appeal for him, then or later.

Synthetic Cubism. By 1910, Cubism was well established as an alternative to Fauvism, and Picasso had been joined by a number of other artists, notably Georges Braque (1882–1963), with whom he collaborated so intimately that their work from this period is difficult to tell apart. Both of them (it is not clear to whom the chief credit belongs) initiated the next phase of Cubism, which was even bolder than the first. Usually called Synthetic Cubism because it puts forms back together, it is also known as Collage Cubism, after the French word for "paste-up," the technique that started it all. Within a year, Picasso and Braque were producing still lifes composed almost entirely of cut-and-pasted scraps of material, with only a few lines added to complete the design. In *Le Courrier* by Braque (fig. 424) we recognize strips of imitation wood graining, part of a tobacco wrapper with a contrasting stamp, half the masthead of a newspaper, and a bit of newsprint made into a playing card (the ace of hearts). Why did Picasso and Braque suddenly prefer the contents of the wastepaper basket to brush and paint? In wanting to explore their new concept of the picture as a sort of tray on which to "serve" the still life to the beholder, they found the best way was to put real things on the tray. The ingredients of a collage actually play a double role. They have been shaped and combined, then drawn or painted upon to give them a representational meaning, but they do not lose their original identity as scraps of material, "outsiders" in the world of art. Their function is both to *represent* (to be a part of an image) and to *present* (to be themselves). In this latter capacity, they endow the collage with a self-sufficiency that no Analytic Cubist picture can have. A tray, after all, is a self-contained area, detached from the rest of the physical world. Unlike a painting, it cannot show more than is actually on it.

The difference between the two phases of Cubism may also be defined in terms of picture space. Analytic Cubism retains a certain kind of depth, so that the painted surface acts as a window through which we still perceive the remnants of the familiar perspective space of the Renaissance. Though fragmented and redefined, this space lies behind the picture plane and has no visible limits. Potentially, it may contain objects that are hidden from our view. In Synthetic Cubism, on the contrary, the picture space lies in front of the plane of the "tray." Space is not created by illusionistic devices, such as modeling and foreshortening, but by the actual overlapping of layers of pasted materials. The integrity of the nonperspective space is not affected when, as in *Le Courrier,* the apparent thickness of these materials and their distance from each other is increased by a bit of shading here and there. Synthetic Cubism, then, offers a basically new space concept, the first since Masaccio. It is a true landmark in the history of painting.

Before long Picasso and Braque discovered that they could retain this new pictorial space without the use of pasted materials. They only had to paint as if they were making collages. World War I, however, put an end to their collaboration and disrupted the further development of Synthetic Cubism, which reached its height in the following decade.

Futurism. As originally conceived by Picasso and Braque, Cubism was a formal discipline of subtle balance applied to traditional subjects: still life, portraiture, the nude. Other painters, however, saw in the new style a special affinity with the geometric precision of engineering that made it uniquely attuned to the dynamism of modern life. The short-lived

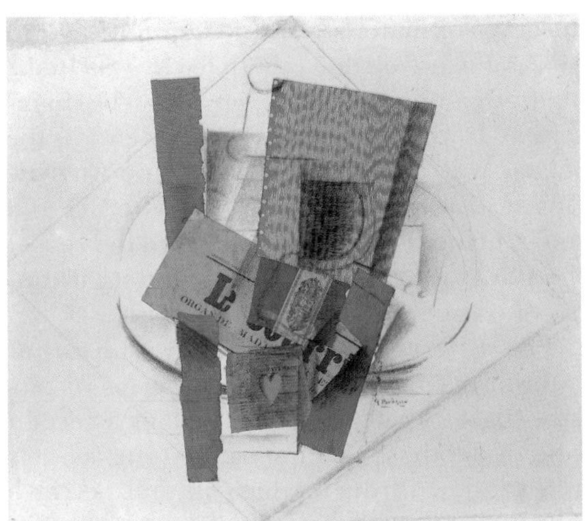

424. Georges Braque. *Newspaper, Bottle, Packet of Tobacco (Le Courrier).* 1914. Collage of charcoal, gouache, pencil, ink, and pasted paper on cardboard, 20⅝ × 25″ (52.4 × 63.5 cm). The Philadelphia Museum of Art. A. E. Gallatin Collection

425. Umberto Boccioni. *Dynamism of a Cyclist.* 1913. Oil on canvas, 27⅝ × 37⅜″ (70.2 × 94.9 cm). Collection Gianni Mattioli, Milan

Futurist movement in Italy exemplifies this attitude. In 1909–10 its disciples, led by the poet Filippo Tommaso Marinetti, issued a series of manifestos violently rejecting the past and exalting the beauty of the machine.

At first they used techniques developed from Post-Impressionism to convey the surge of industrial society, but these were otherwise static compositions, still dependent upon representational images. By adopting the simultaneous views of Analytic Cubism in *Dynamism of a Cyclist* (fig. 425), Umberto Boccioni (1882–1916), the most original of the Futurists, was able to communicate the look of furious pedaling across time and space far more tellingly than if he had actually depicted the human figure, which could be seen in only one time and place in traditional art. In the flexible vocabulary provided by Cubism, Boccioni found the means of expressing the twentieth century's new sense of time, space, and energy that Albert Einstein had defined in 1905 in his special theory of relativity. Moreover, Boccioni suggests the unique quality of the modern experience. With his pulsating movement, the cyclist has become an extension of his environment, from which he is now indistinguishable.

Futurism literally died out in World War I. Its leading artists were killed by the same vehicles of destruction they had glorified only a few years earlier in their revolutionary manifestos, but their legacy was soon taken up in France, America, and, above all, Russia.

Cubo-Futurism. Cubo-Futurism arose in Russia a few years before World War I as the result of close contacts with the leading European art centers. Its style was drawn from Picasso's and its theories based on Futurist tracts. The Russian Futurists were above all modernists. They welcomed industry, which was spreading rapidly throughout Russia, as the foundation of a new society and the means for conquering that old Russian enemy, nature. Unlike the Italian Futurists, however, the Russians rarely glorified the machine, least of all as an instrument of war.

Central to Cubo-Futurist thinking was the concept of *zaum,* a term which has no counterpart in the West. Invented by Russian poets, *zaum* was a trans-sense (as opposed to the Dadaists' non-sense; see p. 432) language based on new word forms and syntax. In theory, *zaum* could be understood universally, since it was thought that meaning was implicit in the basic sounds and patterns of speech. When applied to painting, *zaum* provided the artist with complete freedom to redefine the style and content of art. The picture surface was now seen as the sole conveyer of meaning

426. Liubov Popova. *The Traveler.* 1915. Oil on canvas, 56 × 41½″ (142.2 × 105.4 cm). Norton Simon Art Foundation, Pasadena, California

through its appearance. Hence, the subject of a work of art became the visual elements and their formal arrangement. However, because Cubo-Futurism was concerned with means, not ends, it failed to provide the actual content that is found in other modernist works. Although the Cubo-Futurists were more important as theorists than artists, they provided the springboard for later Russian movements.

The new world envisioned by the Russian modernists led to a broad redefinition of the roles of man and woman. It was therefore in Russia that women achieved an artistic stature not equaled in Europe or America until considerably later. The finest painter of the group was Liubov Popova (1889–1924). She studied in Paris in 1912 and visited Italy in 1914. The combination of Cubism and Futurism that she absorbed abroad is seen in *The Traveler* (fig. 426). The treatment of forms remains essentially Cubist, but the painting shares the Futurist obsession with representing dynamic motion in time and space. The jumble of image fragments creates the impression of objects seen in rapid succession. Across the plane the furious interaction of forms with their environment threatens to extend the painting into the surrounding space. At the same time, the strong modeling draws attention to the surface, lending it a relieflike quality that is enhanced by the vigorous texture.

Suprematism. The first purely Russian art of the twentieth century, however, was that of Suprematism. In one of the greatest leaps of the symbolic and spatial imagination in the history of art, Kazimir Malevich (1878–1935) invented the *Black Quadrilateral* seen in figure 427. How is it that such a disarmingly simple image should be so important? By limiting art to a few elements—a single shape repeated in two tones and fixed firmly to the

427. Kazimir Malevich. *Black Quadrilateral.* c. 1913–15. Oil on canvas, 24 × 17″ (61 × 43.2 cm). Copyright Art Co. Ltd. The George Costakis Collection

picture plane—he emphasized the painting as a painting even more radically than had his predecessors. At the same time, he transformed it into a concentrated symbol having multiple layers of meaning, thereby providing the content missing from Cubo-Futurism. The inspiration for *Black Quadrilateral* came in 1913 while Malevich was working on designs for the opera *Victory over the Sun,* a production that was one of the important artistic collaborations in the modern era. In the context of the opera, the black quadrilateral represents the eclipse of the sun of Western painting and of everything based on it. Further, the work can be seen as the triumph of the new order over the old, the East over the West, humanity over nature, idea over matter. The black quadrilateral (which is not even a true rectangle) was intended to stand as a modern icon. It supersedes the traditional Christian trinity and symbolizes a "supreme" reality, because geometry is an independent abstraction in itself; hence the movement's name, Suprematism.

According to Malevich, Suprematism was also a philosophical color system constructed in time and space. His space was an intuitive one, with both scientific and mystical overtones. The flat plane replaces volume, depth, and perspective as a means of defining space. Each side or point represents one of the three dimensions, with the fourth side standing for the fourth dimension: time. Like the universe itself, the black surface would be infinite were it not delimited by an outer boundary which is the white border and shape of the canvas. *Black Quadrilateral* thus constitutes the first satisfactory redefinition, visually and conceptually, of time and space in modern art. Like Einstein's formula $E=mc^2$ for the theory of relativity, it has an elegant simplicity that belies the intense effort required to synthesize a complex set of ideas and reduce them to a fundamental "law." When it first appeared, Suprematism had much the same impact on Russian artists that Einstein's theory had on scientists. It unveiled a world never seen before, one that was unequivocally modern. The heyday of Suprematism was over by the early 1920s. Reflecting the growing diversity and fragmentation of Russian art, its followers defected to other movements, above all to the Constructivism led by Vladimir Tatlin (see pp. 460–61).

Fantasy

The third current, which we term Fantasy, follows a less clear-cut course than the other two, since it depends on a state of mind more than on any particular style. The one thing all painters of fantasy have in common is the belief that imagination, "the inner eye," is more important than the outside world. Since the artist's imagination is a private domain, the images it provides are likely to be equally private, unless the artist subjects them to a deliberate process of selection. How can such "uncontrolled" images have meaning to the beholder, whose own inner world is not the same as the artist's? Psychology has taught us that we are not so different from each other in this respect as we like to think. Our minds are all built on the same basic pattern, and the same is true of our imagination and memory. These belong to the unconscious part of the mind where experiences are stored, whether we want to remember them or not. At night, or whenever conscious thought relaxes its vigilance, our experiences come back to us and we seem to live through them again.

However, the unconscious mind does not usually reproduce our experiences as they actually happened. They will often be admitted into the conscious part of the mind in the guise of dream images. In this form they seem less vivid, and we can live with our memories more easily. This digesting of experience by the unconscious mind is surprisingly alike in all of us, although it works better with some individuals than with others. Hence, we are always interested in imaginary things, provided they are presented to us in such a way that they *seem* real. What happens in a fairy tale, for example, would be absurd in the language of a news report, but when it is told to us as it should be told, we are enchanted. We need only recall *The Dream* by Henri Rousseau (see fig. 403) to realize that the same is true of paintings.

428. Giorgio de Chirico. *Mystery and Melancholy of a Street.* 1914. Oil on canvas, 34¼ × 28½" (87 × 72.4 cm). Private collection

Why, then, does private fantasy loom so large in twentieth-century art? There seem to be several interlocking causes. First, the cleavage that developed between reason and imagination in the wake of rationalism tended to dissolve the heritage of myth and legend that had been the common channel of private fantasy in earlier times. Second, the artist's greater freedom—and insecurity—within the social fabric give rise to a sense of isolation and favors an introspective attitude. Finally, the Romantic cult of emotion prompted the artist to seek out subjective experience, and to accept its validity. We saw the trend beginning at the end of the eighteenth century in the art of Fuseli (see fig. 348). In nineteenth-century painting, private fantasy was still a minor current. After 1900, it became a major one.

De Chirico. The heritage of Romanticism can be seen most clearly in the astonishing pictures painted in Paris just before World War I by Giorgio de Chirico (1888–1978), such as *Mystery and Melancholy of a Street* (fig. 428). This deserted square with endless diminishing arcades, nocturnally illuminated by the cold full moon, has all the poetry of Romantic reverie. It has also a strangely sinister air. This is an ominous scene in the full sense of the term. Everything here suggests an omen, a portent of unknown and disquieting significance. De Chirico himself could not explain the incongruities in these paintings—the empty furniture van, or the girl with the hoop—that trouble and fascinate us. Later, after he returned to Italy, he adopted a conservative style and repudiated his early work, as if he were embarrassed at having put his dream world on public display.

Chagall. The power of nostalgia, so evident in *Mystery and Melancholy of a Street,* also dominates the fantasies of Marc Chagall (1887–1985), a Russian Jew who went to Paris in 1910. *I and the Village* (fig. 429) is a Cubist fairy tale, weaving dreamlike memories of Russian folk tales, Jewish proverbs, and the look of Russia into one glowing vision. Here, as in many later works, Chagall relives the experiences of his childhood. These were so important to him that his imagination shaped and reshaped them for years without their persistence being diminished.

Duchamp. In Paris on the eve of World War I, we encounter yet another artist of fantasy, the Frenchman Marcel Duchamp (1887–1968). After basing his early style on Cézanne, he initiated a dynamic version of Analytic Cubism, similar to Futurism, by superimposing successive phases of movement on each other, much as in multiple-exposure photography. Soon, however, Duchamp's development took a more disturbing turn. In *The Bride* (fig. 430), we look in vain for any resemblance, however remote, to the human form. What we see is a mechanism that seems part motor, part distilling apparatus. It is beautifully engineered to serve no purpose whatever. The title causes us real perplexity at first. It cannot be irrelevant, because Duchamp has emphasized its importance by lettering it right onto the canvas. The artist evidently intended to satirize the scientific

429. Marc Chagall. *I and the Village.* 1911. Oil on canvas, 75⅝ × 59½" (192.1 × 151.4 cm). Collection, The Museum of Modern Art, New York. Mrs. Simon Guggenheim Fund

430. Marcel Duchamp. *The Bride.* 1912. Oil on canvas, 35⅛ × 21¾" (89.2 × 55.3 cm). The Philadelphia Museum of Art. Louise and Walter Arensberg Collection

outlook on humanity by "analyzing" the bride until she is reduced to a complicated piece of plumbing. The picture, then, may be seen as the negative counterpart of the glorification of the machine, so stridently proclaimed by the Futurists.

Realism

The Ash Can School. In America, the first wave of change was initiated not by the Stieglitz circle but by the Ash Can school, which flourished in New York just before World War I, although it was soon eclipsed by the rush toward a more radical modernism set off by the Armory Show in 1913 (see p. 419). Centering on Robert Henri, who had studied with a pupil of Thomas Eakins at the Pennsylvania Academy, this group of artists consisted mainly of former illustrators for Philadelphia and New York newspapers. They were fascinated with the teeming life of the city slums, and found an endless source of subjects in the everyday urban scene, to which they brought the reporter's eye for color and drama. Despite the socialist philosophy that many of them shared, theirs was not an art of social commentary, but one that felt the pulse of city life, discovering in it vitality and richness while ignoring poverty and squalor. To capture these qualities they relied on rapid execution, inspired by Baroque and Post-Impressionist painting, which lends their canvases the immediacy of spontaneous observation.

Bellows. Although not a founding member of the Ash Can school, George Bellows (1882–1925) became a leading representative of the group in its heyday. His masterpiece, *Stag at Sharkey's* (fig. 431), shows why: no painter in America before Jackson Pollock expressed such heroic energy. *Stag at Sharkey's* still reminds us of Eakins' *William Rush Carving His Allegorical Figure of the Schuylkill River* (see fig. 382), for it continues the same Realist tradition. Both place us in the scene as if we were present, and both use the play of light to pick out the figures against a dark background. Bellows' paintings were fully as

431. George Bellows. *Stag at Sharkey's*. 1909. Oil on canvas, 36¼ × 48¼″ (92.1 × 122.6 cm). The Cleveland Museum of Art. Hinman B. Hurlbut Collection

shocking as Eakins' had been. Most late-nineteenth-century American artists had all but ignored urban life in favor of landscapes, and compared with these, the subjects and surfaces of the Ash Can pictures had a disturbing rawness.

PAINTING BETWEEN THE WARS

Picasso. The end of World War I unleashed an unprecedented outpouring of art after a four-year creative lull. We begin with Picasso, whose extraordinary genius towers over the period, defying ready categorization. As a Spanish national living in Paris he was not

432. Pablo Picasso. *Three Musicians*. Summer 1921. Oil on canvas, 6′7″ × 7′3¾″ (2 × 2.23 m). Collection, The Museum of Modern Art, New York. Gift of Mrs. Simon Guggenheim Fund

involved in the conflict, unlike many French and German artists who served in the military and even sacrificed their lives. This was a time of quiet experimentation that laid the foundation for Picasso's art of the next several decades. The results did not become fully apparent, however, until the early 1920s, following a period of intensive cultivation. *Three Musicians* (fig. 432) shows the fruit of that labor. It utilizes the "cut-paper style" of Synthetic Cubism so consistently that we cannot tell from the reproduction whether it is painted or pasted.

By now, Picasso was internationally famous. Cubism had spread throughout the Western world. It influenced not only other painters, but also sculptors and even architects. Yet, Picasso himself was already striking out in a new direction. Soon after the invention of Synthetic Cubism, he had begun to do drawings in a realistic manner reminiscent of Ingres, and by 1920 he was working simultaneously in two quite separate styles: the Synthetic Cubism of the *Three Musicians,* and a Neoclassical style of strongly modeled, heavy-bodied figures. To many of his admirers, this seemed a kind of betrayal, but in retrospect the reason for Picasso's double-track performance is clear. Chafing under the limitations of Synthetic Cubism, he wanted to resume contact with the classical tradition, the "art of the museums."

A few years later the two tracks of Picasso's style began to converge into an extraordinary synthesis that was to become the basis of his art. The *Three Dancers* of 1925 (fig. 433) shows how he accomplished this seemingly impossible feat. Structurally, the picture is pure Synthetic Cubism. It even includes painted imitations of specific materials, such as patterned wallpaper and samples of various fabrics cut out with pinking shears. The figures are a wildly fantastic version of a classical scheme (compare the dancers in Matisse's *The Joy of Life,* fig. 416). They are an even more violent assault on convention than the figures in *Les Demoiselles d'Avignon* (see fig. 422). Human anatomy is here simply the raw material for Picasso's incredible inventiveness. Limbs, breasts, and faces are handled with the same sovereign freedom as the fragments of external reality in Braque's *Newspaper, Bottle, Packet of Tobacco (Le Courrier)* (see fig. 424). Their original identity no longer matters. Breasts may turn into eyes, profiles merge with frontal views, shadows become substance, and vice versa, in an endless flow of metamorphoses. They are "visual puns," offering wholly unexpected possibilities of expression: humorous, grotesque, macabre, tragic.

433. Pablo Picasso. *Three Dancers.* 1925. Oil on canvas, 84½ × 56¼" (215 × 142.9 cm). The Tate Gallery, London

Abstraction

Picasso's abandonment of strict Cubism signaled the broad retreat of abstraction after 1920. The utopian ideals associated with modernism, which it embodied, had been largely dashed by "the war to end all wars." The Futurist spirit nevertheless continued to find adherents on both sides of the Atlantic.

434. Fernand Léger. *The City.* 1919. Oil on canvas, 7′7″ × 9′9″ (2.31 × 2.97 m). The Philadelphia Museum of Art. A. E. Gallatin Collection

Léger. Buoyant with optimism and pleasurable excitement, *The City* (fig. 434) by the Frenchman Fernand Léger (1881–1955) conjures up a mechanized utopia. This beautifully controlled industrial landscape is stable without being static, and reflects the clean geometric shapes of modern machinery. In this instance, the term abstraction applies more to the choice of design elements and their manner of combination than to the shapes themselves, since these are "prefabricated" entities, except for the two figures on the staircase.

Demuth. The modern movement in America proved short-lived. One of the few artists to continue working in this vein after World War I was Charles Demuth (1883–1935). A member of the Stieglitz group (see pp. 485–90), he had been friendly with Duchamp and exiled Cubists in New York during World War I. A few years later, influenced by Futurism, he developed a style known as Precisionism to depict urban and industrial architecture. *I Saw the Figure 5 in Gold* (fig. 435) incorporates aspects of all of these movements. The title is taken from a poem by Demuth's friend William Carlos Williams, whose name also forms part of the design, as "Bill," "Carlos," and "W. C. W." In the poem the figure 5 appears on a red fire truck, while in the painting it has become the dominant feature, thrice repeated to reinforce its echo in our memory as the fire truck rushes on through the night.

Mondrian. The most radical abstractionist of our time was a Dutch painter nine years older than Picasso, Piet Mondrian (1872–1944). He arrived in Paris in 1912 as a mature Expressionist in the tradition of Van Gogh and the *Fauves.* Under the impact of Analytic Cubism, his work soon underwent a complete change, and within the next decade Mondrian developed an entirely nonrepresentational style that he called Neo-Plasticism. (The movement as a whole is also known as *De Stijl,* after the Dutch magazine advocating his ideas.) *Composition with Red, Blue, and Yellow* (fig. 436) shows Mondrian's style at its most severe. He restricts his design to horizontals and verticals and his colors to the three primary hues, plus black and white. Every possibility of representation is thereby eliminated, although Mondrian sometimes gave his works such titles as *Trafalgar Square* or *Broadway Boogie Woogie,* which hint at some degree of relationship, however indirect, with observed reality. Unlike Kandinsky, Mondrian did not strive for pure, lyrical emotion. His goal, he asserted, was "pure reality," and he defined this as equilibrium "through the balance of unequal but equivalent oppositions."

Perhaps we can best understand what he meant if we think of his work as "abstract collage" that uses black bands and colored rectangles instead of recognizable fragments of chair caning and newsprint. He was interested solely in relationships and wanted no distracting elements or fortuitous associations. By establishing the "right" relationship among his bands and rectangles, he transforms them as thoroughly as Braque transformed the snippets of pasted paper in *Le Courrier* (see fig. 424). How did he discover the "right" relationship? And how did he determine the shape and number for the bands and rectangles? In Braque's *Le Courrier,* the ingredients are to some extent "given" by chance. Mondrian, apart from his self-imposed rules, constantly faced the dilemma of unlimited possibilities. He could not change

435. Charles Demuth. *I Saw the Figure 5 in Gold.* 1928. Oil on composition board, 36 × 29¾″ (91.4 × 75.6 cm). The Metropolitan Museum of Art, New York. The Alfred Stieglitz Collection, 1949

436. Piet Mondrian. *Composition with Red, Blue, and Yellow.* 1930. Oil on canvas, 20″ (50.8 cm) square. Private collection

the relationship of the bands to the rectangles without changing the bands and rectangles themselves. When we consider his task, we begin to realize its infinite complexity.

Looking at *Composition with Red, Blue, and Yellow* we find that when we measure the various units, only the proportions of the canvas itself are truly rational, an exact square. Mondrian arrived at all the rest "by feel," and must have undergone agonies of trial and error. How often, we wonder, did he change the dimensions of the red rectangle to bring it and the other elements into self-contained equilibrium? Strange as it may seem, Mondrian's exquisite sense for nonsymmetrical balance is so specific that critics well acquainted with his work have no difficulty in distinguishing fakes from genuine pictures. Designers who work with nonfigurative shapes, such as architects and typographers, are likely to be most sensitive to this quality, and Mondrian has had a greater influence on them than on painters (see pp. 475–76).

Fantasy

Dada. Out of anguish over the mechanized mass killing of World War I, a number of artists in New York and Zurich simultaneously launched in protest a movement called Dada (or Dadaism), which then spread to other cities in Germany and France. The term, which means hobbyhorse in French, was reportedly picked at random from a dictionary, and as an infantile, all-purpose word, it perfectly fit the spirit of the movement. Dada has often been called nihilistic, and its declared purpose was indeed to make clear to the public at large that all established values, moral or aesthetic, had been rendered meaningless by the catastrophe of the Great War. During its short life (c. 1915–22) Dada preached nonsense and anti-art with a vengeance, yet Dada was not a completely negative movement. In its calculated irrationality there was also liberation, a voyage into unknown provinces of the creative mind. The only law respected by the Dadaists was that of chance, and the only reality that of their own imaginations.

Ernst. Although their most characteristic art form was the ready-made (see p. 461), the Dadaists adopted the collage technique of

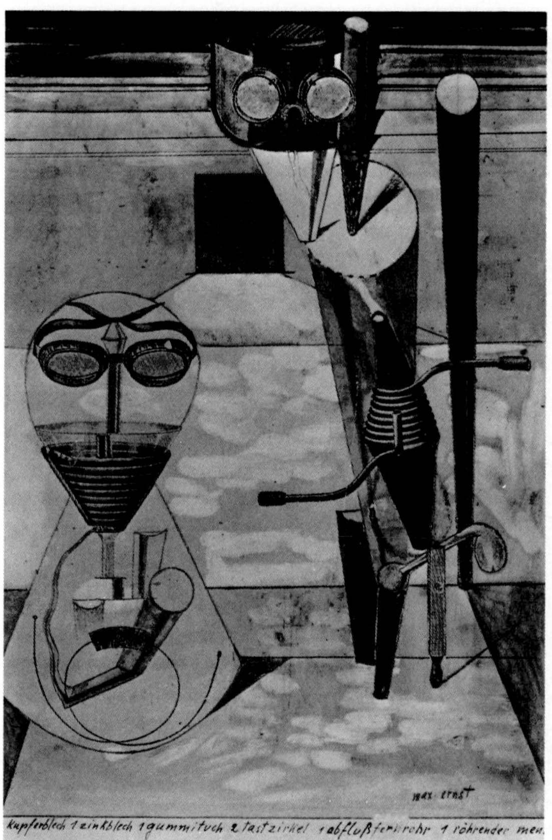

437. Max Ernst. *1 Copper Plate 1 Zinc Plate 1 Rubber Cloth 2 Calipers 1 Drainpipe Telescope 1 Piping Man.* 1920. Collage, 12 × 9″ (30.5 × 22.9 cm). Private collection

Synthetic Cubism for their purposes: figure 437 by the German Dadaist Max Ernst (1891–1976), an associate of Duchamp, is largely composed of snippets from illustrations of machinery. The caption pretends to enumerate these mechanical ingredients which include (or add up to) "1 Piping Man." Actually, there is also a "piping woman." These offspring of Duchamp's prewar *Bride* stare at us blindly through their goggles.

Surrealism. In 1924, after Duchamp's retirement from Dada, a group led by the poet André Breton founded Dada's successor, Surrealism. They defined their aim as "pure psychic automatism . . . intended to express . . . the true process of thought . . . free from the exercise of reason and from any aesthetic or moral purpose." Surrealist theory was heavily larded with concepts borrowed from psychoanalysis, and its overwrought rhetoric is not always to be taken seriously. The notion that a dream can be transposed by "automatic handwriting" directly from the unconscious mind to the canvas, bypassing the conscious awareness of the artist, did not work in practice; some degree of control was simply unavoidable. Nevertheless, Surrealism stimulated several novel techniques for soliciting and exploiting chance effects.

Ernst's Decalcomania. Max Ernst, the most inventive member of the group, often combined collage with "frottage" (rubbings from pieces of wood, pressed flowers, and other relief surfaces—the process we all know from the children's pastime of rubbing with a pencil on a piece of paper covering, say, a coin). He also obtained fascinating shapes and textures by "decalcomania" (the transfer, by pressure, of oil paint to the canvas from some other surface). In *The Attirement of the Bride*

438. Max Ernst. *The Attirement of the Bride.* 1940. Oil on canvas, 51 × 37⅞″ (129.5 × 96.2 cm). Peggy Guggenheim Collection, Venice

439. Joan Miró. *Painting*. 1933. Oil on canvas, 51¼ × 64" (130.2 × 161.3 cm). Wadsworth Atheneum, Hartford, Connecticut. © Wadsworth Atheneum. Ella Gallup Sumner and Mary Catlin Sumner Collection

(fig. 438), Ernst certainly found an extraordinary wealth of images to elaborate on among his stains. The end result has some of the qualities of a dream, but it is a dream born of a strikingly romantic imagination (compare Moreau's *The Apparition*, fig. 397).

Miró. Surrealism, however, has a more boldly imaginative branch. Some works by Picasso, such as *Three Dancers* (see fig. 433), have affinities with it, and its greatest exponent was also Spanish: Joan Miró (1893–1983), who painted the striking *Painting* (fig. 439). His style has been labeled "biomorphic abstraction," since his designs are fluid and curvilinear, like organic forms, rather than geometric. Actually, "biomorphic concretion" might be a more suitable name, for the shapes in Miró's pictures have their own vigorous life. They seem to change before our eyes, expanding and contracting like amoebas until they approach human individuality closely enough to please the artist. Their spontaneous "becoming" is the very opposite of abstraction as we defined it above (see pp. 420–21), though Miró's formal discipline is no less rigorous than that of Cubism—in fact, he began as a Cubist.

Klee. The German-Swiss painter Paul Klee (1879–1940), too, had been influenced by Cubism, but ethnographic art and the drawings of small children held an equally vital interest for him. During World War I, he molded these disparate elements into a pictorial language of his own, marvelously eco-

440. Paul Klee. *Twittering Machine.* 1922. Watercolor and pen and ink on oil transfer drawing on paper, mounted on cardboard, $25\frac{1}{4} \times 19''$ (63.8 × 48 cm). Collection, The Museum of Modern Art, New York. Purchase

nomical and precise. *Twittering Machine* (fig. 440), a delicate pen drawing tinted with watercolor, demonstrates the unique flavor of Klee's art. With a few simple lines, he had created a ghostly mechanism that imitates the sound of birds, simultaneously mocking our faith in the miracles of the machine age and our sentimental appreciation of birdsong. The little contraption is not without its sinister aspect: the heads of the four sham birds look like fishermen's lures, as if they might entrap real birds. It thus condenses into one striking invention a complex of ideas about present-day civilization.

The title has an indispensable role. It is characteristic of the way Klee worked that the picture itself, however visually appealing, does not reveal its full evocative quality unless the artist tells us what it means. The title, in turn, needs the picture: the witty concept of a twittering machine does not kindle our imagination until we are shown such a thing. This interdependence is familiar to us from cartoons. Klee lifts it to the level of high art without relinquishing the playful character of these verbal-visual puns. To him art was a language of signs, of shapes that are images of ideas as the shape of a letter is the image of a specific sound, or an arrow the image of the command, "This way only." He also realized that in any conventional system the sign is no more than a "trigger." The instant we perceive it, we automatically invest it with meaning, without stopping to ponder its shape. Klee wanted his signs to impinge upon our awareness as visual facts, yet also to share the quality of "triggers."

Expressionism

Grosz. The experience of World War I filled German artists with a deep anguish at the

441. George Grosz. *Germany, A Winter's Tale.* 1918. Formerly Collection Garvens, Hanover, Germany

state of modern civilization, which found its principal outlet in Expressionism. George Grosz (1893–1959), a painter and graphic artist, studied in Paris in 1913, then joined Dadaism in Berlin after the end of the war. Inspired by the Futurists, he used a dynamized form of Cubism to develop a bitter, savagely satiric manner that expressed the disillusionment of his generation. In *Germany, A Winter's Tale* (fig. 441), the city of Berlin forms the kaleidoscopic and chaotic background for several large figures, which are superimposed on it as in a collage: the marionettelike "good citizen" at his table, and the sinister forces that molded him (a hypocritical clergyman, a general, and a schoolmaster).

Beckmann. Max Beckmann (1884–1950), a robust descendant of the *Brücke* artists, did not become an Expressionist until after he had lived through World War I. In his triptych *Departure* (fig. 442), completed when he was at the point of leaving his homeland under Nazi pressure, the two wings show a nightmarish world crammed with puppetlike figures, as disquieting as those in Bosch's *Hell* (see fig. 194). Its symbolism, however, is even more difficult to interpret, since it is necessarily subjective. In the hindsight of today, the topsy-turvy quality of these two scenes, full of mutilations and meaningless rituals, has acquired the force of prophecy. The stable design of the center panel, in contrast, with its expanse of blue sea and its sunlit brightness, conveys the hopeful spirit of an embarkation for distant shores. After living through World War II in occupied Holland, under the most trying conditions, Beckmann spent the final three years of his life in America.

442. Max Beckmann. *Departure.* 1932–33. Triptych, oil on canvas, center panel 84¾ × 45⅜" (215.3 × 115.3 cm), side panels each 84¾ × 39¼" (215.3 × 99.7 cm). Collection, The Museum of Modern Art, New York. Given anonymously (by exchange)

Realism

O'Keeffe. After 1920 in the United States, most of the original members of the Stieglitz group concentrated on landscapes, which they treated in representational styles derived loosely from Expressionism. The naturalism that characterized American art as a whole during the 1920s found its most important representative in Georgia O'Keeffe (1887–1986). Throughout her long career, she covered a wide range of subjects and styles. O'Keeffe practiced a form of organic abstraction indebted to Expressionism; she also adopted the Precisionism of Charles Demuth (see p. 431), so that she is sometimes considered an abstract artist. Her work often combines aspects of both approaches. As she assimilated a subject into her imagination, she would alter and simplify it to convey a personal meaning. Nonetheless, O'Keeffe remained a realist at heart. *Black Iris III* (fig. 443) is the kind of painting for which she is best known. The image is marked by a strong sense of decorative design uniquely her own. The flower, however, is deceptive in its treatment. Observed close up and magnified to large scale, it is transformed into a thinly disguised symbol of female sexuality.

443. Georgia O'Keeffe. *Black Iris III.* 1926. Oil on canvas, 36 × 29⅞" (91.4 × 75.9 cm). The Metropolitan Museum of Art, New York. The Alfred Stieglitz Collection, 1949

American Scene Painting. The 1930s witnessed an even stronger artistic conservatism than the previous decade's, in reaction to the economic depression and social turmoil that gripped both Europe and the United States. The dominance of realism signaled the retreat of progressive art everywhere. In Germany, where it was known as the New Objectivity, realism was linked to the reassertion of traditional values. Most American artists split into two camps, the Regionalists and the Social Realists. The Regionalists sought to revive idealism by updating the American myth, defined, however, largely in Midwestern terms. In their pictures, the Social Realists captured the dislocation and despair of the Depression era, and were often concerned with social reform. Both movements, although bitterly opposed, drew freely on the Ash Can school (see pp. 428–29).

Hopper. The one artist who appealed to all factions alike, including that of the few remaining modernists, was a former pupil of Robert Henri, Edward Hopper (1882–1967). He focused on what has since become known as the "vernacular architecture" of American cities—storefronts, movie houses, all-night diners—which no one else had thought worthy of an artist's attention. *Early Sunday Morning* (fig. 444) distills a haunting sense of loneliness from the all-too-familiar elements of an ordinary street. Its quietness, we realize, is temporary. There is hidden life behind these facades. We almost expect to see one of the window shades raised as we look at them. Apart from its poetic appeal, the picture shows an impressive formal discipline. We note the strategy in placing the fireplug and barber pole, the subtle variations in the treatment of the row of windows, the precisely calculated slant of sunlight, the delicate balance of verticals and horizontals. Obviously, Hopper was not unaware of Mondrian.

444. Edward Hopper. *Early Sunday Morning*. 1930. Oil on canvas, 35 × 60″ (88.9 × 152.4 cm). Whitney Museum of American Art, New York. Purchase with funds from Gertrude Vanderbilt Whitney.

PAINTING SINCE WORLD WAR II

Abstract Expressionism: Action Painting

The term Abstract Expressionism is often applied to the style of painting that prevailed for about a dozen years following the end of World War II. It was initiated by artists living in New York City partly in reaction to the anxiety brought on by the nuclear age and the cold war. Under the influence of existentialist philosophy, Action painters, the first of the Abstract Expressionists, developed from Surrealism a new approach to art. Painting became a counterpart to life itself, an ongoing process in which artists face comparable risks and overcome the dilemmas confronting them through a series of conscious and unconscious decisions in response to both inner and external demands. The Color Field painters coalesced the frenetic gestures and violent hues of the Action painters into broad forms of poetic color that partly reflect the spirituality of Oriental mysticism. In a sense, Color Field painting resolved the conflicts expressed by Action painting. They are, however, two sides of the same coin, separated by the thinnest differences of approach.

Gorky. Arshile Gorky (1904–1948), an Armenian who came to America at sixteen, was the pioneer of the movement and the single most important influence on its other members. It took him twenty years to arrive at his mature style, painting first in the vein of Cézanne, then in that of Picasso. We see it in *The Liver Is the Cock's Comb* (fig. 445), his greatest work. The enigmatic title suggests Gorky's close contact with the poet André Breton and other Surrealists who found refuge in New York during the war. Distraught by the carnage, which threatened the very existence of civilization, the early Abstract Expressionists were mythmakers who sought to evoke archetypal images that expressed their sense of impending disaster. Gorky developed a personal mythology that underlies his work; each form represents a private symbol within this hermetic realm. Everything here is in the pro-

445. Arshile Gorky. *The Liver Is the Cock's Comb.* 1944. Oil on canvas, 6′1¼″ × 8′2″ (1.86 × 2.49 m). The Albright-Knox Art Gallery, Buffalo, New York. Gift of Seymour H. Knox, 1956

cess of turning into something else. The treatment reflects his own experience in camouflage, gained from a class he conducted earlier. The biomorphic shapes clearly owe much to Miró, while their spontaneous handling and the glowing color reflect Gorky's enthusiasm for Kandinsky (see figs. 439, 420). Yet the dynamic interlocking of the forms, their aggressive power of attraction and repulsion, are uniquely his own.

Pollock. The most important of the Action painters proved to be Jackson Pollock (1912–1956). His huge canvas entitled *Autumnal Rhythm: Number 30, 1950* (fig. 446) was executed mainly by pouring and spattering the colors, instead of applying them with the brush. The result, especially when viewed at close range, suggests both Kandinsky and Max Ernst (compare figs. 420, 438). Kandinsky's nonrepresentational Expressionism and the Surrealists' exploitation of chance effects are indeed the main sources of Pollock's work, but they do not sufficiently account for his revolutionary technique and the emotional appeal of his art. Why did Pollock "fling a pot of paint in the public's face," as Ruskin had accused Whistler of doing? It was surely not to be more abstract than his predecessors, for the strict control implied by abstraction is exactly what Pollock relinquished when he began to dribble and spatter. Rather, he came to regard paint itself not as a passive substance to be manipulated at will but as a storehouse of pent-up forces for him to release.

The actual shapes visible in our illustration are largely determined by the internal dynamics of his material and his process: the viscosity of the paint, the speed and direction

446. Jackson Pollock. *Autumnal Rhythm: Number 30, 1950.* 1950. Oil on canvas, 8′8″ × 17′3″ (2.64 × 5.26 m). The Metropolitan Museum of Art, New York. George A. Hearn Fund, 1957

447. Lee Krasner. *Celebration.* 1959–60. Oil on canvas, 7′8¼″ × 16′4½″ (2.34 × 4.99 m). Private collection. Courtesy Robert Miller Gallery, New York

of its impact upon the canvas, its interaction with other layers of pigment. The result is a surface so alive, so sensuously rich, that all earlier painting looks pallid in comparison. When he "aims" the paint at the canvas instead of "carrying" it on the tip of his brush—or, if you will, releases the forces within the paint by giving it a momentum of its own—Pollock does not simply "let go" and leave the rest to chance. He is himself the ultimate source of energy for these forces, and he "rides" them as a cowboy might ride a wild horse, in a frenzy of psychophysical action. He does not always stay in the saddle; yet the exhilaration of this contest, which strains every fiber of his being, is well worth the risk. Our simile, though crude, points up the main difference between Pollock and his prede-

cessors: his total commitment to the act of painting. Hence his preference for huge canvases that provide a "field of combat" large enough for him to paint not merely with his arms, but with the motion of his whole body.

The term Action painting conveys the essence of this approach far better than does Abstract Expressionism. To those who complain that Pollock was not sufficiently in control of his medium, we reply that this loss is more than offset by a gain—the new continuity and expansiveness of the creative process that gave his work its distinctive mid-twentieth-century stamp. Pollock's drip technique, however, was not in itself essential to Action painting, and he stopped using it in 1953.

Krasner. Lee Krasner (1908–1984), who was married to Pollock, never abandoned the brush. Although Krasner and Pollock clearly influenced each other, she struggled to establish her artistic identity, and emerged from his long shadow only after undergoing several changes in direction and destroying much of her early work. After Pollock's death, she succeeded in doing what he had been attempting to do for the last three years of his life: to reintroduce the figure into Abstract Expressionism while retaining its automatic handwriting. The potential had always been there in Pollock's work; in *Autumnal Rhythm,* we can easily imagine wildly dancing people. In *Celebration* (fig. 447), Krasner defines these nascent shapes from within the tangled network of lines by using the broad gestures of Action painting to suggest human forms without actually depicting them.

De Kooning. The work of Willem de Kooning (born 1904), another prominent member of the group and a close friend of Gorky, always retains a link with the world of images, whether or not it has a recognizable subject. In some paintings, the image emerges from the jagged welter of brushstrokes. De Kooning has in common with Pollock his furious energy, the sense of risk, of a challenge successfully—but barely—met. What are we to make of his wildly distorted *Woman II*

448. Willem de Kooning. *Woman II.* 1952. Oil on canvas, 59 × 43" (149.9 × 109.3 cm). Collection, The Museum of Modern Art, New York. Gift of Mrs. John D. Rockefeller 3rd

(fig. 448)? It is as if the flow of psychic impulses in the process of painting has unleashed this nightmarish specter from deep within the artist's subconscious. For that reason, he has sometimes been accused of being a woman-hater, a charge he denies. Rather, she is like a primordial goddess, cruel yet seductive, who represents the dark, primitive side of our makeup.

Expressionism in Europe

Action painting marked the international coming-of-age for American art. The movement had a powerful impact on European art, which in those years had nothing to show of comparable force and conviction. One French artist, however, was of such prodigal originality as to constitute a movement all by himself: Jean Dubuffet, whose first exhibition soon after the Liberation electrified and antagonized the art world of Paris.

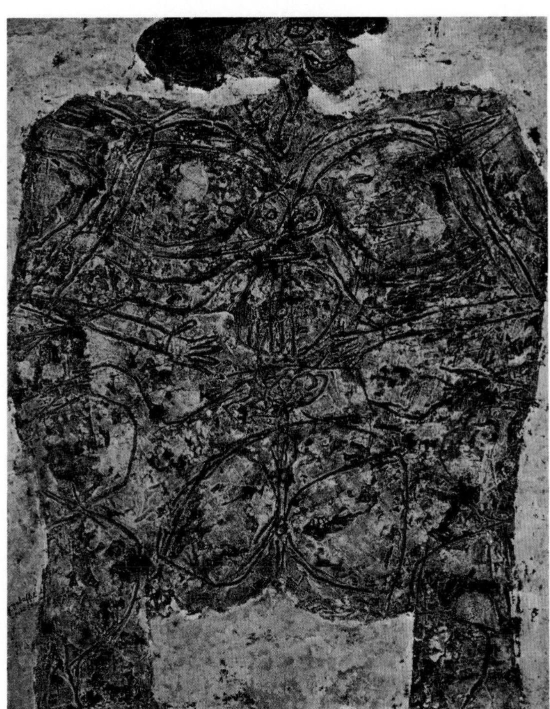

449. Jean Dubuffet. *Le Métafisyx (Corps de dames).* 1950. 45¾×35¼″ (116.2×89.5 cm). Private collection

Dubuffet. As a young man Dubuffet (1901–1985) had formal instruction in painting, but he responded to none of the various trends he saw around him nor to the art of the museums. All struck him as divorced from real life, and he turned to other pursuits. Only in middle age did he experience the breakthrough that permitted him to discover his creative gifts. Dubuffet suddenly realized that for him true art had to come from outside the ideas and traditions of the artistic elite, and he found inspiration in the art of children and the insane. The distinction between "normal" and "abnormal" struck him as no more tenable than established notions of "beauty" and "ugliness." Not since Marcel Duchamp (see pp. 427–28) had anyone ventured so radical a critique of the nature of art.

Dubuffet made himself the champion of what he called *l'art brut*, "art-in-the-raw," but he created something of a paradox besides. While extolling the directness and spontaneity of the amateur as against the refinement of professional artists, he became a professional artist himself. Whereas Duchamp's questioning of established values had led him to cease artistic activity altogether, Dubuffet became incredibly prolific, second only to Picasso in output. Compared with Paul Klee, who had first utilized the style of children's drawings (see pp. 434–35), Dubuffet's art is "raw" indeed. Its stark immediacy, its explosive, defiant presence, are the opposite of the older painter's formal discipline and economy of means. Did Dubuffet perhaps fall into a trap of his own making? If his work merely imitated the *art brut* of children and the insane, would not these self-chosen conventions limit him as much as those of the artistic elite?

We may be tempted to think so at our first sight of *Le Métafisyx* (fig. 449) from his *Corps de dames* series—even De Kooning's wildly distorted *Woman II* (see fig. 448) seems gentle when matched against this shocking assault on our inherited sensibilities. The paint is as heavy and opaque as a rough coating of plaster, and the lines articulating the blocklike body are scratched into the surface like graffiti made by an untrained hand. Appearances can deceive, however. The fury and concentration of Dubuffet's attack should convince us that his demonic female is not "something any child can do." In an eloquent statement the artist has explained the purpose of images such as this: "The female body . . . has long . . . been associated with a very specious notion of beauty which I find miserable and most depressing. Surely I am for beauty, but not that one. . . . I intend to sweep away everything we have been taught to consider—without question—as grace and beauty [and to] substitute another and vaster beauty, touching all objects and beings, not excluding the most despised. . . ."

Color Field Painting

By the late 1940s, a number of artists began to transform Action painting into the style called Color Field painting, in which the can-

450. Mark Rothko. *Ochre and Red on Red.* 1954. Oil on canvas, 7′8⅝″×5′3¾″ (2.36×1.62 m). The Phillips Collection, Washington, D.C.

vas is stained with thin, translucent color washes. These may be oil or even ink, but the favored material quickly became acrylic, a plastic suspended in a polymer resin, which can be thinned with water so that it flows freely.

Rothko. In the mid-1940s Mark Rothko (1903–1970) worked in a style derived from Gorky, but within less than a decade he subdued the aggressiveness of Action painting so completely that his pictures breathe the purest contemplative stillness. *Ochre and Red on Red* (fig. 450) consists of two rectangles with blurred edges on a dark red ground. The pink "halo" around the lower rectangle seems to immerse it in the red ground, while the yellow rectangle stands out more assertively in front of the red. The thin washes of paint permit the texture of the cloth to be seen through the very large canvas. This description hardly begins to touch the essence of the work or the reasons for its mysterious power to move us. These are to be found in the delicate equilibrium of the shapes, their strange interdependence, the subtle variations of hue. Not every beholder responds to the works of this withdrawn, introspective artist. For those who do, the experience is akin to a trancelike rapture.

Louis. Among the most gifted of the Color Field painters was Morris Louis (1912–1962). The successive layers of color in *Blue Veil* (fig. 451) appear to have been "floated on" without visible marks of the brush. Their harmonious interaction creates a delicately shifting balance that gives the picture its mysterious beauty, like the aurora borealis.

Late Abstract Expressionism

Kelly. Many artists who came to maturity in the 1950s turned away from Action painting altogether in favor of hard-edge painting. *Red Blue Green* (fig. 452) by Ellsworth Kelly (born 1923), an early leader of this tendency, abandons Rothko's impressionistic softness. Instead, flat areas of color are circumscribed within carefully delineated forms as part of the formal investigation of color and design problems for their own sake.

451. Morris Louis. *Blue Veil.* 1958–59. Acrylic resin paint on canvas, 8′4½″ × 12′5″ (2.65 × 3.79 m). Fogg Art Museum, Harvard University Art Museums, Cambridge, Massachusetts. Gift of Lois Orswell and Gifts for Special Uses Fund

452. Ellsworth Kelly. *Red Blue Green.* 1963. Oil on canvas, 6′11⅝″ × 11′3⅞″ (2.12 × 3.43 m). Collection San Diego Museum of Contemporary Art. Gift of Dr. and Mrs. Jack M. Farris

Stella. The brilliant and precocious Frank Stella (born 1936) began as an admirer of Mondrian, then soon evolved a nonfigurative style that was even more self-contained. Unlike Mondrian (see pp. 431–32), Stella did not concern himself with the vertical-horizontal balance that relates the older artist's work to the world of nature. Logically enough, he also abandoned the traditional rectangular format, so as to make quite sure that his pictures bore no resemblance to windows. The shape of the canvas had now become an integral part of the design. In one of his largest works, the majestic *Empress of India* (fig. 453), this shape is determined by the thrust and counterthrust of four huge chevrons, identical in size and shape but sharply differentiated in color and in their relationship to the

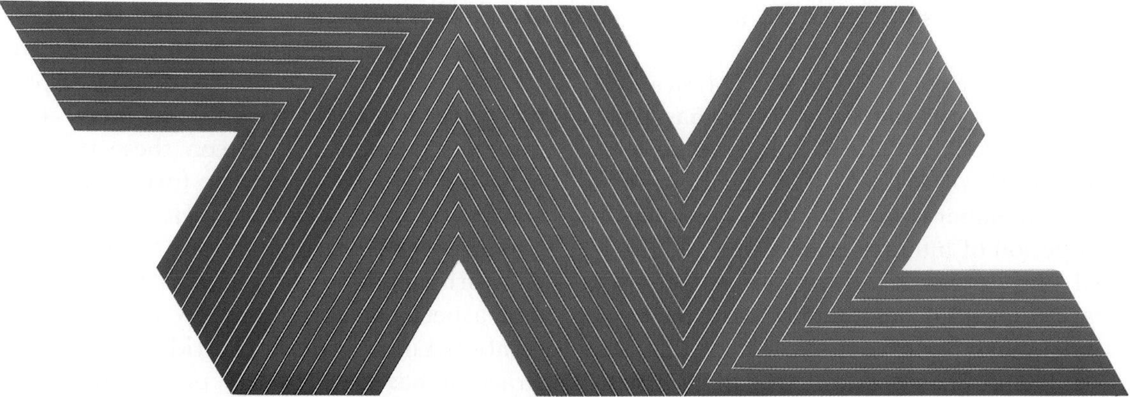

453. Frank Stella. *Empress of India.* 1965. Metallic powder in polymer emulsion on shaped canvas, 6′5″ × 18′8″ (1.96 × 5.49 m). Collection, The Museum of Modern Art, New York. Gift of S. I. Newhouse, Jr.

454. William T. Williams. *Batman.* 1979. Acrylic on canvas, 80 × 60" (203.2 × 152.4 cm). Collection the artist

whole. The paint, moreover, contains powdered metal, which gives it an iridescent sheen. This is yet another way to stress the impersonal precision of the surfaces and to remove the work from any comparison with the "handmade" look of easel pictures. In fact, to speak of *Empress of India* as a picture seems decidedly awkward. It demands to be called an object, sufficient unto itself.

Williams. The contribution of the lyrical Expressionists from the early 1970s has been largely overlooked. Their legacy can be seen in the work of William T. Williams (born 1942), a member of this "lost" generation. After a period of intense self-scrutiny, he developed the sophisticated technique seen in *Batman* (fig. 454). His method can be compared to jazz improvisation, a debt that the artist himself has acknowledged. He interweaves his color and brushwork within a clear two-part structure that permits endless variations on the central theme. Although Williams is concerned primarily with formal issues, the play of color and abstract shapes across the encrusted surface further evokes the patterns, light, and space of nature. But instead of depicting a landscape, the painting seemingly captures, albeit unconsciously, an evanescent memory of the artist's past.

Williams belongs to the generation of African Americans born around 1940 who have brought black painting and sculpture to artistic maturity. In the 1920s, the Harlem Renaissance had produced a cultural revival that unfortunately was short-lived, its promise dashed by the economic catastrophe of the Depression. Following World War II, however, blacks began to attend art schools in growing numbers, at the very time that Abstract Expressionism marked the coming of age of American art. The civil rights movement helped blacks establish their artistic identities and find appropriate styles for expressing them. The turning point proved to be the assassinations of Malcolm X in 1965 and Martin Luther King, Jr., in 1968, which provoked an outpouring of African American art.

Since then, black artists have pursued three major tendencies. Mainstream Abstractionists, particularly those of the older generation, tend to be concerned primarily with seeking a personal aesthetic, maintaining that there is no such thing as African American, or black, art, only good art. Consequently, they have been denounced by activist artists who, stirred by social consciousness as well as by political ideology, have adopted highly expressive representational styles as the means for communicating a distinctive black perspective directly to the people in their communities. Mediating between these two approaches is a very decorative form of art that frequently incorporates African, Caribbean, and sometimes Mexican motifs. No hard-and-fast principles separate these alternatives, and aspects of each have been successfully combined into separate individual styles. Abstraction has nevertheless proved the most fruitful path, for it has opened up avenues of expression that allow the black artist, however

455. Victor Vasarely. *Vega.* 1957. 77×51" (195.6×129.5 cm). Collection the artist

private his or her concerns may be, to achieve a universal, not only an ethnic, appeal.

Op Art

Another trend that gathered force in the mid-1950s was known as Op Art because of its concern with optics: the physical and psychological process of vision. Op Art is devoted primarily to optical illusions. Needless to say, all representational art from the Old Stone Age onward has been involved with optical illusion in one sense or another. What is new about Op Art is that it is rigorously nonrepresentational. It evolved partly from hard-edge abstraction, although its ancestry can be traced back still further to Mondrian (see pp. 431–32). At the same time, it seeks to extend the realm of optical illusion in every possible way by taking advantage of the new materials and processes constantly supplied by science, including laser technology. Much Op Art consists of constructions or "environments" (see pp. 467–72) that are dependent for their effect on light and motion and cannot be reproduced satisfactorily in a book.

Because of its reliance on science and technology, Op Art's possibilities appear to be unlimited. The movement nevertheless matured within a decade of its inception and developed little thereafter. The difficulty lies primarily with its subject. Op Art seems overly cerebral and systematic, more akin to the sciences than to the humanities. And although its effects are undeniably fascinating, they encompass a relatively narrow range of concerns that lie for the most part outside the mainstream of modern art. Only a handful of artists have enriched it with the variety and expressiveness necessary to make it a viable tradition.

Vasarely. Victor Vasarely (born 1908), a Hungarian residing in France, has been Op

456. Richard Anuszkiewicz. *Entrance to Green.* 1970. Acrylic on canvas, 9×6' (2.74×1.83 m). Collection the artist

Art's chief theoretician as well as its most inventive practitioner. Much of his work is in stark black and white, such as the large canvas *Vega* (fig. 455), named after the brightest star in the Lyra constellation. It is a huge checkerboard whose regularity has been disturbed by bending the lines that make the squares. But since many of these squares have been subjected to distortion, their sizes vary considerably. As a consequence, no matter what our viewing distance, our eyes receive contradictory data. The picture thus practically forces us to move back and forth, and as we do so, the field itself seems to move, expanding, undulating, contracting. If *Vega* were a three-dimensional object, the variety of effects would be greater still.

Anuszkiewicz. Op Art involves the beholder with the work of art in a novel, dynamic way. Josef Albers, who came to America after 1933, when Hitler closed the Bauhaus school at Dessau (see p. 477), became the founder of another, more austere kind of Op Art based on subtle color relations among simple geometric shapes. His gifted pupil Richard Anuszkiewicz (born 1930) developed his art by relaxing Albers' self-imposed restrictions. In *Entrance to Green* (fig. 456), the ever-decreasing series of rectangles creates a sense of infinite recession toward the center. This is counterbalanced by the color pattern, which brings the center close to us by the gradual shift from cool to warm tones as we move inward from the periphery. Surprising for such an avowedly theoretical work is its expressive intensity. The resonance of the colors within the strict geometry heightens the optical push-pull, producing an almost mystical power. The painting can be likened to a modern icon, capable of providing a deeply moving experience to those attuned to its vision.

Pop Art

Other artists who made a name for themselves in the mid-1950s rediscovered what the layperson continued to take for granted despite all efforts to persuade otherwise: that

457. Jasper Johns. *Three Flags.* 1958. Encaustic on canvas, 30⅞ × 45½ × 5″ (78.4 × 115.6 × 12.7 cm). Whitney Museum of American Art, New York. 50th Anniversary Gift of the Gilman Foundation, Inc., The Lauder Foundation, A. Alfred Taubman, an anonymous donor, and purchase

a picture is not "essentially a flat surface covered with colors," as Maurice Denis had insisted, but an image wanting to be recognized. If art was by its very nature representational, then the modern movement, from Manet to Pollock, was based on a fallacy, no matter how impressive its achievements. Painting, it seemed, had been on a kind of voluntary starvation diet for the past hundred years, feeding on itself rather than on the world around us. It was time for the artist to give in to this "image hunger"—a hunger from which the public at large had never suffered, since its demand for images was abundantly supplied by photography, advertising, magazine illustrations, and comic strips.

The artists who felt this way seized on these products of commercial art catering to popular taste. Here, they realized, was an essential aspect of our century's visual environment that had been entirely disregarded as vulgar and antiaesthetic by the representatives of highbrow culture, a presence that cried out to be examined. Only Marcel Duchamp and some of the Dadaists, with their contempt for all orthodox opinion, had dared to penetrate this realm (see p. 432). It was they who now became the patron saints of Pop Art, as the new movement came to be called.

Pop Art actually began in London in the mid-1950s with the Independent Group of artists and intellectuals. They were fascinated by the impact on British life of the American mass media, which had been flooding England ever since the end of World War II. It is not surprising that the new art had a special appeal for America, and that it reached its fullest development there during the following decade. In retrospect, Pop Art in the United States was an expression of the optimistic spirit of the 1960s that began with the election of John F. Kennedy and ended at the height of the Vietnam War. Unlike Dada, Pop Art was not motivated by despair or disgust at contemporary civilization. It viewed commercial culture as its raw material, an endless source of pictorial subject matter, rather than as an evil to be attacked. Nor did Pop Art share Dada's aggressive attitude toward the established values of modern art.

Johns. Jasper Johns (born 1930), one of the pioneers of Pop Art in America, began by painting, meticulously and with great precision, such familiar objects as flags, targets, numerals, and maps. His *Three Flags* (fig. 457) presents an intriguing problem: just what is the difference between image and reality? We instantly recognize the Stars and Stripes, but if we try to define what we actually see here, we find that the answer eludes us. These flags behave "unnaturally." Instead of waving or flopping they stand at attention, rigidly aligned with each other in a kind of reverse perspective. There is movement of another sort as well: the reds, whites, and blues are not areas of solid color but are subtly modulated. Can we really say, then, that this is an image of three flags? Clearly, no such flags can exist anywhere except in the artist's head. The more we think about it, the more we marvel at the picture as a feat of the imagination, which is probably the last thing we expected to do when we first looked at it.

Lichtenstein. Roy Lichtenstein (born 1923) has seized on comic strips—or, more precisely, on the standardized imagery of the traditional strips devoted to violent action and sentimental love, rather than those bearing the stamp of an individual creator. His paintings, such as *Girl at Piano* (fig. 458), are greatly enlarged copies of single frames, including the balloons, the impersonal, simplified black outlines, and the dots used for printing colors on cheap paper.

These pictures are perhaps the most paradoxical in the entire field of Pop Art. Unlike any other paintings past or present, they cannot be accurately reproduced in this book, for they then become indistinguishable from the comic strip on which they are based. Enlarging a design meant for an area about six square inches to one no less than 3,264 square inches must have given rise to a host of formal problems that could be solved only by the most intense scrutiny: how, for example, to draw the girl's nose so it would look "right" in comic-strip terms, or how to space the colored dots so they would have the proper weight in relation to the outlines.

458. Roy Lichtenstein. *Girl at Piano.* 1963. Magna on canvas, 68×48″ (172.7×121.9 cm). Private collection

Clearly, our picture is not a mechanical copy, but an interpretation which remains faithful to the spirit of the original only because of the countless changes and adjustments of detail that the artist has introduced. How is it possible for images of this sort to be so instantly recognizable? Why are they so "real" to millions of people? What fascinates Lichtenstein about comic strips, and what he makes us see for the first time, are the rigid conventions of their style, as firmly set and as remote from life as those of Byzantine art.

Warhol. An artist who seized on this very quality was Andy Warhol (1928–1987), who used it in ironic commentaries on modern society. A former commercial artist, he made the viewer consider the aesthetic qualities of everyday images, such as soup cans, that we readily overlook. He did much the same thing with the subject of death, an obsession of his, in silk-screened pictures of electric chairs and gruesome traffic accidents, which demonstrate that dying has been reduced to a banality by the mass media. Warhol had an uncanny understanding of how the media shape our view of people and events, creating their own reality and larger-than-life figures. He became a master at manipulating the media to project a public persona that disguised his true character. These themes come together in his *Gold Marilyn Monroe* (fig. 459). Set against a gold background like a Byzantine icon, she becomes a modern-day Madonna (can it be a coincidence that a Marilyn look-alike singer uses only Madonna as her stage name?). Yet Warhol conveys a sense of the tragic personality that lay behind the famous movie star's glamorous facade. The color, lurid and off-register like a sleazy magazine reproduction's, makes us realize that

459. Andy Warhol. *Gold Marilyn Monroe.* 1962. Synthetic polymer paint, silk-screened, and oil on canvas, 6′11¼″×4′7″ (2.11×1.45 m). Collection, The Museum of Modern Art, New York. Gift of Philip Johnson

she has been reduced to a cheap commodity. Through mechanical means, she is rendered as impersonal as the Virgin that stares out from the thousands of icons produced by hack artists through the ages.

Photorealism. Although Pop Art was sometimes referred to as "the new realism," the term hardly seems to fit the painters we have discussed. They are, to be sure, sharply observant of their sources. However, their chosen material is itself rather abstract: flags, numerals, lettering, signs, badges, comic strips. A more recent offshoot of Pop Art is the trend called Photorealism because of its fascination with camera images. Photographs had been utilized by nineteenth-century painters soon after the "pencil of nature" was invented (one of the earliest to do so, surprisingly, was Delacroix), but they were no more than a convenient substitute for reality. For the Photorealists, in contrast, the photograph itself is the reality on which they build their pictures.

Eddy. Their work often has a visual complexity that challenges the most acute observer. *New Shoes for H* (fig. 460) by Don Eddy (born 1944) shows Photorealism at its best. Eddy grew up in southern California. As a teenager he learned to do fancy paint jobs on cars and surfboards with an airbrush, then worked as a photographer for several years. When he became a painter, he used both earlier skills. In preparing *New Shoes for H,* Eddy took a series of pictures of the window display of a shoe store on Union Square in Manhattan. One photograph (fig. 461) served as the basis for the painting. What intrigued him, clearly, was the way glass filters and transforms everyday reality. Only a narrow strip along the left-hand edge offers an unobstructed view; everything else is seen through two or more layers of glass, all of them at oblique angles to the picture surface. The familiar scene is transformed into a dazzlingly rich and novel visual experience by the combined displacement, distortion, and reflection of these panes.

When we compare the painting with the photograph, we realize that they are related in much the same way as Lichtenstein's *Girl at Piano* (see fig. 458) is to the original comic-strip frame from which it derives. Unlike his photograph, Eddy's canvas shows everything in uniformly sharp focus, articulating details lost in the shadows in the photograph. Most important of all, he gives pictorial coherence

460. Don Eddy. *New Shoes for H.* 1973–74. Acrylic on canvas, 44 × 48" (111.8 × 121.9 cm). The Cleveland Museum of Art. Purchased with a grant from the National Endowment for the Arts, matched by gifts from members of The Cleveland Society for Contemporary Art

461. Don Eddy. Photograph for *New Shoes for H.* 1973. The Cleveland Museum of Art. Gift of the artist

462. Audrey Flack. *Queen.* 1975–76. Acrylic on canvas, 6′8″ (2.03 m) square. Private collection. Courtesy Louis K. Meisel Gallery, New York

to the scene through a brilliant color scheme whose pulsating rhythm plays over the entire surface. At the time he painted *New Shoes for H,* color had become newly important in Eddy's thinking. The H of the title pays homage to Henri Matisse and to Hans Hofmann, an Abstract Expressionist whom Eddy had come to admire.

Photorealism was part of a general tendency that marked American painting in the 1970s: the resurgence of realism. It took on a wide range of themes and techniques, from the most personal to the most detached, depending on the artist's vision of objective reality and its subjective significance. Its flexibility made realism a sensitive vehicle for the feminist movement that came to the fore in the same decade. Beyond the organizing of groups dedicated to a wider recognition for women artists, feminism in art has shown little of the unity that characterizes the social movement. Many feminists, for example, turned to traditional women's crafts, particularly textiles, or incorporated crafts into a collage approach known as Pattern and Decoration. In painting, however, the majority have pursued different forms of realism for a variety of ends.

Flack. Women artists such as Audrey Flack (born 1931) have used realism to explore the world around them and their relation to it from a personal as well as a feminist viewpoint. Like most of Flack's paintings, *Queen* (fig. 462) is an extended allegory. The queen is the most powerful figure on the chessboard, yet she remains expendable in defense of the king. Equally apparent is the meaning inherent to the queen of hearts, but here the card also refers to the passion for gambling in members of Flack's family, who is represented by the locket with photos of the artist and her mother. The contrast of youth and age is central to *Queen*: the watch is a traditional emblem of life's brevity, and the dewy rose stands for transience of beauty, which is further conveyed by the makeup on the dressing table. The suggestive shapes of the bud and fruits can also be taken as symbols of feminine sexuality.

Queen is successful not so much for its provocative statement, however, as for its compelling imagery. Flack creates a purely artistic reality by superimposing two separate photographs. Critical to the illusion is the gray border, which acts as a framing device and also establishes the central space and color of the painting. The objects that seem to project from the picture plane are shown in a different perspective from those on the tilted tabletop behind. The picture space is made all the more active by the play of its colors within the neutral gray.

Post-Modernism

Art since 1980 has been called Post-Modern. The term itself is anomalous: modernity, after all, can never be outdated, because it is simply whatever is contemporary. The word nevertheless suggests the paradoxical nature of the trend, which seeks out incongruity. Post-Modernism is marked by an abiding skepticism that rejects modernism as an ideal defining twentieth-century culture as we have known it. In challenging tradition, however, Post-Modernism resolutely refuses to define a new meaning or impose an alternative order in its place. It represents a generation consciously *not* in search of its identity. Hence, it is not a coherent movement at all, but a loose collection of tendencies which, all told, reflect a new sensibility.

We are, in a sense, the new Victorians. A century ago, Impressionism underwent a like crisis, from which Post-Impressionism emerged as the direction for the next twenty years. Behind its elaborate rhetoric, Post-Modernism can be seen as a stratagem for sorting through the past while making a decisive break with it that will allow new possibilities to emerge. Having received a rich heritage, artists are faced with a wide variety of alternatives. The principal features of the new art are a ubiquitous eclecticism and a bewildering array of styles. Taken together, these pieces provide a jigsaw puzzle of our times. Another indication of the state of flux is the reemergence of many traditional European and regional American art centers.

From all the recent ferment, a new direction in art has begun to appear, at least for the time being. Much recent art has been concerned with appropriation and deconstruction. Appropriation looks back self-consciously to earlier art, both by imitating previous styles and by taking over specific motifs or even entire images. Artists, of course, have always borrowed from tradition, but rarely so systematically as now. Such plundering is nearly always a symptom of deepening cultural crisis, suggesting bankruptcy. The first sign of this historicism actually occurred in the early 1970s with the widespread use of "Neo-" to describe the latest tendencies. Unbound as it is to any system, Post-Modernism is free not only to adopt earlier imagery but also to alter its meaning radically through deconstruction, by placing it in a new context. The traditional importance assigned to the artist and object is deemphasized in this approach, which stresses process over content. Hence, Performance Art (which is discussed with sculpture on pp. 473–74), became perhaps the most characteristic art form of the 1980s.

Clemente. The Italian Francesco Clemente (born 1952) is representative in many respects of his artistic generation. His association with the *Arte Povera* ("Poor Art") movement in Italy led him to develop a potent Neo-Expressionist style. His career took a decisive turn in 1982 when he decided to go to New York in order "to be where the great painters have been," but he also spends much of his time in India, where he has been inspired by Hinduism. His canvases and wall paintings sometimes have an ambitiousness that can assume the form of allegorical cycles addressed directly to the Italian painters who worked on a grand scale, starting with Giotto. His most compelling works, however, are those having as their subject matter the artist's moods, fantasies, and appetites. Clemente is fearless in recording urges and memories

463. Francesco Clemente. *Untitled.* 1983. Oil and wax on canvas, 6′6″ × 7′9″ (1.98 × 2.36 m). Courtesy Thomas Ammann, Zurich

that the rest of us repress. Art becomes for him an act of cathartic necessity that releases, but never resolves, the impulses that assault his acute self-awareness. His self-portraits (fig. 463) suggest a soul bombarded by drives and sensations that can never be truly enjoyed. Alternately fascinating and repellent, his pictures remain curiously unsensual, yet their expressiveness is riveting. Since his work responds to fleeting states of mind, Clemente utilizes whatever style or medium seems appropriate to capturing the transient phenomena of his inner world. He is unusual among Italians in being influenced heavily by Northern European Symbolism and Expressionism with an occasional reminiscence of Surrealism. Here indeed is his vivid nightmare, having the psychological terror of Munch and the haunted vision of De Chirico.

Kiefer. The German artist Anselm Kiefer (born 1945) is the direct heir to Northern Expressionism, but rather than investigating personal moods he confronts moral issues posed by Nazism that have been evaded by other postwar artists in his country. By exploring from a modern perspective the major themes of German Romanticism, he has attempted to reweave the threads broken by history. That tradition, which began as a noble ideal based on a similar longing for the mythical past, ended as a perversion at the hands of Hitler and his followers because it lent itself readily to abuse.

To the Unknown Painter (fig. 464) is a powerful statement of the human and cultural

464. *(opposite above)* Anselm Kiefer. *To the Unknown Painter.* 1983. Oil, emulsion, woodcut, shellac, latex, and straw on canvas, 9′2″ (2.79 m) square. Carnegie Museum of Art, Pittsburgh. Richard M. Scaife Fund; A. W. Mellon Acquisition Endowment Fund

465. *(opposite below)* Elizabeth Murray. *More Than You Know.* 1983. Oil on ten canvases, 9′3″ × 9′ × 8″ (2.82 m × 2.74 m × 20.3 cm). The Edward R. Broida Trust

catastrophe presented by World War II. Conceptually as well as compositionally it was inspired by the paintings of Caspar David Friedrich (see p. 367), of which it is a worthy successor. To express the tragic proportions of the Holocaust, Kiefer works on an appropriately epic scale. Painted in jagged strokes of predominantly earth and black tones, the charred landscape is made tangible by the inclusion of pieces of straw. Amid this destruction stands a somber ruin; it is shown in woodcut to proclaim Kiefer's allegiance to the German Renaissance and to Expressionism. The fortresslike structure is a suitable monument for heroes in recalling the tombs and temples of ancient civilizations (see fig. 31). But instead of being dedicated to soldiers who died in combat, it is a memorial to the painters whose art was equally a casualty of Fascism.

Murray. Neo-Expressionism has a counterpart in Neo-Abstraction, which has yielded less impressive results thus far. The greatest success in the Neo-Abstractionist vein has been achieved by those artists seeking to infuse their formal concerns with the personal meaning of Neo-Expressionism. Elizabeth Murray (born 1940) has emerged since 1980 as the leader of this crossover style in America. *More Than You Know* (fig. 465) makes a fascinating comparison with Audrey Flack's *Queen* (see fig. 462), for both are filled with autobiographical references. While it is at once simpler and more abstract than Flack's, Murray's composition seems about to fly apart under the pressure of barely contained emotions. The table will remind us of the one in Picasso's *Three Musicians* (see fig. 432), a painting she has referred to in other works from the same time. The contradiction between the flattened collage perspective of the table and chair and the allusions to the distorted three-dimensionality of the surrounding room establishes a disquieting pictorial space. The more we look at the painting, the more we begin to realize how eerie it is. Indeed, it seems to radiate an almost unbearable tension. The table threatens to turn into a figure surmounted by a skull-like head that moves with the same explosive force of Picasso's *Three Dancers* (see fig. 433). What was Murray thinking of? She has said that the room reminds her of the place where she sat with her ill mother. At the same time, the demonic face was inspired by Munch's *The Scream* (see fig. 401), while the sheet of paper recalls Vermeer's paintings of women reading letters (see fig. 301), which to her express a combination of serenity and anxiety.

TWENTIETH-CENTURY SCULPTURE

SCULPTURE BEFORE 1945

The three main currents we followed in painting before 1945—Expressionism, Abstraction, and Fantasy—may be found also in sculpture. They are present, however, in different measure. While painting has been the richer and more adventurous of the two arts, sculpture has challenged its leadership by often following a separate path of development.

Brancusi. Expressionism, for instance, is a much less important current in sculpture than in painting. This is rather surprising, since the rediscovery of ethnographic sculpture by the *Fauves* might have been expected to evoke a strong response among sculptors. Only one important sculptor shared in this rediscovery: Constantin Brancusi (1876–1957), a Romanian who went to Paris in 1904. He was more interested in the formal simplicity and coherence of primitive carvings than in their savage expressiveness. This is evident in *The Kiss* (fig. 466), executed in 1909 and now placed over a tomb in a Parisian cemetery. The compactness and self-sufficiency of this group is a radical step beyond Maillol's *Seated Woman* (see fig. 405), to which it is related much as the *Fauves* are to Post-Impressionism. Brancusi has a "genius of omission" not unlike Matisse's. To him, a monument is an upright slab, symmetrical and immobile—a permanent marker, like the steles of the ancients—and he disturbs this basic shape as little as possible. The embracing lovers are differentiated just enough to be separately identifiable, and seem more primeval than primitive. They are a timeless symbol of generation, innocent and anonymous.

466. Constantin Brancusi. *The Kiss*. 1909. Stone, height 35¼″ (89.5 cm). Tomb of T. Rachevskaia, Montparnasse Cemetery, Paris

Moore. Brancusi's "primevalism" was the starting point of a sculptural tradition that still continues today. It has appealed particularly to English sculptors, as we may see in the early works of Henry Moore (1898–1986).

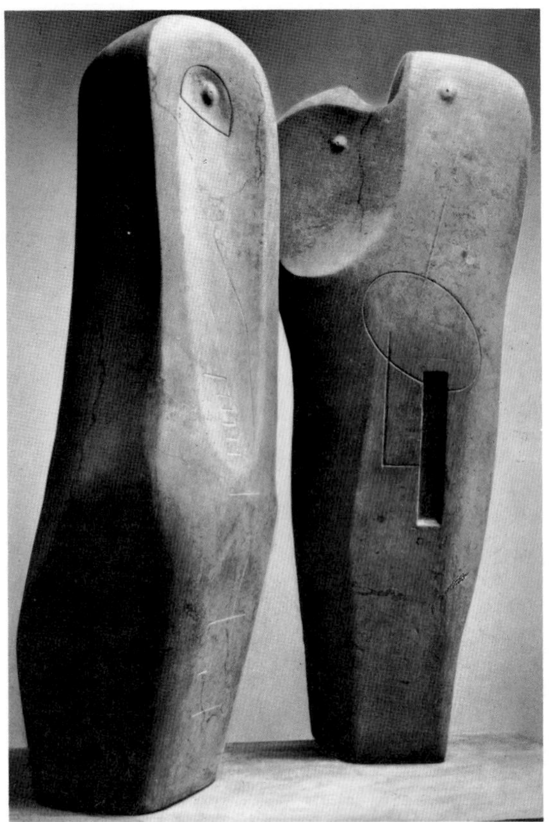

467. Henry Moore. *Two Forms.* 1936. Stone, height c. 42″ (106.7 cm). Philadelphia Museum of Art. Gift of Mrs. H. Gates Lloyd

468. Barbara Hepworth. *Sculpture with Color (Oval Form), Pale Blue and Red.* 1943. Wood with strings, length 18″ (45.7 cm). Private collection

His majestic *Two Forms* of 1936 (fig. 467) are the second-generation offspring of Brancusi's *The Kiss.* More abstract and subtle in shape, they are nevertheless "persons," even though they can be called "images" only in the metaphoric sense. This family group (the forked slab evolved from the artist's studies of the mother-and-child theme) is mysterious and remote like the monoliths of Stonehenge, which greatly impressed the sculptor (see figs. 21, 22).

Hepworth. Barbara Hepworth (1903–1975), for long the preeminent woman sculptor of modern times, was closely associated with Moore during the early 1930s. They became leaders of the modern movement in England and influenced one another. Like Moore's, her sculpture had a biological foundation. With the beginning of World War II, she initiated an individual style that emerged fully in 1943. *Sculpture with Color (Oval Form)* flawlessly synthesizes painting and sculpture, Surrealist biomorphism and organic abstraction, and the molding of space and shaping of mass (fig. 468). Carved from wood and immaculately finished, Hepworth's sculpture reduces the natural shape of an egg to a timeless ideal that has the lucid perfection of a classical head, yet the elemental expressiveness of the face of a primitive mask (compare fig. 24). The colors accentuate the play between the interior and exterior of the hollowed-out form, while the strings seem to suggest a life force within.

Brancusi's *Bird in Space.* Hepworth's egg undoubtedly owes something to Brancusi, although their work is very different in appearance. Brancusi's work had taken another daring step in about 1910, when he began to produce nonrepresentational pieces in marble or metal. (He reserved his "primeval" style for wood and stone.) The former fall into two groups: variations on the egg shape, with such titles as *The Newborn* or *The Beginning of the World,* and soaring, vertical "bird" motifs. Because he concentrated on two basic forms of such uncompromising simplicity, Brancusi has at times been called the Mondrian of sculpture. This comparison is misleading, however, for Brancusi strove for essences, not for relationships. He was fascinated by the

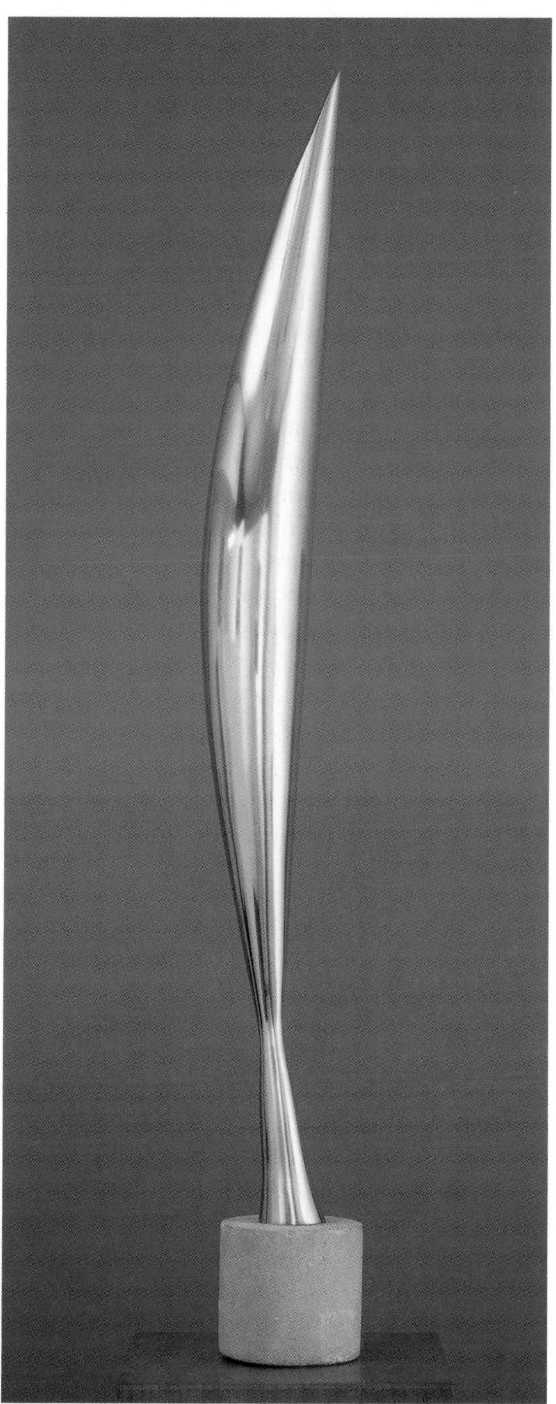

469. Constantin Brancusi. *Bird in Space*. 1928. Bronze (unique cast), 54 × 8½ × 6½" (137.2 × 21.6 × 16.5 cm). Collection, The Museum of Modern Art, New York. Given anonymously

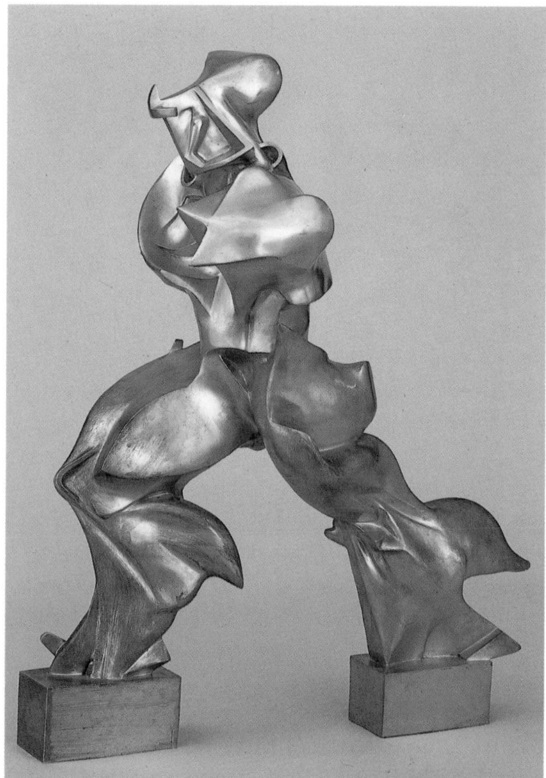

470. Umberto Boccioni. *Unique Forms of Continuity in Space*. 1913. Bronze (cast 1931), 43⅞ × 34⅞ × 15¾" (111.2 × 88.5 × 40 cm). Collection, The Museum of Modern Art, New York. Acquired through the Lillie P. Bliss Bequest

antithesis of life as potential and as kinetic energy—the self-contained perfection of the egg, which hides the mystery of all creation, and the pure dynamics of the creature released from this shell. *Bird in Space* (fig. 469) is not the abstract image of a bird. It is flight itself, made visible and concrete. Its disembodied quality is emphasized by the high polish that gives the surface the reflectivity of a mirror, and thus establishes a new continuity between the molded space within and the free space without.

Boccioni. Other sculptors in the first decade of the century were tackling the problem of body-space relationships with the formal tools of Cubism. The running figure entitled *Unique Forms of Continuity in Space* (fig. 470), by the Futurist Umberto Boccioni (see pp. 423–24), is as breathtaking in its complexity as *Bird in Space* is in its simplicity. Boccioni has attempted to represent not the human form itself, but the imprint of its motion upon the

471. Raymond Duchamp-Villon. *The Great Horse.* 1914. Bronze, height 39⅜″ (100 cm). The Art Institute of Chicago. Gift of Miss Margaret Fisher

medium in which it moves. The figure remains concealed behind its "garment" of aerial turbulence. The statue recalls the famous Futurist statement that "the roaring automobile is more beautiful than the Winged Victory," although it obviously owes more to the Winged Victory (the *Nike of Samothrace*; see fig. 78) than to the design of motorcars.

Duchamp-Villon. Raymond Duchamp-Villon (1876–1916), an elder brother of Marcel Duchamp, achieved a bolder solution in *The Great Horse* (fig. 471). He began with abstract studies of the animal, but his final version is an image of "horsepower," wherein the body has become a coiled spring and the legs resemble piston rods. Because of this very remoteness from their anatomical model, these quasi-mechanical shapes have a dynamism that is more persuasive, if less picturesque, than that of Boccioni's figure.

Tatlin. In Analytic Cubism, we recall, concave and convex were postulated as equivalents. All volumes, whether positive or negative, were "pockets of space." The Constructivists, a group of Russian artists led by Vladimir Tatlin (1895–1956), applied this principle to relief sculpture and arrived at what might be called three-dimensional collage. Eventually the final step was taken of making the works free-standing. According to Tatlin and his followers, these "constructions" were actually four-dimensional: since they implied motion, they also implied time. Suprematism (see pp. 425–26) and Constructivism were therefore closely related, and in fact overlapped, for both had their origins in Cubo-Futurism. They were nonetheless separated by a fundamental difference in approach. For Tatlin, art was not the Suprematists' spiritual contemplation but an active process of formation that was based on material and technique. He believed that each material dictates specific forms that are inherent in it, and that these must be followed if the work of art is to be valid according to the laws of life itself. In the end, Constructivism

472. Vladimir Tatlin. Project for *Monument to the Third International.* 1919–20. Wood, iron, and glass, height 20′ (6.7 m). Destroyed; contemporary photograph

won out over Suprematism because it was better suited to the post-Revolution temperament of Russia, when great deeds, not great thoughts, were needed.

Cut off from artistic contact with Europe during World War I, Constructivism developed into a uniquely Russian art that was little affected by the return of some of the country's most important artists, such as Kandinsky and Chagall. The Revolution galvanized the modernists, who celebrated the overthrow of the old regime with a creative outpouring throughout Russia. Tatlin's model for a *Monument to the Third International* (fig. 472) captures the dynamism of the technological utopia envisioned under communism. Pure energy is expressed as lines of force that establish new time-space relationships as well. The work also implies a new social structure, for the Constructivists believed in the power of art literally to reshape society. This extraordinary tower revolving at three speeds was conceived on a monumental scale, complete with Communist party offices. Like other such projects, it was wildly impractical in a society still recovering from the ravages of war and revolution, and was never built.

Constructivism subsequently proceeded to a Productivist phase, which ignored any contradiction between true artistic creativity and purely utilitarian production. After the movement had been suppressed as "bourgeois formalism," some of its members emigrated to the West and joined forces with the Dutch group, *De Stijl* (see pp. 431–32).

473. Marcel Duchamp. *In Advance of the Broken Arm.* 1945, from the original of 1915. Snow shovel, length 46¾" (118.8 cm). Yale University Art Gallery, New Haven, Connecticut. Gift of Katherine S. Dreier for the Collection Société Anonyme

Duchamp. As it did in the other arts, Dada uncompromisingly rejected formal discipline in sculpture, perhaps even more so, since only three-dimensional objects could become ready-mades, the sculpture of Dada. Playfulness and spontaneity are the impulses behind the ready-mades of Marcel Duchamp (see pp. 427–28), which the artist created by shifting the context of everyday objects from the utilitarian to the aesthetic. He would put his signature, and a provocative title, on "ready-made" objects such as bottle racks and snow shovels and exhibit them as works of art. *In Advance of the Broken Arm* (fig. 473) pushed the spirit of ready-mades to a new height. Duchamp "re-created" the lost original version of 1915 with this one made in 1945. Some of Duchamp's examples consist of combinations of found objects. These "assisted" ready-mades approach the status of constructions or of three-dimensional collage. This technique, later baptized "assemblage" (see pp. 467–70), proved to have unlimited possibilities, and numerous younger artists have explored it since, especially in junk-ridden America (see fig. 482).

474. Julio González. *Head.* c. 1935. Wrought iron, 17¾ × 15¼" (45.1 × 38.7 cm). Collection, The Museum of Modern Art, New York. Purchase

Surrealism. Ready-mades are certainly extreme demonstrations of a principle, but the principle itself—that artistic creation depends neither on established rules nor on manual craftsmanship—was an important discovery. The Surrealist contribution to sculpture is harder to define. It was difficult to apply the theory of "pure psychic automatism" to painting, but still harder to live up to it in sculpture. How indeed could solid, durable materials be given shape without the sculptor being consciously aware of the process? Thus, apart from the devotees of the ready-made, few sculptors were associated with the movement, and the effect produced by those who were cannot be directly compared with Surrealist painting.

González. Surrealism contributed to the astonishing sculptural imagination of Julio González (1872–1942). Trained as a wrought-iron craftsman in his native Catalonia, González had gone to Paris in 1900. Although he was a friend of both Brancusi and Picasso, he produced little of consequence until the 1930s, when his creative energies suddenly came into focus. It was González who established wrought iron as an important medium for sculpture, taking advantage of the very difficulties that had discouraged its use before. *Head* (fig. 474) combines extreme economy of form with an aggressive reinterpretation of anatomy that is derived from Picasso's work after the mid-1920s. As in the head of the figure on the left in Picasso's *Three Dancers* (see fig. 433), the mouth is an oval cavity with spikelike teeth, the eyes two rods that converge upon an "optic nerve" linking them to the tangled mass of the "brain." Similar gruesomely expressive metaphors were later created by a generation of younger sculptors in wrought iron and welded steel, as if the violence of their working process mirrored the violence of modern life.

Calder. Surrealism in the early 1930s led to still another important development, the mobile sculpture of the American Alexander Calder (1898–1976). Called mobiles for short, they are delicately balanced constructions of metal wire, hinged together and weighted so as to move with the slightest breath of air. They may be of any size, from tiny tabletop models to the huge *Lobster Trap and Fish Tail* (fig. 475). Kinetic sculpture had been conceived by the Constructivists. Their influence is evident in Calder's earliest mobiles, which were motor-driven, and tended toward abstract geometric configurations. Calder was also affected early on by Mondrian, but it was his contact with Surrealism that made him realize the poetic possibilities of "natural" rather than fully controlled movement. He borrowed biomorphic shapes from Miró and began to think of mobiles as similes of organic structures: flowers on flexible stems, foliage quivering in the breeze, marine animals floating in the sea. Such mobiles are infinitely responsive to their environment so that they seem more truly alive than any fabricated thing. Unpredictable and ever-changing, they incorporate the fourth dimension as an essential element of their structure.

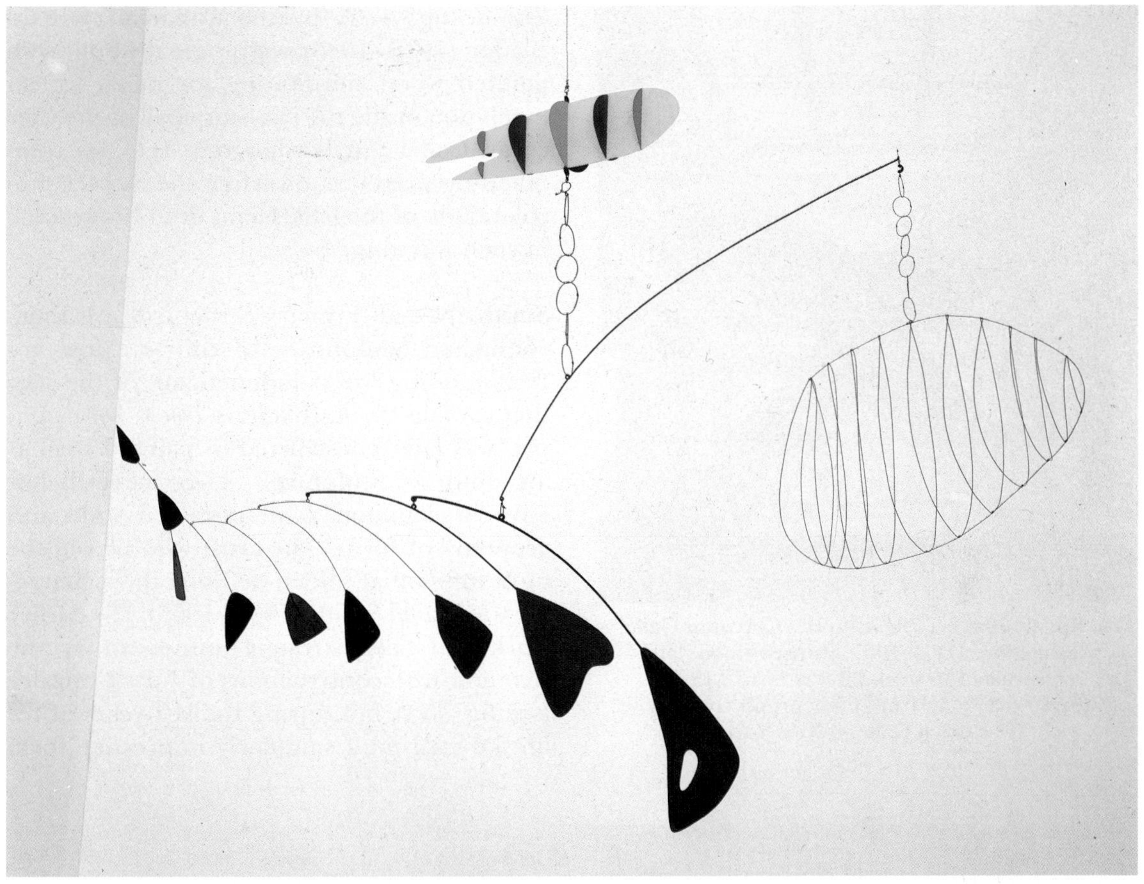

475. Alexander Calder. *Lobster Trap and Fish Tail.* 1939. Hanging mobile: painted steel wire and sheet aluminum, c. 8′6″ high × 9′6″ diameter (2.6 × 2.9 m). Collection, The Museum of Modern Art, New York. Commissioned by the Advisory Committee for the stairwell of the Museum

SCULPTURE SINCE 1945

Primary Structures and Environmental Sculpture

Like painting, sculpture since 1945 has been notable for its epic proportions. Indeed, scale assumed fundamental significance for a sculptural movement that extended the scope—indeed, the very concept—of sculpture in an entirely new direction. "Primary Structure," the most suitable name suggested for this type, conveys its two salient characteristics: extreme simplicity of shapes and a kinship with architecture. The radical abstraction of form is known as Minimalism, which implies an equal reduction of content. Another term, "Environmental Sculpture" (not to be confused with mixed-medium "environments"), refers to the fact that many Primary Structures are designed to envelop the beholder, who is invited to enter or walk through them. It is this space-articulating function that distinguishes Primary Structures from all previous sculpture and relates them to architecture. They are the modern successors, in structural steel and concrete, to such prehistoric monuments as Stonehenge (see figs. 21, 22).

Bladen. Often, these sculptors limit themselves to the role of designer and leave the execution to others, to emphasize the impersonality and duplicability of their invention. If no patron is found to foot the bill for carrying out these costly structures, they remain on paper, like unbuilt architecture, but sometimes such works reach the mock-up stage.

476. Ronald Bladen. *The X* (in the Corcoran Gallery, Washington, D.C.). 1967. Painted wood, later constructed in steel, 22′8″ × 24′6″ × 12′6″ (6.71 × 7.47 × 3.81 m). Photograph courtesy Fischbach Gallery, New York

The X (fig. 476), by the Canadian Ronald Bladen (1918–1988), was originally built with painted wood substituting for metal for an exhibition inside the two-story hall of the Corcoran Gallery in Washington, D.C. Its commanding presence, dwarfing the Neoclassical colonnade of the hall, seems doubly awesome in such a setting.

Smith. Not all Primary Structures are Environmental Sculptures, of course. Most are free-standing works independent of the sites that contain them. (Bladen's *The X,* for example, was later constructed of painted steel as an outdoor sculpture.) They nevertheless have in common a monumental scale and economy of form. The artist who played the most influential role in defining their character was David Smith (1906–1965). His earlier work had been strongly influenced by the wrought-iron constructions of Julio González (see fig. 474), but during the last years of his life he evolved a singularly impressive form

477. David Smith. *Cubi* series. Stainless steel. From left to right: *Cubi XVIII.* 1964. Height 9′8″ (2.95 m). Museum of Fine Arts, Boston; *Cubi XVII.* 1963. Height 9′ (2.74 m). Dallas Museum of Fine Arts; *Cubi XIX.* 1964. 9′5″ (2.87 m). The Tate Gallery, London

of Primary Structure in his *Cubi* series. Figure 477 shows three of these against the open sky and rolling hills of the artist's farm at Bolton Landing, New York (all are now in major museums). Smith has created a seemingly endless variety of configurations using only two basic components, cubes and cylinders. The units that make up the structures are poised one upon the other as if they were held in place by magnetic force, so that each represents a fresh triumph over gravity. Unlike many members of the Primary Structure movement, Smith executed these pieces himself, welding them of sheets of stainless steel whose shiny surfaces he finished and controlled with exquisite care. As a result, his work displays an "old-fashioned" subtlety of touch that reminds us of the polished bronzes of Brancusi.

Minimalism. A younger generation of Minimalists, Bladen among them, carried the implications of Primary Structures to their logical conclusion. In search of the ultimate unity, they reduced their geometry to the fewest possible components and used mathematical formulas to establish precise relationships. They further eliminated any hint of personal expression by contracting out the work to industrial fabricators. Minimalism was a quest for basic elements representing the fundamental aesthetic values of art, without regard to issues of content. It made an important contribution by enabling the sculptor to achieve an elusive perfection through total control over every element. At its most extreme, however, Minimalism reduced art not to an eternal essence but to a barren simplicity.

Shapiro. Confronted by this artistic dead end, a number of artists began to move away from Minimalism without entirely renouncing it. This trend, called Post-Minimalism to denote its continuing debt to the earlier style, has as its leading exponent Joel Shapiro (born 1941). After fully exploring the possibilities of small pieces having great conceptual intensity and aesthetic power, he suddenly began to produce sculptures of simple wood beams that refer to the human figure but do not directly represent it. They assume active "poses," some standing awkwardly off-balance, others dancing or tumbling, so that they charge the space around them with energy. Shapiro soon began casting them in bronze, which retains the impress of the rough wood-grain (fig. 478). These are hand-finished with a beautiful patina by skilled artisans, reasserting the craftsmanship traditional to sculpture. By freely rearranging Smith's vocabulary, Shapiro has given Minimalist sculpture a new lease on life. His work can be regarded as the counterpart to Elizabeth Murray's paintings in combining abstraction and content (see pp. 455–56), and to Bernard Tschumi's architecture in its allegiance to Constructivism (see p. 483). Nevertheless, contemporary sculptors as a whole have found it especially difficult to seek a new direction, and Shapiro's remains one of the few successful responses to Post-Modernism thus far (see p. 453).

478. Joel Shapiro. *Untitled.* 1989–90. Bronze, 101½ × 42 × 78" (257.8 × 106.7 × 198.1 cm). North Carolina Museum of Art, Raleigh. Purchased with funds from various donors, by exchange

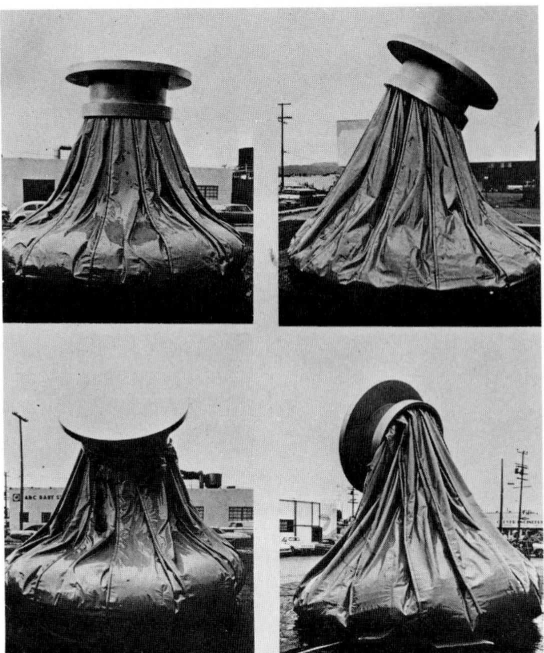

479. Claes Oldenburg. *Ice Bag—Scale A*. 1970. Programmed kinetic sculpture of polyvinyl, fiberglass, wood, hydraulic and mechanical movements, 16 × 18 × 18′ (4.9 × 5.5 × 5.5 m). Collection National Gallery of Art, Washington, D.C.

a mechanism inside to create "movements caused by an invisible hand," as the artist described them. For a piece of outdoor sculpture he wanted a form that combined hard and soft and did not need a base. An ice bag met these demands, so he bought one and started playing with it. As he manipulated the object, he realized "that movement was part of its identity and should be used." He sent the *Ice Bag—Scale A* to the U.S. Pavilion at EXPO 70 in Osaka, Japan, where crowds were endlessly fascinated to watch it heave, rise, and twist like a living thing, then relax with an almost audible sigh.

What do such monuments celebrate? Part of their charm, which they share with readymades and Pop Art, is that they reveal the aesthetic potential of the ordinary and all-too-familiar. But they also have an undeniable grandeur. There is one dimension, however, that is missing in Oldenburg's monuments. They delight, astonish, amuse—but they do not move us. Wholly secular, wedded to the here and now, they fail to touch our deepest emotions.

Oldenburg. On a large scale, Primary Structures are obviously monuments. But just as obviously they are not monuments commemorating or celebrating anything except their designer's imagination. To the uninitiated, they offer no ready frame of reference, nothing to be reminded of, even though the original meaning of "monument" is "a reminder." Monuments in the traditional sense died out when contemporary society lost its consensus of what ought to be publicly remembered; yet the belief in the possibility of such monuments has not been abandoned altogether. The Pop artist Claes Oldenburg (born 1929) has proposed a number of unexpected and imaginative solutions to the problem of the monument. He is, moreover, an exceptionally precise and eloquent commentator on his ideas. All his monuments are heroic in size, though not in subject matter. All share one feature, their origin in humble objects of everyday use.

In 1969 Oldenburg conceived a work shaped like a gigantic ice bag (fig. 479) with

Smithson. The ultimate medium for Environmental Sculpture is the earth itself, since it provides complete freedom from the limitations of the human scale. Some designers of Primary Structures have, logically enough, turned to "Earth Art," inventing projects that stretch over many miles. These latter-day successors to the mound-building Indians of Neolithic times have the advantage of modern earth-moving machinery, but this is more than outweighed by the problem of cost and the difficulty of finding suitable sites on our crowded planet.

The few projects of theirs that have actually been carried out are mostly found (and the finding is itself often difficult enough) in remote regions of western America. *Spiral Jetty*, the work of Robert Smithson (1938–1973), jutted out into Great Salt Lake in Utah (fig. 480) and is now partly submerged. Its appeal rests in part on the Surrealist irony of the concept: a spiral jetty is as self-contradictory as a straight corkscrew. But it can hardly be said to have grown out of

480. Robert Smithson. *Spiral Jetty*. As built in 1970. Total length 1,500′ (457.2 m), width of jetty 15′ (4.57 m). Great Salt Lake, Utah

the natural formation of the terrain. No wonder it has not endured long, nor was it intended to. The process by which nature is reclaiming *Spiral Jetty*, already twice submerged, was integral to Smithson's design from the start. The project nevertheless lives on in photographs.

Constructions and Assemblage

Constructions present a difficult problem. If we agree to restrict the term "sculpture" to objects made of a single substance, then we must put "assemblages" (that is, constructions using mixed mediums) in a class of their own. This is probably a useful distinction, because of their kinship with ready-mades. But what of Picasso's *Bull's Head* (see fig. 2)? Is it not an instance of assemblage, and have we not called it a piece of sculpture? Actually, there is no inconsistency here. The *Bull's Head* is a bronze cast, even though we cannot tell this by looking at a photograph of it. Had Picasso wished to display the actual handlebars and bicycle seat, he would surely have done so. If he chose to have them cast in bronze, this must have been because he wanted to "dematerialize" the ingredients of the work by having them reproduced in a single material. Apparently he felt it necessary to clarify the relation of image to reality in this way—the sculptor's way—and he used the same procedure whenever he worked with ready-made objects.

Nevertheless, we must not apply the "single-material" rule too strictly. Calder's mobiles, for instance, often combine metal, string, wood, and other elements. Yet they do not strike us as being assemblages, because these materials are not made to assert their separate identities. Conversely, an object may deserve to be called an assemblage even though composed of essentially homogeneous material. Such is often true of works known as "junk sculpture," made of fragments of old machinery, parts of wrecked automobiles, and similar discards, which constitute a broad class that can be called sculpture, assemblage, or environment, depending on the work itself.

Rauschenberg. Robert Rauschenberg (born 1925) pioneered assemblage as early as the mid-1950s. Like a composer making music out of the noises of everyday life, he constructed works of art from the trash of urban civilization. *Odalisk* (fig. 481) is a box covered with a miscellany of pasted images—comic strips, photos, clippings from picture magazines—held together only by the skein of brushstrokes the artist has superimposed on them. The box perches on a foot improbably anchored to a pillow on a wooden platform and is surmounted by a stuffed chicken.

The title, a witty blend of "odalisque" and "obelisk," refers both to the nude girls among the collage of clippings (for the original meaning of "odalisque," see p. 359) and to the shape of the construction as a whole, for the box shares its verticality and slightly tapering

481. Robert Rauschenberg. *Odalisk.* 1955–58. Construction, 81 × 25 × 25″ (205.7 × 63.5 × 63.5 cm). Museum Ludwig, Cologne

482. John Chamberlain. *Essex.* 1960. Automobile body parts and other metal, 9′ × 6′8″ × 43″ (2.74 × 2.03 × 1.09 m). Collection, The Museum of Modern Art, New York. Gift of Mr. and Mrs. Robert C. Scull and Purchase

sides with real obelisks. Rauschenberg's unlikely "monument" has at least some qualities in common with its predecessors: compactness and self-sufficiency. We will recognize in this improbable juxtaposition the same ironic intent as in the ready-mades of Duchamp, whom Rauschenberg had come to know well in New York.

Chamberlain. A most successful example of junk sculpture, and a puzzling borderline case of assemblage and sculpture, is *Essex* (fig. 482) by John Chamberlain (born 1927). The title refers to a make of car that has not been on the market for many years, suggesting that the object is a kind of homage to a vanished species. But we may well doubt that these pieces of enameled tin ever had so specific an origin. They have been carefully selected for their shape and color, and composed in such a way that they form a new entity, evoking Duchamp-Villon's *The Great Horse* (see fig. 471) rather than the crumpled automobiles to which they once belonged.

483. Louise Nevelson. *Black Cord.* 1964. Painted wood, 8′ × 10′ × 11½″ (2.44 m × 3.05 m × 29.2 cm). Whitney Museum of American Art, New York. Gift of Anne and Joel Ehrenkranz

Nevelson. Although it is almost always made entirely of wood, the work of Louise Nevelson (1900–1988) must be classified as assemblage, and when extended to a monumental scale, it acquires the status of an environment. Before Nevelson, there had not been important women sculptors in twentieth-century America. Women had traditionally been excluded from this medium because of the manual labor involved. Thanks to the women's suffrage movement in the second half of the nineteenth century, Harriet Hosmer (1830–1908) and her "White Marmorean Flock" (as the novelist Henry James called her and her followers in Rome) had succeeded in legitimizing sculpture as a medium for women. This school of sculpture lapsed, however, when the sentimental, idealizing Neoclassical style fell out of favor after the Philadelphia Centennial of 1876.

In the 1950s Nevelson rejected external reality and began to construct a private one, using her collection of found pieces of wood. At first these self-contained realms were miniature cityscapes. They soon grew into large environments of free-standing "buildings," encrusted with decorations that were inspired by the sculpture on Mayan ruins. Nevelson's work generally took the form of large wall units that flatten her architecture into reliefs (fig. 483). Assembled from individual compartments, the whole is always painted a single color, usually a matte black to suggest the shadowy world of dreams. Each compart-

484. Barbara Chase-Riboud. *Confessions for Myself.* 1972. Bronze painted black and black wool, 10′ × 3′4″ × 1′ (3.05 m × 1.02 m × 30.5 cm). University Art Museum, University of California, Berkeley. Selected by The Committee for the Acquisition of Afro-American Art

ment is elegantly designed and is itself a metaphor of thought or experience. While the organization of the ensemble is governed by an inner logic, the entire statement remains an enigmatic monument to the artist's fertile imagination.

Chase-Riboud. Nevelson's success has encouraged other American women to become sculptors. Barbara Chase-Riboud (born 1939), a prize-winning author who now lives in Paris, belongs to a generation of remarkable black women who have made significant contributions to several of the arts at once. She is heir to a unique American tradition. It is a paradox that whereas black women never carve in traditional African cultures, in America they found their first artistic outlet in sculpture. They were attracted to it by the example set by Harriet Hosmer at a time when abolitionism and feminism were closely allied liberal causes.

Chase-Riboud received a traditional training in her native Philadelphia, the first center of minority artists (see p. 388). In search of an artistic identity, she then turned to African art for inspiration. Her monumental sculpture makes an indelible impression on the viewer. In *Confessions for Myself* (fig. 484) she has conjured up a demonic archetype of awesome power. Its sources can be found in cast bronze figures from Benin and in the Senufo tribe's carved wooden masks, which are sometimes embellished with textiles. From them she developed her highly individual aesthetic, which utilizes a combination of bronze that has been painted black and braided fiber to express a distinctly ethnic sensibility and feminist outlook.

Environments and Installations

Some artists associated with Pop Art have also turned to assemblage because they find the flat surface of the canvas too confining. In order to bridge the gap between image and reality, they often introduce three-dimensional objects into their pictures. Some even construct full-scale models of everyday things and real-life situations, utilizing every conceivable kind of material in order to embrace the entire range of their physical environment, including the people, in their work. These "environments" combine the qualities of painting, sculpture, collage, and stagecraft. Being three-dimensional, they can claim to be considered sculpture, but the claim rests on a convention that Pop Art itself has helped make obsolete. According to this convention, a flat or smoothly curved work of art covered with pigments is a painting (or, if the surface consists mainly of lines, a print or drawing); everything else is sculpture, regardless of medium or size (unless we can enter it, in which case we call it architecture).

Our habit of using the term "sculpture" in this sense is only a few hundred years old. Antiquity and the Middle Ages had different words to denote various kinds of sculpture according to the materials and working processes involved, but no single term that covered them all. Maybe it is time to revive such distinctions and to modify the all-inclusive definition of sculpture by acknowledging "environments" as a separate category, distinct from both painting and sculpture in their use of heterogeneous materials ("mixed mediums") and their blurring of the borderline between image and reality. The differences are underscored by "installations," which are expansions of environments into room-size settings.

Segal. George Segal (born 1924) creates life-size three-dimensional pictures showing people and objects in everyday situations. The subject of *Cinema* (fig. 485) is ordinary enough to be instantly recognizable: a man changing the letters on a movie theater marquee. Yet the relation of image and reality is far more subtle and complex than the obvious authenticity of the scene suggests. The man's figure is cast from a live model by a technique of Segal's invention and retains its ghostly white plaster surface. Thus it is one crucial step removed from our world of daily experience, and the illuminated sign has been carefully designed to complement and set off the shadowed figure. Moreover, the scene is brought down from its natural context, high above the entrance to the theater where we might have glimpsed it in passing, and is presented at eye level, in isolation, so that we grasp it completely for the first time.

485. George Segal. *Cinema*. 1963. Plaster, metal, and illuminated plexiglass, 9′10″ × 8′ × 3′3″ (2.99 m × 2.44 m × 99.1 cm). Albright-Knox Art Gallery, Buffalo, New York. Gift of Seymour H. Knox, 1964

De Andrea. John De Andrea (born 1941) pursues very different ends than Segal understood. *The Artist and His Model* (fig. 4) has the subtle content and almost classical purity that make him a worthy successor to Antonio Canova, but with a difference (see pp. 369–70). Here the Romantic sculptor's dilemma of representation versus duplication is reversed. Without confusing the two, De Andrea's hyperrealism expresses an ideal, while leaving us in just enough doubt to make the illusion convincing.

Kienholz. Some environments can have a shattering impact on the viewer. This is certainly true of *The State Hospital* (fig. 486) by the West Coast artist Edward Kienholz (born 1927), which shows a cell in a ward for senile patients with a naked old man strapped to the lower bunk. He is the victim of physical cruelty, which has reduced what little mental life he had in him almost to the vanishing point. His body is little more than a skeleton covered with leathery, discolored skin, and his head is a glass bowl with live goldfish, of which we catch an occasional glimpse. The horrifying realism of the scene even has an olfactory dimension. When the work was displayed at the Los Angeles County Museum of Art, it exuded a sickly hospital smell. But what of the figure in the upper bunk? It al-

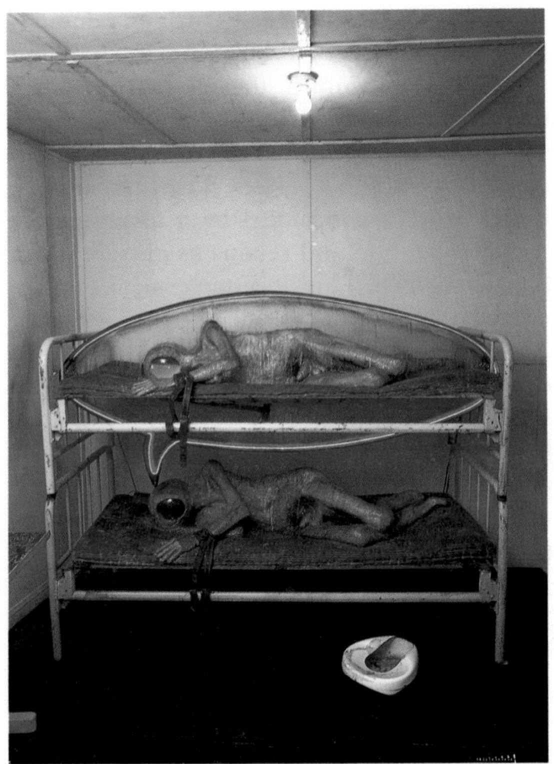

486. Edward Kienholz. *The State Hospital.* 1966. Mixed mediums, 8 × 12 × 10′ (2.44 × 3.66 × 3.05 m). Moderna Museet, Stockholm

most duplicates the one below, with one important difference: it is a mental image, since it is enclosed in the outline of a comic-strip balloon rising from the goldfish bowl. It represents, then, the patient's awareness of himself. The abstract devices of the balloon and the metaphoric goldfish bowl are both alien to the realism of the scene as a whole, but they play an essential part in it: they make us think as well as feel. Kienholz' means may be Pop, but his aim is that of Greek tragedy. As a witness to the unseen miseries beneath the surface of modern life, he has no equal.

Pfaff. The installations of Judy Pfaff (born 1946) can be likened to exotic indoor landscapes. The inspiration of nature is apparent in the junglelike density of *Dragons* (fig. 487), aptly named for its fiery forms and colors. Pfaff uses painting together with sculptural and other materials to activate architectural space. The treatment of the wall surface will remind us of the collage in *Odalisk* (see fig. 481), but Pfaff's playfulness is closer to Calder's whimsy (see fig. 475) than to Rauschenberg's ironic wit. The nearest equivalent to Pfaff's spontaneous energy is the Action painting of Pollock. It is as if the poured paint had been released from the canvas and left free to roam in space. The swirling profusion around the viewer makes for an experience that is at once pleasurable and vertiginous.

Conceptual Art

Conceptual Art has the same "patron saint" as Pop Art: Marcel Duchamp. It arose during the 1960s out of the Happenings staged by Alan Kaprow, in which the event itself became the art. Conceptual Art challenges our definition of art more radically than Pop, insisting that the leap of the imagination, not the execution, is art. According to this

487. Judy Pfaff. *Dragons.* Installation at the Whitney Biennial, February–April 1981. Mixed mediums. Whitney Museum of American Art, New York. Courtesy Holly Solomon Gallery, New York

view, since the works of art are incidental by-products of the imaginative leap, they can be dispensed with altogether; so too can galleries and, by extension, even the artist's public. The creative process need only be documented in some way. Sometimes this is in verbal form, but more often it is by still photography, video, or film shown in an installation.

Conceptual Art, we will recognize, is akin to Minimalism as a phenomenon of the 1960s, but instead of abolishing content, it eliminates aesthetics from art. This deliberately anti-art approach, stemming from Dada (see p. 432), poses a number of stimulating paradoxes. As soon as the documentation takes on visible form, it begins to come perilously close to more traditional forms of art (especially if it is placed in a gallery where it can be seen by an audience), since it is impossible fully to divorce the imagination from aesthetic matters.

488. Joseph Kosuth. *One and Three Chairs.* 1965. Wooden folding chair, 32⅜ × 14⅞ × 20⅞″ (82 × 37.8 × 53 cm); photograph of chair, 36 × 24⅛″ (91.5 × 61.1 cm); and photographic enlargement of dictionary definition of chair, 24 × 24⅛″ (61 × 61.3 cm). Collection, The Museum of Modern Art, New York. Larry Aldrich Foundation Fund

Kosuth. We see this in *One and Three Chairs* (fig. 488) by Joseph Kosuth (born 1945), which is clearly indebted to Duchamp's readymades (see fig. 473). It "describes" a chair by combining in one installation an actual chair, a full-scale photograph of that chair, and a printed dictionary definition of a chair. Whatever the Conceptual artist's intention, this making of the work of art, no matter how minimal the process, is as essential as it was for Michelangelo (see pp. 11–12). In the end, all art is the final document of the creative process, because without execution, no idea can ever be fully realized. Without such "proof of performance," the Conceptual artist becomes like the emperor wearing new clothes that no one else can see. And, in fact, Conceptual Art has embraced all of the mediums in one form or another.

Performance Art

Performance Art, which originated in the early decades of this century, belongs to the history of theater, but the form that arose in the 1970s combines aspects of Happenings and Conceptual Art with installations. In reaction to Minimalism, the artist now sought to assert his or her presence once again by becoming, in effect, a living work of art. The results, however, have relied mainly on the shock value of irreverent humor or explicit sexuality.

Beuys. The German artist Joseph Beuys (1921–1986) managed to overcome these limitations, though he, too, was a controversial figure who incorporated an element of parody into his work. Life, for Beuys, was a creative process in which everyone is an artist. He assumed the guise of a modern-day shaman intent on healing the spiritual crisis of contemporary life caused by the rift between the arts and sciences. To find the common denominator behind such polarities, he created objects and scenarios that, though often baffling at face value, were meant to be accessible to the intuition. In 1974, Beuys spent

489. Joseph Beuys. *Coyote.* Photograph of performance at René Block Gallery, New York, 1974. Photograph © 1974 Caroline Tisdall, Courtesy Ronald Feldman Fine Arts, New York

one week caged up in a New York gallery with a coyote (fig. 489), an animal sacred to the American Indian but persecuted by the white man. His objective in this "dialogue" was to lift the trauma caused to an entire nation by the schism between the two opposing world views.

Paik. The notes and photographs that document Beuys' performances hardly do them justice. His chief legacy today lies perhaps in the stimulation he provided his many students, including Anselm Kiefer (see pp. 454–55), and collaborators, among them Nam June Paik (born 1932). The sophisticated video displays of the Korean-born Paik fall outside the scope of this book; but his installation with a Buddha contemplating himself on television (fig. 490) is a memorable image uniquely appropriate to our age, in which the fascination with electronic media has replaced transcendent spirituality as the focus of modern life.

490. Nam June Paik. *TV Buddha.* 1974. Video installation with statue. Stedelijk Museum, Amsterdam

TWENTIETH-CENTURY ARCHITECTURE

The technical and aesthetic basis for a truly modern architecture was laid by the eve of World War I. Much of twentieth-century architecture is distinguished by an aversion to decoration for its own sake. Instead, it favors a clean functionalism, which expresses the machine age with its insistent rationalism. Yet modern architecture demanded far more than a reform of architectural grammar and vocabulary. To take advantage of the expressive qualities of the new building techniques and materials that the engineer had placed at the architect's disposal, a new philosophy was needed. The leaders of modern architecture have characteristically been vigorous and articulate thinkers, in whose minds architectural theory is closely linked with ideas of social reform to meet the challenges posed by industrial civilization. To them, architecture's ability to shape human experience brings with it the responsibility to play an active role in molding modern society for the better.

Early Modernism

Wright. The first indisputably modern architect was Frank Lloyd Wright (1867–1959), Louis Sullivan's great disciple. If Sullivan and Van de Velde could be called the Post-Impressionists of architecture, Wright took architecture to its Cubist phase. This is certainly true of his brilliant early style, which he developed between 1900 and 1910 and had broad international influence. In the beginning Wright's main activity was the design of suburban houses in the upper Midwest. These were known as prairie houses, because their low, horizontal lines were meant to blend with the flat landscape around them. His last, and his most accomplished, example in this series is the Robie House of 1909 (figs. 491, 492). The exterior, so unlike anything seen before, instantly proclaims the building's modernity. However, its "Cubism" is not merely a matter of the clean-cut rectangular elements composing the structure, but of Wright's handling of space. It is designed as a number of "space blocks" around a central core, the chimney. Some of the blocks are closed and others are open, yet all are defined with equal precision. Thus the space that has been architecturally shaped includes the balconies, terrace, court, and garden, as well as the house itself. Voids and solids are regarded as equivalents, analogous in their way to Analytic Cubism in painting, and the entire complex enters into an active and dramatic relationship with its surroundings. Wright did not aim simply to design a house, but to create a complete environment. He even took command of the details of the interior. Wright acted out of a conviction that buildings have a profound influence on the people who live, work, or worship in them, making the architect, consciously or unconsciously, a molder of people.

Rietveld. The work of Frank Lloyd Wright attracted much attention in Europe by 1914. Among the first to recognize its importance were some young Dutch architects who, a few years later, joined forces with Mondrian in the *De Stijl* movement (see pp. 431–32). Among their most important experiments is the Schröder House, designed by Gerrit Rietveld (1888–1964) in 1924 for a woman artist. The facade looks like a Mondrian painting transposed into three dimensions, for it utilizes the same rigorous abstraction and refined geometry (fig. 493). The lively arrangement of floating panels and intersecting planes is based on Mondrian's principle of dynamic equilibrium: the balance of unequal

491. Frank Lloyd Wright. Robie House, Chicago. 1909

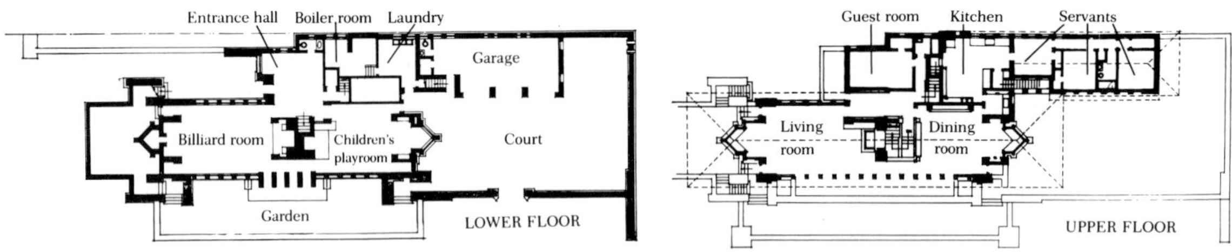

492. Plan of the Robie House

but equivalent oppositions, which expresses the mystical harmony of humanity with the universe. Steel beams, rails, and other elements are painted in bright, primary colors to articulate the composition. Unlike the elements of a painting by Mondrian, the exterior parts of the Schröder House look as if they can be shifted at will, though in fact they fit as tightly as interlocking pieces of a jigsaw puzzle. Not a single element could be moved without destroying the delicate balance of the whole. Inside, the living quarters can be reconfigured through a system of sliding partitions to suit the individual lifestyle of the owner.

The Schröder House proclaims a utopian ideal widely held in the early twentieth century. The machine would hasten our spiritual development by liberating us from nature, with its conflict and imperfection, and by leading us to the higher order of beauty reflected in the architect's clean, abstract forms.

493. Gerrit Rietveld. Schröder House, Utrecht. 1924

The harmonious design of the Schröder House owes its success to the insistent logic of this aesthetic, which we respond to intuitively even without being aware of its ideology. Yet the design, far from being impersonal, is remarkably intimate.

494. Walter Gropius. Shop Block, The Bauhaus, Dessau, Germany. 1925–26. Photograph, Courtesy The Museum of Modern Art, New York

The International Style

The Bauhaus. The Schröder House was recognized immediately as one of the classic statements of modern architecture. The *De Stijl* architects represented the most advanced ideas in European architecture in the early 1920s. They had a decisive influence on so many architects abroad that the movement soon became international. The largest and most complex example of this International Style of the 1920s is the group of buildings created in 1925–26 by Walter Gropius (1883–1969) for the Bauhaus in Dessau, the famous German art school of which he was the director. (Its curriculum embraced all the visual arts, linked by the root concept of structure, *Bau.*) The complex consisted of three major blocks for classrooms, shops, and studios. The most dramatic is the shop block, a four-story box with walls that are a continuous surface of glass (fig. 494). This radical step had been possible ever since the introduction of the structural steel skeleton several decades before, which relieved the wall of any load-bearing function. Sullivan had approached it, but he could not yet free himself from the traditional notion of the window as a "hole in the wall." Gropius frankly acknowledged, at last, that in modern architecture the wall is no more than a curtain or climate barrier, which may consist entirely of glass if maximum daylight is desirable. The result is rather surprising: since such walls reflect as well as transmit light, their appearance depends on the interplay of these two effects. They respond, as it were, to any change of conditions without and within, and thus introduce a strange quality of life into the structure. (The mirrorlike finish of Brancusi's *Bird in Space* serves a similar purpose.) The same principles have been used on a much larger scale for skyscrapers ever since.

495. Le Corbusier. Villa Savoye, Poissy-sur-Seine, France. 1929–30

Le Corbusier's Early Work. In France, the most distinguished representative of the International Style during the 1920s was the Swiss-born architect Le Corbusier (Charles Édouard Jeanneret, 1886–1965). At that time he built only private homes (from necessity, not choice), but these are worthy successors to Wright's prairie houses and Rietveld's Schröder House. Le Corbusier called them *machines à habiter* (machines to be lived in), a term intended to suggest his admiration for the clean, precise shapes of machinery, not a desire for "mechanized living." (The paintings of his friend Fernand Léger during those years reflect the same attitude; see fig. 434.) Perhaps he also wanted to imply that his houses were so different from conventional homes as to constitute a new species.

The most famous of them, the Villa Savoye at Poissy-sur-Seine (fig. 495), resembles a low, square box resting on stilts—pillars of reinforced concrete that form part of the structural skeleton and reappear to divide the "ribbon windows" running along each side of the box. The flat, smooth surfaces, denying all sense of weight, stress Le Corbusier's preoccupation with abstract "space blocks." The functionalism of the Villa Savoye is governed by a "design for living," not by mechanical efficiency. Within the house, we are still in communication with the outdoors, but we enjoy complete privacy, since an observer on the ground cannot see us unless we stand next to a window.

Aalto. Although the style and philosophy of the International Style were codified around 1930 by an international committee of Le Corbusier and his followers, soon all but the most purist among them began to depart from this standard. One of the first to break

496. Alvar Aalto. Villa Mairea, Noormarkku, Finland. 1937–38

ranks was the Finnish architect Alvar Aalto (1898–1976), whose Villa Mairea (fig. 496) reads at first glance like a critique of Le Corbusier's Villa Savoye of a decade earlier. Like Rietveld's Schröder House, Villa Mairea was designed for a woman artist. This time, however, the architect was given a free hand by his patron, and the building is a summation of ideas Aalto had been developing for nearly ten years. He adapted the International Style to the traditional architecture, materials, lifestyle, and landscape of Finland. Aalto's primary concern was human needs, both physical and psychological, which he sought to harmonize with functionalism. The modernist heritage, extending back to Wright, is unmistakable in his vocabulary of forms and massing of elements; yet everywhere there are romantic touches, such as the use of wood, brick, and stone, that add a warmth absent from Le Corbusier's pristine classicism. Free forms are employed to break up the cubic geometry and smooth surfaces favored by the International Style. Aalto's importance is undeniable, but his place in twentieth-century architecture remains unclear. His infusion of nationalist elements in the Villa Mairea has been interpreted both as a rejection of modernism and as a fruitful regional variation on the International Style. Today his work can be seen as a direct forerunner of Post-Modern architecture (see pp. 481–83).

Postwar Architecture

Mies van der Rohe. America, despite its early position of leadership, did not share the exciting growth that took place in European architecture during the 1920s. The impact of the International Style did not begin to be felt on its side of the Atlantic until the end of the decade. When in the 1930s Hitler condemned their work as "un-German," the best German architects emigrated to the United States and greatly stimulated the development of American architecture. Gropius, who was appointed chairman of the architecture department at Harvard University, had a major educational influence. Ludwig Mies van der Rohe (1886–1969), his former colleague at Dessau, settled in Chicago as a practicing architect. The Lake Shore Drive apartment houses (fig. 497), two severely elegant slabs set at right angles to each other, exemplify Mies van der Rohe's dictum that "less is more." Here is the great spiritual heir of Mondrian among contemporary designers, possessed of the same "absolute pitch" in determining proportions and spatial relationships.

497. Ludwig Mies van der Rohe. Lake Shore Drive Apartment Houses, Chicago. 1950–52

Urban Planning

Mies van der Rohe belongs to the same heroic generation as Gropius and Le Corbusier; all were born in the 1880s. In the course of their long, fruitful careers, these men coined the language of twentieth-century architecture. Their successors continue to use many elements of its vocabulary in new building types and materials, and they do not forget its fundamental logic. To some younger architects, the greatest challenge is not the individual structure but urban design, which involves marshaling the political, social, and economic resources of an entire society. Urban planning is probably as old as civilization itself (which, we recall, means "city life"). Its history is difficult to trace by direct visual evidence. Cities, like living organisms, are ever-changing, and to reconstruct their pasts from their present appearances is not an easy task. With the advent of the industrial era two cen-

498. Oscar Niemeyer. Brasília, Brazil. Completed 1960

499. Renzo Piano and Richard Rogers. Centre National d'Art et de Culture Georges Pompidou, Paris. 1971–77

turies ago, cities began to grow explosively. Much of this growth was uncontrolled. The unfortunate result can be seen in the overcrowded, crumbling apartment blocks that are the blight of vast urban areas. Architects, however, have generally failed in their social mandate to replace the slums of our decaying cities with housing that will provide a socially healthful environment for very large numbers of people.

Niemeyer. Nowhere are the issues facing modern civilization put into sharper relief than in the grandiose urban projects conceived by modern architects. These utopian visions may be regarded as laboratory experiments that seek to redefine the role of architecture in shaping our lives and to pose new solutions. Limited by their very scope, few of these ambitious proposals make it off the drawing board. Among the rare exceptions is Brasília, the inland capital of Brazil built entirely since 1960. Presented with an unparalleled opportunity to design a major city from the ground up and with vast resources at its disposal, the design team, headed by the Brazilian Oscar Niemeyer (born 1907), achieved undeniably spectacular results (fig. 498). Like most projects of this sort, Brasília has a massive scale and insistent logic that make it curiously oppressive, so that despite the lavish display, the city provides a chilling glimpse of the future.

Post-Modernism

Spurred by radical social theories, Post-Modernism—as its misleading name implies (see p. 453)—constitutes a broad repudiation of the mainstream of twentieth-century architecture. It represents an attempt to reinstate meaning in architecture, as against the self-contained designs espoused by the modern tradition. Post-Modernism rejects not only the vocabulary of Gropius and his followers, but also the social and ethical ideals implicit in their lucid proportions. As in the visual arts, Post-Modernism includes a variety of tendencies, but acquires a subtly different meaning when applied to architecture.

Piano and Rogers. One approach is to reject the formal beauty of the International Style. The Centre Georges Pompidou (fig. 499), the national arts and cultural center in Paris, looks like the Bauhaus turned inside out (see fig. 494). Selected in an international competition, the design by the Italian-English team of Renzo Piano (born 1937) and Richard Rogers (born 1933) eliminates any trace of Le Corbusier's elegant facades (see fig. 495), exposing the building's inner mechanics while disguising the underlying structure. The interior itself has no fixed walls, so that temporary dividers can be arranged to meet any need. This stark utilitarianism reflects a populist sentiment current in France. Yet it is enlivened by eye-catching colors, each keyed to a different function. The festive display is as vivacious and imaginative as Léger's *The City* (see fig. 434), which, with Paris' Eiffel Tower, can be regarded as the Pompidou Center's true ancestor.

Stirling. The Pompidou Center represents a reaction against the International Style without abandoning its functionalism. Other Post-Modern architects have sought to create more human environments by reverting to what can only be called Pre-Modernist architecture: their chief means of introducing greater expressiveness has been to adopt elements from historical styles rich with association. The Neue Staatsgalerie in Stuttgart (fig. 500) has the grandiose scale befitting a "palace" of the arts, but instead of the monolithic cube of the Pompidou Center, English architect James Stirling (born 1926) incorporates more varied shapes within more complex spatial relationships. There is, too, an overtly decorative quality that will remind us, however indirectly, of Garnier's Paris Opéra (see fig. 360). The similarity does not stop there. Stirling has likewise invoked a form of historicism through paraphrase that is far more subtle than Garnier's opulent revivalism, but no less self-conscious. The primly Neoclassical masonry facade, for example, is punctured by a narrow arched window recalling the Italian Renaissance and by a rusticated portal that has a distinctly Mannerist look.

This eclecticism is more than a veneer—it lies at the heart of the building's success. The site, centering on a circular sculpture court, is designed along the lines of ancient temple complexes from Egypt through Rome, complete with a monumental entrance stairway. This plan enables Stirling to solve a wide range of practical problems with ingenuity and to provide a stream of changing vistas which fascinate and delight the visitor.

501. Bernard Tschumi Architects. Folie P6, Parc de La Villette, Paris. 1983

Deconstructivism

Historicism addresses only the decorative veneer of the International Style, but Deconstructivism, another tendency that has been gathering momentum since 1980, goes much further in challenging its substance. It does so, paradoxically enough, by returning to one of the earliest sources of modernism: the Russian avant-garde. The Russian experiment in architecture proved short-lived, and few of its ideas ever made it beyond the laboratory stage. Recent architects, inspired by the bold sculpture of the Constructivists and the graphic designs of the Suprematists, seek to violate the integrity of modern architecture by subverting its internal structure, which the Russians themselves did little to undermine. Nevertheless, Deconstructivism does not abandon modern architecture and its principles altogether. Unlike some other avant-garde investigations that seek a decisive break with tradition, it remains an architecture of the possible based on structural engineering. As the term suggests, Deconstructivism dismantles modern architecture, which it then puts back together again in new ways.

Tschumi. Although Deconstructivist designs have won major awards, their experimental approach and ambitious scale have discouraged their actual construction. Among the most advanced designs to get off the drawing board is the Parc de La Villette in Paris, an ensemble of brightly colored structures designed by the Swiss Bernard Tschumi (born 1944). The geometry of the Parc de La Villette is derived from the most basic shapes laid out on a simple grid, but broken up and rearranged by Tschumi to create highly unorthodox relationships, both between and within the elements, which give the park a disquieting sense of instability. The individual buildings resemble large-scale sculptures extended almost to the breaking point (fig. 501). Yet the tension between the reality of the built structures and their "impossibility" results in an architecture of rare vitality.

Clearly such buildings push modern architecture to its practical limits. This sort of questioning has gone on before. It happened, for example, under Mannerism, when architects introduced an element of decadence into the classical vocabulary inherited from the Renaissance. Architects, like artists, have repeatedly plundered the past in search of fresh ideas. Deconstructivism is no mere historicism, however, but a transition much like *Art Nouveau* at the turn of the century, which provided the foundation for modern architecture. It is a necessary part of the process that will redefine architecture as we have come to know it.

500. James Stirling, Michael Wilford and Associates. Neue Staatsgalerie, Stuttgart, Germany. Completed 1984

TWENTIETH-CENTURY PHOTOGRAPHY

THE FIRST HALF-CENTURY

During the nineteenth century, photography struggled to establish itself as art but failed to find an identity. Only under extraordinary conditions of political upheaval and social reform did it address the most basic subject of art, which is life itself. In forming an independent vision, photography would combine the aesthetic principles of the Secession and the documentary approach of photojournalism with lessons learned from motion photography. At the same time, modern painting, with which it soon became allied, forced a decisive change in photography by undermining its aesthetic assumptions and posing a new challenge to its credentials as one of the arts. Like the other arts, photography responded to the three principal currents of our time: Expressionism, Abstraction, and Fantasy. But because it has continued to be devoted for the most part to the world around us, modern photography has adhered largely to realism and, hence, has followed a separate evolution. We must therefore discuss twentieth-century photography primarily in terms of different schools and how they have dealt with those often-conflicting currents.

The course pursued by modern photography was facilitated by technological advances. It must be emphasized, however, that these have increased but not dictated the photographer's options. George Eastman's invention of the hand-held camera in 1888 and the advent of 35mm photography with the Leica camera in 1924 made it easier to take pictures that had been difficult but by no means impossible to take with the traditional view camera. Surprisingly, even color photography did not have such revolutionary importance as might be expected. Color, in fact, has had a relatively modest impact on the content, outlook, and aesthetic of photography, even though it removed the last barrier cited by nineteenth-century critics of photography as an art.

The School of Paris

Atget. Modern photography began quietly in Paris with Eugène Atget (1856–1927), who turned to the camera only in 1898 at the age of forty-two. From then until his death, he toted his heavy equipment around Paris, recording the city in all its variety. Atget was all but ignored by the art photographers, for whom his commonplace subjects had little interest. He himself was a humble man whose studio sign read simply, "Atget—Documents for Artists," and, indeed, he was patronized by the fathers of modern art: Braque, Picasso, Duchamp, and Man Ray, to name only the best known. It is no accident that these artists were also admirers of Henri Rousseau, for Rousseau and Atget had in common a naive vision, though Atget found inspiration in unexpected corners of his environment rather than in magical realms of the imagination.

Atget's pictures are marked by a subtle intensity and technical perfection that heighten the reality, and hence the significance, of even the most mundane subject. Few photographers have equaled his ability to compose simultaneously in two- and three-dimensional space. Like *Pool, Versailles* (fig. 502), his scenes are often desolate, bespeaking a strange and individual outlook. The viewer has the haunting sensation that time has been transfixed by the stately composition and the photographer's obsession with textures. Atget's photographs are directly related to a strain of magic realism that was a forerunner of Surrealism, and it is easy to see why he was

502. Eugène Atget. *Pool, Versailles.* 1924. Albumen-silver print, 7 × 9⅜″ (18 × 24 cm). Collection, The Museum of Modern Art, New York. Abbott-Levy Collection. Partial Gift of Shirley C. Burden

rediscovered by Man Ray, the Dada and Surrealist artist-photographer.

Cartier-Bresson. The culmination of the Paris school is no doubt Henri Cartier-Bresson (born 1908), the son of a wealthy thread manufacturer. He studied under a Cubist painter in the late 1920s before taking up photography in 1932. Strongly affected at first by Atget, Man Ray (see p. 493), and even the cinema, he soon developed into the most influential photojournalist of his time. His purpose and technique are nevertheless those of an artist.

Cartier-Bresson is the master of what he has termed "the decisive moment." This to him means the instant recognition and visual organization of an event at the most intense moment of action and emotion in order to reveal its inner meaning, not simply to record its occurrence. Unlike other members of the Paris school, he seems to feel at home anywhere in the world and always to be in sympathy with his subjects, so that his photographs have a nearly universal appeal. His photographs are distinguished by an interest in composition for its own sake, derived from modern abstract art. He also has a particular fascination with motion, which he invests with all the dynamism of Futurism and the irony of Dada. The key to his work is his use of space to establish relations that are suggestive and often astonishing. Indeed, although he deals with reality, Cartier-Bresson is a Surrealist at heart. The results can be disturbing, as in *Mexico, 1934* (fig. 503). By omitting the man's face, Cartier-Bresson prevents us from identifying the meaning of the gesture, yet we respond to its tension no less powerfully.

United States

Stieglitz. The founder of modern photography in the United States was Alfred Stieglitz, whose influence remained dominant throughout his life (1864–1946). From his involvement with the Photo-Secession onward (see p. 413), he was a tireless spokesman for photography-as-art, although he defined this more broadly than did other members of the movement. He backed his words by publishing the magazine *Camera Work* and supporting the other pioneers of American photography through exhibiting their work in his New York galleries, especially the first one, known as "291." The bulk of his early work adheres to Secessionist conventions, treating photography as a pictorial equivalent to painting. During the mid-1890s, however, he took some pictures of street scenes that are harbingers of his mature photographs.

His classic statement, and the one he regarded as his finest photograph, is *The Steerage* (fig. 504). Taken in 1907 on a trip to Europe, it captures the feeling of a voyage by letting the shapes and composition tell the story. The gangway bridge divides the scene visually, emphasizing the contrasting activities of the people below in the steerage, which was reserved for the cheapest fares, and the observers on the upper deck. What it lacks in obvious sentiment it makes up for by remaining true to life.

This kind of "straight" photography is deceptive in its simplicity, for the image mirrors the feelings that stirred Stieglitz. For that reason, it marks an important step in his evolution and a turning point in the history of photography. Its importance emerges only in comparison with earlier photographs such as Steichen's *Rodin* and Riis' *Bandits' Roost* (see figs. 414, 410). *The Steerage* is a pictorial statement independent of painting on the one hand and free from social commentary on the other. It represents the first time that documentary photography achieved the level of art in America.

Stieglitz' straight photography formed the basis of the American school. It is therefore ironic that it was Stieglitz, with Steichen's encouragement, who became the champion of abstract art against the urban realism of the Ash Can school (see pp. 428–29), whose paintings were at face value often similar in

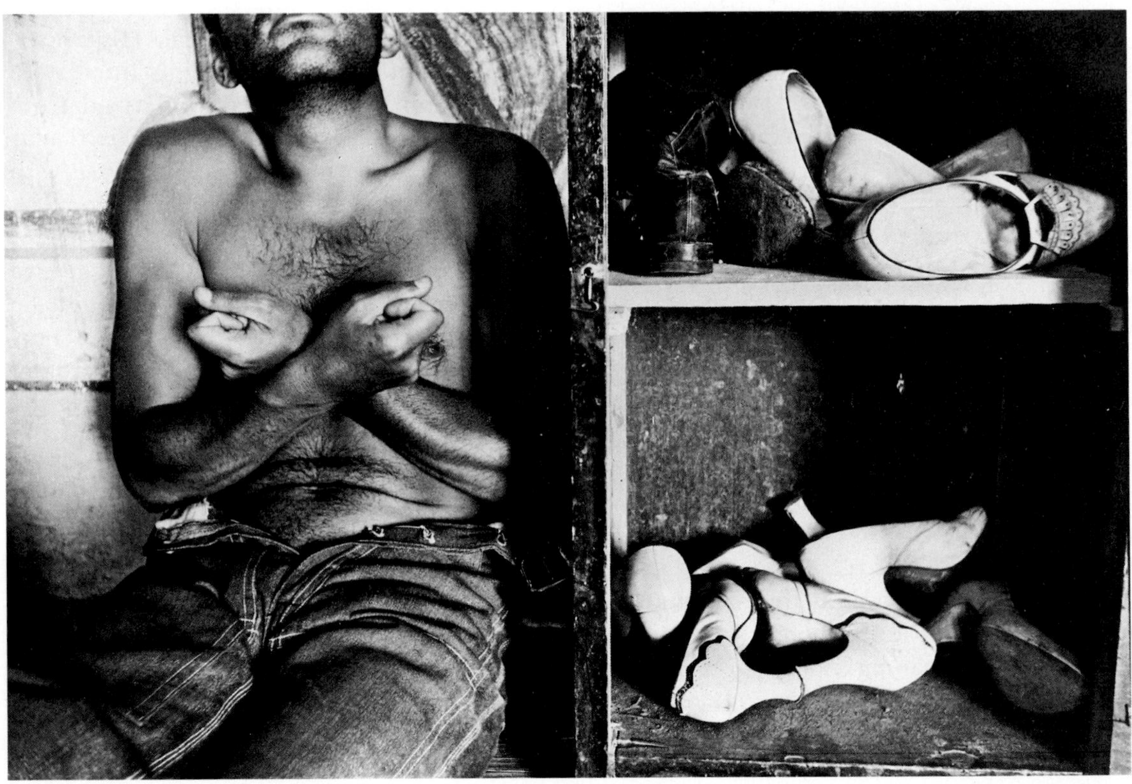

503. Henri Cartier-Bresson. *Mexico, 1934.* Gelatin-silver print

504. Alfred Stieglitz. *The Steerage.* 1907.
The Art Institute of Chicago. Alfred Stieglitz Collection

content and appearance to his photographs. The resemblance is misleading. For Stieglitz, photography was less a means of recording things than of expressing his experience and philosophy of life, much as a painter does.

This attitude culminated in his "Equivalents." In 1922 Stieglitz began to photograph clouds to show that his work was independent of subject and personality. A remarkably lyrical cloud photograph from 1930 (fig. 505) corresponds to a state of mind waiting to find full expression rather than merely respond-

505. Alfred Stieglitz. *Equivalent.* 1930. Chloride print. The Art Institute of Chicago. Alfred Stieglitz Collection

506. Edward Weston. *Pepper.* 1930. Center for Creative Photography, Tucson, Arizona

ing to the moonlit scene. The study of clouds is as old as Romanticism itself, but no one before Stieglitz had made them a major theme in photography. As in Käsebier's *The Magic Crystal* (see fig. 413), unseen forces are evoked that make *Equivalent* a counterpart to Kandinsky's *Sketch I for "Composition VII"* (see fig. 420).

Weston. Stieglitz' concept of the Equivalent opened the way to "pure" photography as an alternative to straight photography. The leader of this new approach was Edward Weston (1886–1958), who, although not Stieglitz' protégé, was decisively influenced by him. During the 1920s he pursued abstraction and realism as separate paths, but by 1930 he fused them in images that are wonderful in their design and miraculous for their detail. *Pepper* (fig. 506) is a splendid example that is anything but a straightforward record of this familiar fruit. Like Stieglitz' Equivalents, Weston's photography makes us see the mundane with new eyes. The pepper is shown with preternatural sharpness and so close up that it seems larger than life. Thanks to the tightly cropped composition, we are forced to contemplate the form, whose every undulation is revealed by the dramatic lighting. *Pepper* has the sensuousness of O'Keeffe's *Black Iris III* (see fig. 443), which lends the Equivalent a new meaning. Here the shapes are intentionally suggestive of the photographs of the female nude that Weston also pioneered.

Adams. To achieve uniform detail and depth, Weston worked with the smallest possible camera lens openings, and his success led to the formation, in 1932, of the West Coast society known as Group f/64, for the smallest lens opening. Among the founding members was Ansel Adams (1902–1984), who soon became the foremost nature photographer in America. Adams was a meticulous technician, beginning with the composition and exposure and continuing through the final printing. His justifiably famous work *Moonrise, Hernandez, New Mexico* (fig. 507) came from pure serendipity which could never be repeated, a perfect marriage of straight and Equivalent photography. As in all of Adams' pictures, there is a full range of tonal nuances, from clear whites to inky blacks. The key to the photograph lies in the low cloud that divides the scene into three zones, so that the moon appears to hover effortlessly in the early evening sky.

507. Ansel Adams. *Moonrise, Hernandez, New Mexico.* 1941. Gelatin-silver print, 15 × 18" (38.1 × 47 cm). Collection, The Museum of Modern Art, New York. Gift of the artist. © 1991 by the Trustees of The Ansel Adams Publishing Rights Trust

Bourke-White. Stieglitz was among the first to photograph skyscrapers, the new architecture that came to dominate the horizon of America's growing cities. In turn, he championed the Precisionist painters (see p. 431), who began to depict urban and industrial architecture around 1925 under the inspiration of Futurism. Several of them soon took up the camera as well. Thus, painting and photography once again became closely linked. Both were responding to the revitalized economy after World War I, which led to an unprecedented industrial expansion on both sides of the Atlantic. During the subsequent Depression, industrial photography continued surprisingly to grow with the new mass-circulation magazines that ushered in the great age of photojournalism and, with it, of commercial photography. In the United States, most of the important photographers were employed by the leading journals and corporations.

508. Margaret Bourke-White. *Fort Peck Dam, Montana, 1936* (first cover of *Life* magazine). Time-Life

Margaret Bourke-White (1904–1971) was the first staff photographer hired by *Fortune* magazine and then by *Life* magazine, both published by Henry Luce. Her cover photograph of Fort Peck Dam in Montana for the inaugural November 23, 1936, issue of *Life* remains a classic example of the new photojournalism (fig. 508). The decade witnessed enormous building campaigns, and with her keen eye for composition, Bourke-White drew a visual parallel between the dam and the massive constructions of ancient Egypt (compare fig. 36). In addition to their architectural power, Bourke-White's columnar forms have a remarkable sculptural quality and an almost human presence, looming like colossal statues at the entrance to a temple. But unlike the pharaohs' passive timelessness, these "guardian figures" have the spectral alertness of Henry Moore's abstract monoliths (see fig. 467). Bourke-White's rare ability to suggest multiple levels of meaning made this cover and her accompanying photo essay a landmark in photojournalism.

Van Der Zee. The nature of the Harlem Renaissance, which flourished in the 1920s (see p. 446), was hotly debated by black critics even in its own day. While its achievement in literature is beyond dispute, the photography of James Van Der Zee (1886–1983) is often regarded today as its chief contribution to the visual arts. Much of his work is commercial and variable in quality, yet it remains of great documentary value and, at its best, provides a compelling portrait of an era. Van Der Zee had an acute understanding of settings as reflections of people's sense of place in the world, which he used to bring out a sitter's character and dreams. Though posed in obvious imitation of fashionable photographs of white society, his picture of the wife of the Reverend George Wilson Becton (fig. 509), taken two years after the popular pastor of the Salem Methodist Church in Harlem was murdered, shows Van Der Zee's unique ability to capture the pride of African Americans during a period when their dreams seemed on the verge of being realized.

509. James Van Der Zee. *The Wife of the Reverend Becton, Pastor of Salem Methodist Church.* 1934. James Van Der Zee Estate

Germany

With the New Objectivity movement in Germany during the late 1920s and early 1930s (see p. 437), photography achieved a degree of excellence that has not been surpassed. Fostered by the invention of superior German cameras and the boom in publishing everywhere, this German version of straight photography emphasized materiality at a time when many other photographers were turning away from the real world. The intrinsic beauty of things was brought out through the clarity of form and structure in their photographs. This approach accorded with Bauhaus principles except with regard to function (see p. 477).

Sander. When applied to people rather than things, the New Objectivity could have deceptive results. August Sander (1876–1964), whose *Face of Our Time* was published in 1929, concealed the book's intentions behind a seemingly straightforward surface. The sixty

510. August Sander. *Pastry Cook, Cologne*. 1928. Courtesy of August Sander Archive and Sander Gallery, Inc., New York

511. Dorothea Lange. *Migrant Mother, California*. February 1936. Gelatin-silver print. Library of Congress, Washington, D.C.

portraits provide a devastating survey of Germany during the rise of the Nazis, who later suppressed the book. Clearly proud of his position, the man in Sander's *Pastry Cook, Cologne* (fig. 510) is the very opposite of the timid figure in George Grosz' *Germany, A Winter's Tale* (see fig. 441). Despite their curious resemblance, this "good citizen" seems oblivious to the evil that Grosz has depicted so vividly. While the photograph passes no individual judgment, in the context of the book the subject's unconcern stands as a strong indictment of the era as a whole.

The Heroic Age of Photography

The period from 1930 to 1945 can be called the heroic age of photography for its photographers' notable response to the challenges of their times. Photographers in those difficult years demonstrated moral courage as well as physical bravery. Under Roy Stryker, staff photographers of the Farm Security Administration compiled a comprehensive photodocumentary archive of rural America during the Depression. While the FSA photographers presented a balanced and objective view, most of them were also reformers whose work responded to the social problems they confronted daily in the field. The concern of Dorothea Lange (1895–1965) for people and her sensitivity to their dignity made her the finest documentary photographer of the time in America.

Lange. At a pea-pickers' camp in Nipomo, California, Lange discovered 2,500 virtually starving migrant workers and took several pictures of a young widow (much later identified as Florence Thompson) with her children. When *Migrant Mother, California* (fig. 511) was published in a news story on their plight, the government rushed in food, and eventually migrant relief camps were opened. More than any Social Realist or Regionalist painting (see p. 437), *Migrant Mother, California* has come to stand for that entire era. Unposed and uncropped, this photograph has an unforgettable immediacy no other medium can match.

Fantasy and Abstraction

"Impersonality," the very liability that had precluded the acceptance of photography in the eyes of many critics, became a virtue in the 1920s. Precisely because photographs are produced by mechanical devices, the camera's images now seemed to some artists the perfect means for expressing the modern era. This change in attitude did not stem from the Futurists, who, contrary to what might be expected, never fully grasped the camera's importance for modern art. The new view of photography arose as part of the Berlin Dadaists' assault on traditional art.

Toward the end of World War I, the Dadaists "invented" the photomontage and the photogram, although these completely different processes had been practiced early in the history of photography. In the service of anti-art they lent themselves equally well to fantasy and to abstraction, despite the apparent opposition of the two modes.

Photomontages. Photomontages are simply parts of photographs cut out and recombined into new images. Composite negatives originated with the art photography of Rejlander (see pp. 411–12), but by the 1870s they were already being used in France to create witty impossibilities that are the ancestors of Dada photomontages. Like *1 Piping Man* (see fig. 437) by Max Ernst (who, not surprisingly, became a master of the genre), Dadaist photomontages utilize the techniques of Synthetic Cubism to ridicule social and aesthetic conventions.

These imaginative parodies destroy all pictorial illusionism and therefore stand in direct opposition to straight photographs, which use the camera to record and probe the meaning of reality. Dada photomontages might be called "ready-images," after Duchamp's ready-mades. Like other collages, they are literally torn from popular culture and given new meaning. Although the photomontage relies more on the laws of chance (see p. 433), the Surrealists later claimed it to be a form of automatic handwriting on the grounds that it responds to a stream of consciousness.

512. John Heartfield. *As in the Middle Ages, So in the Third Reich.* 1934. Poster, photomontage. Akademie der Künste zu Berlin, Heartfield-Archiv. © 1991 VG Bild-Kunst Bonn

Posters. Photomontages were soon incorporated into carefully designed posters as well. In Germany, posters became a double-edged sword in political propaganda, used by Hitler's sympathizers and enemies alike. The most acerbic anti-Nazi commentaries were provided by John Heartfield (1891–1968), who changed his name from the German Herzfeld as a sign of protest. His horrific poster of a Nazi victim crucified on a swastika (fig. 512) appropriates a Gothic image of humanity punished for its sins on the wheel of divine judgment. Obviously, Heartfield was not concerned about misinterpreting the original meaning in his montage, which communicates its new message to powerful effect.

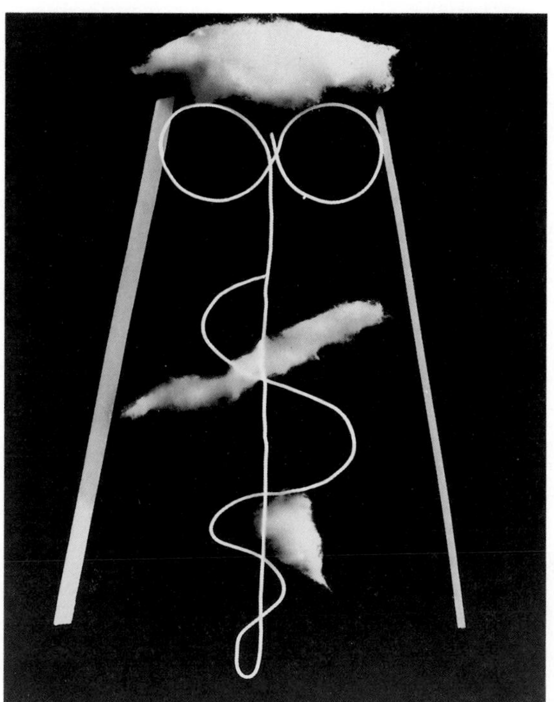

513. Man Ray. *Rayograph.* 1928. Gelatin-silver print, 15½ × 11⅝" (39 × 29.6 cm). Collection, The Museum of Modern Art, New York. Gift of James Thrall Soby

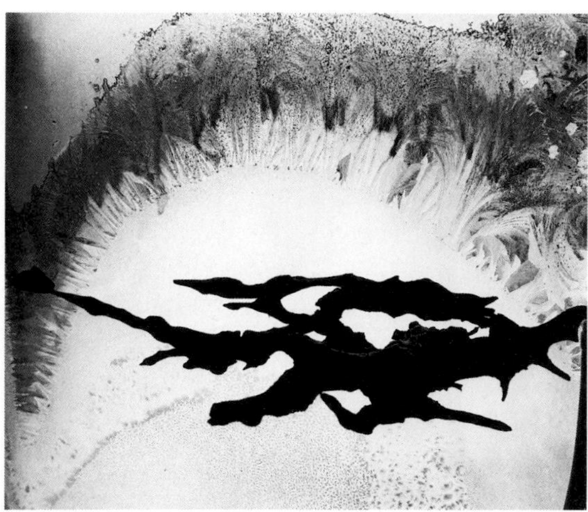

514. Minor White. *Ritual Branch.* 1958. Gelatin-silver print, 10⅜ × 10⅝" (26.4 × 27 cm). Collection of the International Museum of Photography at George Eastman House, Rochester, New York. Reproduction courtesy The Minor White Archive, Princeton University. Copyright 1982. Trustees of Princeton University

Photograms. The photogram does not take pictures but makes them: objects are placed directly onto photographic paper and exposed to light. Nor was this technique new. The Dadaists' photograms, however, like their photomontages, were intended to alter nature's forms, not to record them, and to substitute impersonal technology for the work of the individual. Since the results in the photogram are so unpredictable, making one involves even greater risks than does a photomontage.

Man Ray. Man Ray (1890–1976), an American working in Paris, was not the first to make photograms, but his name is the most closely linked to them through his "Rayographs." Fittingly enough, he discovered the process by accident. The amusing face in figure 513 was made according to the laws of chance by dropping a string, two strips of paper, and a few pieces of cotton onto the photographic paper, then coaxing them here and there before exposure. The resulting image is a witty creation that shows the playful, spontaneous side of Dada and Surrealism as against Heartfield's grim satire.

PHOTOGRAPHY SINCE 1945

White. Photography after World War II was marked by abstraction for nearly two decades, particulary in the United States. Minor White (1908–1976) closely approached the spirit of Abstract Expressionism. He was decisively influenced by Stieglitz' concept of the Equivalent. During his most productive period, from the mid-1950s to the mid-1960s, White evolved a highly individual style, using the alchemy of the darkroom to transform reality into a mystical metaphor. His *Ritual Branch* (fig. 514) evokes a primordial image: what it shows is not as important as what it stands for, but the meaning we sense is there remains elusive.

Frank. The birth of a new form of straight photography in the United States was largely the responsibility of one man, Robert Frank (born 1924). His book *The Americans,* com-

515. Robert Frank. *Santa Fe, New Mexico.* 1955–56. Gelatin-silver print. Courtesy Pace-MacGill Gallery, New York

piled from a cross-country odyssey made in 1955–56, created a sensation upon its publication in 1959, for it expressed the same restlessness and alienation as *On the Road* by his traveling companion, the Beat poet Jack Kerouac, published in 1957. As this friendship suggests, words have an important role in Frank's photographs, which are as loaded in their meaning as Demuth's paintings (see fig. 435); yet Frank's social point of view is often hidden behind a facade of disarming neutrality. It is with shock that we finally recognize the ironic intent of *Santa Fe, New Mexico* (fig. 515): the gas pumps face the sign SAVE in the barren landscape like members of a religious cult vainly seeking salvation at a revival meeting. Frank, who subsequently turned to film, holds up an image of American culture that is as sterile as it is joyless. Even spiritual values, he tells us, become meaningless in the face of vulgar materialism.

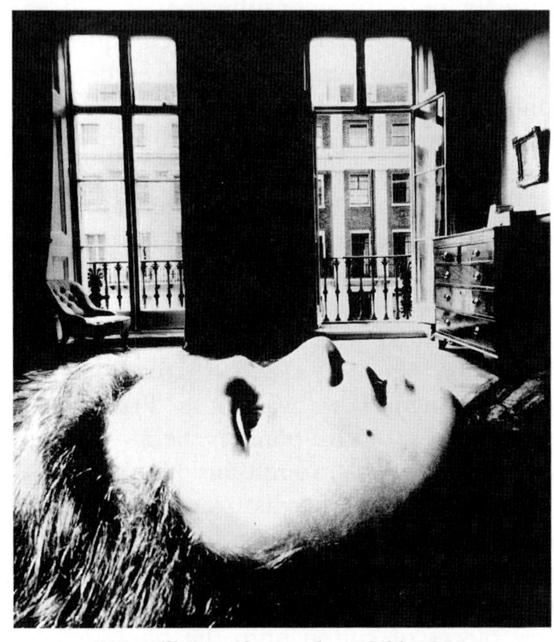

516. Bill Brandt. *London Child.* 1955. Copyright Mrs. Noya Brandt. Courtesy Edwynn Houk Gallery, Chicago

Brandt. Fantasy gradually reasserted itself on both sides of the Atlantic in the mid-1950s. Photographers first manipulated the camera for the sake of extreme visual effects by using special lenses and filters to alter appearances, sometimes virtually beyond recognition. Since about 1970, however, they have employed mainly printing techniques, with results that are frequently even more startling.

Manipulation of photography was pioneered by Bill Brandt (1904–1983). Though regarded as the quintessential English photographer, he was born in Germany and did not settle in London until 1931. He decided on a career in photography during psychoanalysis and was apprenticed briefly to Man Ray. Consequently, Brandt remained a Surrealist who manipulated visual reality in search of a deeper one, charged with mystery. His work was marked consistently by a literary, even theatrical, cast of mind, which drew on the cinema for some of its effects. His early photodocumentaries were often staged as re-creations of personal experience for the purpose of social commentary based on Victorian models. Brandt's fantasy images manifest a strikingly romantic imagination. Yet, there is an oppressive anxiety implicit in his landscapes, portraits, and nudes. *London Child* (fig. 516) has the haunting mood of novels by the Brontë sisters Charlotte, Emily, and Anne. At the same time, this is a classic dream image fraught with troubling psychological overtones. The spatial dislocation, worthy of De Chirico, expresses the malaise of a person who is alienated from both himself and the world.

Leonard. Contemporary photographers often turn to fantasy as autobiographical expression. Both the image and the title of *Romanticism Is Ultimately Fatal* (fig. 517) by Joanne Leonard (born 1940) suggest a meaning that is personal in its reference; it was made during the breakup of her marriage. We will recognize in this disturbing vision something of the tortured eroticism of Fuseli's *The Nightmare* (see fig. 348). The clarity of the presentation turns the apparition at the window into a real and terrifying personification of despair: this is no romantic knight in shining armor, but a grim reaper.

517. Joanne Leonard. *Romanticism Is Ultimately Fatal,* from *Dreams and Nightmares.* 1982. Positive transparency selectively opaqued with collage, 9¾ × 9¼" (24.8 × 23.5 cm). Collection M. Neri, Benicia, California

Hockney. The most recent demonstrations of photography's power to extend our vision have come, fittingly enough, from artists. The photographic collages that the English painter David Hockney (born 1937) has been making since 1982 are like revelations that overcome the traditional limitations of a unified image, fixed in time and place, by closely approximating how we actually see. In *Gregory Watching the Snow Fall, Kyoto, Feb. 21, 1983* (fig. 518), each frame is analogous to a discrete eye movement containing a piece of visual data that must be stored in our memory and synthesized by the brain. Just as we process only essential information, so there are gaps in the matrix of the image, which becomes more fragmentary toward its edges, though without the loss of acuity experienced in vision itself. The resulting shape of the collage is a masterpiece of design. The scene appears to bow curiously as it comes toward us. This ebb and flow is more than simply the result of optical physics. In the perceptual process, space and its corollary, time, are not

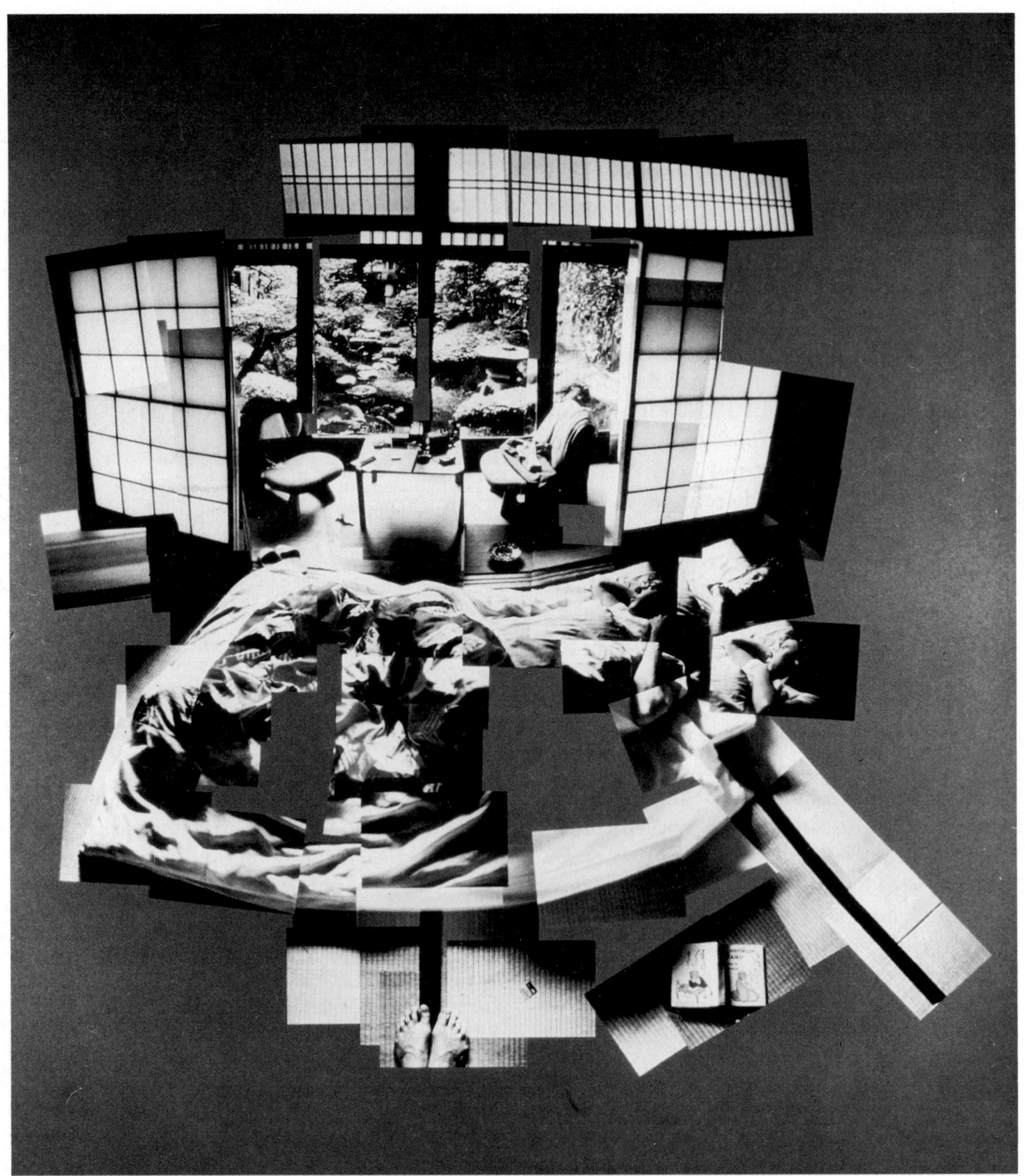

518. David Hockney. *Gregory Watching the Snow Fall, Kyoto, Feb. 21, 1983.* Photographic collage, 43½ × 46½" (110.5 × 118.1 cm). © David Hockney, 1983

linear, but fluid. Moreover, by including his own feet as reference points to establish our position clearly, Hockney helps us realize that vision is less a matter of looking outward than an egocentric act that defines the viewer's visual and psychological relationship to the surrounding world. The picture is as expressive as it is opulent. Hockney has recorded his friend several times to suggest his reactions to the serene landscape outside the door. Hockney's approach is embedded in the history of modern painting, for it shows a self-conscious awareness of earlier art. It combines the faceted views of Picasso and the dynamic energy

519. Annette Lemieux. *Truth.* 1989. Latex and acrylic on canvas, 7′ × 11′1″ × 1½″ (2.13 m × 3.3 m × 3.8 cm). Josh Baer Gallery, New York

of Popova (see figs. 423, 426). *Gregory Watching the Snow Fall* is nonetheless a distinctly contemporary work, for it incorporates the illusionistic potential of Op Art and the fascinating effects of Photorealism (see figs. 455, 460).

Lemieux. Unlike Hockney, most artists today do not take their own photographs but appropriate them from other mediums. Because their pictures are intended as counterparts to paintings, they are enlarged on an unprecedented scale, using commercial processes developed for advertisements, which may also serve as sources. Many of these "rephotographers" are conceptual artists, such as Annette Lemieux (born 1957), whose work conveys a message, served with the aid of texts. Her themes are thought-provoking. Centering on social issues, they address the human condition without engaging in polemic. Lemieux has a gift for perceiving new possibilities of meaning in old photographs and illustrations. *Truth* (fig. 519) is an image about sound—or, rather, the lack of it. The photograph, derived from a book on the history of radio, is a visual counterpart to the saying, "Hear no evil, speak no evil, see no evil." Transferred to canvas, it acquires a very different meaning in its new context. This process is known as deconstruction. Stenciled in bold letters is the Russian proverb, "Eat bread and salt but speak the truth," which means roughly, "Be frank when accepting someone's hospitality." The lettering transforms the image from an amusing publicity photograph into an ominous-looking propaganda poster. Contrary to initial impressions, the issue is neither Russia nor communism—the photograph features the famous American entertainer Jack Benny—but the role of the media in modern life. They enter our homes as guests without being candid: here the performer covers his mouth in order to speak no evil. Shielded by the medium itself, he distorts truth by selectively concealing information, not by telling a deliberate falsehood. Truth emerges as a matter of relative perspective, determined as much by who controls it as by who hears it.

CHRONOLOGICAL CHART IV

	POLITICAL HISTORY	RELIGION, LITERATURE	SCIENCE, TECHNOLOGY
1750	Seven Years' War (1756–63): England and Prussia vs. Austria and France, called French and Indian War in America; French defeated in Battle of Quebec 1769 Catherine the Great (r. 1762–96) extends Russian power to Black Sea	Thomas Gray's *Elegy* 1750 Diderot's *Encyclopedia* 1751–72 Samuel Johnson's *Dictionary* 1755 Edmund Burke, English reformer (1729–1797) Jean-Jacques Rousseau, French philosopher and writer (1712–1778)	James Watt patents steam engine 1769 Priestley discovers oxygen 1774 Coke-fed blast furnaces for iron smelting perfected c. 1760–75 Benjamin Franklin's experiments with electricity c. 1750
1775	American Revolution 1775–85; Constitution adopted 1789 French Revolution 1789–97; Reign of Terror under Robespierre 1793 Consulate of Napoleon 1799	Edward Gibbon's *Decline and Fall of the Roman Empire* 1776–87 Thomas Paine's *The Rights of Man* 1790 William Wordsworth and Samuel Taylor Coleridge, *Lyrical Ballads,* 1798	Power loom 1785; cotton gin 1792 Jenner's smallpox vaccine c. 1798
1800	Louisiana Purchase 1803 Napoleon crowns himself emperor 1804; exiled to St. Helena 1815 War of 1812 Greeks declare independence 1822 Monroe Doctrine proclaimed by U.S. 1823	Johann Wolfgang von Goethe's *Faust* (part I) 1808 George Gordon Byron's *Childe Harold's Pilgrimage* 1812–18 John Keats, English poet (1795–1821) Percy Bysshe Shelley, English poet (1792–1822) Jane Austen, English novelist (1775–1817) Walter Scott's Waverly novels 1814–25	Lewis and Clark expedition to Pacific 1803–6 First voyage of Fulton's steamship 1807; first Atlantic crossing 1819 Stephenson's first locomotive 1814 Faraday discovers principle of electric dynamo 1821
1825	Revolution of 1830 in France Queen Victoria crowned 1837 U.S. treaty with China opens ports 1844 Famine in Ireland, mass emigration 1845 U.S. annexes western land areas 1845–60 Revolution of 1848; fails in Germany, Hungary, Austria, Italy; France sets up Second Republic (Louis Napoleon) Gold discovered in California 1848	Aleksandr Pushkin, Russian writer (1799–1837) Victor Hugo, French writer (1802–1885) Stendahl's *The Red and the Black* 1831 Ralph Waldo Emerson, American essayist (1803–1882) Margaret Fuller, American reformer (1810–1850) Charles Dickens' *Oliver Twist* 1838 George Eliot, English novelist (1819–1880) William Thackeray's *Vanity Fair* 1847 Karl Marx's *Communist Manifesto* 1848 Edgar Allan Poe, American poet (1809–1849)	Erie Canal opened 1825 First railway completed (England) 1825 McCormick invents reaper 1831 Daguerreotype process of photography introduced 1839 Morse perfects telegraph 1844
1850	Louis Napoleon takes title of emperor 1852 Perry's visit ends Japan's isolation 1854 Frederick Douglass (c. 1817–1895) becomes American abolitionist leader Russia abolishes serfdom 1861 U.S. Civil War (1861–65) ends slavery; Lincoln assassinated 1865 Susan B. Anthony (with Elizabeth Cady Stanton) organizes National Woman Suffrage Association 1869 Franco-Prussian War 1870–71 Disraeli British prime minister 1874–80	Herman Melville's *Moby Dick* 1851 Stowe's *Uncle Tom's Cabin* 1851 Thoreau's *Walden* 1854 Walt Whitman's *Leaves of Grass* 1855 Flaubert's *Madame Bovary* 1856 Charles Baudelaire, French poet (1821–1867) Leo Tolstoy's *War and Peace* 1864–69 Feodor Dostoyevsky's *Crime and Punishment* 1867 Karl Marx's *Das Kapital* 1867–94	Darwin publishes *Origin of Species* 1859 Bessemer patents tilting converter for turning iron into steel 1860 Pasteur develops germ theory 1864 Mendel publishes first experiments in genetics 1865 Nobel invents dynamite 1867 First transcontinental railroad completed in America 1869 Suez Canal opened 1869

NOTE: Figure numbers of black-and-white illustrations are in (italics). Colorplate numbers are in **(bold face)**. *Duration of papacy or reign is indicated by the abbreviation* r.

ARCHITECTURE	SCULPTURE	PAINTING	PHOTOGRAPHY	
				1750
Horace Walpole, Strawberry Hill, Twickenham (**357**) Soufflot, Panthéon, Paris *(333)*		Greuze, *Village Bride (325)* West, *Death of General Wolfe* (**328**)		
				1775
Jefferson, Monticello, Charlottesville *(335)*	Houdon, *Voltaire (331)*	Copley, *Watson and the Shark (329)* David, *Death of Socrates* (**326**); *Death of Marat* (**327**) Gros, *Napoleon at Arcole (338)*		
				1800
	Canova, *Pauline Borghese as Venus* (**354**)	Goya, *Family of Charles IV* (**336**) Ingres, *Odalisque* (**340**) Goya, *Third of May, 1808* (**337**) Géricault, *Raft of the "Medusa" (339)* Constable, *Haywain* (**350**) Friedrich, *Polar Sea* (**352**)		
				1825
Barry and Pugin, Houses of Parliament, London *(359)* Labrouste, Bibliothèque Ste.-Geneviève, Paris *(387, 388)*	Rude, *La Marseillaise,* Arc de Triomphe, Paris *(355)*	Delacroix, *Massacre at Chios* (**342**) Corot, *Papigno (345)* Ingres, *Louis Bertin* (**341**) Turner, *Slave Ship* (**351**) Bingham, *Fur Traders Descending the Missouri (353)* Bonheur, *Plowing in the Nivernais* (**347**) Courbet, *Stone Breakers (365)*	Niépce, *View from His Window at Le Gras (361)*	
				1850
Paxton, Crystal Palace *(389)* Garnier, Opéra, Paris (**360**)	Carpeaux, *The Dance (356)*	Rossetti, *Ecce Ancilla Domini* (**377**) Millet, *The Sower* (**346**) Daumier, *Third-Class Carriage (344)* Manet, *Luncheon on the Grass* (**368**); *The Fifer* (**369**) Homer, *Morning Bell* (**381**) Monet, *The River* (**370**) Whistler, *Artist's Mother* (**379**); *Falling Rocket* (**380**)	Rejlander, *Two Paths of Life (411)* Nadar, *Sarah Bernhardt (362)* Gardner, *Home of a Rebel Sharpshooter, Gettysburg (364)* Cameron, *Portrait of Ellen Terry (412)* *Tsar Cannon Outside the Spassky Gate, Moscow (363)*	

	POLITICAL HISTORY	RELIGION, LITERATURE	SCIENCE, TECHNOLOGY
1875	Peak of colonialism worldwide 1876–1914 First pogroms in Russia 1881–82 First Zionist Congress called by Theodor Hertzl 1897 Spanish-American War 1898; U.S. gains Philippines, Guam, Puerto Rico, annexes Hawaii	Mark Twain's *Tom Sawyer* 1876 Henrik Ibsen, Norwegian dramatist (1828–1906) Émile Zola, French novelist (1840–1902) Oscar Wilde, Irish writer (1854–1900) Henry James, American novelist (1843–1916) G. B. Shaw, British writer (1856–1950) Emily Dickinson (1830–1886), poetry published 1890, 1891	Bell patents telephone 1876 Edison invents phonograph 1877; invents electric light bulb 1879 First internal combustion engines for gasoline 1885 Roentgen discovers X-rays 1895 Marconi invents wireless telegraphy 1895 Edison invents motion picture 1896 The Curies discover radium 1898
1900	President T. Roosevelt (1901–9) proclaims Open Door policy; Panama Canal opened 1914 8,800,000 immigrate to U.S. 1901–10 Internal strife, reforms in Russia 1905 Revolution in China, republic set up 1911 First World War 1914–18; U.S. enters 1917 Bolshevik Revolution 1917; Russia signs separate peace with Germany 1918 Gandhi agitates for Indian independence after First World War Woman Suffrage enacted in U.S. 1920; in England 1928; in France 1945 Irish Free State established 1921 Mussolini's Fascists seize Italian government 1922 Turkey becomes republic 1923	Marcel Proust, French novelist (1871–1922) W. B. Yeats, Irish poet (1865–1939) André Gide, French novelist (1869–1951) Gertrude Stein, American writer (1874–1946) T. S. Eliot, British poet (1888–1964) James Joyce, Irish writer (1882–1941) Eugene O'Neill, American dramatist (1888–1953) D. H. Lawrence, English novelist (1885–1930)	Planck formulates quantum theory 1900 Freud's *Interpretation of Dreams* 1900 Pavlov's first experiments with conditioned reflexes 1900 Wright brothers' first flight with power-driven airplane 1903 Einstein's theory of relativity 1905 Victor Victrola available 1906 Ford begins assembly-line automobile production 1909 First radio station begins regularly scheduled broadcasts 1920

ARCHITECTURE	SCULPTURE	PAINTING	PHOTOGRAPHY	
				1875
Sullivan, Wainwright Building, St. Louis *(407)*	Degas, *Little Fourteen-Year-Old Dancer (386)* Rodin, *The Thinker (384); Monument to Balzac (385)*	Moreau, *The Apparition* (**397**) Renoir, *Moulin de la Galette* (**371**) Degas, *Glass of Absinthe (372)* Eakins, *William Rush Carving His Allegorical Figure of the Schuylkill River* (**382**) Cézanne, *Still Life with Apples* (**390**) Redon, *À Edgar Poe (399)* Seurat, *Sunday Afternoon on the Grande Jatte* (**392**) Degas, *The Tub (373)* Morisot, *La Lecture* (**374**) Gauguin, *Vision After the Sermon* (**395**) Van Gogh, *Self-Portrait* (**394**); *Wheat Field and Cypress Trees* (**393**) Cassatt, *The Bath* (**375**) Toulouse-Lautrec, *At the Moulin Rouge* (**400**) Beardsley, *Salome (398)* Munch, *The Scream* (**401**) Tanner, *Banjo Lesson* (**383**) Cézanne, *Mont Sainte-Victoire Seen from Bibémus Quarry* (**391**)	Käsebier, *Magic Crystal (413)* Muybridge, *Female Semi-Nude in Motion (415)* Riis, *Bandits' Roost, Mulberry Street (410)*	
				1900
Gaudí, Casa Milá, Barcelona *(408)* Wright, Robie House, Chicago *(491, 492)* Van de Velde, Werkbund Theater, Cologne *(409)* Rietveld, Schröder House, Utrecht (**493**)	Maillol, *Seated Woman (Méditerranée) (405)* Brancusi, *The Kiss (466)* Barlach, *Man Drawing a Sword (406)* Boccioni, *Unique Forms of Continuity in Space* (**470**) Duchamp-Villon, *Great Horse (471)* Duchamp, *In Advance of the Broken Arm (473)* Tatlin, Project for *Monument to the Third International (472)* Brancusi, *Bird in Space* (**469**) Ancestor figure from New Guinea (**23**) Mask from Cameroon (**24**) Mask from New Britain (**25**) Eskimo mask from Alaska (**26**)	Matisse, *Joy of Life (416)* Picasso, *Demoiselles d'Avignon* (**422**) Monet, *Water Lilies* (**376**) Matisse, *Red Studio* (**417**) Nolde, *Last Supper (419)* Picasso, *Ambroise Vollard (423)* Rousseau, *The Dream* (**403**) Chagall, *I and the Village* (**429**) Duchamp, *The Bride* (**430**) Braque, *Le Courrier* (**424**) Boccioni, *Dynamism of a Cyclist (425)* Kandinsky, *Sketch I for "Composition VII"* (**420**) Malevich, *Black Quadrilateral (427)* De Chirico, *Mystery and Melancholy of a Street (428)* Popova, *The Traveler* (**426**) Rouault, *Old King (418)* Léger, *The City* (**434**) Ernst, *1 Copper Plate . . . (437)* Picasso, *Three Musicians* (**432**) Klee, *Twittering Machine* (**440**) O'Keeffe, *Black Iris III* (**443**)	Steichen, *Rodin with His Sculptures "Victor Hugo" and "The Thinker" (414)* Stieglitz, *The Steerage (504)* Atget, *Pool, Versailles (502)* Man Ray, *Rayograph (513)*	

	POLITICAL HISTORY	RELIGION, LITERATURE	SCIENCE, TECHNOLOGY
1925	Stalin starts Five-Year Plan 1928 Hitler seizes power in Germany 1933 Roosevelt proclaims New Deal 1933 Mussolini conquers Ethiopia 1936 Spanish Civil War 1936–39; won by Franco Hitler annexes Austria 1938 Second World War 1939–45 Atomic bomb dropped on Hiroshima 1945 United Nations Charter signed 1945 Israel becomes independent 1948 Apartheid becomes government policy in South Africa 1948 NATO founded 1949 Communists under Mao win in China 1949	Sinclair Lewis, American novelist (1885–1951) Virginia Woolf, English author (1882–1941) William Faulkner, American novelist (1897–1962) Ernest Hemingway, American writer (1898–1961) Thomas Wolfe, American novelist (1900–1938) Bertolt Brecht, German dramatist (1898–1956) Jean-Paul Sartre, French philosopher (1905–1980) Simone de Beauvoir, French author (1908–1986) Albert Camus, French novelist (1913–1960)	First regularly scheduled TV broadcasts in U.S. 1928, in England 1936 Motion pictures with sound appear in theaters 1928 Margaret Mead's *Coming of Age in Samoa* 1928 Atomic fission demonstrated on laboratory scale 1942 Penicillin discovered 1943 Computer technology developed 1944
1950	Korean War 1950–53 U.S. Supreme Court outlaws racial segregation in public schools 1954 Common Market established in Europe 1957 African colonies gain independence after 1957 Castro takes over Cuba 1959	Wallace Stevens, American poet (1879–1955) Samuel Beckett, Irish author (1906–1989) Jean Genet, French dramatist (1910–1986) Eugène Ionesco, French dramatist (born 1912) Lawrence Durrell, English novelist (1912–1990) Jack Kerouac's *On the Road* 1957	Genetic code cracked 1953 First hydrogen bomb (atomic fusion) exploded 1954 Sputnik, first satellite, launched 1957
1960	Sit-ins protest racial discrimination 1960 Berlin Wall built 1961 John F. Kennedy assassinated 1963 Johnson begins massive U.S. intervention in Vietnam 1965 Great Proletarian Cultural Revolution in China 1965–68 Martin Luther King, Jr., assassinated 1968 Russia invades Czechoslovakia 1968	Jorge Luis Borges, Argentinian author (1899–1986) John Steinbeck awarded Nobel Prize 1962 Betty Friedan's *The Feminine Mystique* 1963	First manned space flight 1961 First manned landing on the moon 1969
1970	Massacre of student demonstrators at Kent State University, Ohio, 1970 Civil war in Pakistan gains independence for People's Republic of Bangladesh 1972–73 Vietnam War ends 1973 Nixon resigns presidency 1974 Death of Franco 1975 Iranian Revolution 1979	Gabriel García Márquez' *One Hundred Years of Solitude* 1970 First non-Italian pope elected since Adrian VI in 1522—Pope John Paul II (from Poland) 1978	First orbiting laboratory (Skylab) 1973 Viking I and II Space Probes land on Mars 1976 Personal computers available 1978 Voyager I Space Probe orbits Jupiter 1979
1980	Socialization of French banks 1981 Lech Walesa, Polish Solidarity leader, wins Nobel Peace Prize 1983 Gorbachev begins implementing reform policy of *perestroika* (restructuring) and *glasnost* (openness) in U.S.S.R. 1985 Tiananmen Square massacre 1989 Reform movements develop throughout Eastern Europe; Romanians overthrow Ceausescu; Havel elected president of Czechoslovakia; Berlin Wall demolished 1989	Alice Walker's *The Color Purple* 1982	AIDS virus recognized 1981 Space shuttle initiated by U.S. 1981 First artificial heart implanted 1982 Compact discs available 1983 Explosion of space shuttle Challenger 1986
1990	Walesa elected president of Poland 1990 Reunification of Germany 1990 Persian Gulf War 1991		

	ARCHITECTURE	SCULPTURE	PAINTING	PHOTOGRAPHY
1925	Gropius, Bauhaus, Dessau *(494)* Le Corbusier, Villa Savoye, Poissy-sur-Seine *(495)* Aalto, Villa Mairea, Noormarkku *(496)*	González, *Head* (**474**) Moore, *Two Forms (467)* Calder, *Lobster Trap and Fish Tail* (**475**) Picasso, *Bull's Head (2)* Hepworth, *Sculpture with Color (468)*	Picasso, *Three Dancers (433)* Demuth, *I Saw the Figure 5 in Gold* (**435**) Hopper, *Early Sunday Morning* (**444**) Mondrian, *Composition with Red, Blue, and Yellow* (**436**) Beckmann, *Departure* (**442**) Miró, *Painting* (**439**) Ernst, *Attirement of the Bride* (**438**) Gorky, *The Liver Is the Cock's Comb* (**445**)	Sander, *Pastry Cook, Cologne (510)* Stieglitz, *Equivalent (505)* Weston, *Pepper (506)* Heartfield, *As in the Middle Ages, So in the Third Reich (512)* Van Der Zee, *Wife of the Reverend Becton (509)* Cartier-Bresson, *Mexico, 1934 (503)* Bourke-White, *Fort Peck Dam, Montana (508)* Lange, *Migrant Mother, California (511)*
1950	Mies van der Rohe, Lake Shore Drive Apartment Houses, Chicago *(497)* Wright, Solomon R. Guggenheim Museum, New York *(14, 15)*	Rauschenberg, *Odalisk* (**481**)	Pollock, *Autumnal Rhythm* (**446**) Dubuffet, *Le Métafisyx (449)* De Kooning, *Woman II* (**448**) Rothko, *Ochre and Red on Red* (**450**) Vasarely, *Vega (455)* Johns, *Three Flags* (**457**) Louis, *Blue Veil* (**451**) Krasner, *Celebration* (**447**)	Brandt, *London Child (516)* Frank, *Santa Fe, New Mexico (515)* White, *Ritual Branch (514)*
1960	Niemeyer, Brasília *(498)*	Segal, *Cinema (485)* Smith, *Cubi* series *(477)* Nevelson, *Black Cord (483)* Kosuth, *One and Three Chairs (488)* Kienholz, *State Hospital* (**486**) Bladen, *The X (476)* Oldenburg, *Ice Bag (479)*	Warhol, *Gold Marilyn Monroe* (**459**) Lichtenstein, *Girl at Piano* (**458**) Kelly, *Red Blue Green* (**452**) Stella, *Empress of India* (**453**)	
1970	Piano and Rogers, Centre National d'Art et de Culture Georges Pompidou, Paris (**499**)	Smithson, *Spiral Jetty*, Great Salt Lake, Utah *(480)* Chase-Riboud, *Confessions for Myself (484)*	Anuszkiewicz, *Entrance to Green* (**456**) Eddy, *New Shoes for H* (**460,** *461)* Flack, *Queen (462)* Williams, *Batman* (**454**)	
1980	Tschumi, Folie P6, Parc de La Villette, Paris *(501)* Stirling, Neue Staatsgalerie, Stuttgart *(500)*	Shapiro, *Untitled* (**478**)	Clemente, *Untitled* (**463**) Kiefer, *To the Unknown Painter* (**464**) Murray, *More Than You Know* (**465**)	Leonard, *Romanticism Is Ultimately Fatal (517)* Hockney, *Gregory Watching the Snow Fall, Kyoto, Feb. 21, 1983 (518)* Lemieux, *Truth (519)*
1990				

GLOSSARY

Cross-references are indicated by words in SMALL CAPITALS.

ABSTRACT. Having little or no reference to the appearance of natural objects; pertaining to the nonrepresentational art styles of the twentieth century.

ACRYLIC. A plastic binder MEDIUM for PIGMENTS that is soluble in water, developed about 1960.

ALTARPIECE. A painted or carved work of art placed behind and above the altar of a Christian church. It may be a single panel, or a triptych or polyptych having hinged wings painted on both sides.

AMBULATORY. A passageway, especially around the CHANCEL of a church. An ambulatory may also be outside a church.

AMPHORA. A Greek vase having an egg-shaped body, a narrow cylindrical neck, and two curving handles joined to the body at the shoulder and neck.

APSE. A large niche facing the NAVE of a church, usually at the east end. See BASILICA.

ARCADE. A series of ARCHES and their supports.

ARCH. A structural member, often semicircular, used to span an opening; it requires support from walls, PIERS, or COLUMNS, and BUTTRESSING at the sides.

ARCHAIC. A relatively early style, as Greek sculpture of the seventh and sixth centuries B.C.; or any style adopting characteristics of an earlier period.

ARCHITRAVE. The main horizontal beam, and the lowest part of an ENTABLATURE.

ASSEMBLAGE. Two or more accidentally "found" objects placed together as a construction. See READY-MADE.

ATMOSPHERIC PERSPECTIVE. A means of showing distance or depth in a painting by changing the tone of objects that are far away from the picture plane, especially by reducing in gradual stages the contrast between lights and darks.

BAPTISTERY. A building or part of a church, often round or octagonal, in which the sacrament of baptism is administered. It contains a baptismal font, a receptacle of stone or metal that holds the water for the rite.

BARREL VAULT. A semicylindrical VAULT.

BASE. The lowest element of a COLUMN, wall, DOME, etc.

BASILICA. In the Roman period, the word refers to the function of the building—a large meeting hall—rather than to its form, which may vary according to its use; as an official public building, the Roman basilica had certain religious overtones. The term was used by the Early Christians to refer to their churches. An Early Christian basilica had an oblong plan, flat timber ceiling, trussed roof, and an APSE. The entrance was on one short side and the apse projected from the opposite side, at the far end of the building.

BAYS. Compartments into which a building may be subdivided, usually formed by the space between consecutive architectural supports.

BLACK-FIGURE. A type of Greek vase painting, practiced in the seventh and sixth centuries B.C., in which the design was painted mainly in black against a lighter-colored background, usually the natural clay.

BOOK OF HOURS. A book for individual private devotions with prayers for different hours of the day; often elaborately ILLUMINATED.

BUTTRESS, BUTTRESSING. A masonry support that counteracts the THRUST exerted by an ARCH or a VAULT. See FLYING BUTTRESS, PIER BUTTRESS.

CAMERA OBSCURA. Latin for dark room. A darkened enclosure or box with a small opening or lens on one wall through which light enters to form an inverted image on the opposite wall. The principle had long been known but was not used as an aid in picture-making until the sixteenth century.

CAPITAL. The crowning member of a COLUMN, PIER, or PILASTER on which the lowest element of the ENTABLATURE rests. See CORINTHIAN COLUMN, DORIC COLUMN, IONIC COLUMN.

CARTOON. A preliminary SKETCH or DRAWING made to be transferred to a wall, panel, or canvas as a guide in painting a finished work.

CASTING. A method of reproducing a three-dimensional object or RELIEF. Casting in bronze or other metal is often the final stage in the creation of a piece of SCULPTURE; casting in plaster is a convenient and inexpensive way of making a copy of an original. See SCULPTURE.

CHANCEL. In a church, the space reserved for the clergy and choir, set off from the NAVE by steps, and occasionally by a screen.

CHAPEL. A compartment in a church containing an altar dedicated to a saint.

CHIAROSCURO. Italian for light and dark. In painting, a method of modeling form primarily by the use of light and shade.

CHOIR. See CHANCEL.

CLASSICAL. Used generally to refer to the art of the Greeks and the Romans.

CLERESTORY. A row of windows in a wall that rises above the adjoining roof.

COLLAGE. A composition made by pasting cut-up textured materials, such as newsprint, wallpaper, etc., to form all or part of a work of art; may be combined with painting or drawing or with three-dimensional objects.

COLONNADE. A series of COLUMNS placed at regular intervals.

COLOR. The choice and treatment of the hues in a painting.

COLUMN. A vertical architectural support, usually consisting of a BASE, a rounded SHAFT, and a CAPITAL.

COMPOSITION. The arrangement of FORM, COLOR, LINE, etc., in a work of art.

COMPOUND PIER. A PIER with COLUMNS, PILASTERS, or SHAFTS attached.

CONTRAPPOSTO (counterpoise). Italian for set against. The disposition of the parts of the body so that the weight-bearing leg, or engaged leg, is distinguished from the raised leg, or free leg, resulting in a shift in the axis between the hips and shoulders. Used by the Greek sculptors as a means of showing movement in a figure.

CORINTHIAN COLUMN. First appeared in fifth-century

Greece, apparently as a variation of the IONIC. The CAPITAL differentiates the two: the Corinthian capital has an inverted bell shape, decorated with acanthus leaves, stalks, and volute scrolls. The Corinthian ORDER was widely used by the Romans.

CORNICE. The crowning, projecting architectural feature, especially the uppermost part of an ENTABLATURE.

CROSSING. In a cross-shaped church, the area where the NAVE and the TRANSEPT intersect.

CUPOLA. A rounded, domed roof or ceiling.

DAGUERREOTYPE. Originally, a photograph on a silver-plated sheet of copper that had been treated with fumes of iodine to form silver iodide on its surface and, after exposure, was developed by fumes of mercury. The process, invented by L. J. M. Daguerre and made public in 1839, was modified and accelerated as daguerreotypes gained worldwide popularity.

DOME. A large CUPOLA supported by a circular DRUM or square BASE.

DORIC COLUMN. The Doric column stands without a BASE directly on the top of the stepped platform of a temple. Its SHAFT has shallow FLUTES.

DRAWING. A SKETCH, design, or representation by LINES. Drawings are usually made on paper with pen, pencil, charcoal, pastel, chalk, etc.

DRUM. One of several sections composing the SHAFT of a COLUMN; also a cylindrical wall supporting a DOME.

ENCAUSTIC. A method of painting in colors mixed with wax and applied with a brush, generally while the mixture is hot. The technique was practiced in ancient times and in the Early Christian period and has been revived by some modern painters.

ENGAGED COLUMN. A COLUMN that is part of a wall and projects somewhat from it. Such a column often has no structural purpose.

ENGRAVING. A design incised in reverse on a copperplate; this is coated with printer's ink, which remains in the incised lines when the plate is wiped off. Damp paper is placed on the plate, and both are put into a press; the paper soaks up the ink and produces a print of the original.

ENTABLATURE. The upper part of an architectural ORDER.

ETCHING. Like ENGRAVING, etching is an incising process. However, the design is drawn in reverse with a needle on a plate thinly coated with wax or resin. The plate is placed in a bath of nitric acid; the etched lines are produced on the plate by the coating. The coating is then removed, and the prints are made as in engraving.

FACADE. The front of a building.

FLUTE, FLUTES. Vertical channels on a column SHAFT; see DORIC COLUMN, IONIC COLUMN

FLYING BUTTRESS. An ARCH that springs from the upper part of the PIER BUTTRESS of a Gothic church, spans the aisle roof, and abuts the upper NAVE wall to receive the THRUST from the nave VAULTS; it transmits this thrust to the solid pier buttresses.

FORESHORTENING. A method of representing objects as if seen at an angle and receding or projecting into space; not in a frontal or profile view.

FORM. The external shape or appearance of a representation, considered apart from its COLOR or material.

FREE-STANDING. Used to refer to a work of SCULPTURE in the round, that is, in full three-dimensionality; not attached to architecture and not in RELIEF.

FRESCO. A technique of wall painting known since antiquity; the PIGMENT is mixed with water and applied to a freshly plastered area of a wall. The result is a particularly permanent form of painted decoration.

FRIEZE. In CLASSICAL architecture an architectural element that rests on the ARCHITRAVE and is immediately below the CORNICE; also, any horizontal band decorated with moldings, RELIEF sculpture, or painting.

GABLE. The triangular part of a wall, enclosed by the lines of a sloping roof. See PEDIMENT.

GALLERY. A roofed promenade. See AMBULATORY, COLONNADE.

GENRE. French for kind or sort. A work of art, usually a painting, showing a scene from everyday life that is represented for its own sake.

GOSPELS, GOSPEL BOOK. Contains the four Gospels of the New Testament that tell the life of Christ, attributed to the Evangelists Matthew, Mark, Luke, and John. Often elaborately illustrated.

GROIN. The sharp edge formed by the intersection of two VAULTS.

GROIN VAULT. A VAULT formed by the intersection at right angles of two BARREL VAULTS of equal height and diameter so that the GROINS form a diagonal cross.

GROUND PLAN. See PLAN.

HIEROGLYPHICS. The characters and picture-writing used by the ancient Egyptians.

ICON. A panel painting of Christ, the Virgin, or saints; regarded as sacred, especially by Eastern Christians.

ILLUMINATION. A term used generally for manuscript paintings. Illuminated manuscripts may contain separate ornamental pages, marginal illustrations, ornament within the text, entire MINIATURE paintings, or any combination of these.

ILLUSIONISM, ILLUSIONISTIC. The effort of an artist to represent the visual world with deceptive reality.

ILLUSTRATION. The representation of an idea, scene, or text by artistic means.

IMPASTO. From the Italian word meaning "in paste." Paint, usually OIL PAINT, applied very thickly.

IONIC COLUMN. The Ionic column stands on a molded BASE. The SHAFT normally has FLUTES more deeply cut than DORIC flutes. The Ionic CAPITAL is identified by its pair of spiral scroll-like ornaments.

JAMB. The side of a doorway or window frame.

KORE. An ARCHAIC Greek statue of a draped maiden.

KOUROS. An ARCHAIC Greek statue of a standing nude youth.

LINE. A mark made by a moving tool such as a pen or pencil; more generally, an outline, contour, or silhouette.

LINEAR PERSPECTIVE. A mathematical system for representing three-dimensional objects and space on a two-dimensional surface. All objects are represented as seen from a single viewpoint.

MASS. The expanse of COLOR that defines a painted shape; the three-dimensional volume of a sculptured or architectural form.

MEDIUM. The material with which an artist works, such as marble, OIL PAINT, TERRA-COTTA, WATERCOLOR, etc.

METOPE. An oblong panel between the TRIGLYPHS on the ENTABLATURE of the DORIC ORDER.

MINIATURE. A painting or drawing in an ILLUMINATED manuscript; also a very small portrait, sometimes painted on ivory.

MOBILE. A type of sculpture made of movable parts that can be set in motion by the movement of air currents.

MODELING. See SCULPTURE. In painting or DRAWING, the means by which the three-dimensionality of a form is suggested on a two-dimensional surface, usually through variations of COLOR and the play of lights and darks.

MONUMENTAL. Frequently used to describe works that are larger than lifesize; also used to describe works giving the impression of great size, whatever their actual dimensions.

MOSAIC. A design formed by embedding small pieces of colored stone or glass in cement. In antiquity, large mosaics were used chiefly on floors; from the Early Christian period on, mosaic decoration was increasingly used on walls and vaulted surfaces.

MOTIF. A distinctive and recurrent feature of theme, shape, or figure in a work of art.

MURAL. A wall painting. See FRESCO.

NAVE. The central aisle of a BASILICAN church, as distinguished from the side aisles; the part of a church between the main entrance and the CHANCEL.

OIL PAINTING. Though known to the Romans, it was not systematically used until the fifteenth century. In the oil technique of early Flemish painters, PIGMENTS were mixed with drying oils and fused while hot with hard resins; the mixture was then diluted with other oils.

ORDER. In architecture, a CLASSICAL system of proportion and interrelated parts. These include a COLUMN, usually with BASE, SHAFT, and CAPITAL, and an ENTABLATURE with ARCHITRAVE, FRIEZE, and CORNICE.

PAINTING MEDIUMS. See ACRYLIC, ENCAUSTIC, FRESCO, OIL PAINTING, TEMPERA, WATERCOLOR.

PANTHEON. A temple dedicated to all the gods, or housing tombs of the illustrious dead of a nation, or memorials to them.

PASTEL. Powdered PIGMENTS mixed with gum and molded into sticks for drawing; also a picture or SKETCH made with this type of crayon.

PEDIMENT. In CLASSICAL architecture, the triangular part of the front or back wall that rises above the ENTABLATURE. The pediments at either end of a temple often contained SCULPTURE, in high RELIEF or FREE-STANDING.

PERISTYLE. A COLONNADE (or ARCADE) around a building or open court.

PERSPECTIVE. See ATMOSPHERIC PERSPECTIVE, LINEAR PERSPECTIVE.

PHOTOGRAM. A shadowlike picture made by placing opaque, translucent, or transparent objects between light-sensitive paper and a light source and developing the latent photographic image.

PHOTOMONTAGE. A photograph in which prints in whole or in part are combined to form a new image. A technique much practiced by the Dada group in the 1920s.

PIER. A vertical architectural element, usually rectangular in section; if used with an ORDER, often has a BASE and CAPITAL of the same design.

PIER BUTTRESS. An exterior PIER in Romanesque and Gothic architecture, buttressing the THRUST of the VAULTS within.

PIETÀ. In painting or SCULPTURE, a representation of the Virgin Mary mourning the dead Christ whom she holds.

PIGMENT. A dry, powdered substance that, when mixed with a suitable liquid, or vehicle, gives color to paint. See ACRYLIC, ENCAUSTIC, FRESCO, OIL PAINTING, TEMPERA, WATERCOLOR.

PILASTER. A flat vertical element having a CAPITAL and BASE, engaged in a wall from which it projects. Has a decorative rather than a structural purpose.

PLAN. The schematic representation of a three-dimensional structure, such as a building or monument, on a two-dimensional plane. A ground plan shows the outline shape at the ground level of a given building and the location of its various interior parts.

PORTAL. An imposing doorway with elaborate ornamentation in Romanesque and Gothic churches.

POST AND BEAM. A system or unit of construction consisting solely of vertical and horizontal elements.

PROPORTION, PROPORTIONS. The relation of the size of any part of a figure or object to the size of the whole. For architecture, see ORDER.

PYLON. In Egyptian architecture, the entranceway set between two broad oblong towers with sloping sides.

READY-MADE. A manufactured object exhibited as being aesthetically pleasing. When two or more accidentally "found" objects are placed together as a construction, the piece is called an ASSEMBLAGE.

RED-FIGURE. A type of Greek vase painting in which the design was outlined in black and the background painted in black, leaving the figures the reddish color of the baked clay after firing. This style replaced the BLACK-FIGURE style toward the end of the sixth century B.C.

RELIEF. Forms in SCULPTURE that project from the background, to which they remain attached. Relief may be carved or modeled shallowly to produce low relief, or deeply to produce high relief; in very high relief, portions may be entirely detached from the background.

REPRESENTATIONAL. As opposed to ABSTRACT, means a portrayal of an object in recognizable form.

RHYTHM. The regular repetition of a particular form; also, the suggestion of motion by recurrent forms.

RIB. An ARCH or a projecting arched member of a VAULT.

RIBBED VAULT. A compound masonry VAULT, the GROINS of which are marked by projecting stone ribs.

SARCOPHAGUS. A coffin made of stone, marble, TERRACOTTA (less frequently, of metal). Sarcophagi are often decorated with paintings or RELIEF.

SCALE. Generally, the relative size of any object in a work of art, often used with reference to human scale.

SCULPTURE. The creation of a three-dimensional form, usually in a solid material. Traditionally, two basic techniques have been used: carving in a hard material such as marble, and modeling in a soft material such as clay, wax, etc. For types of sculpture, see FREE-STANDING and RELIEF.

SHAFT. A cylindrical form; in architecture, the part of a COLUMN or PIER intervening between the BASE and the CAPITAL. Also, a vertical enclosed space.

SKETCH. A rough DRAWING representing the main features of a composition; often used as a preliminary study.

STAINED GLASS. The technique of filling architectural openings with glass colored by fused metallic oxides; pieces of this glass are held in a design by strips of lead.

STILL LIFE. A painting or drawing of an arrangement of inanimate objects.

TEMPERA. A painting process in which PIGMENT is mixed with an emulsion of egg yolk and water or egg and oil.

Tempera, the basic technique of medieval and Early Renaissance painters, dries quickly, permitting almost immediate application of the next layer of paint.

TERRA-COTTA. Clay, modeled or molded, and baked until very hard. Used in architecture for functional and decorative parts, as well as in pottery and SCULPTURE. Terra-cotta may have a painted or glazed surface.

THRUST. The downward and outward pressure exerted by an ARCH or VAULT and requiring BUTTRESSING.

TRANSEPT. In a cross-shaped church, an arm forming a right angle with the NAVE, usually inserted between the latter and the CHANCEL or APSE.

TRIGLYPH. A vertical block with V-cut channels, placed between METOPES on the ENTABLATURE of the DORIC ORDER.

TRUMEAU. A central post supporting the lintel of a large doorway, as in a Romanesque or Gothic PORTAL, where it was frequently decorated with sculpture.

TYMPANUM. The space above the beam and enclosed by the ARCH of a medieval PORTAL or doorway; a church tympanum frequently contains RELIEF sculpture.

VAULT. An arched roof or covering, made of brick, stone, or concrete. See BARREL VAULT, GROIN VAULT, RIBBED VAULT.

VELLUM. Thin, bleached calfskin, a type of parchment on which manuscripts are written or printed.

WATERCOLOR. PIGMENTS mixed with water instead of oil or other mediums, or a picture painted with watercolor, often on paper.

WOODCUT. A printing process in which a design or lettering is carved in RELIEF on a wooden block; the areas intended not to print are hollowed out.

ZIGGURAT. An elevated platform, varying in height from several feet to the size of an artificial mountain, built by the Sumerians to support their shrines.

BOOKS FOR FURTHER READING

This list includes standard works and the most recent and comprehensive books in English. Books with material relevant to several chapters are cited only under the first heading. Asterisks (*) indicate titles available in paperback; for publishers, distributors, and the like, see Paperbound Books in Print *(R.R. Bowker, annual).*

INTRODUCTION

*Arnheim, Rudolf, *Art and Visual Perception,* 2d ed., Univ. of California Press, Berkeley, 1974

*Gombrich, Ernst H., *Art and Illusion,* 4th ed., Pantheon Books, N.Y., 1972

*Holt, Elizabeth G., *A Documentary History of Art,* 2d ed., 2 vols., Doubleday, Garden City, 1981

*Panofsky, Erwin, *Meaning in the Visual Arts,* Doubleday, Garden City, 1955; reprint, Overlook Press, Woodstock, 1974

*———, *Icon and Idea,* Schocken, N.Y., 1965

*Rosenberg, Harold, *The Anxious Object: Art Today and Its Audience,* 2d ed., Horizon, N.Y., 1966

*Taylor, Joshua C., *Learning to Look: A Handbook for the Visual Arts,* 2d ed., Univ. of Chicago Press, 1981

PART ONE: THE ANCIENT WORLD

PREHISTORIC AND ETHNOGRAPHIC ART

*Bascom, William R., *African Art in Cultural Perspective,* Norton, N.Y., 1973

*Gimbutas, Marija, *The Gods and Goddesses of Old Europe, 7000–3500 B.C.: Myths, Legends and Cult Images,* Univ. of California Press, Berkeley, 1974

*Guidoni, Enrico, *Primitive Architecture,* Rizzoli, N.Y., 1987

Leroi-Gourhan, André, *Treasures of Prehistoric Art,* Abrams, N.Y., 1967

Lommel, Andreas, *Shamanism: The Beginnings of Art,* McGraw-Hill, N.Y., 1967

Trachtenberg, Marvin, and Isabelle Hyman, *Architecture: From Prehistory to Post-Modernism,* Abrams, N.Y., 1985

*Wingert, Paul, *Primitive Art: Its Traditions and Styles,* Oxford Univ. Press, N.Y., 1962

EGYPTIAN ART

Aldred, Cyril, *Development of Ancient Egyptian Art from 3200 to 1315 B.C.,* Transatlantic, N.Y., 1975

Fletcher, Bannister, *A History of Architecture,* 18th ed., rev., R. A. Cordingley, Scribner, N.Y., 1975

*Groenewegen-Frankfort, Henriette A., *Arrest and Movement,* Univ. of Chicago Press, 1951; reprint, Hacker Art Books, N.Y., 1972

Lange, Kurt, and Max Hirmer, *Egypt: Architecture, Sculpture, Painting in Three Thousand Years,* 4th ed., Phaidon, London, 1968

Michalowski, Kazimierz, *Art of Ancient Egypt,* Abrams, N.Y., 1969; reprint 1985

*Panofsky, Erwin, *Tomb Sculpture: Its Aspects from Ancient Egypt to Bernini,* Abrams, N.Y., 1969

*Smith, William S., and William K. Simpson, *The Art and Architecture of Ancient Egypt,* rev. with additions, Pelican History of Art, Penguin, Baltimore, 1981

ANCIENT NEAR EASTERN ART

Akurgal, Ekrem, *Art of the Hittites,* Abrams, N.Y., 1962

Amiet, Pierre, *Art of the Ancient Near East,* Abrams, N.Y., 1980

*Frankfort, Henri, *The Art and Architecture of the Ancient Orient,* 4th rev. impression with additional bibliography, Pelican History of Art, Penguin, Baltimore, 1969

*Mellaart, James, *Earliest Civilizations of the Near East,* McGraw-Hill, N.Y., 1965

Porada, Edith, *The Art of Ancient Iran: Pre-Islamic Cultures,* Crown, N.Y., 1965

Strommenger, Eva, and Max Hirmer, *5000 Years of the Art of Mesopotamia,* Abrams, N.Y., 1964

AEGEAN ART

*Graham, J. W., et al., *The Palaces of Crete,* expanded ed., Princeton Univ. Press, 1987

Hampe, Ronald, and Erika Simon, *The Birth of Greek Art from the Mycenaean to the Archaic Period,* Oxford Univ. Press, N.Y., 1981

Hood, Sinclair, *The Minoans: The Story of Bronze Age Crete,* Praeger, N.Y., 1981

Marinatos, Spyridon N., and Max Hirmer, *Crete and Mycenae,* Abrams, N.Y., 1960

Mylonas, George E., *Mycenae and the Mycenaean Age,* Princeton Univ. Press, 1966

*Vermeule, Emily T., *Greece in the Bronze Age,* Univ. of Chicago Press, 1972

GREEK ART

Ashmole, Bernard, *Architect and Sculptor in Classical Greece,* New York Univ. Press, 1972

Beazley, John D., and Bernard Ashmole, *Sculpture and Painting to the End of the Hellenistic Period,* Cambridge Univ. Press, 1966

*Boardman, John, *Greek Sculpture: The Archaic Period,* Oxford Univ. Press, N.Y., 1978

Brilliant, Richard, *Arts of the Ancient Greeks,* McGraw-Hill, N.Y., 1973

*Cook, Robert M., *Greek Art: Its Development, Character and Influence,* Farrar, Straus and Giroux, N.Y., 1973

*Dinsmoor, William B., *The Architecture of Ancient Greece:*

An Account of Its Historic Development, Norton, N.Y. and London, 1975 (reprint of the 1950 ed. [3d rev.] augmented)

*Lullies, Reinhard, and Max Hirmer, *Greek Sculpture,* Abrams, N.Y., 1960

*Moon, Warren G., ed., *Ancient Greek Art and Iconography,* Univ. of Wisconsin Press, Madison, 1983

Papaioannou, Kostas, *The Art of Greece,* Abrams, N.Y., 1988

Richter, Gisela M. A., *A Handbook of Greek Art,* 6th ed., redesigned, Phaidon, London, 1969

———, *Kouroi,* 3d ed., Phaidon, N.Y., 1970

———, *The Sculpture and Sculptors of the Greeks,* 4th ed., rev., Yale Univ. Press, New Haven, 1970

Robertson, Martin, *History of Greek Art,* 2 vols., Cambridge Univ. Press, 1975

Scully, Vincent, *The Earth, the Temple and the Gods: Greek Sacred Architecture,* Yale Univ. Press, New Haven, 1962

Ward-Perkins, J. B., *The Cities of Ancient Greece and Italy: Planning in Classical Antiquity,* Braziller, N.Y., 1974

ETRUSCAN ART

*Boethius, Axel, and J. B. Ward-Perkins, *Etruscan and Early Roman Architecture,* 2d integrated ed., Pelican History of Art, Penguin, Harmondsworth, 1978

*Brendel, Otto J., *Etruscan Art,* Pelican History of Art, Penguin, Harmondsworth, 1978

Pallottino, Massimo, *Etruscan Painting,* Skira, Geneva, 1953

Sprenger, Maja, Gilda Bartolini, Max Hirmer, and Albert Hirmer, *The Etruscans: Their History, Art, and Architecture,* Abrams, N.Y., 1983

ROMAN ART

Andreae, Bernard, *The Art of Rome,* Abrams, N.Y., 1977

*Brilliant, Richard, *Roman Art from the Republic to Constantine,* Phaidon, N.Y., 1974

*L'Orange, Hans P., *Art Forms and Civic Life in the Late Roman Empire,* Princeton Univ. Press, 1965

*MacDonald, William, *The Architecture of the Roman Empire,* Vol. 1, rev. ed., Yale Univ. Press, New Haven, 1982

*Strong, Donald E., *Roman Art,* Pelican History of Art, Penguin, Harmondsworth, 1976

Vermeule, Cornelius C., III, *Greek Sculpture and Roman Taste,* Univ. of Michigan Press, Ann Arbor, 1977

*Ward-Perkins, John B., *Roman Imperial Architecture,* Pelican History of Art, Penguin, Harmondsworth, 1981

EARLY CHRISTIAN AND BYZANTINE ART

*Beckwith, John, *Early Christian and Byzantine Art,* 2d integrated ed., Pelican History of Art, Penguin, Harmondsworth, 1979

Demus, Otto, *Byzantine Art and the West,* New York Univ. Press, 1970

Grabar, André, *Early Christian Art,* Braziller, N.Y., 1971

*Krautheimer, Richard, *Early Christian and Byzantine Architecture,* Pelican History of Art, Penguin, Baltimore, 1965

*MacDonald, William L., *Early Christian and Byzantine Architecture,* Penguin, Baltimore, 1965

*Mango, Cyril, *Byzantine Architecture,* Abrams, N.Y., 1976

*Runciman, Steven, *Byzantine Style and Civilization,* Penguin, Harmondsworth, 1975

*Weitzmann, Kurt, *Late Antique and Early Christian Book Illumination,* Braziller, N.Y., 1977

PART TWO: THE MIDDLE AGES

EARLY MEDIEVAL ART

*Conant, Kenneth J., *Carolingian and Romanesque Architecture, 800–1200,* new ed., Pelican History of Art, Penguin, Norwich, 1974

Duby, Georges, *History of Medieval Art, 980–1440,* new 1-vol. ed., Skira and Rizzoli, Geneva and N.Y., 1986

*Kitzinger, Ernst, *Early Medieval Art in the British Museum,* Indiana Univ. Press, Bloomington, 1964

*Kubach, Hans E., *Romanesque Architecture,* Rizzoli, N.Y., 1988

*Nordenfalk, Carl, *Early Medieval Book Illumination,* Skira and Rizzoli, Geneva and N.Y., 1988

*Pevsner, Nikolaus, *An Outline of European Architecture,* 6th ed., Penguin, Baltimore, 1960

*Snyder, James, *Medieval Art: Painting, Sculpture, Architecture, 4th–14th Century,* Abrams, N.Y., 1989

ROMANESQUE ART

Demus, Otto, *Romanesque Mural Painting,* Abrams, N.Y., 1971

*Duby, Georges, *The Age of the Cathedrals: Art and Society, 980–1420,* Univ. of Chicago Press, 1981

*Focillon, Henri, *The Art of the West in the Middle Ages,* ed. by Jean Bony, 2 vols., Phaidon, N.Y., 1963

*Grabar, André, *Romanesque Painting from the Eleventh to the Thirteenth Century: Mural Painting,* Skira, Geneva, 1958

Kubach, Hans E., *Romanesque Architecture,* Abrams, N.Y., 1975

*Saalman, Howard, *Medieval Cities,* Braziller, N.Y., 1968

Schapiro, Meyer, *Romanesque Art,* Braziller, N.Y., 1977

Stoddard, Whitney S., *Art and Architecture in Medieval France,* Harper and Row, N.Y., 1972

*Swarzenski, Hans, *Monuments of Romanesque Art: The Art of Church Treasures in North-Western Europe,* 2d ed., Univ. of Chicago Press, 1967

Zarnecki, George, *Romanesque Art,* Universe Books, N.Y., 1971

GOTHIC ART

*Baxandall, Michael, *Giotto and the Orators: Humanist Observers of Painting in Italy and the Discovery of Pictorial Composition, 1350–1450,* Clarendon Press, Oxford, 1971

*Bony, Jean, *French Gothic Architecture of the 12th and 13th Centuries,* Univ. of California Press, Berkeley, 1983

*Branner, Robert, and Shirley P. Branner, *Gothic Architecture,* Braziller, N.Y., 1961

Deuchler, Florens, *Gothic Art,* Universe Books, N.Y., 1973

Frankl, Paul, *Gothic Architecture,* Pelican History of Art, Penguin, Baltimore, 1962

Grodecki, Louis, *Gothic Architecture,* Abrams, N.Y., 1977

*Henderson, George, *Gothic Style and Civilization,* Penguin, Baltimore, 1967

*Holt, Elizabeth G., ed., *A Documentary History of Art,* Vol. I, *The Middle Ages and the Renaissance,* 2d ed., Doubleday, Garden City, 1957

Krautheimer, Richard, and Trude Krautheimer-Hess, *Lorenzo Ghiberti,* 2d ed., Princeton Univ. Press, 1970

*Mâle, Émile, *The Gothic Image: Religious Art in France of the Thirteenth Century,* Harper, N.Y., 1958

*Meiss, Millard, *Painting in Florence and Siena After the Black Death,* Princeton Univ. Press, 1951

*Petersen, Karen, and J. J. Wilson, *Women Artists: Recognition and Reappraisal from the Early Middle Ages to the Twen-*

tieth Century, Harper and Row, N.Y., 1976
Pope-Hennessy, John, *Italian Gothic Sculpture,* 2d ed., Phaidon, N.Y., 1970
Sauerländer, Willibald, *Gothic Sculpture in France, 1140–1270,* Abrams, N.Y., 1973
Stubblebine, James H., *Duccio di Buoninsegna and His School,* 2 vols., Princeton Univ. Press, 1979
*Watson, Percy, *Building the Medieval Cathedrals,* Cambridge Univ. Press, 1976
*White, John, *Art and Architecture in Italy, 1250–1400,* Pelican History of Art, Penguin, Baltimore, 1966

PART THREE: THE RENAISSANCE, MANNERISM, AND THE BAROQUE

"LATE GOTHIC" PAINTING, SCULPTURE, AND THE GRAPHIC ARTS

Blum, Shirley N., *Early Netherlandish Triptychs: A Study in Patronage,* Univ. of California Press, Berkeley, 1969
Châtelet, Albert, *Early Dutch Painting,* Rizzoli, N.Y., 1981
*Cuttler, Charles D., *Northern Painting: From Pucelle to Bruegel,* Holt, Rinehart and Winston, N.Y., 1968
Eichenberg, Fritz, *The Art of the Print: Masterpieces, History, and Techniques,* Abrams, N.Y., 1976
*Friedländer, Max J., *From Van Eyck to Bruegel: Early Netherlandish Painting,* Phaidon, N.Y., 1969
*Hind, Arthur M., *History of Engraving and Etching,* 3d ed., rev., Houghton Mifflin, Boston, 1923
*———, *An Introduction to a History of Woodcut,* 2 vols., Houghton Mifflin, Boston, 1935
*Ivins, William M., Jr., *How Prints Look,* Metropolitan Museum of Art, N.Y., 1943
Meiss, Millard, *French Painting in the Time of Jean de Berry: The Limbourgs and Their Contemporaries,* 2 vols., Braziller, N.Y., 1974
*Panofsky, Erwin, *Early Netherlandish Painting,* 2 vols., Harvard Univ. Press, Cambridge, 1958
Snyder, James, *Northern Renaissance Art,* Abrams, N.Y., 1985

THE EARLY RENAISSANCE IN ITALY

*Alberti, Leone Battista, *On Painting and On Sculpture,* Phaidon, N.Y., 1972
*Antal, Frederick, *Florentine Painting and Its Social Background,* Boston Book and Art Shop, 1965
*Baxandall, Michael, *Painting and Experience in Fifteenth-Century Italy,* Clarendon Press, Oxford, 1972
*Berenson, Bernard, *Italian Painters of the Renaissance,* rev. ed., Phaidon, London, 1967
*Blunt, Anthony, *Artistic Theory in Italy, 1450–1600,* Oxford Univ. Press, N.Y., 1956
*Burckhardt, Jacob C., *The Civilization of the Renaissance in Italy,* 3d ed., rev., Phaidon, London, 1950
Clark, Kenneth, *Piero della Francesca,* 2d ed., Phaidon, London, 1969
*Gombrich, Ernst H., *Norm and Form: Studies in the Art of the Renaissance,* Phaidon, London, 1966
Hartt, Frederick, *History of Italian Renaissance Art,* 3d ed., Abrams, N.Y., 1987
Heydenreich, Ludwig, and Wolfgang Lotz, *Architecture in Italy, 1400–1600,* Pelican History of Art, Penguin, Harmondsworth, 1974
*Janson, H. W., *The Sculpture of Donatello,* 2 vols., Princeton Univ. Press, 1957
*Lee, Rensselaer W., *Ut Pictura Poesis: The Humanistic Theory of Painting,* Norton, N.Y., 1967
*Levey, Michael, *Early Renaissance,* Penguin, Harmondsworth, 1967
*Murray, Peter, *Renaissance Architecture,* Abrams, N.Y., 1976
*Panofsky, Erwin, *Renaissance and Renascences in Western Art,* Humanities Press, N.Y., 1970
*Pope-Hennessy, John, *Italian Renaissance Sculpture,* Phaidon, N.Y., 1971
Seymour, Charles, Jr., *Sculpture in Italy, 1400–1500,* Pelican History of Art, Penguin, Baltimore, 1966
Vasari, Giorgio, *The Lives of the Painters, Sculptors and Architects,* tr. by Gaston Du C. De Vere, 4 vols., Abrams, N.Y., 1977
*Wilde, Johannes, *Venetian Art from Bellini to Titian,* Clarendon Press, Oxford, 1974
*Wittkower, Rudolf, *Architectural Principles in the Age of Humanism,* 3d ed., Random House, N.Y., 1965

THE HIGH RENAISSANCE IN ITALY

*Clark, Kenneth, *Leonardo da Vinci,* rev. ed., Penguin, Baltimore, 1967
*Freedberg, Sydney J., *Painting in Italy, 1500 to 1600,* 1st rev. ed., Pelican History of Art, Penguin, Harmondsworth, 1975
———, *Painting of the High Renaissance in Rome and Florence,* 2 vols., Harvard Univ. Press, Cambridge, 1961
*Hibbard, Howard, *Michelangelo,* new ed., Penguin, Harmondsworth, 1978
*Levey, Michael, *High Renaissance, Style and Civilization,* Penguin, Baltimore, 1975
*Panofsky, Erwin, *Studies in Iconology: Humanistic Theories in the Art of the Renaissance,* Harper and Row, N.Y., 1972
Pignatti, Terisio, *Giorgione,* Phaidon, N.Y., 1971
Pope-Hennessy, John, *Italian High Renaissance and Baroque Sculpture,* 3 vols., Phaidon, London, 1963
———, *Raphael,* New York Univ. Press, 1970
Rosand, David, *Painting in Cinquecento Venice: Titian, Veronese, Tintoretto,* Yale Univ. Press, New Haven and London, 1982

MANNERISM AND OTHER TRENDS

*Ackerman, James S., *Palladio,* Penguin, Harmondsworth, 1966
*Friedlaender, Walter F., *Mannerism and Anti-Mannerism in Italian Painting,* Columbia Univ. Press, N.Y., 1957
*Harris, Ann S., and Linda Nochlin, *Women Artists, 1550–1950,* Knopf, N.Y., 1976
*Holt, Elizabeth G., ed., *A Documentary History of Art,* Vol. II, *Michelangelo and the Mannerists: The Baroque and the Eighteenth Century,* 2d ed., Doubleday, Garden City, 1957
*Shearman, John K. G., *Mannerism, Style and Civilization,* Penguin, Baltimore, 1967
Smyth, Craig H., *Mannerism and Maniera,* Augustin, Locust Valley, 1963
Valcanover, Francesco, and Terisio Pignatti, *Tintoretto,* Abrams, N.Y., 1984

THE RENAISSANCE IN THE NORTH

*Benesch, Otto, *The Art of the Renaissance in Northern Europe,* rev. ed., Phaidon, London, 1965
*Blunt, Anthony, *Art and Architecture in France, 1500–1700,* 4th ed., Pelican History of Art, Penguin, Harmondsworth, 1981

Christensen, Carl C., *Art and the Reformation in Germany,* Ohio Univ. Press, Athens, 1979

Ganz, Paul, *The Paintings of Hans Holbein the Younger,* 1st comp. ed., Phaidon, London, 1956

*Panofsky, Erwin, *The Life and Art of Albrecht Dürer,* 4th ed., Princeton Univ. Press, 1955

Pevsner, Nikolaus, and Michael Meier, *Grünewald,* Abrams, N.Y., 1958

*Stechow, Wolfgang, *Pieter Bruegel the Elder,* Abrams, N.Y., 1969

*Waterhouse, Ellis K., *Painting in Britain, 1530–1790,* 4th ed., Pelican History of Art, Penguin, Baltimore, 1978

THE BAROQUE IN ITALY AND SPAIN

Brown, Jonathan, *Francisco de Zurbarán,* Abrams, N.Y., 1974

———, *Velázquez: Painter and Courtier,* Yale Univ. Press, New Haven, 1986

*Freedberg, Sydney J., *Circa 1600: A Revolution of Style in Italian Painting,* Harvard Univ. Press, Cambridge, 1983

*Friedlaender, Walter F., *Caravaggio Studies,* Princeton Univ. Press, 1955

*Haskell, Francis, *Patrons and Painters: A Study in the Relations Between Italian Art and Society in the Age of the Baroque,* rev. and enl. ed., Yale Univ. Press, New Haven, 1980

*Hibbard, Howard, *Bernini,* Penguin, Harmondsworth, 1966

Kubler, George, and Martin Soria, *Art and Architecture in Spain and Portugal and Their American Dominions, 1500–1800,* Pelican History of Art, Penguin, Baltimore, 1959

Moir, Alfred, *The Italian Followers of Caravaggio,* 2 vols., Harvard Univ. Press, Cambridge, 1967

Posner, Donald, *Annibale Carraci,* 2 vols., Phaidon, London, 1971

*Wittkower, Rudolf, *Art and Architecture in Italy, 1600 to 1750,* 3d rev. ed., with corrections and augmented bibliography, Pelican History of Art, Penguin, Harmondsworth, 1980

———, *Gian Lorenzo Bernini: The Sculptor of the Roman Baroque,* 3d rev. ed., Cornell Univ. Press, Ithaca, 1981

THE BAROQUE IN FLANDERS AND HOLLAND

Brown, Christopher, *Anthony van Dyck,* Cornell Univ. Press, Ithaca, 1982

D'Hulst, R.-A., *Jacob Jordaens,* Cornell Univ. Press, Ithaca, 1982

Gerson, Horst, and E. H. ter Kuile, *Art and Architecture in Belgium, 1600–1800,* Pelican History of Art, Penguin, Baltimore, 1978

Haak, Bob, *The Golden Age: Dutch Painters of the Seventeenth Century,* Abrams, N.Y., 1984

Kahr, Madlyn M., *Dutch Painting in the Seventeenth Century,* Icon Editions, Harper and Row, N.Y., 1978

*Rosenberg, Jakob, Seymour Slive, and E. H. ter Kuile, *Dutch Art and Architecture, 1600–1800,* 3d (2d integrated) ed., Pelican History of Art, Penguin, Harmondsworth, 1977

Scribner, Charles, III, *Rubens,* Abrams, N.Y., 1989

Slive, Seymour, *Frans Hals,* 3 vols., Phaidon, N.Y., 1970–74

———, *Jacob van Ruisdael,* Abbeville, N.Y., 1981

*Stechow, Wolfgang, *Dutch Landscape Painting of the Seventeenth Century,* reprint of 1966 ed., Cornell Univ. Press, Ithaca, 1980

Wheelock, Arthur K., Jr., *Jan Vermeer,* Abrams, N.Y., 1981

White, Christopher, *Peter Paul Rubens,* Yale Univ. Press, New Haven, 1987

THE BAROQUE IN FRANCE

Blunt, Anthony, *Nicholas Poussin,* 2 vols., Pantheon Books, N.Y., 1967

Friedlaender, Walter F., *Nicholas Poussin, A New Approach,* Abrams, N.Y., 1966

Nicolson, Benedict, and Christopher Wright, *Georges de La Tour,* Phaidon, London, 1974

ROCOCO

Gaunt, William, *The Great Century of British Painting: Hogarth to Turner,* Phaidon, London, 1971

Hitchcock, Henry-Russell, *Rococo Architecture in Southern Germany,* Phaidon, London, 1968

*Laing, Alastair, et al., *François Boucher, 1703–1770,* Abrams, N.Y., 1986

*Levey, Michael, *Rococo to Revolution: Major Trends in Eighteenth Century Painting,* Oxford Univ. Press, N.Y., 1977

Paulson, Ronald, *Hogarth: His Life, Art and Times,* 2 vols., Yale Univ. Press, New Haven, 1971

Posner, Donald, *Antoine Watteau,* Cornell Univ. Press, Ithaca, 1984

Rosenberg, Pierre, *Fragonard,* Abrams, N.Y., 1988

Wildenstein, Georges, and Daniel Wildenstein, *Chardin,* rev. and enl. ed., New York Graphic Society, Greenwich, 1969

PART FOUR: THE MODERN WORLD

NEOCLASSICISM

Boime, Albert, *The Academy and French Painting in the 19th Century,* Phaidon, N.Y., 1970

Brown, Milton W., *American Art to 1900,* Abrams, N.Y., 1977

Driskell, David C., *Two Centuries of Black American Art,* Los Angeles County Museum of Art and Knopf, N.Y., 1976

*Fried, Michael, *Absorption and Theatricality: Painting and Beholder in the Age of Diderot,* Univ. of California Press, Berkeley, 1980

*Friedlaender, Walter F., *From David to Delacroix,* Harvard Univ. Press, Cambridge, 1952

Gaunt, William, *The Restless Century: Painting in Britain, 1800–1900,* Phaidon, London, 1972

*Hamilton, George Heard, *Nineteenth and Twentieth Century Art: Painting, Sculpture, Architecture,* Abrams, N.Y., 1970

*Hitchcock, Henry-Russell, *Architecture: Nineteenth and Twentieth Centuries,* 2d ed., Pelican History of Art, Penguin, Baltimore, 1971

*Honour, Hugh, *Neoclassicism: Style and Civilization,* Penguin, Harmondsworth, 1968

Janson, H. W., *19th-Century Sculpture,* Abrams, N.Y., 1985

*Novotny, Fritz, *Painting and Sculpture in Europe, 1780–1880,* Pelican History of Art, Penguin, Baltimore, 1971

Pingeot, Anne, et al., *Sculpture: The Adventure of Modern Sculpture in the Nineteenth and Twentieth Centuries,* Rizzoli, N.Y., 1986

*Rosenblum, Robert, *Transformations in Late Eighteenth Century Art,* Princeton Univ. Press, 1967

———, and H. W. Janson, *19th-Century Art,* Abrams, N.Y., 1984

THE ROMANTIC MOVEMENT

Clark, Kenneth, *The Romantic Rebellion: Romantic Versus Classical,* Harper and Row, N.Y., 1974

Daval, Jean-Luc, *Photography: History of an Art,* Skira and Rizzoli, Geneva and N.Y., 1982

Eitner, Lorenz E., *Géricault: His Life and Works,* Cornell Univ. Press, Ithaca, 1982

Gernsheim, Helmut, *Julia Margaret Cameron: Her Life and Photographic Work,* 2d ed., Aperture, Millerton, N.Y., 1975

*Honour, Hugh, *Romanticism,* Icon Ed., Harper and Row, N.Y., 1979

Licht, Fred, *Canova,* Abbeville, N.Y., 1983

*———, *Goya: The Origins of the Modern Temper in Art,* Icon Ed., Harper and Row, N.Y., 1983

Parry, Elwood C., III, *The Art of Thomas Cole: Ambition and Imagination,* Univ. of Delaware Press, Newark, 1988

Powell, Earl A., *Thomas Cole,* Abrams, N.Y., 1990

*Reynolds, Graham, *Constable, the Natural Painter,* Schocken, N.Y., 1969

*———, *Turner,* World of Art, Thames and Hudson; distr. by Norton, N.Y., 1985

Rosenblum, Naomi, *A World History of Photography,* Abbeville, N.Y., 1984

Rosenblum, Robert, *Jean-Auguste-Dominique Ingres,* new ed., Abrams, N.Y., 1985

Shapiro, Michael Edward, et al., *George Caleb Bingham,* Abrams, N.Y., 1990

*Welling, William, *Photography in America: The Formative Years, 1839–1900,* Crowell, N.Y., 1978

Wilton, A., *J. M. W. Turner: His Life and Art,* Rizzoli, N.Y., 1979

REALISM AND IMPRESSIONISM

Breeskin, Adelyn D., *Mary Cassatt: A Catalogue Raisonné of the Oils, Pastels, Watercolors and Drawings,* National Gallery of Art, Washington, D.C., 1970

Cikovsky, Nicolai, Jr., *Winslow Homer,* Abrams, N.Y., 1990

*Clark, T. J., *The Painting of Modern Life: Paris in the Art of Manet and His Followers,* Princeton Univ. Press, 1984

*Elsen, Albert E., *Origins of Modern Sculpture: Pioneers and Premises,* Braziller, N.Y., 1974

Goodrich, Lloyd, *Thomas Eakins,* 2 vols., Harvard Univ. Press, Cambridge, for the National Gallery of Art, Washington, D.C., 1982

Hanson, Ann Coffin, *Manet and the Modern Tradition,* Yale Univ. Press, New Haven, 1977

Herbert, Robert L., *Impressionism: Art, Leisure and Parisian Society,* Yale Univ. Press, New Haven, 1988

*Hilton, Timothy, *The Pre-Raphaelites,* Abrams, N.Y., 1971

Johns, Elizabeth, *Thomas Eakins and the Heroism of Modern Life,* Princeton Univ. Press, 1984

Kelder, Diane, *The French Impressionists and Their Century,* Praeger, N.Y., 1970

*Nochlin, Linda, *Realism, Style and Civilization,* Penguin, Harmondsworth, 1972

Rewald, John, *The History of Impressionism,* 4th rev. ed., New York Graphic Society, Greenwich, for The Museum of Modern Art, N.Y., 1973

Reynolds, Graham, *Victorian Painting,* Macmillan, N.Y., 1966

Weisberg, Gabriel P., *The Realist Tradition: French Painting and Drawing, 1830–1900,* Cleveland Museum of Art, 1981

*Wilmerding, John, *American Art,* Pelican History of Art, Penguin, Harmondsworth, 1976

POST-IMPRESSIONISM

Bunnell, Peter, ed., *A Photographic Vision: Pictorial Photography 1889–1923,* Peregrine Smith, Salt Lake City, 1980

Doty, Robert, *Photo-Secession: Stieglitz and the Fine Arts Movement in Photography,* Dover, N.Y., 1978

Gibson, Michael, *The Symbolists,* Abrams, N.Y., 1988

Haas, Robert Bartlett, *Muybridge, Man in Motion,* Univ. of California Press, Berkeley, 1976

*Hamilton, George Heard, *Painting and Sculpture in Europe 1880–1940,* 3d ed., Pelican History of Art, Penguin, Harmondsworth, 1981

Homer, William I., *Seurat and the Science of Painting,* MIT Press, Cambridge, 1964

Rewald, John, *Post-Impressionism: From Van Gogh to Gauguin,* 2d ed., The Museum of Modern Art, N.Y., 1962

Roskill, Mark, *Van Gogh, Gauguin, and the Impressionist Circle,* New York Graphic Society, Greenwich, 1970

Schapiro, Meyer, *Paul Cézanne,* 3d ed., Abrams, N.Y., 1965

———, *Van Gogh,* rev. ed., Abrams, N.Y., 1982

Scharf, Aaron, *Art and Photography,* Penguin Books, Baltimore, 1974

Schmutzler, Robert, *Art Nouveau,* Abrams, N.Y., 1962

Sutter, Jean, ed., *The Neo-Impressionists,* New York Graphic Society, Greenwich, 1970

TWENTIETH-CENTURY PAINTING

Arnason, H. H., *History of Modern Art: Painting, Sculpture, Architecture, Photography,* 3d ed., Abrams, N.Y., 1986

Arp, Hans, *Arp on Arp: Poems, Memories,* Viking, N.Y., 1972

Baker, Kenneth, *Minimalism,* Abbeville, N.Y., 1989

Barr, Alfred H., Jr., ed., *Cubism and Abstract Art,* reprint of The Museum of Modern Art's 1936 ed., Arno Press, N.Y., 1966

*Braun, Emily, ed., *Italian Art in the 20th Century,* Prestel-Verlag, Munich, 1989

Brown, Milton W., *The Story of the Armory Show,* updated ed., Abbeville, N.Y., 1988

*Celant, Germano, *Unexpressionism: Art Beyond the Contemporary,* Rizzoli, N.Y., 1988

Crichton, Michael, *Jasper Johns,* Abrams, for Whitney Museum of American Art, N.Y., 1977

Daix, Pierre, *Cubists and Cubism,* Rizzoli, N.Y., 1982

De Francia, Peter, *Fernand Léger,* Yale Univ. Press, New Haven, 1983

Doty, Robert, ed., *Contemporary Black Artists in America,* Whitney Museum of American Art, N.Y., 1971

Fine, Elsa H., *The Afro-American Artist: A Search for Identity,* Holt, Rinehart and Winston, N.Y., 1973

*Francis, Richard, *Jasper Johns,* Abbeville, N.Y., 1984

*Frank, Elizabeth, *Jackson Pollock,* Abbeville, N.Y., 1983

*Goldwater, Robert, *Primitivism in Modern Art,* rev. ed., Vintage, N.Y., 1967

*Gowing, Lawrence, *Matisse,* Oxford Univ. Press, N.Y., 1979

*Gray, Camilla, *The Russian Experiment in Art, 1863–1922,* rev. ed., Abrams, N.Y., 1970

Homer, William I., and Violet Organ, *Robert Henri and His Circle,* Cornell Univ. Press, Ithaca, 1969

Hunter, Sam, and John Jacobus, *American Art of the Twentieth Century: Painting, Sculpture, Architecture,* Abrams, N.Y., 1974

Jaffé, H. L. C., *De Stijl, 1917–1931: Visions of Utopia,* Abbeville, N.Y., 1982

*Krauss, Rosalind E., *The Originality of the Avant-Garde and Other Modernist Myths,* MIT Press, Cambridge, 1986

Landau, Ellen G., *Jackson Pollock,* Abrams, N.Y., 1989

Levin, Gail, *Edward Hopper, The Art and the Artist,* Whitney Museum of American Art, N.Y., 1980

*Leymarie, Jean, *Fauves and Fauvism,* Rizzoli, N.Y., 1987

*Lippard, Lucy, *Pop Art,* Praeger, N.Y., 1966

Meisel, Louis K., *Photorealism,* Abrams, N.Y., 1989

*Papadakis, Andreas, et al., *Deconstruction: The Omnibus Volume,* Rizzoli, N.Y., 1989

Pincus-Witten, Robert, *Postminimalism into Maximalism: American Art, 1966–1986,* UMI, Ann Arbor, 1987

*Rose, Barbara, *American Art Since 1900,* rev. ed., Praeger, N.Y., 1975

Rosenberg, Harold, *The De-Definition of Art: Action Art to Pop to Earthworks,* Horizon, N.Y., 1972

*Rosenblum, Robert, *Cubism and Twentieth-Century Art,* rev. ed., Abrams, N.Y., 1976

*Rosenthal, Nan, *Robert Rauschenberg,* Abbeville, N.Y., 1984

Rubin, William, *Dada and Surrealist Art,* Abrams, N.Y., 1968

Sandler, Irving, *The Triumph of American Painting: A History of Abstract Expressionism,* Praeger, N.Y., 1970

———, *The New York School: The Painters and Sculptors of the Fifties,* Harper and Row, New York, 1979

*Vergo, Peter, *Art in Vienna, 1898–1918: Klimt, Kokoschka, Schiele and Their Contemporaries,* Cornell Univ. Press, Ithaca, 1981

*Waldman, Diane, *Mark Rothko, 1903–1970: A Retrospective,* Abrams, N.Y., 1978

TWENTIETH-CENTURY SCULPTURE

*Burnham, Jack, *Beyond Modern Sculpture,* Braziller, N.Y., 1968

*———, *Great Western Saltworks: Essays on the Meaning of Post-Formalist Art,* Braziller, N.Y., 1974

Geist, Sidney, *Brancusi: The Sculpture and Drawings,* Abrams, N.Y., 1975

*Goldberg, RoseLee, *Performance Art from Futurism to the Present,* rev. and enl. ed., Abrams, N.Y., 1988

Hammacher, A. M., *Modern Sculpture: Tradition and Innovation,* Abrams, N.Y., 1988

Krauss, Rosalind E., *Terminal Ironworks: The Sculpture of David Smith,* MIT Press, Cambridge, 1971

Marcus, Stanley E., *David Smith: The Sculptor and His Work,* Cornell Univ. Press, Ithaca, 1983

Melville, Robert, *Henry Moore: Sculpture and Drawings, 1929–69,* Abrams, N.Y., 1970

Read, Herbert, *Henry Moore,* Thames and Hudson, London, 1965

———, with Barbara Hepworth, *Barbara Hepworth: Carvings and Drawings,* Lund Humphries, London, 1952

Withers, Josephine, *Julio González, Sculpture in Iron,* New York Univ. Press, 1978

TWENTIETH-CENTURY ARCHITECTURE

*Bayer, Herbert, *Bauhaus 1919–1928,* New York Graphic Society, Greenwich, for The Museum of Modern Art, N.Y., 1976

*Dal Co, Francesco, *Figures of Architecture and Thought: German Architectural Culture, 1890–1920,* Rizzoli, N.Y., 1986

*Drexler, Arthur, *Ludwig Mies van der Rohe,* Braziller, N.Y., 1960

*———, *Transformations in Modern Architecture,* New York Graphic Society, Boston, 1980

Fitch, James Marston, *American Building,* 2d ed., 2 vols., Houghton Mifflin, Boston, 1966–72

*Hitchcock, Henry-Russell, and Philip Johnson, *The International Style,* Norton, N.Y., 1966

Jencks, Charles, *Post-Modernism: The New Classicism in Art and Architecture,* Rizzoli, N.Y., 1987

Johnson, Philip, *Mies van der Rohe,* 3d ed., rev., New York Graphic Society, Boston, for The Museum of Modern Art, N.Y., 1978

*Kallir, Jane, *Viennese Design and the Wiener Werkstätte,* Braziller, N.Y., 1986

Klotz, Heinrich, *History of Postmodern Architecture,* MIT Press, Cambridge, 1988

*Pevsner, Nikolaus, *The Sources of Modern Architecture and Design,* Oxford Univ. Press, N.Y., 1977

*Scully, Vincent, *Modern Architecture,* rev. ed., Braziller, N.Y., 1974

TWENTIETH-CENTURY PHOTOGRAPHY

Coke, Van Deren, *The Painter and the Photograph from Delacroix to Warhol,* rev. ed., Univ. of New Mexico Press, Albuquerque, 1972

Freund, Gisele, *Photography and Society,* Godine, Boston, 1980

Gidal, Tim N., *Modern Photojournalism: Origins and Evolution 1910–33,* Macmillan, N.Y., 1973

*Goldberg, Vicki, ed., *Photography in Print,* Simon and Schuster, N.Y., 1981

Green, Jonathan, *American Photography: A Critical History, 1945 to the Present,* Abrams, N.Y., 1984

Haus, Andreas, *Moholy-Nagy: Photographs and Photograms,* Pantheon, N.Y., 1980

Hurley, F. Jack, *Portrait of a Decade: Roy Stryker and the Development of Documentary Photography in the Thirties,* Louisiana State Univ. Press, Baton Rouge, 1972

Marzona, Egidio, and Roswitha Fricke, *Bauhaus Photography,* MIT Press, Cambridge, 1987

Szarkowski, John, *Mirrors and Windows: American Photography Since 1960,* The Museum of Modern Art, N.Y., 1978

———, and Maria Morris Hambourg, *The Work of Atget,* 4 vols., The Museum of Modern Art, N.Y., 1981

INDEX

Illustration references, shown in *italic* type, are to figure numbers.

LIST OF CREDITS

The author and publisher wish to thank the libraries, museums, galleries, and private collectors named in the picture captions for permitting the reproduction of works of art in their collections and for supplying the necessary photographs. Photographs from other sources are gratefully acknowledged below.

Alinari, Florence: 59, 76, 83, 93, 96, 98, 106, 192, 200, 202, 203, 204, 205, 209, 210, 222, 226, 231, 234, 235, 236, 281; Courtesy Department of Library Services, American Museum of Natural History: 27; Wayne Andrews, Grosse Pointe, Michigan: 335; Copyright Archives Centrales Iconographiques, Brussels: 143, 286; Art Resource, New York: 377, 433, 477; Arxiu MAS (A. y R. MAS. Barcelona): 191, 194, 285, 288, 336, 337, 408; Bildarchiv Oesterr, Nationalbibliothek, Vienna: 103; Joachim Blauel/Artothek: 261, 287, 294; Hedrich Blessing, Ltd., Chicago: 491; Arnold von Borsig, Berlin: 161; Brassaï, Galerie Louise Leiris, Paris: 2; Bulloz, Paris: 142; Caisse Nationale des Monuments Historiques, Paris: 19, 134, 141, 154, 169, 241, 264, 269, 270, 355, 356, 373; Cameraphoto, Piero Codato, Venice: 176, 250; Ludovico Canali: 9, 62, 80, 81, 91, 99, 100, 105, 110, 112, 139, 180, 181, 207, 213, 214, 224, 238, 243, 246, 247, 251, 266, 271, 273, 274, 275, 276, 279, 354; Canali Bertoni: 172, 201, 208; Canali Rapuzzi: 57; Copyright *Country Life*, London: 334, 358; Courtesy Culver Pictures, New York: 363; Deutscher Kunstverlag, Munich: 121, 167; Deutsches Archäologische Institut, Rome: 40, 111; Jean Dieuzade, Toulouse: 132; Fischbach Gallery, New York: 476; Fotocielo, Rome: 277; Foto Grassi, Siena: 175; Foto-Marburg, Marburg/Lahn: 126, 155, 156, 163, 164, 165, 387; Fototeca Unione, Rome: 82, 84, 85, 86, 89; Alison Frantz, Princeton, New Jersey: 54, 64; Gabinetto Fotografico Nazionale, Rome: 278; G.E.K.S., New York: 15, 97, 113, 152; Copyright Courtesy Gemini GEL, Los Angeles: 479; Giraudon, Paris: 147, 184, 225, 228, 257, 258, 331, 333, 338, 341, 368, 372; Lucien Hervé, Paris: 495; Hirmer Fotoarchiv, Munich: 29, 31, 32, 33, 34, 36, 51, 52, 53, 66, 70, 71, 78, 95, 114; Timothy Hursley, Little Rock, Arkansas: 500; A. F. Kersting, London: 136, 159, 357; Nikos Kontos, Athens: 1, 56, 69, 74; Jannes Linders, Rotterdam, Holland: 493; Copyright Peter Mauss/Esto: 501; Rollie McKenna, Stonington, Connecticut: 212; Ministry of Works, London, Crown Copyright: 332; National Monuments Record, London: 359; Courtesy Oriental Institute of the University of Chicago: 35, 49; Eric Pollitzer, New York; 394; Josephine Powell, Rome: 115; Antonio Quattrone, Florence (Courtesy Olivetti): 215; Mario Quattrone, Florence: 219, 245; Rheinisches Bildarchiv, Cologne: 168; R.M.N., Paris: 45, 178, 179, 196, 221, 227, 289, 302, 311, 312, 314, 325, 339, 340, 342, 343, 347, 366, 369, 371, 379; Roger-Viollet, Paris: 360; Jean Roubier, Paris: 133, 135, 151, 166; Scala, Florence: 177, 217, 237; Helga Schmidt-Glassner, Stuttgart: 322; Marco and Toni Schneiders, Lindau: 324; S. Sunami, New York: 23; Wim Swaan, New York: 3, 39, 138, 153, 160, 162, 173, 254, 282, 308, 309, 321; Copyright Caroline Tisdall, Courtesy Ronald Feldman Fine Arts, New York: 489; Marvin Trachtenberg, New York: 63, 255, 323, 388; Yan Photo Reportage, Toulouse: 140.

ILLUSTRATION COPYRIGHTS